Handbook of Clinical Sexuality for Mental Health Professionals

HANDBOOK OF CLINICAL SEXUALITY FOR MENTAL HEALTH PROFESSIONALS

Stephen B. Levine, MD

Editor

Candace B. Risen, LISW
Stanley E. Althof, PhD

Associate Editors

Brunner-Routledge
New York • Hove

Published in 2003 by
Brunner-Routledge
29 West 35th Street
New York, NY 10001
www.brunner-routledge.com

Published in Great Britain by
Brunner-Routledge
27 Church Road
Hove, East Sussex
BN3 2FA
www.brunner-routledge.co.uk

Brunner-Routledge is an imprint of the Taylor & Francis Group.
Printed in the United States of America on acid-free paper.

10 9 8 7 6 5 4 3 2 1

Library of Congress Cataloging-in-Publication Data

Handbook of clinical sexuality for mental health professionals / Stephen
B. Levine, editor ; Candace B. Risen, Stanley E. Althof, associate editors.
p. cm.
Includes bibliographical references and index.
ISBN 1-58391-331-9 (hbk.)
1. Sexual disorders—Handbooks, manuals, etc. I. Levine, Stephen B., 1942–
II. Risen, Candace B. III. Althof, Stanley E., 1948–

RC556 .H353 2003
616.85′83—dc21

2002152844

Contents

About the Editors

Stanley E. Althof, PhD (Co-editor) is Professor of Psychology in the Department of Urology at Case Western Reserve University School of Medicine in Cleveland, Ohio and is Co-director at the Center for Marital and Sexual Health in Beachwood, Ohio

Stephen B. Levine, MD (Editor) is Clinical Professor of Psychiatry at Case Western Reserve University School of Medicine in Cleveland and is Co-director at the Center for Marital and Sexual Health in Beachwood, Ohio

Candace B. Risen, LISW (Co-editor) Assistant Clinical Professor of Social Work in the Department of Psychiatry at Case Western Reserve University and is Co-director at the Center for Marital and Sexual Health in Beachwood, Ohio

Contributors

Rosemary Basson, MD, MRCP is a Clinical Professor of Psychiatry and Obstetrics/Gynecology at the University of British Columbia in Vancouver, Canada

Sophie Bergeron, PhD is Assistant Professor in the Department of Sexology, Université du Québec à Montréal in Montréal, Québec and Clinical Psychologist at the Sex and Couple Therapy Service at McGill University Health Centre (Royal Victoria Hospital)

Yitzchak M. Binik, PhD is Professor of Psychology at McGill University and Sex and Couple Therapy Service at McGill University Health Centre (Royal Victoria Hospital) in Montréal, Québec, Canada

Al Cooper, PhD is the Clinical Director of the San Jose Marital and Sexuality Centre in Santa Clara, Associate Professor (Research) at the Pacific Graduate School of Professional Psychology, and Training Coordinator for Counseling and Psychological Services at Vaden Student Health, Stanford University in Palo Alto, California

Tiffany Cummins, MD just completed her residency at the Department of Psychiatry at Northwestern University in Chicago, Illinois

Lorraine L. Dennerstein, AO, MBBS, PhD, DPM, FRANCZ directs the Office for Gender and Health and is Professor in the Department of Psychiatry at the University of Melbourne at Royal Melbourne Hospital in Australia

Jennifer I. Downey, MD is Clinical Professor of Psychiatry at Columbia University College of Physicians & Surgeons in New York

Carol Rinkleib Ellison, PhD is a psychologist in private practice in Oakland, California and an Assistant Clinical Professor in the Department of Psychiatry at University of California at San Francisco

Peter Fagan, PhD is Associate Professor of Medical Psychology in the Department of Psychiatry and Behavioral Sciences at The Johns Hopkins University School of Medicine and head of the Sexual Behaviors Consultation Unit in Lutherville, Maryland

J. Paul Federoff, MD is Co-Director of the Sexual Behaviors Clinic and Research Unit Director of the Institute of Mental Health Research at the Royal Ottawa Hospital at the University of Ottawa in Ontario Canada

Richard C. Friedman, MD is Clinical Professor of Psychiatry at Columbia University College of Physicians and Surgeons in New York

Jeffrey W. Janata, PhD is Assistant Professor in the Department of Psychiatry and Director of the Behavioral Medicine Program and University Pain Center at Case Western Reserve University School of Medicine in Cleveland, Ohio

Samir Khalifé, MD is a gynecologist at the Departments of Obstetrics and Gynecology *At McGill University and Jewish General Hospital in Montréal, Québec, Canada*

Sheryl A. Kingsberg, PhD is Assistant Professor the Department of Reproductive Biology at Case Western Reserve University School of Medicine in Cleveland, Ohio

I. David Marcus, PhD is a psychologist at the San Jose Marital and Sexuality Center in Santa Clara, California

William L. Maurice, MD is an Associate Professor in the Department of Psychiatry of the University of British Columbia in Vancouver, Canada

Barry W. McCarthy, PhD is a psychologist in private practice and Professor in the Department of Psychology at American University in Washington, DC

Marta Meana, PhD is Associate Professor in the Department of Psychology at the University of Nevada at Las Vegas, Nevada

Sheldon I. Miller, MD is Professor of Psychiatry at Northwestern University School of Medicine in Chicago, Illinois

Sharon G. Nathan, MPH, PhD, is a psychologist in private practice in New York

Friedemann Pfäfflin, MD is psychiatrist and head of the Department of Forensic Medicine in the University of Ulm in Germany

S. Michael Plaut, PhD is Assistant Dean for Student Affairs and Associate Professor of Psychiatry at the University of Maryland School of Medicine in Baltimore, Maryland

Derek C. Polonsky, MD is a psychiatrist in private practice in Brookline, Massachusetts and is Clinical Instructor in Psychiatry at Harvard Medical School

Raymond C. Rosen, PhD is Professor in the Department of Psychiatry at the Robert Wood Johnson Medical School in Piscataway, New Jersey

David E. Scharff, MD is Co-Director, International Institute of Object Relations Therapy in Chevy Chase Maryland and Clinical Professor of Psychiatry, Georgetown University and the Uniformed Services University of the Health Sciences in Washington, DC

R. Taylor Segraves, MD, PhD is Chairman at the Department of Psychiatry at MetroHealth Center and is Professor at Case Western Reserve University School of Medicine in Cleveland, Ohio

Lynda Dykes Talmadge, PhD is in private psychology practice in Atlanta, Georgia

William C. Talmadge, PhD is in private psychology practice in Atlanta, Georgia

Marcel D. Waldinger, MD, PhD is a psychiatrist in the Department of Psychiatry and Neurosexology at Leyenburg Hospital in The Hague and is in the Department of Psychopharmacology at Utrecht University in The Hague, The Netherlands

Preface

Each mental health professional's life offers a personal opportunity to diminish the sense of bafflement about how health, suffering, and recovery processes work. Over decades of work in a mental health field, many of us develop the sense that we better understand some aspects of psychology and psychopathology. Those who devote themselves to one subject in a scholarly research fashion seem to have a slightly greater potential to remove some of the mystery for themselves and others in a particular subject area. But when it comes to the rest of our vast areas of responsibility, we are far from expert; we remain only relatively informed.

The authors of this handbook devoted their careers to unraveling human sexuality's knots. Their inclusion in this book is a testimony to their previous successes in helping others to understand sexual suffering and its treatment. Because one of the responsibilities of scholars is to pass on their knowledge to the next generation, in the largest sense, passing the torch is the overarching purpose of this book.

We humans are emotionally, cognitively, behaviorally, and sexually changeable creatures. We react, adapt, and evolve. When our personal evolution occurs along expected lines, others label us mature or normal. When it does not, our unique developmental pathways are described as evidence of our immaturity or psychopathology. Sometimes we are more colloquially described as "having problems."

Sexual life, being an integral part of nonsexual life processes, is dynamic and evolutionary. I think about it as having three broad categories of potential difficulties: disorders, problems, and worries. The **disorders** are those difficulties that are officially recognized by the *DSM-IV-TR*—for example, Hypoactive Sexual Desire Disorder, Gender Identity Disorder, and Sexual Pain Disorder. Many common forms of suffering that afflict groups of people, however, are not found in our official nosology and attract little research. I call these **problems.** Here are just two examples: continuing uncertainty about one's orientation and recurrent paralyzing resentment over having to accommodate a partner's sexual needs. **Problems** are frequent sources of suffering in large definable groups of the population—for example, bisexual youth and not-so-happily married menopausal women. Then there are sexual **worries.** Sexual **worries** detract from the pleasure of living. They abound among people of all ages. Here are five examples: Will I be adequate during my first intercourse? Will my new partner like my not-so-perfect body? Does my diminishing interest in sex mean that I no longer love my partner? How long will I be able to maintain potency with my young wife? Will I be able to sustain love for my partner? **Worries** are the concerns that are inherent in the experience of being human.

Sexual disorders, sexual problems, and sexual worries insinuate themselves into the therapy sessions even when therapists do not directly inquire about the patient's sexuality. This is simply because sexuality is integral to personal psychology and because the prevalence of difficulties involving sexual identity and sexual function is so high.

Unlike the frequency of sexual problems and worries, the prevalence of sexual **disorders** has been carefully studied. Their prevalence is so high, however, that most professionals are shocked when confronted with the evidence. The 1994 National Health and Social Life Survey, which obtained the most representative sample of 18- to 59-year-old Americans ever interviewed, confirmed the findings of many less methodologically sophisticated works. In this study, younger women and older men bore the highest prevalence. Overall, however, 35% of the entire sample acknowledged being sexually problematic in the previous 12 months.[1] There are compelling reasons to think that the prevalence is even higher among those who seek help for mental[2] or physical conditions.[3] Although people in some countries have unique sexual difficulties,[4] numerous studies have demonstrated that the population in the United States is not uniquely sexually problematic.[5,6]

To make this point about prevalence and, therefore, the relevance of this book even stronger, I'd like you to consider with me a retrospective study from Brazil. The authors compared the frequencies of sexual dysfunction among untreated patients with social phobia to those with panic disorder.[7] The mean age of both groups was mid-30s. The major discovery was that Sexual Aversion, a severe *DSM-IV* diagnosis previously thought to be relatively rare, was extremely common in men (36%) and women (50%) with panic disorder, but absent in those with social phobia (0%). The sexual lives of those with social phobia were limited in other ways.

I find this information ironic in several ways. This finding probably would not have shocked therapists who were trained a generation or two ago because it was then widely assumed that an important relationship existed between problematic sexual development and anxiety symptoms.[8] Modern therapists, however, tend to be disinterested in sexuality and so are likely not to respond to these patients' sexual problems. Adding insult to injury, the modern treatment of anxiety disorders routinely employs medications with a high likelihood of dampening sexual drive, arousability, and orgasmic expression.

For most of the 20th century, sexuality was seen as a vital component of personality development, mental health, and mental distress. During the last 25 years, the extent of sexual problems has been even better defined, and their negative consequences have been better appreciated. Mental health professionals' interest in these matters has been thwarted by new biological paradigms for understanding the causes and treatments of mental conditions, the emphasis on short-term psychotherapy, the constriction of insurance support for nonpharmacological interventions, the political conservatism of government funding sources, and the policy to consider sexual problems inconsequential.

As a result of these five forces, the average well-trained mental health professional has had limited educational exposure to clinical sexuality. This professional is neither comfortable dealing with sexual problems, skillful in asking the relevant questions, nor able to efficiently provide a relevant focused treatment. It does not matter much if the professional's training has been in psychiatric residencies, psychology internships, counseling internships, marriage and family therapy training programs, or social work agency placements. Knowledgeable teachers are in short supply. The same paucity of supervised experiences focusing on sexual disorders, problems, and worries applies to all groups.

In my community, Cleveland, Ohio, there happens to be a relatively large number of highly qualified sexuality specialists. Most moderate to large urban communities, however, have no specialists who deal with the entire spectrum of male and female dysfunctions, sexual compulsivities, paraphilias, gender-identity disorders, and marital-relationship problems. Although many communities have therapists who deal with one part of this spectrum, the entire range of problems exists in every community.

A remarkable bit of progress occurred in the treatment of erectile dysfunction in 1998. Since then, primary care physicians, cardiologists, and urologists have been effectively prescribing a phosphodiesterase-5 inhibitor for millions of men. But despite the evidence of the drug's safety and efficacy, at least half of the men do not refill their prescriptions. There is good reason to believe that this drop-out rate is due to psychological/interpersonal factors, rather than to the lack of the drug's ability to generate erections. This fact alone has created another reason for mental health professionals to become interested in clinical sexuality. Most physicians who prescribe the sildenafil are not equipped to deal with the psychological issues that are embedded in the apparent failures. The nonresponders to initial treatment need access to us. But mental health professionals need to be better educated in sexual subjects. So there are three reasons for developing this handbook: (1) to pass the torch of knowledge to another generation; (2) to better equip mental health professionals to respond to sexual disorders, problems, and worries as these appear in their current practice settings; and (3) to help patients take advantage of emerging advances in medication treatment by helping them to master their psychological obstacles to sexual expression.

Stephen B. Levine, MD

YOU CAN DO THIS!

We use this exhortative heading for a reason. "You Can Do This!" is our way of saying that the handbook provides coaching, encouragement, and optimism and aims to inspire others to turn their interests to clinical sexuality. Mental health professionals can learn to competently address their patients' sexual worries, problems, and disorders.

How We Created the Handbook

Once the editors decided to say yes to the publisher's invitation to develop a handbook, we set our sights on creating a unique book. We imagined it as a trustworthy, informative, informal, supportive, and highly valued volume that would encourage and enable mental health professionals to work effectively with patients who have sexual concerns. To attain this lofty goal, we knew that the book would have to be a departure from the usual excellent book on clinical sexuality.

We created the handbook through seven steps.

The first step we took was to define the intended audience. We quickly realized, having valued teaching so highly during our careers, that this audience was mental health professionals with little formal clinical training in sexuality. Although we thought some readers might be trainees in various educational programs, we envisioned that most of the readers would be fully trained, competent professionals. We thought that experienced clinicians would have already had many clients who alluded to their sexual concerns and might have already perceived how their sexual problems may have contributed to their presenting depression, substance abuse, or anxiety states. We wanted to help general mental health professionals think about sex in a way that diminished their personal discomfort, increased their clinical confidence, piqued their interest in understanding sexual life better, and increased their effectiveness. We wanted professionals to stop avoiding their clients' sexual problems. We also clarified that we were not trying to create a book that would update sexual experts. We were writing for those who knew that they needed to learn both basic background material and basic practical interventions.

The second step was to realize that because we were writing an educational text, our authors would have to be excellent teachers. Excellence as a researcher or a clinician would not be compelling reason to put a person on the author list.

The third step was to define our strategy for making the handbook unique. We decided it would be through our instructions to the authors about how to compose their chapters. We gave them ten instructions:

1. Use the first person voice—use "I" as the subject of some sentences.
2. Imagine when writing that you are talking privately to the reader in a supervisory session.
3. Reveal something personal about your relationship to your subject—how you became interested in the subject, how it changed your life, how your understanding of the subject evolved over the years.
4. Imagine that you are guiding your readers through their first cases with the disorder you are discussing. Do not share everything that you know about the subject! Try not to exceed your imagined readers' interest in the topic.
5. Keep your tone encouraging about not abandoning the therapeutic inquiry, even if readers are uncertain what to do next.
6. Discuss your personal reactions to patient care as a model for the appearance of countertransference. Illustrate how a therapist might use his or her private responses to better understand the patient.
7. Either tell numerous short patient stories or provide one case in depth. Do not write a conceptual paper without clinical illustrations.

8. Annotate at least half of your bibliography. Your reference list is not there primarily to demonstrate your scholarship; it is there to guide the interested supervisee.
9. Be realistic about the reality of life processes and the limitations of professional interventions. Although we want the readers to be encouraged to learn more, we do not want to mislead them into thinking that experts in the field can completely solve people's sexual difficulties.
10. Be cognizant when writing that you are trying to prepare your reader to skillfully and comfortably approach the patient, to gain confidence in his or her capacity to help, and to rediscover the inherent fascination of sexual life.

The fourth step was the definition of relevant sexual topics. We did not want to deal with uncommon problems—for example, there was not going to be a chapter devoted to females who want to live as men, to female impersonators, or to serial sex murderers. This book was to help with common problems, ordinary ones, the ones that are often lurking behind other psychiatric complaints. This task was relatively easy.

The fifth task was slightly more difficult: to decide what basic information was necessary as background preparation for dealing with the common sexual problems. After this, we set about matching authors to the intended topics.

The sixth step was really fun. We had been told that it was often difficult to get people to write for edited texts and that it might take 6 months or more to complete the author list. The vast majority of our esteemed colleagues who were asked said yes immediately and thought that the idea for the book was terrific. A few needed several weeks to agree. Four pled exhaustion and wished us luck.

The final step—the seventh—involved the review of the manuscripts. It was during this 5-month process that we, the editors, more fully realized what modern clinical sexology is. While reading these 25 chapters, we realized that as a group we vary considerably in our emphasis on evidence-based, clinically-based, or theory-based ideas. All of us authors, however, speak of having been enriched as we struggled to better understand and assist people with various sexual difficulties. All of us have seen considerable progress in our professional lifetimes with our specialty issues. Some of the chapters are stories of triumphs (treatment of rapid ejaculation, erectile dysfunction, female orgasmic difficulties), others of disorders still awaiting the significant breakthrough (female genital pain, sexual compulsivity, sexual side effects of SSRIs). A number of authors address essential human processes that are part of life (boundaries and their violations, menopausal changes, love), whereas others are coaching their readers about how to think of their roles and attitudes (sexual history taking, diagnosis of women's dysfunction, transgenderism). Some chapters focus on grave difficulties (aversion, sexual avoidance, sexual victimization) and yet others on hidden private struggles that tend to remain unseen by those around them (homoeroticism in heterosexuals, paraphilias, unhappy marriages). All in all, we find the field of clinical sexuality fascinating and hope that our readers will rediscover what they used to know: sex is very interesting!

We designed this handbook with the idea that the vast majority of readers will look at only the few chapters that are relevant to their current clinical needs at one sitting. Those who are taking a course in clinical sexuality and reading the entire hand-book, however, will quickly discover some redundancy. In editing, we objected to any redundancy within a chapter; we were reassured by it in the book as a whole. This was because it meant to us that teachers of various backgrounds focusing on different sub-jects shared certain convictions about the importance of careful assessment, how to conduct therapy, the limitations of medications, the possibility of being helpful de-spite not being expert, and so forth.

We are deeply indebted to the authors of the handbook for their years of devotion to their subjects that enabled them to write such stellar educational pieces. As editors, we considered it a privilege to have been immersed in their thinking. We hope that our readers feel the same way.

Stephen B. Levine, MD
Candace B. Risen, LISW
Stanley E. Althof, PhD

NOTES

1. Laumann, E. O., & Michael, R. T. (Eds.). (2001). *Sex, Love, and Health in America: Private Choices, and Public Policies.* Chicago: University of Chicago Press.
2. Kockott, G., & Pfeiffer, W. (1996). Sexual disorders in nonacute psychiatric patients. *Comprehensive Psychiatry, 37*(1), 56–61.
3. Dunn, K. M., Croft, P. R., & Hackett, G. I. (1999). Association of sexual problems with social, psychological, and physical problems in men and women: A cross sectional population sur-vey. *Journal of Epidemiology and Community Health, 53,* 144–148. Another demonstration that the chronically mentally ill have a high prevalence of sexual dysfunction, some of which is medication-induced, some of which is illness-induced, and some of which is simply part of the difficulties of living.
4. El-Defrawi, L. G., Dandash, K. F., Refaat, A. H., & Eyada, M. (2001). Female genital mutilation and its psychosocial impact. *Journal of Sex & Marital Therapy, 27,* 465–473.
5. Dennerstein, L. (2000). Menopause and sexuality. In Jane M. Ussher (Ed.), *Women's Health: Contemporary International Perspectives* (pp. 190–196). Leicester: British Psychological Society Books.
6. Madu, S. N., & Peltzer, K. (2001). Prevalence and patterns of child sexual abuse and victim–perpetrator relationship among secondary school students in the northern province (South Africa). *Archives of Sexual Behavior, 30*(3), 311–321. Childhood sexual abuse is a major concern everywhere. Though in the United States, its prevalence varies widely from one economic group to another, this variation is not likely to be unique to the United States.
7. Figueira, I., Possidente, E., Marques, C., & Hayes, K. (2001). Sexual dysfunction: A neglected complication of panic disorder and social phobia. *Archives of Sexual Behavior, 30*(4), 369–378. Although this is only a retrospective study that awaits confirmation, those highly inter-ested in anxiety disorders will profit from the implications of their data.
8. Freud, S. (1905). *Three Essays on the Theory of Sexuality in the Complete Psychological Works of Sigmund Freud, Volume VII* (p. 149). London: Hogarth. This is an interesting read even today, almost a century after it was written. Freud organized information about sexual life in a new language, which reflected a wonderful grasp of the range of sexualities in the population and what might account for the numerous variations that he categorized.

Part One

ADULT INTIMACY:
HOPES AND DISAPPOINTMENTS

Chapter One

Listening to Sexual Stories

Candace B. Risen, LISW

INTRODUCTION

When I began listening to sexual stories, I was 27 years old, married, and returning to clinical practice after a 10-month maternity hiatus. Prior to the birth of my child, I had been a social worker for 4 years, most of which were spent in an inpatient psychiatric unit. I heard that a psychiatrist, wishing to launch a new subspecialty clinic devoted to sexual issues, was looking for an intake coordinator. It was not exactly what I had in mind, but I needed a job. In that new role I had to screen referrals, ascertain the nature of the sexual complaint, present the intake to the clinic staff for assignment, and see some of the cases myself. I had to talk about sex! I had to know about sex. How was I going to do that? My frame of reference was limited to my own personal life experiences. I had strongly internalized the cultural expectation that I was a "good girl"—that is, I could not be *that* worldly! My mother echoed my concerns when, upon learning of my new position, she asked, "But how do you know so much about sex that you can help people? . . . No, no, don't answer that question. . . . I don't want to know!"

Thus began the next 27 years—a journey of personal growth and discovery, and ever-increasing confidence and competence in helping people tell their sexual stories. Over time, I learned to listen without anxiety, to ask pointed questions without fear of reprisal, and to articulate sexual issues in a manner that was extraordinarily helpful to many of my patients. Book knowledge certainly helped me along the way, but I learned far more from the patients themselves. I have spent thousands of hours hearing about a wider range of sexual experiences, feelings, thoughts, and struggles than I could have ever imagined. I am indebted to those countless patients who taught me through their sexual stories. In this chapter I will share what I believe are the key obstacles to overcome and the necessary skills to acquire in order to develop professional sexual comfort and expertise.

Why Do I Need to Learn This?

Everyone has sexual thoughts, feelings, and experiences that are integral to their sense of who they are and how they relate to the world. Sexual problems often manifest and mask themselves in the major symptoms that bring patients to treatment; depression, anxiety, failure to achieve, low self-esteem, and the inability to engage in intimate relationships. Yet patients are shy about revealing their sexual concerns. It feels so private, so awkward, so potentially embarrassing that many are reduced to paralyzing inarticulateness. They dread being asked, but they long to be asked. They know for sure that they need to be asked if it is ever to come out. Too often, therapists find themselves reluctant to initiate an inquiry. They rationalize, "If my patient doesn't bring up sex, it must not be an issue and I should not be asking about it." At best, this can lead to a missed opportunity to be helpful; at worst, it can lead to the wrong therapy plan.

Why Don't I Want To?

This is often the fundamental question behind "Why do I need to?" The reasons for not wanting to are many.

1. I'm not used to talking about sex . . . my discomfort and awkwardness will be obvious.
2. I don't exactly know why I am asking or what I want to know.
3. I won't know how to respond to what I hear back.
4. I may be unfamiliar with, not understand, or neither be familiar with nor understand something my patient tells me.
5. I may offend or embarrass my patient.
6. I may be perceived as nosy or provocative.
7. I won't know how to treat any problem I hear.
8. I'll be too embarrassed to consult with my colleagues.

The anxiety and discomfort underlying these reasons can be overcome with the courage to try something new. Most of us can recall having some of these concerns about a wide range of issues when we first began our clinical careers. Questions about what to ask, how, when, and why were the ongoing central focus of our learning. Patience, persistence, and a sense of humor helped to get us through the processes of gaining experience. Over time, increasing comfort and expanding knowledge made the job that much easier.

The concerns about being perceived as nosy or intrusive or about offending or embarrassing our patients may be more specific to sexual topics. Although patients may initially react as though you have intruded into territory too personal to be shared, they are usually settled by a simple explanation as to the relevance of the question.

THERAPIST: "You've told me a lot about your ambivalence about marrying Joe . . . your concerns about his lack of ambition and his relationship to his family. You haven't mentioned anything about your sexual life together. Can you tell me about that?"

JILL: "Well, uh . . . it's okay, I guess." (Squirms in her seat.) "What do you want to know?"

THERAPIST: "Sexual intimacy is often a vital part of a relationship. . . . It can really enhance it or can be problematic. How have you felt about your sexual relationship with Joe?"

JILL: "Well, sometimes it feels like he lacks ambition in bed, too. . . . He doesn't seem to be interested that often . . . we are so busy during the week; I can understand . . . but it seems he would rather spend Sunday afternoon visiting his family than being, you know, intimate with me."

THERAPIST: "How do you feel about that?"

JILL: "Well, I haven't told anyone. . . . It's embarrassing to admit that we're not even married yet and already Joe seems disinterested. . . . Isn't it supposed to take several years before that happens? It makes me feel like he isn't attracted to me, like I'm too fat or not sexy enough."

Jill is a little taken aback by the initial question. She doesn't know how to respond because she is not used to articulating aspects of her sexual life. A simple statement by her therapist about sexual intimacy helps Jill to get started.

Sometimes, however, it is the therapist, not the patient, who feels weird or embarrassed by the exploration of sexual material. This is particularly true when the topic is something the therapist has never experienced ("My ignorance will show."), can't imagine experiencing ("That's disgusting!"), or has experienced with ambivalence and conflict ("I don't think I want to go there!"). The therapist may unwisely avoid the subject if it threatens to bring up painful memories.

ALAN: "I can't believe I slept with my roommate's girlfriend! I mean, I've had sort of a crush on her, but I wasn't thinking about that when he asked me to look out for her over the weekend while he was away. We were just talking, drinking some beer, and having a good time. One thing led to another. Now she won't speak to me and my roommate will be back tomorrow. What can I do?"

THERAPIST: (This is making me very anxious. . . . I don't want to remember what I did to Jim in college. . . . It was the end of our friendship. . . . To this day I feel like a worm about it.) "I'm sure everything will be okay. These things happen."

Alan is clearly upset by his behavior and wants to talk about it. The situation, however, reminds his therapist of a similar time in his life. In an effort to ward off his own feelings of guilt, the therapist cuts off the discussion and falsely reassures Alan that everything will work out.

The heterosexual therapist may be most reluctant to bring up sexual issues when dealing with a client of the opposite sex; the homosexual therapist may feel similarly anxious when dealing with a client of the same sex. The gender of the therapist often dictates what the particular worry is about; in other words, the male therapist is more likely to worry about feeling excited if he pursues sexual issues with his client and the female therapist is more likely to worry about being seen as provocative or inviting of her client's sexual interest.

Who Should I Be Asking?

Everyone: Unless the chief complaint is so specific and narrow in focus or the time spent together so short or crisis-oriented, *every* patient should at least be offered the opportunity to address sexual concerns. How will we know whether sexuality is of concern unless we inquire? Because sexuality is a topic that is difficult for patients to bring up, the therapist must assume responsibility for introducing it as an area of possible relevance. If nothing else, the inquiry tells the patient, "This is okay to talk about. . . . I'm interested in hearing about it if you want to tell me. . . . I'll even help you talk about it by taking the lead."

Including Older Persons: Therapists are often reluctant to inquire about the sexual feelings and activities of "the elderly" (often defined as anyone as old as or older than one's parents!). Our culture emphasizes youth and beauty, and there is a tendency to see aging people as asexual or, even worse, to make fun of their displays of sexual interest. Older adults, in turn, may be embarrassed to admit that they still have needs for physical affection, closeness, intimacy, and sexual gratification. They may be told by their physicians that they are "lucky to be alive" and shouldn't fret over sexual concerns.

Even When Your Patient Is the Couple: It is hard to imagine a marital relationship in which sexuality does not play a role. Yet marriage counselors often refer patients to sex specialists and tell us, "Mr. and Mrs. X have done terrific work with me in the past year on their marriage. We were winding down and they brought up a sexual issue. I'm sending them to you to deal with their sex life." This process is neither clinically nor financially efficient and is a result of either the marriage counselor's discomfort with the topic of sex or the assumption that sex is not within the range of marital counseling.

When Should I Ask?

Inquiring about sex when someone shows up in a crisis about his dying mother is not particularly relevant. Early and abrupt questions about sexuality will be off putting unless the chief complaint is of a sexual nature. On the other hand, putting it off indefinitely or waiting until the patient brings it up may reinforce the idea that it is a taboo subject. The situation that offers the most natural segue into the topic is the gathering of psychosocial and developmental information early on in the assessment phase. As one is inquiring about childhood and family-of-origin history, significant events, issues, and problems, this can be a natural lead-in to inquiring about sexual matters.

THERAPIST: "You were telling me about your male friendships growing up. . . . Do you remember when you first became aware of sexual feelings?"

JACK: "Do you mean liking girls? I didn't think much about girls until middle school. . . . I had a crush on a girl in seventh grade. Her name was Judy. She was very popular and hung out with eighth-grade boys. She never knew how I felt. I was geeky. She wouldn't have given me the time of day."

THERAPIST: "How did you handle that at the time?"

JACK: "Not well. I was very self-conscious and it didn't go away in high school. I didn't date although I wanted to. That's when I found my brother's magazines under his bed and I started masturbating. I guess most guys do and it's not a problem but I got 'hooked' on it and I think I still am. I don't know if that is related to why I'm here, but it might be."

Jack's therapist made a smooth transition from the focus on growing up and friendships to a question about the emerging awareness of sexual feelings. The transition made sense to Jack, and he easily picked up on the question. In this case, Jack thinks that the issue of sexuality may be relevant to his seeking therapy. That isn't always so. The advantage of taking a sexual history in the assessment phase, whether or not a sexual problem exists, is that it gives permission to speak of sexual issues in the future. If, however, one has forgotten to do this, it won't hurt to introduce it as a topic at a later date.

How Do I Do This Well?

Using the Right Words: Even when clinicians are convinced of the worthiness of inquiring about sexual matters and are ready to do so, they often stumble over the vocabulary. The task of finding the right words and pronouncing them correctly can intimidate the best of us; we realize that we are far more comfortable reading such words as "penis, vagina, clitoris, orgasm" than saying them out loud.

Nevertheless, it is up to the clinician to go first—that is, to say the words out loud so that the patient can follow suit. Sometimes we may use a word that is confusing or foreign to our patient; sometimes patients will use words we don't understand. Shortly after I began this work, a patient told me his chief complaint was *"I've lost my nature."* I did not know what a "nature" was, never mind how he could lose one! I was too embarrassed to ask. I copped out by replying, *"Tell me more about losing your nature."* I hoped that the subsequent discussion would reveal the definition of the word. Eventually, I figured out that he was using the word to describe his erection. It would have been a lot easier if I had just inquired, *"Tell me what a nature is . . . I haven't heard that expression."* Over time one can build up knowledge of a large repertoire of expressions—some clinical and formal, others slang and street talk. It helps to gain a working familiarity with both kinds.

Allowing the Story to be Told: Though it helps to have an organized approach to the questioning, you should not become an interrogator who is wedded to a predetermined agenda or outline. I have found that the most useful conceptualization for my talking about sexuality is that of helping people tell their "sexual story." Sexual stories, as with any story, have a pattern of flow and a combination of plots and subplots, characters, and meaning. Some stories unfold chronologically from beginning to end; others begin at the end and flash backward to illustrate and highlight the significant determinants to the ending. Either way, the events, characters, and meanings are eventually interwoven into one or two major themes that constitute "the story." Whether or not one begins by asking about current sexual feelings and behaviors and then gathers history or begins by taking a developmental history depends on two factors:

1. the absence or presence of a current sexual issue that requires direct attention; and
2. the client's comfort with addressing current sexual functioning as opposed to historical narrative.

Being Flexible: Open-ended questions that encourage clients to tell their sexual stories using their own language are ideal, but many clients are too inhibited or unsure of what to say. They require more direction. When your open-ended questions are met with blank stares, squirming, blushing, or other signs of discomfort, it's enough to make you regret ever having broached the topic. But do not give up. Patience and calm encouragement, along with the guidance of more specific questions, will usually get the ball rolling. Looking for an aspect of the client's sexuality that is the least threatening—the easiest to talk about first—may provide the direction.

> THERAPIST: "What is your sexual life like these days?"
>
> JOYCE: "I don't know what you mean. . . like, am I seeing anyone?"
>
> THERAPIST: "Sure . . . we can start there."
>
> JOYCE: "Well, I've been dating this guy, Steven, for 3 months. We have been sexual . . ."(long silence).
>
> THERAPIST: "How has that been for you? Are you enjoying the sexual relationship?"
>
> JOYCE: "It's okay" (silence).
>
> THERAPIST: "Is Steven your first sexual partner?"
>
> JOYCE: "No" (silence).

THERAPIST: "Tell me about the first one."

JOYCE: "I was 15 and he was a year ahead of me in high school. My parents didn't approve of him because he smoked and hung out with a crowd they didn't like. But I wasn't having a good year and he was an escape for me. He had a car and we would go driving around after school . . . . I told my mother I had to stay after school for one thing or another."

THERAPIST: "What were the circumstances that led up to your being sexual with him?"

JOYCE: "I didn't really want to, but he did and I didn't want to lose him. The first time was in his car. . . . I didn't really get anything out of it. We went together until he graduated and went to work. We were sexual the whole time, but I never really felt good about it. I didn't trust him. Later, after he broke up with me, I heard he had been with others, and I really felt used and angry with myself. . . . I think it warped me or something. Sex has never been all that good. I don't get much out of it. I think I just do it to stay in a relationship."

In this case, the therapist helped Joyce by being willing to start with whatever Joyce brought up, *"like, am I seeing anyone?"* Even so, Joyce was reticent, and so, rather than push her beyond a question or two, the therapist switched gears and inquired about her earlier experiences. Joyce had an easier time responding to this question and was then able to relax enough to go back to talking about Steven. Had she not seemed more comfortable, her therapist might have chosen to keep the focus on past experiences and inquire about Steven at another time.

Talking with Couples

Talking to a couple about sexuality requires a sensitivity to three issues that do not appear when talking to an individual client:

1. The absence of communication about sexuality in most couples;
2. The distortion of facts that may occur when one or both partners fear correcting the other when telling their sexual story; and
3. The presence of private sexual thoughts, experiences, and secrets.

Many couples, even those who enjoy an active and rich sexual life together, do not necessarily feel comfortable talking about their sexual desires, needs, fantasies, or fears. Youth and good health enable them to *be* sexual without having to talk about it. Inviting partners to describe their sexual life together may produce an embarrassment and inhibition that might not be present if either one was talking to you alone. Partners will usually giggle, look at each other helplessly, or in some other way convey an amused discomfort as they acknowledge, "We never talk about this!"

Talking to partners about their sexuality requires a respect for each person's private feelings, wishes, and behaviors. These should be addressed only in an individual session. Many therapists prefer to begin with a conjoint interview rather than with each person separately, to get a sense of the quality of the relationship between the two people and to establish their role as being responsible for both parties and therefore aligned with neither. However, it is wise to schedule at least one individual session with each partner early in the assessment so that both know from the beginning that they will have some private time in which to discuss those feelings or life experiences that have never been shared with their partner or that cannot be discussed with as much candor in front of their partner. Presenting this format at the first session as "routine" reassures each partner that this is not being suggested because the therapist has gotten the indication that there are big secrets being withheld.

The difference between "private" and "secret" sexual feelings and behaviors is an important but sometimes confusing one. Private sexual thoughts are the myriad of images, fantasies, and attractions that do not impact on one's real sexual relationship, but that one might not want to share with one's partner because to do so would be unnecessarily hurtful and would serve no useful purpose—for example, "I think my neighbor is cute," "I had a dream last night about an old boyfriend," or "I found myself flirting a little with that woman at the sales meeting last week." Secret sexual thoughts or behaviors are those that are impacting the relationship negatively or would be if discovered, or those that represent a betrayal of a vow, agreement, or shared value system—for example, having an extramarital affair or avoiding sex with a partner because of a persistent sexual fantasy that interferes with lovemaking. Some behaviors fall somewhere in the middle. Masturbation, for example, in some couples is a shared and openly accepted behavior; in others, it is a private behavior that one or both partners engage in but do not discuss, and sometimes it is a secret either because it is accompanied by deviant fantasy or because it is a breach of a shared value system that prohibits it.

This distinction between private and secret sometimes poses a dilemma for the therapist, who hears personal and undisclosed sexual information from one or both partners that may be negatively impacting their sexual relationship. Making the correct determination whether that information can harmlessly remain private or whether its privacy will undermine a successful outcome if not shared with the partner is never a certainty. Open and frank discussion with the holder of the information regarding the power of the material being withheld is the proper first step in making the difficult determination.

THERAPIST: "You've told me about seeing another woman right now and your inability to make a decision about whether or not you want to remain in the marriage. Yet you want me to see you and your wife in marital counseling and concentrate on your sexual relationship."

SAM: "I'm hoping that if our sex life improves, it will be easier to give up seeing Janet. Part of the reason I continue to see Janet is because sex with my wife has never been good. She has never expressed any interest in being sexual with me."

THERAPIST: "Marriages usually have little to no chance of improving while there is an affair going on. Your emotional energy is elsewhere. And it would not be right for me to counsel the two of you, withholding this information from your wife. Neither of you can successfully work on your marital sexual relationship if she isn't aware of one of the major issues that is now pulling you away."

SAM: "I'll take your word for it, but I can't tell her. I know she will leave me and I'm not ready to end my marriage. What do I do now?"

I have always been amazed when a spouse presents me with this dilemma. I wonder what people were thinking when they agreed to come to marital counseling, knowing that they were involved in an affair and were neither ready to give it up nor to reveal it. I feel like they are asking me to be a magician and wave my magic wand to make everything turn out okay. That said, I explore the options when we reach this impasse: Tell your partner; stop the affair; leave your marriage; or take a time out and get some individual therapy to sort out ending one relationship or the other before you work on the one remaining.

THE COMPONENTS OF SEXUAL EXPRESSION

Demonstrating interest, asking friendly questions, and being relatively accepting of what clients have to say will go a long way toward helping them tell their sexual story. But these actions are not enough. Sexual stories are comprised of three components that cannot be readily expressed unless facilitated by the educated listener. Just as physical distress is more accurately described only after the physician has guided the patient through a series of questions that reflect the physician's knowledge about what might be wrong, so it is with sexual distress. Obtaining the complete sexual story requires that the therapist have a professional conceptual framework. I propose the following framework: Sexual expression is the product of the interweaving of identity, function, and relational meaning. Each of these three components is multifaceted and requires separate investigation by the therapist.

I. Sexual Identity

Gender identity and orientation merge to create sexual identity. Gender refers to both biological sex—that is, male or female—and the more subjective sense of self as either masculine or feminine. A relatively small number of people are distressed about their biological gender and are confused by their strong, persistent wishes to be the opposite sex. They may express this directly, in their search for a therapist who will help them get hormones or surgery to "correct the gender mistake," or they may present with a host of symptoms, such as cross dressing, body dysmorphia, mutilation of breasts or genitals, and efforts to prevent, delay, hide, or reverse aspects of sexual development—for example, binding or "hiding" the male genitals or breasts. Often there is an accompanying depression and failure to fit in with one's peers.

More frequently, however, gender issues involve a subjective sense of inadequacy and failure to live up to some yardstick of femininity or masculinity. Males express this in a number of ways: dissatisfaction with their body (I'm too short, thin, fat, soft), athletic ability or lack thereof (I am slow, uncoordinated, clumsy, weak), personality (I'm too sensitive, passive, shy, easily intimidated), interests (I am not interested in sports, cars, tools), and sexual prowess (I don't know how to make the move, won't be able to perform, won't satisfy my partner; my penis is too small). Females will also express this in terms of their body (I'm too tall, big, flat-chested) and concerns about sexual desirability and performance, but culture allows for a much wider range of behaviors that, though not strictly feminine, will not damage a feminine self-image. Thus females are more likely to enjoy more "masculine" pursuits such as athletics, interest in sports, a career in business, and so forth, without compromising their sense of femininity.

A negative gender identity sense can lead to low self-esteem, avoidance of partner-related sex and intimacy, and social and emotional isolation. Gentle inquiry about a client's gender identity is illustrated in the following questions:

- How did you feel about the changes in your body that took place during adolescence?
- How do you feel about your body now?
- Do your interests fit in with the interests of your peers?
- Do you feel more comfortable with males or females?
- Do you share interests more with males or females?

Such questions focus on body image, gender preferences, and gender role and will reveal areas of gender conflict.

Orientation refers to the linkage of sexual feelings with an attraction to another person. Orientation does not require actual sexual behavior—that is, one often knows that one is homosexually or heterosexually inclined long before one is ready to participate in partner-related sexual activity. However, the terms *heterosexual* and *homosexual* are often used to indicate either subjective interest or actual behavior or both. This is not a problem if both the subjective and objective aspects of orientation are congruent, but it can be confusing and misleading if the two are not. For example, if a married man has sexual fantasies exclusively about males even when he is making love to his wife, is he a heterosexual because he is engaged in sex with a female or is he homosexual because the objects of his sexual attraction are exclusively male? The following use of language may help differentiate the objective and subjective components of orientation:

Objective	Subjective
Contact with opposite sex partner (heterosexual)	Fantasy about opposite sex (heteroerotic)
Contact with same sex partner (homosexual)	Fantasy about same sex (homoerotic)
Contact with both sex partners (bisexual)	Fantasy about both sexes (bierotic)
Contact with neither sex (asexual)	Fantasy about neither sex (anerotic)

Therapists need to be clear that the subjective and objective aspects of orientation are distinct from each other and cannot be assumed from one another. When talking about orientation, you must always inquire about fantasies and behaviors with both opposite- and same-sex partners. It is best not to assume a heterosexual orientation by asking questions that steer in that direction, such as asking a male, *Who was your first girlfriend?* It's better one should say, *Tell me about your first sexual experience.* After a client has described his or her opposite-sex experiences or feelings, it is appropriate and wise to inquire, *How about same-sex experiences . . . have you ever had any or thought that you might like to?* Although there is a slight risk that your client may be offended, that reaction can be managed by a matter-of-fact reply, *Well, many people do and it's always better to ask.* The goal is to give permission to *everyone* to speak about sexual feelings or behaviors that they may fear revealing.

II. Sexual Functioning

Sexual functioning refers to the actual process of engaging in sexual behavior and the myriad of little and big things that can go wrong. Clients often present with complaints about some aspect of their or their partner's ability to function sexually. We break sexual functioning into three separate but interwoven phenomena; desire, arousal, and orgasm. Desire and arousal can precede or follow each other. An increase in one usually

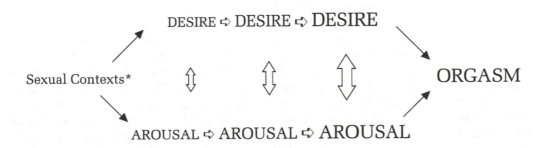

*These may be drive, fantasy, interpersonal, touching, or anything else that leads to sexual excitement.

FIGURE 1.1. The Interplay of Desire and Arousal

augments an increase in the other—in other words, the better it feels, the more I want it, and the more I want it, the better it feels.

Sexual desire is, in turn, composed of the interaction of three elements:

- A biological urge referred to as drive
- A cognitive wish to engage in sexual behavior
- An emotional willingness to allow one's body to respond to a sexual experience

Although men's desire, especially that of young men, is often most determined by drive, women's desire is often more defined by the psychological receptivity to an external sexual overture. Desire is complex, and ascertaining the nature of a patient's desire will take more than the question *How often do you desire sex?* Asking several of the following questions will be necessary.

How often does your body need a sexual release?
How often do you masturbate?
Do you think about making love with your partner when he or she is not around?
How do you feel when your partner initiates sexual contact?
How often would you have sex if you could?

Sexual arousal is a bodily experience, a subjective "horniness" or excitement that may be described as a warm, tingling, and increasingly pleasurable sensation; often, but not always, it is accompanied by increased blood flow to the pelvic area, resulting in an erection and vulvar swelling and lubrication. Arousal, or the lack thereof, is usually easier to describe than desire.

Questions might include:

How does it feel when your partner stimulates you?
Do you experience a pleasurable sensation when your breasts, genitals are touched?
Do you get an erection when exposed to sexual stimulation?
Are you aware of lubricating when your partner stimulates you?
Does sensation build up as the stimulation continues?

Orgasm, the rhythmic contractions and accompanying pleasurable sensations, is the culmination of sexual excitement. The word *climax* is often used instead, as is the more colloquial expression "to come." It is rare to encounter a male who has never experienced an orgasm through self or partner stimulation. Male complaints about orgasm usually center on their inability to control the timing of it. Either they climax too quickly to suit their or their partner's needs, or they find it very difficult to accomplish. The former is a common complaint of young and relatively inexperienced males; the latter of males who may be taking medications that interfere with or delay orgasm. It is not rare, however, to encounter females who have never experienced orgasm. This is most likely due to a number of factors, including females' greater susceptibility to cultural taboos about self-exploration, less biological urge, and greater internal conflict about expressing sexual longings. Female complaints typically center on their inability to build up enough arousal to reach orgasm or a sense of being "left hanging" at a peak of arousal, with no prospect of orgasmic relief.

> AMY: "It feels good, but it doesn't go anywhere. . . . Ken keeps touching me, but after a while I lose the feelings and it actually gets unpleasant. I get frustrated and push his hand away."

Concerns about absent, low, or high sexual desire; difficulties in achieving or maintaining arousal; and problems with the timing or achievement of orgasm are highly prevalent in the general population and are referred to as sexual dysfunctions. When they have always been present, we describe them as "lifelong" or primary; when they reflect a distinct change in sexual functioning, we describe them as "acquired" or secondary. When they occur in all situations—that is, with all partners and self-stimulation—we call them "global," and when they occur only in some situations, that is, with one partner but not another, or with a partner but not with self-stimulation, we describe them as "situational."

> *Rosemary is a 25-year-old single woman who has never been orgasmic with a partner. She is able to bring herself to orgasm through masturbation, but "shuts down" when any partner attempts to stimulate her to orgasm (lifelong, situational anorgasmia).*

> *John is a 60-year-old married man who has not been able to achieve a satisfactory erection for 5 years. Morning erections are nonexistent, erections via masturbation are floppy, and he is no longer able to achieve penetration during lovemaking (acquired, global erectile dysfunction).*

Lifelong dysfunctions reflect some impediment in the development of a comfortable sexual self. Rosemary's ability to stimulate herself to orgasm suggests a mastery of her own sexual sensations, but her inability to be orgasmic with a partner probably represents her inhibition about letting go, a fear of being perceived as "too" sexual if she demonstrates what kind of stimulation she needs, or her unrecognized link between sexual arousal and being "bad." Because this has taken place with all sexual partners, it will not be fruitful to spend too much time exploring the dynamics with a particular partner; it makes more sense to explore childhood and familial sexual experiences, attitudes, messages, and beliefs that may have negatively impacted her comfort level with a partner.

We understand acquired sexual dysfunctions to mean that the person successfully navigated the development of a comfortable sexual self before something undermined his or her success. The destructive force may be a physical change such as illness, injury, medication, radiation, or surgery or an emotional change as a result of personal, partner, or familial discord. Some acquired sexual dysfunctions can be traced to both physical and emotional changes. The emotions that most commonly interfere with sexual functioning are anxiety, guilt, fear, anger, and sadness. John's erectile failure may reflect a change in his physical health, a deterioration in his marriage, a personal depression, guilt over an affair, or other stressors. Therefore, the right approach would be to focus on what was going on 5 years ago, not on John's early childhood and sexual development.

> John reports that 5 years ago he was passed over for a promotion that he was certain he was going to receive. At the same time his physician encouraged him to lose some weight, after a glucose tolerance test suggested borderline diabetes. He lost some of the weight, but it has been a constant struggle.

John's failure to be promoted may have created depression, anxiety about his vocational future, anger at his employer, or guilt over his perceived less-than-stellar work performance. These feelings could negatively impact his ability to relax and receive sexual stimulation. The borderline diabetes presents two concerns; not only is diabetes highly correlated with erectile difficulties, it may well have been a blow to his view of himself as healthy and vital. His ongoing battle to lose weight may be accompanied by feelings of deprivation, the sense of inadequate discipline, and a negative body image. All of these may have contributed to John's acquired erectile problems.

When clients report multiple sexual difficulties, we must obtain an accurate picture of each of these. Ultimately, we want to understand how they relate to each other.

> John now reports a lack of desire for sexual relations. Five years ago he kept trying to have sex and occasionally climaxed with a partial erection. He has not attempted to masturbate or initiate sex with his wife for several years. He avoids spending evenings with his wife and waits until she is asleep before retiring. He reports low self-esteem and a preoccupation with his mortality. "I am an old man."

The Sexual Equilibrium: Understanding the sexual functioning of a couple begins with the realization that the sexual function of one partner always has an impact on the other. Each partner's component characteristics—desire, arousal, orgasm patterns—impact on the other person, whether these components are positive or problematic. His premature ejaculation may bring about her lack of orgasm; her loss of sexual motivation may induce his loss of desire or, conversely, his hyperdesire as he attempts to woo her back. We refer to the balancing act that occurs within every couple's life as the "sexual equilibrium." It continually occurs and accounts for the different outcomes from partner to partner and from episode to episode with the same partner.

III. Relational Meaning

Most people aspire to enter into an intimate, caring, and trusting relationship with another person that will, at some point, lead to a commitment to monogamy and permanency. They bring to each other their respective gender identities and orientation, their ability to function as sexual beings, and any problems accumulated along the way. The decision to be sexual, whether made after 1 night or 2 years, almost always has a relational meaning, conveys something about how the person feels about the other one, and shows the role sexual behavior will play in conveying that feeling. These meanings can promote or prevent intimacy. Consider these 10, usually unstated, relational meanings about having sex.

1. I will have sex with you because I love you.
2. I will have sex with you to see if I love you.
3. I will have sex with you because I don't love you.
4. I will have sex with you so that you will love me.
5. I will have sex with you to get closer to you.
6. I will have sex with you to avoid getting closer to you.
7. I will have sex with you so that you will belong to me.
8. I will have sex with you to prove that I can.
9. I will have sex with you to dominate you.
10. I will have sex with you to hurt you.

When the motivation to be sexual is based on affection, caring, and a genuine desire to be with the other person, the meaning of the sexual exchange will lend itself to emotional satisfaction and increased intimacy. When the motivation to be sexual is, however, based on a need to avoid intimacy or to dominate, control, or hurt the other person, the meaning of the sexual exchange may be experienced by the partner as distressing, uncomfortable, frightening, or traumatic, even if there is no actual coercion.

> ELAINE: "Arthur never wants to have sex with me except when I get home late and he accuses me of being with other men. He badgers me for hours about where I've been, and he persists in wanting sex even though I tell him I am tired and need to sleep. Eventually, I give in because I know he is upset and I feel bad."

You can gain access to your client's relational meaning by both inquiring about the motivation to be sexual with the partner *and* asking about the sexual fantasies that the client relies on during self-stimulation or with the partner. Motivations and fantasies are intensely personal, private aspects of a sexual history and must be approached in the most gentle, nonjudgmental manner.

Here are some questions about motivation:

What determines when you feel ready to be sexual with a partner?
What are you feeling when you wish to be sexual with your partner?
When in the course of a relationship do you usually become sexual with a partner?
How do you feel about being sexual with your partner?
Why do you not feel like being sexual with your partner?

Here are some questions about sexual fantasies:

What do you usually fantasize about when you masturbate?
Do you ever find yourself fantasizing about something else while engaged in sex?
What imagery in pornography are you most drawn to?
Do you ever fantasize about sexual behaviors you would be reluctant to do?

The more conventional the imagery, the easier it will be to reveal it. It is a lot easier to relate a fantasy about walking on the beach, holding hands with an opposite-sex partner at sunset, than it is to talk about fantasies about same-sex partners, a wish to be sexual with a minor, or a desire to force someone to do something unwanted. In those situations, the therapist should not expect that even the gentlest approach will necessarily elicit an honest, accurate response. With time and patience, the trust level may build up enough for the client to feel increasingly willing to reveal more. Periodically revisiting questions about the more personal and private aspects of sexual fantasy and behavior, along with a face-saving comment such as *"I know we've talked about this before, but perhaps other things have come to mind since then,"* will often yield new and valuable information.

Disorders of Relational Meaning: When the meaning or purpose of engaging in sexual behavior is unusual, hostile, dehumanizing, or coercive, therapists term these urges and behaviors *paraphilias*. The paraphilias are characterized by recurrent, intense, sexually arousing fantasies, sexual urges, or behaviors generally involving (1) nonhuman objects, (2) the suffering or humiliation of oneself or one's partner, or (3) children or other nonconsenting persons that occur over a period of at least 6 months. Exhibitionism, voyeurism, fetishism, pedophilia, and sadomasochism are some of the most common. Many therapists recoil in disgust, anxiety, or both when they are initially confronted with a paraphilic disorder. They are quick to say, "I don't treat that!" and refer to a specialist. Although seeking out an expert in paraphilic disorders may be appropriate, especially if the behavior involves legal consequences, the ideal first step is to discuss the topic in a helpful manner. The development of this skill increases the likelihood that the client will accept the referral to an expert. To attain this, we must suspend the anxiety and negative judgments that we have acquired over the years about these matters and put forth our intellectual curiosity. It helps to realize that most clients with these disorders are deeply troubled and ashamed of their behavior. Your willingness to discuss the subject will provide them with an opportunity to come out from hiding and get help.

Patients may voluntarily disclose a paraphilic disorder, but more typically, such disorders are not revealed unless the person is "outed" by the law, a spouse, or an employer. When the disorder is revealed by a spouse in a conjoint session, the therapist should offer additional individual time with the patient to explore the issue further.

AMY: "Ken and I haven't made love in a long time. Yesterday I went into his study to look for a bill and I noticed the computer was on. Ken was upstairs with one of the kids. I looked to see what was on the screen and I was horrified to see pornography. It was a woman tied up and a man standing over her. I looked further and there were dozens of photos of bondage. Our kids could have seen this!"

KEN: "I forgot to turn it off when I left. It's no big deal. I just look occasionally."

AMY: "It is a big deal! You've been spending hours on the computer lately. Last weekend you stayed up until 3 A.M. both nights and you overslept Monday morning and missed a meeting. You used to ask me if I would let you tie me up during sex, but it turned me off. You said it was no big deal then, but sex has been practically nonexistent between us for a long time!"

This interchange is typical, in that Amy reveals Ken's "secret," which he then minimizes or denies. The therapist's initial understanding of the problem will come from Amy's observations, but the establishment of a therapeutic alliance with Ken will come only if Ken is given the opportunity to explore his sexuality with the therapist privately. If this interferes with the therapist's role as a marriage counselor, referral to an individual therapist for Ken is in order. The careful delineation of identity, function, and relational meaning as they evolve and influence each other over a lifetime will yield a sexual story, each one rich and unique. You may feel at times that the book has been opened for you at chapter 10. Just as you settle into the storyline, the pages flip to the beginning . . . or the ending . . . or just about anywhere. Relax. With your interest and guidance, the storyline will come together.

IT'S NOT SO HARD ANYMORE

So here I am, 27 years later, still interested in the complexity of sexual expression and the infinite number of ways people conduct their sexual lives. It's definitely easier now to do this work. For one thing, all of the experiences in my own life have contributed to my ever-expanding frame of reference. No one questions me anymore about how I acquired my knowledge about sexuality. I've earned the badge (and the grey hairs) of maturity.

You don't have to wait until middle age, however, to be good at this work. Your willingness to help clients tell their sexual story for even a few months will catapult you far ahead of the majority of your colleagues who refer out to a sex therapist at the mention of the word *sex* or avoid the subject altogether. You will be rewarded with grateful and appreciative clients, opportunities to help people sort through intensely private and personal issues to gain understanding, and, if you are anything like me, a deeper appreciation of your own sexual expression. Return to this chapter after you have familiarized yourself with the contents of the other chapters. The combination of your expanding knowledge about sexuality, along with the guidelines I've discussed, will place you in an excellent position to do good work.

Chapter Two

What Patients Mean by Love, Intimacy, and Sexual Desire

Stephen B. Levine, MD

PREFACE

For the first 20 or so years of my career, I refused my inclinations to write about love. I knew, of course, that love was important to sexual happiness and disappointment, but I considered myself too young for the task. I thought my decision wise because the psychoanalytic pieces on the subject that I encountered seemed incomprehensible to me. Instead of love, I began to write about sexual desire and several years later about psychological intimacy. When I was finally ready to write about love in the mid-90s, I was delighted to discover that I could comprehend the literature on love.

Two ideas sustain my interest in writing about love. First is my conviction that love is the most cross-culturally honored context from which to view sexual experience.[1] Second is the observation that my patients talk a lot about their love lives.

In this chapter I want to provide a background for understanding the key issues that determine sexual health and psychogenic dysfunction that readers will encounter as they take care of people with sexual concerns. I hope I can prevent some readers from spending as many years as I did before I learned to appreciate what patients mean when they talk about love, desire, and intimacy.

WHAT IS LOVE?

Love Is Far More Than a Feeling

The assumption that love is a feeling is so ubiquitous that it seems unquestioningly correct. Few of us are indicating a discrete feeling, however, when we tell anyone that we love him or her. Love as a feeling is usually synonymous with pleasure. We commonly say, "I love this sweater, this music, beer, or my sister," for instance. When the pleasure from any person, activity, or thing is more intense, love is used to connote joy.

But joyful moments, such as having one's marriage proposal accepted, giving birth, or having one's team win the championship, probably consist of at least four feelings: joy, gratitude, pride, and awe.

Affects are hardwired universal human capacities for feeling.[2] Almost all humans can feel sadness, fear, guilt, anger, sexual arousal, defiance, shame, and so forth. Each of these emotional states exists on a continuum of intensity. The capacity for anger, for instance, ranges from annoyance to rage. Love is the label we give to our transient experiences that combine various degrees of pleasure and interest. The affect of pleasure ranges through joy to exhilaration, whereas that of interest ranges through fascination and excitement. Affects, however, tend to comingle.

Your patients may say, "I don't know if I love my partner." This often means, "On balance, I no longer experience much pleasure with and have little interest in this person."

Love Is an Idealized Ambition

Love is so intensely celebrated in culture that few people can grow up without longing to realize it.[3] We generally aspire to a love that combines mutual respect, behavioral reliability, enjoyment of one another, sexual fidelity, psychological intimacy, sexual pleasure, and a comfortable balance of individuality and couplehood.[4] The ambition is to abide with a person in such a way as to enhance each other's opportunities for mental and physical health, sexual pleasure, vocational accomplishment, financial stability, parenting, and so forth. Partners are chosen with the tacit purpose of accompanying, assisting, emotionally stabilizing, and enriching us as we evolve, mature, and cope with life's other demands.

When your patient declares, "I love my partner!" it may mean, "I have not personally given up on this grand cultural ambition."

Love Is a Commitment

The clergy, who ritualize and sanctify marriage, are very clear about love: it is a commitment. Joy may attend the ceremony for the participants, but their transient emotional intensity is not the main point. The love that is being celebrated is the public commitment of two people to honor and cherish each other through all of life's vicissitudes. It is this love that restructures life and generates a whole new set of meanings and obligations. Committed love is a developmental step.

"I love my partner" often refers more to the commitment to the partner than to the emotions currently felt about that person.

The experience of the partner is a separate matter. After we have made the commitment to love, we gradually come to recognize our partner's limitations for us. The negative emotions that stem from our disappointment do not quickly cancel our love for our partners. This in large part is because our love for them stems from our ambition and commitment to happily abide with them. We buffer our disappointment by focusing on an array of competing life demands ("I have children to raise."), defense mechanisms ("I keep telling myself that no partner is ideal."), and self-management techniques ("Take a deep breath and focus on your work!"). When our buffering works, we think of our experience with our partner, though not continuously or completely harmonious, as good enough.

When your committed patient asserts that "I love my partner, but I am not certain that I am in love with him (her)," what is being communicated is that the patient no longer can idealize the partner.

Love Is a Force of Nature

Love is also something beyond a feeling, an ambition, and a commitment. It is a force in nature that creates a unity out of two individuals. It casts our fates together, organizes reproduction, and then remains vital to human growth and development.[5]

"I love my partner, but I am no longer in love with her (him)" may reflect the sense that we have shared so much of our lives that I know my partner is inextricably part of me. Nature has had its role. It is just that I don't enjoy her (him) very much anymore.

BECOMING A COUPLE

The first phase of establishing a relationship is scripted by culture. The process is supposed to be a wondrous experience of two people finding each other—as Plato put it, two souls finding their missing other halves.[6] Stories of two people overcoming obstacles and falling in love hold an endless charm for us. Many people, however, establish a relationship without following the script. They have to act the part.

One possible meaning of "I will grow to love him (her)" is that the person does not take the dominant Western cultural script as a trustworthy guide. Like cultures that have long arranged marriages, the person hopes that sharing a life will trigger the processes of love. What are these processes?

Falling in Love: One Person

Falling in love is a one-person intrapsychic process stimulated by some, even slight, experience with a would-be partner. These experiences generate a positive assessment of the person's social merits—attractive, employed, similar values, similar life experience, available, comparably intelligent, and so forth. They stimulate a crucial act of imagination. When the would-be partner is privately designated as "the one," three new processes appear: a sense of excitement, motivation to be with this person, and worry about being "crazy." Often such romantic excursions are followed by disappointment, embarrassment, and self-castigation about one's foolishness. Many people, however, do not give up on these one-sided loves. They mentally hold the person as beloved for long periods, sometimes years. Please do not think that this process is rare or confined to adolescence.

Falling in Love: Requited Love: Being in Love

People who fall in love are often keenly aware of the need for something different in their lives. This need for psychological or social change is likely to be the predisposing factor to "falling." Others, watching us, comment on our defenses. Lovers are often privately accused of having exaggerated the capacities and minimized the limitations of their newly beloved. They are thought to be either unrealistically idealizing each other or naively not appreciating the implications of what they do see.

It is difficult to think clearly while falling because we expect love to transform us into a better person and an improved life. Unbridled hope is intoxicating. Clinicians should not be surprised to learn, however, that despite the exhilaration, falling in love is accompanied by anxieties about being damaged from disappointment.

As social experiences reinforce each person's private positive assessment of the other, intimate touching begins to appear. In the uncertain, often-turbulent processes of two people ascertaining whether they are simultaneously falling in love, their willingness to behave sexually often reaches a pinnacle. Whether sexual behavior consists of slow, gradual, tentative explorations of each other's bodies or quickly attained genital union, sex is wanted, is rehearsed mentally, and is experienced with a deliciousness that is long recalled. When these early sexual pleasures enhance the sense of rightness of the union, the partners' attachment to one another deepens. This uncommitted state is often designated passionate love. Therapists need to recognize that while "passionate" conveys the sexual desire inherent in early love, what is passionately desired is far more than sex. It is a desire to be happy, to be understood, to be in agreement about important things, to live an exalted, extraordinary life.[7]

When lovers tell one another that they "love" each other, they are saying, "I have imagined a fine life with you." The lovers cannot then be together too much. The world of others tends to disappear, as they privately relish the idea that they have become their newly beloved's beloved. The recognition that each has idealized the other creates the sense of *being in love*. Exhilaration predominates. Once this has occurred, the attainment of their imagined life becomes the organizing force for much of their subsequent behavior. Their emotional intensity begins to diminish. As they begin to deal with practical matters, they more acutely notice their new partner's coping style. Many couples soon destruct over what they learn about each other in this process. When couples do not run into major dissatisfactions with what seems to be the character of the lover, the issue of commitment begins to loom. They wonder, "Do we move in together? Marry? When? Why not soon?" For many people, the matter of commitment introduces an anxiety that may ruin the relationship, even though the pleasures of the relationship are great. The reasons for not making the commitment are often carefully guarded from the would-be spouse.

Staying in Love

Staying in love is the product of two ongoing hidden mental activities: the assessment of the partner's character (appraisal) and the granting of cooperation (bestowal).[8] People often erroneously assume that their partners simply and constantly love them. But a partner notices the other's behavior, interprets it, and decides whether or not to behave lovingly. When "love" can be genuinely bestowed, it is typically immediately reflected in cooperation, affection, and enjoyment of the partner. The vital unseen consequence of positive appraisal and mutual bestowal is the shoring up of the idealized internal image of the beloved.

Although we do not love our partners constantly, we allow them to think that we do. They make these erroneous assumptions because we do genuinely feel pleasure in their company sometimes. And when we do not, our commitment to behave in a kind, helpful fashion may carry the moment. Our idealized image of our partner enables us to act loving because we do feel loving toward the partner's image—if not to the actual partner sulking upstairs. Continuing negative appraisals, however, interfere with sensations we called love, the commitment to love, and the internal image of the partner as worthy of our affection and cooperation.

Love Is the Private Relationship We Have to the Image of Our Partner

Falling in love, being in love, and staying in love are phases of our internal relationship with our partners. Of course, they are based on transactions with them, but these transactions are mediated through the meanings that we attribute to their behaviors. Meaning making is a profoundly individual process that continually remakes our internal image of our partner. Love exists in privacy.

Falling in Love Again

After divorce, during widowhood, and even during an extramarital affair, a person can fall in love another time. But because time, maturation, and many life experiences have passed, the illusions of falling in love tend to fade away, leaving the person with a practical assessment of the social assets of the partner. Unlike the first time in youth, there is little defense against thinking clearly about the question, "What will this person bring to my life—socially, economically, aesthetically, recreationally, sexually, medically, time to death, and so forth?"

When your patient is considering a new partner and says to you, "I'm not sure I'm in love with him (her)," this often means that "I think I'm too old for the romanticism of my youth, yet I'm uncertain whether this is a required prelude to happiness. Tell me, doctor, what do you think?"

MORE TERMINOLOGY

Sternberg has described six typologies of love, based on how three essential character-istics are arranged:[9]

1. *Infatuation* = passion (sexual desire) without commitment or intimacy (friendship). This corresponds to the one-person falling in love.
2. *Romantic Love* = passion and intimacy. This corresponds to being in love.
3. *Consummate Love* = passion, intimacy, and commitment. This is culture's ideal be-ginning for marriage.
4. *Companionate Love* = intimacy and commitment. This is the ideal picture of older persons' love.
5. *Fatuous Love* = passion and commitment without intimacy. Fatuous means silly.
6. *Empty Love* = commitment without intimacy or passion.

The first four categories represent the usual ideal evolution of love.[10] Companion-ate love eventually emerges from long-lasting consummate love, despite much hard work by couples and prosexual drugs. The timing varies from couple to couple. The fifth and sixth categories are often encountered in our patients at eras of life where regular sexual behavior is expected.

A Glimpse of a Fatuous Sexual Phase

In the last 6 months she was aware that I might be leaving because I told her I was thinking about it. She could not talk about it. Dammit! She never could talk about her inner experience of anything. She began to want to have more sex. At first I went along with it, but because I felt so alienated from her, this became increasingly difficult. When her nightly initiations felt pathetic to me, I refused. Without words, we both knew it was over.

A Glimpse of an Empty Love

SHE: "Yes, I love him, I guess, but how can I know it, how can I feel it when he is so consistently aggravating? And he expects me to have sex with him!"

HE: "I know she loves me. So why can't she have sex with me sometimes? I said I was sorry!"

SHE: "You say you are sorry all the time, but your behavior does not change."

From Love to Sexual Desire

Rather than speak of love, mental health professionals speak of attachment.[11] This is a good-enough objectifying term for the sexualized bond between people and its representation in each person's mind. Sexual desire is both a means of attachment and a reflector of its quality. In the next section, I'm going to discuss desire and only slowly come to define it for you.

UNDERSTANDING SEXUAL DESIRE

The Spectrum

Even during periods of stable happy relationships, sexual desire is remarkably changeable, fluctuating from intensely positive, through neutral, to intensely negative. In the positive range, people feel their desire in their bodies, as when they utter sentences such as "I'm so horny!" In the neutral range people grant sexual behavior primarily because of the other person's expressed desire. This is referred to as receptivity. Negative desires range from the prospect of sex being unappealing to the more intense, "I can't stand the thought of sex with you tonight!"

The ordinary spectrum of sexual desire looks like this:

Aversion—Indifference—Interest—Need—Passion

Sexual desire consists of two components: an interest in behaving sexually and the emotional intensity of that interest. The valence can be either positive or negative.

The ill-defined word *passion* is sometimes referred to with the poorly defined term *lust*. Whereas passion connotes the emotionally rich aspiration to restructure life through love and continued psychological intimacy, lust connotes the intensity of desire generated by high levels of sexual arousal. Although both women and men experience passion and lust, women more often invoke *passion*[12] and men more often invoke *lust*.[13] Either term might be used to anchor the right side of the spectrum. Ultimately, they both convey intensity.

When a patient complains of a desire problem, the spectrum of that person's experience is not usually emphasized.

Sexual Temperament

Clinicians need a word for the strength of desire over long periods of time. We have not agreed what the word should be, but it needs to convey desire's capacity to organize a person's life. It has to communicate that desire can behave like a ferocious tiger or a secretive house cat. Here are four commonly invoked ways of expressing sexual temperament:

"All 20-year-old men's ids are not alike."

"After his wife became psychiatrically ill upon discovery of his 5-year sexual addiction, he entered into a phase in which his libido all but disappeared."

"She never had much sexual energy."

"My third wife was the most sexual woman I have ever known."

The Evolution of Sexual Desire

Sexual desire evolves through the life cycle. Older people often report that they more
or less reside to the left of the middle of the spectrum. Felt episodes of desire occur less
frequently and are less intense. Although clinicians teach that humans are sexual beings from birth to death, we also convey that sex has different qualities during youth
and older age.[14] Youthful sex is intense, impatient, and a bit clumsy; older age sex is
quieter, more skillful, perhaps more emotionally satisfying and is often biologically
limited. In middle age, many people explain their decrement in desire by invoking
partner familiarity or boredom. Repetition with the same partner is a factor, but so is
the weakening of the biology of desire. Many, but not all, men in their 50s report an
increased comfort in *not* having sex as often. Many, but not all, women experience a
decrement in desire within 1 to 2 years of their natural menopause.[15] From a population perspective, the trend toward quieting of sexual desire as we move through the life
cycle is biological in origin. In any individual person's life, however, the cause may be
far more interpersonal or psychological.

Evolving Social Contexts

Clinicians understand sexual desire by first recognizing the relevant social context. As
patients move from being unattached to becoming engaged, happily married, parents,
unhappily married, having an affair, divorcing, divorced, widowed, remarried, and so
forth, their sexual desire often dramatically changes.

When young and single, we often feel an intense, desperate need to connect intimately with others as we search for an ideal life partner. As that connection is established, we celebrate it with exuberant sexual behaviors. Soon, however, despite the
expectation to continue regular and frequent sexual behavior, one or both members'
sexual desire lessens. When the couple wants to get pregnant, intense sexual motivation returns. When we want to reaffirm our love or commitment or want to convey our
remorse for our past bad behavior, sexual desire may intensely reappear. When we
grieve for a partner and later, if no replacement is available, desire may quietly slip
away.

Partner loss can also induce more motivation for sex. In the midst of bitter divorce
processes, numerous men angry at their wives seek sexual behavior at a great rate with
a large variety of partners, keeping secret from those partners and from themselves how
much private anger at "women" they are discharging through sex. After divorce, some

women worry that they have become "oversexed" because they think about sex far more than they have in many years. They have been genitally reawakened to sexual possibilities that they long felt were dead with their husbands. Their desire is a longing for attachment.

Because sexual behavior is a means of expression that does not require words, many an embarrassing sentiment—such as, I'm sorry, I missed you, or I'm angry—is carried on its wings. Most of these sentiments are private from the partner, but some may be not fully known by the person. Clinicians tend to assume that sexual desire may shift without the person being aware of the inciting source, but it simply may be that it shifts without the patient being willing to initially share its source with us. Either way, when we try to unravel the mystery of a desire problem, we get curious about subtle evolutionary processes from happily to unhappily married, from admiration to loss of respect, and from optimism to pessimism about love.

Desire Is a Political Topic

Sexual Desire Is Different for Men and Women. Every account of sexual desire runs into the matter of the differences in patterns of males and females at any given era of the life cycle.[16] This increasingly mentioned subject is not well studied. I assume there are two basic differences.

The first is that males generally have more sexual desire from puberty on. Male desire lasts longer in the life cycle and is far more reliable. Female sexual desire, being weaker, is more easily ignored and eradicated. Sexual desire distorts women's sensibilities far less than it skews men's thinking.[17] If androgenic compounds are the hormone system of desire, female desire is less strongly biologically supported. Normal young women have 10–15% of normal young men's testosterone levels. Women's desire fluctuates in response to the menstrual cycle, pregnancy, lactation, menopause, and fatigue. Women's desire is highly sensitive to subtle positive and negative interpersonal context. Each woman defines this context within her subjectivity.

The second is the differences in how men and women use psychological intimacy. Women aspire to psychological intimacy as a gateway to sex. Men aspire to sex as a gateway to the sense of closeness.

Refining desire: #1 drive. I think of these sex differences as primarily reflecting the biological aspects of desire. I use the term *drive* to describe the subjectively recognized moments of genitally felt, sex-motivating behavior. Sexual drive manifests itself in genital tingling, vaginal wetness, clitoral or penile tumescence, erotic fantasy, focus on physically appealing aspects of people's bodies, plotting for orgasm with a partner or through masturbation, and dreams of sexual activity. Drive generates patterns of sexual initiation and receptivity. The ease with which a person can forgo sexual expression is a manifestation of drive. Almost all biologically intact people have moments of sexual drive. Biological sexual drive occurs within a personality and a culture; these other sources can suppress the awareness of sexual drive.

Refining desire: #2 motive. Although sexual desire has biological underpinnings that involve the cerebral cortex, the limbic system,[18] and the endocrine system, all individuals must manage their drives. In doing so, they discover they have choices, emotions, aspirations, and stated and ulterior motives for bringing their bodies to the sexual experience with a particular person. Sexual motivation derives from individual psychology, interpersonal connection, and culture. Culture provides guidelines for how to be a good person. These are internalized in the conscience and contribute to a style of being a sexual person. How culture, subculture, school, religion, and family shape a person's willingness to know about his or her sexual self and willingness to express it to another is largely uncertain. What is certain is that culture programs the sexual mind and becomes an important part of sexual motivation. Although sexual desire always contains biological, psychological, and cultural elements, the latter two elements often arrange themselves into dilemmas or paradoxes. Chief among these are clashes between conventional pro-marriage values and impulses toward infidelity.

Sexual Temperament Creates Politics. The drive endowments of the individuals within a couple are different from one another. This forces every couple to negotiate for sex. What begins as sexual temperament in individual life becomes a private political matter for every couple. The subjects of the negotiations are the management of each partner's drives and psychological intimacy needs. Many of those who become our patients expect to negotiate with few, if any, words. We therapists need to conceptualize the possibility that inadequate negotiations play a role in generating partners' sexual withdrawal from one another. We get to see people labeled sexually "hypoactive" or "hyperactive," whose disorder ameliorates when we help them negotiate for the necessary conditions for them to conduct a regular sexual life with their partners. The therapist has to be a politically sensitive mediator and educator.

My Definition of Sexual Desire

Sexual desire is the sum of the forces that incline us toward and away from sexual behavior.[19]

PSYCHOLOGICAL INTIMACY

Because psychological intimacy is the key to maintenance of sexual motivation in new and established relationships, clinicians need to know how intimacy is generated and maintained. In a sense, we earn our livings with psychological intimacy because it is what enables us to assess, diagnose, and begin to offer our patients relief from their difficulties. Let's review what we know about how we do this. We want to be able to help others attain psychological intimacy so that they can easily negotiate with their partners for sexual experience.

The First Step

Psychological intimacy begins with one person's ability to share her or his inner experiences with another. This deceptively simple-sounding capacity actually rests upon three separate abilities:

1. The capacity to know what one feels and thinks;
2. The willingness to say it to another; and
3. The language skill to express the feelings and the ideas with words.

The crucial first step is the sharing by one person of something from within the inner self. What is shared need not be elegantly said, lofty in its content, or unusual in any way; it just needs to be from the inner experience of the self—from the continual monologue of our self-consciousness, from our subjectivity.

The Second Step

The listener has to respond to the speaker in a manner that conveys

1. A noncritical acceptance of what is being said;
2. An awareness of the importance of the moment to the speaker;
3. A grasp of what is being said; and
4. The interest in hearing what the speaker has to say.

Clinicians need to be excellent listeners. We have our subtle variations from one professional to another, but when a professional and a patient are in conversation, it is the patient's lack of self-awareness, unwillingness to share, or inability to express what is felt that should be the only obstacles to professional intimacy.

In social interactions, when a listener negatively judges what is being said by saying, "You shouldn't feel that way!" or doesn't acknowledge the significance of what is being said by impatiently remarking, "Can't this wait? Don't you see how busy I am?" or listens, but misses the point of the speaker's words, intimacy will not occur.

Definition

Psychological intimacy is the transient, rarefied pleasure of emotional connection. The pleasure has at least several components. The speaker's pleasure is in large part solace—a form of peace or contentment that results from sharing the inner self, being listened to with interest, and being comprehended. Solace is the response to being seen, known, understood, and accepted. With solace soon come a sense of excitement, energy, and an uplifting of mood. If the listener is a therapist, this combination may be stunning for the speaker because it offers hope for relief. If the listener is a social equal, it offers the hope for friendship. If the social context is dating, it offers the hope of love and sex.

The listener's pleasure results from hearing about the speaker's inner experiences. The listener is trusted enough to be told, competent enough to have enabled the telling, perceptive enough to understand the speaker's story, and wise enough to respond without censure.

Intimacy Has Two Basic Forms. If the conversation continues with the speaker speaking and the listener listening, it is one-sided; but if they switch roles, the intimacy is two-sided. One-sided psychological intimacies are common between children and their parents, patients and health-care professionals, clients and lawyers or accountants, and advice-seekers and clergy. Two-sided intimacies are the basis of friendships and love relationships and are the best day-in-day-out aphrodisiacs ever discovered. Within these two basic forms, there are countless degrees of self-disclosure and nuances of attention and understanding. No two intimacies are quite alike; each relationship is uniquely rich or poor in its possibilities.

The importance of psychological intimacy derives from what it stimulates.

The Bond, Visible and Invisible. On the way to the solace of being understood and to the pleasure and privilege of hearing another person's inner self, internal processes are stimulated within each person. Intimate conversation creates a bond between the speaker and the listener. Thereafter, each regards the other differently. The two people are together in a new way: They glance at each other differently; touch each other differently; laugh together differently; and can continue to readily discuss other aspects of their private selves.

Yet more occurs. In two-sided intimacies, a mutual attachment occurs. Social indifference toward one another is lost as each is designated special. Each listener becomes internalized within the other. Internalization weaves the listener into our psyches. This results in

1. Imagining the person when she or he is not present;
2. Inventing conversations with the person;
3. Preoccupation with the person's physical attributes;
4. Anticipation of the next opportunity to be together—that is, missing the person;
5. Dreaming about the person;
6. Thoughts about that person as a sex partner.

Our new intimate partner is not only reacted to as a unique individual, she or he stimulates thoughts, feelings, and worries that we previously experienced in relationship to others. In one-sided psychotherapeutic intimacies, we designate this as transference and try to use it to help patients understand the source of their overreactions to their partner. But such weaving of the current and past partners is also the ordinary intrapsychic response to two-sided psychological intimacy.

Eroticization. The amount of time required to imagine the person as a sex partner—that is, the speed of the eroticization provoked by intimacy—is modified by age, sex, sexual orientation, social status, purpose in talking together, the nature of other emotional commitments, and the person's attitudes toward private sexual phenomena. If the pair consists of a comparably aged, socially eligible heterosexual man and woman, the eroticization triggered by sharing some aspects of their inner selves can occur with lightning speed—in both of them. Similarly, for a homosexual pair of men or women, eroticization can occur in a flash. The stimulation of the erotic imagination may never occur, may take a long time to occur, or may occur in only a fleeting, disguised way, depending on how these factors line up.

Friendships are valued because they afford an opportunity to share the self without the intrapsychic burden of eroticization. But clinicians need to be quietly alert about friendships. The specific emotional experiences that occur as a result of intimate conversations are usually guarded with extreme care. They can be exceedingly exciting, both generally and erotically. Some individuals who are new to intimate conversations may have fear about their intense responses to their new friend. They feel so excited that they wonder if they are losing their mind. The processes of a new psychological intimacy with a friend are strikingly similar to falling in love.

When people recognize that they are falling in love with a potential sexual partner, they at least have the culture's teaching to understand their general and erotic excitement. Some friendships, however, end abruptly without satisfying explanation because one person cannot tolerate the excitement it creates. In response to the private eroticization of the mutually revealing conversations, the individual may worry that the relationship is "homosexual" or could lead to sexual behavior.

Some individuals are so unnerved by their responses to psychological intimacy that they extol emotional closeness, but subvert it when it is near. The again-disappointed partner hears, "I don't know why I do that." We clinicians need to act as though we know why.

The Long-Term Effects of Psychological Intimacy

Without repetition of the solace/pleasure experience, the positive consequences of intimacy are short-lived. In order for two-sided psychological intimacy to fully blossom, periodic sharing of aspects of the inner self is required. There are good reasons to continue to share over time. Reattaining psychological intimacy provides a sense of security about the relationship. It calms the individuals. Intimacy allows people to be seen, known, accepted, understood, and treated with uniqueness. This is the stuff of friendship, good parenting, and, of course, being and staying in love. Although most friendships are not bothered by eroticization of each other, most sexual partners expect to be dear friends. Dear friendships and good lovers do some of the same things for us: they stabilize us—make us feel secure, happy, good; they create greater self-cohesion, self-esteem, and improved ego function.[20] When psychological intimacies disappear from previously important relationships—no matter whether they involve spouses, lovers, friends, or a parent–child unit—various anxiety, depressive, or somatic symptoms may appear.

Gender and Psychological Intimacy

Women typically require more frequent psychologically intimate experiences—with each other, with children, with lovers, with husbands—than do men.[21] They complain more often about the lack of psychological intimacy in their relationships to men. Men are more typically patterned to more autonomous operational patterns. They have trouble understanding why women complain about their lack of communicating, why women say their marriages do not contain enough intimacy. It is now more broadly recognized by mental health professionals that psychologically healthy women organize their lives to a far greater degree around relationships—to friends, family, lovers, children, and spouses—than do healthy men. Women expect themselves to be relational, to gravitate to connection, and to personally evaluate their successes in terms of psychologically intimate relationships and responsiveness to other person's lives. Men tend to think of themselves as successful more often in terms of the creation of a unique self-sufficient wage earning self.[22] When we generalize about gender differences, we must leave room for the fact that no psychological trait is the exclusive province of either gender. Men also prosper in intimate relationships.

Relationship Between Psychological and Sexual Intimacy

Psychological intimacy lays the groundwork for select people to become lovers. It is often the trigger to falling in love. Once two people become lovers, the sexual behavior creates a further sense of knowing each other. But it is the reattainment of psychological intimacy that enables them to make love again and again over time, to shed their inhibitions during lovemaking, and to eventually discover the limits of their sexual potential with one other.

Over time it becomes increasingly difficult to behave sexually together without psychological intimacy. Lovers may quickly discover that sharing how one thinks and feels about a matter increases their willingness to behave sexually. Psychological intimacy, however, requires partners to set aside time to reestablish it when the sense of distance is felt by either of them. This can be a formidable problem for those who do not intuitively understand these ideas, cannot provide the speaking or listening requirements, are chronically overwhelmed by other external demands, or originally could manage only a meager intimacy. The sexual potential of psychological intimacy then does not get realized.

CONCLUSIONS

Specializing in sexual life has been a wonderful developmental journey for me. I began with an interest in sexual dysfunction. After a few years I realized that without even trying, I had become a relationship therapist. My clinical identity gradually shifted to an enabler of intimacy skills and a teacher who helped people find the words to articulate their private dilemmas. When I began to write about love, I quickly realized that no one's contributions could be more than a modest description of this profound subject. Love is the ultimate multidisciplinary topic; it needs to be reconsidered by every field in every era, even though the tools of every field are insufficient for its richness.

I hope that you have found this chapter useful in organizing aspects of your personal and clinical experiences. If you immerse yourself further in this subject, I think you are likely to discover both how commonly these problems exist in your patients and how much they appreciate your interest in helping them to think about their sexual lives.[23]

NOTES

1. Tresidder, M. (1997). *The Secret Language of Love*. San Francisco: Chronicle Books.
2. Nathanson, D. (1992). *Shame and Pride*. New York: Norton. Donald Nathanson has made more accessible the cross-cultural anthropological work of Silvano Tompkins, who articulated the differences between the hardwired brain capacities for *affect* from the *feelings* that the environment stimulates from the personal meaning of these feelings to the growing person which is emotion. Thus, the reader is apt to learn to use affect, feeling, and emotion as noninterchangeable words thereafter.
3. Ackerman, D. (1994). *A Natural History of Love*. New York: Random House.
4. Levine, S. B. (1998). *The Nature of Love in Sexuality in Mid-Life*. New York: Kluwer Plenum Publications. The first three chapters of this book have a more extensive treatment of love, intimacy, and desire than are found in this chapter. Another chapter deals with the biopsychosocial evolution of sexual physiology through the life cycle, a topic that was briefly touched upon in this offering.
5. Walsh, A. (1991). *The Science of Love: Understanding Love and Its Effects on Mind and Body*. Buffalo, NY: Prometheus Books. How a child is loved early in life creates circuitry that is probably used later in life in adult love relationships. There must be a neurochemical basis of love as well.
6. Plato. (1956). In B. Jowett (Ed.), *The Symposium* (pp. 315–318). New York: Tudor. This is the classic ancient reference to falling in love that is almost always quoted by writers. It is well worth reading these four pages for the flavor of how unchanged the experience is and how at various epochs in history theories are different.
7. Alberoni, F. (1983). *Falling in Love: A Revolutionary Way of Thinking About a Universal Experience*. (Translated by L. Venuti). New York: Random House. A charming, brief, insightful philosophical excursion into this brief phase of some people's lives.
8. Singer, I. (1984). *The Nature of Love: 2, Courtly and Romantic*. Chicago: University of Chicago Press. One of three volumes on love by this philosopher/historian.

9. Sternberg, R. J. (1988). *A Triangular Theory of Love: Intimacy, Passion, and Commitment.* New York: Basic Books. Others have replicated Dr. Sternberg's important concepts about the three basic elements of adult love.

10. Hatfield, E., & Rapson, R. L. (1993). *Love, Sex, and Intimacy: Their Psychology, Biology, and History.* New York: HarperCollins College Publishers. The most extensive research-based treatment of love that I have ever encountered. A prize-winning book.

11. Bowlby, J. (1989). *The Making and Breaking of Affectional Bonds.* London: Routledge. A summary work by one of the major thinkers about the relationship between childhood relationships to parents and adult psychiatric symptoms.

12. Person, E. S., Terestman, N., Myers, W. A., Goldberg, E. L., & Salvadori, C. (1989). Gender differences in sexual behavior and fantasies in a college population. *Journal of Sex & Marital Therapy, 15*(3), 187–198. Ethel Person has written extensively about romantic love and provides readers with a broad cultural perspective to her psychoanalytically informed views.

13. Stoller, R. J. (1975). *Perversion: The Erotic Form of Hatred.* New York: Pantheon Books.

14. Butler, R. N. (1975, September). Psychiatry and the elderly: An overview. *American Journal of Psychiatry, 132*(9), 893–900.

15. McCoy, N. L., & Davidson, J. M. (1985). A longitudinal study of the effects of menopause on sexuality. *Mauritas, 7*(3), 203–210.

16. Basson, R. (2001). Human sex response cycles. *Journal of Sex & Marital Therapy, 27*(1), 33–43.

17. Levine, S. B. (1999). Male heterosexuality. In R. C. Friedman and J. I. Downey (Eds.), *Masculinity and Sexuality* (pp. 29–54). Washington, DC: American Psychiatric Press.

18. Rauch, S. L., Shin, L. M., Dougherty, D. D., et al. (1999). Neural activity during sexual and competitive arousal in healthy men. *Psychiatric Research, 9,* 1–10.

19. Levine, S. B. (2002). Re-exploring the concept of sexual desire. *Journal of Sex & Marital Therapy, 28*(1), 39–52.

20. Frayn, D. H. (1990). Intersubjective processes in psychotherapy. *Canadian Journal of Psychiatry, 35*(5), 434–438.

21. Gilligan, C. (1982). *In a Different Voice.* Cambridge, MA: Harvard University Press. A pathbreaking study about the social differences between girls and boys and their implications for adult life.

22. Jordan, J. V. (1989). *Relational Development: Therapeutic Implications of Empathy and Shame. Work in Progress.* Wellsley, MA: Stone Center Working Paper Series.

23. Levine, S. B. (1997). *Solving Common Sexual Problems.* Livingston, NJ: Jason Aronson.

Chapter Three

Life Processes That Restructure Relationships

David E. Scharff, MD

INTRODUCTION

I first came to see the importance of the crises and transitions that restructure each individual life when, thrown into a particular life crisis of my own, I read a wonderful literate article called "Death and the Mid-Life Crisis" by Elliott Jacques (1965). He documented the changes that occurred in the organization of the lives of so many creative figures at approximately the middle of their lives. Many showed a major shift in the quality of their art or their themes: Shakespeare moved from comedy to tragedy. Some stopped writing or painting; some, like Gauguin, began; some ended their creative careers, as, for instance, van Gogh did through suicide. Jacques's argument that development normally resulted in a major reorganization at midlife illuminated my own struggles, whereas his examples gave me a feeling of being connected to the ages. The article also broadened my understanding of development. I had been accustomed to thinking of *child* development when I trained as a child psychiatrist, but I now saw that my own continued development as a (then) young adult was continuing the process of shifts in life that did not stop after adolescence or getting married—or ever until death. That article had a particularly personal impact on me. Jacques called the transition he was studying a life crisis, and indeed these periods of transition often have the feel of introducing such a radical discontinuity into a life (as that period did in mine) that they feel like a crisis. But these are the ordinary stuff of life, the shifts that mark life's continual growth and that reflect the fact that we all have a reservoir of creativity that lets us take what we have up to a certain point and recreate our patterns in infinite ways that mark our lifelong potential to change the way we live (Levinson, 1978, 1996; Scarf, 1987; Sheehy, 1976; Viorst, 1986). I still think it's a fascinating story that has enhanced my work with patients of all ages—from birth to old age—at every step of my career doing psychotherapy, psychoanalysis, and family, couple, and sex therapy with people whose problems (the life difficulties that bring them to us) always intertwine with their development.

The thing I would most like you to get a sense of is the immediacy of developmental process throughout the life cycle, the importance it has to each of our patients, and the way an understanding of it can put you in touch with what is most important to a patient when you are trying to help. Let me give you an example of the way understanding development can lead to understanding a clinical problem.

> Sally was a cuddly and compliant 2½ year old, the pride and joy of her mother, Mary's, life and her constant companion since Mary had taken leave from her law firm at the time of Sally's birth. She was securely attached to both parents. She would hold hands fondly with her mother, sit in her mother's lap and kiss her, and on the playground, she would run off to play, then turn to see if Mommy was there or come running to show her something and then happily run off again. Sally was fond of her father, Sam, but Mary was clearly her favorite parent. Yet as Sally came close to her third birthday, she began to turn on her mother and bring a new excitement to the relationship with her father. Mary felt spurned, but tried not to let the hurt interfere with her feelings for Sally. At age 3 Sally focused her interest on Sam's genitalia, although he acted modestly around the house. Sometime later Sally said, "Mommy, would you get a divorce from Daddy? I'm going to marry him!" It was too much for Mary. She sought consultation from a child psychiatrist, who explained that this development was one of a number of natural restructurings as children develop. All Mary needed was the steady support of her husband and the reassurance that he understood the primary role of the marital relationship. Mary sought support from Sam, who gladly gave it. It was a long time through to age 6, but by then Mary vastly preferred the company of girls and spurned the "nasty boys" in her first-grade class. Although she still thought her father was important, she was far less excited about him. It never occurred to her that he had once been one of those nasty boys.

Patients seek help at vulnerable points in their lives, but there is a tendency for patients with sexual difficulty to act as though sex is unrelated to other aspects of life and especially to development. Freud and his followers thought the oedipal reorganization from 3 to 6 years of age—the period when Sally focused excitedly and sexually on her father and turned against her mother—was the first time relationships moved to the center for the child. Subsequent research has revised that thinking. I've found it helpful to realize that there are continual reorganizations of mental and emotional processes throughout life, although they occur at a greater pace in early life. The periods of maturational reorganization, however, show great variance and aren't precisely predictable ahead of time because they are mixed both with individual difference and with the influence of external events. Nevertheless, they form a map of development that I try to keep in mind when I'm evaluating a patient and during therapy, because it allows me to recognize the importance of maturational change.

A developmental framework serves to orient assessment and treatment planning for individuals and couples with sexual difficulty. This chapter develops such a framework by highlighting sexual development within the life cycle, along with life events that influence and restructure relationships within the family. As we move through the life cycle, I will describe some of the vulnerabilities often expressed in sexual symptoms and difficulties at various stages.

Then we can use this sense to develop a map of each patient's or couple's life course, and that map lets us locate the meaning of a difficulty or symptom within the narrative of their life course. Seeing them, in this way, as the product of their own development and narrative, enriches our understanding of them and facilitates the process of helping them understand themselves and broaden the options that therapy makes possible. This chapter is structured to give you the outline of such a map. Along the way I will try to give you some sense of how I get the kind of information I want from patients.

LIFE BEGINS IN THE PARENTS' FANTASIES

There's no easy place to begin an exploration of the life cycle, so I'll arbitrarily begin in the mind of the parents after conception occurs, as they learn that they are due to have a child. There's a favorite song of mine from the musical *Carousel*, that the hero sings when he learns his wife is pregnant. "My boy Bill," he dreams, "Tall and strong he'll grow. . . . " And on he dreams, until he is shocked to realize that they might have a girl. He is completely unprepared to be a parent to a girl. It would call on him to offer things he has never considered.

As a married couple hopes for a child, the partners' fantasies and fears begin to form the child, often even before conception. When I see parents, I often ask them, "Were you worried ahead of time that your child would disrupt your relationship?" Or, "Were you having trouble and hoping a baby might bring you closer together?" There are other questions we can ask: Does the future mother yearn for a girl to be a companion or a boy to be what she could not be? These fantasies and the whole realm of dreams about the couple, the child, and the future will influence the growing child. Then, when the child is born, unexpected things can happen. To a father who feels that his wife no longer has time for him, I might ask if he feels shut out from his wife by their son? The parents may get a rude shock when the child seems to fail to meet their expectations—for instance, by not being the girl they wanted—or the child may please them in unexpected ways beyond their wildest dreams.

Because two-parent households are no longer the rule, we also want to think about female or male single parents and other alternate partnerships—same-sex pairs or couples or individuals who adopt or use artificial insemination. These are all variant frameworks for children's growth. The existence or absence of brothers and sisters provides differing situations for growth and determines how experience is embedded in children's memory as the foundation upon which the child's sexual development rests. So I will ask about the role of siblings, how a brother reacted at the birth of his little sister, and how they got along.

Two core elements of early psychological development are not observable by the time we see adults. The first, the quality of early child–parent interaction, is transmitted when parents hold a child in their arms (physically and emotionally) and, within this "arms-around holding," relate to the child, respond to its needs, and provide safety, nourishment, pleasure, and a sense of well-being (D. Scharff, 1982). If parents—or other primary caretakers—provide a sense of well-being and pleasure, they provide the most important ingredient for the child's development and specifically for the growth and maturation of the child's right brain. The right brain, especially the right orbito-frontal area (the part of brain above the right eye) is the main organizer of emotion. In the first 18 months of life, it is the fastest-growing area of brain. A warm, loving relationship between infant and primary caretakers promotes optimal right frontal brain development. Not until the last half of the second year do speech and cognitively oriented brain growth, centered in the executive centers of the left brain, lead the child's neural development. During the 3rd year of life, the more conscious areas of parental influence begin to mean more to the child, building on the foundation of the affectively toned early interactions (Schore, 2001).

Because the emotional aspects of relationships are important before a child has words, later in life it is difficult for words to reach and express the most profound emotions that were stored early on. That's why we need poets and artists to express the feelings that tend to evade our ordinary words. The early feelings also most characterize our sexual lives because the earliest relationship between children and parents is a "psychosomatic partnership," equally physical and psychological (Winnicott, 1971). The child spends his or her first 9 months inside the mother in a bodily relationship, a period that is the platform for everything that will follow. At the moment of birth, the partnership becomes equally physical and psychological. The bodily aspects are more intense than they will ever be again—except in the heightened bodily exchanges of adolescent and adult sexuality. For that reason, these later sexual interactions always echo the profound experience of the earliest child–parent psychosomatic exchanges. By the time children toddle around, they spend much less time in the parents' arms, and by the age of 3 or 4, physical contact diminishes to a small fraction of waking hours. Nevertheless, the psychological partnership between parent and child always hearkens to the original psychosomatic partnership, always there as bedrock to be invoked at times of heightened pleasure or sexual frustration. Information about the earliest relationships in patients' lives is hard to get by verbal questioning alone. We might get it from a parent's description of a child, but when we see adults, we have to assess the quality of their overall capacity for relating in order to even guess at the effects of their earliest family experience. Although we cannot rely on direct questioning for reliable information about early development, over time we can get a sense of patients' basic security in relationships from the transference they develop to us about whether we are trustworthy or not (Scharff & Scharff, 1998).

I have been interested in John Bowlby's work for my whole career, ever since reading one of his early publications on the centrality of the mother–child relationship while I was in college. Ten years later I had the good fortune to take a seminar with him, where I learned firsthand about his attachment theory, which has revolutionized our thinking about mothers and infants and about child development generally. He first used the term *attachment* to characterize a central element of the mother–infant relationship and explored it in his now-famous trilogy *Attachment and Loss* (1969, 1973, 1980). Following object relations theorist Ronald Fairbairn (1952), who taught that every infant needs relationships from the beginning, Bowlby and his colleagues (Ainsworth, Blehar, Waters, & Wall, 1978) described specific patterns of attachment that babies form with their parents. A baby can have one pattern with its mother and a different one with its father. Ainsworth studied attachment relationships in a benign laboratory situation by having 12-month-old children experience brief separations from their mothers, with and without the presence of a kindly stranger. The researchers looked for the behavior and quality of anxiety at reunion—when the mother came back into the room after the separation. Attachment patterns are specific to each relationship. When Bowlby was teaching us, there were only three patterns of attachment that had been identified, but there was a large group that the researchers could not yet classify. That group was later found to include the most traumatized attachment relationships (Main & Solomon, 1986). The four categories that attachment researchers have now identified are:

TABLE 3.1. Types of Attachment

Secure: The infant greets the returning mother (or other primary figure) with relief and confidence.

Preoccupied/Ambivalent: The infant clings and scolds the mother for her absence, but does not reject her.

Resistant: The infant turns its back literally and emotionally on the mother, as though hurt and angry, and may ignore her altogether for a considerable time.

Disorganized/Disoriented/Fearful: The infant looks confused and behaves in an apparently disorganized way. Closer observation of this pattern shows that beneath the disorganization and apparently random behavior of these infants is an acute attention to the mother's eyes and mood. A fearful hypervigilant monitoring of the mother's emotional state characterizes the relationship of these infants to their primary caretakers.

I find it helpful to remember that these attachment categories describe styles of relating, not diagnostic entities, even though the nonsecure categories do carry developmental risk. Furthermore, the Disorganized/Disoriented group contains a large number of infants who either have been subjected to trauma or abuse themselves or whose parents have been traumatized. The wary checking on their parents that these infants demonstrate is a sign of enormous anxiety in the child–caretaker relationship, a sign that something may be far wrong in the relationship, or that the parent may be carrying an overload of anxiety herself from which she is unable to protect the child. The example I give further of Freda and her son illustrates this (Fonagy, 2001).

In assessing the quality of partners' attachment to each other, I ask them how dependent they are on each other, how much they trust the other. Is it hard for them to be apart, and what patterns change or disorganize their relationship? For instance, it is common to find that separations—brief ones or longer ones—produce mistrust and chaos, a pattern of dependent clinging, or a turning against the spouse with a protective detachment. Often we get clues to these issues when one patient in a couple reacts to the therapist's vacations or absences by getting angry, suddenly claiming that he or she no longer needs us, or by decompensating.

These issues from children's early development are relevant to the sexual adolescent or adult because sexual interaction and vulnerability occur in relationships. Even the apparently solo quality of masturbation is centered on internal aspects of relating. The template for attachment patterns formed in the early years is the model each person carries when forming primary emotional relationships in later years. If a woman is capable of secure relating, she is off to a good start, even if she has some specific difficulty with sexual functioning. Ideally, she enjoys relationships, picks partners who are securely attached themselves, and enjoys the sexual aspects of a relationship without feeling that she has to render sex to her partner whenever if he is feeling needy. But I also tell couples that it is all right if one partner can make herself sexually available even when sex is mostly for her partner at that particular moment, precisely because she is not particularly worried about being used. On the other hand, if a woman has an anxious or wary attachment pattern going into a sexual relationship, that tends to undermine her capacity for sexual relating. She may feel that she cannot rely on the relationship, so she had better be sexually available to hang on to a partner. This way of using sex may leave her feeling exploited, resentful that she has to be sexually available for her partners in violation of her own wishes. People with a severely dismissive attachment style may only be able to have sex with a partner to whom they have no emotional attachment. Finally, for those who carry the template of a disorganized, fearful attachment and the need to be constantly checking on the other person for unpredictable moods and intrusive behavior, the vulnerability of the sexual exchange will often be the time they are most frightened and therefore likely to behave unpredictably themselves. Their partners may experience them as suspicious, frightened, untrusting, and unpredictably angry, never suspecting how much they fear for their own existence.

SOME SPECIFIC PERIODS OF SEXUAL DEVELOPMENT

Like all aspects of development, sexual relating grows out of the earliest relationship we have examined so far, but there are some periods of individual and family development in which sex is itself at the leading edge of the reorganizations of personality (Scharff, 1982). The first of these explicitly sexual reorganizations is the period in the 2nd year of life when babies learn to masturbate. Given the prerequisite that mothers hold and handle the babies adequately in the year or so leading up to this period, and given even brief periods of genital nudity, babies will explore their genitals just as they do all other parts of their bodies that they can reach. But exploring the genitals leads to heightened arousal, and so children learn to masturbate. Later, toddlers get interested in the differences between their parents' bathroom behavior and can be seen chasing their parents into the bathroom to look at the parents' genitals and behavior. They look up at their father urinating and open their mouths as if mouthing the urine stream (Riophe & Galenson, 1981). During this period, they are consolidating their core gender identity, their sense that they are either a boy or a girl. This process draws on their anatomical and hormonal makeup. Although there is now some question about the relative weight given to family influence versus the biological givens of the child, I still believe that core gender identity is mostly determined by the parents' treatment of the child as a boy or a girl during the first 2 years (Stoller, 1968).

Then, between 2½ and 2¾, earlier for girls than for boys, children sexualize their relationship to their parents. Freud and most later psychoanalysts called this the "phallic" period, believing that girls thought they were really boys and behaved in ways that focused on discovering their penis (for boys) or its absence (for girls.) I think it is better to call this period "genital"—that both boys and girls discover sexual difference. They already know that they are male or female, but they still try out the behaviors and attributes of the opposite sex. So they leap from the bed to show how high they can jump, try out urinating in the position that does not naturally suit them, and make sexualized assaults on both parents (if they have two) or on the parent of either sex if only one. This sexualization is between the child and one parent at a time and does not yet take the other parent into account.

A few months later, at about 3, children join their new sexualization of relationships with their understanding of her parents' relationship with each other. The child's fervent wish for each of them has a rival—the other parent. Freud (1905) described the way the boy wants an erotic, sexualized relationship with his mother and therefore experiences his father as his rival, fearing father's retaliation for his designs on the mother. Little girls have sexual designs on their fathers and fear rejection and retaliation from their mothers. This is true even if the child only has one parent, when the child's rival is the parent's fantasy of an adult partner.

Freud thought that oedipal reorganization was the centerpiece of development. Although we now see it as one among many major restructurings, I still see his discovery as an amazing piece of research, the first description of this kind of emotional restructuring in psychology. During the oedipal period, emotional and cognitive functions mature at a rapid rate. In this period that extends from about ages 3 to 5, children are sexualized hormonally, shift dominance from right to left brain function, become solidly verbal, recognize the role of relational triangles in their emotional life, and experience a sexualization of primary relationships in the external world and in their mind (Scharff & Scharff, 1987).

Children have always had mixed feeling toward the parents. Now they try to resolve ambivalence toward two parents by assigning the good and exciting aspects of relating to one parent and the forbidding, rejecting aspects to the other parent (Fairbairn, 1952). Most commonly, the child does this along sexual lines in the manner Freud described, assigning the opposite-sex parent the exciting and sexually appealing relationship and the same-sex parent a threatening and rejecting role. However, the child may reverse the pattern and take as its sexual object the same-sex parent and as a threatening object the opposite-sex parent. Furthermore, in health and in the well-functioning family, the child prefers two parents who love each other, rather than winning against either parent.

Children represent their parents-as-a-pair in their mental structure as an "internal couple," a pair that represents the possibility for long-term relating in all modes—sexual, aggressive, committed, and broken. Even children who grow up in a single-parent family have a mental internal couple, built from that parent's representation to them of the possibilities and dangers of relating. A parent can live through the child's whole life as a single parent and still imbue the child with the possibility of loving relationships, whereas two parents can live together in such a painful manner that the child believes that love is impossible.

When we evaluate children, we can ask parents about such things as oedipal development, but seeing adult patients, we do not expect them to have recall for their own development before the age of 6 or 7. Instead, I ask the general questions "Tell me about your parents. How did they get along with each other? Did you get along better with one of them? Did they seem to have a loving relationship?" Then, by the quality of the relationships the patients describe, we get a sense of how they may have split idealization and denigration between their parents, and we check out this early impression as we get to know them better, and with partners, by seeing how they treat each other. Then we might say out loud to a man, "It looks to me that you treat your wife as though she were the mother you feared as a child," and see if this makes sense to the patient.

When children go to school, sexual issues should diminish in prominence, as they invest in intellectual and physical learning and encounter a widening world. Although sexual issues are present, they should not exert the pressure they did earlier if the child is free to invest energy more widely. At about the age of 10 or 11, children often become interested in dirty jokes and a kind of antisexual focus, a reaction as though they were backing up from an onrushing locomotive of sexualization. At 12 or 13, the early adolescent redevelops an interest in sex. Children are usually wary about this shift, interested in the opposite sex but shy. Here again there is a search for sexual identity that causes boys and girls to emphasize aspects of their behavior that confirm their core gender identity and that are also part of their search for sexual partners. The fluidity of adolescent identity includes a fluidity of choice of partner, so that many adolescents have questions about homosexual or heterosexual identity in this period and are open to influence from teachers, parents, and other adolescents. I find that I have to tread lightly when seeing adolescents with this kind of identity diffusion, because they can be touchy lest an adult seem to be trying to influence their choices.

Fifteen-year-old Susan was interested in boys, but also frightened of them. Coming from a disorganized family, she looked to peers for a stability she lacked. As a result, she recklessly threw herself at boys without thinking. When two boys used her roughly sexually and then spurned her, she turned to an older girl for comfort. This motherly girl persuaded Susan that boys were all like that, and that Susan would be safer as a lesbian. Susan sur-

rendered to the persuasion. Only later did Susan question the basis for her decision to become lesbian and begin to notice that not all boys were exploitative.

Adolescents often begin their sexual interests slowly, at first using masturbation to try out their sexual feelings and later talking with same-sex peers with less sense of threat than they feel when confronting possible sexual partners. They often move with peers in groups of several teens, protected against premature intimacy. But some young adolescents, or even preteens, rush headlong into sexual relationships and then feel trapped by the intense intimacy and heightened feeling, or may, perhaps feeling that sex is the only intense feeling they are capable of, learn to substitute sex for intimacy.

WHY SEXUAL SYMPTOMATOLOGY?

Sexual symptoms are signs that a child has internalized relationships in a way that presents sexual behaviors as a solution to problems in relating. A number of factors predispose children and adolescents to develop sexual symptoms instead of other kinds of symptoms (Scharff, 1982).

Here are the factors that I think sexualize symptomatology:

1. Disruptions to safety or health during periods in which sex is a major way of handling things: the period of infantile masturbation, the oedipal period, or during adolescent sexualization.
2. Families that sexualize or strongly suppress sexuality. For some families, everything is sexual, beginning with the identification of the genitals. These parents talk about sex and flaunt sexual life. In other families, nothing is recognized as sexual: oedipal sexualization is unrecognized and denied. The families that oversexualize contribute a sexualizing trend to later symptomatic expression, whereas the families that suppress sexuality tend to raise children for whom sex is feared and avoided.
3. In some love-starved families, parents feel unloved by each other and focus on their children for love. A parent may say openly that the child gives what the spouse denies. The ensuing excitement can sexualize children's growth and contribute to premature sexualization of adolescent relationships.
4. Sexual abuse carries this tendency to a disastrous extreme. The invasion of a child's body by a parent is fundamentally a sexual invasion of the mind. The result skews development, to varying degrees, depending on how closely related the abuser is and the amount of support the child gets in dealing with the abuse. The sequelae vary, from serious disruptions of total personality like multiple personality, to sexualization of all development, or to phobic avoidance of genital sex or all personal intimacy.
5. Trauma to a child's parents, even when not directly communicated to the child, can still influence development through unconscious communication. *Projective identification* refers to the way a part of the parent's mind is unconsciously communi-

cated to the child when a parent cannot tolerate or contain his or her own anxieties (Scharff & Scharff, 1991). When parents have suffered physical or emotional trauma, such as the overwhelming trauma of a parent's own sexual abuse, they often communicate the anxieties of their horror to their children, who then build their minds around the expectation of trauma.

> *Freda came to see me because of persistent pelvic pain for which her gynecologist could find no organic cause. She knew that her parents had been negligent, but it was only in therapy that she began to remember that she had been invited into their bed from the age of 3 to watch them have intercourse. Later she remembered that her father had forced fellatio and intercourse on her from the age of 8. At 14 he stopped when she threatened to kill herself. She had been able to marry. Just as she had psychologically removed herself from her body when her father forced himself on her, she "wasn't there" during sex with her husband. The childhood defense of dissociation led to her adult dissociative disorder. Her children grew up avoiding their grandfather, whom they thought was "a lecher." They were without symptoms themselves, until Freda's 15-year-old son, Tom, hooked up with a disturbed, traumatized girl, who began to threaten him with suicide unless he agreed to have a baby with her. The whole family got involved in caring for this desperate girl, until a family session uncovered the way that Tom was unconsciously trying to repair the damage done to Freda by her father through taking care of this girlfriend. That realization set the whole family free of the spell cast by the girl, whom they persuaded instead to get treatment for herself. Freda had communicated her anxiety about sexuality as a traumatic factor to her children through her inability to discuss her father's seductiveness, despite her obvious distress about having him around her children. Her wordless state of tension communicated her heightened anxiety (that is, it got into him through unconscious projective identification), which put them on guard, but without the words that would have enabled him to understand exactly why she was so constantly on guard against her father. Then Tom undertook to guard another female against sexual trauma, but in a roundabout way that would have exposed him to another version of trauma. Verbalizing the trauma that had happened to Freda then freed the family to think through more appropriate action.*

ADULT DEVELOPMENTAL TRANSITIONS

Development continues during late adolescence and adulthood, including decisions about marriage, having children, marital separation, marital affairs, and divorce. The ticking of the clock is always a part of these developments. Other chapters will consider the biological aspects of adulthood in menopause and its correlates in male development. I mentioned the midlife crisis at the beginning of this chapter. Here I'll consider other transitions that occur or that are marked by not happening. What I mean by this, for instance, is that marriage or pairing with a mate of the opposite or same sex either happens or life is channeled to a significant degree by the fact that it does not happen, so that an individual either chooses to live outside a committed partnership or does so by the default of being unable or unwilling to marry. Having or not having children introduces the same dilemma: either you do it, or your life is partly defined by the fact that you did not have them.

Mate Selection and Marriage

The choice to get married or partnered shapes each person's life in significant ways, although the variety of patterns of married and partnered life is essentially infinite. Each of us carries within our psyche a composite image of an "internal couple"—of what couples are like—loving couples, warring couples, the couple-as-parents, sexual couples, divorced couples. The internal couple plays a significant role in orienting each person during mate selection and the trying-out period of courtship or living together that tests compatibility for relationships intended to be permanent.

> *Michelle and Lenny came to see a cotherapist and me with a strange complaint. Michelle said, "He wants to get married and I want to break up. So we should do something about that. Can you give us something? A pill maybe?"*
>
> *"Would it be to break up or to stay together?" my cotherapist asked.*
>
> *"To break up," said Michelle. "I don't want to stay with him, even though he did ask me to marry him and gave me a diamond ring. I had to try it on. It was so beautiful! But I had to give it back."*
>
> *Michelle and Lenny had a teasing, emotionally perverse relationship in which he clung to her like an infant with a cruel mother while she taunted him mercilessly. They did offer something positive to each other.*
>
> *Lenny said, "I'm the rock in the river for Michelle, there for her while she runs up and down stream."*
>
> *Michelle said, "He's immovable. I have to light a fire under his toosh or he won't move."*
>
> *For Lenny, being the rock meant providing the stability and durability she did not have, whereas she provided the liveliness and vitality he feared that he lacked. Although Michelle hated Lenny's immovability, she secretly leaned on him for the stability and persistence that shored up her shaky self-esteem.*

People seek mates to make up for deficiencies in themselves, and it was this Michelle and Lenny secretly found in each other. They were also looking to repair bad things that have happened to them and the people they have grown up with. When people's lives have been good, they seek mates with whom to continue what has been good and loving in life. In seeking partners, we all generally want someone to support us, and we want someone through whom we can find meaning by giving. At the same time we want someone to give to us; we need someone so that we can find goodness in ourselves by offering things to them. At another level, we look partly for someone like ourselves, who shares our values and interests, as well as our unconscious issues, and we look for someone to provide aspects of ourselves that have been lost to us or about which we feel deficient. Then, through projective identification, we hope to find in our mates and partners help for the parts of ourselves we feel bad about or feel are weak. Michelle could not bring herself to break up with Lenny because he was a convenient receptacle for the badness she unconsciously felt about herself and because, when he offered to suffer her recriminations and insults, he somehow knew that he was doing her a service. He said, "I grew up learning that men could be terrible to women and vowed that I would make up for that." When he offered to be the rock in the river, he felt good about the way he made her feel better, and although he found a vitality in her that he felt he lacked, he also felt an increase in his self-esteem by standing by her.

SEX IN MARRIAGE AND LONG-TERM RELATIONSHIPS

Sexuality plays a central role in adult partnerings, carrying the physical aspect of emotional intimacy and playing a continuing role in renewal of intimacy over the long haul (Scharff, 1982). But I've found that among couples who seek our help, a funny thing has often happened at the moment of marriage or at the moment of commitment—which is not necessarily simultaneous with the wedding in our current Western culture. During the courtship period, as partners woo each other into a long-term relationship, the forces of romance, yearning, and mutual idealization cover over each partner's darker side, the side of fears and anxiety, anger and distrust. If this were not so, many people could not even get married. Indeed, some couples now choose to live together for seemingly endless periods, shunning actual marriage for fear of what will be brought on by the formal seal of commitment.

Couples I have seen have taught me that at the moment of commitment, each person cries out to be fully known by the partner, so I often ask if anything changed at the moment they decided to get married or on the actual wedding day. In primary relationships, the unlikable parts of each person also cry out for recognition—the parts we are afraid others will not tolerate, much less love. Some partnerships are able to tolerate and soothe these aspects of partners, but many are torn by previously repressed forces that now come out from hiding. A man who felt neglected as a child wants his wife to understand and compensate for the deprivation he suffered. A woman who was victim to her father's rage carries unconscious resentment that now, for the first time, is loosed on her lesbian partner as though that partner were the angry father.

Often the spouse is surprised by this previously hidden part of the partner, although there may have been hints overlooked before marriage or committed partnering. But it also often seems that the partner was unconsciously chosen precisely because of the traits that were consciously ignored. For instance, I recently saw a man who had chosen a woman with low self-esteem, who was constantly self-defeating, in order to give himself an opportunity to heal her, filling an unconscious fantasy that he could repair his depressed mother.

Sex is often caught up in this reordering of personality. Under the exciting, come-hither organization of courtship, sex often goes well, only to fall victim to the emergence of disappointment and aggression following marriage or commitment. This may parallel a general deterioration in the relationship, but it may happen for another reason. Often one partner mentally locates the frightening or frightened feelings in the genitals and breasts. That is to say, the person acts as though these parts of the body contain a threat to the self and the partner. We call this a conversion reaction, when a bodily problem comes to stand for an emotional problem. A couple may appear to have a generally loving relationship, but closer examination reveals that sexual incapacity contains a mutual sense of dread. When this happens, an ongoing loving relationship may help partners move past the difficulty, but often couples are unable to overcome the sexual dread without psychotherapy or sex therapy.

For most couples, pregnancy and the birth of children are joyful, despite the troubles children inevitably bring. But for many, children are a significant challenge. A husband may feel displaced by his wife's growing focus on herself during pregnancy or by her obvious love affair with her new child, feeling that there is no room for him. He may feel that he is shut out sexually by her difficulty with reasonably frequent sex. As a child grows older, a mother may be angered by her 4-year-old daughter's oedipal love affair with her husband that shuts her out. For some parents, having a boy may be threatening because it triggers memories of some painful event in the past, whereas for others, a girl baby symbolizes something painful. Or the accumulation of children may overwhelm parents who did well with a smaller family. In the last 20 years, as people get married later and have trouble getting pregnant, I see many more couples for whom not having children and having infertility problems introduces strain. One husband and wife I saw recently were on the verge of divorce after many failures to conceive, when a pregnancy they no longer expected almost miraculously revived their relationship. So far they are doing well, much better than I would have predicted.

For any given couple, it is not that any one event will automatically introduce strain, but that the meaning of any event may be toxic when it would not have been in different circumstances. It is the specific meaning of the event to the couple meeting it that matters. Almost any couple, even those in the heartiest and most loving marriages, can be strained to the breaking point by the serious chronic illness or death of a child. Anyone suffering these tragic events deserves therapeutic help because they cause strain.

The same considerations that apply to these developmental strains in young or middle adulthood continue to exert influence throughout the life cycle. Aging couples continue to experience developmental crises—menopause or the aging processes in men—which cause physical wear and tear, erectile difficulty, or loss of ease in sexual functioning as a woman loses hormonal support and experiences loss of vaginal lubrication. All these events introduce changes in an individual that affect the couple's relationship. Some couples handle these better than others, but as they grow older, all couples have to face challenges that threaten the well-being that the relationship had in their youth.

> *Ed and Maria both grew up in physically abusive families and vowed not to express anger or raise their hands against each other or their children. "If it came to that," Ed said to me, "I'd leave first." So Maria's complete hysterectomy, done to stop hemorrhagic periods from fibroids in the uterus, came as a challenge to them. Having difficulty mourning the loss of her fertility, she became depressed and developed pain during intercourse for the first time. No physical cause could be found, but with vaginal pain she became reluctant to have intercourse, as well as moody, irritable, and depressed. Ed felt her withdrawal, exacerbated by her moodiness and her new angry irritability. He, too, became resentful, but, motivated by his determination not to express the anger, he withdrew. Now Maria felt depressed and abandoned. She told me, "I knew that Ed missed sex, but I got to resenting him for wanting it, even though he never insisted." Over time, their distant and resentful relationship came to bear little resemblance to the loving and cooperative one they had for the first several years of their marriage.*

When Things Don't Go Well

No marriage goes perfectly. In this last part of this chapter, I'll consider some of the elements of the wandering eye and mind that pull many marriages painfully apart.

Let's begin with fantasy because it's important and normal. At the deepest level, we all have unconscious fantasies that guide us through our lives at every stage— hopes to repair the damage of our childhoods, an imagined structure of the future of our lives. These deep fantasies are embedded in our minds, resulting from past experience and structuring our lives and relationships. The derivatives of these deep-structure fantasies are the daydreams and night dreams, and the hopes and fears present from the time a child dreams of becoming a hero or movie star, through the fantasies of being a pop star or having a love affair with one—to the fantasies about sexual partners that are fed by erotic magazines and movies. The fantasies of adolescents, often coupled with masturbation, contain central themes that represent the move from attachments to the adolescents' families and parents to the formation of bonds with new partners who can solve the problems the adolescent now feels.

Some people fantasize a secret life of sexual passion or even of more mundane extramarital affairs from the beginning of their marriage, using these fantasies to live out wishes and to calm fears that they unconsciously feel will contaminate marriage. This may be a minor theme that can be contained by the marriage, but in people who later turn to therapists for help, it often happens that the vitality needed by the marriage is funneled into this fantasy life.

Ian, a mild-mannered man in his 30s, loved his wife, but had no sexual interest in her. He thought he never had, although he knew she was beautiful. His lack of interest seemed inexplicable, as she grew increasingly angry that they had no sex and no children. He masturbated, but felt upset when she suggested sex. In therapy, he told me about a secret fantasy life that excited him greatly. He would fantasize being held in a sultan's prison and that a beautiful wife of the sultan would seek him out. They had passionate sex, but in the end, fearing betrayal and with great regret, he felt he had no alternative but to kill the sultan's wife. The cycle of passion, regret, and violence excited him greatly as he masturbated. The fantasy contained the split-off versions of his experience of his mother. An alluring and unavailable woman, she was also a frightening ballbreaker. His wife didn't stand a chance. Out of fear and concern that she would become the victim of his unconscious fury at his mother, he suppressed his sexual interest in her.

Infidelity

I have found that therapists are often too anxious to ask about extramarital affairs. Most do not know what to think if a patient or a couple has had affairs. Please ask! One of my standard questions to an individual is "Have you had any affairs?" and to a couple, "Have either of you had any affairs?" You may not get a straight answer, but it puts you on record as wanting to know and thinking that this kind of information is important. With familiarity, a therapist can learn to think about affairs with the same clarity as about other marital issues. If a man or woman comes into a partnership frightened of commitment, she may begin to have affairs from the beginning, living out the inability to commit. For most marriages, affairs express disappointment and deprivation that has developed before the affair. One or both partners seek out—or are susceptible to—invitations from someone who offers what the partner does not. These affairs are a living extension of the fantasies I mentioned a moment ago, but when affairs actually happen, they almost inevitably restructure a couple's relationship. Now the partner reacts to the secrecy that almost inevitably accompanies affairs, to the exporting of love and interest that goes with it, and to the sense of violation that comes with discovery. The impact of these forces usually goes beyond that of secret fantasies. Sometimes, the discovery of an affair catalyzes a new awakening for a couple, an opportunity for growth and rediscovery, but all too often it delivers the death blow to a marriage.

Zachary, a successful money manager I saw sometime ago, idealized his wife, Sarah, and felt an emptiness in his own life and career. He saw Sarah as a beautiful, successful doctor and himself as an underachiever and worthless. He could not explain the affair he began a year ago with his office manager, whom he felt had seduced him and then flaunted the af-

fair in front of his friends. Sarah hired a detective who got the goods on him, but still he denied the affair until one day the light dawned. He broke off the affair and begged Sarah's forgiveness. He could see the origins of his actions in his own depression and in a critical mother he carried within, but he felt his wife had done nothing to deserve what he had done to her. When I saw them, I felt no doubt that Zachary was reacting to Sarah's aggressive control. He had no awareness of her domineering style, but underneath the surface, I thought, he was reacting to it. She demanded complete submission and repentance, and that he "submit to therapy." Zachary accepted her terms and admitted to all the blame, and because I agreed that he did need therapy, I referred him to a colleague. Sarah, having no insight into her own role in the marital tension, soon ended the couple therapy, continuing the pattern of placing blame on Zachary and, I thought, dramatically limiting the chances for growth in the marriage.

Divorce and Other Losses

Divorce is usually a result of changes that lead to a bankrupt relationship. So it is a paradox to say that the divorce itself restructures relationships, but each ending is also a beginning. There is the rest of life to be lived, and the failure to invest in what is next is a frequent problem. The divorce is the end point for a marriage that failed, no matter what the reason for the failure. But being a single person again, or being a single parent, forces a new perspective on life, brings on new challenges, and calls on new resources. A man who makes a positive decision to leave an unhappy marriage may nevertheless founder at the prospect of being on his own, or a woman who is bereft when her husband of 25 years leaves or dies may find that the new structure of her life holds opportunities she had never dreamed of. The key to successfully negotiating these adult restructurings is the capacity to mourn.

Thomas came to see me because his second wife complained about his lack of sexual interest in her. He had married her after having an affair with her during his first marriage. Unable to give her up, although more interested in his first wife, he had driven that first wife to distraction until she finally demanded a divorce. Now, 8 years later, he was still preoccupied with the first wife and unable to invest in the second marriage. The divorce should have led to a reconfiguration of his life and, through mourning, to a capacity to invest in someone new. His inability to commit to either woman and his incessant dwelling on his lost first wife, despite the fact that she was happily remarried, were in danger of costing him a second chance.

The incapacity to mourn a lost marriage, regardless of whose fault the divorce was (it's usually the fault of both partners!) can make it impossible to move on. But when the lost marriage can be mourned, sadness gives way to openness for reconnection to the next phase of life, whether single or partnered. Sometimes the difficulty moving on from divorce comes in the form of clinging to children so that there is no room for a new adult partner. And although this is attractive and irresistible for many children, it's no favor to them either, for they soon get the message that they cannot be children because they are supposed to play parent to their own parents.

Losing a mate through death or living with a mate with a chronically debilitating illness impinges on life and the phases of late adult development. These conditions restructure life, and their successful negotiation requires active restructuring in turn. In older couples, one spouse commonly lives for several years with a debilitating physical illness or dementia from Alzheimer's or stroke. Then the relatively healthy spouse has to decide whether to limit his or her own life in order to care for and stay with the debilitated one or whether to carve out time and space for personal interests.

> *A woman in her 70s, married to a man a few years her junior, was able to care for him as he grew weaker from diffuse vascular disease that affected his mobility and strength, although not his mind. For 10 years she was restricted by his disability, punctuated by medical crises requiring hospitalization. In the last 2 years of his life, she could not leave the city to see her children and grandchildren, because each time she did, he went into a life-threatening crisis. He died when she was over 80. She mourned him, saying she had lost her best friend. But she also took the new freedom to travel and to visit children and friends. She said she felt she didn't have much time when she could rely on good health, and she was going to enjoy herself while she could.*

Losing a partner through death is a challenge to everyone who survives a spouse, whether in a young marriage or at the end of a long partnership. Sometimes surviving spouses feel they don't have the energy to reshape life, but that feeling is not limited to older persons. Depression is more frequent in old age, but can immobilize those who suffer loss at any age.

FINAL THOUGHTS

I have said relatively little about how the sexual incapacity that may come with age or disease interacts with the developmental framework I have outlined, but it obviously does. Likewise, the way partners treat each other—as representatives of good or threatening parental images—brings out different capacities in each of them, furthering or impeding growth throughout the adult life cycle. In treatment, as partners learn to be more understanding about each other, they often catalyze growth in each other. Sometimes this effect is so striking that a couple's sexual life may improve as a result of the partners' enhanced care and understanding, even without any direct focus on their sexual difficulty.

Let me return finally to the developmental focus of the chapter. The more a therapist has a developmental framework in mind, the easier it is to locate the difficulties that patients bring us on a kind of life map. When I ask a patient's age, this is an obvious, common starting point in placing that person on the map, and so are the other simple questions about marriage and children, what the patients' own parents were like, and finally what their life has been like at each stage. It's the way I build a story about each patient or couple, and it has a lot in common with writing a short story (a fantasy notion I still nurture about an alternative life for myself as a writer.) Unlike the fiction writer, however, I know I'm trying to build a story about each patient so that I can see where that individual got into difficulty. We all have our own life experience to draw on, so, in a way, the older we get, the more complete our own map. Fortunately, we can draw on more than our own experience. All we have read in school, all the study of development we've done, and all that our patients teach us go into our data bank. As our careers progress, the bank gets richer and richer. I've found that this is one of the most satisfying elements of our profession: Life, in its infinite variability, gets more understandable as we go. It's a big help in the job we all want to do for ourselves personally and to help our patients with: to keep growing and changing in response to all the forces that restructure our lives.

REFERENCES

Ainsworth, M., Blehar, D., Waters, E., & Wall, S. (1978). *Patterns of Attachment: A Psychological Study of the Strange Situation.* Hillsdale, NJ: Erlbaum.

Bowlby, J. (1969). *Attachment and Loss, Volume I: Attachment.* New York: Basic Books.

Bowlby, J. (1973). *Attachment and Loss, Volume II: Separation: Anxiety and Anger.* New York: Basic Books.

Bowlby, J. (1980). *Attachment and Loss, Volume III: Loss: Sadness and Depression.* New York: Basic Books. Bowlby's three volumes are now classics that are too rarely read in the original. He was an exceptionally clear thinker and writer, and a perusal of any of these three volumes continues to be richly rewarding.

Fairbairn, W. R. D. (1952). *Psychoanalytic Studies of the Personality.* London: Routledge. This volume isn't easy going, but it is the foundation of all object relations theory and has re-formed psychoanalysis by making it completely relevant to family and couple therapy and therefore to an understanding of sexuality in relationships.

Fonagy, P. (2001). *Attachment Theory and Psychoanalysis.* New York: Other Press.

Freud, S. (1909). Analysis of phobia in a five-year-old boy. *Standard Edition of the Complete Works of Sigmund Freud:* Volume 7 (pp. 7–122). London: Hogarth.

Freud, S. (1909). Three essays on the theory of sexuality. *Standard Edition of the Complete Works of Sigmund Freud:* Volume 7 (pp. 135–245). London: Hogarth.

Jacques, E. (1965). Death and the mid-life crisis. *International Journal of Psycho-Analysis, 46,* 502–514.

Levinson, D. J. (1978). *The Seasons of a Man's Life.* New York: Knopf. This book and the one below on women's development provide the best research information on adult development in the literature. They are the work on which Gail Sheehy's popular book *Passages* is based.

Levinson, D. J. (1996). *The Seasons of a Woman's Life*. New York: Knopf.

Main, M., & Solomon, J. (1986). Discovery of an insecure/disorganized/disoriented attachment pattern. In T. B. Brazleton & M. W. Yogman (Eds.), *Affective Development in Infancy* (pp. 95–124). Norwood, NJ: Ablex.

Riophe, H., & Galenson, E. (1981). *Infantile Origins of Sexual Identity*. New York: International Universities Press.

Scarf, M. (1987). *Intimate Partners: Patterns in Love and Marriage*. New York: Random House. This book is written for the general public, but is well researched and grounded in solid theory. It is still the best book on couple life development and difficulties for the general public or the beginning therapist.

Scharff, D. E. (1982). *The Sexual Relationship: An Object Relations View of Sex and the Family*. Northvale, NJ: Jason Aronson. In this book, I described development from infancy through adulthood and applied the developmental way of thinking to sexual growth and pathology through the life cycle. This chapter is largely taken from this book, although there are new findings concerning infant attachment and brain functioning that were not available when it was written.

Scharff, D. E., & Scharff, J. S. (1991). *Object Relations Couple Therapy*. Northvale, NJ: Jason Aronson. This book covers the issues of development in couples. It is the place to read about the definition and illustration of projective identification and about how to apply a developmental framework to treating couples.

Scharff, D. E., & Scharff, J. S. (1987). *Object Relations Family Therapy*. Northvale, NJ: Jason Aronson. In this book, we describe the restructuring life transitions throughout the life cycle, seen through the lens of family therapy, where children and adults can be studied in interaction and as their life cycles overlap.

Scharff, J. S., & Scharff, D. E. (1998). *Object Relations Individual Therapy*. Northvale, NJ: Jason Aronson.

Schore, A. N. (2001). The right brain as the neurobiological substratum of Freud's dynamic unconscious. In D. E. Scharff (Ed.), *The Psychoanalytic Century: Freud's Legacy for the Future* (pp. 61–88). New York: Other Press. This paper is a readable version of Schore's invaluable thinking on the way the right brain leads in early affective development, in the description of how the mother and baby have minds that are entrained in early development, and on the importance of chaos theory in understanding both neurological and psychological development.

Sheehy, G. (1976). *Passages: Predictable Crises of Adult Life*. New York: Dutton.

Stoller, R. (1968). *Sex and Gender*. New York: Science House.

Viorst, J. (1986). *Necessary Losses*. New York: Simon & Schuster. A well-researched and well-written popular book on developmental life crises and transitions. This is a wonderful place to start.

Winnicott, D. W. W. (1971). *Playing and Reality*. London: Tavistock. This little classic is one of my all-time favorites, poetically written and continually alive. Winnicott was the British "Dr. Spock" from the 1940s to 1970, when he died, and he was also one of the most influential child analysts of the 20th century, contributing original and intuitive descriptions of the mother–infant relationship as the foundation of all development.

Chapter Four

Infidelity

Stephen B. Levine, MD

INTRODUCTION

All relationships have intuitively felt, affectively sensed boundaries. Culture translates the experiences of these boundaries into the rules for appropriate behaviors. The boundaries and the rules they generate have some leeway, but crossing these boundaries carries a great risk. Fidelity is a conventional rule for relationships, and infidelity is a boundary crossing.

During my formal psychiatric education, I paid little attention to infidelity. After my residency, as my clinical experience with it accumulated, I began to realize how powerful a force it was in rearranging the internal and the interpersonal lives of couples. Now, 30 years after my formal training, I spend at least a part of most work days talking about the subject with individuals who are having an affair, thinking about having one, trying to end one, trying to repair its effects, or coping with a currently unfaithful partner.

I am writing this chapter to assist those who are not yet clinically experienced with infidelity. I will be trying to help you:

1. Recognize the power of your values and life experiences in organizing your clinical perceptions;
2. See the need to remain empathic without certainty as to what the individual or couple should do; and
3. Respectfully clarify the private struggles in people's lives.

Infidelity creates many diverse and volatile clinical situations for mental health professionals. These are so varied, however, that I cannot define many trustworthy guidelines for dealing with them. Instead, I hope to provide you with enough information to make informed decisions with your patients on a case-by-case basis.

IS INFIDELITY SICK?

The question involves our values. For many, it goes to the heart of moral standards—culturally reinforced yardsticks for how people *ought* to behave. Although we mental health professionals avoid terms like *morality* and *sin* in order to remain nonjudgmental and serve people who have different value systems, many of our patients employ these concepts. Unlike our patients, who may be certain that their partner's infidelity is "sick," we may be confused because when we are asked, "Isn't infidelity sick?" we try to answer the question in terms of our personal values and in terms of what we know professionally. Rather than assuming that our values have no place in our clinical work, I want to interest you in this subtle sequence of how our minds actually function: Values—personal and professional—organize meanings for us. Meanings generate our emotional responses. Patients, of course, tell us about their emotional responses, but ours occur in the privacy of our minds during clinical work.

I used to simply think that infidelity was sick. Then I had a number of clinical experiences that convinced me that my view was a personal judgment, not a cross-culturally validated professional one. There are groups in culture that abhor infidelity and others that admire it.[1] I have come to realize that in individual minds, however, both of these elements are often paradoxically present.

FLIRTING

Infidelity is far more diverse, complicated, and widespread than I had imagined.[2] Its occurrence does not surprise me much because I realize that it is very difficult to remain faithful for a lifetime to whatever values one has—personal, religious, or professional. Sexual values are not an exception.

Flirting illustrates the discrepancy between our endorsed values and our behavior.

Flirtation is early courtship behavior, a means of getting the erotic attention of another. Its observable mechanisms involve prolonged eye contact, apparent interest or enjoyment in the person's conversation, standing or sitting close to the person, and a slight excess of innocuous touching.[3] No verbal expressions of personal interest are necessary to create the excitement that comes from the realization that he or she is "interested in me."

For the flirting person, the behavior creates a tantalizing, promising, exciting *uncertainty. The motivation to create such *un*certainty is not necessarily to initiate an affair. It can be to make social occasions less boring; to affirm one's attractiveness, social worth, or power to provoke the interest of others; to pretend to oneself that one has more relationship possibilities than one knows that one has; to celebrate the overcoming of one's former social shyness and sense of social inadequacy; to provoke sexual desire in oneself or another person; or to present a false impression to others of oneself as a comfortable sexual person. These motivations are why some people think flirtation is a harmless social game that is not in conflict with their values.

Flirtation becomes dangerous when its signal is received with serious interest. Intimate talk, arranging for the next intimate talk, and escalation of intrapsychic arousal and erotic imagery can then quickly occur. Soon both individuals know exactly what is transpiring. Men and women who have decided that these liaisons are part of their pleasure of living—their personal value system—can perfect the process of spotting, alerting, and negotiating with another to an impressive degree. For them, flirtation is a means of initiating partner sexual behavior.

TERMS FOR INFIDELITY AND THEIR CONNOTATIONS

Infidelity is one of the most private topics that I can think of. There are a multitude of terms for extra-relationship sex. No matter the label used, the public discussion of it usually causes considerable discomfort.[4]

Cheating

The expectation for fidelity arises from the evolving process of commitment to one another. As dating becomes exclusive to one person, the identity of each person begins to change; both people start to experience themselves as a couple. These identity shifts do not occur at the same rate in each person. Fidelity is widely understood to be inherent in both the process of falling in love and the commitment to try out being a couple. We typically expect it, even without any formal discussion.

Cheating during courtship may be a marker for insufficient commitment to this particular union. "I'm not ready yet." It also may be a reflection of the belief that fidelity rules do not personally apply. This vital distinction can be a difficult discernment to make for both members of the courtship. Once a couple is going steady, cheating is commonly used to describe current undisclosed extra-relationship sex. "Cheaters," of course, may prefer to think of their sexual behaviors as an entitled youthful adventure—"sowing my wild oats," "having enough fun now so I won't regret missed opportunities later, " or "I'm not ready yet."

Philandering, Womanizing

Youthful cheating may give way to thinking that fidelity is not an expectation that applies personally. This value judgment is kept secret from the partner. When a man is thought to have been repeatedly unfaithful to a partner, he may be called a philanderer or womanizer. I know of no comparable term for a woman, although some women live this way. Shall we call them philandering manizers?

Sexual Adventuring

Not all extra-relationship sex is secret. Some partners agree to have sex outside their relationship. Here are some examples: a married couple participates in a swingers club, best friends "swap" partners for an evening, a couple agrees to take on a third person for fun, or two people marry, strongly believing that fidelity is neither possible nor desirable. Crossing the fidelity boundary leaves most people at least a little uneasy, but such open sexual adventurers remind us that people do not have the same value systems when it comes to fidelity.

> *Frank and I are thinking about bringing a woman into our bed as an experiment. The woman, a graduate student in my department, approached me about it. She told me that she was an adventurous bisexual who was sexually attracted to me. Frank has long had a fantasy of being with two women. We have talked about it: we agree it is both weird and intriguing. I have never been with a woman sexually—other than when my older sister introduced me to sex when I was a first-grader. I don't know if I will do it. I don't think I like her. Nonetheless, the idea seems exciting.*

Affairs, Affairs of the Heart, Love Affair

These terms imply an evolving personal attachment between two clandestine lovers. The actual affair usually begins at some moment of psychological intimacy that stimulates both individual's erotic imagination. One or both partners may think that they have fallen in love. When their sexual behavior begins, it usually deepens the bond and begins the processes of more talking, being together, sexual interaction, and a large degree of intimate psychological knowledge of the other.

Very Brief Sexual Liaisons, Just-Sex, Flings, One-Night Stands, Adultery

Many surreptitious unions are quickly sexual, but carry no emotional, social, or sexual obligation beyond the original physical acts. These are "just-sex." Liaisons with prostitutes, pickups at bars or parties, convention flings, or other one-night stands are typical heterosexual examples. Arrangements made at parks, bookstores, or bathhouses are male homosexual counterparts. These secret sexual adventures are of interest to us when the adventurer is in a committed relationship. These adulterous experiences involve little to no intimate psychological knowledge of the sexual partner. Nonetheless, they can be quite influential because of their meaning for the person.

> *I went to Vegas, spent $200 to be with a beautiful young woman. We talked, had lovely unrushed sex, and talked some more. I think I'll remember this for a long time. It reminded me that there are possibilities for me beyond the resentful sex that Sherrie doles out monthly.*

Casual Sex, Relationships of Convenience, Sex-Buddies

Some extra-relationship sexual processes seem to be neither affairs nor just-sex. They may begin as sexual adventuring and become an affair or begin as an affair and not engage the person's heart. These in-between states are sometimes called *casual* or *convenient sex*. These terms convey a relaxation that does not jibe with the anxiety, deception, and guilt that cause the individuals' fits and starts, confusions, advantage-taking, and wavering. After a while, sometimes quite a while, both partners realize that they are ashamed of how they behaved within the relationship and would simply like it to end. Some people, however, come to realize eventually that they are friends who have sex. They both accept what can and what can't be in the relationship. This is quite an accomplishment because each person's understanding of the arrangement keeps evolving.

> *I thought both of us were unhappily situated with our husbands and that we had happened upon a very nice arrangement. We had very intense sex for 4 months. Then she seemed to change the rules. She wanted me to leave Jim because she had decided to leave her guy. It ruined everything.*

Imaginary Partner Sex, Cybersex, Quasi-Imaginary Sex

You will undoubtedly meet patients in committed relationships who have a masturbatory life excited by external sources. Such heterosexual men typically use explicit still pictures, videotapes, or strip shows for this purpose,[5] whereas homosexual men may use explicit male-on-male videos and opportunities for voyeuristic excitement at movies, bathhouses, and parks for the same reason. Until the Internet phenomenon in the 1990s, large numbers of women were not known to be interested in such outlets. The Internet, however, now provides 24-hour, 7-day-a-week sexual stimulation for everyone. This medium allows the imagination to be stimulated by conversations with strangers and by looking at images of men and women engaged in a wide variety of sexual behavioral patterns. Until these people meet for sex, as occasionally happens, this constitutes quasi-imaginary, quasi-extramarital sex. Many people feel uncertain whether quasi-cybersex represents a moral lapse, whereas others interpret it as just another form of cheating.

Acting Out

We mental health professionals have our own vocabulary; we call extra-relationship sex *acting out*. Unfortunately, we use the term *acting out* in five ways. In order to discern which meanings are being invoked, we must pay attention to context clues. This equally applies to our colleagues, our patients, and ourselves.

a. The behavior is disapproved of in a conventional sense. No one says that a man who has sex at home with his wife is acting out. But his sexual behavior with another person will be so labeled. A Catholic priest is thought to be acting out, regardless of his sexual partner, because of the social expectation of celibacy.

b. The behavior expresses a fantasy, typically a long-standing one. Married partners having sex on a beach with the tide washing over their feet may be acting out a fantasy that one of them has long had.

c. The behavior carries a high risk of negative consequences. Here are some of its dangers. Extra-relationship sex can be self-destructive and destructive to the patient's family life. The secret, forbidden nature of the activity can readily become preoccupying or "addicting." When the episode is over, the patient may develop persistent remorse that he or she has behaved badly, without self-control or integrity, and has been of a source of personal, interpersonal, familial, economic, or vocational destructiveness. When the partner discovers these activities, emotional distress usually increases considerably, shockingly so: "I never thought she would be this disturbed by it!"

d. The behavior is created by the psychopathology of major psychiatric disorders. Character disorders (e.g., psychopathic personality disorder and narcissistic personality disorder), paraphilia (e.g., exhibitionism and pedophilia),[6] bipolar states, schizophrenia, and substance abuse are commonly thought to reduce a patient's capacity to remain faithful to a partner. Both the dangerousness and its frequency among people with severe psychiatric disorders support the professional judgment that acting out is a symptom of "sickness." A cocaine-using, intermittently psychotic schizophrenic who exhibits himself while drunk will be thought of as acting out his multiple sicknesses.

e. Unconscious forces motivate the behavior. "She seemed to have no idea that her promiscuity was related to her incestuous experiences with her stepfather; she was acting out for years because of this." When this meaning is invoked, therapists seem to be implying that unconscious forces are the most important of the motives. Freud originally used *acting out* to refer to the behaviors that reflected his patients' unspoken or unrealized feelings about him. He limited the term to the behaviors that reflected the unconscious transference. However, others recognized that children and adolescents routinely act out their feelings because they either have not yet learned what they are feeling or, if they are aware, do not have the vocabulary to express what they feel. It takes many people longer to recognize and describe their sexual feelings than other emotions, so sexual behavior often seems to be unconsciously motivated.

We need to be careful about using the term *acting out* because all five of these connotations tend to run together in the minds of those who listen to us and of those who invoke it. Our aim is to think clearly about infidelity. The multiple meanings of *acting out* inevitably create confusion. When your colleagues invoke the term, try to discern whether they mean that the behavior is disapproved of, stems from fantasy, is related to psychopathology, has a high risk of negative consequences, or is motivated by unconscious factors. If we are not careful, we may be simply colluding with others to find agreement that the infidelity is a sickness—that is, it offends our personal values. We need to aspire to precise explicit meanings in our terminology.

THREE VITAL CLINICAL QUESTIONS

When confronted with a person's extra-relationship sexual behavior, you may find that answering three questions will help you to professionally judge whether the behavior is "sick."

1. Is there evidence for a major psychiatric diagnosis as a significant cause for the infidelity?
2. What are the motivations for extra-relationship sex?
3. What are the consequences of infidelity?

Here are two extreme examples to see how the answers to these questions help you.

> *Joy, a faithful, unhappily tensely married 29-year-old mother of two, worked as a pharmaceutical rep. She has regretted her marriage for at least 3 years and occasionally has fantasies of running away with a kinder man. Joy developed a mania when treated with an SSRI. Before being hospitalized because of grandiosity, boundless energy, and irritability, she had physical intimacies with three men within one week. When she recovered from her mania, she became horrified over her public flirtatious behaviors and was paralyzed by her husband's cold, hostile name calling: "You slut!" She resigned her job, lost her self-respect, and doubted even her minor decision making. She was more depressed after her mania than before she began taking the SSRI.*
>
> *Joy's infidelity was a product of her SSRI-induced mania. Her motivations were to find a man to take her away from her critical husband. Her restraint mechanisms, which previously were intact, failed. The consequences of her infidelities—deeper depression, more marital tensions, and grave personal doubt—were profound. Though others may think of her as immoral, mental health professionals would think that her acting out was a symptom of a toxic brain. Her therapist, when addressing her husband, may choose to speak of her sickness to soften his narcissistic injury and to interest him in considering the more important issue of their long-standing marital tensions.*

Beverly, a highly religious, extremely bright and accomplished mother, and now grandmother, and high-level administrator, is long married to a highly accomplished man she has continuously loved since college. After 35 years together they still emanate warmth, respect, and mutual affection. Beverly, a high sex-drive person, discovered before marriage that her fiancé was nervous sexually and could rarely ejaculate. He improved somewhat over time and even more so in response to therapy, but he continues to have less sexual drive, be less comfortable, and not be able to be sensuous enough to regularly attain orgasm. When I met them 20 years ago, they had long since worked out an arrangement. She has lovers who are her friends. Her husband knows some of them personally, but prefers not to interact with them. Beverly keeps him informed about them. He knows when they are together. Although I had a difficult time believing this arrangement was acceptable to Beverly's husband, having seen them periodically for 2 decades, I continue to conclude that it is. "Beverly is a very sexual woman. I satisfy her in every other way, but not sexually. We love each other very much."

I have never been able to see Beverly as mentally ill. She speaks openly and knowledgeably about her motivations and her ability to be in love with her husband but have sex-friends whom she never loves in that way. She and her husband manage their reactions to her extramarital sex sensitively. Her husband has had no interest in other partners. Beverly did not consider herself "sick," nor did she meet my professional criteria for illness.

MEANING MAKING

It is in the realms of values and meanings that we can find the differences between those who are deeply disturbed by infidelity and those who are not. Our feelings derive from the meanings that events have for us.

In the typical previously clandestine affair of the heart that comes to psychiatric attention, the usual cast of meaning makers includes the person having the affair, the person with whom the affair is conducted, the committed partner, and you, the mental health professional. Each of us finds separate meanings in the affair.

You, the therapist, are apt to repeatedly hear sentences from couples in front of you, such as, "I can't understand how you could do that!" or "Yes, we had a fling, but it was nothing really." Distressed spouses may not be able to pay attention when the partner tries to explain the meanings and motives of the affair. They may argue over whose meanings are correct. Your patient may not feel that you are an ally when you explain that the meanings of events are ultimately private, and one person's meanings cannot be superimposed on the other person's. Even if a spouse has egregiously violated marital norms, his outraged wife does not actually dictate the meaning of the infidelity to him. That is a separate matter. The same is true for an outraged husband.

John may tell his wife in front of you that her affair was despicable, that she is a moral reprobate who is not worthy of being in his children's presence. John may indignantly announce this with the conviction that anyone—man or woman—in a similar situation would feel the same way. When his wife tries to speak, John may interrupt her to tell her the meaning of her affair to him. "You are just talking bullshit rationalizations for your immoral behavior!" What John cannot conceptualize during this session is that some tomorrow he may think differently about her affair— that is, have a different set of meanings at his disposal—just as others interpret her affair differently today.

In our field, we recognize that, over time, perspective on everything changes. Our feelings change, our meanings change, and, whether we like to admit it or not, even our values change. In helping people with their current anguish, we try to prevent them from destroying their possibilities for relating in the future. Here is one trustworthy guideline in dealing with the couple's tumult: Remind both partners that we are trying to work through the meanings of this event so that they can make decisions *in the future* about how they want to relate to one another.

THE PRE-AFFAIR MENTAL PROCESS
IN AN UNHAPPY RELATIONSHIP

From the 50% American divorce rate, it is safe to assume that many individuals are not satisfied in their marriages. They may be disappointed about what does or does not happen within the home, the bedroom, or social activities. Or they may reach their conclusion simply from the frequency and strength of their fantasies or behaviors with others. However they arrive at their judgment, they may find themselves preoccupied with their perception that their love for their partner is diminishing.

What they know with certainty is that they desire something fresher, more exciting. They want something less encumbered by their appraisal of their partner, less burdened by their partner's appraisal of them. They imagine beginning anew, but, of course, the reality of their commitment immovably stands there like a fortress. They flirt a little—that is, they pretend that they are not seriously entrapped within a marriage and family or within a culturally sanctioned commitment.

A friend may have recently decided to divorce or take a lover, but still, such a drastic and serious step may not feel like a realistic personal possibility. A search for safer interests may begin—in work, recreation, children, or the community. An otherwise unexplained period of depression, however, may appear. Because the person may not be willing to acknowledge to him- or herself this state of feeling unhappily married, a clinician may think the patient has a mood disorder. The depression may be induced by the dawning awareness that there is no hope for marital happiness.

Some feel rebellious against what fate has brought to them. The possibility of beginning anew, of revitalizing the self in a new relationship, of behaving differently with someone else keeps appearing in consciousness. The internal voice whispers repeatedly, "Have an affair!" Its pleasures are deliciously imagined; its dangers are minimized.

"But what will happen to my partner and children if the affair is discovered?" "Can the honest me tolerate the tantalizing dishonesty?" "Didn't I always want to be faithful?" Other thoughts may be at war with these. "Oh, stop being so self-depriving! Others do it; it is not the end of the world! It is just a little dalliance, an experience. What if my partner has been doing it and I don't have any awareness of it? Just make the ground rules clear from the beginning. I'll look for somebody who is looking for something that fits with what I am looking for. So, I will no longer think myself as honest a person as I used to be. Since when is honesty an absolute thing?"

The unhappily married person is experiencing the paradox between the self as socially committed and as mentally uncommitted, between honesty and deception, between the wish to have a new life and the need to keep this wish a secret. One needs a sense of humor to bear such paradoxes. One also needs to be able to see that private, subjective life is not always logical. Rather than simply feel, know, and smile about one's paradoxical self, some people decide to have extra-relationship sex. They may come to explain their infidelity as due to some irresistible force or having been overwhelmed by sexual attraction. Such melodramatic concepts lose their appeal as we age—as we come to realize that we have to choose to have an affair.

Temptations to be unfaithful are widespread internal mental dramas that go nowhere. They are part of many committed relationships. Something precipitates an affair. It may be another angry interchange with a spouse, a vocational success or failure, the flirtation of another person, a school reunion, a helpful process by a coworker, the looming death of a family member, or unexpectedly experiencing a deep connection to someone. Whatever the final provocation, the person decides—actively makes a choice to participate at every step along the way.

UNRAVELING

Spouses usually become suspicious because of their perceptions that the partner is talking less, is away more, is increasingly irritable, has less sexual interest, and suddenly is daydreaming. The concerned spouse asks, "What is happening?" The answer is an artless dodge such as, "I'm just working too hard" or "Nothing." The spouse may gradually develop a new anxiety, jealousy, suspicion, increased alcohol consumption, or depression. The spousal consequence of the affair may begin *before* it is discovered! When the evidence of the affair is finally in, the aggrieved spouse often passionately says, "Not only did you deceive me with *that* person, but when I was suffering, when I felt like a crazy person and did not understand why, you willfully allowed my pain to continue! You sacrificed me to your comfort! I don't know which is worse!"

Once an affair becomes known, life really changes. When life is unraveling, you are called.

THE CRISIS OF THE BETRAYED

When you are consulted by a person who has recently discovered the affair of a spouse, you will have the opportunity to observe the thoughts, feelings, defenses, modifying circumstances, and coping strategies of the betrayed. The betrayed feel confused by the intensity of their emotions. They have a large number of questions, many of which arise at the same time.

The Questions

The betrayed, of either sex or any orientation, find their minds swirling with questions. Why did this happen? Does this mean that something is wrong with me physically, sexually, interpersonally, or psychologically? Does this mean that something is wrong with our relationship? Does this mean that something is wrong with my partner? Is this just the way most people are? Why do I feel this roller-coaster of emotions: sadness, anxiety, anger, guilt, desperation, embarrassment, sexual desire for my partner, aversion for my partner, love, vengeance? Who should I tell about this? What else do I not know about my partner's behaviors?

After a while, another set appears: Will I, does anyone, ever get over this? Will I ever be able to forgive my partner? Will I ever be able to forget this? Will I be able to trust my partner again? Will I be able to trust *any* partner again? How can I make my partner realize what I am going through? How do I best manage this? Should I seek counseling? Consult a divorce attorney? Have a retaliatory affair? Refuse to do anything for my partner for a while? Read a book about affairs? Punish him or let this quietly blow over? Shall I think of myself as a fool? Shall I take this opportunity to end this relationship? Does it now matter what I have done wrong in the past?

Many feel uncertain whether they want their partner back. If they clearly do, however, they worry whether they are being disgracefully weak for wanting to preserve the union.

The Therapist's Role

Therapists can helpfully distinguish those feelings that are likely to last a long time and those that are more transient. The emotional swirl the patient is experiencing is, of course, tied to the questions. Whether you pay attention to the emotion or to the question, you help with both because, of course, they are two sides of the same coin. Please realize that although the questions are good ones, you do not actually know the answers to most of them. As long as you listen well, with interest and appreciation of the pain and uncertainty, the betrayed will find some relief with you. You may be tempted to recommend that the patient do something—create a separation, tell the children or in-laws, file for divorce, and so on, but be wary! Such suggestions may increase the social and coping demands on the patient, who is already overwhelmed. It is enough to listen well to the patient and try to help that individual consider the pros and cons of each option. You must also listen well to your own inner reactions. Your goal is to not add to the tumult. Try to slow the pace of the unfolding drama by being calm and supportive of using time as an aid to decision making.

Countertransference

You should expect that your early experiences with the betrayed will be quite emotionally evocative and difficult for you. This may be true even if this is your first personal experience with the subject. But just think of your burden if your parents' marriage broke up over an affair in your adolescence or if your affair devastated your partner. The patient's tumult will likely restimulate your angst for a while—arouse distress that you thought you had worked through.

Several errors tend to recur in dealing with the betrayed, before we gain better self-control and reestablish better boundaries. If our personal values do not endorse extramarital sex, we may privately begin to feel very negatively toward the spouse who is not in the room. We are immersed in the distress that he (or she) has caused. We may find ourselves authoritatively declaring, "He's a scumbag, get rid of him!" Or, "Your partner is sick!" Or, if infidelity has been in our life experience, we may be inclined to say something like, "Believe me, I know what you are going through; my partner did the same thing to me." Or if we have been unfaithful to our partner and feel uncomfortably guilty again, we may be too coolly intellectual and try to quickly bypass the patient's pain with encouraging comments like, "You will get over this."

I still vividly recall the shock I felt when a sheepish, frightened husband brought his disturbed wife to me in mid-July. Their presentation led me to assume for 30 minutes that she had discovered his affair "over Memorial Day weekend." Actually, it had occurred 7 years earlier. I was distressed for days over this because each of them was convinced that she had been mentally well before that holiday weekend.

Sometimes the emotional burden of dealing with the betrayed requires me to comfort myself. So I imagine that if I were paid for the work of holding myself together today, my fee would be doubled. I work hard to be there with the patient's questions and emotions, provide clarification when I can, and allow hope to grow in the patient through my constancy, interest, and calmness. Ironically, it has helped me to keep personal balance and boundaries by spending equal time with those who have done the betraying.

THE MIND OF THE PERSON HAVING THE AFFAIR

It is not easy for some betrayers to talk about what they have done. They are often ashamed or uncertain about what your response may be. Some may never tell you. All of our patients are not honest; some, generally honest, cannot be honest about this. Even when people speak at their first session about having an affair, people rarely tell you *all* about it. In particular, they find it onerous to share details of their pre-affair processes and motives, the direct and indirect promises they made, and the lies they told to the new partner.

When you begin asking questions, you may frequently hear, "I did not think about that," or, " I don't think I had any idea of what this could have brought." On the other hand, you will also encounter those who do not regret their affairs; some, in fact, cherish them and feel that the benefits were worth the conundrums that ensued. Nonetheless, they want to discuss the affairs because so much is cognitively and affectively swirling within them.

The Questions

Eventually, the person confronts his or her motives for the affair. "Am I doing this because my partner is so unsatisfying? Have I lost respect for my partner? Am I angry, deeply resentful, of my partner? Do I simply want to have this, desire to have this, or need to have this? Did it serendipitously begin and I decided to take the opportunity? Do I continue simply because it would be too ugly to directly stop it?" Other questions also occur. "How am I to think of myself now?" "I have become such a liar, yet I am generally an honest person." "Do I really want to stop?" "Whom shall I hurt—my lover or my spouse?" "I am going to hurt somebody." "Should I stay married just for my children?" "Who might be of help to me?" "Was I crazy to begin with or am I just crazy now?"

Such questions can last a very long time, cause considerable suffering, and make you think the patient's basic problem is obsessive-compulsive disorder. It is not.

> *Bill, a 43-year-old politician, originally sought help with his wife because of his indecision about whether to leave the family for his never-married lover of 3 years. Everyone, his wife, three teenage daughters, lover, and himself, had become highly symptomatic. For the last year, he had left each woman twice, with the announcement of having made a final decision. Each time, however, he missed the other too much. He was living on the cell phone, secretly calling the other one. Although "not serious," he was beginning to think of suicide. At his 10th visit, I told him:*
>
> *"I call what you have a dilemma. Some problems have elegant solutions, but a dilemma is a problem without a painless solution. Make no mistake— your dilemma is an unenviable, terrible one: whatever you decide, it will be quite difficult for a long time. But it is time for a real decision. Please remember that whatever you decide, you will have to work everyday to make it a good decision. You may not end up with either women or a family. Go decide! "*
>
> *Bill took my suggestion to go away, contacting no one; to read Solitude;[7] and to weigh his desires against the costs to himself and his family*

and friends. When he returned, he had decided on his lover because he considered that with her, he would have a greater chance of emotional and physical love.

Many men and women in these indecisive situations never are able to make a decision; they waver for years, waiting for the partner to give up on them.

The Therapist

Eventually, most patients ask you for some explanation of why it occurred. The best answer is, "I'm happy to try to figure it out with you." Be wary of single explanations that stem from developmental and remote explanations, such as a repetition compulsion stemming from an early trauma. The trauma may be a parent's infidelity, oedipal excitement, the unconscious oedipal implications of marriage, childhood sexual abuse, family traditions of separations and interpersonal chaos, preoedipal attachment anxiety and distrust, replacement for the mother who died when the individual was young, or replacement for the emotionally distant father. It is not that these ideas have no validity, at least as one of many forces that enter into the mix. When we offer such explanations for extramarital behaviors, we have lost sight of the fact that the patient knows—is aware—of some of the personal considerations that went into the *decision* to begin the extramarital relationship. By invoking an unconscious motivation, we imply that the patient did not have control or responsibility.

We can also hear ourselves offering four two-person system formulations for the background of the affair:[8] (1) The couple was always unable to discuss anything disagreeable. The affair arose to end the partners' locked-in pattern of conflict avoidance. (2) The partners cannot overcome their fear of deep psychological intimacy. The affair helps them to avoid being close. (3) The person having the affair is an addict trying to fill up personal emptiness in a search to soothe his or her abused child within. (4) The couple's children are gone, and the partners exist in a loveless, devitalized marriage. The affair was designed to provoke the spouse to end the marriage, something that the unfaithful one does not have the courage to do.

Each of these may strongly apply to some couple sitting in front of you. But by providing the explanation in your terms, you become the meaning maker. Your role is to understand the patient's meanings first. Temptations to various forms of sexual acting out, after all, are very common, if not nearly universal. Stay with the spouses' meanings and try to keep such elegant, sophisticated summaries to yourself for a while. Eventually, you and your patient(s) will be working together, exchanging concepts of motivations, and moving to deeper explanations than were offered by either of you at the beginning of your relationship.

Countertransference

There are dangers in listening to the sexual experiences of others. It may stimulate your own yearnings for a new partner. You may spend too much time asking for details or encouraging the person to tell of other experiences and may find yourself admiring the courage and risk taking of the patient. Or you may feel disgusted by the patient's "immorality" and find no reason to see him or her further. Just imagine if your father's affair, in your view, broke up your home and you could not talk with him for years. In comes this patient in his 40s who is having an affair. He is not conspicuously ill or character disordered. You learn of his views of his marriage, his failed attempts to emotionally connect through the various stages of his marital development, and how his friendship evolved into sexual behavior with a person he highly regards and understands. Not only do you have to think about his patterns, choices, consequences, and possibilities, but you have to rethink your own life experiences. This can be hard work during and after the session with the patient.

It is far easier to deal with men and women who are having affairs when their acting out is clearly related to long-standing psychopathology and when your own life experiences are quite removed from their behavior. Some patterns of extramarital involvement indicate the presence of chronic difficulties. These include compulsive sexual behavior syndromes—that is, addictions—inability to have sex with a valued partner, though readily attracted to others; paraphilia; repeated infidelity from early in marriage; and attractions that are limited to married or socially unavailable men or women.

Rocco was "easy" to deal with because he did not stimulate any emotionally important memories from my development. He was clearly psychiatrically ill. I had little private struggle, even though he did not accept some of my recommendations.

> *Rocco, a semiliterate tradesman who has been a binge drinker for over 40 years, had failed 12 treatment attempts to gain sobriety. He was referred from an inpatient service where he finally acknowledged his other problem: compulsive exhibitionism. Immediately after he was given naltrexone as a new treatment for his alcoholism,[9] he noticed a "miraculous absence of craving for a drink." Rocco had exhibited himself to 13- to 14-year-old girls three times a week since his early 20s. In early adolescence, he only sporadically exhibited himself, but his other behaviors would have qualified him for a diagnosis of a psychopathic personality. When Rocco was arrested in his 30s, his lawyer plea-bargained so he could pay a fine, and his wife did not learn about the matter. A father of three girls who was rarely home, he had not had sex with his wife for 3 years. I immediately placed him on 60mg medroxy-progesterone acetate daily. Within a few days, he experienced a marked decrease in his urge to exhibit and an increase in his confidence about his ability to control his urges. He was pleased to take it, but he has kept his contacts with me and his medication*

secret from his wife. Sex with prostitutes, adults he met in bars, and women his buddies arranged for him punctuated his adult married life.

We spend our sessions discussing our views about tactics for self-control. I ask many questions about his work, his childhood, his hoodlum days, his courtship. He is pleased to share his history, but without being asked, he does not know what to say. He likes to see me. I like to see him, but infrequently. He taught me what passed as normal in his family: violence, alcoholism, neglect, and no educational encouragement.

When his sexual relationship with his wife restarted, she teased him that his affair must be over now. They both felt a lot better about his newly found time to be with his family at home. At year 3 he went on a bender and started to exhibit his penis, but stopped. He claims to be free of drinking and exhibitionistic behavior since then. The impulses to exhibit persist, but are not acted upon any longer.

QUESTION: WHY ARE EXTRAMARITAL SEX EXPERIENCES SO THREATENING? ANSWER: THEY THREATEN THE STRUCTURE OF OUR LIVES!

They rearrange our individual psyches, our relationships, our children's psyches, and the developmental trajectory of our future. They threaten our partners with abandonment. They assault our identities. They show us that we cannot control our destiny, let alone our partner. They unleash a firestorm of judgment against us. They confront us with the fact that our future is not certain. They humble us by quickly demonstrating to us that our planned sequence for our life is not going to occur. They assault us much like death does, but death is public, is inevitable, and generally carries little shame with it. Affairs convey, however erroneously, personal failure, as if the betrayed one caused the partner to decide and implement the new relationship.

Even if affairs are rarely mentioned, they are not forgotten. They are part of our history as a couple. When other issues are discussed heatedly years later, the again aggrieved person may bring it up. But more important, when affairs are ended for the sake of the marriage, a period of private grief occurs. If it is the man, for instance, who has been having the affair, his wife is not likely to have a large capacity to remain sympathetic to him as he recalls the sweet experiences of the past and feels sad for his loss. Of course, it is exactly the same if it is the woman who has been having the affair.

Affairs are often the prelude to divorce because the feelings, attitudes, and concerns that they generate are beyond both partners' capacities to work through and master—even with our help. Divorce puts all parties on a new developmental trajectory, filled with uncertainties that cause almost all persons, however inherently mentally well, considerable anxiety, guilt, and regret.

I want my patients to think clearly about this subject. I try to help them separate the effect of affairs per se from the effects of the decision to divorce. This is often initially difficult because swirling within the emotional upheaval induced by the knowledge of a spousal affair are the reactions to a potential divorce.

Even though people restructure their lives, beginning with an affair, in the hopes of finding an improved social, sexual, emotional, and interpersonal life, it is not always clear that they have accomplished these goals. A particular heavy burden is the ex-spouse who does not do well after all the dust settles. And, of course, the person who decided to divorce to find happiness is far from guaranteed that happiness will be secured.

NOT-SO-UNIQUE EXAMPLES

A Gay Husband's Affair Is Discovered

When a wife has to deal with her husband's affair with a man, as he rediscovers his homoerotic nature, she often feels that she is in an extremely awkward circumstance. Her questions also include: How do I compete with a man? Is he going to leave me, stay with me and be unfaithful, or stay with me, forever longing for his private desire in a way that I can never compete with? Did he ever really love me? Do I have AIDS? Will I get the disease if I stay with him? After all these good years together, is his right to pursue his desire to love and be loved by a man more important than my desire not to enter into the realm of the divorced? Do I have the right to tell my friends, family, or children about why he has left, or does his wish for not being known as a homosexual person supersede my needs? I love him. I know he loves me in his relatively asexual way. What am I to do?

The Cuckold

Men and women both may become highly symptomatic from their spouses' affairs. The emotional issues are essentially the same. Men, however, may think that they have been particularly humiliated by the affair. Men who are cuckolds think that others are laughing at them. Their idea that there is something unique about their intense embarrassment reflects how little they appreciate what any betrayed person experiences.

What are often different are the coping opportunities. Men do not often have friends who can listen to them or help them process what has occurred to them. They usually do not associate with other men in the same position. Men are not used to relating in this way. They tend to turn inward, drink or abuse substances, overwork, and pretend that they feel better and are functioning better than they are. The alienation that they had from their inner experiences earlier in their lives reaches a crisis point: they either return to it, hiding their emotional realities from themselves or others, or they surrender to the profound sadness, anxiety, and anger and allow this painful experience to assist their maturation. Although some try to replace their wives, many others begin making-do relationships that tide them over until they can regain their internal sense of themselves.

SUMMARY

As we therapists confront the variety of human infidelities, we also confront the knowledge that we cannot rely on behavioral science to tell us what to do. Clinical experience accumulates in us and creates at times a sense of what is helpful. This sense, of course, may be an illusion. My hope was to comfort your initial fears about dealing with these complexities. I did not tell you what to do to manage them in detail because I am still uncertain myself. Your task, as in all crises—infidelity is no exception—is to try to find the opportunities for personal and interpersonal growth from the dangers in which the patients are immersed. With infidelity, however, we often have to be mindful of our separate personal and professional values.

NOTES

1. Fisher, H. E. (1992). Why adultery? In *Anatomy of Love: The Natural History of Monogamy, Adultery, and Divorce* (pp. 75–97). New York: Norton. Fisher provides a nice cross-cultural and anthropological view of the widespread mental interest in extra-relationship sex.
2. Levine, S. B. (1998). *Sexuality in Mid-Life.* New York: Plenum. Chapter 7 provides an incomplete registry of the myriad forms of sexual infidelities. I'm sure the list could be extended. This and the following chapter contain a lengthier discussion of infidelity and are the template from which this chapter was updated.
3. Ackerman, D. (1994). *Natural History of Love* (p. 182). New York: Random House. The description of the facial idioms of female flirtation, seemingly unlearned, combines modesty and sexual availability.
4. Regan, P. C. (2001). Love relationships. In L. T. Szuchman & F. Muscarella (Eds.), *Psychological Perspectives on Human Sexuality* (pp. 232–282). New York: Wiley. In this extensive research-oriented review of normal and problematic aspects of love, infidelity is mentioned only once by inference. This is an indication of how uncomfortable a subject infidelity really is. It has not yet been systematically—that is, scientifically—studied. Nonetheless, this chapter will acquaint you with academic concepts of love and love-style mismatches that may lead to cheating.
5. Levine, S. B. (1999). Male heterosexuality in male sexuality. In R. C. Friedman & J. I. Downey (Eds.), *Annual Review of Psychiatry.* Washington, DC: American Psychiatric Press. This essay contains a diagnostic schema to illuminate the problematic patterns of heterosexual men and explains various sexual fixations in terms of developmental failures.
6. Levine, S. B. (1999). The paraphilias. In B. Sadock & R. C. Friedman (Eds.), *Comprehensive Textbook of Psychiatry.* Baltimore: Williams and Wilkins.
7. Storr, A. (1988). *Solitude: A Return to the Self.* New York: Free Press. A wonderful book extolling the virtues of being by oneself at important life transitions. A psychiatrist, Dr. Storr, writes of the lives of many musical greats and figures from Greek and Roman history to illustrate his points.
8. Brown, E. (1992). *Patterns of Infidelity and Their Treatment.* New York: Brunner/Mazel.
9. Anton, R. F., Moak, D. H., Waid, L. R., Latham, P. K., Malcohm, R. J., & Dias, J. K. (1999). Naltrexone and cognitive behavioral therapy for the treatment of outpatient alcoholics: Results of a placebo-controlled trial. *American Journal of Psychiatry, 156,* 1758–1764. Subsequently, further research has not consistently supported the usefulness of this drug for outpatients.

Chapter Five

Dealing With the Unhappy Marriage

Lynda Dykes Talmadge, PhD
William C. Talmadge, PhD

PREFACE

We were married at 19 in 1968 while we were in undergraduate school. Eventually, after picking several other major areas of study, as most young college students do, we both settled into the study of psychology. Thus began our long-standing and rewarding collaboration. When we were 22, our son was born; he is now completing his doctorate in counseling psychology. Ultimately, we both completed our doctoral degrees in psychology and went on to work in marital and sex therapy. We have worked together closely for over 27 years, logging many hours with couples in distress about their sexual or marital relationships, or both. Over these years, we have come to appreciate the intricate workings of a long-standing sexual relationship such as marriage and how sexual symptoms provide us with information about how to intervene.

INTRODUCTION

In this chapter we hope to help you understand and calmly deal with a frequently underlying aspect of sexual dysfunctions—the unhappy marriage. First, we will share some general comments. Next we'll highlight some of the major findings from marital research. Then we will introduce you to Gary and Sheila, a couple that Lynda saw. Lynda will describe this couple's circumstances in great detail to illuminate the typical complexity found in many cases of psychological sexual dysfunction within an unhappy marriage. Together, we will give you a framework that we hope you find helpful in approaching a sexually dysfunctional couple with an unhappy marriage. We hope Gary and Sheila's circumstance will illustrate the processes that keep a marriage healthy. We tend to think of marriage as a developmental journey, because of both our personal experience and our clinical experience, and hope you find that a useful metaphor in reading this chapter.

We hope you find this chapter helpful upon your first reading and will want to return to it as a reminder and a support when you feel you need to get some "supervision" with future cases. We realize that you, the readers, will have varying comfort levels and expertise in working with couples. We are assuming that all, however, will be relatively new to trying to understand the psychological and interpersonal origins of sexual dysfunction in unhappy relationships.

Often, in working with sexual problems, it becomes painfully obvious that the problem is not only in sexual functioning. Lynda recently had a session with a patient who, in the course of her therapy for sexual dysfunction, has gotten a divorce. She has been through much soul searching and personal growth to arrive at this place. Feeling better, she laughed and said, "What must you have thought when we came to you for my desire and orgasm problems? You must have thought, 'That's the least of this couple's problems!'" In truth, that is exactly what Lynda thought! This, of course, is true of much of psychotherapy. Human beings' functioning and feelings do not fall into neat categories, regardless of our needs to categorize so that we do not become overwhelmed by the messiness and intricacy. There may be Axis II diagnoses for one or both partners, and, certainly, there may be marital issues flowing from those or other sources. As the therapists, we are called upon to sort these issues, to determine how they interact and how they manifest in the complaints as the partners conceptualize them.

RESEARCH FINDINGS ABOUT UNHAPPY MARRIAGES

Let's review briefly what some of the marital research tells us about the nature of marital happiness and unhappiness. By age 45, 90% of both men and women have been married once. According to statistics compiled during the 1980s and early 1990s, almost one third of all marriages fail within the first 5 years (National Center for Health Statistics, 1991), and ultimately, between one half and two-thirds end in divorce (Cherlin, 1992; Karney & Bradbury, 1997). Much research demonstrates that couples who start out with more love, care, affection, sense of humor, commitment, and optimism will be more satisfied in their marriages (Adams & Jones, 1997; Bradbury, Beach, Fincham, & Nelson, 1996; Brunstein, Dangelmayer, & Schultheiss, 1996; Carrere, S., Buehlman, Gottman, Coan, & Ruckstuhl, 2000; Carstenesen, Gottman, & Levenson, 1996; Christensen, Russell, Miller, & Peterson, 1998, Fincham, Harold, & Gano-Phillips, 2000; Gottman, Coan, Carrere, & Swanson, 1998; Haynes, et al., 1992; Johnson & O'Leary, 1996; Perrone & Worthington, 2001; Talmadge & Talmadge, 2001; Vansteenwegen, 1996). Carrere et al. (2000), in a longitudinal study of 95 newlywed couples, found that the perceived marital bond of the partners predicted which couples would remain married or would divorce within this vulnerable first 5 years of marriage. These observations may seem self-evident, but it is important not to simply rely on our own biases and assumptions as we are confronted with something so complex as marriage.

Marital Developmental Milestones

We also know from research that some developmental milestones are predictable. Around the 4th year of marriage, the honeymoon appears to be over. The rose-colored glasses are off and the satisfaction falls, to some extent, seeming to plateau at that level. For many couples this is also the time the first child is born. Perhaps a disturbing fact is that couples without children have higher marital quality (Hampson, Prince, & Beavers, 1999). This, too, seems intuitively plausible when we consider the demands and adjustments of bringing the first child into the marital union.

Another developmental milestone where marital happiness decreases is at year 8. We are all aware of the so-called 7-year itch, and this seems validated by the research (Kurdek, 1999). In psychological terms, we see this period as one in which the partners' views of one another, the conscious or unconscious fantasies about "How will I feel with him? Who will she be for me? Who will he be for me? How will she alleviate all my emotional pain and make me feel happy with myself and my life?" is challenged, if not shattered. The vicissitudes of intimacy require courage, stripping oneself to the bone emotionally, revealing vulnerabilities we did not even know about in ourselves. The old cliché "You always hurt the one you love" does have some merit. We are at our most needy and vulnerable in a love relationship such as marriage. We are required to encounter and expose the carefully guarded and disowned parts of ourselves as we bump up against our beloved. This is not a conscious intention; it just happens in our interaction. Instead of seeing this painful process as necessary to emotional and spiritual maturation, it may be experienced as a betrayal by the partner.

Here is a conceptual example of unhealthy dependency and its bad potential marital consequences. A woman becomes disillusioned as she sees that her spouse is not rescuing her from her vocational dilemmas. She perceives that he is making her situation more difficult because she feels that he is deliberately, viciously hurting her. Although he attempts to soothe and comfort her, and she conceptually knows that he should not take responsibility for her distress, she feels betrayed because part of her expects that of a husband. Ultimately, her anger over her dependence on him may lead to contemplation of divorce.

In these situations, savvy marital therapists warn the partners that although you can leave the relationship, you take yourself, including these immature fantasies, with you into the next relationship. We have often wondered whether or not Elizabeth Taylor, in her eight marriages and liaisons, personifies pernicious serial monogamy. Marital problems are moments when the partners can choose to look deeper into themselves as individuals and into the relationship to enhance their development. It is a time when they can choose once again to be committed to one another, to choose from a self that is likely different from the one who first chose 8 years ago. They may also choose to dissolve the relationship as a result of looking deeper. Our concern is not so much the outcome, as the process by which they arrive there. If the decision is thoughtful and respectful, involving self-responsibility, though a loss, it is based on healthier processes than if people are running from something.

The next developmental stage clinicians have observed is around the 17th or 18th year, as the children are leaving home. At that point, the marital happiness can increase or decrease. This is obviously dependent on the care the partners have provided for their relationship. One of the crucial things that many married couples overlook is the need for maintenance of their relationship. We recently encountered a cartoon that showed a husband approaching his wife in the living room as she was reading, saying, "Now that the kids are grown and gone, I think we should have sex." Obviously, they have not attended to their relationship, perhaps organizing themselves exclusively around their children. The outlook for their marital happiness is not promising. They will have a difficult adjustment period, if they make it at all, because the glue that held them together is gone.

"Communication Problems"

Whenever you ask couples what issues have brought them to you, many will say, "We have a communication problem." This formulation is rarely useful to us as therapists because it can mean anything. What does this particular couple mean by saying this? Do the partners mean they do not know how to resolve conflict? They never fight? They fight all the time? They don't talk at all, or they can't talk about particular subjects like children, sex, or money? They can't express tenderness? They can't have sex? It could be any, all, or none of the above. Our job is to ferret out what specifically happens or does not happen between them that affects their marital or sexual happiness—or both.

Four Major Contributors to Unhappy Marriages

John Gottman, after years of prospective research on the same married couples over an 18-year period, determined four major contributors to marital unhappiness. These are processes of defensiveness, criticism, contempt, and stonewalling (Gottman, 1994, 1999). In fact, divorce can be reliably predicted, based on the presence of these elements in a couple's "communication problems." A study of 130 newlywed couples was designed to explore marital interaction processes that are predictive of divorce and processes that discriminate between happily and unhappily married couples. Support was not found for anger as a dangerous emotion, active listening as a helpful communication tool, or reciprocity of negative affect. In predicting divorce, support was found for the husband's rejecting his wife's influence, negative start-up by the wife in interactions, the husband's failing to de-escalate the wife's low-level negative affect, and a lack of physiological soothing in the male (Gottman et al., 1998). Other studies have found that it is the wife whose physiological arousal is correlated with negative marital interaction (Groth, Fehm-Wolfsdorf, & Hahlweg, 2000).

We also know from research that husbands are affected more adversely by their wives' negativity—specifically, "demandingness"—and wives are affected more adversely by their husbands' withdrawal. When the men habitually withdrew during discussions of issues raised by the wives, the wives' relationship satisfaction reliably declined (Heavey, Christensen, & Malamuth, 1995, p. 797). Many times a couple can get into a negative cycle where the more negative the wife is, the more the husband withdraws, and thus the more negative she becomes. These systemic dances that couples move into need to be interrupted and processed in therapy (Middleberg, 2001). You will often see this pattern in your therapy sessions with distressed marriages.

Context

The Marital Developmental Context: One of the first questions therapists tend to formulate for themselves is, "What is primary, the sexual dysfunction, or the marital distress?" Though this question may be necessary to get yourself organized, in some ways it is naïve. If you are ruled too much by your hypothesis, you may narrow your focus on one area primarily, assuming the other will magically recover. In our experience, this is rarely the case. As we listen to couples, we are listening for the context in which they are struggling to be emotionally intimate and sexually satisfied. It is hard to over-emphasize context in a long-term committed relationship.

The developmental context is an important aspect of this. One of the important factors in marital unhappiness involves how couples respond to outside stressors, including predictable ones that are a result of developmental milestones. These stressors and marital distress have health consequences with each individual (Kiecolt-Glaser & Newton, 2001). Part of the skills required for marital psychological health is resilience in the face of stressors (Cowen, 1991). Here are four questions that we use to think about the development of our clients' marriages:

1. How long have they been married?
2. What developmental milestones are they attempting to negotiate as individuals and as a couple?
3. Where are they in relation to life demands, such as pregnancy, career development and economic survival, illness, losses, raising children, launching children, relationship to extended family? (Barnett, Raudenbush, Brennan, Pleck, & Marshall, 1995)
4. Where is each partner with psychological development and emotional maturation that allows for self-definition and intimacy with another?

We view the same symptom differently, depending on whether the partners are in their first 2 years of marriage, their 10th year, or their 30th year. In general, the longer they have had to "calcify" their problems, the harder it is to effect change. Cowen (1991) has conceptualized psychological wellness as including resilience and competence and being influenced by cultural institutions, both public and private. These contextual variables will impact the external, interpersonal, and intrapsychic stressors the partners are managing. These, in turn, affect the level of marital happiness and sexual intimacy.

The Family-of-Origin Context: This brings us to the important variable of family of origin, the most private of cultural institutions that affects our development. Our families, and all they were and were not for us, leave profound marks on our ability to be intimate (Cassidy & Shaver, 1999; Klohnen & Bera, 1998; Lopez & Brennan, 2000). In understanding marital unhappiness, we believe it is crucial to understand the emotional contexts within which each partner developed. We want to know what type of family this was. We lead the individual through his or her history with the family, using questions designed to ascertain the general climate, emotional and physical.

1. What were the relationships like with each parent, siblings; where were the alliances and estrangements?
2. How were feelings handled? We are particularly interested in affection and conflict because these have great impact on later ability to form and sustain a satisfying intimate bond that includes sexual energy.
3. What was the marriage like that this person grew up in? Or, was there one? Here, we are looking for modeling of what adult pair bonding is for this person.
4. What kinds of significant events or losses occurred for the patient, especially at early critical developmental times? We are not only looking for dramatic or traumatic events, but also the subtleties of existence in this particular family. Our view is that the child is essentially bathed in this emotional environment, and its effects may not be obvious to this patient or the therapist at first glance.

Intimacy and Sexuality Contexts: In the next portion of this chapter Lynda will illustrate in great detail how the individual, marital development, and family-of-origin contexts can paralyze or damage the intimacy and sexuality contexts. We will look at the story of Sheila and Gary. We are deeply grateful to them for helping us as teachers to illustrate these vital points.

History of the Couple

Sheila and Gary, in their 40s, married 4 years, came to me for therapy because they did not have a sex life. Both of their individual therapists referred them. The symptom they presented was that Gary could not maintain an erection. His physician had already ruled out physiological problems. This has been a very painful and contentious issue for them. To make matters worse, they wanted to have a baby and were undergoing infertility treatment.

It became obvious as I listened to this couple's story that the marriage was not mutual. It was imbalanced, with Gary questioning himself and being fearful of asserting himself in his own life, as well as in the relationship, and Sheila feeling anxious, angry, a great need to control, and the burden that follows from that. Essentially, Gary felt like her little boy. You can imagine how that would impact their sexual relating.

Gary's Family of Origin: His mother and his aunt raised Gary. His father left when he was quite young, and his mother and her sister made a home together, with Gary as their charge. So, he basically had no consistent male influence growing up and had become quite attached to Sheila's father. Gary became very devoted to his mother, taking his dad's place as her husband. He did not date in high school, but throughout his development concentrated on being a good boy. His mother did not express her displeasure with him in an overt way. Instead, when he was not doing her bidding, he would get subtle messages about how that hurt her, through her withdrawal. He mostly was controlled by guilt. His mother was not very affectionate, but his aunt, her younger sister, was. He clearly thought of her as his second mother and in some ways was more at ease with her. Generally, he developed the strong sense that in order to get what he needed in the way of support and approval, he must please women. It was never acceptable and was even threatening to be in conflict with them.

Sheila's Family of Origin: She was the oldest of three girls and was her perfectionist dad's favorite. She did not respect her mother and decided she would never be such a "doormat." Her father was bright, competent, and domineering. Sheila experienced him as emotionally distant, demanding, angry, and rigid. Her mother was subservient to her dad, though the mother was also bright and competent. She was nurturing with Sheila and her siblings, but placating and dependent with Sheila's father. Sheila lost respect for her mother in this role in the marriage and vowed never to give her power away to a man. It has only been in recent years that she has become appreciative of her mother's wisdom and become closer to her. She thought her dad really wanted her to be a son, and she developed some competitive qualities, which served her well as she grew in mastery and competence. What she did not get was a sense of how to receive and give tenderness and affection. Having rejected her mother at such an early age, she is only now integrating those feminine aspects her mother seems to have to offer her.

The Partners' Sexual Histories Before Meeting: Gary had little sexual experience compared to Sheila. His relationships were few and the longest was 2 years. He felt awkward with women and did not even attempt romantic involvement until college. It is probably no surprise that his longest involvement was with a young woman who was very dominating. He was very fond of her brother, being starved for male companionship and attention. He stayed with that relationship for 2 years, but could never quite establish his own will with her, except to ultimately refuse to marry her. Sheila, on the other hand, had a passionate sex life with several men. Only one was important to her, and she still fantasizes about what it would have been like to be married to him rather than to Gary. In the others, she seems to have had some trouble establishing an emotionally intimate connection, bailing out because she felt "suffocated" by the closeness.

THE PARTNERS' INDIVIDUAL DEVELOPMENTAL CONTEXTS

Here are some of the developmental issues for Gary and Sheila as individuals and as a couple.

Gary is struggling on several fronts. He has not been able to claim his manhood with women. He does not feel competent emotionally, sexually, or professionally. He feels inadequate with Sheila in all these areas, and it does not help that she makes more money and has more family money than he does. He is still motivated by trying to be a "good boy," which makes him largely ineffective at asserting himself or initiating his own agenda. Guilt is his primary motivator. He is poorly defined as an individual, in that he does not even know what his agenda is in many areas. Vocationally, he is developing some dreams, which involve being an entrepreneur. However, he will be hampered in those activities and may not succeed unless he learns to develop his own sense of purpose and desire. One of the major questions we, as his therapists, must continue to confront him with is "What do you want?" Individuals like Gary have enormous difficulty focusing on the self and automatically take the other person's point of view in determining how they "should" feel and behave. This is very destructive for him, as well as for the marriage. He, not surprisingly, approaches sex the same way, focusing on Sheila's experience: "Is she approving? Am I doing it right?" As Bill and I discussed this case, we were not at all surprised by his erection difficulties. The same things happen in the partners' daily interactions about how to run their lives and how they feel with each other. Gary is so conflict avoidant that it requires enormous concentration and commitment on his part to tell the truth from his perspective. He fears being abandoned in close relationships, because in different ways both his parents abandoned him—his father literally, and his mother, emotionally, every time she punitively withdrew when he asserted his own will.

Sheila is a very competent individual in the business world. She learned well from her father how to perform and succeed. She is very successful in her career. However, in relationships, she also has some difficulties as a result of gaps in her emotional development. Though she is very comfortable with her sexuality, she is not able to really combine it with emotional intimacy. Sheila mistakes sexual activity for emotional intimacy. She developmentally negotiates sexual interest and functioning, but lacks the ability to be vulnerable. She tends to lead with aggression rather than openness, having a chip on her shoulder with men. When she is hurt or fearful, she is apt to attack. Anger is her primary emotion. She is competitive and thinks that is the way you get what you want. She has internalized the hard edge of her father well, but it does not serve her any better in matters of the heart than it did her father. She does not understand the concept of being strong enough to be vulnerable. She wants what she wants when she wants it and can feel betrayed when it does not happen her way. This is not to say she is not a generous person; she is. It is important to understand that beneath her hard-driving edge, she feels fearful and sad. No matter how well she performed to earn her dad's affection, she did not get it, because he is emotionally constricted and cannot give it. She has not learned how to negotiate disappointment and loss as a fact of life and does not even realize how much emotional loss she has incurred. She tries to ward it off by being in control. Thus, she is prone to manage others, rather than be intimate with them. She is frightened to take risks, working hard to control her environment and the people in it who might present some risk. Intimacy involves risk and vulnerability. She is heartbroken that she does not have the emotional and sexual closeness she craves with Gary, but sees him as the source of her disappointment, rather than understanding her own limitations. Sheila has always feared being consumed in close relationships, as she saw her mother consumed by her father and as she experienced herself struggling not to be obliterated by his overwhelming personality and demands of her.

THE COUPLE'S DEVELOPMENTAL CONTEXT

How do these issues affect their developmental status as a couple? We see how conflicted they must be, both individually and as a couple, as we note how unresolved developmental issues of the past insert themselves into the current developmental context. Psychologically, both seem in their early teens, though Sheila may be precocious sexually for an early teen. In a sense, Sheila has an underdeveloped feminine aspect and Gary an underdeveloped masculine aspect. Viewing them as this young helps us see the developmental issues in the marriage. Though they are in their 40s, it is a young marriage, and the individuals in it are emotionally young. However, because Sheila is in midlife, her biological clock is running out, so pressure is on to have a baby. Yet we can see that they were not prepared for parenthood as individuals or as a couple when they entered marital therapy. It would be like asking two 13-year-olds to become competent enough to be parents. They could not even negotiate a sexual relationship in which to procreate. To make matters worse, their marriage is subjected to the further stress of infertility procedures to increase the chance of pregnancy. This is an external stressor that can harm even the most resilient and mature relationships. I confronted Gary about his desire to have a child, telling him it could easily be just another part of Sheila's agenda with which he felt compelled to comply. I wondered if he was ambivalent, and, if so, whether that ambivalence would affect his ability to get erections sufficient for intercourse. He vehemently denied ambivalence and said he very much wanted to be a father and felt terrible for his failure to impregnate her "the natural way" that she wanted it to happen. He simultaneously realized that whether or not he got erections might have had little impact on Sheila's fertility, as she would probably have to undergo in vitro fertilization with a donor egg anyway because of her age and the decline of her egg quality. He fervently wished he could have intercourse so that she could not hold him responsible for the infertility.

The Present Developmental Context

Because it is early in the marriage, as well as being each person's first marriage, Sheila and Gary are still defining their roles and trying to become a couple. This includes everything from how money is handled (and who provides it) to trying to make a home together. For a while they lived in Sheila's house, which hurt their mutuality even more. Now they have bought a home together and are trying to make it theirs as a couple. As is always the case in a new marriage, extended family relationships have to be negotiated. Gary has done a good job over the last year of backing off his intrusive mother, setting limits on her, and insisting she treat his wife with respect. This has earned him more respect from both his wife and his mother. To his mother's credit, she has responded well to these boundaries and is cooperating. She seems to be trying to let go of her "good boy." Sheila is much closer to her mother now and uses her as a confidante. She is now able to have those mother–daughter talks that are characteristic of the preteen and early teenage girl. She still respects her father, but has taken him off his pedestal and is developing an adult relationship with him. She sees his flaws and limitations, and admires Gary for having more emotional depth and access to that than her father does. Gary, being starved for male guidance and attention, has sought some of that from her father. Lately, that has felt less satisfying to him because he detects subtle criticism that he is not competent.

APPROACHING THE THERAPY OF UNHAPPY MARRIAGES

How does a therapist begin to untangle such a web? Our approach from the beginning with a couple allows us to create a purposeful, incisive frame for the problems and their solutions. We do not just accept the problems as the couple defines them. We explain in a phone call before we ever see the couple that the first four sessions are devoted to assessing the situation. The first meeting is ideally with both partners, where we get a description of the problems, how they are affected by them, how each feels about his or her dilemma, a natural history of the problems, and an opportunity to view their marital interaction. Many times couples will not agree on how the problem began and the course of its development. Though this is not unusual, it is one sign of more acute marital distress: The partners do not have a common understanding and will tend to be more at odds. The next two meetings are with each partner individually, where we get a social and sexual history. We take the sexual history as we are taking the developmental history, so that it does not stand out or feel intrusive. That approach also communicates that sexuality is a natural part of development and increases the comfort level with the subject matter as it is integrated into the therapy, the person, and the marriage. Usually, by the fourth meeting we have enough information to reconvene with both partners and give them feedback. This is an important therapeutic intervention, our opportunity to define the problem in a way that allows us to explore avenues we find important. It also helps us to define problems in ways that make them solvable. Because couples feel stuck when they come to therapy, many do not initially present their issues this way.

Gary and Sheila: As they presented their feelings in their initial interview, Sheila felt betrayed by Gary's inability to have an erection and distraught over having her own sexuality dampened; she questioned his desire to be committed in this 4-year marriage. She also had a lot of grief over the possibility that she would never carry a pregnancy. Because she was in her 40s and they had sexual dysfunction, she felt that repeated attempts at intercourse or engaging in vitro fertilization seemed beyond them at this point in their lives. She had difficulty not blaming this loss entirely on Gary.

Gary felt beaten down by the whole sexual interaction in their relationship, afraid of disappointing again, yet knowing that avoiding sex was also a disappointment to her. As in most of his relationships, especially with women, he placated and did not assert himself. He was and is especially intimidated by female anger. Further imbalance results from the fact that Sheila was wealthy in her own right, and he was struggling to make a small business work. They don't sleep together, and affection had stopped.

They did not agree on the genesis of these problems. He felt, though this has always been somewhat of an issue, that they regressed when she stopped being supportive as he worked on his erectile difficulties. She felt that the problem was largely his and he should get it fixed if he loves her.

There was a grain of truth in both views. One good sign for their union, which may be a result of their each having had considerable individual therapy, was that they spoke relatively openly in front of one another with these concerns. In the individual history interviews where I probed deeper, each was more frank and forthcoming, stating that there was no need to be unduly hurtful to the other. Where do the individual issues intersect with the marital struggles?

So, how do we handle all this data in giving them feedback and framing the problems and solutions? We have all heard the adage that most marital problems involve sex, money, or children. We have referred to the imbalances in this relationship in sex, money, initiative, and assertiveness. And there is the disappointment in being childless. It would be tempting to focus on these content areas, but our view is that educating the partners about the underlying processes contained in their struggles is most helpful to them and to us as directors of the therapeutic process.

In the feedback interview I told Gary and Sheila that Gary's erection problem was not their only problem. I explained to them that any couple would be having sexual problems when the partners were so unhappy with themselves and their marriage. I told Sheila that she has intimacy issues in allowing Gary to be close and in forming an emotional attachment with him. I directed Gary to concentrate on how he wanted to run his life and make a marriage he could live in. Furthermore, I said they needed to focus on what they liked about each other, to resume sharing the same bed, and to begin daily expressions of verbal and physical affection. Of course, I was not at all surprised that they were not willing or able to do these things to improve their marital happiness. I am patient. I am willing to sit and wait with them as they struggle. So, why would I give them all these instructions if I expected them to fail? Because this framework provides the grist for the therapy mill, as we examine their obstacles to making these changes. When they returned for subsequent interviews, I did not disapprove or judge. In fact, sometimes when I thought it would help lighten the intensity, I would joke about their obstinacy and power struggles. I was giving them a model for not blaming each other and confronting their individual responsibilities in staying stuck.

Access and Control

What all intimate couples have to negotiate can be broken down into two broad categories: access and control. Here is what we mean by access to the other: It is the need to feel the partner's availability to us with individual resources (money, time, energy) and the heart (acceptance, attention, love, sex). Partners need to feel one another's commitment to offer access in these ways. When that commitment is uncertain, trust erodes and motives are questioned. The importance of the perceived marital bond has already been noted (Carrere et al., 2000). Whenever we feel denied access, we may feel hurt, afraid, angry, and usually that our marital bond is weakened.

Sheila has been generous with her financial resources, but Gary is loathe to accept them because it makes him feel worse about his contribution, his mutuality, and his power in the marriage. They do not struggle over issues of time or energy, do not have arguments about who is working too much or spending too much time away. They do, however, have other significant access problems. Gary feels shut out of Sheila's heart because he feels she does not accept him. They both see him as inadequate. Sheila feels shut out of Gary's heart because he denies her sex. He has a problem, so why doesn't he care enough about her to just fix it and give her what she wants? She feels it as a lack of commitment. Of course, the more she takes a demanding stance, the more he withdraws, as has been noted previously in the research we cited by Heavey et al. (1995). This pattern of demand on the part of the wife and withdrawal on the part of the husband is a very common tendency in unhappy marriages. Sheila and Gary both feel little access to the other for affectionate touch and tenderness. They stay physically apart. They do not sleep together. Gary wants to start sleeping together, but Sheila is not ready. He has suggested that he could come into the bed for at least some time on weekend mornings. She continues to stonewall him on this. She has the sense that until they have successful sex, she does not want him in their bed with her. He, on the other hand, says that until they can begin to build back some affectionate touch, he does not see how they can bridge the sexual gap. We tend to agree with Gary about what the sequence needs to be. Though Sheila and Gary like each other at many levels, both feel unloved in these ways and wonder if their marriage can survive. We have noted that in the family history, as well as in the present context, we are very interested in affection. This is a physical expression of allowing your partner access to your loving, tender side and also a way of seeking that access. When the affection has broken down, the couple is in danger of creating more marital unhappiness. We see restoring affectionate touch as a building block for this access to tenderness and intimacy and a bridge to repairing sexual problems. As it stands now with these partners, they are at a stalemate regarding affectionate touch. The importance of this and the obstacles to it are primary concerns for the therapeutic interventions.

One of the things that we know does *not* work, from the research as well as practical experience, is to demand access when one feels denied it (Heavey et al., 1995). Coercive approaches in a marriage produce unhappiness. Sheila especially needs to learn the concept of invitation and request. One of the ways she could do that would be her willingness to risk more affectionate touch and sleeping together. Yet, at this point, she is unwilling to take that chance. She is afraid of the feelings of pain and disappointment it will evoke in her to know that the contact stops with affection and does not culminate in sexual intercourse. Gary cannot produce an erection for her on demand. They actually tried that recently on a day when she was ovulating and the results were predictably disastrous. Sheila would need some individual work to explore her vulnerability to the affection, to understand how to invite and receive, to acknowledge her need of his love. Gary, on the other hand, will not gain access to Sheila's heart by withdrawing from her emotionally and sexually and blaming her for not being available to him. He must learn to be a "worthy opponent," pushing back when appropriate to define himself and his limits, requiring respect by having more self-respect, and behaving according to his personal integrity instead of constantly selling out for fear she will disapprove.

In addition to access to the other as a factor in marital unhappiness, access to the self is very important. Here is what we mean by access to the self: Individuals must develop some awareness of their emotional processes, so that they know how they are responding and can define the self and then share that information with their intimate partners. This is where individual development is crucial to the skills needed in an intimate relationship. Gary has had particular trouble accessing his agenda, his desires. He often does not know what he wants, let alone how to go after it. He also has had trouble accessing his personal power, particularly as that is expressed with male energy. Sheila, as we have noted, has had difficulty accessing her softer, vulnerable side. She is only now becoming aware of this aspect of herself, and because it contains a lot of pain and emotional deprivation, she will find it hard to tolerate. This limitation has prevented her from being open in a way that would give her more emotional nurturing, for which she is so hungry, and it keeps her from helping to create the intimacy that would increase marital happiness and sexual satisfaction.

Another important point of struggle in unhappy marriages is control. By control of oneself, we mean a mastery of the self, a basic human need to be in control of oneself, feeling effective in maintaining one's physical and psychological boundaries. Some people stay out of relationships altogether because they are so threatened about their boundaries. Others, like Sheila and Gary, have managed to make some connections as they have developed, but are encountering major problems with how to manage their personal control and still develop and sustain closeness. Many times individuals focus on controlling the relationship or the partner as a way to develop this safe zone for the self. This is not only misguided, but also ineffective. It is the source of many power struggles we see in couples and results in problems handling conflict. Sheila has this tendency, and it can manifest in a range from appropriate assertiveness to aggression. Gary, on the other hand, deals with threats to his personal control by abdicating it entirely to the other person. He fears being abandoned more than he fears being violated. So, they developed a pattern where Sheila would approach him directly, sometimes in his face, and he would usually withdraw to protect himself. Again, we see the demand/withdrawal pattern. Sometimes it is helpful to conceptualize it for the couple as an issue of physical space.

I have said, "For example, take this office as your relationship. Gary, it seems all the space you occupy is this one corner over here, while Sheila is wandering through the entire room looking for you, feeling lonely and desperate. How could you expect to have an erection in such a circumstance, when you are hiding out? So, Gary, you have to learn to take up more space, be more of a presence."

"Sheila, you have to learn more about surrendering and yielding space as he does that. You need to learn how to invite him rather than hunt him down. Otherwise, even if he comes out and gives you what you want, you wonder, 'did he really want to or did he do it because I made him do it?' and it feels unsatisfying, as though it is not meeting your need to be loved. Being obeyed and being loved are not the same things. Your father did not know that, and you still need to learn the lesson."

Such a spatial metaphor is graphic and nonblaming. It shows them each how they contribute individually to their marital unhappiness and sexual problems. It is especially important for Sheila to take some ownership here, as both she and Gary can easily make him the primary problem because he carries the obvious symptom. Notice how, in the phrasing to Gary, I touched on Sheila's vulnerability in feeling lonely and desperate. I literally put words in her mouth. I did this to bring up her vulnerability in an indirect way and have it in the room. She did not argue, as she felt my empathy and some relief to have it spoken for her, because she is so poor at conveying it herself. Likewise, in speaking to Sheila, I touched on Gary's sense of coercion. I also gave him a message that he was not loving her by obeying her as a way to empower himself.

The other aspect we have mentioned as important, both in development and in the current relationship, has to do with how conflict is handled. In many ways, this is an expression of the control factor. What we see in this couple is that Sheila raises an issue, often in anger, and Gary avoids in some fashion. He may get silent, change the subject, or placate her to get her to stop. No matter which he chooses, he is withdrawing his genuine self from the interaction and from his wife. She, on the other hand, in her effort to gain access to him and maintain control over her own boundaries, leads with anger and accusations, which does not help her get what she wants.

The real control any individual can each have involves mastery of the self, a real access to and knowledge of the self that allows us to take responsibility for our own emotional well-being, leaving behind the immature fantasy that we can be rescued from ourselves by another. If we feel we have our internal house in order and have some way to regulate how we experience the self with others, we don't need to focus on controlling those around us to maintain our internal equilibrium. Both Gary and Sheila need to be more introspective as a way to take responsibility for the self, to search within for fears and limitations that maintain this marital and sexual unhappiness. The ability for such introspection and self-responsibility helps develop the emotional skills of regulating one's feelings and expressing them in a constructive way. In

Sheila's case, it would help her regulate her anger, if she can see that in many respects it is loss, disappointment, and grief she feels, not just about her current situation, but about her whole development. Her fear is largely about experiencing this pain. This is acutely available to her in her grief over not being a mother and possibly never being one. Though it is acutely available, it is so devastating that she finds it hard to stay with this process of introspection and experience the vulnerable feelings that fuel her anger.

Gary's introspection needs to take the form we have already alluded to: He needs to look within and examine his fear of abandonment so that it is not such a strong, unconscious motivator for his actions. He needs to do as the lion did in *The Wizard of Oz* and search for the courage to be himself. He only compounds his feelings of shame and inadequacy by failing to be true to himself, selling out his integrity. He needs to be able to take control of his own boundaries and say to Sheila, "I will not accept your contempt about my erection problems. I am done with that. You also need to look at your part as I am. We need to fix this problem together." And he needs to say it with the force of some conviction, with some feeling behind it, rather than just repeating it because his therapist tells him to. If he would take himself out of the scapegoat, identified-patient position, the stalemate would be broken.

Access and Control: A Summary

Access and control involve both commitment to the self and commitment to the relationship. Access issues can often be experienced as problems with commitment to the relationship, whereas control issues can be experienced as problems with commitment to the self. Marriage is an intimate connection where one must have the desire and the ability to do both. There is a dynamic tension between the needs of the individual and the needs of the relationship. People in unhappy marriages tend to see these needs at odds more than they really have to be. These couples tend to have a rigid, black or white view that involves a winner and loser. They have difficulty constructing win-win scenarios.

Our role as marital therapists is to attend to both individuals, as well as to the relationship. Ideally, we see marriage as a container for the growth of both partners, as well as for their offspring. Adult development does not stop at the wedding altar. In fact, this intimate container can challenge individuals in ways they never dreamed of. Marriage is both a theater where the individual's script is revealed and an incubator for the new emotional life breathed into the individuals. The individual growth, in turn, brings richness and depth to the marriage. These are not causal or linear processes, but circular and interwoven. That is why we are ever mindful in doing marital therapy with couples like Gary and Sheila that we must track where individual issues are blocking couple progress and vice versa. This knowledge will guide us in structuring the treatment, which almost always includes individual as well as couple sessions. They each need some individual therapy in the context of this marital therapy. Gary needs to be propped up enough to assume a more mutual stance with her, to use his personal power; what we are constructing here is a stronger sense of self. Sheila needs the individual therapy to help her with introspection into her pain, her vulnerability, and to take responsibility for these without shame. We doubt that either can do this deep psychological work in the presence of the partner right now, because they do not feel safe enough. The individual sessions are part deep exploration of these individual issues and part coaching on how to bring the new awareness, vulnerability, and definition into the marriage. As each person incrementally learns the emotional skills to be in control of the self and allow access to the other, we put them together in sessions so they can practice. This is using the marriage as the incubator for experiencing the self differently and as the theater for expressing the self differently. Both this experience and this expression help to integrate the psychological changes. Having access to the individual dynamics and the couple gives the therapist several routes toward breaking up negative, entrenched cycles. If the marriage won't budge, meet individually and turn up the heat on the individual dysfunctions. As system theorists note, it only takes a shift in one part of the system to get movement.

CONCLUSION

In this way, the marriage becomes a powerful tool for changing the individuals and vice versa. Because this therapy structure can intensify healing and involves such intricate complexity, we find working within the context of marriage both a taxing and a rewarding endeavor. Viewing marriage and the partners in their developmental contexts, while being mindful of issues of access and control, is a potent way to organize what can be overwhelming data in the face of marital unhappiness.

It would be a mistake to read this chapter and think that this formulation has healed Gary and Sheila, either individually or as a couple. In fact, they were so overwhelmed by their current stressors related to the infertility that they suspended marital therapy after about eight sessions. For such a couple, eight sessions is hardly enough time to try to establish the framework we have discussed. We had barely scratched the surface of what they needed. Perhaps they will return. Perhaps enduring this stress without the marital therapy as a support will be their undoing.

Nevertheless, we feel confident that our 27-plus years of evaluating and treating marriages helped this couple. We hope that Gary and Sheila were able to take the framework Lynda gave them and reduce their blaming of one another and maybe even become supportive of each other in the stressful infertility treatment process. Lynda spoke with both individual therapists during the evaluation period and feels certain that if Gary and Sheila continue in those treatments, their therapists will support these same objectives.

We consider that whatever the outcome for couples, as there will be those who choose divorce, our work is to help them clarify their dynamics, both individually and together, and help them be more self-aware and self-responsible as they seek intimacy. Usually, this is not a quick fix. It tends to take years rather than weeks. We encourage you not to be disheartened as you encounter the pain and the complexity in unhappy marriages and to draw on this chapter for ideas to support your healing endeavor.

REFERENCES

Adams, J., & Jones, W. (1997). The conceptualization of marital commitment in integrative analysis. *Journal of Personality and Social Psychology, 72*, 1177–1196. This is an empirical study of three types of commitment in marriage. The study is significant because it is one of the few empirical works on this important aspect of marriage.

Barnett, R. C., Raudenbush, S. W., Brennan, R. T., Pleck, J. H., & Marshall, N. L. (1995). Change in job and marital experiences and change in psychological distress: A longitudinal study of dual-earner couples. *Journal of Personality and Social Psychology, 69*(5), 839–850. Well-done study on one of the major stressors in marriage of dual-career partners.

Bradbury, T. N., Beach, S. R. H., Fincham, F. D., & Nelson, G. M. (1996). Attributions and behavior in functional and dysfunctional marriages. *Journal of Consulting and Clinical Psychology, 64*, 569–576. These authors are leaders in the marital research field, particularly in the area of attributions. Beach's contribution is the relationship between depression and marital distress.

Brunstein, J. C., Dangelmayer, G., & Schultheiss, O. C. (1996). Personal goals and social support in close relationships: Effects on relationships, mood and marital satisfaction. *Journal of Personality and Social Psychology, 71*, 1006–1019. This article examines the importance of social support in encouraging partners to pursue their personal goals and how this impacts the marital relationship.

Carrere, S., Buehlman, K. T., Gottman, J. M., Coan, J. A., & Ruckstuhl, L. (2000). Predicting marital stability and divorce in newlywed couples. *Journal of Family Psychology 14*(1), 42–58. More data from the Gottman researchers on what accounts for marital stability.

Carstenesen, L., Gottman, J., & Levenson, R. (1995). Emotional behavior in long-term marriage. *Psychology and Aging, 10*, 140–149. Major article that examines marital couples who have been together for a long period.

Cassidy, J., & Shaver, P. (Eds.). (1999). *Handbook of Attachment Theory, Research and Clinical Applications*. New York: Guilford. Very good new volume of articles by the top theorists, clinicians, and researchers in attachment theory.

Cherlin, A. (1992). *Marriage, Divorce, and Remarriage*. Cambridge, MA: Harvard University Press.

Christensen, L. L., Russell, C. S., Miller, R. B., & Peterson, C. M. (1998). The process of change in couples therapy: A qualitative investigation. *Journal of Marital and Family Therapy, 24*, 177–188. One of the few empirical process articles on couples psychotherapy.

Cowen, E. L. (1991). In pursuit of wellness. *American Psychologist, 46*(4), 404–408.

Fincham, F. D., Harold, G. T., & Gano-Phillips, S. (2000). The longitudinal association between attributions and marital satisfaction direction of effects and role efficacy expectations. *Journal of Family Psychology, 14*, 267–285.

Gottman, J. (1994). *What Predicts Divorce? The Relationship Between Marital Processes and Marital Outcomes*. Hillsdale, NJ: Erlbaum. The foremost marital researcher presents his findings on what the behaviors are in couples that predict divorce.

Gottman, J. (1999). *The Seven Principles for Making Marriage Work.* New York: Crown.

Gottman, J., Coan, J., Carrere, S., & Swanson, C. (1998). Predicting marital happiness and stability from newlywed interactions. *Journal of Marriage and the Family, 60*, 5–22. More data from the University of Washington research group on discriminating variables between divorcing couples, stable/unhappy couples, and stable/happy couples.

Groth, T., Fehm-Wolfsdorf, G., & Hahlweg, K. (2000). Basic research on the psychobiology of intimate relationships. In K. B. Schmaling & T. G. Sher (Eds.), *The Psychology of Couples and Illness: Theory, Research & Practice* (pp. 13–42). Washington, DC: American Psychological Association. Excellent summary of the psychophysiology of couples.

Hampson, R. B., Prince, C. C., & Beavers, W. R. (1999). Marital therapy: Qualities of couples who fare better or worse in treatment. *Journal of Marital and Family Therapy, 25*, 411–424. Another good article on the variables related to who does better or worse in couple psychotherapy.

Haynes, S. N., Floyd, F. J., Lemsky, C., Rogers, E., Winemiller, D., Heilman, N., Werle, M., Murphy, T., & Cardone, L. (1992). The marital satisfaction questionnaire for older persons. *Psychological Assessment, 4,* 473–482. Good study of what the important factors that contribute to marital satisfaction are in older couples.

Heavey, C., Christensen, A., & Malamuth, N. (1995). The longitudinal impact of demand and withdrawal during marital conflict. *Journal of Consulting and Clinical Psychology, 63*, 797–801. Outstanding empirical work on the demand/withdrawal dynamic in couples.

Johnson, P. L., & O'Leary, K. D. (1996). Behavioral components of marital satisfaction: An individualized assessment approach. *Journal of Consulting and Clinical Psychology, 64,* 417–423.

Karney, B. R., & Bradbury, T. N. (1997). Neuroticism, marital interaction, and the trajectory of marital satisfaction. *Journal of Personality and Social Psychology, 72,* 1075–1092.

Kiecolt-Glaser, J. K., & Newton, T. L. (2001). Marriage and health: His and hers. *Psychological Bulletin, 127,* 472–503. Another excellent review of the psychophysiology of couples.

Klohnen, E., & Bera, S. (1998). Behavioral and experiential patterns of avoidantly and securely attached women across adulthood: A 31 year longitudinal perspective. *Journal of Personality and Social Psychology, 74,* 211–223. An empirical attachment study on women in long-term marriages, comparing those who are avoidant to secure.

Kurdek, L. A. (1999). The nature and predictors of the trajectory of change in marital quality for husbands and wives over the first 10 years of marriage. *Developmental Psychology, 35,* 1283–1296. Good study on the process of change in marriages during the first 10 years.

Lopez, F., & Brennan, K. (2000). Dynamic process underlying adult attachment organization: Toward an attachment theoretical perspective on the healthy and effective self. *Journal of Counseling Psychology, 47,* 283–300.

Middleberg, C. V. (2001). Projective identification in common couple dances. *Journal of Marital and Family Therapy, 27,* 341–352. Practical application of the object relations of projective identification in systems theory approach.

National Center for Health Statistics. (1991). *Advance Report of Final Marriage Statistics, 1988* (Monthly Vital Statistics Report 39). Hyattsville, MD: Public Health Service.

Perrone, K. M., & Worthington, E. L. (2001). Factors influencing ratings of marital quality by individuals within dual-career marriages: A conceptual model. *Journal of Counseling Psychology, 48,* 3-9. Multi-factorial study of dual-career couples—what are the factors that make for a good relationship/love?

Talmadge, L. D., & Talmadge, W. C. (2001). Integrative Approach: Advances in couples therapy. *Presentation at annual Georgia Psychological Association Meeting, Atlanta, Georgia.*

Vansteenwegen, A. (1996). Who benefits from couple therapy? A comparison of successful and failed couples. *Journal of Sex & Marital Therapy, 22,* 63–67.

Part Two

WOMEN'S SEXUAL ISSUES

Chapter Six

When Do We Say A Woman's Sexuality is Dysfunctional?

Sharon G. Nathan, PhD, MPH

The question "When do we say a woman's sexuality is dysfunctional?" has in-trigued—and confused—me ever since the late 1970s. I encountered it for the first time when I disquietingly undertook simultaneous postdoctoral fellow-ships in psychiatric epidemiology and in sex therapy. In the epidemiology program, I reviewed previously published sex surveys to learn about the distribution of dysfunc-tion in the population. Conducting that research, I became convinced that we needed highly explicit criteria to define dysfunction—for example, has orgasms all of the time, most of the time, some of the time (or better still: has orgasms 95–100% of the time, 75–94% of the time, etc.). Only with this degree of specificity could we use surveys to establish base rates of functioning in the population, a step I believed crucial for defin-ing sexual dysfunction scientifically (Nathan, 1986). But in my clinical work in the sex therapy program, I found that these highly refined criteria were less useful, telling me both more and less than I needed to know. They told me more than I wanted to know because distinctions between, say, "has orgasms occasionally" and "has orgasms fre-quently" were usually clinically unimportant. A woman who had orgasms only occa-sionally, I learned, might be content, whereas a woman who had orgasms frequently might not be. And they told me less than I wanted to know because, in order to treat a patient, I needed to understand when, how, and why she had orgasms, even more than I needed to know how often she did.

I did not know 25 years ago that my dilemma was actually one of choosing be-tween two classic approaches to defining sexual dysfunction. The "objective approach" compares the woman's behavior with established standards of sexual functioning, demarking a point where good functioning ceases and dysfunction begins. The "func-tional approach," on the other hand, is not concerned with how this woman's sexuality compares with that of others but with how it promotes satisfaction, or causes prob-lems, for her, her partner, or both of them.

In this chapter I am going to show you what an objective approach can tell us. I will discuss where our norms come from and describe their limitations in clinical practice. Then I will examine the functional approach to assessing dysfunction. I will try to convince you that despite the softness of its criteria, it is a far better standard for you to employ and the one that sex therapists actually rely on in practice.

THE SEARCH FOR OBJECTIVE STANDARDS OF DYSFUNCTION

When we use the objective approach to say a woman's sexuality is dysfunctional, we are implicitly or explicitly measuring it against some standard, compared to which her performance is found to be deficient or lacking. But where do our standards come from? In deciding what level of functioning is normal, we can consult sources such as the *Diagnostic and Statistical Manual of Mental Disorders* (*DSM-IV*) (*Diagnostic and Statistical Manual*, 1994), clinical judgment, population data, laboratory studies, and common knowledge.

DSM-IV

In theory, assessing female sexual dysfunction using the *DSM-IV* seems straightforward. A woman presents a sexual complaint (e.g., "I don't have orgasms," "I have no sexual desire") that approximates one of the *DSM-IV* disorders, and the clinician, considering the woman's problem in light of the diagnostic criteria provided by the *DSM*, formalizes the diagnosis—"Female Orgasmic Disorder"; "Hypoactive Sexual Desire Disorder"—or fails to find a diagnosis warranted. In practice it is almost never that simple.

Problems arise because the *DSM-IV* criteria for Sexual Dysfunctions are not operationally defined in the way the criteria for, say, Major Depressive Episode are. For Major Depressive Episode, the clinician is directed to determine whether the patient has experienced five or more of nine listed symptoms over a period of 2 consecutive weeks; furthermore, many of the symptoms themselves are defined, or at least exemplified, rather specifically. In contrast, the diagnostic criteria for the Sexual Dysfunctions are vague to the point of being tautological. Thus Hypoactive Sexual Desire is defined as "deficient (or absent) fantasies or desire for sexual activity" (*DSM-IV*, p. 496), a criterion that really doesn't go much beyond saying that Hypoactive Sexual Desire is desire for sex that is hypoactive. It's certainly not much help in deciding whether a particular woman qualifies for the designation.

Recognizing the vagueness of the criteria it provides, the *DSM-IV* turns the matter of operationalizing them over to "clinical judgment." Thus for Hypoactive Sexual Desire Disorder, the "*judgment of* deficiency or absence is made by *the clinician*, taking into account factors that affect sexual functioning such as age and the context of the person's life" (*DSM-IV*, p. 498). And for Female Orgasmic Dysfunction: "The diagnosis of Female Orgasmic Disorder should be based on *the clinician's judgment* that the woman's orgasmic capacity is less than would be reasonable for her age, sexual experience, and the adequacy of the sexual stimulation she receives [italics mine]" (*DSM-IV*, p. 506). But clinical judgment cannot do all it is called upon to accomplish.

Clinical Judgment

Clinical judgment, whatever else it may be useful for, cannot be utilized to establish norms. And yet that is explicitly what the *DSM-IV* is calling upon it to do: "Because of a lack of normative age- or gender-related data on frequency or degree of sexual desire, the diagnosis must rely on clinical judgment based on the individual's characteristics, the interpersonal determinants, the life context, and the cultural setting" (*DSM-IV*, p. 496). In other words, the clinician must decide, for example, whether a particular level of sexual desire is appropriate for a 51-year-old, happily married, lower-middle-class, Greek-American woman—when, and *because*, nothing is known about what level of sexual desire is normal for a woman with any one of these characteristics, let alone with all four in combination. What knowledge or experience would equip the clinician to make such a judgment, even if the clinician were a seasoned practitioner and not, as might also be the case, a 1st-year resident? Lest you think that making such an assessment might in some way be easier than I am suggesting, let me present you with some actual clinical examples requiring correlating sexual desire with the variables the *DSM-IV* says are relevant to it:

Individual Characteristics: David insisted that his fiancée Emily's level of sexual desire was not only low in an absolute sense but lower than she was capable of because she was someone with a highly refined appreciation of other sensual pleasures such as food, wine, and art. (Sounds logical, but do we really have any evidence supporting the notion that sensuality is a dimension of personality such that if someone appreciates some sensual pleasures, she can appreciate all?)

Interpersonal Determinants: Sally had always been puzzled why her mother had stayed with her father, a man who had been physically and verbally abusive to her throughout the marriage. After her father's death, Sally asked her mother about it and was stunned to hear in reply, "Ah, yes, but the sex was perfect." (When we read in the *DSM-IV* that sexual desire should be assessed in light of "interpersonal determinants," the chances are that our first thought is that sexual desire should be higher in good relationships than in bad ones. So why do we see so many couples—like Sally and her husband, for that matter—where the relationship is great and the sex is minimal? And, certainly, Sally's parents' marriage doesn't stand alone as a bad relationship with good sex. What, if any, are the interpersonal determinants that sexual desire actually correlates with?)

Life Context: Yesterday I found myself relying on my clinical judgment to confidently reassure a couple not to worry about having sex only on the weekends because "couples with two careers and two kids just don't have sex during the week." (I believed it—or rather, I believed a less emphatic version of it—when I said it, and, truth to tell, I believe it now, but I cannot say on the basis of any evidence that it is true.)

Cultural Setting: By coincidence, a few years ago I was seeing two couples with sexual desire problems, each of which consisted of a Jewish man and an Italian-American woman. In one case it was the Jewish man who had the desire problem, and in the other case it was the Italian-American woman. What was fascinating was that the nondysfunctional partner in each couple explained the couple's problem in cultural terms. Couple A: "What do you expect? He comes from a scholarly, cerebral Jewish tradition, and I'm a passionate Mediterranean type." Couple B: "What do you expect? I'm from a liberal Jewish background and she's grown up as a typically repressed Italian Catholic." And you know what? They were both right, as far as their own individual situations were concerned. (The lesson: A cultural setting is not unidimensional, and therefore, assessing sexual desire in light of it is complicated.)

Population Data

What if we did have good epidemiological data about how sexual functioning variables, like sexual desire and frequency of orgasm, were distributed in the population? What if we actually could consult a table and find out what the average level of sexual desire is for a 51-year-old, happily married, lower-middle-class, Greek-American woman? How far would that go toward solving our problem of determining if a woman's sexuality is dysfunctional? It certainly would be of some help, I think, but it would not solve all the problems by a long shot.

Most sexual functioning variables are probably arrayed in the population the way other population characteristics, like height and intelligence, are—that is, in a bell-shaped, or normal, distribution, with most people clustered around the mean and fewer and fewer people the further out from the mean you go.[1] So here's the first problem: It is simply an unalterable statistical fact that for any characteristic we select, *half the population is going to be below average.* Half the women are going to have fewer than average orgasms, less than average sexual desire. Surely, we are not willing to call half the female population dysfunctional—not on the basis of statistical prevalence alone, at any rate. But an individual woman might see herself as dysfunctional for just this reason. We live in a culture where average equals mediocre and below average equals deficient. Everyone wants to be at least above average (indeed, surveys of motorists show that most do rate themselves as above-average drivers) and outstanding, if possible. Being statistically outstanding has become the goal, and even the expectation, of some contemporary women, particularly those who have been exceptionally high achievers in other areas of their lives. We need to make it clear that the failure to be above average is not the definition of dysfunctional.

So where do we draw the line? Perhaps more important, *on what basis* do we draw the line? With a characteristic like intelligence we draw a dysfunction-indicating line where we expect a person will actually have difficulty functioning; with an IQ of, say,

70 or lower, a person will not be able to function independently in society. The IQ score of 70 is two standard deviations below the mean, but it is not its statistical placement but the actual consequences of having an IQ that low that makes it a dysfunctional score. A woman who is 4'11" tall, a height that is also a good two standard deviations below the population mean, would not logically be labeled dysfunctional because this height does not seriously handicap her functioning; she is statistically deviant but not dysfunctional.[2] Thus dysfunctionality can only be defined *in terms of something*. We must then ask how her persistent or recurrent delay in, or absence of, orgasm handicaps her. After all, female orgasm is not needed for conception, as is male orgasm, with its accompanying ejaculation of semen, and from our clinical experience we also know that women who don't have orgasms can desire and enjoy sex (and that some women who do have orgasms may dislike and avoid it). Statistical norms can take us only so far in our attempts to diagnose when a woman's sexuality is dysfunctional.

Laboratory Studies: Masters and Johnson

Masters and Johnson's laboratory studies (Masters & Johnson, 1966) provide us with very important information about female sexual functioning. By showing how similar men and women are in what Masters and Johnson identified as the four stages of the human sexual response cycle—arousal, plateau, orgasm, and resolution—they showed women to have the same capacity for sexual response that men have. This was very definitely news when they published *Human Sexual Response*. What they did not address (because it was outside the scope of a laboratory study of sexual physiology) was whether the meaning and import of sexual functioning were the same for men and women. Just because women are at least as capable as men of arousal and orgasm doesn't mean that men and women value them and seek them out to the same extent. To what extent should our norms for sexual desire, sexual arousal, and orgasm be based at all on women's capacity (except, of course, to make sure they are not higher than what is possible)? There is a fine line between what Masters and Johnson did—give women the opportunity to fulfill their sexual potential—and a standard that turns that opportunity into an obligation (and then into a dysfunction if they fail to achieve it).

Common Knowledge

At the beginning of my first social science course in graduate school, the professor stood at the front of the classroom and extolled the value of studying human behavior scientifically. Why, within the last decade alone, he proclaimed, social science had made some remarkable discoveries; and he went on to enumerate half a dozen significant findings. Someone's hand shot up impatiently from the back of the classroom. Called upon, the student said what many of us had been thinking: "With all due respect, sir, I think all that research was a waste of time. It only showed what everybody already knows." Having gotten the response he hoped for, the professor smiled and responded, "Actually, it is the exact opposite of all of those statements that has been proven in the past 10 years." I instantly became a whole lot more skeptical about common knowledge.

Subsequent experience as a sex therapist has further reinforced the notion that it is wise to question what everybody knows. When I graduated from college, it was common knowledge—at least, for those who thought about such things—that women had two kinds of orgasms, clitoral and vaginal, and that vaginal orgasms were better (in the sense of being the orgasms that more mature women, who had overcome masculine striving, etc., had). Soon afterward came Masters and Johnson and their tiny cameras to prove that all orgasms were not only equal but actually the same; whether occurring during direct clitoral manipulation or intercourse, orgasms were produced by stimulation of the clitoris. It became common knowledge that all orgasms were clitoral and that vaginal orgasms were a myth. But within the last two decades, common knowledge on this matter has allowed for some variety of experience. Women are now allowed to have vaginal and "blended" orgasms as long as they do not proclaim these orgasms to be superior to the other kind. Thus, had I used common knowledge to assess female orgasm dysfunction in 1965, 1975, and 1995, I would have come up with quite different answers. Of course, we have no choice but to be limited by the state of knowledge at the time we make our assessment; it's just that it behooves us to be aware that our current notions may not represent eternal truths.

A NOTE ON STIMULATION

Although the *DSM-IV* requires the clinician to assess the adequacy of stimulation only when making a determination of Female Orgasmic Disorder, in fact adequacy of stimulation is a critical variable in evaluating each of the female sexual dysfunctions. I think stimulation is mentioned only for Female Orgasmic Disorder because stimulation is meant to be understood narrowly as physical stimulation. But psychological and situational stimulation are critical for a woman's feeling sexual desire and arousal, and they may play a role in some cases of sexual aversion, dyspareunia, and vaginismus, too. By psychological and situational stimulation I mean that the woman is motivated to be sexual because of ideas about who she and her partner are to one another and about the meaning of their sexual encounter.

Matt and Kitty had been husband and wife for 34 years, business partners for 32 years, and parents for 28 years. They also had had a barely detectable sex life for 27 years. Over that time period, due to Kitty's lack of sexual desire, the couple had had sex an average of twice a year—and even this was with Kitty's only nominal participation. In sex therapy, Kitty was able to design a scenario that engendered in her a genuine desire for sex: a quiet dinner with Matt in a lovely restaurant that served good food and wine. Kitty thought this scenario worked for her because it enacted courtship, a feature that was otherwise little in evidence in their lifestyle of constant partnership and togetherness.

Frequently, the woman's sexual desire is triggered by intimacy with her partner—the exchange of confidences, the sharing of hopes and dreams and fears. Men are often baffled that factors like courtship behavior and intimacy trigger sexual interest in their partners because their own desire is elicited so differently, but many women cannot be said to have received adequate stimulation unless these features are present.

These differences between men and women highlight the problem of using introspection to decide what is functional or dysfunctional in another, particularly when the other is of the opposite sex. In a recent therapy session where partners were dealing with their greatly discrepant levels of desire, the husband fumed at the wife, "I don't think you have any desire at all. Do you ever see a handsome man on the street, and undress him with your eyes, and want to go to bed with him?" This was exactly the analogue of his desire experience, but it is not a pattern frequently found in women. Clinicians, too, do this sort of thing. I recall at a professional meeting a decade ago a presenter expressed puzzlement about one of his research findings: Most of the women in his study with low sexual desire had orgasms when they did have sex. So why wouldn't they want to have sex more often in order to experience this pleasure? The women in the audience exchanged meaningful looks with one another, looks that said, "Doesn't he know that female sexual desire is about how the woman feels about herself that day, about how she feels about her partner (not just in the long run but at that very moment), about half a dozen factors more immediate and important than the prospect of orgasm?"

Overall, when we assess how little normative data about female sexual functioning we have from the *DSM-IV*, clinical judgment, laboratory studies, common knowledge, and introspection—and how difficult it is to draw a dysfunction-defining line even when we do—it becomes apparent that we need some other standard to guide us in making diagnoses, either as a supplement to the objective approach or as a replacement for it.

ASSESSING THE SYSTEM'S FUNCTIONING: A PROBLEM IS A PROBLEM IF IT'S A PROBLEM

As we have seen, the *DSM-IV* strives mightily to define sexual dysfunction in objective terms. However, it does also include a second criterion for each disorder that points toward a functional approach to diagnosing dysfunction. For each of the *DSM-IV* Sexual Disorders, a diagnosis is not to be made unless "the disturbance causes marked distress or interpersonal difficulty," a criterion that requires the clinician to look at what, if any, effect the disturbance is having on the system.

I must admit that I did not always look on this criterion with approval. For a long time it annoyed me, first, because it seemed motivated by political correctness—"No, no, if you're not bothered by your vaginismus, who am I to say it's a dysfunction?"—and, second, because it would be such an obviously absurd requirement were we talking about a medical condition—"No, no, if you're not troubled by your serum cholesterol of 383, who am I to say it's a dysfunction?" Even most of the other *DSM-IV* diagnoses, let alone medical diagnoses, allow for objective impairment to be a criterion for diagnosis, even if the condition doesn't cause marked distress or interpersonal difficulty. (Indeed, for some psychiatric conditions, the lack of concern about the condition is part of the pathology; that's one of the things we can mean when we talk about poor judgment, lack of insight, or inappropriate affect.) If "marked distress or interpersonal difficulty" was to be considered at all, I thought it should be a way of defining sub-types—the way "Lifelong Type" and "Acquired Type" are—rather than part of the main diagnosis itself.

It seemed especially inappropriate to have this criterion be a part of the diagnoses if we were thinking about doing epidemiological studies of the general population. Surely, we would be interested in knowing what percentage of the population suffered from "recurrent or persistent genital pain associated with sexual intercourse," whether or not the pain caused distress or difficulty. Knowing what percentage of the affected experienced marked distress or interpersonal difficulty on account of it would be an interesting additional fact—an interesting *additional* fact. But I no longer object to distress or interpersonal difficulty being part of the very definition of a disorder be-cause I have come to realize that, from a clinical perspective, the reaction to a sexual situation is actually more important than the objective situation itself in determining the sexual system's functionality and in determining when someone will seek treatment.

Let's take a look at the ways the objective and subjective criteria can co-vary. For this purpose, just as a way of having terms to refer to these two aspects of an overall situation, let's refer to the objective sexual pattern of the woman (e.g., delayed orgasm) as the putative "disorder" and the distress, interpersonal difficulty, or both, as the "problem." By separating these two aspects of the overall situation (just as the *DSM-IV* does in labeling them Criterion A and Criterion B), we can construct a fourfold table based on whether one, both, or neither is present. The table below represents the four possible situations; in this case, the dysfunction in question is Hypoactive Sexual Desire:

HYPOACTIVE SEXUAL DESIRE

CRITERION A
"DISORDER"
(Deficient or absent desire)

	+	−
CRITERION B "PROBLEM" (Distress) +	A	B
−	C	D

The situations represented by Cells A and D are the straightforward ones. In A, the woman has little interest in sex, and she, her partner, or both of them are troubled by it; this couple, other things being favorable (belief in seeking professional help for problems, ability to pay for therapy, etc.) is likely to present for treatment. In D, the woman's level of sexual desire is satisfactory and she and her partner are content with it; this is a satisfied couple we are unlikely to see in clinic. Situations B and C are more interesting because they represent discordant conditions: sexual problems that aren't caused by disorders (B) and disorders that don't cause sexual problems (C).

The *DSM-IV* itself anticipates situation B, a problem without a disorder, and suggests that in some cases it can be caused by "two people in the normal range at different ends of the continuum" (*DSM-IV*, p. 497). A sophisticated presentation of this problem is the couple that comes into treatment saying "we are sexually incompatible," but not all partners exhibit this much self-awareness and generosity toward each other:

> *John and Sarah had levels of desire that were normal but incompatible. John would have enjoyed having sex with Sarah almost every day, but Sarah was interested in sex perhaps once a month. (The designation of this as a normal level of desire was Sarah's own, but John did not contest it.) Sarah used the fact of her desire's presumed normality to dismiss out of hand John's wishes for more frequent sex. (It had never occurred to John that he could likewise assert his normality and demand that Sarah meet his level; this was in part because John was less certain that he was normal and in part because he would never have sought a solution that required his wife to do all the compromising.) Interestingly, I did not see John and Sarah as a couple. I saw John individually when he presented with concern about his increasing preoccupation with Internet sex chatrooms. It was only in the course of discussing John's problem that I became aware of this desire disparity as a contributing factor.*

The *DSM-IV* also warns that a couple can present for treatment of a woman's Hypoactive Sexual Desire when the real cause is "excessive need for sexual expression by the other partner" (*DSM-IV*, p. 497).

> *Although the presenting problem was his wife's lack of sexual desire, Mike came to see me alone for the first session. He told me that he was on the verge of divorcing his wife of 17 years because she wasn't interested in sex. Mike had an intense craving to feel wanted by his partner, something he had experienced in an affair he had had the previous year. The contrast with his marriage was so striking as to be almost unbearable. With Mike's description of the situation, I was totally unprepared for meeting his wife, Millie, the next week. She was stunning, warm, and sensual. She said that the couple usually made love twice a week and that she enjoyed sex and almost always had at least one orgasm. The problem was, she said, that it was never good enough for Mike. If she enjoyed an hour's*

*lovemaking and felt satisfied, Mike was furious that she didn't want to
have intercourse again. If they were having an intimate dinner as a prelude to sex, the whole evening could be ruined if she mentioned something about one of the children, a sign to Mike that she was not really
"into it."*

Other situations in which a clinician can be presented with a problem in the absence of true dysfunction stem not from interpersonal difficulty with the partner but
from the "marked distress" of the woman herself. These are cases of the "worried well,"
often with unrealistic expectations.

*When 30-year-old Maria, a fellow in a surgical subspecialty, sought treat-
ment for her purported orgasmic dysfunction, she had had intercourse
exactly seven times. Brought up by conservative European Catholic parents, Maria had decided early on to save her virginity for her husband.
When she became engaged about 3 weeks before I saw her, she decided
the circumstances were finally right to have intercourse. Maria had enjoyed intercourse, just as she had enjoyed the foreplay the couple had
experimented with previously, but she was terrified that she would never
have an orgasm. I tried allaying her fears by saying that it often took a bit
more practice and experimentation before orgasms occurred during intercourse. For once I even had objective data to back me up: I cited Kinsey's
1953 data showing how the percentage of women having orgasms increased
month by month throughout the 1st year of marriage (back in the days
when the start of marriage and the start of sexual activity were more likely
to coincide than they do today) (Kinsey, Pomeroy, Martin, & Gebhard, 1953).
But Maria, who had never failed to be precocious at anything she did, was
too anxious to let things happen naturally—she was already developing
performance anxiety and "spectatoring"—and so I felt I had to treat her
for Female Orgasmic Disorder even though I didn't think she had it.[3]*

The last cell in the fourfold table, C, is the case of deficient or absent desire on the
woman's part that doesn't create a problem for either her or her partner. Because these
are women we don't see in treatment, I cannot present any illustrative case material
from my own experience. I can speculate that these may be women whose partners also
have low desire.[4] Or mistresses. These may be relationships where the woman's lack of
sexual desire is considered normal and expected, and where the partner doesn't mind—
as long as she doesn't use her lack of sexual desire as an excuse not to have sex. As sex
therapists we may feel sad for these women, who don't know or care what they're
missing,[5] but as the good liberals the *DSM-IV* requires us to be, we have to acknowledge their right to choose their own goals, their right *not* to fulfill their sexual potential. (It is certainly the case that many of us do not fulfill our potential in other areas,
and we may leave, say, the fitness gurus and personal trainers of the world similarly
shaking their heads at our value systems.)

HOW AND WHY IS A SEXUAL PROBLEM A PROBLEM? OR WHAT ARE THE CAUSES OF "MARKED DISTRESS" OR "INTERPERSONAL DIFFICULTIES"?

Why Is This Complaint a Cause of "Marked Distress" for the Dysfunctional Woman?

It seems like a silly question, doesn't it? The reason is obvious: A sexual complaint is a problem because it diminishes the woman's sexual pleasure. But the obvious answer is the correct answer only a fraction of the time. There are many other ways in which a sexual complaint can constitute a problem. Here are some of them:

Sexual dysfunction can make a woman feel flawed and abnormal.

> *Luz avoided getting close to people, male and female, because she believed that to do so was to chance revealing how peculiar she was. Although most of the ways in which Luz felt odd were being explored in an excellent psychotherapy, her psychotherapist referred Luz for sex therapy because she believed that Luz's unusual way of having orgasms—they would happen spontaneously while watching someone enact a repetitive motion, such as tapping a pencil—was adding to her sense of being abnormal.*

By the time we see some of these women, their sense of being abnormal has often been exacerbated by previous psychotherapies, which, unlike Luz's, posit serious psychopathology as the cause of their sexual problems—thus, their vaginismus has been interpreted as a rejection of the female role and their anorgasmia as derivative of abandonment fears and an inability to trust.

Some women believe that not enjoying sex will be a handicap in the race for a relationship, where being eager for sex and performing it ably are advantages. Better sexual functioning in these cases is sought out in the same way that cooking lessons or breast implants might be, not because they provide pleasure in and of themselves but because they are seen as instrumental in achieving something else—marriage—that is desirable.

A sexual complaint can also be a problem because the woman's sexual functioning is in conflict with her other goals. A not rare presentation is that of a woman who enters sex therapy after years of unconsummated marriage, with the goal of achieving not pleasure but pregnancy.

> *Tricia was in the 3rd year of her second unconsummated marriage. According to Tricia, the absence of intercourse was not the reason her first marriage ended, and her second, happier marriage seemed quite stable. Although her current husband wanted to have intercourse, he had known about Tricia's difficulty before he married her and accepted it because he loved her and because the couple did enjoy other types of sexual activity.*

> *Tricia had never been motivated to seek treatment for her vaginismus (the problem preventing consummation) for her own pleasure or for her husband's; what motivated her to seek out sex therapy was that at 34, she had decided she wanted to have a baby.*

A woman's distress about her sexual functioning can stem even from a cause that is quite remote from sexuality itself.

> *Grace and Paul had not had sex since they conceived their now 8-year-old daughter, Sasha. Paul was bothered by the situation, but Grace was not—until she realized that soon Sasha would learn the facts of life and would ask her parents if they "did it." Grace could not bear either lying to her daughter or admitting to such a humiliatingly abnormal sex life. To develop a sex life that would allow her to say yes truthfully to Sasha's anticipated question was the entire reason Grace sought sex therapy for her Sexual Aversion Disorder.*

An even more extreme case of someone seeking sex therapy for a goal other than increased sexual pleasure is Linda, who had no problems that fell into any category of dysfunction, but who nonetheless had a serious problem with her sex life.

> *After 20 years of "vanilla sex" in an unhappy marriage, Linda felt freed by her divorce to seek out partners who were enthusiasts, as she was, of D&S (domination and submission) sex. This kind of sex was highly exciting and gratifying for Linda, but it was so largely because for her it enacted a fantasy of being so precious to a man that he had to subordinate and control her to keep her his. Linda was shocked to find that this was not the fantasy her D&S partners were entertaining—for them, the fantasy was of degrading a woman. To make matters worse, Linda's goal was not only sex that focused on her preciousness but a relationship with the same premise. Her sex partners, who were turned on by demeaning her, were poor candidates for such a partnership.*

Why Is the Complaint a Cause of "Interpersonal Difficulty"?

Oftentimes the complaint about the woman's sexuality is voiced not by her but by her partner. The partner's distress is perfectly understandable in the many cases where the woman's sexual functioning prevents her partner from having an enjoyable sex life or, in some cases, a sex life at all.

> *Elizabeth and Frank had lived together in a virtually sexless relationship for 10 years. From the outset, Elizabeth, who had had no previous sexual experience, was both uninterested in and phobic about sex. She did not*

become aroused with foreplay and had such severe dyspareunia that in-
tercourse was not even attempted after the first few tries. At Frank's angry
insistence, she had made desultory attempts at having the possible medi-
cal causes of her dyspareunia investigated, but she seemed unconcerned
that his sexual needs were thwarted, and she was unaware that she her-
self might be missing anything at all.

This lack of concern about a nonexistent sex life is not unique to Elizabeth. Some women who have no sexual desire of their own seem unable to understand how important sex might be to their partners. (Indeed, I have seen couples where the woman acted as if her partner's not putting his dishes in the dishwasher constituted a greater threat to the relationship than did their lack of a sex life.) Sometimes the first few sessions of sex therapy are devoted just to getting the woman to take her partner's wishes seriously. As one exasperated husband fulminated, "Try to understand that this is as important to me as shoe shopping is to you."

Although we refer to men like Frank as "invested partners" and feel sympathy for them, there is also a category of "overinvested partners," who evoke different responses. These overinvested partners are men who require the women they are with to function at a particular level for the man's self-esteem or self-image, rather than for his sexual satisfaction. One not uncommon presentation is the man who comes into treatment insisting that his partner must have orgasms or orgasms during intercourse. Ostensibly, this is for the woman's own pleasure or good (even though the woman herself is satisfied with the status quo), but the man's anger at his partner's "dysfunction" betrays a more complex motivation.

Newlyweds William and Courtney presented for sex therapy because Wil-
liam was enraged that Courtney didn't have orgasms during intercourse.
Every partner whom he had been with before marrying Courtney was or-
gasmic in this way, he said, and he was quite insistent that there was
something wrong with his wife that needed to be fixed. In an individual
session, Courtney told me what she was afraid to say in front of her hus-
band: She had always had orgasms during intercourse before, but William
ejaculated prematurely, within 1–2 minutes of intromission (an estimate
that William did not dispute), too little time for her to reach climax (or for
most women to reach climax, she added with a note of suspicion regard-
ing the accuracy of William's previous partners' reports).

Sometimes there can be a Catch-22 flavor to the partner's demand:

Marla's level of sexual interest was admittedly lower than Peter's, but she
was glad to engage in sex with him even when she was not feeling particu-
larly interested herself. Peter would not accept this. He had grown up in a
home where a tyrannical father terrorized the family into constantly seek-
ing to placate him by doing whatever he wanted, and he saw Marla's hav-

ing sex with him when she wasn't interested as her trying to placate him as if he were a tyrant like his father. He was slower to realize why his angry insistence that Marla develop a higher intrinsic level of sexual desire so he wouldn't feel that he was forcing her to have sex to placate him was in itself perceived by her as a need to do something to placate him.

WHAT'S A CLINICIAN TO DO?

Despite all the complexities discussed, a few considerations can take the clinician a long way toward deciding if a woman's sexuality is dysfunctional:

1. *Work backward.* Examine Criterion B first. Before focusing on any objective assessment of dysfunction, examine the "marked distress" and "interpersonal difficulty." It is highly unlikely that the patient is consulting you on account of mere intellectual curiosity about her sexual functioning. Start with what's really bothering her or her partner.
2. *Use rough standards to evaluate dysfunction objectively.* No orgasms, painful sex, absent desire, inability to "get into" sex mentally or physically, problems achieving penetration—these are complaints that would seem to make a prima facie case for dysfunction. With subtler manifestations, the dysfunction-determining line is a matter of debate, a debate that is probably not worth engaging in the consulting room. (Even when presenting feedback to the patient, the clinician does not have to dwell on whether or not she has a sexual dysfunction. "I think you can enjoy sex more than you do now" not only fudges the dysfunction issue, but tells the patient what she probably really wants to know.)
3. *Determine the adequacy of stimulation.* Inadequate stimulation, broadly understood to include psychological and situational, as well as physical, stimulation is the major cause of female dysfunction, as well as the most obvious place to begin intervention and treatment. Dysfunction cannot be understood apart from it.
4. *The relationship of dysfunction and distress is not always obvious.* Even if a dysfunction is present, its connection to the individual's or couple's distress needs to be determined. A dysfunction is a nice concrete problem to present to a clinician, but it is the presumed *effect* of the dysfunction that has actually led the patient to seek help.

But the best advice I can give to someone new to the sexuality field is simply to be patient and stay with it. In my clinical psychology graduate program, we students were always debating whether it was better to become immersed in "book learning" about psychopathology before beginning to see patients or to get some clinical experience first before dealing with psychological topics academically. Neither approach seemed satisfactory. When we saw patients first, we felt we didn't have enough knowledge to be competent diagnosticians and therapists. But when we started with theory, we realized that we didn't have enough clinical experience to make the concepts meaningful.

I imagine that you, too, will experience a similar disquiet as you begin to see women with sexual complaints. Please remain patient because we all go through this discomfort until theory and practice come together. Eventually, you will experience that wonderful moment when you realize you are no longer self-consciously assessing sexual dysfunction; you're just absorbed in listening to the patient tell her story—and you're a better diagnostician for it.

NOTES

1. This is probably not the correct model for the distribution of dyspareunia and vaginismus (and perhaps not for sexual aversion either). We might better conceptualize the distribution of these variables as bimodal: Either you have dyspareunia, or you don't. Of course, some women with dyspareunia may have more pain than others do, but the most important distinction for determining dysfunction is between those who have any pain at all and those who have none.
2. There is also the consideration of how someone got to where she is in the distribution. A woman can be 4'11" because that is her genetic destiny or because something stunted her growth. Similarly, a woman can have little sexual desire because of inborn factors (or rather, putative inborn factors—we don't really know anything about what these might be) or because her expected level of desire was inhibited by negative experiences. Does it matter in determining dysfunction how a woman got to be where she is in the distribution, or is it only her absolute placement that counts?
3. The situation of a sex therapist treating a dysfunction that doesn't meet the *DSM-IV* criteria for it is actually extremely common, particularly in the case of Female Orgasmic Disorder. That is because a woman cannot be said to have Female Orgasmic Disorder if her deficient orgasmic response can be attributed to inadequate sexual stimulation. And yet many (most?) of the anorgasmic women we see are anorgasmic precisely because they are receiving inadequate stimulation. Indeed. increasing the adequacy of the stimulation is usually the first thing we focus on in treating the problem.
4. The only cases I have seen of a couple seeking treatment because both partners have low sexual desire have been lesbian couples. In these instances, even though neither woman wants sex, both want to want it.
5. We actually do see women who don't know or care what they're missing. They're women with egosyntonic Hypoactive Sexual Desire, and we see them when their lack of interest presents "interpersonal difficulties" for their partners, rather than "marked distress" for them. They are usually dragged into treatment by their disgruntled partners. The hallmark of their presentation is the statement, "If I never had sex again for the rest of my life, I wouldn't miss it."

REFERENCES

American Psychiatric Association. (1994). *Diagnostic and Statistical Manual of Mental Disorders* (4th ed.). Washington, DC: Author.

Kinsey, A. C., Pomeroy, W. B., Martin, C. E., & Gebhard, P. H. (1953). *Sexual Behavior in the Human Female.* Philadelphia & London: W. B. Saunders.

Masters, W. H., & Johnson, V. E. (1966). *Human Sexual Response.* Boston: Little, Brown.

Nathan, S. G. (1986). The epidemiology of the *DSM-III* Psychosexual Dysfunctions. *Journal of Sex & Marital Therapy, 12,* 267–281.

Chapter Seven

Women's Difficulties with Low Sexual Desire and Sexual Avoidance

Rosemary Basson, MD

PREFACE

Beginning my career in sexual medicine after 15 years in internal medicine and family practice, I was honored to be asked to be involved in the teaching of human sexuality and its problems to medical students—teaching I myself had never received. We taught them how to respectfully and diligently enquire about their patients' sexual function and dysfunction. We taught them how to manage erectile dysfunction, orgasm problems, and dyspareunia, but we made little mention of problematic low sexual desire, especially in women. I was advised by some colleagues that this is basically untreatable. Laumann's published data were still some 8 years away—but I knew that in Vancouver, at least, concerns about their apparently abnormally low sexual desire were highly prevalent among women—were they really "untreatable"?

As I spoke with women who did and did not have desire concerns, some themes were readily apparent.

1. A minority, but only a minority, spoke of their sexual desire in terms of a physical wanting—rather, the overriding wanting was to be emotionally closer to the partner. It followed that poor emotional intimacy was often associated with loss of desire—but women largely found this logical and not a sign that they had any "dysfunction."

2. Sexual stimuli and sexual context were vital. Thus fatigue, nothing sensual or erotic happening through the day, or lack of attractive behavior by their sexual partners, all had the expected negative effect on sexual desire. Conversely, a new partner was typically a powerful sexual stimulus, sometimes causing women who had self-diagnosed as having "low libido," unable to be aroused, to become problem-free.

3. Not being able to focus on the moment, on the sexual stimulation, or on the emotions associated with being so close to another person was commonly a component of the difficulties of women labeling their dysfunction as low sexual desire.

I learned the traditional human sexual response of Masters, Johnson, and Kaplan and was soon requested to teach it—but to me, it did not contain the vital elements. So, after some 10 years of listening and checking, moving on to presenting these themes to colleagues at conferences, and hearing their feedback, I started to do what my patients had repeatedly encouraged—to write it down! So began the so-called alternative models.

INTRODUCTION

Even before the media blitz on safe and effective medication for men's erectile dysfunction, women frequently couched their most common sexual concerns—those of low sexual desire—in medical terms: "I know I have some kind of hormone imbalance," or "I have had no desire since my tubal ligation, second pregnancy, hysterectomy, menopause." Ready access to the Internet further aided these various self-proposed etiologies, but these beliefs were conveyed to me from the early 1970s onward in clinics of internal medicine, family practice, and sexual medicine. Women usually acknowledge that an unhappy relationship, emotional or physical abuse, drug or alcohol addiction, and depression would logically interfere with their sexual desire. However, when they examine their own relationships and feel none of this is relevant for them, they conclude that their lack of desire must be something other than a psychological or interpersonal issue—that is, presumably something "medical" (even if previous health professionals have not been able to identify it). A recent promotion in the North American media of "previously ignored biological causes of women's sexual dysfunction" further fuels these beliefs. The reality is that there are usually multiple compounding factors, both biological and psychological, underlying women's low sexual desire and avoidance.

THE CHANGING NATURE OF DESIRE
THROUGH ONE RELATIONSHIP

Women often recall desire early on in relationships when they were caught up in the excitement of the "chase," likely idealizing their (potential) partners and having many motivations to be sexual, in addition to fulfilling any innate sexual hunger. For any one woman, these may have included the enjoyment of feeling attractive, attracted; perhaps playing a role, fulfilling an expectation, feeling better about herself, or wanting to cement the relationship; wanting the relationship in order to feel loved, to feel "normal," to not be lonely; wanting to leave the family of origin, even to further a career or to distance herself from a culture, church, or extended family. Perhaps women were oblivious of these various motivations—it seemed easy for them to accept the sexual activity, often to enjoy it—because, typically, the novelty and presence of many sexual triggers and settings conducive to sexual awareness made this desire for sex appear easy and even "spontaneous." Provided the sexual outcome was rewarding, the wanting of shared sexual sensations and the mutual vulnerability increased. Within the context of desirable erotic stimuli, the woman was consciously aware of a desire for sex and all that it fulfilled. In some relationships, the secrecy of the liaison, its uncertainty, even its lack of societal approval may have enhanced the potency of the stimuli. The experiences resulted in increased emotional intimacy, such that some women, even in the very early stages of their relationships, state that their main reason for agreeing to or instigating sex is to feel closer to the partner.

When women speak of why they agree to or initiate sex with their long-term partners, they emphasize nurturing of the emotional intimacy with that partner as being very important.[1,2,3,4] To show that the partner is wanted, loved, missed, or appreciated; to give something to the partner; to show that an argument is over; to increase the sense of bonding, commitment, trust, and confidence in the relationship—these aspirations become cemented by sexual experiences with the partner, assuming those experiences are satisfying. Accessing sexual arousal becomes more clearly a deliberate choice.[5] Initially, during any experience, the woman may be sexually neutral, but motivated by these intimacy-based reasons. The key question is, How can a woman's mindset repeatedly be changed from one of sexual neutrality to one of sexual desire?

ALTERNATIVE SEXUAL RESPONSE CYCLE FOR WOMEN

The following diagram is a model of an alternative sexual response cycle frequently confirmed by women as reflective of their experiences. Unlike the traditional model of the human sexual response stemming from the writings of Masters, Johnson, and Kaplan (of a linear sequence of discrete events with a predominant genital focus), this alternative model is circular, and within it, arousal precedes and then accompanies an accessed or "developed" form of desire.[6]

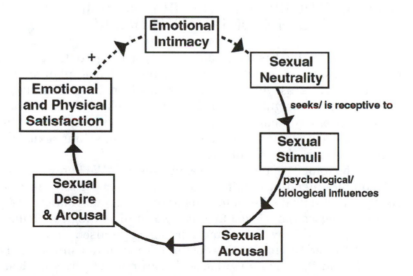

FIGURE 7.1. Alternate Model of the Female Sexual Response Cycle

EMOTIONAL INTIMACY AS THE MOTIVATING FORCE BEHIND THE CYCLE AND THE INTEGRAL ROLE OF SEXUAL STIMULI

As Stephen Levine has clarified in his chapter, growing psychological intimacy can breed a wanting of sexual intimacy. However, for very many women, the psychological intimacy—though vital—is, I would suggest, by itself insufficient. Although emotional intimacy can fuel a willingness to move on from sexual neutrality to a state of sexual arousal, useful sexual stimuli and appropriate context are vital. Entities external to the woman are, in fact, integral components of her sexual response cycle—moving her from sexual neutrality to sexual arousal. The needed stimuli are both mental and physical, and the context may be more important than the actual stimuli themselves—for instance, visually explicit sexual stimuli out of context, although possibly causing a fairly prompt genital vasocongestive response of which the woman is relatively unaware, are typically not considered subjectively arousing. Women speak frequently of the need for caring, attractive behavior from their partner throughout the day, which will determine the effectiveness of the specific sexual stimuli when the time comes to sexually interact.

When sexual stimuli and an appropriate context are missing, despite psychological intimacy, the woman's feelings for her partner are typically those of affection, love, and caring. A women often discusses her likely contentment if she and her partner could be just "soul mates," but adds that any contentment would be marred by guilt: "I know this sounds awful—but I wouldn't care if we never have sex again." There is sadness that this is not what society expects, and there is fear that the relationship will suffer. These feelings tend to counterbalance any positive thoughts of "no more sex."

RESPONSIVE DESIRE IS PROBABLY MORE IMPORTANT THAN SPONTANEOUS DESIRE

The previous alternative cycle has focused on women's capacity to access desire during a sexual experience. This is not a new concept—Helen Kaplan spoke of desire triggered by external factors, as well as a desire arising from internal biological events, including thoughts[7] (these thoughts presumably arise somehow "spontaneously" rather than in response to the environment). More recently, Roy Levin has argued that women do indeed have the capacity to begin an experience with conscious sexual desire, then to (in addition) access more desire after arousal.[8]

What, then, is the role of "spontaneous sexual desire"? We know that sexual function is a highly complex blending of mind and body and that certain neurotransmitters and hormones "permit" sexual stimuli to register unconsciously and thereby alter autonomic nervous responses. This leads to a number of physiological changes, including increased genital blood flow. The stimuli are also appraised as mentally sexually arousing/attractive, triggering a responsive desire. The neurotransmitters and hormones permit this process, but there is no evidence that in normal physiological amounts, these neurochemical agents actually generate a feeling of sexual desire. It could be argued that all of sexual desire is responsive to something—be it a thought, a memory. The term *spontaneous desire* is usually meant to describe a seemingly innate neediness of the experience that builds sexual tension and its release, preferably with someone else, and which appears not to be triggered by anything in the current environment or by deliberate focusing of the mind on sexual matters.

This brings us to the difficulties with the traditional markers of women's spontaneous sexual desire,[9] as reflected in the definition of Hypoactive Sexual Desire Disorder in the *DSM-IV*. Sexual fantasies, self-stimulation, and spontaneous thinking about sex have been considered correlates of healthy sexual desire. However, women tell of their using fantasy in order to become aroused or in order to stop being distracted during the sexual experience.[10] For them, the presence of fantasies is hardly a reflection of a high innate spontaneous desire. Spontaneously thinking about sex would appear to be rather uncommon for women who are nevertheless living satisfying sexual lives, according to both British and American community studies. One study by Cawood and Bancroft showed that of premenopausal women over 40 years of age, almost 50% thought about sex once a month or less or never. Figures for the peri- and postmenopausal groups showing similar infrequency of sexual thinking were 56 and 77%, respectively.[11] Studying why women are sexual, Gayler et al. focused on women who had undergone hysterectomy from 18 months previously versus those with nongynecological surgery. The majority of both groups reported engaging in sexual activity without awareness of sexual desire.[12]

Using self-stimulation as a marker of spontaneous desire is also problematic. Women will give many reasons other than to release sexual tension for their self-stimulation—to soothe, to get to sleep, to relax, and even "to prove it still works" are reasons frequently offered to me. Laumann's study showed not only far fewer autoerotic practices in women compared to men, but also a much wider spectrum of frequency.[13]

Studies that ask women specifically about spontaneous desire are few, but very interesting. A careful study of a random sample of 225 40-year-old sexually experienced Danish women, the majority of whom always or mostly experienced orgasm, showed that 32% claimed to never experience spontaneous desire.[14]

I would suggest that more useful criteria for low sexual desire are:

1. There may be a lack of receptivity to sexual activity or other sexual stimuli.
2. There may also be a marked absence of sexual thinking, fantasizing, self-stimulation, or conscious yearning for the physical sexual experience—that is over and beyond a normative lessening with relationship duration.
3. There may be a coexistent arousal disorder, such that lack of receptivity is stemming from that lack of ability to become aroused (and, subsequently, access desire)

AROUSABILITY

Given the premise that arousal often precedes desire, what alters the ease or difficulty with which the woman becomes aroused? Biological and psychological factors influence *arousability*—a term used in the past by Whalen and Bancroft. Currently, Bancroft and the Kinsey team, using psychometric means, are seeking to prove the existence of an inherent but highly variable tonic inhibition of arousability in both men and women.[15] Other researchers, including Karama, using brain imaging with PET scans, have shown areas of reduced brain activity with sexual arousal, as well as areas of increased activity.[16] Clearly, any inhibition can be partly programmed by life's experiences, but the postulate is that some of it is inherently "set," that is, "biological." Knowledge of neurotransmitters, neuropeptides, and hormonal central control of sexual arousal is rudimentary. Medications with partly or completely known mechanisms of action may have pro- or antisexual effects. Broadly speaking, prosexual neurotransmitters and hormones include dopamine, oxytocin, centrally acting noradrenalin, serotonin acting via 5HT1A and perhaps 5HT2C receptors, LHRH, and androgens.[17] On the other hand, serotonin acting via some 5HT2 and 5HT3 receptors, β endorphin, prolactin, and GABA are sexually negative, with opioids potentially increasing sexual wanting, but lessening the ability to be physiologically aroused. Depression alters the balance of these neurotransmitters and is commonly associated with reduced arousability, which may be the woman's main symptom of depression. Needless to say perhaps, screening for depression is necessary for all women presenting their sexual desire complaints.

The question of the role of androgens is frequently raised. Sudden complete loss of all ovarian androgen can lead to a typical picture whereby mental and physical stimuli become minimally effective—then, arousal can only be very slowly reached with deliberate focusing on the stimuli and no intense arousal is experienced. Sometimes a brief low-intensity orgasm may occur, shutting off further arousal—a concept totally foreign to the woman who previously likely had the potential for continued arousal after orgasm, with or without further orgasmic release.

For other women, losing both ovaries results in no sexual changes—presumably, their adrenal production of testosterone, which does not "pick up the slack" when the ovaries are removed or destroyed by chemotherapy, is nevertheless sufficient. An enormous current problem is the lack of available sensitive accurate assays of serum testosterone—the available assays are designed to be accurate in the male range. "Androgen deficiency" in women does not have the same scientific accuracy as, for example, thyroid deficiency or estrogen deficiency. Testosterone production during and after natural menopause appears to be quite variable. We have studies suggesting that testosterone values drop, stay the same, and increase.[18,19,20,21,22] Ovarian production of androstenedione—a precursor of testosterone—seems to always reduce, but production of testosterone is variable. The important issue is that sex hormone-binding globulin (SHBG) usually decreases through the menopausal transition (although it may increase again in the late 60s and 70s). This protein attaches itself to testosterone (and estrogen), rendering these sex hormones largely unavailable to the tissues—only the free portion is useful. So with the SHBG decreasing, a bigger fraction (albeit of a smaller total amount) of testosterone is available to the tissues, such that free testosterone may actually rise. To complicate matters further, if estrogen replacement therapy is given, especially by the oral route, SHBG again rises and so free testosterone falls. So the picture of menopause is complex, and sometimes lack of available testosterone is one of the biological factors determining arousability. The alternative model can usefully show this effect, reducing the effectiveness of sexual stimuli such that neither arousal nor desire might be reached.

Fatigue is a very common biological factor affecting arousability. This may be from poor sleep due to small children, chronic pain, debility from any cause, or sleep disturbance from chronic stressors. The most common medications associated with reduced arousability that I encounter include serotonergic antidepressants, tranquilizers, beta-blockers, and analgesics that include codeine.

Frequently, psychological factors have a negative impact on arousability.[23] Included are negative sexual self-image or feeling guilt or shame—these negative emotions modulate and possibly preclude any subjective arousal. Negative cognitions include nonsexual distractions; concerns of being sexually substandard, sexually naïve, inexperienced, or infertile; fear of dyspareunia; concerns for emotional safety, physical safety, or safety from sexually transmitted disease and unwanted pregnancy.

COMPLEXITIES OF SEXUAL AROUSAL FOR WOMEN

Women's subjective arousal appears to be largely reflective of how sexually exciting they find the stimulus and context.[24,25] This correlates to an extremely variable degree with objective genital engorgement; in other words, there is high variability between different sexually healthy women. This is in marked contrast to sexually healthy men—their subjective sexual arousal correlates closely with their degree of genital congestion (erection). Objective measurement of female genital congestion resulting from an erotic (usually visual) stimulus has, to date, mainly stemmed from the use of the vaginal photoplethysmograph. This is a tampon-like probe placed in the vagina, which contains a light source and a phototransistor, that is, a light detector. Light is back-scattered by the blood in the vaginal vascular plexus, and changes in vaginal congestion cause changes in the output from the light detector. Short-term changes in vaginal engorgement are reflected by changes in the vaginal pulse amplitude (VPA); in other words, with each heartbeat there is a phasic change in blood content of the vaginal tissues.

The results of studying women with arousal disorders are very interesting. When watching an erotic video, women will typically report no subjective arousal or minimal arousal accompanied by negative emotions, but they are found to have plethysmograph studies identical to those of women who are acting as controls and who are subjectively aroused by the video.[26,27,28,29,30,31] The same increase in VPA is shown by both groups of women. Note that it is the accessing of *subjective* arousal that I am suggesting will allow a developed form of desire—see figure 7.1. The degree of awareness of genital tingling, throbbing, swelling, and lubrication is also highly variable among sexually healthy women, correlates rather poorly with objective measurement of that congestion, and is not the main influence determining their subjective state.[32,33,34,35]

Recent work has shown that increasing sexually healthy women's physiological genital vascular response to erotic stimulation by heightening sympathetic nervous system activity pharmacologically (as with ephedrine) or nonpharmacologically (e.g., with exercise or hyperventilation) has no effect on the *subjective* experience of arousal when watching the erotic video.[36,37,38]

This is not to say that genital engorgement is unimportant. For many women, it is vital:

1. To allow a genital stimulus to move them from neutral to sexually aroused.[39] Physical massage of engorging vulval erectile tissue can be increasingly pleasurable, leading to intense sexual sensations with or without orgasms, whereas physically massaging nonengorged vulval erectile tissue is unpleasant, irritating, or painful.
2. In the absence of vulval and vaginal engorgement, vaginal entry by penis, finger, or vibrator is not associated with pleasure and frequently is associated with pain or discomfort.

The important point is that the genital response is an involuntary unconscious reflex—a rapid autonomic nervous system response. The response confirms that the woman's mind has recognized the sexual nature of the stimulus, but does not itself confirm that the appraisal of the stimulus and context is subjectively arousing.[40,41]

Vulvar and vaginal engorgement is dependent on a minimum amount of estrogen activity. For some women, when they are postpartum or postmenopausal, or they receive a GnRH agonist for endometriosis, for instance, estrogen is insufficient to permit the increased vasocongestion needed to allow genital caressing to be pleasurable and vaginal lubrication to be adequate for painless vaginal stimulation and intercourse.

The safety of long-term hormone replacement therapy (HRT) after menopause remains unclear. The 2002 Women's Health Initiative (WHI) study results add new data to the body of evidence suggesting that the use of HRT for prevention of chronic conditions requires reevaluation by physicians and their patients. Based on some but not all previous observational studies, HRT was thought to reduce the risk of cardiovascular disease, osteoporosis, colon cancer, and dementia and was likely causing a slight increase in incidence (but not mortality) of breast cancer, venothrombotic episodes, and cholecystitis. Before the WHI study, the option of providing long-term systemic estrogen for its sexual and urological benefits appeared reasonable.

The WHI prospectively assessed data on the risks and benefits of 0.625 mg conjugated equine estrogens and 2.5 mg medroxyprogesterone acetate daily to 16,608 women of different ages (average age 63 years at study onset). The 8-year study was stopped after 5.2 years, as the data demonstrated that for every 10,000 postmenopausal women taking HRT for 1 year, there would be 8 more venothrombotic events, 7 more coronary heart-disease events, 8 more strokes, and 8 more cases of breast cancer, along with 6 fewer cases of colorectal cancer and 5 fewer hip fractures. While hazard ratios of 1.0 represent no difference between the treatment group and controls, the ratios were 1.22 for cardiovascular disease, 1.03 for total cancer, 0.76 for fractures, and 0.98 for mortality (not significant). Both a previous and a subsequent large prospective trial of HRT in women with known coronary artery disease have shown that HRT was not beneficial in this population and one suggested a possible increased risk of heart disease in the 1st year.

So, as clinicians, we are still lacking very important data to guide our recommendations about HRT. We would like to have data that focus on women who are

1. Beginning HRT during the perimenopause or close to menopause;
2. Known not to have coronary artery disease;
3. Using other formulations of HRT, particularly non-oral estrogen and progesterone, rather than a synthetic progestin; and
4. Taking estrogen by any route, who do not need progesterone. Data on this group will be forthcoming from the WHI within several years.

The WHI study did not address the issue of quality of life in women—particularly, the question of sexual and urological health. Some physicians may choose to advise women to switch from systemic estrogen to local estrogen in the form of a tablet of estradiol of only 25 μg, which is placed in the vagina and minimally absorbed systemically, or to use a ring that is placed high in the vagina and that slowly releases estradiol over the subsequent 12 weeks, where there is even less (almost zero) systemic absorption. Others will explain the results of the recent study and will emphasize that it sheds no light on the use of various other formulations of HRT, beginning at the time of menopause.[42,43]

IMPORTANCE OF A REWARDING EMOTIONAL AND PHYSICAL OUTCOME

Despite accessing arousal and desire and enjoying both, if the ultimate outcome is negative, neither the original goal (to be emotionally close to the partner) nor the accessed goal (to enjoy more intense sexual sensations with ultimate sexual satisfaction) is reached. Instead, emotional distancing or feelings of being used, even of being abused, can surface. Common causes of negative outcome include chronic dyspareunia, partner sexual dysfunction, lack of sexual skills, or inability to communicate the type of sexual stimulation required.[44,45,46] Clearly, one break in the cycle usually leads to others—an unrewarding outcome weakens the "motor"—the emotional intimacy with the partner. The woman no longer finds or focuses on sexual cues and stimuli—she is distracted when they are present such that arousal is not experienced.[47]

WHERE DOES "SPONTANEOUS" SEXUAL DESIRE FIT IN?

Typically, early on in relationships; for some women mid-cycle, around the time of ovulation; perhaps when the partners have been apart; or when sex is infrequent—especially when the woman is single—seemingly "spontaneous" or innate sexual neediness or hunger does occur. This can augment the intimacy-based cycle by further motivating the woman to be increasingly receptive to stimuli and indeed can lead directly to arousal, as in the traditional Masters, Johnson, and Kaplan model. Then the two response cycles will merge,[48] as shown in Figure 7.2.

Marked loss of this "innate" desire, rather than a gradual lessening with relationship duration, needs assessment. Depression is the most frequent cause, but other causes include medication effects, hyperprolactinemia, or physical or emotional stress (e.g., recently recalled childhood abuse, loss of a loved one, or absorption in studies or work).

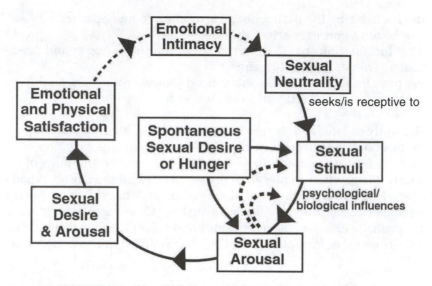

FIGURE 7.2. Blended Spontaneous Intimacy-Based Cycles

This apparently spontaneous sexual neediness, as mentioned, often gradually lessens as the years and decades go by, even in healthy, rewarding relationships, sometimes to be rekindled should a new relationship follow. This lessening is mostly not seen to be problematic, simply because of the woman's ready sexual arousal and her ongoing receptivity.

I likened the innate or spontaneous desire to Stephen Levine's sexual drive component of his former tripartite model of desire—drive, motivation, and wish.[49] However, Stephen's current definition of drive as "the subjectively recognized moment of genitally felt, sex motivating behaviour . . . sexual drive manifests itself in genital tingling, vaginal wetness, clitoral or penile tumescence, erotic fantasy . . . " is far more genitally focused than descriptions I hear from women. They are speaking of a wanting of sexual physical sensations (preferably shared with an attractive partner)—the sensations being nongenital, as well as genital, that would often require physical stimulation in order to be felt. This wanting is an emotion only minimally modulated by any current directly perceived physical (genital) sensations.

CASE OF JENNY

Presentation

Jenny, now 39 years of age, reported 3 years of enjoyable sex when her desire was fine. She even recalled sometimes herself and her partner having sex more than daily and that she would sometimes instigate this. That was up until her pregnancy 9 years ago.

Jenny said she has had minimal sexual desire ever since then. She and Bob have a second child, Karli, now aged 5, sister to her brother Damian. Jenny suggested that sexual times are very infrequent (less than monthly) since Karli's birth and were already down to once a week between the two pregnancies. Jenny spoke of being deliberately avoidant—staying up late, hoping that Bob would already be asleep.

Clarifying the Chief Complaint

Jenny never thinks about sex (other than in a guilty manner of it being so infrequent). She said she doesn't miss it. Jenny does not masturbate (she did this fairly infrequently as a teen and when single). When there is an opportunity to be sexual with Bob, she finds herself too tired.

Jenny's verdict: Jenny has read about testosterone deficiency and feels this should be considered for her.

Medical Background

Jenny has regular periods. She has found that taking or not taking birth control pills made no difference to her low desire. Two years ago, Bob had a vasectomy. This had been discussed fully. Jenny felt at that time that perhaps the pill was partly to blame. She did not want to have an IUD. Neither partner particularly trusted or enjoyed using condoms.

Jenny has no history of depression or any chronic illness. She takes no medication, but had tried various supplements from a naturopath about 3 years ago, which made no difference to her complaint of low sexual desire.

Brief Preliminary Feedback to Facilitate Further Questioning

It was explained to Jenny that her regular menses indicates normal production of estrogen, and that because testosterone is an essential precursor of estrogen, her body must be producing testosterone. I outlined that to date, there is no known pathway that will make estrogen without also making testosterone and that there is no disease that will stop the ovary from releasing testosterone. In addition, Jenny has no medical condition impairing testosterone from adrenal glands (such as prolonged cortisone administration). I told of my experience of women typically presenting with infertility or irregular periods, who are found to have slightly high testosterone levels, but do not have particularly strong sexual desire. I explained that it seems testosterone simply allows sexual stimuli to be more effective in causing arousal and that there are many other factors involved, as well as a minimum amount of testosterone. I admitted that giving her male levels of testosterone would likely increase her sexual hunger, as female-to-male transsexuals prescribed such doses do develop increased sexual wanting, along with their deep voice, beard, and other male characteristics. I added that, nevertheless, there is not a lot known about biochemical mechanisms in the female sex response and much has to be learned. However, at this point in time, the knowledge that there is no simple correlation between testosterone levels in the physiological range and sexual desire meant that we needed to clarify the situation in some more detail. Jenny agreed that we could continue.

Chief Complaint in More Detail

Jenny had never been in a long-term relationship of more than a year before meeting Bob. The couple met when she was 27, he 36. He then had a 12-year-old son living mainly with the ex-wife, but visiting frequently. Jenny described Bob as a successful person who was very attentive to her and not critical (like her last partner and like her parents, especially her mother). Bob and Jenny dated for 6 months, and they moved in together and married 1 year later. They had met at work, but did not continue to work in the same department. There was some traveling involved for both—occasionally together, which she described as very exciting. Once living together, they still had times apart—often from 6 to 10 days—and she did remember looking forward to seeing Bob again and specifically to being sexual with him. I then gently asked what was so good about sex then that she looked forward to it so much. Jenny said it made her feel wanted, attractive, and very feminine, affirming in her mind that she was holding down their very good and much-envied relationship. On a physical level, Jenny recalled that the interaction was very much focused on intercourse. Often Jenny did not reach orgasm but, nevertheless, afterward, she felt good emotionally and physically. When they were together for many weeks without a break and sex was frequent, often daily—yes, from the physical standpoint, it definitely was less rewarding physically. Was it still emotionally rewarding? "Of course," said Jenny—after a pause, adding, "Well, maybe not always." Would she have liked to have somewhat less activity? It looked as if Jenny was about to say something, but changed her mind and said, "No, like I said, it was all fine up until I had Damian."

Did Jenny recall fantasizing more in those first 3 years? She said, "Yes, perhaps, a bit." When? "Well, during sex." And why? "To try to get more excited." Did she masturbate in those days—when Bob was away or when she was away? "Very rarely." How about the other aspects of sexual activity, exclusive of intercourse—touching the rest of her body, touching her breasts, genital stimulation that was not in the vagina—was this enjoyable? Jenny confirmed it was. And did it happen most times? "Some of the time" was the answer. Was there enough of this for her needs? "Well, maybe not, but I didn't mind—I had desire then—it wasn't a problem." How about being kissed and caressed when definitely intercourse would not have happened? (other people around, etc.). Jenny confirmed that was highly enjoyable. Asking Jenny about the times she was or was not orgasmic with Bob in those first 3 years—what was different? Jenny stated that she stimulated herself before or during intercourse and that Bob particularly liked that. Did Jenny like that? Jenny said that initially she was very hesitant, but physically, it did feel good and, again, it was confirming to her that she was "up to standard."

I then asked Jenny to tell us about sex during the pregnancy. "That wasn't a problem. Bob seemed to lose his desire then." Was the lack of sex a problem for her? "It puzzled me a bit, but I was quite tired much of the time. It didn't really concern me. Bob said it happened to him with his first wife—it was just the way he was and he was looking forward to having the baby as much as me." Bob also said he thought it wasn't a good idea to have sex while she was pregnant—that he had read about this and thought it was for the best to be cautious. The labor was long and finally resulted in a cesarean section. Jenny agreed that she was very disappointed, particularly that her milk supply stopped at about 2 weeks. Jenny was told it was from the general anesthetic. How did that make her feel? "Inadequate." But Jenny's philosophy is always to not only make the best of things, but to be as near perfect as possible. So she focused very much on the optimal way of feeding babies, researched the subject intently, read various parenting books, studied early childhood development, and so forth. She described how she loved having baby Damian, who was a good baby. She enjoyed him as a toddler and a child, described the relationship as still extremely close, and went on to explain how important being a mother was to her. She was puzzled why, with this much contentment with her baby and with Bob ("an ideal family"), her sexual desire should have disappeared.

I clarified that Jenny and Bob still had sex together (approximately monthly), which was very much intercourse-focused and often Jenny did not become aroused. So, sexual activity began without desire, but often Jenny could not access desire during the experience, whereas she had done so previously. Reflecting back to the frequent sex before the pregnancies, Jenny agreed quite definitely that sometimes then she began sex feeling "neutral," but, more often than not, became aroused quite quickly and then sensed desire to continue. She agreed then that she very much did "want to want." Jenny was now very troubled by her dislike of Bob's touching her breasts or genital area—for instance, when they were in the kitchen (even when the children were not around) and wondered why this was not only not arousing to her but annoying and negative. When asked about kisses, affectionate sensual hugs, and caresses through the day, Jenny said she did not initiate them and tended to push Bob away—if she behaved differently, she believed he would think she wanted sex.

When asked about the emotional intimacy with Bob, Jenny said she thought it had increased with the children, especially after Damian's birth, as Bob adored Damian and they were a great threesome. Jenny added that the only problem was with sex. With much sadness and guilt, Jenny admitted that in the past, she had sometimes deliberately provoked tension between her and Bob or even an argument at bedtime, to avoid having to say "no." This happened less often recently—it seemed that Bob was simply asking far less often. When I explained to Jenny about true emotional intimacy, being able to really share our thoughts, our fears, our insecurities, and to be vulnerable with each other and totally trusting that we could say these things, Jenny suggested that emotional intimacy certainly was not growing. Jenny then added that in the recent past, she had begun to sense some criticism from Bob that she didn't sense before and remembered that at work all of his staff members said he was super-critical of them. She added that she didn't blame him—"It is probably because he is so frustrated with so little sex."

Jenny's second pregnancy was not planned, but both partners were fine about it and in some ways delighted. This was an elective cesarean section; she was able to nurse Karli for 6 months. She became very involved with both children and, in fact, discontinued her then part-time work.

SUMMARY OF CASE

Jenny, now 39, says, "From the outside we are the perfect family." In many ways she is very content. She very much enjoys motherhood and is going back to part-time work, but not because she feels bored or underchallenged by the various activities she is involved with in the children's schools and the community. She has an extremely close relationship with her son and finds Karli more difficult, but nevertheless describes the relationship as warm and Karli as mostly affectionate to her. She portrays a picture of gaining a semblance of emotional intimacy with Bob from their frequent sexual activities in the first 3 years and perhaps some fulfillment of her need to be very close to another human being from her closeness to Damian (and, to a lesser degree, Karli). Motherhood has been very confirming for her. In the first 3 years, Jenny had been seeking that type of confirmation from the frequent (and never declined) sexual activity. Jenny and Bob are not emotionally intimate.

FEEDBACK

I explained women's responsive cycle to Jenny and focused on the importance of emotional intimacy as the "motor" behind the response and the importance of stimuli and context. Jenny realized that by pushing Bob's affectionate hugs away for fear of giving the wrong message, this in fact deprived her of a sense of emotional closeness that can accompany those physical gestures, and she agreed that maybe Bob did not necessarily expect intercourse if she were to give him a hug. Jenny now recognized her dislike of direct genital or breast touching when she was "at neutral" as being perfectly normal. Once arousal has been accessed, these very same stimuli of genital or breast touch can be very welcome and can move a woman onto further arousal. I explained that I needed to see Bob to discuss these issues and to hear of his own response and his perspective. Jenny was hesitant—"I'm not sure I can ask him to take that time off from the office to work out my problems." I asked Jenny if that was really what she was taking away from this interview and she admitted it was not. She did now see her low desire as a couple entity, but her old fears of being criticized, of being inadequate, were again surfacing.

OUTCOME

Jenny canceled the next visit without leaving a reason and called back 2 weeks later, asking for another appointment. Jenny explained that as she thought over our discussion, she realized that, in fact, she had not had a healthy sexual desire ever and this had frightened her. Losing desire after two babies and being busy and absorbed by children's lives somehow seemed "normal" or almost normal, but never having a healthy sexual desire—only using sex to feel close—she felt must be very abnormal. I went over again women's responsive cycle and told her that a relative lack of innate sexual neediness is normal for many women, especially once their relationships become long term. I explained that there is no certain knowledge of the percentage of women who are the way Jenny is, but that I thought it was a relatively high percentage. These women can and do have rewarding sexual lives, based very much on responding to their environment and, in particular, being influenced by a wanting to respond because of the potential of increasing emotional closeness. Jenny wanted to know why, prior to the pregnancies, their frequent sex did not, in fact, bring her emotionally closer to Bob. I gently suggested that perhaps it was because having frequent sex was all they were doing to attempt to nurture emotional closeness. Jenny readily agreed that they had not developed an openness whereby it was safe to share their worries, and their inadequacies, their vulnerabilities. They were perhaps beginning to do that when they were dating, but that was so long ago. Now they focused much more on the day-to-day events, such that she felt there would be an awkwardness if they were to start now. More and more, Jenny realized that she and Bob needed to address this aspect of their lives as a couple, and an appointment was set up for them both.

Two further visits were productive in clarifying Bob's background, particularly his fear of loss—likely stemming from his mother dying when he was 4. He admitted that he did use sex in the first 3 years to confirm in his mind that this was a very strong marriage. Bob admitted that he found it quite disarming to learn of the many motivations that women (including his wife) have for agreeing to or for instigating sex. On the second visit, he was willing to tell more of his own insecurities, including his very real fear that harm would be caused by having sex during pregnancies and his feelings of devastation at having sex and affectionate physical touching so infrequently. Bob spoke of his source of comfort that sexual infrequency did seem to happen to other couples and of his definite willingness to try and find with Jenny a way toward emotional closeness that did not have to begin with sex, but might well lead to sex on some occasions, providing he and she made the effort to make the context appropriate, the time not too late, and the experience varied and not so intercourse-focused.

This particular couple managed without ongoing formal relationship counseling. Bob and Jenny were able to continue interrelating at home in the same way as in the joint interviews in the office. In time, Jenny believed that she was not abnormal to deliberately need to organize a specific context that was conducive to being sexual. Baby-sitters, "dates," and simply organizing family life so there was time to be together with the children asleep or with Damian not yet asleep, but understanding that if his parents have gone to bed, he would knock on the bedroom door only if there were some major problem. Physical touching and kisses, "no strings attached," were deliberately brought back into the marriage. Changes were gradual. Jenny feared that Damian would feel that she was pushing him away by changing the rules regarding access to their bedroom. Because she understood that she and Damian as a unit had to be echoed by she and Bob forming a unit, the necessary changes were made. Jenny found she could begin again to self-stimulate before and during intercourse if she had initially read something erotic. Later she was able to read erotica with Bob such that she could view it as part of lovemaking, rather than as a sign that she had some dysfunction.

I used the model during the interviews with Jenny and Bob, explaining the various breaks in Jenny's cycle as shown in Figure 7.3.

Rather than being overwhelmed that the cycle had so many areas of weakness or breaks, Jenny, typical of many women when this model is discussed, determined that there were many areas to address, each of them being attainable. She and they would have "preferred" a hormonal explanation—feeling that not only would the problem be easier to fix, but that it would safely distance the partners from *the,* as opposed to *their,* problem.

CONCLUSION

You will see very many women with complaints of low desire, many looking for a medical solution (even if there is no identified medical etiology). Sharing with them this model of their sexual response, which reflects their many motivations to be sexual over and beyond any innate sexual hunger, provides logic to their situation, which in itself is therapeutic. The importance of the degree of emotional intimacy becomes ob-

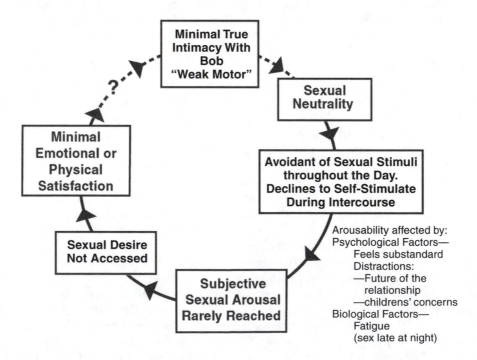

FIGURE 7.3. Model of Jenny's Sexual Response Cycle

vious. When this is lacking, the willingness and ability of both partners to address this lack clearly governs the effectiveness of addressing any problematic context or paucity of sexual stimuli and any psychological and interpersonal (and sometimes biological) issues affecting the woman's arousability. Moreover, addressing any cause of negative outcome, such as partner sexual dysfunction or chronic dyspareunia, requires true motivation from both partners, which will also be dependent on a minimum degree of emotional closeness.

Thus, improving the emotional intimacy per se, although often necessary, may well be insufficient. Deliberately giving some priority to sexual times and finding suitable contexts and types of mental and physical stimulation are also often needed. Some couples will need information regarding women's sexuality in longer-term relationships, including the need for the partners to guide each other, as physical responding changes with age and hormonal milieu. The frequent need for more nongenital and genital nonintercourse pleasuring can be emphasized. Less healthy habits of perfunctory intercourse associated with previous fertility testing or her being exhausted with young children may need to be addressed. The key element to the woman's sex response cycle is that it is a response—not an automatic entity stemming from some biological mechanism. Thus it can be nurtured and can potentially increase, rather than decrease, with the relationship duration.

NOTES

1. Tiefer, L. (1991). Historical, scientific, clinical and feminist criticisms of "the human sexual response cycle." *Annual Review of Sex Research, 2,* 1–23. *Annotation:* This is a very readable critique of "the human sex response cycle" and its historical background, emphasizing the narrow genital focus that has developed since the model of Masters and Johnson was first published. The subjects selected to study, and Masters and Johnson's definitions of "normal human sexual responding" are discussed in detail. The author questions why some sexual difficulties but not others are taken seriously and given title of "disorder."
2. Hatfield, E., & Rapson, R. L. (1993). *Love, Sex and Intimacy: The Psychology, Biology and History.* New York: HarperCollins.
3. Basson, R. (2000). The female sexual response: A different model. *Journal of Sex & Marital Therapy, 26,* 51–65. *Annotation:* I outlined the need for a model of women's sexual responding that can reflect issues important to women's sexuality, including trust, the ability to be vulnerable, respect, communication, affection, and pleasure from sexual touching. A woman's sexual cycle can begin without innate desire. Rather, she is willing to make a deliberate choice to become sexually aroused in order to access some sexual desire "en route." The major underlying motivation to do this is to increase emotional intimacy with her partner. However, she does also enjoy and come to hunger for more sexual sensations, with or without orgasmic release, as the whole experience continues. Factors external to her are, in fact, integral to her sexual cycle, including suitable sexual stimuli and context.
4. Regan, P., & Berscheid, E. (1996). Belief about the states, goals and objects of sexual desire. *Journal of Sex & Marital Therapy, 22,* 110–120.
5. Basson, R. (2000). The female sexual response: A different model. *Journal of Sex & Marital Therapy, 26,* 51–65.

6. Basson, R. (2001). Human sex response cycles. *Journal of Sex & Marital Therapy, 27,* 33–43. *Annotation:* The alternative model of sexual responding, whereby initially there is an intimacy-based motivation, rather than an innate, even "biological," sexual hunger or sense of sexual deprivation, is applied to the sexual experiences of men and women. The augmentation by apparent innate sexual desire is discussed and the model further developed to allow cycles within the basic simple cycle presented in this article. The concept of feedback cycles is introduced, commenting on the feedback from emotions, cognitions, and genital events in both men and women.

7. Kaplan, H. S. (1979). *Disorders of Sexual Desire.* New York: Brunner/Mazel.

8. Levin, R. J. (1998). Sexual desire and the deconstruction and reconstruction of the human female sexual response model of Masters and Johnson. In W. Everaerd, E. Laan, & S. Both (Eds.), *Sexual Appetite, Desire and Motivation: Energetics of the Sexual System.* (Proceedings of the Colloquium, Amsterdam, May 1998). Koninklijke Nederlanse Akademie van Wetenschappen Verhandelingen (Royal Netherlands Academy of Arts and Sciences), Afd. Letterkunde, Nieuwe Reeks, deal 184, Amsterdam, The Netherlands, 2001. *Annotation:* Following an interesting historical background, the author critiques the sex response cycles of Masters, Johnson, and Kaplan and discusses sexual desire. He focuses particularly on the multiple levels of potential genital feedback but little on the variability or relevance of the same. Levin suggests that although a woman's "spontaneous" desire initiates her being sexual alone or with a partner, she could experience more desire during the excitation (arousal) phase. "A galaxy of stimuli" is postulated as causing the endogenous desire— implying that the word *spontaneous* likely should not be used. That endogenous desire is perhaps absent initially, such that the only desire experienced results from arousal and external stimuli, is not suggested by this author.

9. Andersen, B. L., & Cyranowski, J. M. (1995). Women's sexuality: Behaviours, responses, and individual differences. *Journal of Consulting Clinical Psychology, 63,* 891–906. *Annotation:* This is a thorough and critical review of previous concepts of women's sexual behaviors and sexual responses. The authors also emphasize the need to consider individual differences—the focus of recent cognitive and personality research. A sexual self-schema scale is described. This measures inclination to experience passionate romantic emotions and openness to involvement in sexual relationships. Embarrassment and conservatism are also measured. Women with positive schema report high levels of arousability, many positive sexual experiences, and extensive histories of positive romantic ties. In contrast, women with negative schema describe themselves as unromantic, self-conscious, embarrassed, lacking in sexual/social confidence, and restricted in their sexual behaviors. Being unable to define one's schema is shown to lead to less arousability and love for the sexual partner. Women endorsing aspects of both positive and negative schema tend to show higher levels of sexual anxiety, yet high levels of romantic attachment (love) for the partner. The authors advocate assessing women's sexuality in all three domains—behavior, responses, and individual differences (self-schema).

10. Lunde, I., Larson, G. K., Fog, E., & Garde, K. (1991). Sexual desire, orgasm, and sexual fantasies: A study of 625 Danish women born in 1910, 1936 and 1958. *Journal of Sex Education Therapy, 17,* 111–115.

11. Cawood, H. H., & Bancroft, J. (1996). Steroid hormones, menopause, sexuality and wellbeing of women. *Psychophysiological Medicine, 26,* 925–936.

12. Galyer, K. T., Conaglen, H. M., Hare, A., & Conaglen, J. V. (1999). The effect of gynecological surgery on sexual desire. *Journal of Sex & Marital Therapy, 25,* 81–88.

13. Laumann, E. O., Paik, A., & Rosen, R. C. (1999). Sexual dysfunction in the United States: Prevalence and predictors. *Journal of the American Medical Association, 10,* 537–545.

14. Garde, K., & Lunde, I. (1980). Female sexual behaviour. A study in a random sample of 40-year-old women. *Maturitas, 2,* 225–240.
15. Bancroft, J. (1999). Central inhibition of sexual response in the male: A theoretical prospective. *Neuroscience Biobehavioal Review, 23,* 763–784.
16. Karama, S., Lecours, A. R., Leroux, J. M., Bourgouin, P., Beaudoin, G., Joubert, S., & Beauregard, M. (2002). Areas of brain activation in males and females during viewing of erotic film excerpts. *Human Brain Mapping, 16,* 1–13.
17. Herbert, J. (1997). Sexuality, stress, and the chemical architecture of the brain. *Annual Review of Sexual Research, 7,* 1–43.
18. Bancroft, J., & Cawood, E. H. (1996). Androgens in the menopause: A study of 40–60-year-old women. *Clinical Endocrinology (Oxf), 45,* 577–587.
19. Longcope, C., Franz, C., Morello, C., Baker, R., & Johnston, Jr., C. C. (1986). Steroid and gonadotropin levels in women during the perimenopausal years. *Maturitas, 8,* 189–196.
20. Zumoff, B., Strain, G. W., Miller, L. K., & Rosner, W. (1995). Twenty-four hour mean plasma testosterone concentration declines with age in normal premenopausal women. *Journal of Clinical Endocrinology & Metabolism, 80,* 1429–1430.
21. Burger, H. G., Dudley, E. C., Cui, J., Dennerstein, L., & Hopper, J. L. (2000). The prospective longitudinal study of serum testosterone, dihydroepiandrosterone sulfate, and sex hormone binding globulin levels through the menopause transition. *Journal of Clinical Endocrinology & Metabolism, 85,* 2832–2838. *Annotation:* This gives a useful background to the physiology of androgens in women and highlights the uncertainties to date, especially regarding postmenopausal values of androgens.
22. Jiroutek, M. R., Chen, M. H., Johnston, C. C., & Longcope, C. (1998). Changes in reproductive hormones and sex hormone-binding globulin in a group of postmenopausal women measured over 10 years. *Menopause, 5,* 90–94.
23. Andersen, B. L., & Cyranowski, J. M. (1995). Women's sexuality: Behaviours, responses, and individual differences. *Journal of Consulting Clinical Psychology, 63,* 891–906.
24. Laan, E., Everaerd, W., van der Velde, J., & Geer, J. H. (1995). Determinants of subjective experience of sexual arousal in women: Feedback from genital arousal and erotic stimulus content. *Psychophysiology, 32,* 444–451.
25. Everaerd, W., Laan, E., Both, S., & van der Velde, J. (2000). Female sexuality. In L. T. Szuchman & F. Muscarella (Eds.), *Psychological Perspectives of Human Sexuality.* New York: Wiley. *Annotation:* This is a comprehensive review of the literature on women's sexual arousal. It is clear and detailed in its descriptions, as well as in its theoretical explanation for the observed desynchrony between objective genital physiological congestion in women and their total experience of sexual arousal. This is followed by a discussion of the definitions of female sexual dysfunction, plus a brief review of assessment methods.
26. Laan, E., Everaerd, W., van der Velde, J., & Geer, J. H. (1995). Determinants of subjective experience of sexual arousal in women: Feedback from genital arousal and erotic stimulus content. *Psychophysiology, 32,* 444–451.
27. Everaerd, W., Laan, E., Both, S., & van der Velde, J. (2000). Female sexuality. In L. T. Szuchman & F. Muscarella (Eds.), *Psychological Perspectives of Human Sexuality.* New York: Wiley.
28. Palace, E. M., & Gorzalka, B. B. (1990). The enhancing effects of anxiety on arousal in sexually dysfunctional and functional women. *Journal of Abnormal Psychology, 99,* 403–411.
29. Heiman, J. R. (1980). Female sexual response patterns: Interactions of psychological, affective and contextual cues. *American Journal of Psychiatry, 37,* 1311–1316.
30. Morokoff, P. J., & Heiman, J. R. (1980). The effects of erotic stimuli on sexually functional and dysfunctional women: Multiple measures before and after sex therapy. *Behavior Research Therapy, 18,* 127–137.

31. Laan, E., & van Lunsen, R. H. W. (2003). Soma or stimulus? Etiology of female sexual arousal disorders. *Journal of Sex & Marital Therapy* (in press).

32. Andersen, B. L., & Cyranowski, J. M. (1995). Women's sexuality: Behaviours, responses, and individual differences. *Journal of Consulting Clinical Psychology, 63,* 891–906.

33. Laan, E., Everaerd, W., van der Velde, J., & Geer, J. H. (1995). Determinants of subjective experience of sexual arousal in women: Feedback from genital arousal and erotic stimulus content. *Psychophysiology, 32,* 444–451.

34. Everaerd, W., Laan, E., Both, S., & van der Velde, J. (2000). Female sexuality. In L. T. Szuchman & F. Muscarella (Eds.), *Psychological Perspectives of Human Sexuality*. New York: Wiley.

35. Heiman, J. R. (1998). Psychophysiological models of female sexual response. *International Journal of Impotence Research, 10,* S94–97.

36. Meston, C. M., & Gozalka, B. B. (1995). The effects of sympathetic activation on physiological and subjective sexual arousal in women. *Behavior Research & Therapy, 33,* 651–664.

37. Meston, C. M., & Heiman, J. R. (1998). Ephedrine-activated physiological sexual arousal in women. *Archives of General Psychiatry, 55,* 652–656.

38. Brotto, L., & Gorzalka, B. (2002) Genital and subjective sexual arousal in postmenopausal women: Influence of laboratory induced hyperventilation. *Journal of Sex & Marital Therapy, 28,* supplement, 39–54.

39. Basson, R. (2000). The female sexual response: A different model. *Journal of Sex & Marital Therapy, 26,* 51–65.

40. Everaerd, W., Laan, E., Both, S., & van der Velde, J. (2000). Female sexuality. In L. T. Szuchman & F. Muscarella (Eds.), *Psychological Perspectives of Human Sexuality*. New York: Wiley.

41. Basson, R. (2002). A model of women's sexual arousal. *Journal of Sex & Marital Therapy, 28,* 1–10. *Annotation:* I attempt to construct a simple model capable of reflecting the modulation of the woman's subjective sexual arousal by her cognitions, emotions, and highly variable genital feedback—the latter being potentially direct (throbbing, tingling) and indirect—sexual pleasure from massaging physically engorged genital structures, breasts, and other body areas. I also offer subtyping of female sexual arousal disorder to promote further understanding and improve therapy of the same.

42. Writing group for WHI. (2002). Risks and benefits of estrogen plus progestin in healthy postmenopausal women: Principal results from the Women's Health Initiative randomized control trial. *Journal of the American Medical Association, 288,* 321–333.

43. Hulley, S., Grady, D., & Bush, T. (1998). Randomized trial of estrogen plus progestin for secondary prevention of coronary heart disease in postmenopausal women. *Journal of the American Medical Association, 280,* 605–613.

44. Basson, R. (2000). The female sexual response: A different model. *Journal of Sex & Marital Therapy, 26,* 51–65.

45. Writing group for WHI. (2002). Risks and benefits of estrogen plus progestin in healthy postmenopausal women: Principal results from the Women's Health Initiative randomized control trial. *Journal of the American Medical Association, 288,* 321–333.

46. Hulley, S., Grady, D., & Bush, T. (1998). Randomized trial of estrogen plus progestin for secondary prevention of coronary heart disease in postmenopausal women. *Journal of the American Medical Association, 280,* 605–613.

47. Writing group for WHI. (2002). Risks and benefits of estrogen plus progestin in healthy postmenopausal women: Principal results from the Women's Health Initiative randomized control trial. *Journal of the American Medical Association, 288,* 321–333.

48. Basson, R. (2001). Human sex response cycles. *Journal of Sex &Marital Therapy, 27,* 33–43.

49. Writing group for WHI. (2002). Risks and benefits of estrogen plus progestin in healthy postmenopausal women: Principal results from the Women's Health Initiative randomized control trial. *Journal of the American Medical Association, 288,* 321–333.

Chapter Eight

Painful Genital Sexual Activity

Sophie Bergeron, PhD
Marta Meana, PhD
Yitzchak M. Binik, PhD
Samir Khalifé, MD

As you read the title and authorship of this chapter, you might be wondering why four of us wrote it. So let us begin by telling you a bit about who we are and why we often write papers as a group. Ten years ago, Marta Meana—then a graduate student in psychology at McGill University in Montreal—wanted to do her doctoral dissertation on the biopsychosocial characteristics of women with dyspareunia. She and Irv Binik, her then thesis adviser, decided that if they were going to do this right, a gynecologist should be involved in the process. In search of this *perle rare*, they sent out letters to all gynecologists affiliated with McGill University's Faculty of Medicine. Only one answered positively: Samir Khalifé. He not only collaborated with Irv and Marta, but stayed on board for Sophie's dissertation, which focused on the treatment of dyspareunia. Even though Marta and Sophie have now moved on to faculty positions of their own, all four of us have continued to collaborate and exchange ideas on a regular basis. We feel that our current treatment approach is the result of this fruitful collaboration and thus chose to write about it as a group.

Beyond theoretical considerations, we hope that this chapter will impart to you our enthusiasm for working with women suffering from painful genital sexual activity, as well as for using a multidisciplinary approach. It is more than just a "how to" manual; we will try to convey the challenges that we have encountered and give you the kind of guidelines that we wished would have been available when we were just starting out with this population. Ultimately, we find that you do not need to be a specialist of pain during intercourse to work with women who suffer from it. All it takes is an eagerness to learn more about the various aspects of painful genital sexual activity, ranging from the underlying physical pathologies to the therapeutic issues involved—knowledge that we hope this chapter will provide.

INTRODUCTION

Following the use of antibiotics for a bad throat infection, Laura, a successful lawyer in her late 20s, began to suffer from repeated yeast infections about 3 years ago. It seemed that no prescription or over-the-counter cream could help alleviate her symptoms. Over time, she noticed that intercourse had become more and more painful. It felt as though her entire vagina was on fire, and she became increasingly apprehensive about sexual activity. Laura used to very much enjoy sex with her husband, but now hardly has any desire for it, not even for nonpenetrative activities. When she does have sex, it is prompted by the insistence of her frustrated husband and the terrible guilt she feels about not being the lively sexual partner she used to be. Needless to say, under these conditions, she experiences very little sexual arousal, which further contributes to her pain. Laura wonders whether she will ever enjoy sex again and worries that she may never be able to have children. Her gynecologist—the fifth one she has consulted since the development of her problem and the first to tell her that it was not "all in her head"—recently diagnosed her with vulvar vestibulitis. She recommended that Laura take part in a pain-relief therapy program involving group psychotherapy, combined with individual physical therapy for the treatment of pain and sexual dysfunction.

Ten years ago, when a woman came to us complaining of painful genital sexual activity, our treatment consisted of sex therapy focusing mostly on psychosexual and relationship issues, with some vaginal dilatation. We seldom asked about the characteristics of the pain, probably because we felt that there was little we could do about it. However, as more and more of these women began to appear in our clinic, the limits of our treatment approach became apparent and we started to question the theoretical bases of standard treatments and the extent to which these were valid. Our team realized that nobody had really studied painful sex in any systematic way, let alone attempted to treat all of its dimensions. We thus embarked on a journey that has taken us from questions about sex to questions about pain; from sex therapy to pain management, physical therapy, and gynecological surgery; and from unidimensional clinical interventions to a multidisciplinary and individually tailored treatment approach.

What we have learned will be recounted in the following sections: (1) the varied clinical presentations of painful sex; (2) the typical consequences of this problem for women; (3) current and past conceptualizations of painful sex; (4) an overview of current therapeutic options and our multidisciplinary treatment approach; and (5) the strategies we have developed to work with individual women, couples, and groups of women afflicted with this problem, as well as the challenges that one can encounter when dealing with this population.

THE MANY FACES OF PAINFUL SEX

A couple consults their family doctor because they want to conceive a child, but have been unable to have intercourse for the past 2 years; a young woman complains to her doctor that she has been having repeated yeast infections that consist mostly of a burning sensation; a couple consults a sex therapist because the woman has lost interest in sex and says she experiences intense pain after intercourse; a woman in her 50s suffers from depression and anxiety attributed by her to the development of a chronic vulvar pain that interferes greatly with her daily activities. Most probably, all of the previous are among the 8 to 21% of American women who suffer from painful genital sexual activity (Laumann, Paik, & Rosen, 1999), yet this problem often goes undiagnosed and, when diagnosed, is often left untreated. A recent epidemiological study showed that only 60% of women who reported suffering from chronic genital pain sought treatment for this symptom, and 40% of those never received a formal diagnosis (Harlow, Wise, & Stewart, 2001). This finding highlights the importance of making questions concerning painful sex a routine part of medical and mental health assessment interviews. It also explains why the majority of women who end up in our offices are generally well educated and persistent: it is difficult to find a doctor or a psychologist who can diagnose and treat the many conditions associated with painful sex.

Within the mental health professions, painful genital sexual activity has traditionally been diagnosed as either dyspareunia or vaginismus (or both), two sexual disorders classified under the category of sexual pain in the *DSM-IV* (American Psychiatric Association, 1994). In addition to the fact that it is unclear why painful genital sexual activity is considered a sexual dysfunction any more than other pain syndromes interfering with sexual activity (e.g., low back pain) (Meana, Binik, Khalifé, & Cohen, 1997a), one of the main problems with this classification is that there is considerable overlap between dyspareunia and vaginismus. In fact, two recent studies showed that the only factor differentiating women with dyspareunia from those with vaginismus was the avoidance of penetration by the latter (de Kruiff, ter Kuile, Weijenborg, & van Lankveld, 2000; Reissing, Binik, Khalifé, & Cohen, 2002). Furthermore, dyspareunia and vaginismus can encompass a broad array of underlying physical pathologies, ranging from endometriosis and a retroverted uterus, resulting in deep dyspareunia, to vulvar vestibulitis, resulting in entry dyspareunia (Meana et al., 1997b). Normal developmental events such as vaginal birth delivery and menopause can also be a source of painful sex. Finally, many vulvar diseases classified under the umbrella term of *vulvodynia*—a general condition characterized by chronic, unexplained vulvar pain and minimal physical findings—are a source of painful genital sexual activity (McKay, 1988). The main vulvodynia subtype is vulvar vestibulitis (VVS), a syndrome characterized by a burning pain that is elicited via pressure to the vulvar vestibule or attempted vaginal penetration, for which there are no known physical causes. Vulvodynia also includes vulvar dermatoses, cyclic vulvovaginitis, and essential vulvodynia, a debilitating syndrome involving chronic burning of the vulva. Regardless of the often-elusive initial cause, pain during sexual activity diminishes overall quality of life. It impacts negatively on all phases of the sexual response cycle for the woman and sometimes for her partner; it puts a strain on otherwise stable relationships, while rendering more difficult the establishment of new ones; and, after years of unresolved pain, it can also result in mood disturbances and their attendant negative functional impact.

WHAT'S WRONG WITH ME? ASSOCIATED DIFFICULTIES

The difficulties associated with genital pain or any health problem affecting one's sex life are inevitably linked to the sociocultural context within which the problem occurs. A young woman unable to take part in what continues to be the most valued sexual activity—that is, intercourse—can experience devastating consequences, especially if the pain dates back to the first attempt, as is the case for about half the women suffering from dyspareunia (Bazin et al., 1994). At some point during the course of this problem, most will question their worth as women, wonder what is wrong with them psychologically and sexually, and doubt their love and attraction for their partner.

Research conducted in our laboratory showed that as an undifferentiated group, women with dyspareunia had more psychological distress, more negative attitudes toward sexuality, more sexual dysfunction, and more relationship problems than no-pain controls (Meana et al., 1997b). Contrary to clinical lore, they did not report more current or past sexual abuse. However, when this sample of women was subtyped based on physical pathology, a different picture surfaced. Women in whom no physical findings were found had significantly higher rates of psychological symptomatology and relationship maladjustment, although they were no different than controls in their sexual functioning. In contrast, women diagnosed with VVS reported that all aspects of their sexual response cycle were negatively affected: they had significantly lower intercourse frequencies, lower levels of desire and arousal, and less orgasmic success with intercourse and partner manual stimulation than normal controls (Meana et al., 1997b).

Some clinicians have reported that a third to a half of their samples of women with dyspareunia had difficulties with penetration to the point of warranting a diagnosis of vaginismus (Schover, Youngs, & Cannata, 1992; van Lankveld, Brewaeys, ter Kuile, & Weijenborg, 1995), a presumed spasm of the outer third of the vagina making intercourse impossible. Following these clinical accounts, we investigated more closely the pelvic floor hypertonicity often reported as a correlate of painful genital sexual activity (Reissing, Binik, Khalifé, Cohen, & Amsel, 2002). Results of this study demonstrated that women with vaginismus showed significantly higher average muscle tension than those with VVS, who in turn showed higher muscle tension than no-pain controls. These findings suggest that hypertonicity is probably contributing to the pain experienced during intercourse and should be dealt with in the context of a multidisciplinary treatment approach.

As with other pain syndromes, there are multiple mediating factors that contribute to exacerbate and maintain pain (Gatchel & Turk, 1999). Interestingly, women with dyspareunia who attribute their pain to psychosocial factors report higher levels of pain, more sexual dysfunction, as well as more psychological and marital distress, than those who attribute their pain to physical factors, regardless of actual etiology (Meana, Binik, Khalifé, & Cohen, 1999). In addition, as is also the case for other pain problems, anxiety is positively correlated with pain intensity during intercourse, and there is a negative correlation between painful intercourse and relationship satisfaction (Meana, Binik, Khalifé, & Cohen, 1998). It is possible that well-adjusted couples adapt more flexibly to the presence of pain during intercourse, thereby reducing anxiety and overall distress surrounding sexual activities. Thus, both cognitive factors, as well as relational ones, are likely to have an impact on the experience of pain, even if neither completely accounts for the pain's initial onset.

A BRIEF HISTORICAL OVERVIEW

The history of approaches to understanding and treating pain during sexual intercourse is disjointed and confusing. There are at least three important potential reasons for this. First, several different disciplines, including gynecology, the mental health professions, and, most recently, pain specialists, have attempted to develop theories and treatments appropriate to the problem. Typically, there has been controversy within each discipline and little communication between them. Second, there is much confusion concerning whether pain during sexual intercourse is a syndrome, as suggested by the *DSM*, or a symptom of underlying pathology, as suggested by many gynecology texts. Third and perhaps most curious is that until very recently, this problem did not appear to be a major concern for clinicians or researchers from any discipline. The only very clear historical point is that the problem of pain during intercourse and penetration has been known for many centuries (Meana & Binik, 1994).

Gynecologists have traditionally been the front-line clinicians and researchers in this area. In general, 20th-century gynecologists have demonstrated a fairly straightforward dualistic approach. They have attempted to either equate the pain with some known physical pathology or, in its absence, have assumed a psychogenic origin and referred the patient to the mental health professions. There are very long lists in many gynecology texts of possible physical causes to pain during intercourse (e.g., Baram, 1996). The presumption has been that if you treat the physical cause, the pain will disappear. If this is not effective, patients are typically referred to mental health professionals. There has been very little controlled research that supports this view or method of treatment. Very recently, a different "biopsychosocial" view is emerging among gynecologists interested in chronic pelvic pain (e.g., Steege, Metzger, & Levy, 1998). This view conceptualizes all forms of pelvic pain, including pain during intercourse, as multidetermined and relies heavily on research and models from pain research and health psychology. Within gynecology, the one notable exception to this dualistic history is the assessment and treatment of vaginismus. Since Masters and Johnson and perhaps before, vaginismus has been considered a "psychosomatic disorder." Gynecology's primary role was to diagnose vaginal spasm and to then refer the patient for sex therapy, including vaginal dilatation.

For most of the last century mental health professionals shared the dualistic attitude and approach of gynecologists, although the emphasis was different. Mental health professionals would be much more likely to assume psychogenic causation. The specific treatment approach depended primarily on the reigning theoretical model of the time. For at least half of the 20th century, pain during intercourse was likely to be considered a hysterical symptom and treated accordingly. Other approaches saw the pain as the result of faulty couple interaction/communication, poor sexual technique, inadequate arousal, vaginal atrophy, sexual abuse, or some combination of these. There was little attempt to differentiate treatment depending on different locations, types, or qualities of pain. In practice, mental health professionals have only recently become involved in the treatment of dyspareunia. On the other hand, sex therapists are probably the primary practitioners for the treatment of vaginismus.

The current terms *dyspareunia* and *vaginismus* did not enter the psychiatric nosology until the *DSM III* (1980), when they were formally classified as sexual disorders. This presumably occurred because of the enormous influence on mental health practice of Masters and Johnson, Helen Singer Kaplan, and early sex therapists. The *DSM-IV* places dyspareunia and vaginismus in a separate subcategory termed the *sexual pain disorders*. It assumes that dyspareunia and vaginismus are discrete syndromes, and recent consensus conferences concerning sexual problems have retained these terms (Basson et al., 2000). The concept of "sexual pain," as separate from other pain problems, is a confusing one. It suggests that there is a special type of pain called *sexual* and thus implies that there might be other such categories such as work pain, eating pain, sleep pain, and so forth. In fact, "sexual pain" is the only pain left in the *DSM* outside of the category of pain disorder, and it is not clear why pain during intercourse is defined by the activity with which it interferes, rather than by the characteristics of the pain.

In the last 10 years, pain during intercourse has begun to interest the pain research and treatment community (e.g., Wesselman, Burnett, & Heinberg, 1997). Vaginismus and dyspareunia have been included in the International Association for the Study of Pain (IASP) classification of chronic pain, along with other forms of urogenital and pelvic pain (Merskey & Bogduk, 1994). This classification and approach relies heavily on models of pain suggested by the gate control theory (Melzack & Wall, 1983) and its descendants, all of which suggest complex interactions of biopsychosocial determinants in the experience of pain. The treatment models assume multidisciplinary teams, including physicians, mental health professionals, physical therapists, acupuncturists, and so on.

The "pain" approach is currently avoiding the major problems listed previously, because it is multidisciplinary by nature, focuses on the pain, and provides a new multiaxial approach to classification. It has also resulted in some interesting new research ideas that have important clinical implications. For example, Pukall, Binik, Khalifé, Amsel, and Abbott (1996) recently demonstrated that both vulvar pain and touch thresholds are dramatically lower in women suffering from VVS than in matched controls. This finding was not surprising because it reflected the clinical phenomenon. What was remarkable was that nonvulvar pain thresholds were also similarly affected in VVS sufferers. This suggests that peripheral conceptions and perhaps therapies for

VVS may not be sufficient to explain the problem. In another study, Reissing et al. (2002) found that women suffering from vaginismus were indistinguishable from matched VVS controls on measures of pain. These data suggest that pain is an essential part of the diagnosis of VVS, but may be insufficient to distinguish vaginismus from VVS. Whether the "pain approach" will stand the test of time remains to be seen.

CURRENT THERAPEUTIC OPTIONS

In recent years, clinical and scientific interest in treating painful genital sexual activity has increased dramatically. Current therapeutic options include medical, cognitive, behavioral, and surgical interventions. However, most efforts to date remain unidimensional, as they aim to alleviate only one aspect of the complex array of symptoms that characterize painful sex. Moreover, empirically validated treatments are still the exception: There are no randomized clinical trials for vaginismus and only one for dyspareunia (Bergeron et al., 2001). We have suggested that a multimodal treatment approach may be the most fruitful, if we are to provide optimal care for a set of conditions that impact on different areas of functioning (Bergeron et al., 1997a).

Medical interventions are recommended during the first stage of treatment for entry dyspareunia. Physicians typically begin by suggesting minimally invasive treatments, such as the topical application of different types of antifungal, corticosteroid, or estrogen creams. It has been our experience that corticosteroid creams are the most commonly prescribed first-line treatment for superficial dyspareunia, with or without vaginismus, and that many women self-medicate with or are prescribed antifungal agents. There is no published evidence, however, that any of these creams are effective. Barring symptomatic relief from the aforementioned measures, systemic treatments, including oral corticosteroids and antifungals, have been suggested as the next treatment stage. Only one controlled study examined the use of an oral medication for VVS (systemic antifungal), and results show that it is no more effective than placebo (Bornstein, Livrat, Stolar, & Abramovici, 2000). There are typically no medical treatments for the single diagnosis of vaginismus.

Behavioral interventions include sex therapy, pelvic floor physical therapy, and cognitive-behavioral pain management. Sex therapy has been conducted, based on the assumption that increases in desire and arousal, as well as a decrease in vaginismic muscle contraction, would impact on some of the mechanisms that might mediate painful genital sexual activity. Success with a combination of sex therapy and behavioral pain management has been reported in two recent studies, although these did not include control groups (Abramof, Wolman, & David, 1994; Weijmar Schultz et al., 1996). Therapeutic effectiveness was reported in one uncontrolled study of pelvic floor biofeedback in a mixed group of women with vulvar pain. The presence of vaginismus was not formally assessed in this sample, but its frequency was probably high, considering that an important proportion of participants was not engaging in intercourse at the beginning of the study (Glazer, Rodke, Swencionis, Hertz, & Young, 1995). Although retrospective, this study is interesting because there is evidence that biofeedback is beneficial for other pain conditions. Furthermore, the use of other physical therapy techniques (e.g., soft tissue mobilization) appears to be increasingly popular with patients, as seen on Internet sites devoted to genital pain and in newsletters of vulvar pain support networks.

We have recently completed an evaluation of the effectiveness of physical therapy, including biofeedback, in the treatment of 35 women suffering from VVS (Bergeron et al., 2002). Physical therapy was successful for 51.4% of women and unsuccessful for the rest. Prospective measures of pain during gynecological examination showed a significant decrease from pre- to post-treatment. Self-reported pain during intercourse was also significantly reduced pre- to post-treatment. In addition, there were significant increases in frequency of intercourse, sexual desire, and sexual arousal. This pattern of results suggests that physical therapy can be a potentially successful noninvasive treatment option for painful genital sexual activity. Furthermore, it has been our experience that patients usually enjoy this intervention and feel quite satisfied with both the treatment delivery and resulting improvements.

Vestibulectomy is the most commonly reported treatment for one of the main syndromes associated with painful sex—that is, VVS. Usually recommended following the failure of less invasive treatment strategies, this minor surgical intervention is also the treatment most consistently reported as achieving the best therapeutic outcome. It consists of an excision of the hymen and of all the sensitive areas of the vestibule to a depth of about 2 mm, most frequently located in the posterior fourchette. The vaginal mucosa is then sometimes mobilized and brought downward to cover the excised area (Friedrich, 1987). This intervention is done under general or epidural anesthesia (e.g., Goetsch, 1996). Women are instructed to gradually resume intercourse about 6 weeks postsurgery. Bergeron, Binik, Khalifé, and Pagidas's (1997b) and Bornstein, Zarfati, Goldik, and Abramovici's (1999) critical reviews of the VVS surgery literature reveal vestibulectomy success rates ranging from 43 to 100%, with average success rates typically surpassing 65–70%.

Despite this reported success, surgical interventions for genital pain have been the source of much controversy, strong opinions, and understandable puzzlement as to the basic mechanism by which surgery produces its effect. Part of the controversy stems from the fact that until recently, there were no randomized treatment outcome studies evaluating the efficacy of vestibulectomy. In order to address empirically some of the issues surrounding the use of surgery for genital pain, we conducted the first randomized treatment study of VVS comparing vestibulectomy, group cognitive-behavioral therapy, and biofeedback (Bergeron et al., 2001). The main results of this study are striking. There were no changes in pain during the 6-week baseline period but significant improvements at post-treatment and at the 6-month follow-up for all treatments. Vestibulectomy resulted in approximately twice the pain reduction (47–70%, depending on pain measure), as compared with the two other treatments (19–38%). These findings need to be interpreted with caution because 7 women refused to go ahead with the surgery after randomization, and 2 out of the 22 who had the surgery reported being worse at post-treatment. There were significant improvements in overall sexual functioning at the 6-month follow-up, with no treatment differences. However, there were no changes in frequency of intercourse, which remained well below national averages for this age group, with a mean frequency of four times per month, in comparison to the average of eight times per month reported in a recent epidemiological study (Laumann, Gagnon, Michael, & Michaels, 1994). Unfortunately, we were not able to identify any predictors of outcome.

Recently, we carried out a 2.5-year follow-up of these study participants (Bergeron, Binik, Khalifé, Pagidas, & Glazer, 2002). All treatments had effected significant improvements in pain over time. Vestibulectomy remained superior to the other two conditions in its impact on clinically assessed vestibular pain, but was equal to group cognitive-behavioral therapy in terms of self-reported pain during intercourse. This suggests that the effects of cognitive-behavioral therapy may be slower to appear, and that if one is patient, surgery can be avoided. There were no changes in frequency of intercourse or overall sexual functioning between the 6-month and 2.5-year follow-up.

Considering the absence of predictors of treatment outcome, how do we help a patient choose between the widely varied existing interventions? Despite the superior outcome results of the vestibulectomy condition in our randomized study (Bergeron et al., 2001), our overall clinical approach to the treatment of painful sex begins by recommending less invasive behavioral treatments, considering the risks involved with the surgery. After careful evaluation and diagnosis, the gynecologists on our team typically recommend that the woman choose between cognitive-behavioral sex therapy/ pain management (group, couple, or individual format) and physical therapy. If one or a combination of these treatments is not effective, that is, to the satisfaction of the patient, the gynecologist will consider performing a vestibulectomy in the case of VVS only. The traditional medical approach postulates that we should always offer the more conservative treatment first. However, in many cases of genital pain, (1) conservative medical treatments such as corticosteroid creams typically do not help, and (2) many of the patients who come to us have already tried a number of creams, without success.

HOW TO WORK WITH WOMEN WHO SUFFER FROM PAINFUL GENITAL SEXUAL ACTIVITY

Addressing Therapists' Issues and Assumptions: Our Recommendations

The treatment of women suffering from painful genital sexual activity is hard work. Despite the fact that their problem is very specific, and our training has led us to believe that the more well-defined the problem, the more amenable it is to intervention, such is rarely the case for either dyspareunia or vaginismus, and most certainly not for VVS. The presenting problem may be simple enough—pain with intercourse—but it exists within a complex constellation of both physical and psychological etiologic and mediating factors that will challenge even experienced therapists. Sex is a complicated union or disunion of physiology, psychology, and social mores. Adding pain to the mix does not simplify it, nor does the frustration of multiple failed attempts at professional help. The end result is almost always a complicated case that will demand all of your therapeutic talents, but will also provide immense satisfaction when the ripple effect of improvement in one area spreads to the complex whole. Prior to even meeting the patient, it is helpful for therapists to do preparatory work on themselves.

It is likely, although not certain, that your patient will be frustrated about the fact that she has consulted multiple professionals who did not help. Many will tell stories about being dismissed as either imagining their pain or even needing it as an excuse for not dealing with some relational or intrapsychic conflict. Others will recount treatments that produced iatrogenic harm (i.e., chasing supposed repressed memories of sexual abuse or laser treatments that have resulted in even more pain). Be ready for both cynical patients and extremely hopeful ones. In both cases, *avoid the trap of setting yourself up as the savior*. You can empathize with their frustration at treatment failures without creating the impression that you will be the one to solve the problem completely. Often, the main problem in past treatment attempts was a failure to provide either a true validation of their pain or an honest appraisal of treatment expectations. Make that your starting point, and you probably will have done more for them than prior therapists have.

Escaping the dualism that has plagued many attempts at both understanding and treating painful genital sexual activity is easier said than done. In session you may still find yourself trying to pin the pain down to a single cause. Or you may find the patient trying to do just that. After all, both you and the patient would dearly love a simple explanation that would indicate a straightforward treatment direction. Unless it really does jump out at you or them, and this is rarely the case, *avoid attempts to attribute the pain to a single cause*. Doing so will more often than not lead to a cul-de-sac and a retracing of steps. Coherent but inaccurate narratives about the origins of our problems are satisfying only temporarily.

Truly adopting a multidisciplinary approach to the conceptualization, assessment, and treatment of a disorder requires some humility unless you happen to represent all of the disciplines implicated. A mental health professional can be responsible only for the mental health aspect of the problem being treated. This means that you should assume that treatment success is not entirely within your control. You can do your part and you can even coordinate access to the other disciplines, but, ultimately, *you can control only the dimension of the problem you are treating*. This is a challenge to many health professionals, who are not accustomed to coordinating their efforts with other professionals. In the case of painful genital sexual activity, you should be part of a team, and you can own only the part that falls under your purveyance.

However, if you have indeed adopted a multidisciplinary approach to the conceptualization, assessment, and treatment of painful genital sexual activity, *you have a responsibility to educate yourself about what the other disciplines do*. The optimal coordination of multidisciplinary treatment requires that all team members have at least some basic knowledge about what everyone is working on. This means that, as a therapist, you need to educate yourself about the gynecological conditions that are implicated in genital pain, as well as medical and surgical treatment options. You also should inform yourself about the physical therapy component of this treatment approach.

The other challenge in the treatment of painful genital sexual activity is that unlike the case of most other supposedly well-defined problems, you have to *aim your treatment at multiple targets simultaneously*. By the time you see them in your office, women with painful genital sexual activity are very likely to have deficits in desire and arousal and somewhat likely to have problems with their relationships and, maybe, their mood and self-esteem. Our recommendation is to attempt to target all problem areas simultaneously with reasonably modest goals, as one area is not likely to improve without a commensurate improvement in the others. So, a small increase in desire, coupled with a small improvement in arousal, coupled with slightly enhanced partner communication and a somewhat reduced level of hopelessness, is likely to have surprising additive effects, despite the very modest gains in any one single target area.

Our final recommendation for therapists is to *expect treatment gains to come in relatively small increments*. We have often found that therapists new to this area are surprised by the fact that their patients are pleased with relatively small improvements. All of us would love to solve our patients' problems definitively, but what seem to us small improvements can mean a world of difference to our patients. Although we have had cases of women with VVS who experienced complete resolution of their pain, the more common outcome is improvement, as is the case with the treatment of most chronic pain syndromes. Remember that improvement can be exhilarating for women who had lost all hope of ever enjoying sexual activity.

Multidimensional Assessment

In keeping with our biopsychosocial model, we find that a multidimensional assessment of genital pain—that is, the assessment of the organic, cognitive, affective, behavioral, and relationship factors as either causal or maintenance factors—is crucial. Factors that initiated the onset of the pain condition may be different from those maintaining it, and overly simplistic, dualistic etiological frameworks are of little utility in the case of painful sex. Unfortunately, the comprehensive evaluation of women with dyspareunia has traditionally been a neglected dimension of the overall health-care delivery for this population. Still today, too many of these women are not taken seriously, with the resulting effect that physicians do not necessarily perform all the routine medical tests that would help in establishing the proper diagnosis. These include (1) a careful gynecological history; (2) a thorough gynecological examination involving the cotton-swab palpation of the vestibular area, with the woman rating her pain at various sites; and (3) vaginal and cervical cultures to exclude the possibility of infection-related pain. Additional testing may include an endovaginal ultrasound and a colposcopy. It is not uncommon for improper medical evaluation to lead to iatrogenic harm via the recommendation of inappropriate interventions. Such an evaluation should thus constitute the first step in the diagnostic process.

The second step focuses on assessing the quality, location, duration, onset, elicitors, and intensity of the pain, all of which can be done by a mental health professional. These variables have been shown to be the best predictors of underlying physical pathology, in a study conducted with women suffering from different types of dyspareunia (Meana et al., 1997a). Asking about pain characteristics not only informs the health professional as to potential etiologies, but also serves the purposes of validating the patient's suffering and establishing the therapeutic alliance early on. We have found that the use of a 0 to 10 scale, with 0 representing *no pain at all* and 10 representing *the worst pain ever,* to be a useful tool for assessing the intensity of the pain. We use a similar scale to evaluate the degree of emotional distress associated with the experience of genital pain. These scales also constitute invaluable tools for monitoring progress throughout the therapy. Finally, because many women also suffer from genital pain during other, nonsexual activities, such as urination, tampon insertion and removal, and so forth, it is important to inquire about these as well.

After having obtained a good description of the different aspects of the pain, we concentrate the remainder of the assessment on the cognitive, behavioral, and affective reactions that usually accompany the pain, and this for both the woman and her partner. The assessment of behavioral factors is particularly relevant when attempting to establish whether the woman might suffer from what sex therapists traditionally refer to as vaginismus, because it has been shown that only avoidance of penetration differentiates between women suffering from vaginismus and those with dyspareunia (de Kruiff et al., 2000; Reissing et al., 2002). Because these disorders often overlap and co-occur (van Lankveld, Brewaeys, ter Kuile, & Weijenborg, 1995), we have suggested that they might best be viewed along a continuum, rather than as qualitatively distinct diagnostic entities (Meana & Binik, 1994). Nevertheless, knowledge of the extent to which penetration is avoided provides some important clues concerning the role played by psychosocial factors in the sexual dysfunction resulting from painful intercourse. Studies have shown that there is no correlation between pain intensity and extent of disability, and degree of disability is usually predicted by such cognitive and affective factors as catastrophizing and fear of pain (e.g., Turk, Rudy, Kubinski, Zaki, & Greco, 1996).

A major part of the assessment should focus on the impact of pain on sexual functioning. We tend to ask fairly detailed questions about the couple's typical sexual scenario, past and current frequency of intercourse, frequency of masturbation, and who usually initiates sex, how, and for what reason. Women who experience painful genital sexual activity rarely initiate sex, and if so, it is out of guilt rather than out of desire. This is not surprising, in view of the fact that the aspect of sex that is still considered by many as its main component—intercourse—has become a source of pain, not pleasure. The frequency of intercourse for these couples has thus usually taken a downward slope. Other negative impacts on sexual functioning include diminished sexual arousal and reduced orgasmic capacity, which may in turn worsen the pain (Meana et al., 1997b).

We believe that there are two categories of cognitive factors that may play a role in the maintenance of pain during intercourse, although empirical evidence for this as it relates specifically to dyspareunia is lacking. A first type of cognitive distortion has to do with thoughts concerning the overall pain condition—for example "I will be stuck with this problem for life" or "No man will ever want me because I cannot give him the sexual pleasure he desires." Such thoughts are characteristic of pain catastrophizing, a cognitive style that involves magnification, rumination, and helplessness and is related to higher pain intensity (Sullivan, Bishop, & Pivik, 1995). Changes in catastrophizing have been shown to correlate with better treatment outcome following cognitive-behavioral therapy for chronic pain (Turner & Clancy, 1986).

Another type of cognitive distortion concerns the experience of pain per se, more specifically, thoughts immediately preceding and following the pain experience and those occurring during the pain experience. Examples include "I know I will be in terrible pain in a couple of minutes; it will be a horrible experience that will end badly for both myself and my partner," and "The pain I am feeling now is so intense, it's like a knife piercing through my vagina." These thoughts can be targeted with the pain-management component of our program via cognitive restructuring.

Much like its cognitive counterpart, the affective component of the pain experience can take on a more general form, such as an elevated degree of anxiety concerning the disorder in general, common prediagnostically, and a more situational one, such as fear of pain during a given sexual encounter. Fear of engaging in the activities that generate pain is a common response in chronic pain sufferers and can lead to an avoidance of such activities (Linton, Melon, & Götestam, 1985). Furthermore, anxiety is related to higher pain intensity (Gatchel & Turk, 1998).

Although a routine component of all sex therapy evaluations, inquiries about past treatments are of utmost importance in the case of painful genital sexual activity because there is such a wide array of interventions, a preponderance of ineffective ones, and numerous misconceptions about the condition. This unfortunate state of affairs can lead to a loss of hope regarding the chances of ever improving, a difficulty in trusting health professionals, and a more or less skeptical approach to treatment.

Initial Phase of Therapy: Alliance Building, Education, and Goal Formulation

Many traditional sex therapy interventions for dyspareunia and vaginismus have been used for the last 30 years without empirical validation (Heiman & Meston, 1997). Vaginal dilatation, which involves the vaginal insertion of progressively larger dilators by the woman herself, and Kegel exercises, which are series of contraction/relaxation exercises for the pelvic floor, have been the cornerstones of the treatment of painful genital sexual activity, yet we know nothing of their effectiveness. Furthermore, it appears that the main goal of treatment for sexual pain has always been the reduction of the fear of penetration, but never the reduction of the pain. This view is nonsensical, considering that it ignores the main symptom of these disorders—pain. We have thus attempted to develop a new approach that has modified some of the traditional sex therapy interventions and integrated a pain-management component (Binik, Bergeron, & Khalifé, 2000).

The main purpose of the initial phase of therapy is to help the patient reconceptualize her genital pain as a multidimensional problem, influenced by a variety of factors, including her thoughts, emotions, behaviors, and couple interactions (Turk, Meichenbaum, & Genest, 1983). During the first few sessions, we try to develop a collaborative working relationship with the individual patient, couple, or group of patients. We clarify any potential misconceptions about treatment by raising and discussing them openly; we feel it is only normal that a patient be skeptical in the beginning, considering the typical history of her genital pain problem and the counterintuitive aspect of what we are offering her, that is, using psychological means to alleviate a condition that is experienced primarily as a physical one. Providing education about a multidimensional view of painful genital sexual activity, in addition to education about a specific underlying physical pathology, when relevant, is a very effective means of engaging the patient in the therapy process. This usually includes the use of written didactic materials that are subsequently discussed in therapy. Furthermore, we have consistently found that adopting a pain perspective to treatment enhances the development of the therapeutic alliance. The women feel validated, and the overall treatment approach sounds more relevant to them, in comparison to traditional sex therapy. Pain is, after all, the main symptom and primary complaint of women suffering from dyspareunia and vaginismus. It only makes sense that we make it the central focus of therapy.

One of our first treatment objectives is to get the patients to think about how different cognitive, affective, behavioral, and relationship factors affect their pain experience, as well as to notice the variations in their current pain. For example, one woman may notice that when she engages in sexual activity to please her partner, she tends to feel more pain, or that when she has sex during the week following her period, the pain is often less intense. A tool that is most useful in this process is a pain diary, as is used in the treatment of other pain syndromes; we have devised a diary that is specific to painful genital sexual activity. Apart from a pain intensity rating, the diary contains questions about women's menstrual cycle stage; what they were thinking and feeling before, during, and after the pain; what they did to try to cope with the pain; and how aroused/relaxed they were before taking part in the pain-generating event. This diary often becomes the basis for many subsequent interventions because it allows us to gather a wealth of information concerning the different dimensions of the patient's pain experience.

In terms of therapeutic objectives, we try to help our patients formulate two or three short-term, realistic goals that will guide our interventions, as well as contribute to further engaging and motivating the patient. These often consist of at least one pain-reduction goal and one sexual functioning–improvement goal. However, we avoid making the complete elimination of pain an absolute goal, as it is highly improbable that our treatment alone will ever provide this. We emphasize that even though some women do not always notice a reduction in their pain, they usually feel that it has less of a negative impact on their life following the therapy. In addition, we do not make the increase in frequency of sexual activities a goal per se, which would only further stigmatize and alienate the woman suffering from genital pain. In the case of couple therapy, helping the partners to see how they have each contributed to the current polarization of sexual roles and resulting lowered frequency of intercourse creates a more balanced alliance between the therapist and each member of the dyad (Schnarch, 2000). We also try to steer the focus away from intercourse and to help the couple find enjoyment and fulfillment in other, nonpenetrative sexual activities.

Treatment Strategies for Reducing Pain and Sexual Dysfunction

Once the patient recognizes that she has more control over her pain than previously thought, we suggest ways in which she can use this newly acquired awareness in order to actually reduce the pain. A first exercise we propose is the self-exploration of the woman's genitals. Common to many sex therapies, we give it a different twist—that is, an emphasis on the localization of the pain. The woman is not exploring for the sake of exploring, but rather is attempting to delineate the painful area in order to know exactly where it hurts and to show it to her partner when relevant. Education about sexual anatomy is provided at this point when necessary.

We also introduce some form of breathing/relaxation exercise fairly early on in the treatment, with the following rationale: "As you have noticed in your diary entries and in our discussions, the anticipation of pain creates anxiety, which has two consequences: (a) it inhibits arousal, which in turn inhibits lubrication, which increases your pain upon penetration; and (b) it often contributes to an involuntary contraction of the vaginal muscles, which again makes penetration a lot more painful and sometimes impossible. For these reasons, an important part of the treatment is to learn to reduce your anxiety. One major way in which you can learn to do this is via breathing/relaxation techniques." If the woman already practices some form of relaxation, we simply focus on helping her see how it can be used to reduce her pain and encourage her to really make it an integral part of her daily routine. We also suggest that she use this technique during her physical therapy sessions, where she experiences some pain, and during gynecological examinations.

We have learned from our close collaboration with physical therapists that Kegel exercises prescribed by a sex therapist who can never know whether the woman is doing them correctly is practically useless. For all we know, she may be contracting her thighs and her abdomen, rather than the relevant pelvic floor muscles. For this reason, we always recommend that the woman see a physical therapist at least once or twice so that she can be coached as to the proper way to perform these exercises. We then recommend that she practice them everyday and particularly prior to any form of vaginal penetration, so as to relax the pelvic floor as much as possible. Similarly, vaginal dilatation done in the context of a hypertonic pelvic floor is not very useful and can even be counterproductive because the chances of experiencing pain are then very high. Again, a physical therapist can be very useful here, and we can then coordinate a systematic desensitization program together that will help break the association between pain and penetration.

Cognitive restructuring focusing on pain is probably one of the most successful components of our approach. We divide it into the three following steps: (1) preparing for the onset of pain: anticipation of pain; (2) confronting and handling the sensations:

pain during and after intercourse; and (3) handling feelings after an episode of painful intercourse. The woman is encouraged to begin to identify her automatic thoughts, to jot them down in her pain diary, and also to communicate them to her partner and to the therapist. When done in a group format, this strategy is particularly powerful and serves to break the isolation of individual suffering.

An issue that often needs to be discussed at length is the avoidance of penetration and of other forms of sexual activities. We try to work at breaking the avoidance habit by helping patients (1) acknowledge that they have been avoiding sex, (2) raise their awareness regarding the fact that pain is probably only one of many reasons at this point why they are avoiding sex, and (3) identify unrealistic beliefs, inhibitions, or less adaptive attitudes about pain and sex. We eventually help them get reacquainted with painless sexual activities. Sensate focus exercises have sometimes been useful in this context. Again, the emphasis here is not on blaming the woman for her normal reaction of not wanting to engage in a painful activity, but rather for her and her partner to become cognizant of other factors, such as relationship ones, that might have led to the current reduction or absence of pleasure, creativity, and passion during sexual activities.

A related and very important issue is that of the nearly universal decreases in sexual desire and in sexual arousal observed in this population. Because many of our patients are young women, we find that focusing on the identification of sexual needs is often quite productive. What sexual activities/moods/scenarios/ambiances/fantasies really arouse the woman? Can she communicate these to her partner? Sometimes we find that assertiveness has to be improved in order to enable the woman to communicate her sexual preferences to her partner. An extensive overview of how to deal with sexual desire problems is beyond the scope of this chapter. We have found that a systemic conceptualization has been extremely helpful in dealing with desire issues and in working on the relationship issues of women with dyspareunia in general.

The last component of the therapy consists of a review and consolidation of learned strategies and progress with the goal of (1) facilitating internal attributions of improvement and (2) identifying what will need continued attention once therapy is terminated. This may include recommending some readings or another treatment when the present one has not resulted in the desired improvements. Some women will at this point opt for a surgery or for an alternative treatment such as acupuncture. The treatment of painful genital sexual activity is generally a lengthy process, with our psychosocial approach being only one of many available options.

Therapeutic Issues Common to the Treatment of Painful Sex

Most of the therapeutic issues that arise in the treatment of women suffering from painful genital sexual activity are similar to those found in psychotherapeutic approaches to other pain and sexual problems. However, there are at least five therapeutic issues that we have found to be fairly prominent in the treatment of these women. Anticipating these and preparing for their management can be very helpful to the therapist embarking on this treatment.

Resistance to psychological interventions for pain is not uncommon. After all, many of these women have long been told that the problem was emotional or mental, as a way of dismissing the seriousness of the issue. In our research, the most well-adjusted women seem to be relatively convinced that there is a physical component to their pain, despite repeated assertions from gynecologists that there is no obvious pathology (Meana et al., 1998). It is thus understandable that the first reaction to a mental health professional may be a defensive one. It behooves the therapist to validate the pain as it is experienced by the patient and then educate her about the ways in which psychosocial factors can impact the pain experience and how the pain itself, even pain with a strictly physical etiology, can result in psychosocial disturbances. Working on the credibility of psychological treatments for pain is an important part of the initial phase. The patient has to believe that this treatment holds some promise.

As with any treatment that consists of cognitive-behavioral techniques, compliance with monitoring and homework assignments is a therapeutic issue of great importance. Some patients can initially be resistant to these assignments for a variety of reasons, ranging from a lack of belief in their effectiveness, to an inability to make the assignments a priority in an otherwise busy day, to an unwillingness to spend that much time on a topic that is disturbing to them. Whatever the underlying reason, it needs to be explored with the patient and her partner, as it often reflects some degree of ambivalence regarding change; uncompleted homework can sometimes be as informative to the therapist's conceptualization of the pain problem as are diligently performed exercises. One strategy that often helps patients understand the importance of homework is to give a rationale explaining how a given exercise will have a direct impact on their pain. We have also found that the timing in prescribing homework is a key factor in its successful implementation; for example, a prescribed ban on intercourse may prevent a woman from asserting herself with her partner by refusing to continue intercourse when she is in too much pain, as opposed to having the therapist do that for her. Finally, in some cases patients need to be confronted about their commitment to making the resolution or improvement of pain a major priority during the course of treatment.

Another therapeutic issue that we have found prevalent in our work is what we call the "exhilaration/disappointment roller coaster." Initial gains can produce a feeling of joy and unbounded optimism in some patients, who finally envision the possibility of having pain-free intercourse. However, these initial gains are sometimes situational and not maintained with every attempt at intercourse, or, more commonly, they are quickly adapted to and expectations of further improvement rise exponentially. This can lead to feelings of disappointment and defeatism, which can constitute a significant therapeutic setback. It is key to explain to patients that treatment for vulvar pain is more like a marathon than a sprint. The speed of progress throughout treatment will vary from slow to fast to sometimes being at a standstill. It is best to maintain a guarded optimism and steady emotional stance to avoid the pitfalls of negatively impacting reactivity.

Partners are often the big unknown when we first meet a patient complaining of painful genital sexual activity. Although we believe in the active involvement of partners to enhance treatment outcome, one never knows beforehand the extent to which the partner will be helpful or not. A supportive partner who actively participates in the treatment can be the most powerful component of the treatment plan. On the other hand, not all partners are willing to be active in the treatment. Recently, at one of our clinics, a woman's unusually large improvements in sexual function and pain reduction were met with very lukewarm reinforcement from her partner. Before his resistance could be investigated (i.e., sexual dysfunction of his own? the threat of a sexually functional wife who might leave him? etc.), he pulled her out of treatment. Because such relationship dynamics can play a major role in the final outcome of therapy, we always recommend that partners be involved, from the very first sessions. In cases in which partners do not wish to be involved, despite attempts to involve them, the therapist must accept that limitation and do her or his best with the woman only. In the case of actively sabotaging partners, an exploration of the partners' resistance to improvement is indicated. The much more common case is that in which the partner is only too happy to actively engage in a treatment that has the potential to improve both his and his wife's quality of life.

Finally, the multidisciplinary nature of our treatment approach can sometimes give rise to an interesting therapeutic dilemma posed by simultaneous care provided by different health professionals, all working toward the same end. This dilemma can best be described as the potential for the patient to attribute improvement to one of the disciplines exclusively and consequently to lose interest in the others. First, it is crucial that all team members have a similar conceptualization of the disorder so that the patient does not get one message about etiology and treatment from one team member and a different one from another. Second, all team members should reinforce the contribution of all aspects of treatment and their interdependence. Patients looking for a quick cure and wanting to reduce the amount of time devoted to treatment will be motivated to drop treatment ingredients as surplus. Our biopsychosocial conceptualization of painful genital sexual activity and supporting research indicate that this kind of paring down of treatment components will diminish the effort and outcome.

EXPECTED OUTCOMES IN CLINICAL SETTINGS

Susan, an investment banker in her early 30s who has been living with her partner for 1 year, has had pain during intercourse since her first sexual experience when she was a teenager. According to her, this pain often made penetration impossible. Because she also had pain during manual stimulation and had almost no sexual desire, her partner did not know how to approach and how to touch her anymore; he was becoming increasingly frustrated. She was afraid that he would leave her and decided to seek treatment. She first took part in a pain-management group at a local hospital, where two cotherapists provided the women in the group with tools to cope with their pain and to improve their sex lives and romantic relationships. Susan saw only a modest improvement following the end of this therapy and felt that her partner was not very supportive of her efforts to get better. About 6 months later, she decided to seek help again, this time in individual therapy. She had a lot of family issues that she wanted to work on, and she thought these might be related to her pain and sexual difficulties. Besides, her partner felt that this was her problem and was not interested in taking part in the therapy. After about a year of therapy focusing on her familial and individual issues, Susan again saw only a modest improvement in her pain. She finally convinced her partner to come to couple therapy with her, and the last we heard, their sex life had improved, but the pain was still present, albeit somewhat less intense.

This case reflects one of the many possible outcomes of psychosocial treatments of painful genital sexual activity. In this example, the patient is motivated to work on the psychological and relational dimensions of her pain, which results in only limited success. Other patients prefer undergoing a surgery and are not interested in time-consuming and costly therapy; they will come to see us because their physician recommended a few consultations, but will quickly drop out once they see the work that is involved. Sometimes they will actually have a successful surgery and that will be the end of their pain. However, our studies to date show that their sexual functioning will have improved but not their frequency of intercourse (Bergeron et al., 2001).

A combination of treatments is ultimately what appears to bring the most pain relief, improved sexual functioning, reduced psychological distress, and satisfying relationships to the majority of women with painful genital sexual activity. Thus a multidisciplinary treatment approach should be implemented whenever possible. In the meantime, factors such as the impact of length of treatment, patient degrees of self-efficacy, and other patient and therapist characteristics need to be further studied if we are to predict treatment outcome with greater accuracy and eventually recommend what treatment or combination of treatments will work best for each patient we see (Bergeron, Binik, & Khalifé, in press).

WHAT WORKING WITH WOMEN WHO SUFFER FROM PAINFUL SEX HAS MEANT TO US

Our experience of treating this population has been both challenging and highly rewarding: Challenging because it has called upon our ability to be humble, yet ambitious and rewarding because we have been in a unique position to help a group of women who had known nothing but failure in their attempts to address this very important part of their quality of life. The very issues that make painful genital sexual activity so challenging are also the ones that make it one of the most interesting sexuality-related problems to work with: The complexity of the clinical picture and the interrelation of the many factors involved, the necessity to think multidimensionally and to integrate not only multiple theoretical mental health perspectives (e.g., cognitive-behavioral and systemic), but also multiple health professions—plus, the opportunity to learn so much from these other health professionals—all of these have contributed to keep our interest in treating and researching painful sex very much alive.

The other element that keeps us working in this area is the fact that there are still so many unanswered questions, and we lag so far behind other equally prevalent sexual problems (e.g., erectile dysfunction), in terms of our understanding of what causes and maintains this highly prevalent women's health issue. We believe that research that focuses on the characteristics of the pain and that uses other pain syndromes as parallels will undoubtedly be the most fruitful in filling in some pieces of the puzzle. Furthermore, the search for causes needs to move away from unidimensional models and single organic or psychological causal pathways and, rather, to focus on examining the many variables that appear to maintain and exacerbate the pain and sexual dysfunction that are the source of much distress in women suffering from painful genital sexual activity.

REFERENCES

Abramof, L., Wolman, I., & David, M. P. (1994). Vaginismus: An important factor in the evaluation and management of vulvar vestibulitis syndrome. *Gynecological & Obstetrical Investigation, 38,* 194–197.

American Psychiatric Association. (1980). *Diagnostic and Statistical Manual of Mental Disorders* (3rd ed.). Washington, DC: Author.

American Psychiatric Association. (1994). *Diagnostic and Statistical Manual of Mental Disorders* (4th ed.). Washington, DC: Author.

Baram, D. A. (1996). Sexuality and sexual function. In J. S. Berek, E. Y. Adashi, & P. A. Hillard (Eds.), *Novak's Gynecology* (12th ed.). Baltimore, MD: Williams & Wilkins.

Basson, R., Berman, J., Burnett, A., Derogatis, L., Ferguson, D., Fourcroy, J., Goldstein, I., Graziottin, A., Heiman, J., Laan, E., Leiblum, S., Padma-Nathan, H., Rosen, R., Segraves, K., Segraves R. T., Shalosigh, R., Sipski, M., Wagner, G., & Whipple, B. (2000). Report of the international consensus development conference on female sexual dysfuction: Definitions and classifications. *Journal of Urology, 163,* 888–893.

Bazin, S., Bouchard, C., Brisson, J., Morin, C., Meisels, A., & Fortier, M. (1994). Vulvar vestibulitis syndrome: An exploratory case-control study. *Obstetrics and Gynecology, 83,* 47–50. One of the first rigorous etiological studies on vulvar vestibulitis syndrome.

Bergeron, S., Binik, Y. M., & Khalifé, S. (2002). In favour of an integrated pain relief treatment approach for vulvar vestibulitis syndrome. *Journal of Psychosomatic Obstetrics and Gynecology, 23,* 7–9.

Bergeron, S., Binik, Y. M., Khalifé, S., Meana, M., Berkley, K. J., & Pagidas, K. (1997a). The treatment of vulvar vestibulitis syndrome: Toward a multimodal approach. *Sexual and Marital Therapy, 12,* 305–311.

Bergeron, S., Binik, Y. M., Khalifé, S., & Pagidas, K. (1997b). Vulvar vestibulitis syndrome: A critical review. *Clinical Journal of Pain, 13,* 27–42.

Bergeron, S., Binik, Y. M., Khalifé, S., Pagidas, K., Glazer, H. I., Meana, M., & Amsel, R. (2001). A randomized comparison of group cognitive-behavioral therapy, surface electromyographic biofeedback, and vestibulectomy in the treatment of dyspareunia resulting from vulvar vestibulitis. *Pain, 91,* 297–306. The first randomized treatment outcome study of dyspareunia, focusing on one of its main subtypes—vulvar vestibulitis.

Bergeron, S., Binik, Y. M., Khalifé, S., Pagidas, K., & Glazer, H. (2002). (A 2.5 year follow-up of a randomized comparison of group cognitive-behavioral therapy, surface electromyographic biofeedback, and vestibulectomy in the treatment of dyspareunia from vulvar vestibulitis). Unpublished raw data.

Bergeron, S., Brown, C., Lord, M. J., Oala, M., Binik, Y. M., & Khalifé, S. (2002). Physical therapy for vulvar vestibulitis syndrome: A retrospective study. *Journal of Sex & Marital Therapy, 28,* 183–192.

Binik, Y. M., Bergeron, S., & Khalifé, S. (2000). Dyspareunia. In S. R. Leiblum & R. C. Rosen (Eds.), *Principles and Practice of Sex Therapy* (3rd ed.). New York: Guilford. Another chapter on the treatment of dyspareunia, mainly geared toward practicing sex therapists. A good complement to the present chapter.

Bornstein, J., Livrat, G., Stolar, Z., & Abramovici, H. (2000). Pure versus complicated vulvar vestibulitis: A randomized trial of fluconazole treatment. *Gynecologic & Obstetric Investigation, 50,* 194–197.

Bornstein, J., Zarfati, D., Goldik, Z., & Abramovici, H. (1999). Vulvar vestibulitis: Physical or psychosexual problem? *Obstetrics and Gynecology.* 93, 87–-880.

de Kruiff, M. E., ter Kuile, M. M., Weijenborg, P. Th. M., & van Lankveld, J. J. D. M. (2000). Vaginismus and dyspareunia: Is there difference in clinical presentation? *Journal of Psychosomatic Obstetrics and Gynecology, 21,* 149–155.

Friedrich, E. G. (1987). Vulvar vestibulitis syndrome. *Journal of Reproductive Medicine, 32,* 110–114.

Gatchel, R. J., & Turk, D. C. (1999). *Psychosocial Factors in Pain: Critical Perspectives.* New York: Guilford.

Glazer, H. I., Rodke, G., Swencionis, C., Hertz, R., & Young, A. W. (1995). The treatment of vulvar vestibulitis syndrome by electromyographic biofeedback of pelvic floor musculature. *Journal of Reproductive Medicine, 40,* 283–290.

Goetsch, M. F. (1996). Simplified surgical revision of the vulvar vestibule for vulvar vestibulitis. *American Journal of Obstetrics and Gynecology, 174,* 1701–1707.

Harlow, B. L., Wise, L. A., & Stewart, E. G. (2001). Prevalence and predictors of chronic lower genital tract discomfort. *American Journal of Obstetrics and Gynecology, 185,* 545–550. The only epidemiological study to date on the prevalence of vulvar pain and its associated features, such as early menarche.

Heiman, J. R., & Meston, C. M. (1997). Empirically validated treatment for sexual dysfunction. *Annual Review of Sex Research, 8,* 148–194.

Laumann, E. O., Gagnon, J. H., Michael, R. T., & Michaels, S. (1994). *The Social Organization of Sexuality.* Chicago: University of Chicago Press.

Laumann, E. O., Paik, A., & Rosen, R. C. (1999). Sexual dysfunction in the United States. Prevalence, predictors and outcomes. *Journal of the American Medical Association, 281,* 537–545.

Linton, S. J., Melin, L., & Götestam, K. G. (1985). Behavioral analysis of chronic pain and its management. In M. Hersen, R. Eisler, & P. Miller (Eds.), *Progress in Behavior Modification.* New York: Academic.

McKay, M. (1998). Vulvodynia. In J. F. Steege, D. A. Metzger, & B. S. Levy (Eds.), *Chronic Pelvic Pain: An Integrated Approach.* Philadelphia: W. B. Saunders.

Meana, M., & Binik, Y. M. (1994). Painful coitus: A review of female dyspareunia. *Journal of Nervous and Mental Disease, 182,* 264–272. A thorough review of the descriptive/diagnostic, etiological, and treatment aspects of dyspareunia.

Meana, M., Binik, Y. M. Khalifé, S., & Cohen, D. (1997a). Dyspareunia: Sexual dysfunction or pain syndrome? *Journal of Nervous and Mental Disease, 185,* 561–569.

Meana, M., Binik, Y. M., Khalifé, S., & Cohen, D. (1997b). Biopsychosocial profile of women with dyspareunia. *Obstetrics and Gynecology, 90*, 4, 583–589. The first controlled study of the biological, psychological, and relationship characteristics of women with dyspareunia.

Meana, M., Binik, Y. M., Khalifé, S., & Cohen, D. (1998). Affect and marital adjustment in women's rating of dyspareunic pain. *Canadian Journal of Psychiatry, 43*, 381-385.

Meana, M., Binik, Y. M., Khalifé, S., & Cohen, D. (1999). Psychosocial correlates of pain attributions in women with dyspareunia. *Psychosomatics, 40*, 497–502.

Melzack, R., & Wall, P. D. (1983). *The Challenge of Pain.* New York: Basic. This textbook is written by two of the world's foremost leaders in pain research. Accessible to the novice reader, it covers everything one needs to know about pain, from etiological theories and purported basic mechanisms to the main treatments for acute and chronic pain.

Merskey, H., & Bogduk, N. (1994*). Classification of Chronic Pain* (2nd ed.). Seattle, WA: IASP.

Pukall, C., Binik, Y. M., Khalifé, S., Amsel, R., & Abbott, F. (1996). Vestibular tactile detection and pain thresholds in women with vulvar vestibulitis syndrome and matched controls. *Pain, March 96*(1–2), 163–175.

Reissing, E. D., Binik, Y. M., Khalifé, S., Cohen, D., & Amsel, R. (2002). *Vaginal spasm, pain and behaviour: An empirical investigation of the reliability of the diagnosis of vaginismus.* Manuscript submitted for publication.

Schnarch, D. M. (2000). Desire problems: A systemic perspective. In S. R. Leiblum & R. C. Rosen (Eds.), *Principles and Practice of Sex Therapy* (3rd ed.). New York: Guilford. An invaluable resource for gaining a greater understanding of the systemic issues that may contribute to maintain desire problems in couples in which the woman suffers from painful genital sexual activity.

Schover, L. S., Youngs, D. D., & Cannata, R. (1992). Psychosexual aspects of the evaluation and management of vulvar vestibulitis. *American Journal of Obstetrics and Gynecology, 167*, 630–636.

Steege, J. F., Metzger, D. A., & Levy, B. L. (Eds.). (1998). *Chronic Pelvic Pain: An Integrated Approach.* Toronto: W. B. Saunders. A comprehensive book covering a wide range of dimensions of chronic pelvic pain, ranging from pelvic neuroanatomy to overcoming the mind–body split.

Sullivan, M. J. L., Bishop, S., & Pivik, J. (1995). The Pain Catastrophizing Scale: Development and validation. *Psychological Assessment, 7*, 524–532.

Turk, D. C., Meichenbaum, D., & Genest, M. (1983). *Pain and Behavioral Medicine: A Cognitive-Behavioral Perspective.* New York: Guilford. A great book for learning more about the clinical management of chronic pain.

Turk, D. C., Rudy, T. E., Kubinski, J. A., Zaki, H. S., & Greco, C. M. (1996). Dysfunctional patients with temporomandibular disorders: Evaluating the efficacy of a tailored treatment protocol. *Journal of Consulting and Clinical Psychology, 64*, 139–146.

Turner, J. A., & Clancy, S. (1986). Strategies for coping with chronic low back pain: Relationship to pain and disability. *Pain, 24*, 355–366.

van Lankveld, J. J. D. M., Brewaeys, A. M. A., Ter Kuile, M. M., & Weijenborg, P. Th. M. (1995). Difficulties in the differential diagnosis of vaginismus, dyspareunia and mixed sexual pain disorder. *Journal of Psychosomatic Obstetrics and Gynecology, 16*, 201–209.

Wesselmann, U., Burnett, A. L., & Heinberg, L. J. (1997). The urogenital and rectal pain syndromes. *Pain, 73*, 269–294. An extensive review of the literature on the various types of urogenital and rectal pain in both women and men.

Weijmar Shultz, W. C. M., Gianotten, W. L., van der Meijden, W. I., van de Miel, H. B. M., Blindeman, B., Chadha, S., & Drogendijk, A. C. (1996). Behavioural approach with or without surgical intervention for the vulvar vestibulitis syndrome: A prospective randomized and non-randomized study. *Journal of Psychosomatic Obstetrics and Gynecology, 17*, 143–148.

Chapter Nine

The Sexual Aversions

Sheryl A. Kingsberg, PhD
Jeffrey W. Janata, PhD

PREFACE

We are both clinical psychologists who specialize in behavioral medicine. Sheryl is an assistant professor in both the Departments of Reproductive Biology and Psychiatry at Case Western Reserve University (CWRU) School of Medicine. Jeff is an assistant professor in the Department of Psychiatry at CWRU School of Medicine. We chose to write this chapter together because of the synergy between our areas of specialization. Together, we felt we could better teach therapists new to sexual dysfunction about the theory and the treatment of sexual aversion.

Jeff: Sheryl completed a 2-year postdoctoral fellowship in sexuality with the editors of this book. She devotes a great deal of her clinical practice to treating female sexual dysfunction and of her teaching efforts to educating medical students, residents, and physicians about sexual dysfunctions.

Sheryl: Jeff runs the Behavioral Medicine Program in Psychiatry and the Pain Management Program in the Department of Neurology and focuses much of his clinical work and teaching on the topic of cognitive behavior therapy, particularly as it relates to the function of anxiety in the maintenance of avoidance.

Because any independent writing that each of us does invariably get edited by the other, we decided to suffer through the writing process together. We hope that our pain is now not evident and we can help you understand the serious problem of aversion and how you may help a woman to get over it.

PROLOGUE

Sex, like eating, is an appetitive behavior. Healthy human behavior includes an appetite for food, as well as for sexual intimacy. We all find it a bit hard to comprehend when someone develops an aversion to food because eating is a primary drive and most of us relate more to the struggle with overeating than with food refusal.

Yet the second author remembers with nauseating clarity the fast-food fish sandwich he ate at age 13 and the long, unhappy night he spent experiencing the effects of food poisoning. Jeff has not eaten a fast-food fish sandwich since! He suffers a one-trial food aversion, in which a fish sandwich has become paired with nausea and vomiting. This aversion, were he so inclined, is treatable. Sheryl has offered such treatment at no charge. Nevertheless, despite this specific aversion, Jeff's appetite for food, to the groaning consternation of his bathroom scale, remains fully intact.

The fact that appetite remains intact despite aversion applies equally well to sexual behavior as it does to eating. A sexual aversion can develop in much the same way when sex and discomfort (either physical or psychological) are paired. And, as with the fish sandwich, despite the aversive response, sexual appetite can remain intact.

We will discuss this phenomenon over the next few pages and remind you, the reader, ad nauseum, that sexual aversion does not need to imply absent sexual drive.

INTRODUCTION

It has been our experience that Sexual Aversion Disorder is an often misunderstood diagnosis in the spectrum of sexual disorders. It is also the most recent of the disorders, first appearing in the *DSM-III-R* (1987). Although, technically, sexual aversion could be considered an anxiety disorder, it was not included in any of the earlier *DSM* editions as an example of a simple phobia. Though it finally achieved legitimate status as a sexual disorder in 1987, it is often ignored or pushed to a secondary status within the field of sex therapy. In preparing this chapter we browsed the chapter headings from some of the most widely used sex therapy handbooks. We could not find any texts that devote a chapter solely to sexual aversion. Most include some explanation of aversion in the context of understanding hypoactive desire, the impact of sexual abuse, or vaginismus and dyspareunia. Likewise, there is a dearth of literature on the etiology and treatment of sexual aversion.

We credit Theresa Crenshaw for publishing the first landmark manuscript describing what she labeled the sexual aversion syndrome. Published in 1985, it remains one of the two comprehensive manuscripts describing this disorder, joined only by Helen Singer Kaplan's 1987 book *Sexual Aversion, Sexual Phobias and Panic Disorder*. Kaplan suggested that sexual aversion may be better understood as encompassing a dual diagnosis, sexual anxiety and panic disorder, and she believed that one must treat the underlying organic panic disorder with medication before addressing the sexual aversion. Interestingly, her conceptualization served to deemphasize the aversion aspect in favor of the panic component. Seen in historical context, however, she was beginning to orient to the biological underpinnings of the sexual disorders in ways that current conceptual formulations take for granted. Recently, others have underscored the relationship between sexual aversion and panic disorder (Figueira, Possidente, Marques, & Hayes, 2001).

Given that the criteria for sexual aversion disorder overlap with both panic disorder and hypoactive sexual desire disorder, it is understandable that many clinicians, even experts in treating sexual disorders, remain somewhat unclear when to diagnose sexual aversion. For example, according to the *DSM-IV-TR* criteria, sexual aversion does not require the physiological responses that clinicians often associate with aversion. Although sexual aversion certainly can encompass these responses (e.g., nausea, revulsion, shortness of breath), aversion can also be expressed as simple avoidance of partnered sexual behavior and a panic response to engaging in such activity.

DIAGNOSTIC CRITERIA AND OVERVIEW

DSM-IV includes sexual aversion disorder in its Sexual and Gender Identity Disorders classification.

TABLE 9.1. *DSM-IV* Criteria for Sexual Aversion Disorder (302.79)

A. Persistent or recurrent extreme aversion to, and avoidance of, all (or almost all) genital sexual contact with a sexual partner.
B. The disturbance causes marked distress or interpersonal difficulty.
C. The sexual dysfunction is not better accounted for by another Axis I disorder (except another sexual dysfunction).

More recently, the first Consensus Development Panel on Female Sexual Dysfunction proposed a revision of the classification system for female sexual disorders.

TABLE 9.2. 1999 Consensus Classification of Female Sexual Dysfunction

    I. Sexual Desire Disorders
       A. Hypoactive sexual desire disorder
       B. Sexual aversion disorder
    II. Sexual Arousal Disorder
    III. Orgasmic Disorder
    IV. Sexual Pain Disorders
       A. Dyspareunia
       B. Vaginismus
       C. Other sexual pain disorders

The Sexual Function Health Council of the American Foundation for Urologic Disease convened the panel, due to its belief that the *DSM-IV* is too narrowly limited to mental disorders and thus is not able to provide a useful diagnostic framework or classification for female sexual dysfunction. We believe that two of the panel's proposed amendments to the *DSM-IV* criteria are relevant to sexual aversion. First are the inclusion of "personal distress" and the specific exclusion of "interpersonal difficulty" as critical to the diagnosis. Second is the development of a classification system that would include both psychogenic and organically based disorders. In this classification system, sexual aversion is listed under the category of sexual desire disorders, along with hypoactive sexual desire disorders.

The consensus panel developed a very detailed document to describe and justify its new classification system. However, as has been the case historically, sexual aversion was given little attention, and by virtue of being placed in the category of sexual desire disorders, we think it is likely to be missed by many clinicians and misdiagnosed by others.

Aversion is a conditioned response that applies to behaviors beyond sexual. Outside the arena of sexual dysfunction, you may best recognize aversion as the conditioned response that develops in response to cancer chemotherapeutic agents. In this context, aversion implies more than phobic avoidance; aversion is characterized by nausea and vomiting. However, others writing on sexual aversion (Katz & Jardine, 1999) maintain that sexual aversion is equivalent to sexual phobia—the essential diagnostic feature is persistent fear and avoidance.

From our perspective, conditioned aversion is arguably best understood using Mowrer's two-factor avoidance theory (Mowrer, 1947). He proposed that two separate learning processes were involved in avoidance conditioning: a conditioned emotional response (CER) and a conditioned avoidance response (CAR). The CER results from pairing a previously neutral or positive stimulus (sexual behavior) with a painful or traumatic event (and is therefore classically conditioned). When paired with discomfort, the sexual stimuli acquire the capacity to produce aversive emotional reactions (e.g., fear, anxiety, nausea, dizziness) in the absence of the original painful stimulation. The later response (CAR) is operantly conditioned, in that avoidance of sexual stimulation eliminates or reduces the aversive response. Sexual aversion, from the two-factor avoidance perspective, can be conceptualized as a behavioral avoidance response.

DIAGNOSTIC CLASSIFICATION CRITIQUE

DSM IV-TR differentiates lifelong and acquired sexual aversion. These distinctions are confusing to those of us who were trained to understand the fundamental concepts of learning theory. The concept of primary or lifelong aversion is inherently insensible because, by definition, aversion to specific stimuli must be acquired. Crenshaw defines aversion as a negative or unenthusiastic response to any and all sexual interactions from earliest memories to present. However, no matter how young the patient or how absent the memory of life before the aversion, the aversion was certainly learned, either directly or vicariously. Crenshaw notes that people with primary aversion were raised in strict religious and moral environments, validating the concept that the aversion was learned. She also mentions that there may be some form of psychosexual trauma, which again argues against the lifelong or primary aspect of aversion. It is possible that Dr. Crenshaw may have intended primarily to reflect that the aversion developed so early in one's development that the individual never had a chance to experience a normal partnered sexual experience before developing the aversion.

If you read cases in the literature described as examples of primary aversion (e.g., Kaplan, 1987, cases of Bridgitte, Ms. C.; Crenshaw, 1985, case histories 1 and 2), you will notice that they typically involve early, presexual exposure to negative or fear-inducing views of sexual behavior. The distinction seems to be that primary aversion is a diagnosis that applies to negative conditioning of sex in childhood, mediated by environmental learning but not by sexual abuse. Secondary aversion, by contrast, would be diagnosed either if the patient has specific recollection of abuse as a child or later negative experience with sex that seems to be the proximate cause of current sexual aversion.

It may be that the lifelong or secondary distinction has been maintained in the taxonomies because sexual aversion has been confounded with hypoactive sexual desire. In the latter case, it is possible that hypoactive sexual desire, a conceivably more biological than psychological condition (the drive component), may have been present since birth or early age. Furthermore, it follows that a patient with hypoactive sexual desire may become avoidant of sexual activity, and sexual disinterest could evolve into irritation and anger or agitation that is similar to aversion. However, that presentation would be critically absent the fear and anxiety response to sexual behavior.

Although neither the *DSM-IV-TR* nor the 1999 Consensus Classification address gender differences in prevalence, our experience is consistent with Ponticas (1992), in that it has been primarily women who meet the criteria for sexual aversion disorder. Ponticas (1992) hypothesizes that men with sexual aversion disorder do not enter relationships and thus avoid the resulting relationship conflict caused by sexual aversion that might lead them into therapy. We suggest that in addition to this, you will see more women with aversion due to the overlap in etiology and diagnostic criteria with hypoactive sexual desire disorder, which has a much greater prevalence in women than in men.

PROPOSED CRITERIA REVISION

Given the difficulties inherent in the current classification systems for sexual aversion disorder (*DSM IV-TR* and the 1999 Consensus Classification), we propose a revised classification system that is based on a modification of their taxonomies.

TABLE 9.3. Elements of the Current Classification System (*DSM-IV-TR*) for Sexual Aversion Disorder and a Proposed Revision of the Classification System

Diagnosis	Current *DSM-IV-TR* Criteria
Lifelong (Primary sexual aversion)	Lifelong anxiety, fear, or disgust to sexual stimuli
Acquired (Secondary sexual aversion)	Acquired anxiety, fear, or disgust to sexual stimuli.
Diagnosis	Proposed Revised Criteria
Primary sexual aversion	Acquisition of fear, anxiety, or disgust **before** the development of healthy sexual interactions with a partner.
Secondary sexual aversion	Acquisition of fear, anxiety, or disgust **after** the development of healthy sexual interactions with a partner.

This proposed classification maintains the distinction between primary and secondary sexual aversion. However, this distinction will be useful to you only for the diagnostic differentiation of the acquisition of aversion early in life and the lifelong presence of hypoactive sexual desire.

With this modified taxonomy tentatively in place, we will describe two cases of sexual aversion.

CASE EXAMPLE: ALLISON

Allison is a 34 year-old woman who has been married for 17 years and is a mother of three. She presents with mild anorexia, is currently approximately 10% underweight, and menstruates regularly. Allison describes a history of being overweight and successfully participating in a structured weight loss program, losing weight to her ideal body weight. However, her anticipatory anxiety about regaining weight led her to continue to follow a strict reducing caloric intake level. Her preoccupation with avoiding perceived caloric excess led to continued weight loss, body image distortion, and the spectrum of symptoms accompanying an emerging eating disorder.

In the course of describing her sexual history, Allison reveals that she and her husband, Mark, had not had sexual contact of any kind within the past 2 years. After determining that her sexual avoidance was not related to discomfort about exposing her body to her husband (as a function of the body image disturbance that can accompany eating disorders), we took a more complete sexual history.

Allison was raised in a rather strict Catholic home. Although she felt close to her father growing up, she recalls his being particularly strict as she began to date in high school. Her mother is described as emotionally unstable and not as active a participant in parenting as was her father. This oppressive environment led Allison at 18 to pursue a way out of her home life, and she became engaged to Cory, a man who was verbally and emotionally abusive.

Her dating behavior to that point had included sexual behavior, but never intercourse. She recalls those prior experiences as pleasurable. However, despite Allison's moral desire to postpone intercourse until she was married, Cory forced the issue. She is clear that their intercourse was nonconsensual and continued over a period of some months. Allison felt sure that her father, if he knew the truth, would become enraged. "He'd have killed Cory," she is certain.

These sexual interactions were painful, demeaning, and traumatizing to Allison. She associated sex with violation and helplessness. Cory forced her, through strength of will and verbal intimidation, to engage in sexual behavior that quickly became aversive to her.

Ultimately, she was able to break off her engagement to Cory and began dating her future husband, Mark, relatively soon thereafter. Mark, by contrast, was patient and loving and she began to positively recondition sexual behavior. After a period of adjustment, Allison began to enjoy sexual behavior again. Intercourse slowly began to be more pleasurable, and she was able to achieve orgasm.

However, Allison never completely got over her aversion response. After several years of marriage, as nonsexual tensions developed in the relationship, Allison began to withdraw from sex. Mark, frustrated, began to be more sexually insistent, which recapitulated Allison's experience with Cory. Allison again felt intimidated, and sex for her resumed its aversive association. When Mark caressed her one night, awakening her, she "went ballistic" with rage and a sense of violation. They had had no sexual interaction since that night, 2 years prior to entering treatment.

Case Discussion

Allison is someone likely to present to a general mental health professional and, therefore, we think she is a good teaching example of how to diagnose sexual aversion. She meets the *DSM-IV* criteria, evidencing persistent and recurrent avoidance of sexual genital contact with her husband. Genital contact causes marked personal and interpersonal distress and is not better accounted for by another psychiatric disorder. Allison also meets the Consensus Panel criteria, which emphasize personal rather than partner distress as the relevant feature. Moreover, her symptoms are clearly related to an acquisition of fear and subsequent avoidance. Despite her morally strict upbringing, she did not evidence particular fear or avoidance of sexual interactions until her sexual behavior was paired with abuse, pain, and victimization. Allison's previously healthy response to sexual interaction became negatively conditioned; she acquired an aversion response that then was maintained by sexual avoidance.

It is important to note that Allison's sexual desire remained intact throughout her sexual development. Even when experiencing symptoms of aversion in partnered sexual contact, Allison was orgasmic when she masturbated and fantasized about sexual activity with a male partner.

CASE EXAMPLE: KELLY

Kelly, a 26-year-old married mother of 18-month-old Colleen and 16 weeks pregnant, was referred by her obstetrician for treatment of situational vaginismus. He was unable to complete a pelvic exam during her first pregnancy. He had assumed that the physical discomfort during labor would override her anxiety and cure her vaginismus. However, during labor Kelly experienced such an intense feeling of panic that the obstetri-

cian decided to use a general anesthesia and deliver her baby with forceps. When she presented with her second pregnancy, the obstetrician (finally!) referred her for psychological treatment. His goal was to be able to examine her vaginally, prenatally and during labor and delivery. Kelly's goal was to get through this next delivery with minimal pain and anxiety.

In addition to Kelly's chief complaint of situational vaginismus, we quickly learned that she suffered from aversion to her genitals, panic and revulsion in response to almost all sexual activity, and an aversion response to navels. She reported becoming nauseated and lightheaded when she or anyone else touched her navel.

Kelly's aversion to pelvic exams, sexual activities, and vaginal penetration was so intense that simply imagining those events during a therapy session resulted in nausea, muscle weakness, and lightheadedness.

Kelly was able to articulate that vaginal penetration did not need to hurt. She also recognized that any discomfort she did experience was simply due to her anxiety reaction, resulting in her vaginal muscles contracting upon insertion.

Although all of her complaints seemed consistent with childhood sexual abuse, she denied any such memory. Her only relevant memory was of her mother scrubbing her genitals with a rough washcloth while bathing her at age 5. She described her mother as compulsive about bathing and keeping clean.

Kelly remembered being a fearless daredevil and tomboy prior to age 8. When she was 8, her father bought her a dirt bike. She used to race it against neighborhood high school boys. She recalled once crashing into a shed and immediately riding again. She starkly contrasted this behavior with what soon became of her: generalized anxiety, fearfulness, and queasiness when faced with blood. She fainted while visiting a family friend in the hospital, due to the sight of the IV needle moving in his arm.

Kelly thought that she probably discovered masturbation by the age of 8. However, she has no memory of ever having masturbated or stimulating her clitoris. She reached menarche at age 12. She learned about menstruation from a book that her mother gave her around this age (the same book her sister was given a few years prior). Her first experience attempting vaginal insertion was at age 13 when she attempted to teach herself how to use tampons. She used up her sister's entire box in the attempt. She remembered feeling very frightened and anticipating tremendous pain. That was her last attempt at tampon use.

Kelly was aware that all her high school friends were going to the gynecologist for pelvic exams. Her mother also suggested it, but she avoided it because the thought of it induced panic and dread. Kelly was very active in high school sports, but she recurrently worried that she would have to have a pelvic exam to qualify to play on a varsity team.

Kelly reports that she did have sexual desire and felt it was consistent with the level of interest her friends described. However, she refused to have intercourse with her high school boyfriend, primarily because she could not tolerate a pelvic examination in order to obtain oral contraceptives. At age 19, she dated another boy with whom she decided she wanted to have intercourse. Her recollection of her first intercourse is vague. She thought that either she was drunk or she dissociated because she did not notice when his penis was in her vagina. Because she did not feel pain or disgust with penile penetration, she claims never to have avoided or disliked penetration by a penis per se. It is other means of penetration that stimulate disgust and fear of pain; she does not allow her husband's finger or tongue or her own finger in her vagina.

Kelly reported that her sexual desire has gradually declined since she married 5 years ago. She currently has very little sexual desire, but is quite easily orgasmic with intercourse. She would like to limit intercourse to once a month. She never initiates sex. As it is occurring, she is always thinking, "Let's get this over with so that I can go to sleep." Her husband, Steve, is always on top because it is the only intercourse position she will allow.

With her due date as a deadline, we were quite worried that time would run out before we were able to at least treat her vaginismus. To everyone's great relief, Kelly was treated in 11 sessions over a 5-month period. The strategy we used might seem familiar to those of you who have used cognitive-behavioral treatment strategies for an anxiety disorder. As is typical, we began by teaching Kelly the theory and methods of systematic desensitization, including the use of counterconditioning by pairing a relaxation response with increasingly anxiety-producing images.

Session-by-Session Case Summary

Session 1: A history and assessment of her presenting problems was taken, and a description of her sexual disorders and subsequent treatment plan were developed. We explained the theory and methods that underlie systematic desensitization, and Kelly agreed to the treatment plan.

Session 2: Kelly created a hierarchy of aversion- and anxiety-provoking images. The least anxiety-producing image was getting into her car to drive to her obstetrician's office. The most anxiety-producing image was Kelly in stirrups, with her obstetrician poised to insert a speculum. The most aversive image was her husband, Steve, touching her navel.

Session 3: Kelly was taught diaphragmatic deep breathing and a progressive muscle-relaxation technique.

Session 4: Kelly was desensitized to anything related to genitals. Between sessions Kelly had noticed that she was frightened by Colleen's innocent exploration of her own genitals. Homework included daily observation and touching her own naked body, particularly her pubic hair, labia, and clitoris.

Session 5: The first evidence of significant success was reported. Kelly remained relaxed throughout a pelvic exam while the obstetrician inserted a finger. Kelly was instructed to insert one of her fingers at home, using a lubricant.

Session 6: She was unable to insert her own finger at home. Kelly was taught how to do Kegel exercises—to contract her vaginal muscles intensely, followed by relaxing these same muscles.

Session 7: Kelly reported feeling like a failure because she was still unable to insert her finger.

Session 8: As Kelly became less anxious and more relaxed when thinking about her body and sexual activity, she was able to recall memories from her childhood. For example, it was at this point that Kelly recalled her mother using a rough washcloth on her genitals and her navel. Kelly reported that she was making some progress, was able to insert the tip of her finger, and was generally more relaxed. However, she admitted that although her anxiety and fear of pain had diminished, her aversion had not. She felt so disgusted that she took a shower after every self-touching homework assignment.

Session 9: Kelly progressed up the gradual desensitization hierarchy. She reported using new cognitive skills to cope better in all areas of her life. She has become better aware of her irrational thoughts and subsequent muscle tightening when imagining having a pelvic exam. All anxiety has disappeared from using the visual images in her hierarchy. She was also significantly less disgusted by sexual thoughts or images.

Session 10: She reported that her coping skills continue to improve: She has no aversion or fear of pain with vaginal penetration using a finger or a speculum. However, she was still only able to insert her finger to the first joint. She was no longer bothered by the sight or thought of navels. After this session, she called to report that she had her first fully successful vaginal exam. She was calm and experienced no pain or discomfort; her obstetrician was able to use a regular-size speculum. Kelly was still unable to insert her own finger, however.

Session 11: Kelly had 3 successful pelvic exams with no anxiety and even with a little pregnancy-related discomfort during her last exam. She had no anxiety about labor and delivery. She was now able to completely insert her own finger. Kelly was easily able to discuss her feelings about her own sexuality and her sense of guilt and shame regarding her sexual feelings and her body.

After this session, Kelly proudly called to report her successful delivery, without an epidural, of a healthy 8-lb. son.

At a follow-up session, Kelly appeared far more self-confident and relaxed. She reported that this confidence and absence of anxiety were present in all domains of her life. She now had more sexual desire and could enjoy a variety of sexual activities without any sign of aversion or panic. She and Steve plan to have at least one more child.

Case Discussion

Kelly, like Allison, is an example of a case of sexual aversion that under the current *DSM-IV-TR* classification system would be described as *lifelong* aversion. Her aversions and fears developed in childhood, long before she became sexually active. Why is the distinction of lifelong of importance? If it were not for the fact that Kelly was able to express sexual desire and pleasure with penile penetration, her early onset of symptoms would make it difficult to distinguish between hypoactive sexual desire disorder and aversion disorder.

It is important to note that Kelly presented with the chief complaint of vaginismus, not aversion disorder. You will rarely see aversion disorder as the initial presenting complaint. Remember, seeking treatment is as avoided as the sexual contact. Kelly came for treatment only because of pressure from her obstetrician and her own worry about having a safe delivery. Otherwise, her conditioned avoidance response would have included avoiding confronting her aversions in therapy. We were quite fortunate that treatment also resulted in a global counterconditioning to all potentially frightening situations.

TREATMENT CONSIDERATIONS

For those of you who prefer a more psychodynamic theoretical base, the persistence of avoidance behavior was articulated first by Freud (1936). Mowrer (1948) described the phenomenon as the *neurotic paradox.* The common observation that avoidance behavior is remarkably difficult to extinguish has been explained by the theory of *conservation of anxiety.* In essence, the argument is that individuals learn rapid avoidance over time, which prevents the elicitation of fear. Moreover, the theory goes, if fear is not elicited, it will not extinguish.

Consider the two cases of sexual aversion that we presented for you. Both women reported that sexual behavior became synonymous with aversion, but that their eventual avoidance of sexual behavior allowed their aversion response to remain relatively untriggered. Aversion was not elicited in situo because they had learned to avoid sexual behavior so successfully. However, in Kelly's case, when a desensitization hierarchy was created, exposure to sexual stimuli specifically elicited her aversion responses. We suggest that the relative rapidity with which her aversion responses were extinguished is a function of the patient's willingness to engage in graduated exposure to aversion responses and defeat the negative reinforcement function of avoidance (and not due to our brilliant clinical skills).

The theory of conservation of anxiety explains why sexual aversion rarely abates on its own, and, similarly, why it can be treatment-resistant. Crenshaw (1985) states that the sexual aversion syndrome is progressive and rarely reverses spontaneously. Patients like Kelly are treatable insofar as they are willing to expose themselves rather unblinkingly to the anxiety accompanying sexual behavior. We have found that the following can help this exposure process along:

1. The clinician's willingness and ability to conceptualize the patient's sexual aversion in clear behavioral terms, emphasizing how aversion is acquired and maintained;
2. The patient's ability to verbalize an understanding of aversion acquisition and maintenance and, most important, to generate specific examples of the process of exposure;
3. The patient maintaining records of anxiety and aversion symptoms during the treatment process and referring to those records frequently during sessions. Patients will adhere to record-keeping instructions to the degree that clinicians make those records an integral part of the psychotherapy; and
4. Emphasis on maintenance and generalization as the therapy draws to a close to address relapse issues.

CONCLUSION

We believe that sexual aversion disorder has been a neglected topic by sex researchers and clinicians. This neglect has been, in part, because the diagnostic criteria for sexual aversion disorder are vague enough that even most experts in the area are often prone to confuse it with hypoactive sexual desire disorder. We define sexual aversion as the acquisition of fear and anxiety, with accompanying symptoms of disgust, toward sexual activity with a partner.

Primary aversion is diagnosed when one's first sexual experience, either directly or vicariously, is negative. Secondary aversion is diagnosed when the patient has had normal or pleasurable sexual development and experiences, until a traumatic or painful experience, either direct or vicarious, negatively reconditions sexual interactions with a partner.

Despite improved clarity in the criterion for aversion, clinicians may continue to have difficulty with diagnosis and treatment. By virtue of the definition of aversion, most individuals with sexual aversion disorder tend to generalize avoidance behaviors to include even addressing the aversion in a therapy setting. Therefore, many individuals with sexual aversion will not present for treatment and those who do have often presented with a different chief complaint. However, the clinicians reading this chapter are not going to be misled by this false presentation. It is up to the astute clinician to ferret out an aversion disorder as the primary problem. In addition, be sure that the diagnosis includes ruling out hypoactive sexual desire disorder because, as our first case demonstrates, aversion can exist in the context of intact desire.

REFERENCES

American Psychiatric Association. (1987). *DSM-III-R*: *Diagnostic and Statistical Manual of Mental Disorders* (3rd ed.–rev.). Washington, DC: Author.

American Psychiatric Association. (2000). *DSM-IV-TR*: *Diagnostic and Statistical Manual of Mental Disorders* (4th ed., text tevision). Washington, DC: Author.

Basson, R., Berman, J., Bernett, A., Derogatis, L., Ferguson, D., Fourcroy, F., Goldstein, I., Graziottin, A., Heiman, J., Laan, E., Leiblum, S., Padma-Nathan, H., Rosen, R., Seagraves, K., Seagraves, R., Shabsigh, R., Sipski, M., Wagnor, G., & Whipple, B. (2000). Report of the international consensus development conference on female sexual dysfunction: Definitions and classifications. *Journal of Urology, 163,* 888–893.

Crenshaw, T. L. (1985). The sexual aversion syndrome. *Journal of Sex & Marital Therapy, 11,* 285–292. First and most-often-cited article describing the syndrome of sexual aversion and the concepts of primary and secondary aversion.

Figueira, I., Possidente, E., Marques, C., & Hayes, K. (2001). Sexual dysfunction: A neglected complication of panic disorder and social phobia. *Archives of Sexual Behavior, 30,* 369–377. Retrospective study that looked at the comorbidity of sexual dysfunctions with anxiety disorders.

Freud, S. (1936). *The Problem of Anxiety.* New York: Psychoanalytic Quarterly Press, W. W. Norton. Freud. What does that name mean to you? Need we say more?

Kaplan, H. S. (1987). *Sexual Aversion, Sexual Phobias, and Panic Disorder.* New York: Brunner/Mazel. Kaplan's primary focus is her theory that sexual aversion may be better understood as encompassing a dual diagnosis, sexual anxiety and panic disorder, and she believed that one must treat the underlying organic panic disorder with medication before addressing the sexual aversion.

Kaplan, H. S. (1988). Intimacy disorders and sexual panic states. *Journal of Sex & Marital Therapy, 14,* 3–12. Kaplan addresses the question of whether sexual avoidance is a manifestation of an intrapsychic barrier to emotional intimacy.

Katz, R. C., & Jardine, D. (1999). The relationship between worry, sexual aversion, and low sexual desire. *Journal of Sex & Marital Therapy, 25,* 293–296. Study looking at the relationship between worry, sexual aversion, and inhibited sexual desire using a variety of scales, including the Sexual Aversion Scale, which the authors developed. Much of the focus is on fear of contracting a sexually transmitted disease. Subjects were college students.

Mowrer, O. H. (1947). On the dual nature of learning—A reinterpretation of "conditioning" and "problem-solving." *Harvard Educational Review, 17,* 102–148.

Mowrer, O. H. (1948). Learning theory and the neurotic paradox. *American Journal of Orthopsychiatry, 18,* 571–610.

Ponticas, Y. (1992). Sexual aversion versus hypoactive sexual desire: A diagnostic challenge. *Psychiatric Medicine, 10*(2), 273–281.

Chapter Ten

Facilitating Orgasmic Responsiveness

Carol Rinkleib Ellison, PhD

There seems to be a reasonable basis for assuming that the human female's capacity for orgasm is to be viewed much more as a potentiality that may or may not be developed by a given culture, or in the specific life-history of an individual, than as an inherent part of her full humanity.

—Margaret Mead, 1949, p. 219, 1968 edition

PREFACE

I'm delighted to have this opportunity to talk with you about women's orgasms. For over 25 years, I've been a psychologist and marriage and family therapist specializing in issues of sexuality and intimacy. I received postdoctoral training in the Human Sexuality Program of the medical school at the University of California in San Francisco. Although that sexuality program no longer exists, I continue to be affiliated with UCSF and available to supervise residents who want to learn my intimacy-based model of sex therapy. I also regularly teach sexuality courses for mental health professionals and therapists-in-training.

I am certified by the American Association of Sex Educators, Counselors & Therapists (AASECT) as a sex educator and as a sex therapist, and I am a fellow of the Society for the Scientific Study of Sexuality (SSSS). My research has included in-depth interviews and, with a colleague, a nationwide survey of 2,632 women. I'm particularly interested in variations in how we experience and express our sexualities and in how sexuality fits into the various ages and contexts of our lives. How do we become who we are? What makes sex meaningful and satisfying? And what detracts from sexual well-being and a positive sexual self image?

I wear three hats when doing sex therapy. I am a (1) sexual choreographer, in which I am a coach, facilitator, and instructor for creating erotic pleasure; (2) sexual detective/problem solver, in which I try to figure out what is going on in—diagnose—the sexual problems my clients bring to me; and (3) sexual adviser, in which I assume the role of mentor, knowledgeable teacher, trainer, guide, educator, counselor, tutor, and consultant. As sexual adviser, I provide solutions to problems and other relevant and appropriate information. I hope that our time together as you read this chapter will give you some ideas about assuming these roles in your own work.

A Sexual Detective Considers Women's Orgasmic Difficulties

Difficulty in reaching orgasm is not a simple condition with one solution for all. Orgasmic difficulties often reflect a complex combination of causal factors. They can be arrived at by many different routes. If a woman resents her partner or can't relax during sex because she is preoccupied with work, for example, she may get only minimally aroused, experience very little vaginal lubrication, feel discomfort during intercourse, and not reach orgasm. Difficulties with orgasm and arousal may be related to a woman's distraction, her health, or her partner's difficulties (e.g., her partner's inability to relax or to sustain arousal); to relationship issues; to a history of trauma; or to numerous other factors.

If you are talking with a woman who is currently nonorgasmic or experiencing difficulty in reaching orgasm, put on your detective hat and consider the questions that follow as you take her history. It is not a matter of going down the list and asking these questions, but rather, to get the woman talking about her situation, guiding her as she goes along so that you get the information you need. I might start by saying something like, "How can I be helpful to you?" or "You said you would like to talk about orgasms. Can you tell me more about what is concerning you?"

Your client may be nervous, but she is expecting to talk about details of her sexual life. You want her to feel that this is perfectly natural; it's no big deal. It is up to you to create an atmosphere of safety and comfort for talking about these very personal matters. You may have to talk, for example, about details of how she touches herself or is touched by her partner, so you can make suggestions about how to make stimulation more effective. You may find that you feel uncomfortable or perhaps aroused by her responses; that sometimes happens. Still, you will recall that it is your role to create the atmosphere of safety and comfort. If you do this and act accordingly, your client may remain unaware of your feelings, and you will be able to help her stay focused on her own issues. The therapist must be interested only in the woman making progress toward her therapy goals.

When I teach sexuality courses for mental health professionals, I begin by asking the students to consider: Who are you? How does your sexuality fit into who you are? Later, in a written assignment, I ask: Is there a theme in your sexual development that might affect your work with therapy clients or patients? Are there any kinds of sexual issues that clients/patients might bring to you that you don't feel ready to work with in a professional role? These are questions for each of us to consider. Are you ready to work with a woman's orgasm issues? If not, what further training or life experiences might you need?

If you haven't worked with sexual issues before, I hope you will have an opportunity to participate in some desensitizing role-play. Also—whatever your gender—if you have never carefully looked at and attended to pleasuring your own genitals or experimented with building and diminishing waves of sexual energy/arousal, it is likely that you need to develop further your own capacity for erotic artistry if you wish to be comfortable and effective in helping others with their sexual issues.

For a variety of reasons, many women with orgasm difficulties will prefer to work with a woman therapist. They may feel, for example, able to talk more freely with a woman, a sense of shared experience, no need to concern themselves with a male's sexual boundaries or imagined "fragile male ego," or no need to deal with a man who symbolizes other males who have violated their emotional or physical boundaries; distrust of men may be activated by a male therapist. This is such an individual issue, however, that some women may prefer working with a man, and for others, the gender of the therapist won't be important. In my own psychotherapy practice, I, a woman, frequently see men who have sexual difficulties.

The following are questions that will help you to understand a woman's difficulties with orgasm. Other questions will occur to you as you interview her.

- Are there physical factors, such as, for example, pain, cardiovascular problems, diabetes, or medications (e.g., SSRIs, blood pressure and allergy meds) she is taking that are diminishing her capacity for arousal and orgasm? Is she depressed? Is she taking birth control pills? (If so, she may be on a pill that does not provide as much estrogen as her body needs for optimum sexual responsiveness.)
- Is being sexually aroused pleasurable for her? Can she comfortably experience arousal and let it intensify? Does she "leave her body" or begin to experience such emotions as anxiety, shame, or anger as her arousal builds?
- Is a history of sexual abuse or trauma currently affecting her sexual responsiveness? If so, how?
- Has she ever experienced orgasmic release? (If she says she has not, you might suggest that a sexual orgasm is an involuntary release of tension, just as a yawn or sneeze is.)
- Does she know how to create orgasmic experiences for herself? Can she comfortably pleasure herself while alone? Can she comfortably stimulate herself during sex with her partner?
- How does she think of/imagine/describe orgasm? Is she aware that there is no one right way to have an orgasm and that, in fact, there is tremendous variability in women's experiences of orgasm?
- Is she blocking her orgasms because she is trying too hard to have them? Does she experience pressure to have an orgasm from herself or partner? During sex, does it seem to her that she has all the time she needs to relax, become aroused, reach orgasm, or any combination of these?
- Is her partner a skillful/satisfying lover? Is there anything she would like her partner to know about his or her lovemaking?
- Is her partner comfortable with becoming aroused and sustaining arousal? Does her male partner have ejaculatory control?
- Are she and her partner effective at initiating sex and in creating a sense of connectedness when they begin their sexual episodes? Can they readily shift from their not-doing-sex selves into their doing-sex selves?

- Can she and her partner comfortably show each other how they like to be pleasured? Do they understand that how they like to touch and be touched may vary from occasion to occasion?
- Has she frequently faked orgasm with her partner?
- Is she resentful or angry at her partner? Does she sometimes have sex when she doesn't fully consent to do so?
- Are there concerns about pregnancy or sexually transmitted diseases?

Usually, the answers to these questions will deepen your understanding of the woman's orgasm difficulties and suggest interventions that might begin to enhance her orgasmic potential.

I find Annon's PLISSIT model (1974, pp. 56–58) useful when I think about how to proceed. Some women and couples can be helped with *permission* (to touch herself during partner sex), *limited information* (about her body and how other women release their orgasms), and *specific suggestions* (about breathing, making sounds, doing various "experiments" with her partner, changing medications), but some situations call for more *intensive therapy*. For a woman who is contemplating divorce because she doesn't respect or trust her partner or a woman who dissociates during sex because of a history of sexual trauma, therapy may be focused primarily on issues other than orgasm. Still, either woman might benefit from specific suggestions, tailored to her situation, that enhance her skills for sexual self-pleasuring, if she then could use masturbation to feel comforted and empowered (whether or not she reached orgasm). The key, whatever the circumstances, is to start with the situation as it is and to facilitate movement in the direction the woman or couple wishes to go. The many complicated circumstances of their lives will determine the direction and outcomes, which may include orgasms or not. Sometimes you may find it useful to consider, as does the *DSM-IV*, whether a woman's difficulties are situational (i.e., "limited to certain types of stimulation, situations, or partners") or generalized (i.e., not limited in this way) and whether they are lifelong or acquired (*DSM-IV*, p. 494).

HOW WOMEN EXPERIENCE ORGASM

A 52-year-old woman consulted with me for sex therapy because she couldn't have orgasms with her partner without using her vibrator. Wearing my sexual detective hat, I asked for details so I could know more clearly what she did experience. She told me that when she didn't use her vibrator, she usually experienced a wave of sensation, like energy moving gently through her body, when her partner reached orgasm with his penis inside her; afterward, she felt relaxed. I suggested that she was probably having orgasms, but orgasms so different from those she had with her vibrator that she wasn't recognizing them. After thinking about this, she agreed, quite relieved.

What is an orgasm? As a physical event, an orgasm is a discharge or release of physical and energetic arousal. It is a process that returns a woman's body to a less-aroused or nonaroused state. But an orgasm is not simply a physical event. Orgasm is an experience: one that potentially may involve all of the senses, the imagination, emotions, a transpersonal dimension, a spiritual dimension, possibly more.

Often women describe orgasm as their perception of a release, a peaking of intensity, relaxation, pleasure, or any combination of these. For example, "a peak clitoral sensation of some kind; it didn't last very long"; "something wonderful . . . a release, like an explosion. I feel it in the vagina and then the relaxation spreads over my whole body." There is, however, tremendous variability in how women experience their orgasms. It is important that you facilitate a woman's understanding that her own experiences are valid, even if they differ from someone else's or those she sees or reads about in the media.

When working with a woman's orgasm concerns, lead her to understand that she does not have to notice any one thing in particular in having an orgasm. She does not have to be aware of a specific physical response, such as vaginal contractions. She doesn't even have to enjoy orgasms or have them regularly: "I prefer to 'ride the highs' rather than orgasm. I have fibroids that sometimes hurt when I contract in orgasm." Experiences of orgasm might range—even for one woman—from explosive releases to gentle rushes of warmth or sensations of tingling. One woman told me that her orgasms vary from "very much a pumping sensation" to "whole body . . . an overall general feeling"; from "just a feeling of well-being" to "a very soft, rhythmic kind of thing." They vary in intensity from "like a wave washing over me" to "real hard, intense." Sometimes she feels her face contort. Sometimes she wonders if she's orgasming "because it's so generalized" and she feels "release afterward," but doesn't "actually feel the pumping." On those occasions: "It's very soft . . . feels good, very pleasurable . . . it's an overall feeling of well-being . . . a sense of release."

Cultural Messages—How We Think About Orgasm

The ideas many of us have about achieving orgasms and the kinds of orgasms we should be having underlie many of the problems I see in sex therapy. We live in a culture that frequently defines a woman's sexual success in terms of orgasm and her partner's success in terms of producing one for her, sometimes with quite detailed specifications. I call this the *manufacturing orgasms* sexual script.

In this script, orgasm is the goal of sex. To be sexually successful, you *must* have an orgasm. Typically, the orgasm *must* occur in intercourse. And according to some 20th-century marriage manuals and the popular media, the stakes can be even higher: A woman and her partner *must* have not just any orgasms, but must *achieve*, for example, vaginal, clitoral, G-spot, multiple, simultaneous, or extended orgasms, or any combinations of these. Cultural and medical establishments have been telling women for over 100 years that there are right ways for us to experience our sexualities and to have orgasms, thereby creating an ever-changing series of fads in the women's division of the orgasm olympics.

Please reflect for a moment on how often we think or say *achieve orgasm,* as if those two words inevitably belong together. This association reflects the *manufacturing orgasms* sexual script. Unless we think about it, we easily overlook how strongly the phrase implies that sex is work and orgasm is a performance goal. The idea that sex is about achieving orgasm is just that: an *idea* about how sex should be. It is a problematic script that has so permeated our culture that many people take it for granted and believe it to be true. (You may have been believing it, too, up to now.) But trying to *achieve* any particular physical response distracts from pleasure and intimacy. It is a setup for frustration, because it is a goal that most of us can't—and perhaps don't really want to—always meet.

A college student interviewed in the 1990s talked of a sexual episode in which she wasn't interested in having an orgasm. Notice how her boyfriend asked her, in essence, *What's the use, if I can't manufacture an orgasm for you?* She said, "I reach orgasm very, very easily. At first, it wasn't as easy or often, but now I reach orgasm at least once every time we make love. I can think of only one experience with my boyfriend when I didn't orgasm. I wasn't feeling well and I wasn't sure I really wanted sex. I enjoyed the experience, but I couldn't even get close to orgasm. He was very upset. He wanted to stop partway through because he's like, *If you're not getting anything out of this, it's not worth it.* But I wanted to continue. It wasn't a big deal for me; I had a good time anyway." This young woman was having an enjoyable sexual experience. On that particular occasion she didn't need or want orgasm. It was her boyfriend's beliefs (that it was his job to give her one and, perhaps, that he was inadequate if he didn't) that frustrated them both.

A Liberating Alternative. One of my first interventions with most individuals and couples with sexual problems is to offer my answer to the *manufacturing orgasms* sexual script. My definition of sexual success does not define success in a sexual interlude in terms of physical functioning. I define success, instead, in terms of creating erotic pleasure with outcomes of intimacy, satisfaction, mutual pleasure, and self-esteem. This redefinition of success in sex has become the cornerstone of the intimacy-based sex therapy I do.

I typically describe the *manufacturing orgasms* script to those who seek my advice and tell them that, in contrast, I think of partners as sexually successful when they create mutual erotic pleasure, to whatever level and in whatever form they desire on any particular occasion. The goals of this pleasure are to have both partners feel good about themselves and about the other, to have had a good time, and to have enhanced their relationship. An orgasm may occur—or not.

I note that my definition includes the word *create*, but not the word *achieve*. I point out, too, that this definition doesn't say anything about having intercourse or how stimulation occurs, nor does it mention lubrication, achieving erections, lasting longer, achieving orgasms, or any other particular aspect of physical responsiveness. I tell them that I can't promise orgasms right away, but I think we can come up with some ideas about how they can have more satisfying sex and create pleasure together.

Thinking of sex as *creating mutual erotic pleasure in whatever form that might take* means, of course, that whether or not a woman wants to have an orgasm during sex and how she might reach it are choices she can make, not requirements for success-ful lovemaking. I often tell women and their partners that the key existential question during sex is not "How am I doing?" "Am I wet enough?" "Am I going to make it?" or "Is this taking too long?" but "Am I enjoying what's happening right this moment?" If a woman's answer is "Yes," she can continue to pay attention to the pleasure she is feeling. If the answer is "No," that is a sign to consider: "How could I change what's happening to pleasure me more?" or "Do I want to stop for right now?"

SOME FACTORS IN ORGASMIC RESPONSIVENESS

In 1993–1994, Dr. Bernie Zilbergeld and I surveyed a nationwide sample of conve-nience, asking women how they experienced and expressed their sexualities. The 2,632 women who responded to our 16-page questionnaire were born between 1905 and 1977; 556 were age 50 or older. Most had attended college; 40% had done some graduate work or had a graduate degree. With respect to sexual orientation, 7% described them-selves as lesbian, 5½% as bisexual, the remainder as heterosexual. The survey was preceded by in-depth interviews of about 100 women; I did about 70 of these, the rest were done by others. For additional details of this research, see Ellison (2000) or www.womenssexualities.com.

Among our survey respondents who had had partnered sex in the last year, 25% experienced "difficulty in reaching orgasm" and 17% experienced "inability to have an orgasm" all or most of the times they had sex. Of the orgasmic women who had engaged in partnered sex in the preceding 3 months, 30% were not satisfied with the frequency of their orgasms with their partners.

The interviews and survey, and my practice as a psychologist specializing in is-sues of sexuality and intimacy, all have contributed to and enhanced my understand-ing of how women experience and facilitate their orgasms. The women quoted in this chapter were respondents in the research unless I indicate otherwise.

FACTORS THAT FACILITATE ORGASMS

For most women, orgasmic responsiveness tends to develop over time. And because orgasm in partner sex evolves out of the erotic dance of two people, orgasmic responsive-ness can be different in different partnerships or at different stages of a relationship. The potential is there, but different histories, different partners, and different interests in sexual variety and experimentation all contribute to whether a woman is regularly or easily orgasmic.

The research demonstrated that a woman's most satisfying sexual experiences, when she is in an ongoing relationship, tend to be associated with feeling close to her partner before sex, feeling loved, knowing that her partner will provide the physical stimulation she needs, feeling really attuned with her partner during sex, and knowing that her partner is accepting of her desires, preferences, and responses. These are among the conditions that will facilitate orgasms for many women. One theme of our therapeutic interventions, therefore, is to assist a couple in creating these conditions.

"Kathy" told me about the sexual conditions and stimulation that are especially satisfying for her:

> *My partner has to be really into me, into doing what he's doing. It's not any particular kind of stroking—fast or slow—as much that my partner's being attentive to what's feeling good. I have to feel comfortable and really bonded with my partner, at least for that time, and my partner is really paying attention to my needs and what's making me feel good. He'll slow down and then he'll speed up or he'll pull his cock out so just the head's in there for a little bit and tease me and then thrust hard. He'll vary what's he's doing. He kisses me. There's recognition of my whole being, my whole body.*

Kathy and her partner don't just start out and go straight for orgasm, but rather they *tease;* they vary the movements and rhythms of intercourse in ways that allow their arousal to build in waves. The stimulation is intense and less intense, intense and less intense. Kathy and her partner kiss during sex, and each is attentive to what's feeling good to the other. They are caught up in a mutual trance.

As therapist you start with what is, and you hold the intention of assisting your clients in moving, a step at a time, in the direction they want to go. One way to do this is through suggesting experiments partners might try that are particularly suited to them and their life circumstances. One purpose of such experiments is to move them in the direction of more arousing, orgasmic experiences. Another is that both you and they gather information about what they experience. Often I seek a couple's input in creating the experiments. There is no right or wrong outcome, or success or failure. Even not doing a recommended activity is not failure, but rather an opportunity to consider the busyness of their lives, difficulties with initiation, or resistances they might be experiencing. If planned activities have not been done between sessions, I might say something like, "Perhaps we have to think up another experiment for you to try; this one didn't seem to fit your situation right now." Note that I offer "experiments" to couples, rather than "assignments"; "assignments" tend to be laden with performance expectations.

You will need to facilitate with a couple not only what experiments they will do, but also an important step along the way: their transition into these activities. How will they decide when an experiment will happen? How will they create feelings of connection as they begin?

TRANSITIONS

Some people believe that when it comes to sex, rubbing is where you start and how you make it happen. This is much too simplistic. One of the keys to partnered orgasmic sex—and fulfilling therapeutic experiments, and good communication—is the transition the woman and her partner make from separateness to togetherness.

I typically will tell a couple that a sexual experience begins with a shift of attention and consciousness. Most of us go around most of the time in our not-doing-sex selves. Our bodies, our attention, our emotions are not in a doing-sex mode. Something happens—or many things happen—one thing leads to another, and sexual arousal and erotic feelings begin to occur. A transition into one's doing-sex self can be practically instantaneous or can occur gradually, over hours or even days. It may be stimulated primarily through something outside of oneself or from hormones, physical changes, longings, and images within.

Point out to a couple that in partner sex, both individuals will personally shift from their not-doing-sex selves into their doing-sex selves and also, with each other, shift from feeling separate to experiencing a sense of connection—togetherness. These personal and interpersonal transitions may seem to happen spontaneously or be made with effort.

As "Amanda" explained, "Sometimes you just start fooling around and you'll be just so excited, you'll just be like, *Okay, right now, right here.* But other times I've felt like, *No, I need foreplay, I need everything. I need to feel close to you before actually engaging in sex.* If it's a nice day, or if we've maybe gone out and done some exercise together, or something really special, maybe had dinner or romance, there's that sense of coming closer together. Conversation and flirtation definitely play into it, too."

TRANSITION ACTIVITIES

You will find that many individuals and couples can suggest their own transition activities. As their therapist you can help them discover their own, as well as make such suggestions as, "Individually, you might warm up for sex by taking a bath or shower, stretching, and breathing deeply—or you could bathe or shower together. Doing something as a couple that isn't specifically sexual can be an excellent way of starting to feel close. It might be a date or sharing a walk, a meal, exercise, dancing, or a TV program. It could even be weaving in sexual innuendos and play as you clean up the kitchen together. Activities like these can give your sexual interest and arousal time to build into full desire."

Among activities mentioned by survey respondents as great ways both to feel closer and to build arousal were play, talking, laughter, and spiritual practices. For example, "We tussle a bit first, before being more quiet and cuddly"; "We engage in playful chatter; we form a conscious intention of knowing we want to connect in heart, spirit, and body"; or, "We talk to each other, creating a different psychic space to move into"; or, "We pray together before intercourse—believe it or not! A satisfying spiritual oneness is naturally followed by a satisfying oneness."

The transition into sex is more likely to proceed smoothly and effectively if distracting details have been taken care of ahead of time. These might be related to, for example, privacy, contraception, disease protection, music, or the woman talking something over with her partner. Sometimes reducing distractions can be as simple as locking a door, unplugging a phone, getting a pillow, preparing a beverage, or opening a condom package.

Building Arousal Through Simmering and Teasing

Some couples, like those in the following examples, are adept at *simmering*, that is, lighting a pilot light of arousal and keeping their arousal fueled—simmering—in anticipation of later sex. Their preferences provide suggestions you might make in your work with individuals and couples. One woman noted, "A word or a touch can let me look forward to sex. I like to anticipate, be looking forward to something, before you actually ever get there." Another said, "I like flirting, verbal foreplay, innuendoes, and physical, kissing on the neck over a period of time before we get to the bedroom; I can turn it on in the bedroom, but it's just not as easy." And a third reported, "My desire is highest when I know we'll be having sex eventually, but I have to wait. Like we'll be out, close to each other, getting more and more excited, like in the car just waiting to get home."

The ease with which we make sexual transitions and how we go about them change as we move through our lives. Sex—and orgasms—don't have to go away as we get older, but they do change form with, for example, changes in our age, partner, health, and the circumstances under which we are able to have sex. As therapists, we need to adapt our suggestions to a couple's ages and life situation.

Whereas a newlywed in her 20s may find her transitions practically instantaneous, a married woman at 40 may report, "We know we're slowing down, yet it's important for us not to let sex go away or to go through long periods of time without sex. So we set up dates, like *Do you want to have a date tonight?* And that can be anything. We might dress up in nice clothes, even if we stay in the house all dressed up having a cocktail. We just set the time and place to do it. It might mean pulling out some erotica, it might mean lingerie, or playing strip poker. But we'll actively ask each other." A woman in her 70s, who had been with her current husband for about 5 years, needed more transition time: "I don't have the sexual drive I had in my 40s and 50s. The way I like to have sex now is that it's preplanned, a time when we can be totally alone with no interruptions. We usually do getaways, go somewhere for a couple of nights or so. If you only go for one night, it's not enough time. I have a sack of goodies—candles, a fur mitt, feathers, all those nice things—and we give each other foreplay in a very loving, very pleasurable way."

An important factor in orgasmic responsiveness for many women is knowing that they can take as much time as they need. Emphasize to the women and couples you work with that no matter how much time they actually have, they are likely to enjoy sex most when it feels to them that there is absolutely no reason to hurry, that they have all the time they need to become turned on and let their attention be drawn into sex. On one occasion that might be only a few moments in which a look or verbal suggestion triggers a sharp rush of sexual desire. Another time, it might be an hour during which there is a relaxed, unhurried buildup of sexual tension. Sometimes the pressure of a time limit does indeed make sex exciting. *Quickies* can be very arousing and a lot of fun. Typically, though, feeling rushed and pressured to hurry interferes with the physical and psychological changes involved in sexual arousal. In fact, a woman may find that if a partner's touches are too specifically genital or sexual before she feels ready, she will protectively pull away, which will hinder rather than facilitate the unfolding of her arousal and feelings of connection.

One way to demonstrate to a woman how she might surrender to what she is feeling is to suggest that she imagine that she is having sex and feeling hurried or pressured; she's focusing on her genitals and *trying* to make something physical happen. Suggest that she feel in her body how this would be. Then, suggest that she imagine instead—in contrast—that there is no hurry, she can *surrender* to feeling whatever is happening at the moment; all she has to do is *enjoy* what she is feeling; she can *let go* of control and *allow* sexual sensations to develop throughout her entire body. Sometimes I suggest an image of a dog or cat surrendering as it is having its belly rubbed or scratched.

Some Things Orgasmic Women Do to Facilitate Their Orgasms

In the Ellison/Zilbergeld survey, we asked the respondents who had at some time reached orgasm during sex with a partner to consider what, in addition to getting specific physical stimulation, they had done often during sex with a partner to help them reach orgasm. In the survey, 2,371 women marked 1 or more items as applying to them from a list of 14 we provided. Here is our list, with the most frequently selected first, the least frequent last. When appropriate, any or all can be suggested to women with whom you work.

In addition to getting specific physical stimulation, I often have done the following to help me reach orgasm during sex with a partner . . .

Activity	N of women doing it	% N = 2,371
Positioned my body to get the stimulation I needed	2,145	90%
Paid attention to my physical sensations	1,960	83%
Tightened and released my pelvic muscles	1,780	75%
Synchronized the rhythm of my movements to my partner's	1,778	75%
Asked or encouraged my partner to do what I needed	1,756	74%
Gotten myself in a sexy mood beforehand	1,686	71%
Focused on my partner's pleasure	1,612	68%
Felt/thought how much I love my partner	1,548	65%
Engaged in a fantasy of my own	1,331	56%
Engaged in eye contact with my partner	1,080	46%
Engaged in a fantasy shared with my partner	777	33%
Detached from thinking about anything	758	32%
Synchronized my breathing to my partner's breathing	543	23%
Thought or imagined that I might become pregnant	272	11%

In the questionnaire margins, many women wrote in additional information about how they reach orgasm. I found that their suggestions for increasing erotic pleasure and enhancing orgasmic potential fell into four categories: focus of attention; physical stimulation and techniques; the setting and other sensory enhancements; and communication and interaction with her partner.

Focus of Attention

Shifting Attention from Performance to Pleasure. A woman concerned about orgasm may occupy her attention during sex with such questions as, "How am I doing?" or "Am I going to make it?" As therapist, you can make suggestions that encourage her to consciously turn—or return—her attention to one of the images suggested here by other women or to shift her attention to the previously mentioned more useful question "Am I enjoying what's happening right now?"

There are many places a woman can focus attention during sex that address her enjoyment. Women have told me that they facilitate orgasm by paying attention to their physical sensations and pleasure, focusing on their partners' pleasure, feeling and thinking how much they love their partners, engaging in fantasy, or detaching from thinking about anything ("I don't worry about having an orgasm, I just have fun"; "I let go and float"; "I get into total quiet and sense the rhythmic movement"), for example.

In enhancing a woman's ability to focus on the question "Am I enjoying this?" you may want to talk with her about erotic pleasure as a composition of sensations. You might suggest that she pay attention to, for example, scents, tastes, visual images, the varying qualities of the touches she gives and receives, feelings emanating from her muscles and internal organs, and the voluntary and involuntary sounds she and her partner make.

You might tell her that during sex her attention may shift between her sensations, her breathing, fantasies, mental impressions, and a variety of emotional feelings. Can she sense physical tension developing, expanding, and releasing? Is she able to notice sexual energy intensifying, moving, and releasing—or not releasing? She may report becoming aware of memories, judgments, performance expectations, and other mental images. When relevant to her progress in becoming or being orgasmic, these can be addressed in your work with her.

Erotic Stimulation—Creating a Composition of Sensations

In giving touch and in being touched ourselves, we can feel variations in temperature, pressure, texture, shape, shading, tone, intensity, and location of the touch. In making love we can also vary the mood and the setting. The possibilities for varying these in erotic experiences are endless. You may want to show a woman and her partner an erotic massage video or recommend that they take a couples' massage class.

You also may need to inform them that for most people, pleasure is enhanced by varying touch. One reason for this is a physical effect called *habituation*, the numbing effect caused by steadily stimulating one place. Habituation occurs when nerve receptors become fully activated and no longer able to transmit more sensations. This effect is very useful. It lets us, for example, feel a shirt against our skin as we put it on, but it protects us from being continuously bombarded with sensations from the shirt until we take it off again.

Because of habituation, continual unvarying stimulation of one place, even the clitoris, is usually not the most effective way to generate arousal and create erotic pleasure. Sometimes short-term continual steady clitoral stimulation is exactly what a woman wants to enhance her arousal or release her orgasm, but often ongoing steady rubbing of the clitoris by a woman or her partner, or the continual application of a vibrator or a stream or water to the clitoral area, can have a numbing effect. When numbing occurs, arousal may seem to reach a plateau and go no further, or an orgasm may occur but be less intense than the woman desires.

Because, however, different locations and different qualities of touch have their own nerve receptors, touch can be imaginatively varied. Allowing the intensity of stimulation and arousal to build and diminish—or a tension between *Will we?* or *Won't we?* to develop—may take longer than rubbing one place continuously to reach orgasm, but also may create more engorgement of tissues and richer sensations of arousal.

Survey respondents described various specific kinds of stimulation that helped them to reach orgasm during sex with a partner, including, for example, manual stimulation from their partners, cunnilingus, and mutual body massage. Some women enhanced their pleasure and facilitated orgasm by stimulating themselves during partner sex. Some stimulated themselves as their partners watched. Some respondents mentioned using a vibrator or sex toys, whereas others reported they had never tried them or didn't like using them.

A woman can learn a lot about how she experiences pleasure and orgasm through self-exploration and self-pleasuring. Recommend to a woman with orgasm difficulties that she experiment with various ways of stimulating herself. You also might suggest that she look at her vulva and vagina with a hand mirror. Do honor her sensitivities, however; find alternatives if such experiments are contrary to her values.

Don't assume that because a woman is older, masturbation is not for her. It may surprise you to learn that one of the oldest women I interviewed first tried masturbation when she was 81, after her husband's health problems made him uninterested in sex. She told me, "Some of the best orgasms I've ever had were the ones that I gave myself in the last few years. . . . I had read about what a release masturbation is, so I just decided, well, I might as well try it. If my husband can't give me what I need, maybe I can give myself what I need."

Sexual Arousal

A woman's sexual arousal involves the filling with blood of erectile tissues that are very similar in structure to the erectile tissues in a penis. During sexual arousal, a woman's body goes through an internal transformation in size and shape that, if we could watch it, would be as remarkable as the dynamic transformation of a penis in becoming erect.

Some of a woman's erectile tissues become firm, others more elastic or spongy. When a woman becomes sexually excited, her entire clitoris, including the part we don't see because it's inside, becomes engorged with blood, swells, and becomes firm. The more elastic erectile tissues around her vaginal opening, her vaginal lips, and the areas that are sometimes described as the *urethral sponge* and *perineal sponge* also engorge. If we think of the aroused vagina as a cave—a cave that is potential space until it is opened and entered—the *urethral sponge* is the soft, spongy tissue that extends inward along its ceiling, where it surrounds the urethra. If this *sponge* is fully filled during sexual activity, then it can transmit sensations and protect the urethra from irritation. You might suggest to a woman that when she is turned on, she can locate this spongy area by inserting a finger into her vagina and pressing up and forward toward her pubic bone. This is the area sometimes called the G-spot. The *perineal sponge* is the floor of this cave; it can be felt by pressing downward. As these spongy tissues swell, they serve to tighten the vaginal entrance. As arousal heightens, other internal tissues, including the woman's uterus, also may become engorged and expand.

When this *erotic complex*—the vulva, vagina, uterus, and all their associated skin, muscles, connective tissue, nerves, and blood vessels—is fully engorged and distended, a woman's whole internal shape changes. Her uterus and expanded vagina become more accessible to the stimulation of an entering penis, finger, or whatever else is desired. In their aroused sponginess, these tissues can transmit sensations of pressure and compression, as well as perceptions of friction. As a woman becomes highly aroused and her pelvic erotic complex literally becomes differently shaped, she can experience sensations not available to her when she is internally less expanded and spongy. When the erotic complex is quite engorged and distended, a woman may experience, in the words of one woman I interviewed who became very aroused through oral stimulation, "an *aching feeling* for penetration." One function of the rhythmic pulsations of her orgasms is to massage the accumulated fluids out of her erotic tissues, helping to return her body to its nonaroused shape. (Note: The term *erotic complex* was coined by Dr. Eric Golanty and myself to describe the various aspects of the pelvic region that contribute to one's ability to create and experience erotic pleasure.)

Sexual arousal is a very important element in a woman's orgasmic potential, as well as in the pleasure most women can have from intercourse or other internal stimulation. Stimulation of an unaroused vagina is not the same as a penis or dildo moving in the fully engorged vagina of a sexually aroused and actively participating woman. A 30 year old once told me, "When I'm highly aroused by my partner and the situation, those intercourse movements are highly pleasurable. If I'm moderately aroused, the internal stimulation may feel good, but not nearly so good and intense as it does after we've been doing intercourse for awhile and I'm really into it—or after we've done a lot of very arousing foreplay—for example, oral stimulation to orgasm or to the verge of orgasm" (Ellison, 1984, p. 330).

Some women find that at times during the deeper sensations of intercourse, the sensations of direct clitoral stimulation are not what they want. That is the experience of this woman, who also demonstrates that a woman's orgasms may change over time: "I like clitoral stimulation and I like vaginal with intercourse. From a man I want one or the other, but not both at the same time. If he's using his hand, I do like having his finger in my vagina. But not the penis and hand at the same time. In the last 2 years my orgasms have been changing. Clitoral orgasms were easy for me to have. Intercourse orgasms are new, still developing. I feel them deeper inside of me, more in my whole body; they last longer. Orgasms before didn't come up as high; they were shallower, less satisfying."

Full-body arousal typically takes more time to develop than genitally focused surface excitement. To become fully aroused, a woman's (or man's) body needs to make physiological and neurological shifts that usually can't be rushed, but can be enjoyed and experienced as relaxation, sensual pleasure, and building arousal. I often describe full-body arousal as like reaching one's *second wind* in running. When a woman and her male partner reach this arousal level in synchrony, her orgasmic potential is much enhanced, and he is likely to have enhanced ejaculatory control.

The potential richness and fullness of this more deeply aroused kind of erotic experience is missed by couples who always rush to intercourse or only direct their stimulation toward orgasm. Individuals and couples can experiment to discover their own preferences and develop more variability in their love-making. One survey respondent said that for her, "*extensive* foreplay . . . leads to a more on-going eroticism throughout the relationship (that is) sensuous, loving . . . very 'spiritual' in an unusual way . . . and to a much deeper release at orgasm."

A woman in her late 20s described her best times as "when I'm not worried about anything that has to get done and we've got a good stretch of several hours and time afterward to take a little nap and a shower." Realistically, however, everyday life may rarely provide circumstances in which an afternoon or an evening can be devoted to sex. As another in her late 30s explained, "My best sexual experience would be one that would last, including foreplay and everything, an hour. Before we had a child (now two) . . . there would be a lot of foreplay: kissing, caressing, music . . . just everything nice and slow. Everything now is so rushed for us. There's usually not enough time unless we're away." As therapists, we need to emphasize that it's an important part of relationship maintenance to schedule time away—away from kids, job, phone, whatever gets in the way.

Some Factors That Affect Arousal

Although the clitoris is truly unique in that, as far as I know, it is the only human organ devoted entirely to the generation of sexual pleasure, and many women report oral or manual stimulation of it as their most typical or preferable way to reach orgasm, still, orgasm depends on a great deal more than where or what is stimulated. A woman's partner, mood, hormones, health, and the circumstances under which she is having sex are factors that also are important. A woman's experience of orgasm varies, too, according to her partner's skill as a lover, the nature of their relationship, her age, her sexual history, how armored she is against emotions, and more.

For postmenopausal women who are not on hormone replacement, the absence of estrogen can radically diminish the potential of the vaginal tissues for engorgement; this consequently makes it more difficult to create orgasm. Certain medications, such as some SSRIs and SSRI-like compounds, may make orgasm practically impossible. Younger women on birth control pills can experience diminished orgasmic potential if their pills do not provide as much estrogen as their bodies need; they may have such "menopausal" signs as vaginal dryness and even hot flashes. I recommend that you get manufacturers' samples of sexual lubricants to give to women who are experiencing vaginal dryness. For women not on contraceptive pills, you also might recommend, when appropriate, an estrogen cream that could be applied directly to the vaginal tissues.

An older woman with a male partner is likely to be with a man whose arousal and erections are not what they once were; this factor, too, may make reaching orgasm more difficult for her. You might recommend that a woman (of any age) experiment with using a vibrator or lubricated dildo to enhance stimulation and facilitate orgasm. Not every couple will accept these suggestions. If a couple doesn't want to experiment with using a vibrator or dildo, that's okay, too.

The Setting and Other Sensory Enhancements

The setting in which a sexual episode occurs can help facilitate arousal, pleasure, and orgasm. You might suggest to partners, for example, that they have sex in a favorite or novel setting. They might wear special clothing and bring in other sensory enhancements. For example, "We take the phone off the hook, have a glass of wine"; "I wear lingerie and have my husband wear sexy male stuff"; "Our mutual favorite is making love outdoors in the sunshine when we know we'll not be discovered"; "We use candles, music, massage each other." I often recommend that partners use music to create a mood and synchronize their attention.

Communication and Interaction With Her Partner

Women can also facilitate orgasm by communicating and interacting with their partners in a variety of ways. You might model for a woman words to use to ask or encourage her partner to do what she wants or needs during sex; you can give her some ideas, too, about how she might do this without words, such as by guiding her partner's hand to where she wants to be touched.

Let her know that talking or making sounds during sexual activity can be helpful. Women noted on their questionnaires: "I say my partner's name"; "I say 'I love you' over and over"; "I yell out to express my pleasure." Talking about sensations or feelings of the moment also may be an orgasm facilitator. One woman noted that she asks her partner to share erotic fantasies about them while engaged in sex, and others mentioned "talking dirty," reading with their partners other people's fantasies, and otherwise sharing erotica. Other arousal and orgasm enhancers with a partner included going to new places, "parking" after years of marriage, role-playing, eating sensual foods before sex, and taking pictures of each other.

Differences in sexual style are a relationship factor that can interfere when a couple wants to create arousal and feelings of connection. Partners may differ, for example, in what most effectively turns each one on. Sex will become more satisfying if they can find a bridge between their styles. Just as there are many styles of dancing, there are many different sexual scripts and turn-ons. You can help partners to teach each other the styles they know or together experiment with and develop another or others, thereby enhancing their abilities to be sexually aroused and to arouse each other.

Imagery for Learning to Be Orgasmic

The following is an adaptation of guided imagery used by my teacher, Richard Olney, who developed Self-Acceptance Training. You might want to adapt it to fit your situation. Perhaps there will be an occasion in which your client can listen to these or similar words when she is relaxed, with her eyes closed.

> Listen to my words. As you approach orgasm, don't let yourself go too fast. Hold on, let go, hold on, let go—like that. Don't let go any more than feels safe. It's like swimming—or walking down—or up—a staircase. It's not necessary to try. Your body is capable of so many things. These body signals can have a new and joyous meaning to you now.
>
> Stop worrying about having an orgasm. Instead, often imagine yourself experiencing orgasm. Don't go toward or into the orgasm all at one time. Go only in little tiny steps you can control—like going down a staircase toward a bottom door beyond which everything is bright and cheerful. Go down these steps pausing to feel comfortable—pausing to know you are only going to go one little step more. And in no circumstances go beyond the step in which you feel comfortable. If the steps are one to ten, and if the level where you feel comfortable ends at five, go to four. If it ends at eight, go to seven. This way you won't go beyond the point where you feel secure and you can feel comfortable—and you can feel so secure and comfortable doing it that way that you can forget about yourself if you want to. At no point are you going to take a deep plunge. You'll move to your orgasm step by step as you choose to move.
>
> These three things you can put aside: panic, critical judgment, and self-consciousness. So you don't have to hold yourself back from pleasure of any kind any more. Every day it will be easier and easier—not to be overcome—but to choose to surrender yourself to pleasure.
>
> Are you aware of the power you have—the power that only you have—to enter into this experience? Only you have the choice—I have only one power—to point it out to you. You can get to orgasm if you don't give a darn or not.

CONCLUSION

A woman's sexuality is a lifelong work in progress. Learning about the responsiveness of her body and how to create orgasm by herself and with a partner is a process that occurs over time. We all continue to learn, change, and adapt throughout our lives. Erotic pleasure and orgasm with a partner depend on a great deal more than where or what is stimulated, particularly upon qualities of our partner and relationship. With a compatible, involved partner, visual images, mutual sounds, shared emotions and images, the rhythms created by giving and receiving touch, and the mutual building and movement of sexual energy may become as important to the release of orgasm as the physical stimulation of any particular body part.

Keep in mind that there is great variety in women's orgasmic experiences. Women have many different ways of finding their way to orgasmic release. There is no one right way; there is a multitude of ways. There is uniqueness in each sexual-self. You will find that what is arousing for one woman can turn another off. Any absolute standard about orgasm—that a certain kind or number or way is better than another—denies the incredible and wonderful variety in the ways women can experience orgasm—or not—and enjoy sex.

I wish you well.

REFERENCES

Much of the material in this chapter is from my book *Women's Sexualities: Generations of Women Share Intimate Secrets of Sexual Self-Acceptance* (Oakland, CA: New Harbinger Publications, 2000). Based on research with over 2,600 women, *Women's Sexualities* is filled with their quotes, addressing variations in our sexual selves, development, the path to sexual womanhood, and erotic pleasures, solo and with a partner. Included are chapters on satisfaction, sexual problems and concerns, orgasm, sexual choreography, and sexual self-acceptance.

American Psychiatric Association. (1994). *Diagnostic & Statistical Manual of Mental Disorders* (4th ed.). Washington, D.C.: Author.

Annon, J. S. (1974). *The Behavioral Treatment of Sexual Problems.* Honolulu: Enabling Systems.

Ellison, C. R. (2000). *Women's Sexualities. Generations of Women Share Intimate Secrets of Sexual Self-Acceptance.* Oakland, CA: New Harbinger.

Ellison, C. R. (1984). Harmful beliefs affecting the practice of sex therapy with women. *Psychotherapy, 21*(3), 327–334.

Mead, M. (1969). *Male and Female. A Study of the Sexes in a Changing World.* Quote is from New York: Dell, Laurel edition, 1968.

For Additional Reading

Anand, M. (1989). *The Art of Sexual Ecstasy*. Los Angeles: J. P. Tarcher. (1995). *The Art of Sexual Magic*. New York: G. P. Putnam's Sons. (Based on Anand's workshops in which she adapts Eastern practices for Western lovers; can give you many ideas for nonthreatening "experiments" couples can try.)

Barbach, L. G. (1975). *For Yourself: The Fulfillment of Female Sexuality*. New York: New American Library. (This classic offers many useful suggestions for facilitating women's orgasms; the values of the *manufacturing orgasms* sexual script are apparent.)

Dodson, B. (1987). *Sex for One. The Joy of Selfloving*. New York: Crown. (Another classic; the title says it all.)

Ellison, C. R. (2000). *Women's Sexualities. Generations of Women Share Intimate Secrets of Sexual Self-Acceptance*. Oakland, CA: New Harbinger.

Haines, S. (1999). *The Survivor's Guide to Sex. How to Have an Empowered Sex Life After Child Sexual Abuse*. San Francisco: Cleis. (A sex-positive and pleasure-promoting guide to healing the wounded sexual self by a somatics practitioner who specializes in healing trauma and sexual abuse.)

Loulan, J. (1984). *Lesbian Sexuality*. San Francisco: Spinsters/*Aunt Lute*. (1987). *Lesbian Passion. Loving Ourselves & Each Other*. San Francisco: Spinsters Ink. (*Lesbian Sexuality* is a must-read to understand how women experience their sexualities and orgasms; I sometimes recommend it to heterosexual couples.)

Maltz, W., & Boss, S. (2001). *(Private Thoughts). Exploring the Power of Women's Sexual Fantasies*. Novato, CA: New World. (Shows the variety in women's fantasies and steps a woman can take when her fantasies trouble her.)

Montagu, A. (1971, 1983). *Touching. The Human Significance of the Skin*. New York: Columbia University Press. (A classic; provides a strong foundation for understanding the significance of touch in sexual issues.)

Ogden, G. (1999). *Women Who Love Sex. An Inquiry into the Expanding Spirit of Women's Erotic Experience*. Cambridge: Womanspirit. (A book about saying "Yes" to pleasure.)

Resnick, S. (1997). *The Pleasure Zone: Why We Resist Good Geelings and How to Let Go and Be Happy*. Berkeley, CA: Conari. (A how-to book about letting go and saying "Yes" to pleasure.)

Chapter Eleven

The Sexual Impact of Menopause

Lorraine L. Dennerstein, AO, MBBS, PhD, DPM, FRANZCP

INTRODUCTION

My interest in the effect of the ovarian sex steroids on female sexual functioning was triggered by the women patients who consulted me when I was a young general practitioner in the early 1970s. A number of women asked me whether the oral contraceptive pill could have affected their mood and sexual functioning, which they perceived to have deteriorated with the use of the oral contraceptive pill. In trying to answer their questions, I embarked on a journey that has led to a career in academic research with clinical training in psychiatry and a PhD in reproductive endocrinology. For the last 30 years I have studied the effects of changes in endogenous or exogenous sex steroid hormones on sexuality. Thus our studies have examined changes in mood, sexuality, or both with the menstrual cycle (Dennerstein, Smith, Morse, & Burger, 1994), oral contraceptive pill use (Dennerstein, 1999), postpartum (Dennerstein, Lehert, & Riphagen, 1989), hysterectomy (Dennerstein, Wood, & Burrows, 1977; Ryan, Dennerstein, & Pepperell, 1989), with the natural menopausal transition (Dennerstein, Dudley, & Burger, 2001; Dennerstein, Randolph, Taffe, Dudley, & Burger, 2002), and with use of estrogen and progestin after bilateral oophorectomy (Dennerstein, Burrows, Hyman, & Sharpe, 1979, 1980). Our studies have involved double-blind randomized clinical trials, observational studies, bioavailability studies, and critical literature reviews—the full gamut of research. These approaches are complementary and will be drawn on in this chapter, which focuses on the menopausal transition.

There is a high incidence of sexual problems reported by women attending menopause clinics (Sarrel & Whitehead, 1985). How representative is this of most women's experience of the menopausal transition? If there is a deterioration in sexual functioning experienced by mid-aged women, is this related to menopause or simply to aging? The menopausal transition is a time of psychosocial, as well as biological, change. If there are adverse changes in sexuality, do these reflect ill health, hormonal changes, or psychosocial factors? Sorting out this issue is of concern to clinicians, because if there is a decline in sexual functioning specifically related to the hormonal aspects of the menopausal transition, then hormone therapy could be expected to play a role in therapy of such sexual problems.

Of course, reports derived from clinic or convenience samples are known to be based on a small proportion of self-selecting, predominantly ill women and may not be representative (McKinlay, McKinlay, & Brambilla, 1987; Morse et al., 1994). We can learn more about possible links between menopause and sexuality from population-based surveys. Yet relatively few of the population studies of the menopausal transition in mid-aged women have inquired about sexual functioning. Even fewer have used a validated questionnaire to assess the different aspects of sexual functioning. Cross-sectional studies are unable to establish a difference between cohort membership (effects of social change on different age groups) and aging. Aging and length of the relationship are both known to affect sexual functioning of both men and women. For example, James (1983) used cross-sectional and longitudinal data to show that coital rate halved over the 1st year of marriage and then took another 20 years to halve again. The role of aging per se has to be disentangled from that of menopause, with which it is often confounded. Longitudinal studies of samples derived from the general population are in the best position to sort out whether there is a change in sexual functioning, and if so, whether this reflects aging, health status, hormonal, or psychosocial factors.

Other methodological issues include the need for an appropriate age band that covers the menopausal transition; use of standardized objective definitions of menopausal status; distinctions between naturally menopausal women and those with an induced menopause; separation of women who are taking exogenous hormones from those who are in the natural menopausal transition; inclusion of physical measures of hormonal change, rather than subsuming this by menstrual status; limitations imposed on women by questionnaire design; and need for appropriate data analysis techniques (Dennerstein, 1996).

With these limitations in mind, I utilize the results of population-based surveys to address the impact of the menopause on women's sexual functioning. In this chapter I will refer extensively to results from our decade-long observational study of the menopausal transition, the Melbourne Women's Midlife Health Project. This study provides important data, as the data were derived by population sampling rather than by using convenience samples, and we obtained, prospectively and concurrently, hormone measures and information from a validated sexuality questionnaire. The following review is based on my previous review (Dennerstein, 2000) and updated to include more recent findings. I first examine changes in sexual functioning with aging relevant to midlife, then concomitant effects of the menopausal transition, differential effects of hormones and psychosocial factors, determination of the roles of androgens versus estrogens, and then the implications for the clinician.

Is There a Change in Female Sexuality in Midlife?

A number of studies report a decline in aspects of sexual functioning in mid-aged women.

The early work of Pfeiffer and Davis (1972), using cross-sectional data from the Duke University study, found a pattern of declining sexual activity in both men and women. These results relied on coital or orgasmic rates or both, which may reflect availability of partner rather than the woman's own sexuality. When Pfeiffer, Verwoerdt, and Davis (1972) reported results on sexual interest, they found that 7% of women in the 46–50 year group reported no interest compared to 51% in the 61–65 year group, whereas the incidence of no sexual interest reported by men of the same age rose from 0 to 11%. The sharpest decline in interest for women occurred between the 45–50 and 51–55 year groups, which encapsulates the mean age of menopause in the United States. The Duke study sample of 502 married men and women, initially aged 46–71, was followed at 2-year intervals for 4 years (George & Weiler, 1981). Analysis was restricted to those who attended all interviews and remained married (278). Only 57 of the sample were women aged 46–55 at the beginning of study. Despite the authors' conclusions that sexual activity remained more stable over time than was previously suggested, inspection of their data reveals that 20% of the total group reported a decrease in activity, whereas 5% reported an increase. A limitation of the Duke study was that it obtained the sample from people enrolled with an insurance company and so was biased to middle- and upper-class employed people with few health problems, and most people of the sample were aged over 55 years.

These problems were overcome by the Swedish study of Hallstrom (1977), who used population sampling in Gothenburg to find 800 subjects aged 38, 46, 50, and 54. He found a dramatic decline in sexual interest, capacity for orgasm, and coital frequency with increasing age. Not all women reported a decrease, but the majority of the postmenopausal women did. The number reporting an increase in interest or orgasmic capacity was small and less likely with rising age.

Hallstrom and Samuelsson (1990) carried out a prospective study, utilizing the women in the Hallstrom (1977) cross-sectional study. The women were surveyed about their sexual desire on two occasions, 6 years apart. Data from 497 women, married and cohabiting on both occasions, was analyzed. The study found significantly decreased sexual desire between ages 46 and 60. After the age of 50 years, no subject was aware of a strong sexual desire; 27% reported a decrease in desire between the interviews and 10% an increase.

The Oxford study of Hawton, Gath, and Day (1994), involving 436 women aged 35–59 who had sexual partners, was derived from general practice registers. Interviewer–administered questions found that frequency of sexual intercourse, orgasm, and enjoyment of sexual activity with a partner were most closely associated with younger age.

Osborn, Hawton, and Gath (1988) used the same community sample and operationally defined sexual dysfunction, which affected one third of the 436 women, aged 35–59. Sexual dysfunction was significantly associated with increasing age.

A Danish study (Koste & Garde, 1993) utilized a general population sample of 474 women born in 1936, who were examined at the ages of 40, 45, and 51 years. Interviews were conducted in 1976 and 1981, and postal questionnaires were used for the last follow-up. Of the 51-year-old women, 59% reported no change in sexual desire over the study period of 11 years, 30% reported decreased desire, and 11% reported an increase. However this was based on an exceptionally long retrospective recall period (11 years).

Thus there is a consensus for a decline in sexual functioning in midlife.

Does Change in Female Sexuality Relate to Menopausal Status or to Increasing Age?

The Gothenburg study of Hallstrom (1977) was in a better position to disentangle the effect of age on women's sexuality, because it was age-stratified instead of having age groups. Within each age group were pre-, peri- and postmenopausal women. When age was controlled, the relationship between menopausal status and decreased sexual functioning remained highly significant, but when climacteric phase was held constant, the relationship between age and sexual functioning was not significant. These findings indicate a contribution from the climacteric independent of the age factor alone.

A significant, but small, independent adverse effect of menopausal status on female sexual interest and frequency of intercourse was also reported by Pfeiffer and Davis (1972), using stepwise regression on their cross-sectional Duke University study.

A postal survey of 474 women attending an ovarian screening program in London (Hunter, Battersby, & Whitehead, 1986) reported that the sexual functioning factor (dissatisfaction with sexual relationship, loss of sexual interest, vaginal dryness) increased significantly from pre- to peri- to postmenopausal. Sexual interest significantly decreased in peri- and postmenopausal women. Age was associated with reduced interest, but menopausal status was more important. The stepwise reduction in sexual interest from pre- to peri- to postmenopausal status remained when the effects of age were controlled for. Vaginal dryness was more frequently reported in the postmenopause. Sexual satisfaction did not change significantly with menopausal status. Multiple regression found that sexual functioning (like vasomotor symptoms) was significantly associated with menopausal status only, unlike other factors, which were also associated with social class or employment status.

Conflicting evidence was reported by Hawton et al. (1994). Little difference was found between age-matched subgroups of 34 women (still menstruating) and 34 women (not menstruating for 6 months or more) in frequency of sexual behavior and attitudes to their sexual relationships. The lack of menopausal effect may have related to small sample sizes in the age-matched groups. Using the same community sample, Osborn et al. (1988) reported that sexual dysfunction was not associated with menopausal symptoms of hot flushes or sweats, vaginal dryness, or cessation of menses of at least 3 months.

The Melbourne Women's Midlife Health Project set out to overcome many of the methodological limitations of previous research by utilizing a population-derived sample of 2001 women aged 45 to 55 years and following the menstruating women through the menopausal transition with annual assessments. We questioned women at baseline about changes in sexual interest in the past 12 months, reasons for any changes, occurrence of sexual intercourse, and unusual pain on intercourse (Dennerstein et al., 1994). Logistic regression was used to identify explanatory variables for change in sexual interest. The majority of women (62%) reported no change in sexual interest; 31% reported a decrease. Decline in sexual interest was significantly and adversely associated with natural menopause ($p < 0.01$); decreased well-being ($p < 0.001$); decreasing employment ($p < 0.01$); and symptomatology (vasomotor, $p < 0.05$; cardiopulmonary,

$p < 0.001$ and skeletal, $p < 0.01$). The factor of 11 to 12 years of education was associated with a lowered risk of decreased sexual functioning ($p < 0.01$). Heterogeneous results were reported by users of hormone therapies. Only 7% of women reported an increased sexual interest, which was usually attributed by them to having a new partner. The results of this randomly derived population study of Australian-born women are strongly suggestive that the sexual functioning of some women is adversely affected by the natural menopause transition. The baseline cross-sectional analysis did not use a detailed or validated sexuality questionnaire. Nor were any hormonal measures available. These measures were introduced into our prospective study of 438 women who were still menstruating at baseline (Dennerstein et al., 2001). Of these, 197 women who passed through the menopausal transition during 8 years of observation could be studied for effects of the natural menopausal transition. Their results were compared with two subgroups within the cohort: Control Group A ($n = 44$) who remained pre- or early perimenopausal for 7 years, and Control Group B ($n = 42$), who remained postmenopausal over 5 years. The main outcome measure was the shortened version of the Personal Experiences Questionnaire. By the late menopausal transition there was a significant decline in sexual responsivity and the total score of sexual functioning and an increase in partner's problems. By the postmenopausal phase there was a further decline in sexual responsivity, frequency of sexual activities, libido, and the total score and a significant increase in vaginal dyspareunia and partner's problems. Only sexual responsivity was found to significantly decline in both control groups, indicating that sexual responsivity is adversely affected by both aging and the menopausal transition. The other domains of female sexual functioning were significantly adversely affected by the menopausal transition. The relationship with the partner and his ability to perform sexually are also adversely affected by the menopausal transition. To me this suggests, somewhat intriguingly, that passing through the menopausal transition may alter the way women feel toward their partner and about sex.

How do these findings relate to what women themselves say? The sexuality questionnaire used does have a place for further comments. All the comments provided by the women relating to changes in their sexual behavior during the longitudinal phase of the study were downloaded and subjected to a preliminary content analysis. There were a variety of responses listed, but these fell predominantly into four groups. Some comments that are typical of women in each of these groups are described as follows (Dennerstein, Lehert, Burger, Garamszegi, & Dudley, 2000):

No Partner: "No current partner"; "I have been widowed for 2 years"; "Have been divorced for some time—no partner for the last 5 years."

Husband's Problems: "My partner is impotent so I don't have sex with him"; "Some things have changed since my husband's operation for bowel cancer 1 year ago"; "Husband is currently working overseas with infrequent visits home."

Her Decreased Interest: "The last 5 years have been quieter in the sex department than were the previous years"; "We seldom have sex. Our relationship is good but not sexual these days"; "Sexual intercourse is less exciting now than in earlier years and I seem to find other things take time partner & I spend together, e.g., children, friends, work. Put less effort into making it 'fun.'" "At 47 I don't feel like instigating sex."

Increased interest: "I was separated 3 years ago. I have a new partner (9 months' duration). My new partner has transformed my life and love life"; "I don't think I have changed. The difference between now and 5 years ago is that I have a different partner"; "My sex life with the same partner has improved greatly from being satisfactory before in the past 5 years because we have deliberately made time for each other, such as going away for weekends once or twice a year."

Does Change in Female Sexuality in the Menopausal Transition Reflect Hormonal Change or Psychosocial Factors?

Clearly, sexual functioning is affected by a range of health status and psychosocial variables, in addition to hormonal factors.

Pfeiffer and Davis (1972), using the Duke University data and stepwise multiple regression, found that the variables contributing to sexual enjoyment, sexual interest, and frequency were past sexual experience, age, gender (male positively correlated), income (positively), social class (positively), and objective physical function rating. Regression analyses carried out separately on women, after eliminating previous sexual experience (in order to see effect of other independent variables), showed that variables affecting (1) sexual interest were marital status, age, education, postmenopause, and employment status (being employed—positively); and (2) sexual enjoyment were marital status, age, and education (positively).

The Gothenburg study of Hallstrom (1977) found that social class and mental health status were the two most important variables associated with declining sex interest. Sex may be protected for those in higher social classes because of better educational standards, greater freedom to express individuality, and increased freedom from traditional stereotyped sex roles. Other factors characterizing the group with low interest included high age, advanced climacteric phase, low mental health status, high depression, frequent dyspareunia, insufficient emotional support from husband, negative marital relationship, poor health of husband, high number of stressors, unhappy with work outside home, and some personality factors: low extroversion, exhibition, and rational dominance factors. No relationship was found between impaired interest and total 24-hour estrogen output in 146 postmenopausal women. Hallstrom concluded that sexuality is affected by the advancement of the climacteric but also by other factors, particularly social class, mental health status, personality, and other psychosocial factors.

The Gothenburg follow-up study of Hallstrom and Samuelsson (1990) found that decrease in desire was predicted by age, high desire at first interview, lack of a confiding relationship, insufficient support from spouse, alcoholism in spouse, and major depression. Correlates of decreased desire at second interview included degree of mental disorder, anxiety neurosis, psychopathology rating scale score, use of psychotropic medications, duration of mental disorder between visits, and life-event stress. This follow-up study did not appear to examine the role of menopause.

The Oxford study (Hawton et al., 1994) found significant effects on female sexual functioning of marital adjustment, partner's age, and the duration of relationships. Higher neuroticism scores were associated with lower frequency of sexual intercourse. These authors concluded that aging of both women and their partners, length of a relationship, and marital adjustment were the more important influences on female sexual behavior, response, and enjoyment. Sexual dysfunction (Osborn et al., 1988) was significantly associated with increasing age, psychiatric disorder, neuroticism, and marital disharmony.

The longitudinal Danish study of Koste and Garde (1993) found that infrequent sexual desire at age 51 was predicted by baseline (at age 40) variables of coital activity less than once weekly, marital status single, physical fitness worse than peers, lower social status, and anticipation of decreased desire as a consequence of menopause; and by variables recorded at age 45, of coital activity less than once weekly, marital status single, poor self-rated health, and anticipation of symptoms during the menopause. The 51-year-old women's experience of frequency and change in sexual desire was not related to menopausal status but only to anticipation of declining sexual desire as a consequence of menopause. Low frequency in sexual desire correlated with women who reported " weak nerves," were single, and belonged to social class V. No variables were significantly associated with change in desire in this study, which may have reflected the 11-year time frame of the question.

In the Melbourne Women's Midlife Health Project, we found a significant association at baseline between decline in sexual interest and advanced menopausal status, decreased well-being, hormone therapy use, less than full-time paid employment, and presence of bothersome symptoms. Increased years of education were associated with a lower risk of declining sexual interest (Dennerstein et al., 1994).

Which Hormones Relate to the Decline in Sexual Functioning During the Menopausal Transition?

There is much controversy about the relative contribution of androgens and estrogen to female sexual functioning. Low libido, lack of well-being, blunted motivation, and fatigue are listed as major features of the proposed syndrome of female androgen deficiency (Davis, 1999; Davis & Burger,1996). We have indicated that there are several problems in relation to the syndrome as described previously (Randolph & Dennerstein, 2001). The symptoms are vague and difficult to operationalize and all can occur in other syndromes, such as major depressive disorder. As well, there is currently no definition of what comprises low levels of testosterone, reflecting variation in assays and lack of sensitivity. We do know that there are pronounced age-related and phase-related changes in androgens. Testosterone reaches an apparent peak in the early reproductive years (3rd decade) and then declines with age, so that women in their 40s have approximately half the level of circulating total testosterone as that of women in their 20s (Zumoff, Strain, Miller, & Rosner, 1995). The rate of age-related decline in total testosterone then seems to slow and is not specifically related to menopause (Burger, Dudly, Cui, Dennerstein, & Hopper, 2000). As described previously, the amount of bioavailable testosterone actually increases as women become postmenopausal because of the decrease in SHBG (Burger et al., 2000). Dehydroepiandrosterone sulphate (DHEAS) shows similar changes to those described for testosterone, but has an even more pronounced age-related decline after the early reproductive years, which continues through to later life (Carlstrom et al., 1988; Ravaglia et al., 1996). There are both diurnal- and menstrual cycle–linked changes in testosterone and androstenedione (Judd & Yen, 1973). Testosterone (and androstenedione) levels are highest in the morning before 10:00 A.M. (Ankarberg & Norjavaara, 1999) and in the middle third of the menstrual cycle (Sanders & Bancroft, 1982). The menopausal transition is associated with a marked decrease in estradiol and increase in gonadotrophic hormones (Burger et al., 1999).

Although some small observational studies provide suggestions that there is a link between androgens and sexual functioning in women, there is no body of substantial evidence based on large samples and using validated questionnaires to confirm these findings.

The longitudinal phase of our Melbourne Women's Midlife Health Project included annual hormone determinations (Burger et al., 1995). I was stunned to find that from early to late menopausal transition the percentage of women with Short Personal Experiences Questionnaire scores indicating sexual dysfunction rose from 42% to 88% (Dennerstein et al., 2002). There were no significant changes in mood scores. In the early menopausal transition, those women with low total scores on the Short Personal Experiences Questionnaire had lower estradiol ($p = 0.052$) but similar androgen levels to those with higher scores (Dennerstein et al., 2002). Decreasing scores on the Short Personal Experiences Questionnaire correlated with decreasing estradiol but not with androgens. We did not find any direct relationships of hormone levels to mood scores (Dennerstein et al., 2002).

The most reliable way of determining response to hormones is via the randomized double-blind clinical trial. But many trials that have assessed effects on sexual functioning have had relatively small sample sizes. The stage of menopausal transition of the women participants has not always been clarified. There are also some difficulties in extrapolating results from studies of women who have undergone hysterectomy and bilateral oophorectomy to women who have retained their ovaries. Many of the trials failed to use validated and reliable assessments of mood and sexual functioning.

In a classic study I carried out nearly 3 decades ago (Dennerstein, Burrows, Hyman, & Sharpe, 1980), 50 oophorectomized women were randomized to receive 3 months' each of ethinyl estradiol 0.05mgm, norgestrel 250 ugm, the combination of the ethinyl estradiol and norgestrel (Nordiol), and placebo in randomized order. No androgen comparison was included in the study design, which nevertheless demonstrated powerful effects of ethinyl estradiol on mood and sexuality. I found that ethinyl estradiol had a beneficial effect on female sexual desire, enjoyment, and vaginal lubrication (all measured by ordinal scales) and on orgasmic frequency (recorded daily). The combination pill was less beneficial than estrogen alone, but norgestrel was found to be more inhibitory. Thus these results suggest that women on continuous combined preparations of HRT may not have as beneficial a result as those on estrogen therapy only and that the addition of a progestin has an inhibitory effect on sexuality.

Oophorectomized women have lost the important contribution of ovarian production to the total androgen pool. They have also lost ovarian production of estrogens and progesterone. The incremental improvement for oophorectomized women of adding androgen to estrogen replacement has been assessed (Davis, McCloud, Strauss, & Burger, 1995; Sarrel, Dobay, & Wiita, 1998; Sherwin, Gelfand, & Brender, 1985). These studies have found testosterone to have significant positive incremental effects over that of estrogen alone on mood, on aspects of sexual functioning, or both. It was not clear from these studies whether testosterone was acting physiologically or as a pharmacological agent with a pronounced psychotropic effect. Whereas earlier trials used doses that were often above physiologic levels, later trials used lower doses of hormones, similar to the upper end of laboratory ranges (Davis, 1999; Schifren et al., 2000).

There have been relatively few negative trials, suggesting that whatever the role of testosterone physiologically on mood and female sexuality, testosterone administration can have a powerful pharmacological effect (Dennerstein, 2001).

IMPLICATIONS FOR CLINICIANS

Population-based studies such as our Melbourne Women's Midlife Health Project have found a deterioration in several aspects of female sexual functioning associated with the midlife years. The analysis also demonstrates that hormonal change is only one aspect of the many factors that impact on sexual functioning. These include the woman's own premorbid level of sexual functioning, presence of bothersome symptoms, well-being, stress, and the presence and quality of the sexual relationship with a partner.

When mid-aged women report sexual problems, I take a detailed history involving the woman and her partner, alone and together. Given the range of factors affecting sexual functioning and the significantly more powerful effect of partner factors over that of hormonal factors, I utilize a broadly based biopsychosocial approach. I specifically ask for bothersome symptoms that are known to be responsive to hormone therapy. These should be treated, as they impact on aspects of sexual functioning, as well as cause distress in their own right. I give consideration to supplementation with estrogen if the woman has other indicators of estrogen deficiency (hot flashes, genital atrophic changes, oophorectomy) and the deterioration in sexual functioning is time related by the woman to the menopausal transition, natural or induced. Bilaterally oophorectomized women may benefit from the addition of testosterone to estrogen. With each woman I discuss contraindications (absolute and relative) to the use of either hormone and risks and side effects of hormone therapies. But hormonal prescription alone is rarely enough! I give particular attention to the assessment of the relationship with the partner and other stressors in the woman's life. Recall that we found from women's own comments that the midlife transition allows the opportunity for positive change in sexual relationships, if couples increase their intimacy at this time.

Finally, reflecting on my 30 years of research on this topic, I can conclude that sex steroids such as estrogen, progestins, and androgens have subtle but important effects on female sexual functioning. These effects can be overridden by powerful psychosocial factors, such as a new relationship or the effects of past learning, which affect premorbid functioning. With every patient presenting to my practice, an individual approach is needed to sort out the relative role of these factors so that appropriate therapy can be planned.

BIBLIOGRAPHY

Ankarberg, C., & Norjavaara, E. (1999). Diurnal rhythm of testosterone secretion before and throughout puberty in healthy girls: Correlation with 17betaestradiol and dehydroepiandrosterone sulfate. *Journal of Clininical Endocrinology and Metabolism, 84,* 975–984.

Burger, H. G., Dudley, E. C., Cui, J., Dennerstein, L., & Hopper, J. L. (2000). A prospective longitudinal study of serum testosterone, dehydroepiandrosterone sulfate, and sex hormone–binding globulin levels through the menopause transition. *Journal of Clinical Endocrinology and Metabolism, 85*(8), 2832–2838. This paper from the Melbourne Women's Midlife Health Project details androgen levels across the menopausal transition.

Burger, H., Dudley, E., Hopper, J., Groome, N., Guthrie, J. R., Green, A., & Dennerstein, L. (1999). Prospectively measured levels of serum FSH, estradiol, and the dimeric inhibins during the menopausal transition in a population-based cohort of women. *Journal of Clinical Endocrinology and Metabolism, 84,* 4025–4030. This paper from the Melbourne Women's Midlife Health Project details changes in estradiol and the gonadotrophins across the menopausal transition.

Burger, H., Dudley, E., Hopper, J., Shelley, J., Greene, A., Smith, A., Dennerstein, L., & Morse, C. (1995). The endocrinology of the menopausal transition: A cross-sectional study of a population-base sample. *Journal of Clinical Endocrinology and Metabolism, 80*(12), 3537–3545.

Carlstrom, K., Brody, S., Lunell, N. O., Lagrelius, G., Mollerstrom, A., Pousette, G., et al. (1988). Dehydroepiandrosterone sulphate and dehydroepiandrosterone in serum: Differences related to age and sex. *Maturitas, 10,* 297–306.

Davis, S. R. (1999). Androgen treatment in women. *Medical Journal of Australia, 170,* 545–549.

Davis, S. R., & Burger, H. G. (1996). Androgens and the postmenopausal woman. *Journal of Clinical Endocrinology and Metabolism, 81,* 2759–2764.

Davis, S. R., McCloud, P., Strauss, B. J. G., & Burger, H. (1995). Testosterone enhances estradiol's effects on postmenopausal bone density and sexuality. *Maturitas, 21,* 227–236.

Dennerstein, L. (1996). Well-being, symptoms and the menopausal transition. *Maturitas, 23*(2), 147–57. This is a review paper prepared for the World Health Organization.

Dennerstein, L. (1999). Psychosexual effects of hormonal contraception. *Gynaecology Forum, 4*(3), 13–16.

Dennerstein, L. (2000). Menopause and sexuality. In Jane M. Ussher (Ed.), *Women's Health: Contemporary International Perspectives* (pp. 190–196). Leicester: British Psychological Society Books.

Dennerstein, L. (2001). Female androgen deficiency syndrome—Definition, diagnosis and classification. An international consensus conference. June 29, 2001, Princeton, New Jersey.

Medscape Women's Health, 2001. To view: http://www.medscape.com/viewarticle/416448 This is a conference summary prepared for Medscape.

Dennerstein, L., Burrows, G. D., Hyman, G., & Sharpe, K. (1979). Hormone therapy and affect. *Maturitas, 1*, 247–259. This is a classic double-blind randomized clinical trial of the effects of the components of the oral contraceptive pill on mood.

Dennerstein, L., Burrows, G. D., Hyman, G. J., & Sharpe, K. (1980). Hormones and sexuality: Effects of estrogen and progesterone. *Obstetrics and Gynecology, 56,* 316–322. This is a classic double-blind randomized clinical trial of the effects of the components of the oral contraceptive pill on sexuality.

Dennerstein, L., Dudley, E., & Burger, H. (2001). Are changes in sexual functioning during midlife due to aging or menopause? *Fertility and Sterility, 76*(3), 456–460. This paper from the Melbourne Women's Midlife Health Project details how female sexual functioning changes with aging and with menopausal stages.

Dennerstein, L., Gotts, G., Brown, J. B., Morse, C. A., Farley, T. M. M., & Pinol, A. (1994). The relationship between the menstrual cycle and female sexual interest. *Psychoneuroendocrinology, 19*(3), 293–304. Observational study, prospective using daily diaries and daily hormone levels.

Dennerstein, L., Lehert, P., Burger, H., Garamszegi, G., & Dudley, E. (2000). Menopause and sexual functioning. In T. Aso et al. (Eds.), *The Menopause at the Millennium. Proceedings of the 9th International Menopause Society World Congress on the Menopause* (Yokohama, 1999) (pp. 46–53). New York: Parthenon. This chapter includes the qualitative data from the Melbourne Women's Midlife Health Project.

Dennerstein, L., Lehert, P., & Riphagen, F. (1989). Post partum depression—Risk factors. *Journal of Psychosomatic Obstetrics and Gynaecology, 10,* 53–67. Prospective study of changes in mood from pregnancy to postpartum.

Dennerstein, L., Randolph, J., Taffe, J., Dudley, E., & Burger, H. (2002). Hormones, mood, sexuality and the menopausal transition. *Fertility and Sterility, 77,* Supplement 4, 42–48. This paper from the Melbourne Women's Midlife Health Project details how changes in female sexual functioning are related to hormone levels.

Dennerstein, L., Smith, A., Morse, C., & Burger, H. (1994). Sexuality and the menopause. *Journal of Psychosomatic Obstetrics and Gynaecology, 15,* 59–66. This paper from the Melbourne Women's Midlife Health Project details the results from the baseline phase (cross-sectional) on sexuality.

Dennerstein, L., Wood, C., & Burrows, G. D. (1977). Sexual response following hysterectomy and oophorectomy. *Obstetrics and Gynecology, 49,* 92–96.

George, L. K., & Weiler, S. J. (1981). Sexuality in middle and later life: The effects of age, cohort, and gender. *Archives of General Psychiatry, 38,* 919–923.

Hallstrom, T. (1977). Sexuality in the climacteric. *Clinics in Obstetrics and Gynaecology, 4*(1), 227–239.

Hallstrom, T., & Samuelsson, S. (1990). Changes in women's sexual desire in middle life: The longitudinal study of women in Gothenburg. *Archives of Sexual Behavior, 19*(3), 259–268.

Hawton, K., Gath, D., & Day, A. (1994). Sexual function in a community sample of middle-aged women with partners: Effects of age, marital, socioeconomic, psychiatric, gynecological, and menopausal factors. *Archives of Sexual Behavior, 23*(4), 375–395.

Hunter, M., Battersby, R., & Whitehead, M. (1986). Sexual dysjunction among middle aged women in the community. *Maturitas, 7,* 217–228.

James, W. (1983). Decline in coital rates with spouses' ages and duration of marriage. *Journal of Biosocial Science, 15,* 83–87.

L

Judd, H. L., & Yen, S. S. C. (1973). Serum androstenedione and testosterone levels during the menstrual cycle. *Journal of Clinical Endocrinology and Metabolism, 36,* 475–481.

Koste, A., & Garde, K. (1993). Sexual desire and menopausal development. A prospective study of Danish women born in 1936. *Maturitas. 16,* 49–60.

McKinlay, J. B., McKinlay, S. M., & Brambilla, D. J. (1987). Health status and utilization behavior associated with menopause. *American Journal of Epidemiology, 125*(1), 110–121.

Morse, C. A., Smith, A., Dennerstein, L., Green, A., Hopper, J., & Burger, H. (1994). The treatment-seeking woman at menopause. *Maturitas, 18*(3), 161–173.

Osborn, M., Hawton, K., & Gath, D. (1988). Sexual dysfunction among middle aged women in the community. *British Medical Journal, 296,* 959–962.

Pfeiffer, E., & Davis, G. (1972). Determinants of sexual behavior in middle and old age. *Journal of the American Geriatric Society, 20*(4), 151–158.

Pfeiffer, E., Verwoerdt, A., & Davis, G. (1972). Sexual behaviour in middle life. *American Journal of Psychiatry, 128*(10), 1262–1267.

Randolph, J. F., & Dennerstein, L. (2001). Female androgen deficiency syndrome: A hard look at a sexy issue. *Medscape Women's Health, 6*(2). To view: http://www.medscape.com/viewarticle/408940 This is an editorial discussing some of the methodological issues that need to be resolved before the role of androgens in female sexual functioning can be ascertained.

Ravaglia, G., Forti, P., Maioli, F., Bernardi, M., Pratelli, L., et al. (1996). The relationship of dehydroepiandrosterine sulphate (DHEAS) to endocrine-metabolic parameters and functional status in the oldest-old. Results from an Italian study on healthy free-living over ninety-year-olds. *Journal of Clinical Endocrinology and Metabolism, 81,* 1173–1178.

Ryan, M., Dennerstein, L., & Pepperell, R. (1989). Psychological aspects of hysterectomy—A prospective study. *British Journal of Psychiatry, 154,* 516–522.

Sanders, D., & Bancroft, J. (1982). Hormones and the sexuality of women—The menstrual cycle. *Journal of Clinical Endocrinology and Metabolism, 11,* 639–659.

Sarrel, P. M., & Whitehead, M. I. (1985). Sex and menopause: Defining the issues. *Maturitas, 7,* 217–224.

Sarrel, P., Dobay, B., & Wiita, B. (1998). Estrogen and estrogen-androgen replacement in postmenopausal women dissatisfied with estrogen-only therapy. *Journal of Reproductive Medicine, 43,* 847–856.

Sherwin, B. B., Gelfand, M. M., & Brender, W. (1985). Androgen enhances sexual motivation in females: A prospective, crossover study of sex steroid administration in the surgical menopause. *Psychosomatic Medicine, 47,* 339–351.

Shifren, J. L., Braunstein, G. D., Simon, J. A., Casson, P. R., Buster, J. E., Redmond, G. P., et al. (2000). Transdermal testosterone treatment in women with impaired sexual function after oophorectomy. *New England Journal of Medicine, 343,* 682–688.

Zumoff, B., Strain, G. W., Miller, L. K., & Rosner, W. (1995). Twenty-four hour mean plasma testosterone concentration declines with age in normal premenopausal women. *Journal of Clinical Endocrinology and Metabolism, 80*(4), 1429–1430.

Part Three

MEN'S SEXUAL ISSUES

Chapter Twelve

Young Men Who Avoid Sex

Derek C. Polonsky, MD

Men between the ages of 18 and 30 inevitably confront sexual developmental challenges. Some have trouble mastering these tasks and avoid sexual opportunities. My psychiatric training in Boston in the early 1970s led me to assume that any sexual impairment was due to unresolved developmental conflicts or repetitions related to the family of origin. I believed that therapy required a patient exploration of these issues. Treatment outcome rarely supported this approach. Using a method that encompassed both the traditional model and a more directed sexual format, I was able to treat many young men with considerable success. I understood the young men's personal histories in a new way and provided them with specific suggestions. In order to overcome their patterns of avoidance of sex with partners, these single men had to confront their social awkwardness and discomfort and their inordinate focus on their sexual performance. Men in committed relationships were often surprised by changes in sexual desire and were helped to understand the sources of their declining interest. Gay young avoidant men have some special challenges. I will describe in detail what I say to my patients in my attempt to model for you how to be helpful to your patients. I hope this will help you to use your psychodynamic understanding of your patients to speak practically to them, enabling them to get better.

In this book, our hope is to stimulate your awareness of the positive impact you can have on your patients without having to be experts in sex therapy. My own interest in the field came out of an unanticipated necessity. One of my residency supervisors encouraged me to see couples; I enjoyed seeing both partners together and was excited by the theoretical constructs of Dicks,[1] Framo,[2] and Sager,[3] regarding the dynamics of couples. I was totally unprepared for what happened as the couples began to form a trusting relationship with me: they began to raise questions about sex and talked with concern about their sexual problems. To me! In the 3 years of my psychiatric residency there had not been a single discussion about sex. It did not make sense to me to say, "Oh, I get it, you have a sexual problem—let me refer you to a sex therapist." I hurriedly read Helen Singer Kaplan's *The New Sex Therapy*[4] and took a 2-day crash seminar on Sexual Dysfunction with Masters and Johnson. For a while I felt like I was flying by the seat of my pants, often keeping just one chapter ahead of my patients. What was remarkable to me, though, was that despite my belief that "underlying conflicts needed to be addressed before any change sexually could take place," many couples' sexual lives improved with some direct talk and some specific guidance.

I have been seeing individuals and couples for 30 years. The threads of sexuality have almost always been present with each patient. When I first began to talk about my work in sexuality, I was aware that many of my colleagues thought I was strange and labeled me the "sex therapist." I never felt comfortable with this title because it did not recognize my integrating individual psychological factors with the dynamics in couples. Nor did it appreciate the serious study of sexuality by urologists, gynecologists, endocrinologists, and those in mental health. I picked up subtle clues that suggested the couples therapy was considered on a par with "group" (clearly inferior to individual therapy), and sex therapy was bordering on perversion. How things have changed! I now frequently get calls from former co-residents asking for advice regarding their patients' sexual difficulties. Giving them clear information about sexual physiology, with some specific suggestions to help their patients, has been a pleasure. My colleagues are appreciative, and I am grateful for this additional avenue of being helpful. I am aware that without guidance, many therapists feel intimidated when their patients ask about sexual problems. I hope I will be able to encourage you to ask more direct questions of your patients and to treat some of the problems you may have thought of referring to the "expert." I believe you will be enriched when you do.

In his book, *The New Male Sexuality*, Bernie Zilbergeld[5] reflects on the fact that a great deal of attention was focused on the psychological development and needs of girls and women in the late 1960s. This resulted in a richer, more sophisticated awareness of the tasks and experiences that are particular to girls and women. The emphasis on female development followed the many years in which the mental health field had been much influenced by psychoanalysis and theories that were put forward by men. Zilbergeld observed the assumption that the needs of young boys were obvious, but, in fact, boys' development had also been a neglected topic. He observed that up to about age 6–8, boys were able to express fears openly; their dependency was noticed and responded to. However, as they got older, they were taught to hold in their feelings and to admit to little vulnerability and were discouraged from crying; boys were now expected to assume a more independent, self-sufficient style. Zilbergeld makes a cogent case for the price that we paid for this in terms of our adult relationships and our sexual expectations: expressing uncertainty and vulnerability comes to be seen as unmasculine. We feel a pressure to enter into sexual relationships with a burdensome, unrealistic bravado and pseudo-mastery. Although large numbers of men and women are able to separate from their families, see themselves as sexual beings, and master the challenges in acquiring some sexual skills and competence, many clearly are lost along the way. Levine[6] likens sex for the first time or with a new partner to be like a two-horse race: one called Excitement, the other called Fear. Sometimes Fear wins, sometimes Excitement wins by a nose, and with more runnings the horse Fear weakens. I have seen many young men for whom Fear dominates, although the culture demands that the race be run as if Fear did not exist.

What this means for us mental health professionals is that we can play an affirming role, while treating young men by guiding them to embrace sexual and relational pleasures without hiding their anxiety and worry about sexual inadequacy. I used to be surprised by the impact of my discussions about sex on my younger patients. As I reflect on my early training in the 1970s, my teachers emphasized the search for "problems"—for example, unempathic parents and unconscious conflict. No one taught me about being an encouraging mentor who provided sexual information and guided young people to find their own resources to grow and develop sexually and emotionally.

TALKING ABOUT SEX

When I attempted to treat couples in the 1970s who had sexual difficulties, I was struck by the number of couples who would say, "We've bought all the books, and we've tried all the exercises, and nothing helps!" As a resident I wondered what I might offer that would make a difference. I soon found that the process of talking about sex with an encouraging "parental" figure had dramatic effects. In many instances, I was not providing any more information than the individuals already had, but saying the words out loud in my presence and having me calmly and confidently inquire, inform, and discuss all matters sexual in exquisite (sometimes they would say excruciating) detail had a profound impact. I openly, directly talked about sexual development, patterns of touch in families, pleasures of masturbation, sexual physiology, and sexual myths. My doing this was reinforced time and again when patients said, "You know, I've often wondered about that" or "I thought it was weird/abnormal," and so forth. Or when giving real-life examples of people's reactions, I often heard, "What a relief to know that my feelings are within the normal range." People are obsessed with being normal, and as the titles of so many popular magazines attest, many people are drawn to evaluating sexual functioning and performance. There is a painful lack of instruction for the medical community when it comes to taking a sexual history and talking about sex. Leiblum[7] has noted that the time medical schools are devoting to a sexual health curriculum is declining, and residency programs are not much better. So for many therapists, the idea of talking directly about sex is uncomfortable. This is to be expected! I would blush when I said "penis" and "clitoris" with my patients and felt that my embarrassment and discomfort were obvious. With practice, and learning from my mistakes, I grew more comfortable. I continue to be impressed with the way my patients take on my direct approach in their own lives.

When Masters and Johnson described their novel sexual treatments in 1970, they perceived that the couples suffered from sexual performance anxiety. Their approach was to provide structure and guided exercises to overcome this. By the late 1970s, as more understanding about sexual dysfunction accumulated, therapists began invoking the concept of "inhibited" or "low sexual desire." The typical treatment began to take longer and seemed more complicated. However, treatment was still conceived as involving only the couple. For young men who were not in a committed relationship or men for whom sex with another person was a scary, unmasterable challenge, there was no new sex therapy. Our treatments left them out and thereby encouraged their sexual avoidance.

THREE CLINICALLY APPARENT REASONS FOR AVOIDING SEX

1. Lack of Information

The media saturates us with images of attractive, sexual, and anxiety-free couples. This creates the impression that to be uncertain of oneself is not cool. But real young people are uncertain, and they are hungry for good, accurate sexual information. They want to know what behaviors are normal and how to talk openly with a partner about sex. Suggesting books may be in some instances helpful, but such recommendations are more useful after people have discussed their concerns with me. I particularly like to recommend *The Guide to Getting It On.*[8]

2. Fearfulness of Close Relationships

It is sometimes difficult initially to predict whether this fear represents a transient "hesitation" in growing up or a more entrenched characterological style. Many young men misidentify their difficulties as sexual when, in fact, their actual struggle is about getting closer to and vulnerable with another individual. They present with sexual performance concerns, such as worries about losing an erection, being chronically impotent, or coming quickly. Our dual therapeutic challenge is to nurture their ability to form an attachment outside of their family while mastering their sexual concerns.

Typically, the young patient conveys his sense of urgency over dealing with his sexual concern, but he actually needs to pay more attention to how to develop a relationship with another individual. This process may be limited because he may not have yet developed enough distance from his family to realize what he may be reenacting with a new partner. He may not recognize that his new partner may have characteristics that are similar to a parent (or parents) with whom he has a serious conflict.

I've found it helpful to talk about how one develops trust, how important it can be to reveal one's doubts and uncertainties, and that doing so usually makes things easier. I talk about the burden so many carry, in assuming that sex is simply "doing what comes naturally." I have found that providing elements of what I think of as "Relationship 101" is a valuable part of the treatment. Laying out a roadmap of the many elements of a relationship may seem obvious, but for many of our young patients it is helpful and often gratefully received.

Once I talked with a group of high school students about the needs of their sexual education curriculum. They wanted to hear more about how to make relationships—how to say "no" in a variety of situations (not wanting to lend someone a prized possession, not wanting to go to a certain movie, how to say "no" in a sexual situation) and how to end relationships (whether it be with a friend with whom one has had a major falling out, or an intimate relationship that no longer is working). These students were quite clear about their need for guidance about the "rules" and wanted suggestions that they could apply to their lives. We discovered that role-playing a resolution of conflict was helpful because it taught them to define their wishes in relation to someone with a different agenda.

3. Internet-Stimulated Pseudohypoactive Sexual Interest Versus Hypoactive Sexual Desire

The third reason that some young men avoid sex is actually an illusion. Some young couples seek treatment with the complaint that the man has low sexual interest. Treating low desire is usually a complicated endeavor, involving longer therapies and requiring a variety of approaches. Focus may need to be on individual developmental issues, on the couple's dynamics, or both. If the low desire represents a change from a previous pattern, understanding what has changed usually clarifies how treatment might proceed. However, for lifelong low desire you should consider a referral to a therapist specializing in sexual problems after you have considered the following differential diagnosis:

- low self-esteem
- conflicts around competence and assertiveness
- depression
- retreat from performance problems (premature ejaculation or erectile difficulties)
- childhood sexual abuse (about 10% of men)
- hypothyroidism
- low testosterone (hypogonadism and prolactin-secreting pituitary tumor)

You can be very helpful to men or couples caught in what I call "pseudohypoactive interest." (In *DSM-IV* terms, my "pseudohypoactive interest" is situational hypoactive sexual desire disorder.) These men have little expressed sexual interest with their partner, but have considerable sexual drive, as evidenced by their frequent masturbation, stimulated by their computer use. The Internet has introduced a seismic change in the easy availability of sexual material in the home. No longer are there social constraints on going to the local adult bookstore; *infinite* truly describes what is available on the Net. Although I believe that the actual content does not represent much that has not been part of the human range of interests related to sexuality, what is different is that more people are exposed to and become obsessed with the stimulation. It is now an essential part of any psychiatric history to ask about interest in sexual websites. What may be labeled "low desire" may really be high levels of website masturbation. What can be simple about such pseudohypoactive desire is that when this pattern is pointed out, some men can find the motivation to desist because of the negative impact on the partner and their wish to be free of their recent "addiction." Some cases, however, are complicated and not amenable to easy interventions. Here are a few informal guidelines that may be predictors of poor outcomes.

- If he has never been in a committed relationship
- If he is, but you cannot get a clear sense of the couple's dynamics
- If he uses the Internet to avoid relationships, social anxiety, or his phobia of emotional closeness to others
- If he has paraphilic interests; that is, he uses sites related to bondage, domination,

sadism and masochism, or children. Because paraphilic men occasionally masturbate up to 10 times daily, their low sexual desire is not the problem. Having a relationship is.
• If the man is not deeply conflicted about his use of the Internet or feels entitled to it,
  in the face of his partner's distress

The treatment may be frustrating for the therapist who sees "success" as the patient entering into a more gratifying, reciprocal relationship. Some of these men don't
seem to grasp the reasons for your suggesting that they restrict their Internet use. Although they may be aware that their sexual pattern is different from that of others, they
may think that sex therapy can provide them with an "easy fix" that will make them
great in bed with their (complaining) partner, while allowing them to continue to use
the Internet. You, the therapist, should push these men quite directly to explain what
they hope to achieve through therapy. In so doing, you may clarify that for the patient,
sexual enjoyment is not associated with a deeply committed intimate relationship.

For therapists who were trained in the pre-digital age, it is a useful exercise to surf
the Net, using a search engine such as Google or Yahoo and typing in a variety of sex
words. In an instant, you will learn of the remarkable variety of sites and you will be
able to have more informed discussions with your patients. The *Journal of Sex Education and Therapy* comprehensively covered Sexuality and the Internet in a helpful
way.[9]

TEACHING VIA CASE HISTORIES

Avoidance Due to Anticipated or Actual Erectile Difficulties

Alan was a 19-year-old college junior who had a "sexual problem" that was painful
and embarrassing, and he avoided seeking out any dating relationships because of his
worry and anxiety. He became focused on performance early in any relationship with a
woman, and "erectile sufficiency" became his predominant thought. The first time he
attempted to have intercourse, he could not get an erection, and this defined his expectations with every subsequent try. By the time I saw him, he was reluctant to go on
dates and was preoccupied with his sexual "inadequacy."

It is easy for a young man to view his sexuality as defective, a view that may be
incorporated in his psyche forever. Although an understanding of psychological factors provides a schematic understanding that can be helpful to the individual, the key
to change is provided by the therapist's direct suggestions, information, and guidance
as he takes steps in a new relationship.

Alan came from a middle-class family. He described his father as an extremely
successful businessman. From the language he used, it was clear that he was in awe of
his father and admired what he viewed as his father's accomplishments. I am often
impressed how, in the first few meetings, patients in their late teens and early 20s will
give a more idealized account of their parents. They are in the middle of the process of

separation and feel it is disloyal to describe parents negatively to a "stranger" thera-pist. However, when listening between the lines, the therapist will often pick up threads that suggest a different picture. As Alan described more interactions with his father, what emerged was an aggressive man who gambled recklessly with his own and his client's money, dismissed Alan's mother as incompetent, and criticized Alan relent-lessly. I pay attention to what I characterize as a marker issue to give me a sense of what might have happened on a day-to-day basis. Alan was sensitive about his thinning hair. His father missed no opportunity to point out that Alan's hairline was receding.

As Alan talked more about interactions with his father, the parallels with his sexual performance became clearer. He truly believed that he was incompetent and inferior to his father, and his sexual failures confirmed this. I felt that my approach needed to incorporate his getting a better understanding of his relationship with his father, which involved seeing the father's critical behavior and also noticing that the father was far less competent than he presented himself. At the same time, I needed to address con-cretely Alan's sexual concerns and develop a strategy that he might find helpful.

I told him that sexual concerns were very common, and I presented these statistics to him: 10% of guys have trouble getting or keeping a hard-on and about 35% of guys come very quickly. I talked about the unrealistic expectations that are often promoted in the media and the fact that guys almost never share their sexual concerns with each other. In fact, it is quite the opposite: they exaggerate with a hyperbolic bravado that makes genuine discussion of problems with age-mates almost impossible. This discus-sion helped to reduce Alan's anxiety and sense that he was abnormal. It provided his basis for trusting me to help him as he struggled to feel more competent sexually.

We discussed the details of what happened with a partner when he was embar-rassed sexually. I asked about the woman's response and whether he was able to talk about it, either before or after the "failure." I explained that women may worry that the erectile difficulty may be caused by their not being skilled. On the other hand, men are embarrassed and ashamed of their limp penises, and both partners may define him as impotent and defective, coming to an erroneous conclusion that the relationship is doomed. Women may have the same kind of performance difficulties, but it is often less obvious because if they are not aroused, they may still be able to have intercourse. For the guy, having no erection is an obvious, humiliating worst-fantasy experience. At the time I initially saw Alan, he was not dating and was frightened of starting up with anyone. I linked his avoidance of relationships to the critical undermining comments of his father. He began to understand the power these had on his self-esteem and began confronting his father more directly.

He then met a woman whom he liked, and we talked about how to precede. I encouraged him to ask her out and raised the idea that there were two people "evaluat-ing" at this time. He was focused on her opinions of him, and I encouraged him to form some opinions of her. This sounds simple, but where an individual has a poor sense of self, it is much easier to assume that the relationship involves only a one-way negative judgment. In Alan's case, this exactly paralleled his father's negative evaluation of him. After his first date we talked about what he liked about her. I encouraged him to see her again and to focus more on getting to know her (and she him), rather than thinking about what the next sexual move would be. They went on a few more dates, and the pressure began to mount for something sexual. I encouraged Alan to try and keep the focus on the developing connection with Susan and be guided by what felt good physically. I also encouraged him to tell Susan that he was worried about getting an erection, and that it had been a problem for him in the past. By rehearsing it with me, it began to seem a little less crazy to say, and he was surprised by her reaction, which was to ask if there was anything that she might do that would be helpful. Within a few weeks, they had begun to have intercourse, and although Alan worried about performance, he did not lose his erection.

I believe that the combination of my being the benevolent, encouraging "parent" that he needed and my assistance in helping him reject some of his father's negative characterizations made for a new intrapsychic climate that enabled him to succeed and admire himself.

Alan wrote to me a while later: *"I am slowly beginning to feel better about myself. And now that I see that being aggressive about my life is working—I want more each day."* I wrote back: *"Congratulations!"*

ORGASM PROBLEMS AND SEXUAL AVOIDANCE

When I received the call from Brad, an 18-year-old sophomore, I was intrigued. He had been directed by his parents to call me, after tearfully telling them that he had a serious sexual problem—he had never been able to come with any of the women he had dated and was fearful of entering another relationship. I had been seeing his parents, who had been married for nearly 25 years, for the same problem—the father had enormous difficulty coming with his wife during intercourse. I wondered whether I was dealing with some genetic problem. When Brad came into the office, the admonition never to assume anything once again was clear. Brad was tall, muscular, and good-looking, with an outgoing personality that I could imagine made people feel at ease. He talked about how he had many friends and had not had difficulty establishing relationships with both men and women. However, he found that whenever the relationship became sexual and he had intercourse, he was unable to come, and he was now reluctant to "hook up" with anyone.

I knew that I would have only two sessions with Brad before he was to return for the fall term in college. Nothing in his history stood out as problematic. I told Brad that I suspected that many of his friends were probably talking about how often they were getting laid, which would only add to his stress. I added that I thought most of it was exaggeration, but there was no way that he could know that. I said that for him, things would have to be different; that is, that he could not expect to follow in the mode of "scoring" on the first date. In fact, I said, he needed to get to know the person he was with *before* he even thought of moving the relationship to a sexual level. I might add that as I said this, I was thinking that I was not sure if this "mini-lecture" was helpful. Then I added, "I'm going to tell you something that you will probably think is totally nuts; when you are with a woman you have gotten to know, you will need to say to her

'I have a sexual problem—when I start to have intercourse, I get anxious and it is hard for me to come.'" Once I said this, I immediately thought of my two children, who were around the same age, and imagined them rolling their eyes at this suggestion, with a sarcastic tone, saying, "Yeah, right, Dad, tell someone you have sexual problem at our age!" At that point, though, I felt buoyed by the fact that Brad had not walked out of the office, and I continued, "Look, if you don't say anything, you and I know that you are faking it; you will be pretending that you are cool and competent; we know that you are not. It will be a huge burden to shoulder and will only add to making it even less likely that you will come. If you are with someone you know and have begun to trust, it is likely that she will be supportive and will ask if there is any way she could be helpful. If she 'freaks out' and says that she does not want to be with someone so weird, you are better off ending the relationship at that point."

I saw Brad again the next week, and I repeated some of what I had said. I talked more about sexual responses and physiology—I encouraged him to let me know how things were going for him. A few months later, he e-mailed me that he had a new girlfriend—that he had talked with her. The "problem" had disappeared.

I was so moved by the impact of these two meetings to effect change because I had seen the pain and struggle that his parents had experienced throughout their marriage. Rather than seeing the retarded ejaculation as a familial, genetically based problem, I began to better understand how the father, in the absence of an encouraging sexual coach when young, got stuck and incorporated this difficulty into his view of himself sexuality.

With another man who had trouble having an orgasm with his partner, a discussion about masturbation proved to be curative. He was convinced that masturbating would make the problem worse. I corrected his conclusion and added that masturbation was important in learning about the pleasure one could derive from one's body, adding that it might actually help by getting him to focus more on the idea of enjoyable feelings, rather than performance. He left relieved and within a month had solved the problem.

PREMATURE EJACULATION AS A CAUSE FOR SEXUAL AVOIDANCE

Premature ejaculation is one of the most common sexual complaints, affecting roughly 35% of young men. In 1955 a urologist, Semans,[10] described a treatment that became known as the "squeeze technique." It involved collaboration with the wife, who would manually stimulate the penis. As orgasm approached, she was encouraged to squeeze the base of the head of the penis between her thumb and forefinger. Gradually, the man was able to learn better control with this approach. Masters and Johnson incorporated this technique in their program. They emphasized the importance of the collaboration of the couple. When I began to treat people with sexual difficulties in the 1970s, I naively told the single young men who struggled with PE to come back when they were in a relationship and I would be happy to treat them. Boy, was I wrong! This advice inadvertently allowed them to further incorporate their dread of being sexual with a partner into their psyche. To expect the person to feel confident enough to establish a relationship and then ask that partner to come to a therapist was unrealistic, and now I see that it was also unkind.

Phil was a 20-year-old junior. The first time he had intercourse, he felt anxious and incompetent, had little ability to talk much with his partner, came almost immediately, and felt humiliated. It is quite typical of young men to not be able to discuss their performance patterns with their partners. Phil became preoccupied with his lack of control and dated infrequently because of it. I told Phil that PE affects between 35 and 45% of men. I explained how worry about coming became preoccupying and all the usual suggestions to try and distract oneself, use anesthetic jelly, or think of a baseball game never work. I suggested a program[11] that involves masturbating regularly, with some specific instructions as follows:

- Masturbate until you feel that an orgasm is approaching. Then stop and, using the second hand of a watch, wait 1 minute. Resume masturbating and time how long it takes to get to the point just before orgasm. Stop again and wait 1 minute. Repeat this 4 or 5 times, and then allow the sensations to build and come. (The purpose of the timing is twofold. It provides something specific for the guy to "do." Men often feel reassured when there is a defined task. With increased practice, the guy will notice that it takes longer, after first getting to the pre-orgasm place, to get there again, and he is able to notice improvement and be encouraged.) I emphasize the need to do this exercise frequently, not less than twice a week.
- Once the beginnings of more control are felt, I suggest that he masturbate until he feels he is getting closer to orgasm (7.5 on a 1–10 scale, where 10 is orgasm). Then he needs to slow the masturbation down and try and keep the level of arousal constant, and stay at that level for about 10–15 minutes. With increased practice, the threshold for orgasm begins to rise and more stimulation is required to get there. The therapist often needs to provide encouragement to keep doing this, but often, the guy will notice the changes and be motivated to continue.
- The third phase is to use a lubricant (K-Y jelly, Astroglide, Lubriderm) because this more closely approximates the sensations of being inside a vagina. The same technique applies, with the idea of maintaining the high level of arousal for 15 minutes or longer. (Men will be surprised that the intensity of their orgasm is enhanced. This practicing is helpful and undoes the inadvertent training many teenagers have in racing to get to the big "O" as soon as possible because another erection is easy to attain at that age.)
- When a partner enters the picture, I encourage the guy to talk with her (or him) about the concern with PE and to enlist the partner's help. The same kind of practice is required with penetrative sex as outlined previously. The partners need some encouragement to deal with the frustration of it being less spontaneous and passionate, and they benefit from suggestions that might foster taking turns initially in giving each other sexual pleasure.

Phil, however, did not complete the program. It is not uncommon for men to give up the treatment. I believe in his case he was socially awkward and found the masturbating more of a chore than something that gave him pleasure. I have found, though, that the advice and the suggestions remain with the men, and on their own time, they may practice and develop more of the control they want.

HOMOSEXUAL MEN

The sexual problems of young men, it must not be forgotten, include those of gay young men. When writing about sex or talking to patients about sex, it's important not to make the error of assuming that everyone is heterosexual. Therapists should ask the patient if he is attracted to women, men, or both.

Eric was a 19-year-old freshman who had come out in the 10th grade. He described confusion about noticing that he would have sexual reactions in the presence of other boys and the total absence of sexual responses when he was with girls. He searched the Internet, found a number of gay teen sites, and spoke with a teacher about his idea that he might be gay. She responded in a thoughtful, caring way, confirming that she had thought that he was gay and, in her quiet acceptance, facilitated his coming out to his mother and then to his class. Although he appeared to be doing well in letting people know he was gay, he was scared and frightened of engaging in any sexual relationships.

It is ironic that some straight teenagers have more same-sex experimentation during their initial explorations of their sexual feelings and masturbation than gay teenagers do. For gay teenagers, the idea of revealing these interests is filled with shame, fear, and possible negative repercussions. What complicated Eric's story was the fact that his father had died of cancer when he was 15, around the time that he was beginning to come out. When I initially saw Eric, he was quite depressed and talked about the dilemma posed by being gay. He did not want to lead a segregated existence and wanted to go to the same clubs as his straight friends. However, he was painfully aware that for the straight kids, "hitting on people" was fair game and was part of the evening's activity. For him, if he saw a guy he found sexy and attractive, he had to be vigilant in reading the signals correctly, knowing that if he was mistaken, the consequences could be dire.

The therapy involved addressing three main issues simultaneously: the one related to his father's illness and death, the second to his feelings about being gay, and the third to his fear about engaging in sexual activity with other guys. It was in the realm of helping him date that my relationship with him was valuable. I noticed that he would come up with a variety of rationalizations for not experimenting sexually. He would talk about the guys being boring, stupid, unattractive, and not worthy of his time. He could not admit that he felt frightened and incompetent about initiating sexual activity with another person. I was struck that his worries were similar to those of many of the straight young adults. He felt vulnerable about not knowing what to do sexually and was immobilized by possible partner rejection. When he described going out with one guy and talking about how he just wasn't attracted to him, I pushed Eric with "Did you kiss him?" Eric turned bright red and playfully told me I was embarrassing him with my directness. I went on, saying, "Well, if you don't actually try, and see what it might feel like for you to kiss him, how would you know?" I was matter of fact in this discussion and felt that the implicit acceptance and encouragement of his exploring his sexuality was important in Eric's growth.

He came back the next week and said that he had felt very uncomfortable with my confrontations, but that he had welcomed my being direct and challenging him. We talked more about his fear of being rejected, and we rehearsed some possibilities of how he might handle himself when meeting some guy he was interested in. A few weeks later, he talked about being invited to go on a date with a guy he had met and liked. He was apprehensive. I asked him to imagine what might occur on a date and then pushed the issue of what he thought might happen if they were to touch each other. Eric initially did not want to think about it, but I tried to help him walk through the possibilities, and in the process he began to feel a little mastery that I predicted would help him quiet his fears.

He went on the date and was invited back to Jim's apartment. He did feel attracted to Jim, but felt anxious and sweaty. Jim suggested they lie on the bed and began to hold him. Eric nearly jumped out of his skin, and Jim said, "You're so tense—try and calm down." Eric was unable to settle himself, tried kissing Jim, and then said that he needed to go home. Much like many of my straight young adults, as soon as he left Jim's place, he was self-critical about his tentativeness. In our next meeting, Eric went through the details and I reassured him, telling him that he had made progress in going out on a date and kissing the guy, and I encouraged his efforts. I pointed out that there would be another opportunity and that he had probably been through the worst. He called Jim and set up another date, where he was able to focus more on his feelings for Jim and be less preoccupied with what he anticipated would be the negative judgments on the part of Jim. They kissed, held each other, and engaged in some genital play that Eric enjoyed. As we talked about the possibilities for where this might go, Eric was clear that he was not ready to "have sex." It is always important to know what people mean by their terms, and for Eric, genital play, mutual masturbation, or even oral sex was not "having sex"—that was reserved for anal intercourse, which he was clear he wished to delay.

Over time, Eric became more self-accepting and confident and began to seek out relationships in a more comfortable way—getting to know the person, deciding whether he liked him, and then engaging in more sexual experimentation. My role as an accepting, encouraging "parental" figure was the unspoken validation that young adults soak up like sponges.

COUPLES

Dicks observed the reciprocity of conflicts in couples. He describes unconscious repetitions related to the families of origin and collusions whereby each partner agrees to play out behaviors he or she may find distressing. I am often struck by the uncanny match between couples who complain of sexual difficulties, where the problem one partner has may dovetail and reinforce the difficulty of the other.

John seemed uninterested in sex, and Lisa was at the end of her rope. I meet with couples together, initially, and then with each partner alone. This format is sometimes quite revealing. In the joint meeting, John talked about how he was not into the mental/physical thing and did not feel much sexual interest. Lisa described frustration and increasingly loneliness. Alone, John blamed Lisa's weight for his sexual disinterest but said that he could not bring it up with her because it would be too hurtful. He often visited sex sites and masturbated twice a day. After a number of sessions, it became clear to me that nothing would change because of his two secrets. I met with him alone to tell him that. I tried to rehearse with him what he might say about his feeling about her weight. I suggested framing it as something that he could no longer avoid and tried to reassure him that our meetings could be a place in which to process any fallout. He did bring it up with his wife. She was upset, but soon discussed her own negative feelings about her weight. She said that she wanted to have him collaborate with her to lose weight and how inadequate she felt seeing him in such good shape. I pointed out that he felt terribly inadequate about his career failure. I tried to draw on the possibilities of mutual support of each of their perceived inadequacies. This resulted in their talking more with each other at home, setting up times where they would have "tea" to talk. Lisa suggested, with trepidation, that they take a bath together. I commented that each was taking risks. John then revealed for the first time that he had a lot of anxiety about performance and often lost his erection. When I asked how he managed with this, he talked about working to "block everything out" so that he could concentrate on getting an erection—an endeavor that never worked. We were able to laugh when he talked about "blocking everything out," as we had begun discussions about his style of creating emotional distance in most relationships. I asked whether he talked with Lisa about his worry ("No") and whether he had ever let her know how she might fondle his penis in a way that might feel pleasurable. ("No.") I "raised my eyebrow" and asked whether his penis came with instructions. ("No.") I pointed out that without the user manual, Lisa would have little idea about what might feel good, and that as long as he was so focused on blocking everything out, mastering his anxiety, and muscling through an erection, the idea of pleasure was not even on the screen. I emphasized that it was the possibility of sharing pleasure and revealing himself to his wife that might free him from the anxiety and let him focus more on enjoyment. They are continuing in treatment with me, as a couple.

UNCONSUMMATED MARRIAGE:

A colleague of mine had been seeing the husband (of a couple) in therapy twice a week for 5 years. The husband and wife had never had intercourse or seen each other naked. Both were in the health-care field. They appeared socially as an attractive, "together" couple. My colleague described his patient's never acted-upon homosexual preoccupations. I decided to take the focus away from the homosexuality. I indicated to the husband that one possible explanation of his homoerotic preoccupations was his wish for a close relationship to a man, given his very distant and unavailable father. I wanted to focus on the sexual relationship with his wife.

I was interested in his wife's understanding accommodation to his sexual avoidance. I talked with the partners about the kind of touching in each family and suggested that to relieve their pressure to have intercourse, they should use sensate focus exercises. The term *sensate focus* was originally coined by Masters and Johnson and referred to an exercise where the partners were encouraged to focus their attention on their physical and sexual sensations in a reciprocal way. Master and Johnson noted that partners rarely shared likes and dislikes about physical and sexual touch with each other, and this exercise was designed to address that. The husband and wife were told to take turns, one being the touchor and the other the touchee. They were to let each other know what they liked and disliked, and they were encouraged to map or explore each other's bodies, trying to discover sensations of touch that they had either avoided or not known. The exercise also provides an opportunity for the therapist to learn something about their negotiating styles and helps start a conversation about their being more direct about sexual feelings.

I modified the approach for them because the man felt uncomfortable being in his wife's presence without clothes, and she said, "I am certainly not going to go first!" They were to initially do the touching with clothes on and lights off. This went well.

We talked about ways to make more direct skin touching acceptable—and the husband talked about feeling angry that he had to allow his wife to touch him. Rather than trying to interpret this, I suggested that he be the one to guide his wife's hand and thereby feel a little more control over the situation. This, too, worked. What impressed me was the fact that in other areas of their relationship, they collaborated, shared values and interests, and genuinely liked each other.

The couple described their enjoyment of these activities and began to do them in dim lighting. The wife was easily responsive sexually and encouraged the husband to touch her genitals. He maintained control over how much they could do, but was surprised that he obtained an erection quite easily.

I told them I was impressed with how brave they had been in continuing these explorations and said that they were clearly moving into new territory. I explained how for many people, adolescence was a time of experimenting with sharing sexual feelings with another person, and for reasons that I did not understand, the husband had felt blocked at that time—and had a lot of catching up to do.

His appearance strikingly changed during therapy. When he first came in, he was hunched, apologetic, and sallow. After five meetings, he sat more upright and his face came alive. I saw him blossom before my eyes! Their behavioral adventure continued. I remember the session where they came in, filled with smiles, and said, "We didn't follow your instruction—we DID it!!" Their success in having intercourse occurred about 2 weeks before a scheduled cruise—and the two were delighted and happy. I congratulated them and said I wished that I had a bottle of champagne to celebrate. I saw them a few times after the cruise, which was filled with relief and openness. They stopped regular visits and then returned for a 6-month follow-up. They were happy and described a comfort with sex that they had never anticipated.

CONCLUSION

As I reflect on the treatments of these young men, it is evident that for some, guidance, encouragement, and insight can produce remarkable changes. The treatments are often quite brief, and the changes dramatic. For others, though, the outcomes may be less positive, and the symptoms and complaints are more intractable. Although it is often difficult to predict outcome, I have found that the following are associated with making significant changes in sexual functioning.

1. "Good enough" family of origin—if home was a connected and caring place, it is likely that the individual will be able to tolerate the uncertainty and anxiety as he tries to become more confident sexually.
2. Valuing personal connections and long-term friendships. Does he try to work out conflicts? Are other relationships sources of pleasure? When relationships are valued and lasting, sex is a means for deeper and more exciting connections.
3. Having a positive connection with me—that is, people who make eye contact, who are able to account for relationships in depth and reveal nuances as they describe themselves. If the interactions with me are animated, lively, and interactive, it is much easier to encourage risk taking and adventure with relationships.

There are a few observations I have found to be negative predictors:

1. How do I feel with the patient? Am I feeling tense and anxious? Is it really hard to keep the conversation going? Is there no humor? Do I feel unconnected, as if I am in the room alone? Is there is no joy and pleasure in his life?
2. Schizoid character style: If he has little appetite for closeness, the "goal" of being successful sexually may represent a misguided hope for filling a void. I confront this quite directly, with statements like "It seems to me that you don't have much need to be close to another person. . . . You may be struggling to do something you think you ought to, yet at a profoundly deep level you don't want to."
3. The presence of unconflicted paraphilic interests. Partner sex is too complicated for him; he prefers the ease of computer sex, with its limitless variety.

I have indicated through clinical cases that for many of our patients, "doing what comes naturally" is filled with dread and worry. Their pressure to succeed leads them to numb themselves into submission to the presumed cultural standard, with little success. By your incorporating some of the sexual approaches I've outlined, I believe that you will be rewarded with dramatic changes in some of your patients' sexual relationships. Learning to talk more openly and directly with young men about their sexual struggles feels strange at first, but I've found that it is soon replaced by a comfort and confidence that are truly rewarding.

NOTES

1. Dicks, H. V. (1964). Concepts of marital diagnosis of therapy as developed at the Tavistock Family Psychiatric Clinic, London. In E. M. Nash, L. Jessner, & D. W. W. Abse (Eds.), *Marriage Counseling in Medical Practice*. Chapel Hill, NC: University of North Carolina Press.
2. Framo, J. L. (1982). *Explorations in Marital and Family Therapy*. New York: Springer.
3. Sager, C. J. (1981). Couples therapy and marriage contracts. In A. S. Gurman & D. P. Kniskern (Eds.), *Handbook of Family Therapy*. New York: Brunner/Mazel.
4. Kaplan, H. S. (1974). *The New Sex Therapy*. New York: Brunner/Mazel.
5. Zilbergeld, B. (1999). *The New Male Sexuality*. New York: Bantam.
6. Levine, S. B. (1988). *Sex Is Not Simple*. Columbus: Ohio Psychology Publishing Company.
7. Leiblum, S. R. (2001). An established medical school human sexuality curriculum: Description and evaluation. *Sexual and Relationship Therapy, 16*(1), 59–70.
8. Joannides, P. (2000). *The Guide to Getting it On*. Saline, MI: Goofy Foot Press.
9. (1997, June). *Journal of Sex Education and Therapy, 22*(1).
10. Semans, J. H. (1955). Premature ejaculation: A new approach. *Southern Medical Journal, 49,* 353–358.
11. Polonsky, D. C. (2000). Premature ejaculation. In S. R. Leiblum & R. C. Rosen (Eds.), *Principles and Practice of Sex Therapy* (3rd ed.). New York: Guilford.

Chapter Thirteen

Psychogenic Impotence in Relatively Young Men

Peter Fagan, PhD

PREFACE

I am a clinical psychologist who has directed the Sexual Behaviors Consultation Unit in the Department of Psychiatry and Behavioral Sciences of the Johns Hopkins School of Medicine since 1986. My supervisory work stresses an initial proper formulation of the patient's presenting problem. Because the dynamics in each case are so multifactorial, I believe it is crucial for the reader who is new to the treatment of sexual disorders to have a methodology of organizing his or her thinking about the case. For this reason, I emphasize the perspectives model as a rational approach to the treatment of persons with sexual problems. Although I focus on a case of psychogenic impotence in a young man in this chapter, my larger hope is that readers will learn a clinical approach that is helpful for other sexual dysfunctions as well.

> He sat there fidgeting, clearly uncomfortable and looking at me only when he had to. It was bad enough that his wife had left him for another man; now he had to sit here and tell me, a stranger, that when he tried to have sex with the woman he had been dating, he was unable to get an erection. Anxiety, resentment, and a fear that perhaps nothing would help pervaded his demeanor. At one point, he glanced at the door to my office as if he were going to end this self-imposed ordeal with a hasty retreat. But Bill did not leave. After 5 minutes of raging ambivalence, he decided that he might as well tell me what his problems were. "Go, ahead. Ask me what you want to know. . . . I've come this far. I may as well tell you what you want to know." He shifted and settled back a bit more in his chair. I began to ask my questions: first, to get a sense of the problem that brought him to seek help; second, to obtain a full history and mental status examination to get a fuller understanding of the biographical context in which the sexual problem arose.

Bill was a 35-year-old divorced man who for the past 8 months had been having problems maintaining an erection. An associate manager in retail sales, Bill described himself as a hard-working, conscientious man who had devoted himself to his family. He said that he was "devastated and totally surprised" by his wife's infidelity and breakup of their 12-year marriage 2 years ago. He had had episodic problems with maintaining an erection in the final stages of the marriage, but no problems prior to that. He had some fleeting thoughts of suicide at the time he learned of his wife's infidelity, but when he thought of his three children, suicide was so abhorrent to him that these thoughts quickly subsided. He did not want the children to grow up thinking that he had abandoned them.

Bill started to date about a year ago and initially experienced no sexual problems with the women he dated. His present partner, Maria, was "different than the others" and he gave some thought about marriage to her. But as he became more serious about the relationship, his erectile dysfunction occurred more frequently. They are now avoiding sex, and Bill is worried that he will lose Maria. His children get along well with her, so the loss of Maria would be especially hurtful to him.

Bill's primary care physician suggested that he take Viagra, but Bill refused to take the medication saying, "I want to do it on my own." The PCP said that Bill was in good health. He was not taking any medications. In response to my questions about his sexual functioning, Bill reported that he had full morning and masturbatory erections.

I completed the history and mental status examination, but I knew at this point that unless I heard about problems relating to mental illness or substance abuse, my presumption was that Bill had psychogenic impotence.

WHAT'S IN A TITLE? PSYCHOGENIC IMPOTENCE IN RELATIVELY YOUNG MEN

Psychogenic Impotence

Psychogenic impotence is a term used to describe erectile dysfunction that is caused by psychological factors, as contrasted with biological causes such as prostate cancer surgery. Psychological factors can be multiple or single, but the final result is a level of anxiety in the man that prevents the somatic conditions necessary for an erection.

Consider this example from the reptilian world. A pet turtle is walking confidently, albeit slowly, across the floor. You tap its shell lightly with a letter opener. The confident progress stops; the legs and the head disappear into the shell. The "anxious" turtle is protecting itself against whatever slings and arrows of fate just came its way.

In the sexual encounter, if the man's anxiety level is sufficiently high, the effect will be the same. His penis will beat a protective retreat to the flaccid state or, in extreme cases, may begin to withdraw into the pelvic cavity. He is highly anxious; his penis reflects his affect.

Why is this? Why are high anxiety and erection incompatible? Anxiety is adaptive in certain circumstances. It signals that the person should either "fight or flee" the conditions or persons that are causing the anxiety. In a "fight or flight" response, the human body responds by pulling the blood supply back from the peripheral vessels where bleeding might occur (in the fight) and utilizes it in the main organs for the necessary oxygen (for the flight). Just as the turtle reflexively pulls its extremities within the shell, the man pulls his blood supply back into his body in response to his anxiety.

The obvious conflict occurs when an erection is desired and the "fight or flight" response is in process. A penis becomes firmly enlarged in the parasympathetic state of arousal. If there is no increased blood flow and retention of the blood in the penis, there will be no erection. Relaxation and a warm feeling throughout the extremities of the body mark the parasympathetic arousal. That warm feeling is the increased flow of blood. The "fight or flight" reaction is a sympathetic arousal. In this circumstance the alert status of the sympathetic system overrides the "at ease" status of the parasympathetic system. An erection is not possible until the parasympathetic system can regain control of the situation. This will happen only when the high anxiety is attended to and decreased.

Thus when the term *psychogenic* is used to refer to the type of causality involved in erectile dysfunction, we are not referring to a magical telepathy between the man's head and his penis. There are the intermediary somatic responses as the entire body reacts to the high anxiety the man is experiencing and, in some cases, he is unwittingly fostering. Psychogenic means that the process has its origins in cognitions and affects.

In Relatively Young Men

Any man who comes for treatment of erectile dysfunction considers himself to be "relatively young." The difference between a relatively young man and a relatively old man is the direction in which he is looking: toward the future or toward the past. A man who is concerned about having intercourse is looking to the future. He may give nodding assent to the fact that he is in his 70s, but he considers his sexuality a sign and expression of his relativity youthful old age.

That being said, however, for our purposes, relatively young men are those men up to age 50 (or so) who are basically healthy and who are experiencing problems with erections in those sexual situations when they desire to have them.

WHAT IS THE PROBLEM? MALE ERECTILE DISORDER

The Diagnosis

The most universally employed definition of erectile dysfunction is found in the *Diagnostic and Statistical Manual of Mental Disorders IV-TR* (*DSM IV-TR*).[1] The diagnostic criteria for Male Erectile Disorder are

A. Persistent or recurrent inability to attain or maintain an adequate erection until completion of the sexual activity.
B. The disturbance causes marked distress or interpersonal difficulty.
C. The dysfunction is not better accounted for by another Axis I disorder (other than sexual dysfunction) and is not caused exclusively by the direct physiological effects of a substance (e.g., a drug of abuse, a medication).

It is important that there be agreement among clinicians when talking about a sexual dysfunction (technically called inter-rater reliability), so I will briefly comment on these three criteria.

Criterion A alerts us to the fact that the problem must be of some duration and that it occurs on a frequent basis. An "occasional" loss of erection should be considered normal and not focused on by the therapist or the individual as an indication of a more systemic (psychogenic or biogenic) problem. To do so risks actually causing a problem that, if the doctor were to be responsible for the focusing, would be labeled iatrogenic erectile dysfunction.

Criterion A also requires that there is an inability to attain or maintain an erection until the completion of the sexual activity. Sexual activity is not limited to penile–vaginal intercourse. Rather, "sexual activity" is an open category. Therefore, inability to complete anal or oral intercourse or manual stimulation should be considered when making this diagnosis. The one caveat to this openness is to be wary of an unrealistic expectation on the part of the individual with the problem. For example, a man may be quite convinced that he has male erectile disorder because he cannot maintain an erection within his partner for 60 minutes (as his friends have reported doing). For him, the loss of erection interferes with the completion of the sexual activity he has as a model. In this situation it is the model that is a misperception of the average length of penetration (less than 15 minutes). The problem is in the sexual script, not in the sexual response. I'll say more about sexual scripts.

Criterion B was added to the *DSM-IV* series to indicate that male erectile disorder—indeed, all sexual dysfunctions—have an interpersonal context and effects. It is difficult to imagine any man or couple presenting for an evaluation of erectile disorder who does not meet Criterion B.

Criterion C is perhaps the most difficult to ascertain and meet because it requires a careful and complete psychological/psychiatric evaluation of the individual. This evaluation should consist of a full family and personal history, a mental status examination, and an elaboration of the sexual problem in a comprehensive manner. Only through such procedures can one know that there is no other psychiatric disorder that is primary to, and therefore causing, the sexual disorder. Likewise, only with a careful substance and medical history is the presence of a likely agent of dysfunction identified. If the clinician does not feel competent to make such a complete evaluation, then the individual should be evaluated by another professional prior to the treatment of the sexual dysfunction.

MORE DIAGNOSTIC INFORMATION: SUBTYPES

I shall review *DSM-IV*'s subtype qualifiers as they apply to young men with psychogenic impotence because they give us clinicians ideas about treatment modalities and strategies.

Onset: Lifelong Versus Acquired

If the erectile dysfunction has been present since the first attempts at sexual functioning, then the onset is described as lifelong. It is extremely rare that a young man cannot get full erections under some circumstances—for example, masturbation or during sleep. If a man has never had an erection, then a referral to his medical or urological physician is in order.

The more common lifelong male erectile disorder occurs in the man who can attain or maintain full erections under some circumstances—for example, masturbation—but who has never been able to have an erection that lasted long enough to complete the sexual activity with his partner. In a stigmatizing tone, such a man will often refer to himself as a "virgin."

The man with acquired erectile dysfunction, on the contrary, has typically been able to complete sexual activity with a partner in the past, but now is having difficulty doing so. It is important to delineate further the acquired erectile dysfunction by inquiring whether the onset of the problem was sudden, or whether it had a slow, insidious emergence. If it is the former, one should inquire about what other events were occurring at the onset to hypothesize about the cause of dysfunction. If it has an insidious onset, one again may start to wonder about a biological cause of the dysfunction.

> In the case of Bill, described previously, his erectile dysfunction was acquired and had a relatively rapid onset in the context of a relationship that was starting to become more serious in terms of possible commitment to marriage.

Sometimes *lifelong* is referred to as *primary,* whereas *acquired* is referred to as *secondary.*

Context: Generalized Versus Situational

Does the erectile dysfunction occurs with all types of stimulation, situations, and partners, or is it limited to certain types of these contextual elements? If the dysfunction is not limited to specific contexts, it is labeled generalized; if it is limited to certain conditions, it is said to be situational.

By far the more common presentation of a young man with psychogenic impotence is that of situational erectile dysfunction. In this scenario, as was the case with Bill, the man is able to have full erections at some times—for example, masturbation, sleep/awaking, prior to attempting penetration with a partner, or with some partners—but he will also experience erectile dysfunction in other circumstances.

Psychogenic factors can be responsible for both generalized and situational erectile dysfunction. It is more likely that the psychological factors in the situational dysfunction are reactive to environmental cues—for example, perceived hostility in the partner or anxiety to please the partner—whereas the generalized erectile dysfunction may indicate that the sexual conflicts have been internalized and can be activated in any sexual situation. In Bill's case, I hypothesized that the erectile dysfunction was caused by his fear of repeating with Maria the traumatic breakup that he had with his former wife. If sexual intercourse would promote further commitment to Maria, it would also promote a higher risk of eventual emotional hurt. Bill was in an approach–avoidance conflict that his penis mirrored, by both attaining erection and then failing to maintain it.

Etiology: Psychological Versus Combined

In one of the rare instances when the *DSM-IV* has encouraged a statement about the causality of the disorder, the etiology subtype for sexual dysfunction does just that. Perhaps because sexual activity is so much the blending of psychological and somatic realities, it is important to qualify a sexual diagnosis with a statement about what the presumed causative factors are. Such is the goal of the etiology subtype.

Due to Psychological Factors is the appropriate etiology subtype when the "psychological factors are judged to have the major role in the onset, exacerbation or maintenance of the Sexual Dysfunction, and general medical conditions and substances play no role in the etiology of the Sexual Dysfunction."[2] This category applies to most healthy young men.

But it does not apply for those who are using illicit drugs or alcohol in an abusive manner. For these men, the ingestion of such substances or even a medical condition may play a contributory role in the cause and maintenance of the erectile dysfunction. In such cases, the subtype **Due to Combined Factors** should be employed. The substances or illness are not sufficient by themselves to cause the dysfunction, but when combined with the psychological factors that are present in the man, the synergy is sufficient to result in erectile dysfunction.

The coincidence of drugs—even prescription drugs—and sex should not be overlooked when taking the evaluation history. When the erectile dysfunction is suspected to be due to combined factors, then the substance or medical conditions should also be targeted as situations to be addressed in the treatment plan.

BEYOND DIAGNOSIS: FORMULATION

Diagnoses are important tools for communication between clinicians and between clinicians and third-party payers. With a codified three-digit number (extended to two decimal points) and a text label, much information can be conveyed. In some diagnoses, such as the ones for sexual disorders, the addition of subtypes further amplifies the data conveyed. However, what is not conveyed in the *DSM* diagnosis is the complexity of the person who carries the diagnosis. Absent are the wonderful depth and texture of the human psyche, its embodied expressions in sexual gestures and attempted bondings, and its interactions with the equally complex persons labeled mother, father, lover, or spouse. This is not the task of the diagnosis; it is the task of the formulation.

The formulation of the patient is a paragraph statement in which the clinician describes the factors in the patient's life that have combined to bring him to this disorder. It is, of course, professional grandiosity to think that one could do this in a mere paragraph. But the discipline of attempting to do it over and over again teaches us to think critically, to describe the interaction of biological, psychological, and social factors. The formulation is the clinician's understanding of the patient. In concise clarity, it supports the diagnosis and gives direction to the treatment plan. Most important, it protects both the novice and the experienced clinician from acting upon a treatment plan without all the information being considered.

THE PERSPECTIVES

I and most of my colleagues in the Department of Psychiatry employ a methodology called the perspectives. It is based on a biopsychosocial understanding of sexual dysfunction.[3,4] The perspectives methodology provides a structured approach to the biopsychosocial model, helping the clinician utilize the essential insight that human sexual behavior is the result of the interaction of multiple factors in the biological, psychological, and social/cultural domains.

The perspectives methodology was developed by Paul McHugh, formerly chair of the Department of Psychiatry at Hopkins and the director of Residency Training.[5] The methodology emerged from nearly 15 years of teaching residents, psychologists, and social workers about psychiatric disorders. It structures the formulation by providing four perspectives with which to examine a clinical case: disease, dimension, behavior, and life-story. (see table 13.1) By employing each of these perspectives, you can garner complementary and comprehensive information. I will go over this with you one perspective at a time.

Disease Perspective

This perspective looks for any somatic bases of psychiatric disorders as they lead to abnormal physiology. Bipolar Disorder is a clear example of how irregular central nervous system functioning results in the affective illness. Applied to erectile dysfunction, the disease perspective looks for somatic causes. Is some quiet disease process starting in this apparently healthy young man? Is he taking or abusing any substances—for example, alcohol or nicotine—that would contribute to poor erectile functioning?

TABLE 13.1. An Overview of the Perspectives[6]

Perspective	Logic	What the Patient___	Treatment
Disease	Categories	Has	Alleviate or cure
Dimension	Gradation and quantification	Is	Assist in adaptation and response
Behavior	Goal directed, teleological	Does	Interrupt, replace behaviors
Life Story	Narrative	Encounters and gives meaning to	Reinterpret or reconstruct narrative

If a man has not had a complete physical examination in the past 2 years (not merely a routine pre-employment physical), it is good practice to advise him to have a complete physical with his primary care physician (PCP). This should clear up any concern that a disease process is implicated and should allow both the therapist and the man to focus on the psychological and behavioral aspects of treatment. Establishing a relationship with the PCP in connection with a sexual problem also lays the ground for further collaboration between a nonphysician mental health provider and the PCP, should a somatic treatment such as Viagra be incorporated in the treatment.

Regarding the taking of substances that may interfere with erectile dysfunction, it is necessary that the clinician inquire about these behaviors in the initial evaluation and history. You should assume that alcohol consumption will be underreported and that drug use will be downplayed, if not hidden altogether. Thus if there is any use of substances whose level as reported is suspicious, presume that it is a contributing factor to the erectile dysfunction. As one asks questions about substance use, it is a good opportunity to use the information to "remind" the man that alcohol and nicotine consumption are risk factors for developing erectile dysfunction.

> In taking Bill's history, I learned that his father may have been depressed and that, in any case, his father had a problem with drinking too much. For his part, Bill had no neurovegative signs of major depression—for example, poor sleep, poor appetite, anhedonia. But he did say that from time to time, he wondered whether his alcohol consumption was beginning to be problematic. He was drinking three or four glasses of wine when out socially with Maria. I took the opportunity to tell him that alcohol might very well decrease his ability to maintain an erection and, given his father's history, limiting himself to one or two 4-ounce glasses an evening was in order. He did not smoke or use illicit drugs, except for using cannabis in college on about 20 to 30 occasions.
>
> Because the erectile dysfunction did not occur only after consuming alcohol, I did not think that alcohol had a significant contributing role in the problem. Although there was a history of possible depression in Bill's

family, neither his past history, nor his reaction to the breakup of his mar-
riage, nor his mental status examination indicated that he had a major
depression in the past or at present.

In Bill's case, the disease perspective sounded some warnings, but did not indicate to me that his erectile dysfunction was caused by biological factors. I would have to keep a watch on his alcohol consumption during the course of therapy.

Dimension Perspective

The dimension perspective measures traits and behaviors and gives a quantified result to the clinician and patient. Ideally, it measures constructs such as personality traits, intelligence, and frequency, intensity, and duration of behaviors and compares them to normal samples when available. The dimension perspective is useful in identifying the strengths and vulnerabilities of the patient, especially in specific stressful situations. For the man with erectile dysfunction, sex is obviously a stressful situation.

> *Bill completed three inventories that provided information helpful to un-*
> *derstanding his sexual and relational problem: the Brief Symptom Inven-*
> *tory (BSI) to measure current emotional distress,[7] the NEO-PI-R for a*
> *five-factor personality measurement,[8] and the CAGE Questionnaire[9] for*
> *alcohol consumption behaviors.*
>
> *On the BSI, Bill indicated that he was anxious during the past 7 days*
> *but not at a level that suggested he had a severe anxiety problem. Rather,*
> *the self-report BSI seemed to support the impression he had made on me*
> *and the way he had described his emotions to me in the mental status*
> *examination: he was worried about his sexual function and the future of*
> *the relationship with Maria, but his anxiety was not interfering with his*
> *work or his sleep patterns. It was reassuring to have the confirmatory in-*
> *formation.*
>
> *Bill's CAGE confirmed his question whether or not he was tending to*
> *drink too much when he was out socially with Maria. He responded nega-*
> *tively to the CAGE's last three questions, positively only to the first ques-*
> *tion, "Have you ever felt you should cut down on your drinking?" This*
> *suggested that the drinking should be monitored as therapy progressed,*
> *but also that Bill was probably a reliable informant on his drinking behav-*
> *ior.*
>
> *It was on the personality inventory that using the dimension perspec-*
> *tive yielded important information I had not gleaned during my evalua-*
> *tion interview with Bill. Bill's NEO-PI-R profile was notable for his average*
> *neuroticism scores, his high extroversion, and his low agreeableness. The*
> *average neuroticism scales again confirmed that Bill did not chronically*
> *have negative emotions such as depression, anxiety, and vulnerability.*

His high extroversion was concordant with my impressions of him as he described his occupational work, sale management. His low agreeableness indicated that he was quite self-centered and sought to take care of his own needs prior to those of other persons. Suddenly, I recalled Bill saying how surprised he was by his wife's infidelity and that he thought they had a very happy marriage. He obviously had not been paying attention to his wife's probable unhappiness. Also, the suicidal thoughts were blocked not by the harm his suicidal abandonment would inflict upon the children, but by the more self-directed need to have them think well of him. The personality trait of narcissism seemed to fit Bill. Without the NEO-PI-R, it may have taken several sessions to see this trait in him and how it may have affected his relationship not only with his ex-wife, but also with Maria.

Personality measurements such as the NEO-PI-R suggest how much the therapy should focus on interpersonal issues, as compared to a narrower focus on sexual issues. Although on the group level little correlation has been shown between specific personality profiles and specific sexual dysfunctions, my colleagues and I have suggested that individual profiles can contribute greatly to the formulation and treatment.[10,11]

In every evaluation, there should be some measure of the patient's intelligence. In the days of health dollar affluence, a full psychological battery would have included a Weschler Adult Intelligence Scale (WAIS), which would have given a comprehensive measurement of how the subject used his intelligence to engage with his world. Today, however, formal measurements of intelligence are limited mainly to forensic and mental retardation cases. This does not mean that the level of intelligence should not be assessed in every treatment case. This can be done by noting educational level achieved, use of vocabulary, and with some persons who are deficient in these two for social reasons, other evidence from the patient's occupation or "street smarts."

Intelligence level, as applied to psychogenic impotence in relatively young men, will dictate much of the treatment modality. The free use of images, such as the turtle spoken of previously, are helpful with both the bright and the low normal patient. The lower the intelligence, however, the more behavioral and concrete the therapy should be. Thus clear behavioral goals, with minimal theoretical explanation, will typify treatment of a man with lower intelligence. The higher the intelligence, the more the therapy can utilize abstract concepts, such as those involved in discussion of relationship, and can elaborate on the multiple factors in the erectile dysfunction.

Bill's bachelor's degree in business and marketing, as well as his occupational success since graduating, supported the fact that his intelligence was above average, probably in I.Q. range of 115 to 120. To the extent that his defense systems—especially those that served to protect narcissistic insult—would allow, I would be able to move the psychotherapy in directions that required ability to process abstract and subtle aspects of relations.

Behavior Perspective

The behavior perspective is concerned about what a person does. To the extent that the behaviors are maladaptive or problematic, the behavior perspective seeks to replace the behaviors with ones that are more in keeping with the individual's desired goals. If desired behaviors are absent, the perspective seeks to set the conditions that would facilitate their emergence. For example, relaxation is a requisite condition for sexual arousal. Specific attitudes and behaviors will facilitate that relaxation—for example, a nondemanding and trusting cognitive mindset and gentle, sensual touching and caressing of the body. To the extent that these prerequisites are absent, the behavior perspective would seek to suggest methods to bring them into the sexual setting.

The behavior perspective employs traditional behavioral methods and seeks to identify the antecedents and consequences of the behaviors in question. This means that the man must describe to the therapist exactly what he means by, "I cannot get/ keep an erection when I try to have sex." To give a further behavioral description, the man will be aided by a structured series of questions that have been generically called the sexual status exam. (A sample form is found in table 13.2.) This can be adapted and modified according to the circumstances of the case. I offer it to suggest the type of questions that should be asked to gain a full picture of what behaviorally happens when the sexual dysfunction occurs. Please don't try to memorize these questions.

A semistructured interview such as the sexual status examination quantifies the behaviors that are present. Once identified, the antecedent behaviors that trigger intrapsychic anxiety or interpersonal tension are labeled as ones to be avoided. The preconditions that facilitate arousal should be amplified or introduced. Can you see how the consequences of the failure in sexual activity—for example, increased interpersonal tension and lowered self-esteem—become the antecedent factors in the subsequent sexual activities?

There is a distinction between the factors that initially cause a behavior and those factors that maintain it as a patterned behavior. A clear example of this is often seen in erectile dysfunction. A man may have attempted sex with a desirable (and perhaps new) partner after having consumed much alcohol. Though the desire was high, the erection was not. He may have experienced much embarrassment and shame. That may have been the "first straw" that broke off the relationship. Subsequently, the man thinks about this grand failure each time he thinks about having sex. He becomes preoccupied with it and thinks more about not getting an erection or losing it then he does about the attractiveness of his partner. His impotence continues.

The factor that started the dysfunction was his excessive alcohol ingestion. The factor that keeps the impotence going is his performance anxiety. Although the man may wish to focus on the original traumatic event, it is more effective to address the anxiety in the present sexual encounters.

What, you might ask, are the treatment aspects of the behavior perspective? What does one do with the information that one obtains from the sexual status examination? The most elaborate development of the behavioral treatment of psychogenic impotence is sensate focus therapy. Originally developed in the 1960s by William Masters

TABLE 13.2. The Sexual Status Exam

Please recall the last time you tried to have sex with your partner.

Before sex: How long ago did you last try to have sex? What time was it? Were you tired? Had you been drinking alcohol or using drugs? Where were you? Did you have any concerns about privacy? Were the lights on? Were there any possible distractions—for example, telephone, television, children, pets? Was any contraception involved? Did you have any concerns about sexually transmitted disease? Concerns about pregnancy or desire for pregnancy? What was your emotional relationship with your partner like, prior to attempting to have sex? Did either one of you want to have sex more than the other did?

During sex: Who initiated the sexual activity? By what means; what were the signals or words? How much clothing/nudity were involved? Please describe the type of touching and sexual contact that occurred between you. What was the reaction of your partner to these contacts? How long did the activity go on? What were you thinking about? Was your penis starting to get firm? How firm? (At this point, I hold a pen between his thumb and index finger and gradually bring it from a 6 o'clock straight down position up to an 11 o'clock position. Doing this, I ask, " If you were standing up with that erection, at what point would the erection be?" This is a much more reliable method of assessing tumescence than asking the man what percentage of fullness the erection was. Quite honestly, I am not sure what to make of the report of a 60% full erection.) Do you think the erection was firm enough for penetration? How long did the erection last? What was happening between both of you when the erection started to go down?

If penetration was attempted or occurred: Who decided that penetration would be attempted? How was this communicated between you and your partner? How long did the penetration last? Were there repeated penetrations? If so, how was this decided between you and your partner? During this sexual engagement, how many erections did you have?

Did either you or your partner have an orgasm? If so, by what means did each of you experience your orgasm? Did your orgasm occur within your partner?

After sex: What did you do after you lost/did not attain an erection? What did your partner do? How did each of you feel? Was anything said? Did you discuss or mention this or other failures at a subsequent nonsexual time?

What do you think went wrong?

and Virginia Johnson[12] and later adapted by others,[13,14] sensate focus therapy facilitates learning how to give and receive sensual and sexual pleasure between partners. It helps couples identify the helpful antecedents of sexual pleasure as well and the behaviors that facilitate it for each partner. I will say more about this type of treatment later.

Life Story Perspective

In the case of psychogenic impotence in a relatively young man, the life story perspective inquires about the sexual scripts that the man uses when thinking about sex or when involved in sexual activity. Developers John Gagnon and William Simon offered the following description, "Scripts are involved in learning the meaning of internal states, organizing the sequences of specifically sexual acts, decoding novel situations, setting the limits on sexual responses and linking meanings from nonsexual aspects of life to specifically sexual experience."[15,16]

Although the sexual status examination focuses primarily on the behaviors involved in sexual activity, sexual scripts focus on the perception and interpretation of the sexual behaviors. In general, the life story perspective asks, "What does this sexual activity mean to you? Why are you attempting to do it? What does it say about you and the rest of your life?" The sexual script is the response the man makes to those questions.

The sexual script cannot be assessed in a single meeting between therapist and patient. A careful listening to the sexual status examination can generate hints or hypotheses. But it takes a full and oft-revisited psychosexual history for the man to tell the narrative of his sexuality. He tells the story in therapy. He discovers the story's limitations and, perhaps, its lack of meaning for his future. The therapist works with him to develop a new narrative, a new sexual script that will both give authentic meaning to his sexual efforts and give direction to his future. In this process of listening and eliciting meaning, the therapist will be careful to ensure that the new script and the new narrative are based on what emerges from the constructs of the man meeting his real world, rather than from an imposition of meaning from the narrative world of the therapist. A very helpful and enjoyable example of a skilled therapist and author who describes this role is found in *The Pornographer's Grief and Other Tales of Human Sexuality*.[17]

There are developmental issues that most men face in their younger adulthood that may be expressed in erectile dysfunction. Erection problems are more likely if there is a high level of conflict and anxiety about one of these development tasks. The principal tasks facing heterosexuals are developing a sexual relationship with the other gender, commitment and marriage, and the generativity of having children. Emotional conflicts in any of these issues are obscured when problems with erections occur. The erectile dysfunction provides a secondary gain of not having to more intimately face the particular task.

If the man with erectile problems has a relationship with a woman that is colored by fear, dislike, or an excessive desire to please her, then those issues must be addressed. It often happens that the man presents himself as a "feminist," a gentle guy who is concerned about the welfare of his wife or girlfriend. Behind this persona may lie many conflicts about his role with women. The assertiveness required in sexual activity may be bringing these conflicts too close to his awareness. Erectile dysfunction provides a compromise cover. In any case, the woman—wife or girlfriend—often reacts to him as being a "nice boy" rather than a "good man." With this appreciation, her sexual attraction to him wanes accordingly.

Similarly, the man who fears commitment and entering marriage may have his ambivalence disguised by erectile dysfunction. The sexual problem becomes the focus of the man's attention and the rationale why he cannot make further commitment to the woman he loves. Erection and intercourse on an emotional level appear to the man as plunging him into the abyss of committed possession by the other. In the initial stages of therapy, the penis may have a better appreciation of this fear than the brain does. The turtle knows when to pull its head in.

Finally, the developmental task of generativity requires that a young adult man ask and answer the question of whether he will attempt to have children or not. Although in the broader sense, generativity refers to all fruits of life's labor a person gives to successive generations, in the biological sense it refers to children. One certainly need not have children to be generative. But one must answer the question of whether one actively wants to have children or not. Ambivalence about assuming the state of fatherhood may underlie erectile dysfunction in some men. In this case, as in the instances of fear of women and of commitment, it makes more clinical sense to address these questions of meaning in individual or group therapy (without the partner). In couple therapy, candor may be impeded.

In summary, the life story perspective is concerned primarily with the story that the man is telling and making in therapy. For our patients with psychogenic impotence, the perspective beckons the therapist and the man to explore the sexual scripts and meaning that he has been bringing to his sexual encounters.

BEYOND FORMULATION: TREATMENT

I have given considerable attention to the formulation issues involved in impotence in relatively young men. You might be asking, "What about treatment?" And rightly so. The purpose of this book is to encourage general mental health practitioners to treat many, if not most, sexual dysfunction problems that they encounter in their clients or patients.

My emphasis on formulation—that is, thinking about the particulars of the case, which for me is structured by the four perspectives—is the foundation of any treatment regimen. Treatment follows formulation and diagnosis. When it precedes formulation, it often rushes headlong into failure.

I suggest, then, that you take a complete history, a mental status examination, and a sexual status examination and use that information to construct a careful formulation. If you do this, developing a treatment plan will follow easily for you. Treatment of psychogenic impotence in relatively young men will parallel many of the main decisions that are made at the start of any course of psychotherapy. In those areas of psychotherapy that are particular to erectile dysfunction treatment, I cannot think of a better introduction than the chapter "Erectile Dysfunction: Psychotherapy with Men and Couples."[18]

TABLE 13.3. Bill's Formulation, Diagnosis, and Treatment Recommendations

Formulation history: Bill is a 35-year-old white heterosexual divorced male who presents for evaluation with erectile dysfunction of 8 months' duration. Two years prior, his wife left him and their three children for another man. This "devastated and totally surprised" Bill. After the divorce he began dating and being sexually active without sexual dysfunction. Early in the relationship with his present partner, Maria, he likewise had no sexual problem, but as this relationship has gotten more serious, he has experienced episodic erectile dysfunction. This disturbs him greatly because he fears losing Maria.

On personality and psychological inventories, Bill reports himself to be the extroverted interpersonal style with moderately high state anxiety. Notably, his low agreeableness strongly suggests narcissistic personality traits.

Bill has no medical problems. He has refused Viagra, wanting to have intercourse without any medical aid. He drinks moderately, but does not become intoxicated.

Upon mental status examination, Bill was casually dressed, cooperative, with slightly agitated movements. His speech was goal directed, with slightly rapid rate. Neurovegetative symptoms and suicidality were denied, as well as any cognitive problems and obsessions, compulsions, and phobia. His intelligence was above average. His psychological mindedness was average at best.

Formulation impression: Bill's impotence appears to be psychogenic and reactive to the emotional trauma (narcissistic injury) caused by his wife's infidelity. As the relationship with Maria has gotten more serious, issues of trust and past trauma (infidelity and divorce) have become more salient and conflicted for Bill. He was able to accept this understanding of his impotence and would like to address it in individual therapy. He has limited awareness that he may have been too self-absorbed to see signs of his wife's dissatisfaction with him and their marriage. His prognosis is good for therapy collaboration and for the resolution of his erectile problem.

Diagnosis: Axis I: Male Erectile Disorder, 302.72, Acquired Type, Situational, Due to Psychological Factors Axis II: deferred, narcissistic personality traits

Recommended treatment: Brief individual cognitive behavioral therapy to address the acquired impotence (< 20 sessions). Then, if desired and can be afforded, open-ended insight-oriented therapy to address personality trait issues such as narcissism (> 1 year).

Treatment Modalities: Individual, Couple, and Group Therapy

Individual or **group therapy** or both are usually employed when the issues that contribute to the erectile dysfunction were present in the life of the man prior to any present relationship he may be having. Individual and group therapy are also the treatments of choice by default, of course, when the man is not in a relationship. The theoretical orientation of the therapist may be any of the established systems, such as psychoanalytic, existential, cognitive-behavioral, or any theory that can address the issues that were identified in the formulation. For example, if the etiology of the impotence has been hypothesized as rooted in avoidant personality traits, the theoretical orientation should provide the therapist with a way to assist the avoidant man to approach the person whom he both desires and fears.

Couple therapy is probably the treatment of choice when there is a willing partner and the preexisting conditions in the man are contributory but not sufficient in themselves to cause the erectile dysfunction. In couple therapy, relationship issues, such as emotional engagement versus distancing, are addressed, and in most situations a directed sensate focus therapy is used as one of the treatment components. What I suggest is a set of parameters that I use to qualify a couple as appropriate for sensate focus therapy. They are

1. Both partners are willing to participate in sensate focus therapy, with the agreed-upon goal of alleviating the sexual dysfunction(s) (and thereby increasing the sexual satisfaction of the couple).
2. The partners' level of estrangement or hostility is not so great as to prevent their collaboration in the sensate focus exercises. (If it is, then couple therapy without sensate focus therapy should be recommended to them.)
3. There is no untreated substance abuse disorder or untreated major mental illness in either partner.
4. There is no secret sexual relationship or paraphilic behavior that is continuing.
5. The couple is in a committed, cohabitating relationship. (My experience is that when this condition is not met, the sexual dysfunction is a distraction from the primary issues relating to partner choice and commitment to the relationship.)
6. The couple can and does pay for the therapy. (With nearly all third-party payers excluding marital and sexual therapy, the fees are a considerable financial commitment for most couples. They may be prohibitive for some; for others, the decision to pay may be the first step in committing to the therapeutic process.)

There is no reason why individual, group, and couple therapy cannot be used as concurrent treatment arms. There must, however, be a reason for each arm. If there are multiple therapists, they should have established patterns of communicating about their part of the treatment to the other therapist(s). Although many therapists treat their clients/patients in concurrent individual and couple therapy, I prefer to see couples as a couple and ask another therapist to assume the individual treatment of the partners. This helps me view them as an interactive system and not get overinvested in either partner, to the detriment of my concern for the other.

What About Somatic Treatments of Psychogenic Impotence?

If psychogenic impotence is, by definition, a condition caused primarily by the psyche, the question arises, "What about those medical interventions that have physiological effects?" Can they, should they be used for psychogenic impotence? Isn't it a medical or somatic treatment for a condition that is essentially psychological?

The fact is that they are being used, and used successfully, by men with psychogenic impotence. The oral agents, such as Viagra, Uprima, Cialis, and others in development, will continue to be used. So will vacuum devices, penile injections, and urethral suppositories employed by men who are uncertain as to why they are impotent. They will use them because somatic interventions work. At least, most of the time . . . .

When they don't work, the mental health clinician will be consulted because the sexual problem persists. Also, when an initial evaluation is completed, the question of their use will be "in the air" and should be addressed.

When They Don't Work

Although the somatic interventions have efficacy rates ranging from 44% to 91%, sometimes as high as 50% of the men discontinue treatment in some cases.[19] Thus, in terms of overall effectiveness in the bedroom, perhaps less than half of the men who start oral medications, injections, vacuum pumps, and urethral suppositories continue using them. In addition to the anxiety that can override the effectiveness of the pharmacology, clearly there are also problems in the integration of these aids into the sexual scripts of the couple. For example, the use of the somatic intervention may be the idea of one partner only. In a common scenario, the man unilaterally initiates treatment that produces an erection reliably. Unfortunately, his partner—usually his wife—has grown accustomed to a marriage without penetrative intercourse. Now *he* has the erection; *they* are not in agreement about what to do with it.

My experience with the successful integration of somatic treatments into the sexual scripts of couples results from the successful resolution of two issues. First, when the couple has a committed relationship, the decision to use the somatic aid is jointly made by the couple. Second, the couple has recognized the need for external assistance for sexual arousal. For the man, this means accepting help in doing something that almost all men consider their responsibility to achieve on their own. For the partner, this means accepting that the arousal is not caused totally by the man's desire to be sexually engaged with her or him.

When They Should Be Integrated into Therapy

Stanley Althof has suggested helpful guidelines for the integration of somatic interventions into the psychotherapy of erectile dysfunction.[20] Those men who are appropriate for the adjunctive medical interventions have any of the following: (1) lifelong or primary erectile dysfunction; (2) low self-confidence as a sexual partner and poor communication skills (here I would add that they are alexithymic, i.e., have emotions, but do not have words to express them); (3) some biological or medical factors that contribute to the erectile dysfunction; or (4) past psychotherapy that has been competent but not effective. Those who are not appropriate candidates for somatic aids are (1) men whose impotence has been recent, sudden, and without any biogenic factors; (2) couples with severe marital discord; (3) young men with performance anxiety; and, of course, (4) those who have objection to using the somatic aids.

In practice it is helpful to review the somatic options with the man at the conclusion of the evaluation. Mental health clinicians should have a working knowledge of what those options are. A resource for this is the excellent chapter "Medical and Psychological Interventions for Erectile Dysfunction: Toward a Combined Treatment Approach," by Raymond Rosen (2). Beyond the working knowledge of the options, it is also helpful for the mental health clinician to have a good working relationship with a primary care physician or a urologist who has an interest in or, better still, a specialty in the urological treatment of erectile dysfunction.

SUMMARY

Psychological impotence in relatively young men is a problem that can cause great distress to a man and his partner. When considering treating this problem, the mental health clinician should first to take a comprehensive history, a sexual status examination, and a mental status examination in the initial evaluation. The impressions of these three procedures should be organized and stated in a formulation of the case. I have suggested that one methodology for organizing the formulation is the four perspectives model. Treatment modalities should reflect the content of the formulation. At the risk of not treating psychological problems that will persist, adjunctive medical interventions should be used only with those men for whom such somatic aids are appropriate.

NOTES

1. American Psychiatric Association. (1994). *Diagnostic and Statistical Manual of Mental Disorders*. Washington, DC: Author.
2. Ibid.
3. Rosen, R. C. (2000). Medical and psychological interventions for erectile dysfunction. In S. R. Leiblum & R. C. Rosen (Eds.), *Principles and Practice of Sex Therapy* (pp. 276–304). New York: Guilford.
4. Ackerman, M., & Carey, M. (1995). Psychology's role in the assessment of erectile dysfunction: Historical precedents, current knowledge and methods. *Journal of Consulting Clinicial Psychology, 63,* 862–876.
5. McHugh, P. R., & Slavney, P. R. (1998). *The Perspectives in Psychiatry* (2nd ed.). Baltimore and London: Johns Hopkins University Press.
6. McHugh, P. R. (2001, June 15). Managed care and the four perspectives. (Report). Academic Behavioral Healthcare Consortium, editor. 6-15-2001.
7. Derogatis, L. R. (1993). *Brief Symptom Inventory (BSI (c)): Administration, Scoring and Procedures Manual*. Minneapolis: National Computer Systems.

8. Costa, P. T., & McCrae, R. R. (1992). *The NEO-PI-R: Professional Manual.* Odessa, FL: Psychological Assessment Resources.
9. Ewing, J. A. (1984). Detecting alcoholism: the CAGE Questionnaire. *Journal of the American Medical Association, 252*(14), 1905–1907.
10. Costa, P T., Fagan, P. J., Piedmont, R. L., Ponticas, Y., & Wise, T. N. (1992). The Five-Factor Model of personality and sexual functioning in outpatient men and women. *Psychiatric Medicine, 10,* 199–215.
11. Fagan, P. J., Wise, T. N., Schmidt, C. W., Ponticas, Y., Marshall, R. D., & Costa, P. T. (1991). A comparison of five-factor personality dimensions in males with sexual dysfunction and males with paraphilia. *Journal of Personality Assessment,* 434–448.
12. Masters, W. H., & Johnson, V. E. (1970). *Human Sexual Inadequacy.* New York: Little, Brown.
13. Hawton, K. (1985). *Sex Therapy: A Practical Guide.* Northvale, NJ: Aronson.
14. Wincze, J. P., & Carey, M. P. (2001). *Sexual Dysfunction: A Guide for Assessment and Treatment* (2nd ed.). New York: Guilford.
15. Gagnon, J. H., & Simon, W. (1974). *Sexual Conduct* (pp. 17). Chicago: Aldine.
16. Gagnon, J. H. (1990). The explicit and implicit use of the scripting perspective in sex research. *Annual Review of Sex Research, 1,* 1–43.
17. Glenmullen, J. (1993). *The Pornographer's Grief and Other Tales of Human Sexuality.* New York: HarperCollins.
18. Althof, S. (2000). Erectile dysfunction: Psychotherapy with men and couples. In S. R. Leiblum & R. C. Rosen (Eds.), *Principles and Practice of Sex Therapy* (pp. 242–275). New York: Guilford.
19. Althof, S., Turner, L., Levine, S., Risen, C., Bodner, D., & Resnick, M. (1989). Why do so many men drop out of auto-injection therapy for impotence? *Journal of Sex & Marital Therapy, 15,* 121–129.
20. Althof, S. (2000). Erectile dysfunction: Psychotherapy with men and couples. In S. R. Leiblum & R. C. Rosen (Eds.), *Principles and Practice of Sex Therapy* (pp. 242–275). New York: Guilford.

Chapter Fourteen

Erectile Dysfunction in Middle-Aged and Older Men

Raymond C. Rosen, PhD

PREFACE

I have long been involved with sexual research, sexual education, and sexual therapy. For the last several decades my interests have heavily focused on sexual pharmacology. I have had the privilege to participate in the design and the conduct of clinical trials of sildenafil and other prosexual drugs. In this chapter, I hope to share my experiences with you as a "supervisor," to assist you in the evaluation and conduct of your early cases of older single men and couples with erectile dysfunction (ED). Although I use only heterosexual examples in my discussion, please remember that older homosexual men are not in any way exempt from the biological, psychological, and interpersonal forces discussed here.

CASE VIGNETTE #1

Dan B. is a 58-year-old married accountant with a 4-year history of erectile dysfunction. He reports increasing difficulty in achieving or maintaining erections and has not had sexual intercourse for the past 18 months. Sexual desire has also declined, although he misses the physical and emotional intimacy of sex. His wife, Betty, has also experienced a loss of sexual desire and has difficulty in becoming sexually aroused since the onset of her menopause 5 years ago. However, she reports some improvement in these symptoms since she began taking hormone replacement therapy in the past year. The couple has two grown children. The two enjoy a close relationship in other respects.

Dan's medical history is significant for hypertension for the past 10 years. He has been treated with several medications, including diuretics and beta-blockers, and has been attempting to lose weight (current weight = 215 lbs.). He has also been diagnosed with hypercholesterolemia and is

currently taking a lipid-lowering medication (lovastatin) for this problem.
Dan's work situation is moderately stressful, particularly since the account-
ing investigations of recent months. He is mildly depressed and has expe-
rienced sleep difficulties and loss of energy for the past year.

     Dan's erectile difficulties were uncovered during an office visit with
his family physician. After ordering routine blood tests (testosterone, blood
sugar), his physician prescribed Viagra (50–100 mg) and scheduled a re-
turn visit 1 month later with Dan and Betty. On their return, the couple
reported that the medication had been partially successful in restoring
Dan's erections, but that the couple was having difficulty initiating sex.
Betty, in particular, had little interest in sex and felt guilty in rejecting
Dan's initiatives. At this point, the couple was referred for conjoint sex
therapy.

Background and Overview

Erectile dysfunction is a common sexual complaint in middle-aged and older men that
has received increasing public and professional attention since the approval of sildenafil
citrate (Viagra) in 1998. In the Massachusetts Male Aging Study (MMAS), a community-based survey of men between the ages of 40 and 70 years (Feldman et al., 1994),
52% of respondents reported some degree of erectile difficulty. Complete erectile dysfunction, defined as the total inability to obtain or maintain erections during sexual
stimulation, as well as the absence of nocturnal erections, occurred in 10% of respondents. Lesser degrees of mild and moderate erectile dysfunction occurred in 17% and
25%, respectively. A strong relationship to age was observed in both the frequency and
the severity of erectile problems. Although the prevalence of mild ED remained constant (17%) between the ages of 40 and 70, there was a doubling in the number of men
reporting moderate erectile dysfunction (17% to 34%) and a tripling of complete ED
(5% to 15%) in the older age group. Similar findings have been reported in other large-
scale epidemiological studies (Dunn, Croft, & Hackett, 1999; Laumann, Paik, & Rosen,
1999). If the MMAS data are extrapolated to the general population, there are an estimated 18 to 30 million American men who are affected by ED.

    Erectile dysfunction is strongly related to both physical and psychological risk
factors. Among the main predictors of ED observed in the MMAS (Feldman et al., 1994),
diabetes mellitus, heart disease, hypertension, and decreased HDL levels were all associated with increased risk for the disorder. Recent studies have shown a strong association between ED and benign prostatic hypertrophy (BPH), another common disorder in
older men (Brookes et al., 2002). Medications for diabetes, hypertension, and cardiovascular disease are other major risk factors. In addition, there is a higher prevalence of
ED among men who have undergone radiation or surgery for prostate cancer (Goldstein
et al., 1984; Quinlan, Epstein, Carter, & Walsh, 1991). The psychological correlates of
erectile dysfunction include anxiety, depression, and anger (Araujo et al., 1998; Feldman
et al., 1994). Lifestyle factors, such as smoking and lack of exercise, have also been

implicated. One large-scale epidemiological study found a higher rate of erectile difficulties among men who reported poor to fair health and among men experiencing stress from unemployment or other causes (Laumann et al., 1994). Despite its increasing prevalence among older men, ED is not considered a normal or inevitable part of the aging process. It is rarely (in fewer than 5% of cases) due to aging-related hypogonadism (Korenman et al., 1990; Schiavi, 1990), although the relationship between ED and age-related declines in androgen remains controversial (Zonszein, 1995).

How bothered or distressed are middle-aged or older men by their erectile difficulties? Although half or more of all men older than 50 suffer from ED, the amount of psychological distress or motivation for treatment varies widely. According to one recent study, the level of distress associated with ED is much higher in the 50 to 59-year-old group, compared to men in their 60s or 70s (Blanker et al., 2001). Thus, although there is a positive correlation between age and the occurrence of ED, the amount of psychological distress or bother associated with the disorder is inversely related to age. In this study, less than 25% of men older than 70 were sufficiently distressed to seek treatment for their erectile difficulties. In the author's experience, partner needs and availability are major determinants of the amount of psychological distress associated with ED in older men. Men without partners, or those whose partners are not sexually interested or available, are much less likely to seek treatment for ED. This observation needs to be taken into account in interpreting the results of the previously mentioned epidemiological studies.

Major changes have taken place in the medical management of ED since the approval of sildenafil (Viagra). The advent of Viagra has greatly increased the number of older men seeking treatment and has significantly altered the medical and psychological management of the disorder. Historically the province of urologists and sex therapists, ED is now managed predominantly by primary care practitioners. In recognition of this trend, simplified assessment and treatment models have been proposed by several authors (Jardin, Wagner, Khoury et al., 2000; Process of Care Consensus Panel, 1999). These new treatment models strongly emphasize the need for sexual inquiry in all middle-aged and older men but deemphasize the value of intensive medical or psychological assessment in most cases. Costly and potentially invasive diagnostic procedures, such as penile cavernosography or cavernosometry, once the mainstay of urological assessment of ED, are seldom performed nowadays. Nocturnal penile tumescence (NPT) testing, another common procedure of the 1980s and early 1990s, is infrequently performed. Instead, new management guidelines emphasize the need for a brief sexual and medical history, a physical examination, and standard laboratory tests to rule out diabetes, dyslipidemia, or hypogonadism (Process of Care Consensus Panel, 1999). Specialized diagnostic testing is reserved for more complicated or treatment-resistant patients. In reality, most middle-aged men with ED now receive a prescription for Viagra, with little or no systematic evaluation. Further diagnostic studies are usually reserved for those patients who fail to respond to an initial trial of Viagra.

On the treatment side, the vast majority of men receive oral therapy (i.e., Viagra) as first-line treatment for ED. Although treatment guidelines recommend sex or marital therapy or the use of vacuum pump devices (VCDs) as alternative first-line therapies, these are far less widely used. The simplicity and ease of use of an oral therapy are major advantages, particularly for primary care physicians with little training or interest in sexual dysfunction. Referral to a sex therapist or a mental health professional is likely to occur only when couples or psychological issues present a major obstacle to treatment or when Viagra fails. Referrals for other urological treatments (e.g., intracorporal injection, penile implant surgery) are similarly reserved for Viagra treatment failures, for the most part.

Returning to our previous case vignette, we see a number of these current trends at play. Dan's problem was first identified by his primary care physician in the context of a follow-up visit for hypertension and cholesterol management. After taking a brief sexual history and ordering some simple laboratory tests, the physician recommended a trial of Viagra. Little or no attempt was made to identify the specific cause of the patient's ED. Was it due to his cardiovascular disease (hypertension, hypercholesterolemia), mild depression and work stress, or couples' issues? Could his cardiovascular medications be contributing to the problem? How important were psychological factors? No attempt was made to pursue these questions before starting Dan on Viagra. Had he responded positively to the drug, it is unlikely that these questions would ever have been addressed. On the other hand, his physician deserves credit for seeing Dan and his wife, Betty, together at the follow-up visit. This is relatively uncommon in clinical practice today. At this follow-up visit, it became evident that Betty's sexual difficulties were contributing to her husband's ED, and the physician responded appropriately with a referral for couples' counseling. Because middle-aged or older men with ED are treated predominantly with medical or surgical treatments, we will consider these briefly before discussing the role of couples' or psychological approaches.

Oral Erectogenic Agents

Phosphodiesterase Type-5 Inhibitors (Sildenafil).   Normal penile erection depends on the relaxation of smooth muscles in the penile corpora (Burnett, 1995; Rajfer, Aronson, Bush, Dorey, & Ignarro, 1992). In response to sexual stimulation, cavernous nerves and endothelial cells release nitric oxide, which stimulates the formation of cyclic guanosine monophosphate (GMP) by guanylate cyclase, which in turn causes vasodilation and relaxation of the coporal smooth muscle tissue. Sildenafil citrate is a selective inhibitor of cyclic GMP-specific phosphodiesterase type-5. By selectively inhibiting cyclic-GMP catabolism in cavernosal smooth-muscle cells, sildenafil restores the natural erectile response to sexual stimulation but does not cause erection in the absence of sexual stimulation. Sildenafil is rapidly absorbed, with maximal plasma concentrations occurring within 1 hour after oral administration and a mean terminal half-life of 3–5 hours. Cardiac safety does not appear to be a major concern, based on current evidence, except for patients receiving nitrates in any form, or who have other cardiac risk factors associated with sexual activity itself (DeBusk et al., 2000). Sildenafil is contraindicated for men receiving nitrate therapy, including short- or long-acting agents delivered by oral, sublingual, transnasal, or topical administration. The drug's side effects include headaches, flushing, dyspepsia, and nasal congestion. A small percentage of men (2–3%) may also experience mild alterations in color vision (blue hue), visual brightness or sensitivity, or blurred vision.

The safety and efficacy of sildenafil have been investigated in a large number of controlled clinical trials in middle-aged and older males with ED of varying etiologies (see Rosen & McKenna, in press). In two large-scale, multicenter trials sildenafil was administered in doses of 25 mg, 50 mg, and 100 mg, compared to placebo, in either a fixed dose or flexible dose regimen (Goldstein et al., 1998). The majority of patients in both studies was judged to have ED of organic etiology (70%), with fewer patients having psychogenic (11%) or mixed (18%) etiologies. Both studies showed significant dose-related improvements for all measures of erectile function and treatment satisfaction with each of the sildenafil doses, compared to placebo. Headache, flushing, and dyspepsia were the most common adverse effects in the dose-escalation study, occurring in 6% to 18% of the men. Other studies have evaluated the safety and efficacy of sildenafil in patients with cardiac disease, diabetes, spinal cord injury and other neurological diseases, and depression (Rosen & McKenna, in press).

Based upon results of these and other controlled clinical trials, meta-analyses have been performed on treatment outcome with sildenafil as a function of age, severity of erectile dysfunction, and type of etiology. Age was not a significant predictor of treatment responsiveness. Patients over the age of 65 show approximately the same ratio of treatment efficacy, compared to placebo, as do patients under the age of 65. Regarding the effects of disease severity on treatment outcome, patients with mild ED showed a slightly higher rate of improvement with sildenafil treatment, compared to patients with moderate or severe ED. On the other hand, patients with mild or moderate ED also showed higher rates of response to placebo than did patients with severe ED. If one takes into account the relative placebo response compared to active treatment in each group, there is no evidence of improved treatment outcome as a function of disease severity. In other words, sildenafil is highly effective in older men (>age 65) and in patients with more severe degrees of ED. Regarding etiology, patients with ED due to psychogenic factors or spinal-cord injury were found to have the most positive treatment response (approximately 80% improvement), whereas those with chronic diabetes or radical prostatectomy responded least favorably (<50%).

Sildenafil's safety has been the topic of much controversy and debate. Based upon adverse events reported in the main clinical trials, the drug has an acceptable overall safety profile. To date, the most frequent adverse events reported were headache, flushing, dyspepsia, rhinitis, and visual disturbances. In the dose escalation and open label studies, these side effects were observed in less than 20% of patients and rarely resulted in drug discontinuation. Approximately 1–2% of patients withdrew from treatment due to drug side effects. Since approval, increasing concerns have been raised regarding the potential cardiac risks associated with sildenafil use. These risks have been reviewed by a consensus panel of the American College of Cardiology (ACC) (ACC/ AHAA Expert Consensus, 1999). The main conclusion of this panel was that sildenafil poses no special cardiac risk for the large majority of patients. However, the drug is absolutely contraindicated for patients taking nitrates in any form, due to the likely potentiation of hypotensive effects with these drugs. Sildenafil should also be used with caution in patients with a recent history of myocardial infarction (MI) or other significant cardiac conditions (e.g., unstable angina, congestive heart failure). Caution was also recommended in patients using multiple antihypertensive agents.

Other Oral Agents. Other orally administered drugs for ED are currently in advanced stages of development. Two additional PDE-5 inhibitors (tadalafil, vardenafil) have been developed and are currently under regulatory review. Tadalafil is a long-acting PDE-5 inhibitor, which is effective for up to 36 hours in the majority of men. Vardenafil has a similar duration of action to that of sildenafil but is more potent and selective biochemically. Both drugs appear to be highly effective and well-tolerated, with a similar side-effect profile to sildenafil. Both drugs are effective in older men with ED and may have superior efficacy in the treatment of men with comorbid medical conditions such as diabetes and prostate cancer. However, there are no controlled comparison studies with Viagra to date.

Other drugs in development are based on different mechanisms of action. For example, apomorphine is a dopamine agonist that is active in both D1 and D2 receptors. It is a well-known drug that has been used in the treatment of Parkinson's disease and other medical disorders since 1869. However, a novel sublingual formulation has been developed that appears to be both effective and safe for treatment of ED. The drug is available in Europe but has not yet been approved in the United States. The main side effects are nausea, which occurs in up to 20% of patients at higher doses, and syncope, which occurs in <2% of patients. Sublingual apomorphine is in advanced stages of clinical testing and may be available in 2003. Its efficacy in middle-aged and older men is uncertain. Again, there are no controlled comparison studies with Viagra.

Approval of these drugs in the near future is likely to further increase the number of men seeking treatment for ED and to reinforce the use of oral agents as first-line treatment for the disorder. Based on results of clinical trials to date, it is unclear whether any of these agents will offer significant advantages compared to Viagra in the treatment of middle-aged or older men with ED. The relative safety of these agents is also uncertain.

Local Pharmacological Therapies

In addition to oral drugs, locally applied pharmacological agents are also available. These treatments consist of intraurethral administration or intracavernosal injection of alprostadil. Although widely utilized, these treatments are associated with variable efficacy, a high patient discontinuation rate, possible risk of side effects, and moderately high cost. In the author's experience, local therapies, particularly injections, are generally preferred by younger men (i.e., <age 50) with ED.

Intracavernosal Injection Therapy. Prior to the approval of sildenafil, intracavernosal self-injection was the most common medical therapy for erectile dysfunction (Fallon, 1995; Linet & Ogrinc, 1996). The two FDA-approved drugs for intracavernosal injection, alprostadil sterile powder and alprostadil alfadex, are both synthetic formulations of prostaglandin E$_1$. Injection therapy is effective in most cases of ED, regardless of etiology. It is contraindicated in men with a history of hypersensitivity to the drug employed, in men at risk for priapism (e.g., sickle cell disease, hypercoagulable states), and in men receiving monoamine oxidase inhibitors (MAOIs). In general, intracavernosal injection therapy with alprostadil is effective in 70%–80% of patients, although discontinuation rates are high in most studies. Side effects include prolonged erections or priapism, penile pain, and fibrosis with chronic use. In addition to single-agent injection therapy, various combinations of alprostadil, phentolamine, and papaverine are widely employed in urological practice (Fallon, 1995).

Intraurethral Alprostadil (MUSE).   Alprostadil (prostaglandin E$_1$) may be administered intraurethrally in the form of a semisolid pellet inserted by means of a special applicator (MUSE). In a mixed group of patients with organic erectile dysfunction, 65% of men receiving intraurethral alprostadil responded with a firm erection when tested in the office, and 50% of administrations to that subset resulted in at least one episode of successful intercourse in the home setting (Padma-Nathan et al., 1997). Side effects associated with the intraurethral administration of alprostadil include penile pain and hypotension. Prolonged erections and penile fibrosis are rare (Spivak et al., 1997), although the clinical success rate is low (Fulgham et al., 1998).

Vacuum Constriction Device (VCD) Therapy

VCD therapy is a well-established, noninvasive treatment that has been approved by the FDA for over-the-counter distribution (Korenman & Viosca, 1992; Lewis & Witherington, 1997). It provides a useful treatment alternative for older patients for whom pharmacological therapies are contraindicated or who do not desire other interventions. Vacuum constriction devices apply a negative pressure to the flaccid penis, thus drawing venous blood into the penis, which is then retained by the application of an elastic constriction band at the base of the penis. Efficacy rates of 60%–80% have been reported in most studies. Like intracorporal injection therapy, VCD treatment is associated with a high rate of patient discontinuation. The adverse events occasionally associated with VCD therapy include penile pain, numbness, bruising, and delayed ejaculation (Lewis & Witherington, 1997).

VCD therapy can be combined with Viagra in patients who do not have a sufficient response to the drug alone. It is also a preferred medical option for patients who do not wish to use systemic drugs or surgical intervention. VCD therapy can be combined with sex therapy and requires significant education and support in most cases in order to be effective.

Surgical Treatments

Third-line therapy, according to current guidelines, consists of surgical implantation of a penile prosthesis. For select cases of severe treatment-refractory ED, for patients who fail pharmacological therapy, or for those who prefer a permanent solution to the problem, surgical implantation of a semi-rigid or inflatable penile prosthesis is available (Lewis, 1995). Various types of surgical prostheses have been described in the literature. The inflatable penile prosthesis provides a more aesthetic erection and better concealment than semi-rigid prostheses, although there is an increased rate of mechanical failure and complications (5–20%) with the former. Despite the cost, invasiveness, and potential medical complications involved, penile implant surgery has been associated with high rates of patient satisfaction in previous studies (Lewis, 1995; Pedersen, 1988). It should be noted, however, that these studies were conducted prior to the advent of newer forms of therapy (e.g., sildenafil).

In summary, pharmacological therapies for ED are the primary treatment option selected in most cases. This trend has increased markedly since the availability of Viagra and is likely to increase further with approval of additional oral agents. As illustrated by our previous case vignette, most cases are identified and now treated in a primary care setting. Few patients are referred for psychological or couples' therapy for ED, and referrals are usually limited to complicated or treatment-refractory cases. On the other hand, clinical experience suggests that many patients discontinue Viagra use or achieve less than optimal outcomes, and that greater attention to individual psychological or couples' issues might lead to better outcomes. In the next section, we will consider the role of psychological interventions and the potential value of combining medical and psychological approaches.

PSYCHOLOGICAL OR SEX THERAPY APPROACHES TO ED IN MIDDLE-AGED AND OLDER MEN
CASE VIGNETTE #2

Fred C. is a 62-year-old married hospital administrator with end-stage renal disease. Mr. C. has been treated with kidney dialysis for the past 2 years and has been hospitalized several times in the past year for his illness. He suffers from chronic fatigue, muscle weakness, and moderate depression. Mr. C. has had increasing difficulty in achieving erections during the past year and has not initiated sexual intercourse for several months. His libido is also significantly reduced. His wife, Martha, is in good overall health and continues to be sexually interested and available. The partners, who have three grown children, have enjoyed a close and affectionate marriage for the past 34 years.

Fred has major difficulty adjusting to his illness in several areas. Previously a physically active man, he now tires easily with minimal exertion. He experiences unpleasant side effects from several medications he takes daily and is sometimes noncompliant. He is socially withdrawn and frequently noncommunicative and depressed. His physician has recommended consideration of a kidney transplant, but Fred is reluctant to undergo surgery and has been postponing the decision for several weeks. He feels embarrassed about his sexual difficulty and has avoided the issue with his wife. On questioning, he reveals that he misses their sexual relationship greatly and that his inability to perform sexually contributes significantly to his depression.

Psychological Reactions to Aging and Illness

Loss of erection is one of the most salient losses or impairments experienced by many men in response to illness or aging. Men vary greatly in their ability to compensate for or adjust to such losses and in the psychological coping style they display. The significance of the loss is also highly variable, as some men experience ED as equivalent to a loss of masculinity or male identity. As illustrated in Case Vignette #2, Fred C.'s ED, which most likely had a medical or physiological basis due to kidney failure, was greatly complicated by his psychological difficulty in adjusting to his medical condition. The feelings of depression and demoralization, along with the pattern of social and emotional withdrawal that accompanied his illness, contributed significantly to Fred's sexual dysfunction. These issues need to be a major focus of treatment if the patient's sexual and interpersonal difficulties are to be adequately addressed.

There is a complex and clinically important relationship between depression and ED in older men. In general, older men are susceptible to a variety of depressive disorders, including major depressive disorder (MDD), minor depression, and dysthymic mood disorder. In some men, these mood disorders are a reaction to physical illness (as in the previous case), medication effects, sleep disorders, or other biological aspects of the aging process. Other men may have a depressed mood in response to major losses or lifestyle changes, such as loss of a spouse, retirement, or physical disability. The experience of aging itself, with the associated loss of physical strength and mental acuity, may be an additional source of demoralization for many men. Along with depressed mood, aging men typically have declining androgen levels and decreased vascular tone—additional risk factors for ED—which might interact with depression to cause or exacerbate their ED. Although the mechanisms are multifactorial and not well understood, there is increasing evidence of a strong association between depression and ED in older men. From a clinical perspective, this is a central issue to be addressed in most cases.

Several factors need to be taken into account. First, the nature and severity of the patient's depression should be carefully assessed. Potential suicide risk, vegetative symptoms, and other aspects of the patient's depression need to be considered. A psychiatric consultation should be obtained whenever indicated. Because ED may be a presenting symptom of major depression, the first priority should be a more complete mental status assessment and appropriate referral as needed. Following this, specific aspects of the patient's erectile, other sexual difficulties, or any combination of these, should be evaluated and their relationship to the patient's depression explored. Did the sexual problems appear before or after onset of the mood disorder? Is there a loss of libido in addition to ED, and if so, did these problems develop in any particular order? Older depressed men commonly experience loss of libido as a component of their depression, and this may lead to a secondary loss of erectile function over time. Did the sexual problem or problems develop or increase in response to antidepressant medication use? SSRIs and other anti-depressant drugs have a high rate of adverse sexual side effects, including loss of orgasm, decreased desire, and erection difficulties. If the sexual difficulties appear to be directly related to medication effects, a consultation with the prescribing physician may be indicated.

Relationship conflicts can be a contributing factor to the patient's depression or ED, or they may be a consequence or a result in some cases. Depression or dysphoric mood impacts negatively on social and interpersonal relationships in most cases. Depressed men typically avoid making new relationships or may withdraw emotionally or physically from their ongoing relationships. They are less likely to initiate positive social activities and often become sexually or socially unassertive. Men with both ED and depression are especially likely to withdraw from all forms of sexual expression or physical intimacy. Partner reactions may be more or less accepting of these changes, which may in turn elicit a range of partner responses from rejection to anger and hostility. These and other couples' issues can exacerbate or mitigate the effects of depression and associated ED in the older man.

Despite the complex dynamics involved, recent studies support the value of direct treatment of erectile difficulties in men with both depression and ED. In one study involving middle-aged men with ED and subsyndromal depression, we found that direct treatment of ED with Viagra led to marked improvements in both erectile function and mood. Partner relationships were also improved, and a high rate of positive response to Viagra (>70%) was observed overall in the study. Other recent studies have shown that depressed men being treated with SSRIs who develop sexual problems in association with their antidepressant medication also respond well to treatment with Viagra. Overall, these studies suggest that direct treatment of ED in men with both depression and ED is likely to be effective and may have significant positive effects on both mood and sexual function in these patients. Whatever the specific causal relationship involved, it appears that treating ED directly has positive effects on both sexual function and mood in these men. On the other hand, the presence of ED in older men should always be regarded as a potential marker or symptom of depression, which should lead to further clinical investigation in all cases.

In considering psychological or couples' approaches for ED in older men, traditional male attitudes to sexuality also need to be considered. Men with erectile difficulties (and their partners) are often resistant to psychological interventions. As noted by Zilbergeld (1992), men with ED typically experience both shame and guilt in association with their sexual dysfunction, and organic explanations of the disorder are obviously appealing. For this reason, it is frequently necessary to "bypass" the male's resistance by stressing the value of psychological or sex-therapy interventions for the partner relationship. Some men are also more likely to accept psychological treatments, in the author's experience, when combined with medical treatments (see furthermore).

Sexual Communication and Stimulation Needs

It has frequently been observed that ED is most sexually debilitating for couples with limited sexual repertoires and few alternatives to intercourse (Gagnon, Rosen, & Leiblum, 1982; Leiblum & Rosen, 1991). In particular, performance demands and fear of failure are increased markedly for individuals or couples who lack alternative means of sexual satisfaction to penile–vaginal intercourse. For these individuals, the male's inability to achieve a firm and lasting erection typically results in a complete cessation of all sexual activity. This, in turn, may lead to diminished sexual desire in one or both partners and increased distance or conflict in the relationship (Leiblum & Rosen, 1991). A "vicious cycle" phenomenon frequently ensues, as the loss of sexual or affectionate interaction is associated with increased performance demands and interpersonal distress. In one early study, sexual communication training was found to be superior to sensate focus in the treatment of secondary ED (Hawton, Catalan, & Fagg, 1992).

LoPiccolo (1991) has emphasized the critical role of the female partner's attitude toward nonintercourse forms of sexual stimulation in middle-aged and older men. According to this author, the partner's willingness to be satisfied by manual or oral stimulation may be a critical determinant of treatment outcome in most cases of erectile dysfunction: "Far more effective than sensate focus in reducing performance anxiety is the patient's knowledge that his partner's sexual gratification does not depend on his having an erection. If the patient can be reassured that his partner finds their lovemaking highly pleasurable, and that she is sexually fulfilled by the orgasms he gives her through manual and oral stimulation, his performance anxiety will be greatly reduced" (LoPiccolo, 1991, p. 190). From this perspective, treatment is often focused on the sexual receptivity of the partner to nonintercourse forms of stimulation.

Increased genital stimulation may also be necessary for the male partner to achieve an adequate erection and may augment the effects of pharmacological therapy. Among older men, in particular, there is an increasing need for direct, tactile stimulation of the penis, along with a decreasing responsiveness to psychogenic forms of stimulation (Leiblum & Segraves, 1989). Thus, the older male may require extended manual or oral stimulation of the penis in order to achieve adequate erection for intercourse. The female partner is frequently unaware of this important physiological change in her partner and may misattribute his lack of arousal to sexual disinterest or to her loss of sexual attractiveness to her partner. When informed of the need for change in this area, older couples frequently have difficulty in modifying or adapting their traditional sexual scripts (Leiblum, 2000). Many of these couples have minimal experience of foreplay or nonintercourse forms of sexual stimulation.

Combining Medical and Psychological Approaches

pite the availability and widespread use of medical treatments for ED in middle-d and older men, there is growing recognition of the limits of pharmacological therapy and the need for combining medical and psychological treatment approaches. At times, treatment of ED with sildenafil or other medical therapy serves only to reveal or highlight other sexual problems, such as lack of sexual desire or anorgasmia. Sexual problems in the partner or other couples' issues may come to light following successful (or unsuccessful) use of sildenafil. Leiblum (2002) has proposed that success rates with sildenafil may be significantly lower in couples for whom there has been chronic sexual or marital conflict, lack of desire in one or both partners, or significant psychiatric illness in either partner. Although this concern applies equally in the use of any medical or surgical treatment for ED (Althof et al., 1998), in light of the sheer numbers of men taking sildenafil (>10 million, at the time of writing) and the widespread use of the drug, the role of concomitant psychological or interpersonal problems has been highlighted dramatically. Several authors have recommended combined use of sildenafil and sex or marital therapy interventions, particular in cases of low desire, sexual initiation difficulties, or the presence of other sexual dysfunctions in either partner (Weeks & Gambescia, 2001). Controlled trials of combination drug and nondrug therapy have not been performed to date. Despite its overall effectiveness in restoring erectile function for many men, sildenafil should not be regarded as a panacea or a "magic bullet" for achieving sexual happiness.

Problems of Initiation

In couples with long-standing ED, initiating or resuming sexual activity may be difficult following an extended period of sexual abstinence. Leiblum (2002) notes that chronic ED typically leads to sexual apathy or avoidance in one or both partners, and that specific interventions may be required to assist the couple in resuming sexual activity. Sexual avoidance in these cases may be related to embarrassment or fear of failure on the part of the male, unrealistic beliefs or expectations, relationship conflicts, and low sexual desire in one or both partners. Older couples make adjustments in their relationships or lifestyles to the absence of sexual activity, and the availability of the drug may not be a sufficient stimulus to overcome the sexual inertia that permeates their relationship. Few physicians assess the sexual relationship beyond the male's ability to achieve satisfactory erection or orgasm, and problems of initiation are unlikely to be addressed in this setting. In one follow-up study of patients being treated with sildenafil, Pallas, Levine, Althof, and Risen (2000) reported that about one fourth of their sample were unable to sustain initial improvements with the drug. Many of these individuals appeared to have difficulty in resuming or maintaining an active sexual relationship. This problem is evident in the first case vignette in this chapter (Dan and Betty).

How should problems of initiation be managed clinically? We have previously advocated the use of a "sexual script" approach (Rosen & Leiblum, 1992; Rosen, Leiblum, & Spector, 1994) in treating sexual abstinence or initiation problems in ED generally, and this approach can be combined with pharmacological therapy in most cases. At the simplest level, physicians prescribing sildenafil (or other drug therapy) should be encouraged to inquire whether couples have maintained a degree of sexual activity or involvement despite the male's erectile difficulties, and whether any problems are anticipated in resuming sexual activity. This is an important topic for exploration in every ED case, and particularly with older patients. Simple encouragement or advice about the importance of sexual stimulation and the need for foreplay may be adequate in some cases, whereas others may require referral for more in-depth couples' or sex therapy. Sexual stimulation is necessary for Viagra efficacy to be achieved, and older men typically require a greater degree of stimulation. Again, this issue is frequently not addressed by primary care physicians.

After long periods of abstinence, the sexual script is invariably limited to a narrow and restricted range of sexual activity, which the couple typically engages in without interest or enthusiasm. Older couples may have had a limited sexual script prior to the onset of ED, and this script is likely to be further narrowed as the problem develops. An important focus for therapy in these cases is to explore new options and approaches to lovemaking with the couple and to encourage a degree of experimentation in the partners' sexual script. The use of sildenafil can be viewed as an opportunity for the male to regain his sexual confidence, which should in turn facilitate a more open and experimental approach to sexual encounters. Partners should similarly be encouraged to adopt a more relaxed and, if possible, playful approach to lovemaking.

I discussed these issues with Dan and Betty during their initial sex therapy visit. I encouraged them to take turns in initiating sexual activity and to experiment with alternatives to intercourse. I focused our conversation on feelings of embarrassment and shame about initiating sex and gave them reading assignments on the topic for further discussion. Each partner made a commitment to initiate sexual activity at least once during the coming week.

Problems of Low Desire

Middle-aged and older men with ED frequently have concomitant low desire, as either a cause or a consequence of their erectile dysfunction. In some cases, the lack of desire may be sufficiently severe to warrant a secondary diagnosis of hypoactive sexual desire disorder (HSDD). In other instances, a generally low level of sexual interest or enthusiasm is evident, even though the full criteria for an HSDD diagnosis are not met. Although precise data are not available on the proportion of ED cases that have concomitant HSDD, or diminished desire, at least one third of ED cases seen in our clinic in recent years have low desire to a significant degree. Interestingly, this represents a marked discrepancy from the published clinical trial data on sildenafil (Goldstein et al., 1998; Osterloh, Eardley, Carson, & Padma-Nathan, 1999), in which relatively few patients had less than adequate sexual desire. The discrepancy can be explained by the fact that patients needed to be highly motivated to gain entry into the clinical trials, and that they were also recruited on the basis of their being involved in an active sexual relationship. In this sense, conclusions about the effectiveness of sildenafil based on results from clinical trials may significantly overestimate the efficacy of the drug in individuals or couples with desire disorders.

How should problems of low desire be approached in this context? First, a careful assessment of the previous sexual history of the couple should be conducted, with special attention to each partner's past sexual feelings and desires. For men, sexual intercourse may have long-standing associations with performance anxiety or an overall sense of inadequacy. Such individuals may feel threatened or insecure at the prospect of having to "perform" again sexually. Similarly, female partners frequently have sexual performance difficulties or lack of desire, and the loss of erectile ability in the male may be associated with feelings of relief in the female partner. These problems in the partner may or may not be related to menopausal changes, as in our hypothetical case example. If the problems appear related to menopausal changes, a course of hormone replacement therapy may be considered.

Other Sexual Dysfunctions

Older men with ED or their partners frequently have other sexual dysfunctions, such as anorgasmia or delayed ejaculation in the male and arousal or penetration difficulties in the female. Although precise data are lacking on the relative prevalence of these problems in older couples presenting for treatment of ED, many cases present with concomitant sexual problems in one or both partners. Again, a careful assessment is important in determining the history of these problems and their temporal relationship to the ED. In some instances, ED may develop secondary to anorgasmia in the male or in response to chronic penetration difficulties (i.e., dyspareunia) in the female partner. Treatment of the male's erectile difficulties with sildenafil (or other medical therapy) may serve only to reinitiate or exacerbate these underlying problems. Whenever possible, these problems should be clearly identified and addressed prior to the initiation of medical treatment with sildenafil. In many instances, however, the presence of other sexual problems becomes apparent only in the form of "resistance" or failure of drug therapy. At such times, the couple should be referred for more intensive couples' or sex therapy. Again, this pattern was evident with Dan and Betty.

Clinicians can safely address women's penetration or lubrication difficulties prior to initiation of treatment for the man's ED. In cases of dyspareunia or vaginismus, in particular, a complete medical and sex therapy evaluation for the woman is recommended at the outset. Depending upon the severity of the problem and results of the physical and psychosexual evaluation, medical or sex therapy interventions should be initiated, and the couple should be counseled to avoid attempting intercourse initially. The man may wish to try sildenafil in conjunction with manual (either self- or partner-stimulation) or oral stimulation but should be strongly discouraged from attempting intercourse until sufficient progress has been made in treating the sexual dysfunction in the partner. Some women report a recurrence of the penetration problem when the male begins to use sildenafil (or other medical therapy) and intercourse is resumed. Although less debilitating generally than dyspareunia or vaginismus, arousal or lubrication difficulties might also make resumption of intercourse difficult or painful for the partner. This is particularly common in postmenopausal women not taking hormonal replacement. Again, these problems should be separately addressed prior to the introduction of sildenafil.

CASE VIGNETTE #3

John Smith is a 54-year-old accountant, married for 26 years and with two children ages 21 and 19, neither of whom is living at home. He presents for treatment complaining of increasing erectile difficulties for the past 6 years. He states, "I can't remember when last I had a good erection. No matter how hard we try, it never gets more than half way. My wife is ready to quit on me!" The patient's medical history is generally unremarkable. He has been a smoker since his early 20s but is otherwise in good health. The physical exam and laboratory tests were essentially normal.

Sexual history taking reveals that Mr. Smith has experienced little interest or desire for sex since the early days of his marriage. His early medical history was unremarkable. He began masturbation late (age 15) and had few, albeit successful, sexual experiences before marriage. He recalls feeling more physically attracted to his wife prior to their marriage and to the birth of their two children. "During that period [of childbirth and its aftermath], our sex went really downhill. I don't know if it was my problems with erection, or the other way around, but I starting wanting it less, and having it much less often also. It's hard to know which was the chicken and which was the egg!"

Mrs. Smith generally agrees with her husband's description of the problem. She blames part of the problem on the stresses of his family. His mother "leaned on him a lot" recently as she passed through a long bout with cancer. Mrs. Smith feels that the loss of his mother has affected him more than he recognizes. She denies difficulty with arousal or orgasm herself and claims to have been approached sexually by other men but not to have acted on any invitations thus far. She feels frustrated and angry at the loss of sexual activity, as well as at the loss of a great deal of the affectionate exchange that used to characterize her relationship.

During the final session of the evaluation, the Smiths were seen together and a discussion took place about their therapy options. They chose to continue couples' therapy, at the same time that Mr. Smith requested a trial of sildenafil. It was decided to schedule several sessions of counseling, prior to beginning the medication. Mr. Smith was evaluated for a clinical trial of sildenafil and was accepted.

Sex therapy focused initially on communication issues. It was important for each of them to develop a clearer understanding of the problem and their options. It is important for couples to discuss feelings openly at this phase, if possible, and to begin to have more physical exchange. The importance of combining sexual stimulation with the administration of the drug was discussed.

Sildenafil was introduced following the fourth session by the clinic urologist, in conjunction with a clinical trial. Mr. Smith showed a slight response at 50 mg and improved erections at 100 mg. He reported occasional flushing at this dose. His cardiac history was negative. Additional improvement was reported when the patient was regularly treated with 100 mg.

The couple was seen intermittently during a 1-year period following this. The partners continued to make steady progress, although other marital issues surfaced. She felt that he had been emotionally unavailable for her at many times in the marriage. He resented her criticism in this and other areas. Couples' therapy focused on their resentments, their sexual scripts, and the impact of adding sildenafil.

Comment: Although medication played a major role in the recovery of Mr. Smith's erectile capacity, couples' therapy opened the door on a number of issues to prepare them psychologically and practically for the use of the drug and to continue to improve their relationship once sex was reintroduced. Mr. Smith's desire level increased over the 1-year period, most likely due to a combination of sildenafil's effects and the improvements in other areas. He was strongly encouraged to act more confidently and assertively in the bedroom situation, and therapy sessions focused on reinforcing this attitude.

Relationship Problems

Although generally more common in younger couples, relationship problems may be either a cause or a consequence of ED in middle-aged or older couples. This is illustrated in the previous case vignettes #2 and #3. In either event, couples with more severe relationship conflicts or communication difficulties are unlikely to benefit from the use of sildenafil or other medical or surgical treatments for ED. Again, these individuals were excluded from the main clinical trials on sildenafil (Osterloh et al., 1999), and information is lacking on the percentage of treatment failures that may be attributed to problems in the relationship (Leiblum, 2002). Among the more frequent problems encountered are long-standing anger or resentment over unfulfilled sexual or nonsexual needs, power struggles in the relationship, and a loss of physical or emotional intimacy. Changes in physical appearance (e.g., significant weight gain) and loss of sexual attractiveness are also important factors to be considered in middle-aged and older couples. Many individuals or couples adjust well to changes in physical appearance in one or both partners, but this may be a particular issue for some couples.

Clinical judgment needs to be exercised in advising a couple whether or not to begin using sildenafil (or other medical treatment) prior to, or in conjunction with, couples' therapy for one or more of the previously mentioned problems. There is no clear-cut rule to be followed. In each case, a careful assessment should be conducted of the type and degree of relationship distress, as well as the likely impact on the couple of beginning medical treatment for ED. In some instances, a resumption of sexual activity may lead to reduced tension in the relationship, thereby facilitating more effective communication and problem-solving around couples' issues. In other cases, however, attempts at sexual intercourse are likely to dramatically increase underlying conflicts or tensions and should be postponed until significant progress has been made in other areas. Particularly in cases involving extramarital affairs or sexual activity outside of the primary relationship, the introduction of sildenafil (or other medical therapy) should be handled with special care. Unfortunately, due to the increasing prescription of sildenafil by primary care physicians with little experience or knowledge of relationship dynamics, as well as the increasing trend toward Internet prescription of these drugs, this problem is likely to increase significantly in the future.

For couples with less severe relationship problems, physicians or therapists are advised to provide simple guidelines for enhancing relationship satisfaction and for improving communication around sexual issues. For example, partners should be encouraged to communicate directly with one another about their sexual likes and dislikes, preferences, and priorities. Simple suggestions for increasing emotional and physical intimacy can be offered, such as taking more time to talk about personal issues and sharing personal feelings more frequently. Many couples experience a loss of romance along with sexual intimacy, and suggestions can be made for developing a more romantic sexual script. Some of these interventions may be offered by the primary care physician in conjunction with prescription of the drug. Referral for more specialized couples' or sex therapy is advised when physicians are uncomfortable in addressing couples' issues or if more serious problems are encountered.

Conclusion

Erectile dysfunction is a common sexual problem in middle-aged and older men, which has significant consequences on mood, quality of life, and interpersonal relationships. Since the approval of sildenafil, millions of men have sought treatment for ED, and the drug is now widely used as first-line therapy. Practice patterns in this area have also changed dramatically, as most men now seek treatment from primary care physicians for the disorder. In reality, little attention is paid in most instances to psychological or couples' issues, and most men are given a trial of sildenafil as first-line therapy for the disorder. Despite the overall safety and effectiveness of sildenafil, treatment is not always successful, because key psychological and interpersonal barriers to treatment have been identified. Sex therapy and other forms of treatment (e.g., intracorporal injections, penile implants) are likely to be used nowadays after initial treatment with sildenafil has been unsuccessful.

In this chapter I have discussed the current medical and sex therapy approaches for ED in middle-aged and older men. As your "supervisor" for your early clinical experiences with these individuals and couples, I have especially emphasized the combination of medical and psychological approaches to treatment because I believe this provides you and your patients with the best opportunities for success. Unfortunately, there are few studies to date of combined sex therapy and pharmacological treatment for ED in older men. I have drawn your attention in particular to the importance of initiation problems, low desire in one or both partners, the presence of other sexual dysfunctions, and couples' interpersonal problems. I have shared several of my cases with you in order to make the concepts recognizable to you as they present in your practices. In each of these instances and in those that you will encounter, an individualized treatment approach is the best approach. Because depression is both an important cause and a consequence of ED in older men, I have spent time sharing my concepts about this commonly encountered complexity with you. It is my hope that the time you have spent with me in this chapter will help you gain your moorings with older men with ED so that you can confidently proceed to offer them appropriate treatment that enables them to resume mutually satisfying lovemaking.

REFERENCES

ACC/AHA Expert Consensus Document. (1999). Use of sildenafil (Viagra) in patients with cardiovascular disease. *Circulation, 99,* 168–177. Cardiovascular safety of sildenafil is a major consideration in clinical practice. Consensus guidelines were developed by the American College of Cardiology to address these concerns.

Althof, S. E. (1998). New roles for mental health clinicians in the treatment of erectile dysfunction. *Journal of Sex Education Therapy, 23*(3), 229–231.

Araujo, A. B., et al. (1998). The relationship between depressive symptoms and male erectile dysfunction: Cross-sectional results from the Massachusetts Male Aging Study. *Psychosomatic Medicine, 60,* 458–465. An important study of the relationship between ED and depression. The study shows that depression is a risk factor for ED, independent of cardiovascular disease and other comorbid conditions.

Blanker, M. H., Bosch, J. L., Groeneveld, F. P., Bohnen, A. M., Prins, A., Thomas, S., & Hop, W. C. (2001). Erectile and ejaculatory dysfunction in a community-based sample of men 50 to 78 years old: Prevalence, concern, and relation to sexual activity. *Urology, 57*(4), 763–768.

Braun, M., Wassmer, G., Klotz, T., et al. (2000). Epidemiology of erectile dysfunction: Results of the "Cologne Male Survey." *International Journal of Impotence Research, 12,* 305–311.

Brookes, S. T., Donooan, J. L., Peters, T. J., Abrams, P., & Neal, D. E. (2002). Sexual dysfunction in men after treatment for lower urinary tract symptoms: Evidence from randomized controlled trial. *British Medical Journal, 324*(7345), 1059–1061.

Burnett, A. L. (1995). The role of nitric oxide in the physiology of erection. *Biological Reproduction, 52*(3), 485–489.

DeBusk, R., Drory, Y., Goldstein, I., Jackson, G., Kaul, S., Kummel, S. E., Kostis, J. B., Kloner, R. A., Lakin, M., Meston, C. M., Mittleman, M., Muller, J. E., Padma-Nathan, H., Rosen, R. C., & Stein, R. A. (2000). Management of sexual dysfunction in patients with cardiovascular disease: Recommendations of the Princeton Consensus Panel. *American Journal of Cardiology, 86,* 175–181.

Dunn, K. M., Croft, P. R., & Hackett, G. I. (1998). Sexual problems: A study of the prevalence and need for health care in the general population. *Family Practice, 15*(6), 519–524.

Fallon, B. (1995). Intracavernous injection therapy for male erectile dysfunction. *Urologic Clinics of North America, 22,* 833–845.

Feldman, H. A., et al. (1994). Impotence and its medical and psychosocial correlates: Results of the Massachusetts Male Aging Study, *Journal of Urology, 151*, 54–61. The Massachusetts Male Aging Study is a comprehensive epidemiological study of prevalence and risk factors associated with erectile dysfunction. It is the most widely cited reference on this topic.

Fulgham, P. F., et al. (1998). Disappointing results with transurethral alprostadil in men with erectile dysfunction. (Erectile dysfunction) in a urology practice setting. *Journal of Urology, 159*, 237.

Gagnon, J. H., Rosen, R. C., & Leiblum, S. R. (1982). Cognitive and social aspects of sexual dysfunction: Sexual scripts in sex therapy. *Journal of Sex & Marital Therapy, 8*, 44–56.

Goldstein, I., et al. (1984). Radiation-associated impotence. A clinical study of its mechanism. *Journal of the American Medical Association, 251*, 903–910.

Goldstein, I., Lue, T. F., Padma-Nathan, H., Rosen, R. C., Steers, W. D., & Wicker, P. A. (1998). Oral sildenafil in the treatment of erectile dysfunction. *New England Journal of Medicine, 338*, 1397–1404. The classic clinical trial data on sildenafil (Viagra). This article describes results of two randomized, controlled trials of sildenafil's effects on men with ED of mixed etiologies.

Hawton, K., Catalan, J., & Fagg, J. (1992). Sex therapy for erectile dysfunction: Characteristics of couples, treatment outcome, and prognostic factors. *Archives of Sexual Behavior, 21*, 161–176.

Jardin, A., Wagner, G., Khoury, S., et al. (2000). Recommendations of the 1st International Consultation on Erectile Dysfunction. In A. Jardin, G. Wagner, S. Khoury, et al. (Eds.), *Erectile Dysfunction* (pp. 711–726). Plymouth, U.K.: Plymbridge Distributors. An international consensus group developed world-wide guidelines for definition, assessment, and treatment of ED in 1999. Provides guidelines for all aspects of assessment and treatment of ED.

Korenman, S. G., et al. (1990). Secondary hypogonadism in older men: Its relationship to impotence. *Journal of Clinical Endrocrinology & Metabolism, 71*, 963–969.

Korenman, S. G., & Viosca, S. P. (1992). Use of a vacuum tumescence device in the management of impotence in men with a history of penile implant or severe pelvic disease. *Journal of American Geriatric Society, 40*, 61–64.

Laumann, E. O., Gagnon, H., Michael, R. J., & Michaels, S. (1994). *The Social Organization of Sexuality: Sexual Practices in the United States.* Chicago: University of Chicago Press.

Laumann, E. O., Paik, A., & Rosen, R. C. (1999). Sexual dysfunction in the United States: Prevalence and predictors. *Journal of the American Medical Association, 281*(6), 537–544. This article provides a recent reanalysis of the National Health and Social Life Survey and was the most comprehensive national survey of sexual behavior in the United States in the 1990s.

Leiblum, S. R. (2002). After sildenafil: Bridging the gap between pharmacologic treatment and satisfying sexual relationships. *Journal of Clinical Psychiatry, 63*(Suppl. 5), 17–22. A strong clinical discussion of psychosocial and relationship factors that influence the effectiveness of sildenafil treatment.

Leiblum, S. R., & Segraves, R. T. (1989). Sex therapy with aging males. In S. R. Leiblum & R. C. Rosen (Eds.), *Principles of Practice of Sex Therapy: Update for the 1990s* (pp. 352–381). New York: Guilford.

Lewis, R. W. (1995). Long-term results of penile prosthetic implants. *Urologic Clinics of North America, 22*, 847–856.

Lewis, R. W., & Witherington, R. (1997). External vacuum therapy for erectile dysfunction: Use and results. *World Journal of Urology, 15*, 78–82.

Linet, O. I., Ogrinc, F. G., for the Alprostadil Study Group. (1996). Efficacy and safety of intracavernosal alprostadil in men with erectile dysfunction. *New England Journal of Medicine, 334,* 873–877.

LoPiccolo, J. (1992). Postmodern sex therapy for erectile failure. In R. C. Rosen & S. R. Leiblum (Eds.), *Erectile Disorders: Assessment and Treatment* (pp. 171–197). New York: Guilford.

Osterloh, I., Eardley, I., Carson, C. C, & Padma-Nathan, H. (1999). Sildenafil: A selective phosphodiesterase 5 inhibitor for the treatment of erectile dysfunction. In C. C. Carson, R. S. Kirby, & I. Goldstein (Eds.), *Textbook of Erectile Dysfunction* (pp. 285–308). Oxford, U.K.: Isis Medical Media.

Padma-Nathan, H., et al. (1997). Treatment of men with erectile dysfunction with transurethral alprostadil. *New England Journal of Medicine, 157,* 792A.

Pallas, J., Levine, S. B., Althof, S. E., & Risen, C. B. (2000). A study using Viagra in a mental health practice. *Journal of Sex & Marital Therapy, 26*(1), 41–50.

Pedersen, B., et al. (1988). Evaluation of patients and partners 1 to 4 years after penile prosthesis surgery. *Journal of Urology, 139,* 956–958.

Process of Care Consensus Panel. (1999). The process of care model for evaluation and treatment of erectile dysfunction. *International Journal of Impotence Research, 11,* 59–74. A Consensus Panel's recommendations on the assessment and treatment of erectile dysfunction. This report has been used as the basis of subsequent guidelines for management of ED.

Quinlan, D. M., Epstein, J. I., Carter, B. S., & Walsh, P. C. (1991). Sexual function following radical prostatectomy: Influence of preservation of neurovascular bundles. *Journal of Urology, 145,* 998–1002.

Rajfer, J., Aronson, W. J., Bush, P. A., Dorey, F. J., & Ignarro, L. J. (1992). Nitric oxide as a mediator of relaxation of the corpus cavernosum in response to nonadrenergic, noncholinergic neurotransmission. *New England Journal of Medicine, 326,* 90–94.

Rosen, R. C., & Leiblum, S. R. (1992). Erectile disorders: Historical trends and clinical perspectives. In R. C. Rosen & S. R. Leiblum (Eds.), *Erectile Disorders: Assessment and Treatment* (pp. 3–26). New York: Guilford.

Rosen, R. C., Leiblum, S. R., & Spector, I. (1994). Psychologically-based treatment for male erectile disorder: A cognitive-interpersonal model. *Journal of Sex & Marital Therapy, 20,* 67–85.

Rosen, R. C., & McKenna, K. (in press). PDE-5 Inhibition and sexual response: Pharmacological mechanisms and clinical outcomes. *Annual Review of Sex Research.* A comprehensive, up-to-date review of physiological mechanisms and clinical trial results of PDE-5 inhibitors in the treatment of male and female sexual dysfunction.

Schiavi, R. (1990). Sexuality and aging in men. *Annual Review of Sex Research, 1,* 227–250. A major text on sexuality and aging in men. Describes the results of a 5-year NIH study on biological and psychosocial determinants of sexuality in aging men.

Spivak, A. P., et al. (1997). Long-term safety profile of transurethral alprostadil for the treatment of erectile dysfunction. *Journal of Urology, 157,* 792A.

Weeks, G. R., & Gambescia, N. (2000). *Erectile Dysfunction: Integrating Couple Therapy, Sex Therapy and Medical Treatment.* New York: Norton.

Zilbergeld, B. (1992). *The New Male Sexuality.* New York: Bantam.

Zonszein, J. (1995). Diagnosis and management of endocrine disorders of erectile dysfunction. *Urologic Clinics of North America, 22,* 789–802.

Chapter Fifteen

Rapid Ejaculation

Marcel D. Waldinger, MD, PhD

INTRODUCTION

In 1992, a 30-year-old man visited me at my outpatient office and asked me to treat him for premature ejaculation. After taking his medical and sexual history, I told him about the usual treatment for premature or rapid ejaculation. This treatment consisted of the so-called squeeze technique, a behavioral treatment in which a man learns how to delay his ejaculation using masturbation exercises. The technique requires the cooperation of a female partner, but this young man became extremely upset by this requirement. He was sure that his girlfriend never would agree to it. He told me that he thought she was the woman of his life. They had known each other now for 6 months, but the relationship was threatened. She was very angry with him because he always ejaculated so quickly that she had no chance to get sexually aroused herself. She warned him that she would leave him if he did not seek help. He refused the behavioral therapy and insisted that I look for medication to treat him. At that time I had heard that some depressed patients were experiencing a delayed ejaculation or even an absence of ejaculation after being treated with the new antidepressant paroxetine. After some consideration, I told this despairing man about the phenomenon, and that it was worth trying this new antidepressant to see whether it could also delay his ejaculation. He agreed. After 3 weeks he came back to see me. But now he was cheerful, very happy, and very grateful to me for prescribing this drug. To his and also to my own amazement, his ejaculations became very retarded. His girlfriend was also very satisfied with the change that had come about within only a few weeks. Their relationship did not break down after all, and 6 months later they invited me to their wedding.

That was the start of my interest in rapid ejaculation. At that time I didn't understand anything about why paroxetine delayed ejaculation. It was generally thought in those days that only drugs that impaired certain peripheral nerves to the genitals (i.e., with sympatholytic side effects) were able to delay ejaculation. But paroxetine had only a minimum of sympatholytic actions. How were we able to explain this clinical effect? It was only after I looked closely into animal research literature that I gradually began to understand what was probably happening. Since 1992 I have undertaken quite a number of psychopharmacological and other types of studies on men suffering the problem of rapid ejaculation, as well as on the sexual behavior of male rats. Now we have the largest outpatient clinic in Europe for the treatment of and research into rapid ejaculation. In this chapter, I shall tell you more about the subject of rapid ejaculation, its history, its treatment, and the way we can scientifically approach it.

PSYCHOLOGICAL TREATMENT

In the past 100 years or so, rapid ejaculation has been treated as a psychological disorder. Let me tell you a little of its history, because this will help you to understand more of the current debate on this intriguing male disorder.

The phenomenon of too rapid ejaculation is likely to have existed throughout the history of mankind. But has it always been a problem? That is a question we cannot know the answer to. In our own time, the capability for delaying ejaculation and therefore also intercourse provides man with the means to make love in a more intimate and satisfactory way. Therefore, in general, men like to control ejaculation until the male and his female partner feel that the right moment has come for him to ejaculate.

We may speculate that this has always been the case, but the fact of the matter is that it was not until 1889 that the first report of rapid ejaculation appeared in medical literature. About 30 years later, Karl Abraham, at that time a well-known psychoanalyst, wrote an article arguing that rapid ejaculation is a manifestation of a man's unsolved unconscious conflicts (Abraham, 1917). This rapidity, in his own view and that of other psychoanalysts, carried a psychological significance. It meant, for example, that a man unconsciously wanted to punish a woman by giving her no chance to reach orgasm. Karl Abraham termed rapid ejaculation in Latin *ejaculatio praecox*. Soon this was translated as *premature ejaculation* and a difficult debate was born. The logical question was "Premature for whom?" Was it premature for the man or for his partner? Possibly, it was not for the man but only for his partner? This issue led to much unfruitful discussion among physicians, preventing investigators from reaching a clinically satisfying definition of *premature* ejaculation. A better term that does not carry this negative connotation is *rapid ejaculation*. Because that's what it is all about. Rapid has a more neutral meaning, and this is a better starting point for scientific research. But in the past decade people have continued to use the phrase *premature ejaculation*. In the first half of the 20th century, psychoanalysts accepted the idea of Karl Abraham that rapid ejaculation was a symptom of a neurosis. Accordingly, they argued, it had to be treated by classical psychoanalysis. And that's exactly what happened but with poor results. By the psychoanalytic method men probably achieved better insight into their unconscious conflicts, but there are no scientific reports that psychoanalysis in general was an adequate therapy in achieving delayed ejaculation.

In 1943 Bernard Schapiro, a German psychiatrist—for many years, head of the well-known Institut für Sexual Wissenschaft in Berlin, until he escaped from Germany to the United States—wrote an important article about his extensive dealings with men presenting with rapid ejaculation (Schapiro, 1943). He argued that rapid ejaculation was not a *neurosis* but a *psychosomatic disturbance.* In accordance with the accepted ideas of his time, he was of the opinion that men with rapid ejaculation had an emotional problem that was translated into a physical genital symptom because they possessed weak genital mechanisms to ejaculate. Schapiro's article is important because he was the first to try to reconcile both psychological and somatic factors in the pathogenesis of rapid ejaculation. But his publication was also important for other reasons. He mentioned other characteristics that only many years later were recognized by others. For example, he described two types of premature ejaculation. Men with Type B premature ejaculation have always suffered from being rapid, ever since their first act of intercourse. Men with Type A premature ejaculation developed rapid ejaculation later in life and often also experienced erectile dysfunction. Many years later, both types became distinguished as the primary (lifelong) and the secondary (acquired) form of premature ejaculation (Godpodinoff, 1989).

In this chapter I shall concentrate on presenting details of the treatment of and research into the primary (lifelong) type of rapid ejaculation. At the end of the chapter I will go into the characteristics of the secondary form.

Bernard Schapiro also noticed that men with rapid ejaculation had family members who experienced the same complaint. Having seen so many men with rapid ejaculation myself, I asked my patients whether they knew if any other members of their family had rapid ejaculation. It will probably not come as a surprise to you when I say that the majority of my patients did not have any such knowledge of their family members, as the rapidity of making love is not something that people—and even less so, something that members of a family—would be likely to talk about. It is one of the most strongly taboo topics in sexual discussion. But some men spontaneously did tell me that they already knew this about some family members or would be willing to ask male relatives whether they were sexually rapid. It then emerged that a relatively high percentage of male family members also suffered from rapid ejaculation. In 1998, we published the results of that first study on a possible genetic influence on lifelong rapid ejaculation (Waldinger, Rietshel, Nothen, & Olivier, 1998).

Let's now go back to the psychological approach. Very little has been published on this subject for many years now. In 1956 there was a small article by an American urologist (Semans, 1956). He described a method of learning how to control the penis from being rapid. Semans' approach became known as the stop-start method. It includes manual stimulation of the penis by the female partner until just prior to ejaculation, at which point the man feels pre-ejaculatory sensations and removes his partner's hand. When the pre-ejaculatory sensations cease, the woman begins with manual stimulation again. After practicing this procedure, men are instructed to lubricate the penis during stimulation, because ejaculation occurs more rapidly when the penis is wet.

Semans's publication did not attract much attention. It was not until 1970 that this behavioral approach gained any notice, when two well-known American sexologists, Masters and Johnson (1970), reported using his method but adding a small variant and calling it the squeeze technique. Today this technique is practiced all over the world. Masters and Johnson claimed that the method is more effective if the man tells his partner about the sensations experienced pre-ejaculation, and she then squeezes the coronal ridge of the penis between her thumb and first two fingers for about 4 seconds.

This then leads to a loss of the premonitory sensations and a partial reduction in the erection. After waiting for a further 30 seconds or so, manual stimulation begins again. The couple is told not to have intercourse during this period until there is progress in the man's ability to delay ejaculation. Gradually, vaginal containment of the penis is allowed but without pelvic thrusting. Later, pelvic thrusting and other coital positions may be attempted (Tanner, 1973).

Masters and Johnson argued that premature ejaculation arose out of anxiety and was a learned activity. For example, it could be associated with hurried contact in nonprivate places, such as the backseat of cars. Treatment should thus be a matter of training the man to lose his performance anxiety.

In addition to the squeeze technique, all sorts of psychotherapies have been suggested, ranging from Gestalt therapy, to transactional analysis, group therapy, and bibliotherapy. Unfortunately, the effectiveness of these therapies has only been alluded to in case reports but has never been investigated in well-designed controlled studies. For example, the assumption of initial hurried sexual contacts mentioned by Masters and Johnson has never been demonstrated by evidenced-based data (Waldinger, 2002).

Yet the squeeze method is the only psychological treatment known to produce even any short-term effectiveness. Two studies did confirm initial effectiveness in this method but also showed that the ejaculatory control initially achieved had virtually been lost after a 3-year follow-up (DeAmicis et al., 1985; Hawton, Catalan, Martin, & Fagg, 1988).

PHARMACOLOGICAL TREATMENT

Alongside the psychoanalytic approach in the beginning of the 20th century, physicians with a urological focus held the opinion that rapid ejaculation was caused by any of the following list: hypersensitivity of the glans penis, too short a frenulum of the foreskin, or changes inside the urethra. Therefore, their treatment took the form of prescribing anesthetizing ointments, incision of the frenulum, or operations on the urethra. Since the 1940s, case reports occasionally appeared concerning drugs that could delay ejaculation. Apart from reducing penile sensation by applying local anesthetics to the glans penis, other physicians tried to inhibit the nerves that stimulate the genitals (sympathetic nerves) in order to delay ejaculation by prescribing sympatholytic drugs. In the 1960s there were case reports describing the ejaculation-delaying effects of some neuroleptics, which are drugs usually prescribed to psychotic patients, and monoamine oxidase inhibitors (MAOIs), which are used for the treatment of severe depression. It is not difficult to imagine that men with rapid ejaculation, who are in general completely physically and mentally healthy, were not so keen to use these psychiatric drugs, which also have some quite disturbing and even dangerous side effects. But come the 1970s there was a new development. In 1973, Eaton published the first report on clomipramine, a classical antidepressant, describing it as an effective treatment for rapid ejaculation (Eaton, 1973). Later case reports and double-blind placebo-controlled studies now repeatedly demonstrated that low daily doses of clomipramine are effective in delaying ejaculation. In 1993, the American psychiatrist Taylor Segraves published a double-blind placebo-controlled study demonstrating that clomipramine in low doses of 25–50 mg, taken approximately 6 hours prior to coitus, is also effective in delaying ejaculation. The on-demand treatment was replicated in later studies (Segraves, Saran, Segraves, & Maguire, 1993).

In the mid1980s, a new class of antidepressant drugs, the so-called selective serotonin reuptake inhibitors (SSRIs), was introduced on the market. The introduction of SSRIs meant a revolutionary change in the understanding and treatment of various psychiatric disorders, particularly depression, anxiety, and obsessive-compulsive disorder. As I wrote in the introduction to this chapter, just by coincidence in 1992 I noticed the delaying effect of paroxetine, one of the five SSRIs that are currently on the market. In 1994, we published the first placebo-controlled study demonstrating that 40 mg/day of paroxetine successfully treated rapid ejaculation (Waldinger, Hengeveld, & Zwinderman, 1994). The efficacy of paroxetine in daily doses of 20–40 has been replicated in independent studies, both on a regular daily dose and through an "on-demand" regimen. In addition, the efficacy of other SSRIs, such as sertraline in a 50–200 mg/day dose and fluoxetine in a 20 mg/day dose, has also been demonstrated in delaying ejaculation (Waldinger, Hengeveld, Zwinderman, & Olivier, 1998).

DEFINITIONS

As I mentioned earlier, the term *premature ejaculation* produced much debate, and as a result, sexologists were unable to satisfactorily reach an agreement on a definition. The American sexologists Masters and Johnson (1970) and Helen Kaplan (1974) suggested that qualitative descriptions, such as the female partner's satisfaction or the man's voluntary control, have to be at the core of the syndrome. Masters and Johnson, for example, defined premature ejaculation as the man's inability to inhibit ejaculation long enough for his partner to reach orgasm 50% of the time (Masters & Johnson, 1970). But it is obvious that their definition in terms of a partner's response is inadequate. This is because it implies that any male partner of a female having difficulty in reaching orgasm could be labeled a premature ejaculator, given their premise that females *should* reach orgasm in 50% of occasions of intercourse.

Another way to define rapid ejaculation is by using quantitative measures such as the duration of ejaculatory latency or the number of thrusts prior to ejaculation. In the sexology literature we find a wide range in the definitions of the length of time prior to ejaculation: between 1 and 7 minutes after vaginal intromission. Imagine or try it out yourself, using a clock to comprehend what that means. Can we seriously accept that men who maintain thrusting for 5 to 7 minutes are *rapid?* It is important to consider how these writers achieved these figures. Did they measure with a stopwatch? Certainly, they did not! The cut-off points of 1 to 7 minutes were not derived from objective measurements; they were subjectively chosen by the authors. Equally subjective cut-off points have been proposed for the criterion for rapid ejaculation: ejaculation within 8–15 thrusts.

The *DSM-IV* classification of mental diseases tried to solve the problem by defining premature ejaculation as "persistent or recurrent ejaculation with minimal sexual stimulation before, upon, or shortly after penetration and before the person wishes it." But let's be a little bit critical. Is this a satisfying definition? In my own view and that of others, too, it isn't, because the *DSM-IV* definition raises other questions (Waldinger, Hengeveld, Zwinderman, & Olivier, 1998). For example, what is the meaning of "persistent," "recurrent," "minimal," and "shortly after"? How long precisely is "shortly after"? Is it 1 minute or 2 minutes?

For our psychopharmacological treatment studies it was imperative to have an empirically found definition of rapid ejaculation. We had to be sure that the men whom we wanted to treat did indeed suffer from true premature ejaculation.

Then the solution arrived in the form of a simple instrument—the stopwatch. In 1973, the psychoanalyst Tanner (1973) used a stopwatch to measure the ejaculation time. From a methodological perspective, this was a splendid idea, but in the next 20 years there were only two publications about the use of a stopwatch. In 1984 the stopwatch was reintroduced in a pharmacological study by Al Cooper and Ralph Magnus from the University of Western Ontario in Canada, and in 1995 the American psychologist Stanley Althof and psychiatrist Stephen Levine used the stopwatch in a clomipramine study (Althof et al., 1995). Our group in the Netherlands used the stopwatch to get an empirically operationalized definition of rapid ejaculation in a study that included 110 consecutively enrolled men with lifelong rapid ejaculation (Waldinger, Hengeveld, Zwinderman, & Olivier, 1998). In this study, I instructed the female partners of men with a complaint of rapid ejaculation to use a stopwatch at home during each coitus for a period of 4 weeks. The study demonstrated that 90% of these men ejaculated within 1 minute of intromission, with 80% actually ejaculating within 30 seconds (figure 15.1). Thus, assessment by stopwatch reveals that rapid ejaculation is a matter of seconds and not of minutes. Our study in Dutch men was the first stopwatch study done in a Western European Caucasian population. Other patient populations need to be investigated on a clinical basis for any cultural differences and associated behavior that are linked to complaints of rapid ejaculation. For example, do men in other countries or cultures think of themselves as being premature when they ejaculate within 4 minutes?

THE NEUROBIOLOGICAL APPROACH

It's only in the last 10 years that more insight into the background of rapid ejaculation has been gained. I can imagine that psychotherapists don't like to hear this, but although various psychological and psychotherapeutic hypotheses have been postulated, there is a serious lack of well-designed psychological studies that have tested out the validity of the hypotheses. Indeed, most of the psychological hypotheses have never even been investigated or been proved in a scientific way. Still, many therapists insist on using psychotherapy or behavioral therapy for the treatment of rapid ejaculation.

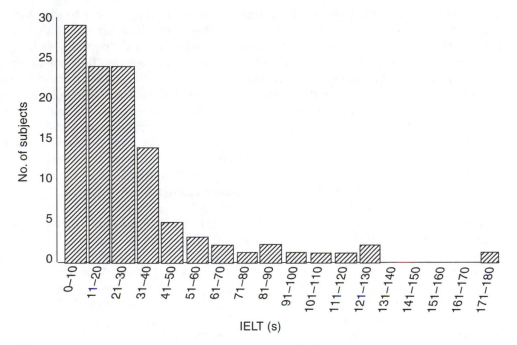

FIGURE 15.1. Intravaginal ejaculation latency time (IELT), measured with a stopwatch in 110 men with lifelong histories of rapid ejaculation. Ninety percent of men ejaculate within 1 minute after vaginal penetration, with 80% actually ejaculating within 30 seconds. (With permission of copyright: Waldinger et al. [1998]. *International Journal of Psychiatric Clinical Practice, 2*, 287–293.)

Personally, I believe this is the critical moment to undertake such psychotherapeutic studies. We may even be in a now-or-never situation, because if these studies are not undertaken, it will become more and more difficult to maintain the assumption that rapid ejaculation is in general related to psychological disturbances.

In the current decade, evidence-based medicine is the key feature of a scientific medical approach. In contrast to the lack of psychological evidence, there is a reasonable amount of neurobiological evidence of how the central nervous system is involved in eliciting rapid ejaculation (Waldinger, 2002). The evidence is based on psychopharmacological human and animal studies.

Animal Studies

Neuroscientists were already investigating the role of serotonin and dopamine in ejaculation in the 1970s. Serotonin and dopamine are compounds in the brain that are involved in transferring messages from one nerve or neuron to another. They are called neurotransmitters, and the process of sending messages from one nerve to the other is called neurotransmission. Around 1990, the important neurobiological data known to neuroscientists were hardly known to the clinicians who saw male patients with rapid ejaculation. So the paradox existed that although clinicians were practicing behavioral therapy for rapid ejaculation, neuroscientists had completely different information about the ejaculation process. In the last decade this has changed. Basic neurobiological knowledge has become integrated with clinical practice. What we have learned so far from animal studies is that serotonin (also called 5-hydroxytryptamine, abbreviated 5-HT) is probably the most important neurotransmitter that is involved in the ejaculatory process. From the various serotonin subtype–receptors that exist in the central nervous system, it is probably the 5-HT_{2C} and 5-HT_{1A} receptors that are crucial for ejaculation. In male rats activation of the 5-HT_{2C} receptor delays ejaculation, whereas activation of the 5-HT_{1A} receptor results in a shorter ejaculation latency.

Based on 5-HT_{2C} and 5-HT_{1A} receptor data in animals, I formulated the hypothesis that in rapid ejaculation there is either a hyposensitivity of the 5-HT_{2C} or a hypersensitivy of the 5-HT_{1A} receptor (Waldinger & Olivier, 2000). I found evidence for this hypothesis by performing various stopwatch studies in men with rapid ejaculation. Investigation of five different SSRIs, which all activate the 5-HT_{2C} receptor, showed that all SSRIs— albeit with different intensity—delay ejaculation, whereas Nefazodone and Mirtazapine, two antidepressants that impair the 5-HT_{2C} subtype receptor, do not result in any delay of ejaculation (Waldinger, Zwinderman, & Olivier, 2001).

Neuroanatomy

So far, I've recounted the history and treatment of rapid ejaculation. But wouldn't it be interesting to know where ejaculation is mediated in the brain? Fortunately, neuroscientists have gained much knowledge of the areas in the brain that are specifically involved in ejaculation. This knowledge did not come from human brains but from male rat studies. For a good understanding, one has to distinguish between brain, brain stem, and spinal cord regions that become activated before and following ejaculation (figure 15.2). Talking about neuroanatomy, we cannot avoid using technical language if we are to have any useful discussion. So here we go. The medial preoptic area (MPOA) in the hypothalamus and the nucleus paragigantocellularis (nPGi) in the medulla are important players in the process leading toward ejaculation. For example, electrical stimulation of the MPOA promotes ejaculation. In addition, serotonergic receptors have been found to be present in the nPGi. The discovery of serotonergic neurons in the nPGi and the well-known ejaculation delay induced by serotonergic antidepressants suggest that SSRIs delay ejaculation by actions on the nPGi. However, the precise location in the central nervous system on which SSRIs act to inhibit ejaculation has not yet been demonstrated.

Around 1995, Lique Coolen and Jan Veening (1998), two Dutch neurobiologists, made some very interesting discoveries. They found that after ejaculation occurred, specific tiny areas in the brain become activated. Here again, some technical language. Let's talk about the posteromedial part of the bed nucleus of the stria terminalis (BNSTpm), a lateral subarea in the posterodorsal part of the medial amygdala (MEApd),

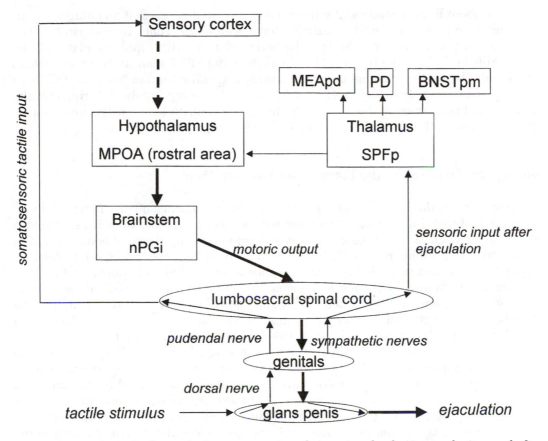

FIGURE 15.2. Areas in the central nervous system that are involved prior to, during, and after ejaculation. Somatosensory fibers reach the sensory cortex. Efferent pathways run from the hypothalamus down to the sacral spinal cord and genitals. After ejaculation, information transmits back from the genitals to various areas in the cerebrum. For full names of abbreviations, see text.

the medial preoptic area (MPOA), and the medial part of the parvicellular subparafascicular nucleus (SPFps) of the thalamus. It is suggested that these areas become activated to inform the brain that an ejaculation has occurred and that the brain has to pause a moment before it can stimulate the genitals again for an ejaculation. Men and women may not like this pause, but it is inevitable from a neurobiological perspective.

By the way, did you know that male rats start to sing after ejaculation? They do. It is a low-frequency song, called the postejaculatory song. And as long a male rat is singing, his female partner rat stays silent and immobile. She only gets lively again when he stops singing, and then she shows she is willing to copulate with him again.

The studies of Veening and Coolen and various other animal studies have clearly shown the existence of a neural circuitry for ejaculation in mammals. This neural circuitry is now partially understood and explained.

How about human studies? It will not come as any surprise that no neuroanatomical studies on men with rapid ejaculation have been done. That's logical, isn't it. The only way in which we can look into the brains of men with rapid ejaculation is by performing brain-imaging studies. Thus by performing a PET-scan study, we are able to investigate the brain areas that are active during a specific human function. PET-scan studies enable us to investigate which areas in the brain are involved during ejaculation. These brain-imaging studies may in the future contribute to a better understanding of the part of the circuitry that is disturbed during rapid ejaculation.

Biological Variation of the Ejaculation Latency Time

In performing animal studies, my colleague the neuropharmacologist Berend Olivier and I noticed that during each experiment with a specific number of male rats, there is always a certain number in the group where there is very rapid sexual behavior and in the remainder a number where it is very slow. About 70%–80% of the rats perform copulation in the same period of time. That phenomenon led us to postulate that possibly there might also exist such a biological variation of the intravaginal ejaculation latency time with men. We defined intravaginal ejaculation latency time (IELT) as the time between the start of vaginal penetration and the start of intravaginal ejaculation (Waldinger, Hengeveld, & Zwinderman, 1994). In other words, in each random sample of men there is a range among men in their speed of ejaculation. The range is from those who ejaculate rapidly, to those who do so at a normal or, let's say, average speed, to those who ejaculate slowly or don't even do so at all. Considered in this way, it is just bad luck for a man who is born with a rapid rate of ejaculation. Unfortunately, due to a lack of epidemiological (stopwatch) research, we do not know the distribution of the mean and range values of the normal intravaginal ejaculation latency time in the totality of the male human population. The assumption of a population-based variability of the ejaculation time implies that rapid ejaculation should be considered a biological phenomenon, rather than a psychological-behavioral abnormality. This biological phenomenon most probably carries different connotations, according to individuals, populations, and cultures. There are men and women who cope very well with rapid ejaculation and do not find it a major problem. But for other men and their sexual partners, rapid ejaculation may become a psychological or emotional problem. This problem may become so severe that psychotherapeutic intervention may be beneficial in helping the man or the couple to cope with rapid ejaculation. The psychology of lifelong rapid ejaculation is therefore a secondary problem, rather than the primary cause.

Ejaculation Threshold Hypothesis

In order to understand the suggested biological variation of the intravaginal ejaculation latency time in relation to the serotonergic system, delaying effects of SSRIs, and suggested genetics, we have proposed the existence of a threshold of the IELT. The threshold is set in the central nervous system.

In the case of a low setpoint of the threshold, men can sustain only a low sexual arousal prior to ejaculation. Whatever these men do or fantasize about during intercourse, any control of ejaculation remains marginal, and these men ejaculate easily even when they are not fully aroused.

I have postulated that the low threshold is probably associated with a low 5-HT neurotransmission and a hypofunction of the 5-HT_{2C} receptor, as mentioned earlier (Waldinger, 2002). In the case of a higher setpoint, men will experience more control over their ejaculation time. They can sustain more sexual arousal before ejaculating. In these men 5-HT neurotransmission varies around a normal or averaged level, and the 5-HT_{2C} receptor functions normally. The mean and range values of the setpoints that are considered to be normal or averaged are not known, due to a lack of epidemiological research.

In the case of a high or very high setpoint, men may experience difficulty in ejaculating or are unable to ejaculate at all, even when fully sexually aroused. At a high setpoint, 5-HT neurotransmission is supposed to be increased, the 5-HT_{2C} receptor sensitivity is enhanced or both of these occur.

According to this threshold hypothesis, it appears to be the level of 5-HT_{2C} receptor activation that determines the setpoint and associated ejaculation latency time of an individual man. In the case of men with rapid ejaculation or any man using serotonergic antidepressants, the SSRIs and clomipramine activate the 5-HT_{2C} receptor. This can therefore switch the setpoint to a higher level, leading to a delay in ejaculation. The effects of SSRIs on the setpoint appear to be individually determined; some men respond with an intense delay, whereas others experience only a small delay with a given dose of the drug. Moreover, cessation of treatment results in a uniform reset of the setpoint within 3–5 days to the lower individually determined reference level—that is, at the level that is, according to my opinion, genetically determined.

It is supposed that the threshold is mediated by serotonin neurotransmission and 5-HT receptors in the brainstem or spinal cord and may consist of serotonergic fibers that inhibit the neurons that convey somatosensory (e.g., tactile) information from the genitals. It is suggested that SSRIs enhance the inhibitory effects of these serotonergic neurons. However, the cerebral cortex may also mediate inhibitory impulses, but, currently, this has not been demonstrated. Apart from a suggested SSRI-induced increase in the inhibition of sensory input, the SSRIs might also delay ejaculation by interfering with spinal cord motoneurons of peripheral neurons that inhibit the internal genitals. Further studies are needed to unravel this important and intriguing question.

Course of Rapidity

It is generally believed that aging delays ejaculation. This assumption might be true for men with a normal or average ejaculation time but has never been investigated in men with rapid ejaculation. Men with rapid ejaculation told me that they were often reassured by their general physicians that the problem would become better as they became older. As there was no evidence on which this reassurance was based, I started a stopwatch study to investigate the tendency in the history of rapidity. The study informed us with new and important data. Of 110 consecutively enrolled men (aged 18 to 65 years) with lifelong rapid ejaculation, 76% reported that throughout their lives, their speed of ejaculation had remained as rapid as at the first sexual contacts in puberty and adolescence; 23% reported that it had even gradually increased in speed with aging. Only 1% reported that it had become slower. These data lend support for my view that in lifelong rapid ejaculation, there is a fixed rate of rapidity across a lifespan and even a paradoxical shortening of the ejaculation latency time. This fixed and paradoxical pattern while getting older should be recognized as a part of the pathogenetic process of rapid ejaculation. Taken together with our hypothesis of a biological variation of the intravaginal ejaculation latency time, I believe that the phenomenon of rapid ejaculation is an inevitable consequence of a normally occurring biological variation of the ejaculation time in men. However, I consider its fixed and even paradoxical course through life as being pathological. In other words, when a man occasionally suffers from rapid ejaculation, this has not to be considered as pathological. It can be explained as being the result of too much arousal or due to some psychological mechanisms. However, when a man is rapid with each intercourse on a continuing basis, then rapid ejaculation has to be considered as a symptom of the clinical syndrome of primary (lifelong) rapid ejaculation. As yet, there is no real cure for lifelong rapid ejaculation, though serotonergic drugs may alleviate the symptoms, but only as long as they are being taken.

RAPID EJACULATION AND ERECTILE DYSFUNCTION

It is important to know that some men with rapid ejaculation may express their complaint as an erectile disorder. In that case, they do not mention the rapidity of ejaculation but focus on the immediate detumescence of the penis after ejaculation. For the clinician, it is therefore always important to ask about rapid ejaculation in men complaining of erectile disturbances. On the other hand, a true erectile dysfunction may be superimposed on the existence of a lifelong pattern of rapid ejaculation, either because of the efforts of these men to minimize their sexual excitement or due to general causes of erectile dysfunction. One may wonder whether rapid ejaculation itself is associated with an increased neurobiological risk to develop erectile dysfunction. As yet, there is no evidence for such an associated risk. To study whether there is such a risk, longitudinal prospective studies in men with rapid ejaculation and matched controls are necessary but not yet undertaken.

I would like to emphasize that the majority of men with a lifelong history of rapid ejaculation do not suffer from concomitant erectile difficulties, and that most of these men do not seek help for being rapid. However, there are some men who look for help only when they also begin to suffer from erectile difficulties. This may bias the population of men with rapid ejaculation that presents at a urological clinic.

In our studies, we recruited men with rapid ejaculation through advertising. The majority of the responding men (75%) had never sought help for rapid ejaculation, mostly out of embarrassment, and 95% did not suffer from erectile difficulties

(Waldinger, Zwinderman, & Olivier, 2001). On the contrary, many of these men reported having an erection very quickly. In 1943, Bernard Schapiro, of whom I have written previously, called this phenomenon *erectio praecox*. Although this term has never been quoted or referred to in literature, I would like to introduce and use it again, as I have heard over and over again, both from men with rapid ejaculation and from their partners, that erection occurs very quickly. However, we need controlled studies before we can state that *erectio praecox* is a true concomitant symptom of *ejaculatio praecox*.

The proven effectiveness of SSRIs in serotonergic-related disorders, like depression, anxiety disorders, obsessive-compulsive disorder, and increased impulsivity, may pose the question whether men with rapid ejaculation are at risk because of these disorders. Our studies, using a clinical interview and the Symptom Check List with 90 items (SCL-90), have repeatedly and clearly demonstrated that men with lifelong rapid ejaculation are in general mentally and physically healthy individuals and as healthy as the average for the age controls of the general (nonpsychiatric) male population.

SUMMARY: LIFELONG RAPID EJACULATION

As you now, I trust, understand, that the primary (lifelong) form of rapid ejaculation has the following characteristics:

1. The rapidity of ejaculation is noticed on the first or earliest sexual encounters, usually around puberty or adolescence.
2. The man experiences rapid ejaculation in more than 90% of acts of intercourse with the woman.
3. The man is likely to experience rapid ejaculation with all sexual partners, not just with one individual woman.
4. The rapidity remains while aging and can even become faster.
5. 90% of the men ejaculate within 1 minute, and 80% within 30 seconds after vaginal penetration.
6. In most cases paroxetine and clomipramine delay ejaculation, but as soon as they are no longer taken, speed of ejaculation increases again within 2–5 days.
7. Psychotherapy is indicated only in cases where the man or the woman experiences problems, as a result of the rapidity, that begin to interfere with their daily lives or the relationship. With the poor prognosis for spontaneous recovery, the aim of psychotherapy is first of all *how to cope* with rapid ejaculation, *not how to delay* ejaculation.

In the next part I shall tell you more about the other form—that is, the secondary form of rapid ejaculation.

With regard to the lifelong form, I would like to underline that neurobiological research in the last decade has demonstrated that the classical psychological view of lifelong rapid ejaculation is no longer tenable as the only theory. In contrast to the behavioristic view, it is the neurobiological approach that has gained support because of its clinically and preclinically based evidence. According to the latter view, rapid ejaculation should be considered part of the normally distributed ejaculation latency time in the general male population, neglecting the natural course of aging-induced ejaculation delay. Paradoxically, ejaculation latency remains similar or becomes even quicker with age. Rapid ejaculation seems to be related to disturbed or maladaptive 5-HT_{2C} receptor properties in specific brain areas, which can be restored by serotonergic agents. Cognitive and emotional influences are certainly interacting with ejaculation, but psychological disturbances must be accounted as a secondary reaction in the case of lifelong rapid ejaculation. Based on various methodologically well-designed studies, psychopharmacotherapy should be recognized as the primary method of treatment of lifelong rapid ejaculation. Psychotherapy is indicated in cases when a man or his partner suffers so much from the syndrome that it disturbs their general well-being or the relationship in too much extent. The aim of psychotherapy is then to help the man, his partner, or both cope with rapid ejaculation. Concise information to educate users about the new neurobiological knowledge should accompany the prescription of the drugs.

SECONDARY RAPID EJACULATION

The secondary or aquired form of rapid ejaculation has a different pattern from the primary form. First of all, these men have not usually suffered from rapid ejaculation throughout their lives, but at some point ejaculation became rapid, with a sudden or gradual onset. This may be due to underlying urological problems, such as prostatitis or an erectile disorder, but certainly could also be due to psychological or relationship problems. I will give you a typical example of secondary rapid ejaculation.

About 3 years ago, a 43-year-old man was referred to me by his general physician. He complained of having rapid ejaculation for about 1 year. He had never previously complained about rapid ejaculation. The rapidity manifested itself within 2 months. He became worried and looked for help. He had no complaints about erectile function. His micturition was undisturbed. I asked him about his life, work, and relationship. He was a manager in a computer company, worked hard, and was satisfied with his job. He was married to a 40-year-old woman, and they had two children, ages 10 and 7 years. The relationship with his wife was good, but the tone with which he talked about his wife led me to seek details about their relationship. And it was fortunate that I did, because he told me, with embarrassment, how a year and a half previously his wife admitted to having had a 6 month affair that was now over. She told him that she had fallen in love with this other man because he paid her attention and listened to her worries. These were things she had not had from her husband for a very long time. After performing a physical examination and a blood analysis, which were both normal, I started sessions with the partners to learn more about their feelings. The man told me that he was completely upset by what his wife had told him and was extremely afraid that it would all end with her leaving him. So he avoided any argument with her and instead tried to give her a lot of attention. As he talked about these details, he became aware that his ejaculations had become rapid at the time she had told him about her affair. In the weeks that followed, I talked with the couple about the impact that a man's busy life may have on marriage. I pointed out that as a young mother who is busy all day long with the children and family, she would have feelings of loneliness if her husband has ceased listening to her. I also pointed out that he would naturally feel embarrassment and anger when he heard about the sexual affair. Both partners valued these discussions, and they were motivated to change some of their attitudes and start paying more attention to each other. However, the man gradually started to realize that he felt an enormous amount of anger against and even disgust with his wife, given that she had "betrayed" him. He even felt that he no longer wanted to make love to her, but he had continued doing so because he was afraid that she would return to her "lover" if there was no more sex between them. Moreover, he was afraid to talk about his anger with her. In becoming aware of his anger, he started to understand that the rapidity of his ejaculation was no coincidence but had a meaning. The rapidity meant that the intercourse lasted only a short while, and that was exactly what he unconsciously or perhaps half-consciously wished as an expression of his anger. As soon as he became aware of this meaning, his experience of having intercourse with his wife generally felt better, although his ejaculations stayed more or less rapid. He took paroxetine for about 3 months. Ejaculation became retarded again, and after he stopped taking this drug, ejaculation did not became rapid again.

This case contains the very characteristics of secondary (aquired) rapid ejaculation:

1. The rapidity of ejaculation can occur at any time in a man's life and is not present from the first or early sexual encounters with the advent of puberty or in adolescence.
2. A physical and blood examination is always necessary in cases of secondary rapid ejaculation.
3. The rapidity is due either to psychological/relationship problems or to urological (for example, prostatitis) causes and erectile dysfunction.
4. Usually, when the rapidity is psychologically determined, it occurs with only one particular partner. However, when it is urologically determined, rapidity is present with most women.
5. Treatment consists of psychotherapy, psychotherapy combined with medication or medication without psychotherapy, in case of a urological cause. The choice of psychotherapy depends on various factors, like the patient's motivation for psychotherapy and the psychological contraindications for psychotherapy.
6. The aim of psychotherapy is to treat the underlying psychological problems. The aim is not learning how to delay ejaculation but how to cope with rapid ejaculation.
7. In cases of a urological cause or underlying erectile dysfunction, treatment has to consist of treating the underlying disorders. In these cases one may prescribe paroxetine or clomipramine as well, with the premise that after 3–6 months the dosage will be gradually reduced, to determine whether the rapidity is not reoccurring.
8. Paroxetine and clomipramine delay ejaculation in most cases. Then—when no longer taken—the speed of ejaculation usually does not become rapid again, if the underlying psychological and urological problems have been adequately treated.

Does all of this make you feel perplexed? Take a break and then start reading again, because I will now write about an interesting trap that clinicians can fall into.

Do you remember that I described how lifelong rapid ejaculation may become worse somewhere in later life? Okay! That's the trap, if you are not aware of this phenomenon. I'll tell you why. Some men who have this subform of the lifelong state may hardly ever or may not at all have realized or been confronted by others that they were at the margins of being very rapid. Only when the rapidity becomes worse during aging do they seek help. If the patient focuses on telling you that it is rapid now where it was not before, and if the clinician does not explicitly focus on the ejaculation latency time before the man noted his current ejaculation time, then the clinician may mistakenly conclude that this particular man suffers from secondary rapid ejaculation. So he can make an incorrect diagnosis, and this usually means an inappropriate treatment. Personally, I believe that the lack of awareness of this trap is one reason that so many men with lifelong rapid ejaculation ended in noneffective psychotherapy in the last century and gave up because it had no effect. But, of course, the unwillingness of many therapists to use medication and their almost obsessive focus on finding a psychological cause has also contributed to this tragic historical fact.

Ejaculation Time Measurement

By comparing open-ended questions, answers on questionnaires, and stopwatch measurements, I have noticed that most men and women are unable to judge time properly. Try it yourself; try to estimate with a random task, for example, walking three times from your house to a particular street corner, how precisely you can judge that time. First estimate or guess at it and write the time on a bit of paper; then repeat this task again, but this time check it using a clock or stopwatch. Now try a second task—I mean, you should really try to do this—if you are a male reader, estimate the time that you take to have an ejaculation after vaginal penetration of your partner. If you are a female reader, estimate this time as well for your male partner or for yourself until you have an orgasm. Then, check it with a stopwatch. Perhaps it sounds a bit strange, but by performing this task yourself, you will better realize how subjective a patient's answer on time estimation is. So what to do? It is obvious that a clinician can't provide a stopwatch for each patient who has rapid ejaculation. But neither can he rely just on a guess about the ejaculation time. I have found the following method to be more accurate to get an estimation of the ejaculation latency time: First, I ask the patient to estimate or guess the duration of the time that he gets an ejaculation after vaginal penetration of his female partner. The answer is written down.

Then I take a stopwatch from my desk and explain the following test to him. I ask the patient to imagine having foreplay with this partner. I tell him that at a certain moment, I will say "now" and that this means that foreplay is over and vaginal penetration starts. He then has to imagine that he penetrates and thrusts with his penis and has to say "yes" when he thinks or feels that he would have an ejaculation at home. I press the start button of the stopwatch at the moment I say "now" and the stop button when the patient says "yes." In the majority of men, I have found that there is a clinically important difference from his first spontaneous answer. Then I tell him the time—for example, 15 seconds—that was measured by the stopwatch and then the time that he had told me earlier: for example, 1 minute. In addition, I say to him, "Now let's check the time that you first mentioned. You told me 1 minute." I start the stopwatch and after 1 minute, I say, "One minute." I then suggest, "Try to find out whether this is the time that you can manage to keep up your ejaculation at home." Very often, the answer I get is "No, I think I overestimated the time." This imaginative time-assessment procedure, checked by stopwatch, is very helpful in achieving a better knowledge of the ejaculation time and is also very helpful for the man himself in realizing the subjectivity of his own time assessment. But, of course, this method is also not very exact. It is nevertheless better than just a wild guess by the patient. Be aware that this test may be embarrassing, as it confronts the man with the likely reality that he is even more rapid than he thought. I also use this method for men's partners, to get an impression of a man's ejaculation time. After an initial talk, I usually ask one of the partners to leave the room so that I can talk to the other individually. I perform, with each of them separately, this "imagined time with a stopwatch test." As tests must have a name, let's call it the ITS-test. The ITS-test is also helpful to get an impression of the validity of each person's estimate. After I have seen each of them individually, I then bring them both back together in my room and explain my diagnosis and choices of treatment.

CONCLUSION

Finally, looking to the future, I would like to make a comment. The daily use of paroxetine and clomipramine has been proved highly effective in delaying ejaculation. But it would be more convenient for some men to take a fast-acting drug. Therefore, in the coming years, research will probably focus on the development of serotonergic drugs that can be taken within an hour before intercourse and that can delay ejaculation effectively.

I hope that you have noticed that rapid ejaculation is a serious problem for those who are affected. Your reassurance and diminishing the severity of it by superficial remarks are not at all helpful for these men. On the contrary, these remarks contribute to more feelings of loneliness for the man or his partner. In the last 10 years I have found conducting research into the subject of rapid ejaculation very satisfying and rewarding, knowing the remarkable effects on and the enthusiastic response of couples using the medication. I hear their expressions of gratitude toward me for taking a serious interest in this problem. Many of these couples were very willing to cooperate in scientific studies that use a stopwatch, for which I am very grateful.

In case you, your partner, or one of your patients suffers from rapid ejaculation, I hope that you will use, advise, or prescribe a drug, as it can make such a difference in your or your patients' lives.

REFERENCES

Abraham, K. (1917). Ueber ejaculatio praecox. *Zeitschrift fur Aerztliche Psychoanalyse, 4,* 171.

Althof, S. E., Levine, S. B., Corty, E. W., Risen, C. B., & Stern, E. B. (1995). A double-blind crossover trial of clomipramine for rapid ejaculation in 15 couples. *Journal of Clinical Psychiatry, 56,* 402.

Cooper, A. J., & Magnus, R. V. (1984). A clinical trial of the beta blocker propranolol in premature ejaculation. *Journal of Psychosomatic Research, 28,* 331.

DeAmicis, L. A., Goldberg, D. C., LoPiccolo, J., Friedman, J., & Davies, L. (1985). Clinical follow-up of couples treated for sexual dysfunction. *Archives of Sexual Behavior, 14,* 467.

Eaton, H. (1973). Clomipramine in the treatment of premature ejaculation. *Journal of International Medical Resarch, 1,* 432.

Godpodinoff, M. L. (1989). Premature ejaculation: Clinical subgroups and etiology. *Journal of Sex & Marital Therapy, 15,* 130.

Hawton, K., Catalan, J., Martin, P., & Fagg, J. (1988). Prognostic factors in sex therapy. *Behavioral Research Therapy, 24,* 377.

Kaplan, H. S. (1974). *The New Sex Therapy.* New York: Brunner-Mazel.

Masters, W. H., & Johnson, V. E. (1970). *Human Sexual Inadequacy.* Boston: Little, Brown.

Schapiro, B. (1943). Premature ejaculation: A review of 1130 cases. *Journal of Urology, 50,* 374.

Segraves, R. T., Saran, A., Segraves, K., & Maguire, E. (1993). Clomipramine vs placebo in the treatment of premature ejaculation: A pilot study. *Journal of Sex & Marital Therapy, 19,* 198.

Semans, J. H. (1956). Premature ejaculation: A new approach. *Southern Medical Journal, 49,* 353.

Tanner, B. A. (1973). Two case reports on the modification of the ejaculatory response with the squeeze technique. *Psychotherapy and Research Practice, 10,* 297.

Veening, J. G., & Coolen, L. M. (1998). Neural activation following sexual behavior in the male and female rat brain. *Behavioral Brain Research, 92,* 181.

Waldinger, M. D. (2002). The neurobiological approach of premature ejaculation (review article). *Journal of Urology, 168,* 2359.

Waldinger, M. D., & Olivier, B. (2000). Selective serotonin reuptake inhibitors (SSRIs) and sexual side effects: Differences in delaying ejaculation. In E. Sacchetti & P. Spano (Eds.), *Advances in Preclinical and Clinical Psychiatry, Vol. 1* (pp. 117–130). Milan, Italy: Excerpta Medica.

Waldinger, M. D, Hengeveld, M. W., & Zwinderman, A. H. (1994). Paroxetine treatment of premature ejaculation: A double-blind, randomized, placebo-controlled study. *American Journal of Psychiatry, 151,* 1377.

Waldinger, M. D., Hengeveld, M. W., Zwinderman, A. H., & Olivier, B. (1998). An empirical operationalization study of DSM-IV diagnostic criteria for premature ejaculation. *International Journal of Psychiatry in Clinical Practice, 2,* 287.

Waldinger, M. D., Hengeveld, M. W., Zwinderman, A. H., & Olivier, B. (1998). Effect of SSRI antidepressants on ejaculation: A double-blind, randomized, placebo-controlled study with fluoxetine, fluvoxamine, paroxetine and sertraline. *Journal of Clinical Psychopharmacology, 18,* 274.

Waldinger, M. D., Rietschel, M., Nothen, M. M., Hengeveld, M. W., & Olivier, B. (1998). Familial occurrence of primary premature ejaculation. *Psychiatric Genetics, 8,* 37.

Waldinger, M. D., Zwinderman, A. H., & Olivier, B. (2001). Antidepressants and ejaculation: A double-blind, randomized, placebo-controlled, fixed-dose study with paroxetine, sertraline, and nefazodone. *Journal of Clinical Psychopharmacology, 21,* 293.

Part Four

SEXUAL IDENTITY STRUGGLES

Chapter Sixteen

Male and Female Homosexuality in Heterosexual Life

Richard C. Friedman, MD
Jennifer I. Downey, MD

PREFACE

We are psychiatrists-psychoanalysts who have collaborated in teaching and scholarship for more than a decade. Before becoming a team, each of us carried out research on the biological and behavioral aspects of human sexuality. Dr. Friedman's 1988 book *Male Homosexuality: A Contemporary Psychoanalytic Perspective* helped revise traditional psychoanalytic paradigms of sexual orientation. Dr. Downey, while working on an NIMH Career Investigator Grant, was the first to demonstrate that the hormonal profiles of lesbians and heterosexual women did not differ.

We realized through our research, teaching, and clinical experience that the topic of human sexuality provokes anxiety in many clinicians—psychotherapists, medical/surgical physicians, and nurses. We discovered that teaching together enabled us to more effectively overcome our students' tendencies to avoid sexual topics in their clinical work. We currently teach a course in human sexuality for psychiatric residents at the College of Physicians and Surgeons, Columbia University, New York State Psychiatric Institute, in New York City.

We are pleased to tell you that the *Journal of the American Psychoanalytic Association* awarded a prize to our article on female homosexuality for the best submission of 1997. In that article, in our recent book *Sexual Orientation and Psychoanalysis: Sexual Science and Clinical Practice*, and in this chapter, case material was written by the author of the same gender as the patient. The rest of this chapter, including discussion of the case vignettes, was written by both of us together.

HOMOSEXUAL PHENOMENA IN HETEROSEXUAL PATIENTS

Sara: A Political Lesbian

Sara came for consultation because she was bewildered about her sexual orientation. A 20-year-old student at a woman's college, she had decided to "renounce" men during her sophomore year of college. Majoring in women's studies, she concluded that women were discriminated against by men throughout the world, and that most societies were organized around "patriarchal" values. An ardent and outspoken feminist, Sara joined a group of feminist/lesbian political activists. They believed that "penetrative sex" placed the woman in an inferior power relationship with her lover and was inherently humiliating. Men used this type of sexual interaction to dominate and exploit women. Only women themselves could provide truly equal, mutually supportive sexual partnerships with other women.

During her pre-college life, Sara had experienced developmental milestones typical of girls on a heterosexual track. She had crushes on boys and men, never on girls. When she began masturbating, in her late teens, the objects of her erotic fantasies were always men. Her only sexual partner prior to beginning college was a boyfriend. They became sexually active during the latter part of her senior year, and after an initial period of awkwardness, she became orgasmic during sexual activity, including sexual intercourse, which she found pleasurable. She and he were not in love, however, and broke off their relationship when they went to different colleges.

Coincident with adopting a role as feminist/lesbian, Sara began having sexual relations with women. She was fully sexually responsive and during a 1-year period participated in sexual activity with two female partners, neither of whom she fell in love with, however. One evening she found herself engaged in a political discussion with a male graduate student and, to her surprise, when he proposed that they become lovers a few days later, she accepted. She was drawn to him, despite intellectual reservations about heterosexuality. Sara felt guilty about this relationship, believing that she had betrayed her political convictions. During the next few months they became deeply involved, and their erotic life was profoundly satisfying to them both. Even so, Sara found herself objecting to many of her lover's traits, which she attributed to "innate masculinity." He seemed more action-oriented than emotionally communicative, was not particularly nurturant, and was deeply competitive with other men, both at sports and in intellectual activities. Sara decided again that she preferred the company of women to men, yet "almost against my will, my emotions drew me to him." For reasons that she was unaware of, the quality of sex with him was more satisfying than with female lovers, despite the fact that she condemned it for political reasons. The conflict between what she experienced sexually and what she believed she should experience led her into therapy.

> *Psychotherapeutic exploration (by J.I.D.) uncovered many of the un-conscious factors contributing to Sara's complex sexual adaptation. It is important to note that the therapist did not express an opinion about whether Sara was "really" homosexual or heterosexual. Nor did she dis-agree with or affirm Sara's political beliefs. Sometimes Sara would seek direct feedback, "Am I a true lesbian or what?" and the therapist would reply, "Our job here is to help you understand yourself—let's see what comes to mind." J.I.D. did not reveal whether she herself was married or not, or what her sexual orientation was. Sara ultimately fell in love with a man whom she married. J.I.D. saw her again briefly, after the birth of their second child years later. Sara had anxiety symptoms as a result of some (minor) congenital abnormalities of the baby. These improved after only a few sessions. With respect to her sexual orientation, Sara enjoyed a loving heterosexual relationship and saw herself as heterosexual. Looking back at her college years, she felt that her sexual experiences with women were authentic, as was her sense of lesbian identity during that phase of her life. She was comfortable with the awareness, however, that she had "moved to a different place" subsequently.*

Discussion

We discuss this vignette with the goal of reviewing questions of general clinical relevance that it raises.

Psychiatric Diagnosis. No matter what a patient's chief complaint, it is important to establish whether significant psychopathology is present or not. The meanings underlying the patient's request for therapy differ across different psychiatric diagnoses. Often, the patient attributes the cause of difficulties to factors that are different than those that the therapist might. In Sara's case, her psychopathology was not severe. For example, she did not have any Axis I disorders according to the *DSM* (*Diagnostic and Statistical Manual of the American Psychiatric Association*, 1994). She also was not borderline, either by *DSM* standards (Borderline Personality Disorder) or using a more global psychodynamic referent (borderline level of personality organization (Kernberg, 1975), nor did she meet criteria for other types of Personality Disorder.

Sara needed psychotherapy because important motivational issues influencing her sexuality were unconscious—but not because her sexual conflicts led to severe psychiatric symptoms. Thus, the problem that perplexed her at the outset of her treatment—"Am I homosexual or heterosexual?"—did not appear to disguise deep difficulties with identity consolidation, self-representation, or affect regulation. The therapist decided that was what she appeared to be—a young adult whose political value system was not fully integrated with her erotic responsivity. Her self-representation had not yet been fully fashioned in a way that seemed to her to be authentic.

Feminist Lesbianism. Feminist lesbianism is common and certainly not inherently psychopathological. Feminist/lesbian patients sometimes seek psychotherapeutic assistance, however, as did Sara. Sara happened to be the kind of person who left lesbianism behind and continued through life on a heterosexual pathway. Her course is best understood as being the product of her particular and idiosyncratic motivations. Someone with her "profile" might just as easily have continued through life on a lesbian track. As is true in many other areas of female psychology, there is great diversity with respect to the different types of women who become feminists/lesbians (Downey & Friedman, 1998; Friedman & Downey, 2002). Sara saw herself as heterosexual until she left home to attend college. There she became a feminist, and she decided that it was better to interact sexually with women than with men for political reasons. Sara's erotic fantasies and activities also became directed at women, however, a point not to be minimized. This type of psychosexual profile, in which a political value system seems to influence erotic responsivity, is much less common among men. Gay men, for example, tend to experience sexual attraction toward males from childhood. Their sexual desire profile tends, as a general rule, to remain in place for life (Friedman & Downey, 2002). Although some also experience some degree of sexual desire for women and participate in heterosexual activity, there is no real counterpart of feminist lesbianism among men. Men don't tend to change sexual orientations for political reasons during young adulthood. This is but one example of the difference between men and women in sexual plasticity, the degree to which erotic responsivity is fixed and rigid or may be modified in keeping with changing social and emotional context.

The Therapist's Stance

J.I.D. helped Sara understand different unconscious psychological conflicts that appeared to influence her sexual experience. She did this by being accepting, nonjudgmental, and relativistic. Thus, the therapist's personal sexual value system was not expressed. She was bounded, yet empathic. In considering this, it is important to stress the distinction between the *therapeutic process* and the specific features of the patient's sexual adaptation (e.g., the way in which her sexual orientation is experienced). Sara's psychotherapeutic experience reached termination because Sara accomplished her fundamental goal—to establish a sense of self-authenticity that included integration of her philosophical beliefs and her sexual experience. A different patient working with the same therapist might well have become as productively engaged in therapy as Sara and accomplished similar *process* goals with a different *outcome* with respect to sexual orientation. Psychotherapeutic exploration may have revealed that the patient's erotic desires for men masked underlying unconscious conflicts that when explored, resulted in diminution of her heterosexual motives. Such a patient may have discovered that her sexual life with women was more profoundly satisfying and meaningful than with men. The solution to sexual orientation difficulties of the type experienced by Sara is frequently not possible to predict at the outset of psychotherapeutic treatment. Thus, the search for identity might lead to lesbianism or to heterosexuality (or to some type of bisexuality), without the specific outcome being considered innately healthy or pathological by the therapist. A sense of identity coherence and ego integration, however, should ideally be achieved, no matter what type of sexual orientation outcome results. Although Sara's course is not "typical" (no course is), it is common enough and illustrates important general issues about sexuality. A key ingredient in the psychotherapeutic treatment of patients like Sara is the therapist's capacity to tolerate the patient's anxiety about "being" homosexual or heterosexual. Without directly saying so, the therapist ideally should convey acceptance of the patient as a *person* whose struggle for self-authenticity requires joint exploration, which, if all goes well, leads to a sense of self-authenticity and security.

A MIDDLE-AGED HETEROSEXUAL WOMAN FALLS IN LOVE WITH ANOTHER WOMAN

We have elsewhere described a marital relationship in which a heterosexual woman became passionately involved with another woman in a sexual-love relationship. We reproduce our description of the relationship here—the wife's pattern of sexuality illustrates homosexual responsiveness in someone who had considered herself heterosexual. Her sexual desire for another woman occurred later in life than in the situation of the young woman described previously and for reasons that were deeply personal, not political.

Consider the psychology of each partner in a marriage in which each experiences a loss of passionate vitality. The 50-year-old wife is struggling to cope with feelings of "emptiness" that have become insistent and persistent in recent years. At work she experiences loss of ambition and energy, a tendency to withdraw from social interactions, and irritability. Although her appearance has not outwardly changed, she feels unattractive. Her efforts to obtain solace and support from her mate are frustrated by his attitude toward her. She experiences him as emotionally unavailable, and she feels lonely in his presence. She complains that his idea of being together is to participate in activities at the same time, such as watching television or socializing with friends. He offers her little sense of emotional connection or empathic understanding.

The husband experiences his wife as increasingly clinging, dependent, and self-preoccupied. He feels bewildered by her criticism that he is emotionally not present when he is physically in her company. His attempts to hug and hold her are angrily rebuffed when he becomes sexually aroused. She interprets his initiating physical intimacy as manipulative. "All you want is sex," she tells him. She begins to find intercourse invasive and intrinsically devaluing. He interprets her sexual withdrawal as infantile and frustrating. He complains that she wants him to relate to her as if she were a child.

The husband spends more and more time at work, where he is perceived as being energetic and effective. It seems to his wife that the more she complains about her loneliness, the more he withdraws. Soon he begins a sexual affair with one of his women colleagues. At this point, his wife begins to have lengthy conversations with a widow who lives nearby. The women meet each other frequently and commiserate about sex differences in behavior. Each feels that the other is warm, supportive, understanding, empathic, expressive, and caring. The friendship deepens and the women discover sexual feelings for each other. The emergence of these is a surprise to both. Each is heterosexist in attitude, has not experienced homosexual desire before, and has never engaged in homosexual activity. After a period of shock, turmoil, and mutual revelation, they realize that they have fallen in love and allow themselves to express their feelings sexually. Although their love relationship becomes fully sexual and deeply satisfying to each, neither considers herself a lesbian. In fact, neither feels it necessary to label their same-sex passionate relationship in terms of a particular sexual orientation/social role.

In this instance, intense intimacy kindled sexual desire in two women. Once this occurred, each felt attractive and desirable. The depression experienced by the first woman remitted. This type of "kindling" rarely occurs in men except in special situations. "A lifelong heterosexual man may develop intensely close friendships during middle or later life, but these are not likely to alter the sex of the object of his fantasies" (Downey & Friedman, 1998).

In women, much more frequently than men, sexual feelings emerge in the context of trusting, empathic, intimate relationships. This is compatible with differences between the sexes in the *onset* of erotic feelings during childhood and adolescence. In females, erotic feelings tend to emerge early in life in the context of meaningful relationships; in males, they tend to be triggered by visual stimuli and do not necessarily emerge in a relational context (Friedman & Downey, 2002).

MALE SEXUAL FANTASY

In males, feelings of sexual desire usually emerge during mid- and late childhood. Boys are usually aware of feelings of sexually lustful desire prior to puberty, and the imagery associated with such stimuli are summoned up during masturbation. Sexual fantasies, experienced during masturbation and at other times as well, consist of visual imagery of females, males, or both (in different men) and a rudimentary story line. These fantasies motivate men to be interested in pornography depicting their fantasies and to participate in sexual activity. The images and story line tend to act as a limit— that is, stimuli that are outside the pattern are not experienced as being sexual. Exclusively heterosexual men will not be aroused by homosexual stimuli, and exclusively homosexual men will not be aroused by heterosexual stimuli. Epidemiological studies indicate that a majority of men is heterosexual, a minority is exclusively homosexual, and a somewhat larger minority, bisexual (Billy, Tanfer, Grady, & Klepinger, 1993; Laumann, Gagnon, Michael, & Michaels, 1994). Thus, the most common time line of psychosexual male development is that a boy is erotically attracted to girls and women from mid-childhood. By puberty he masturbates to fantasies of nude women and is interested in heterosexual pornography. During adolescence, he participates in interpersonal sexual activity with young women, and he then maintains his heterosexual fantasy profile during the rest of his life. Gay men tend to follow a similar time line, except that the sexual object is male and not female.

HOMOSEXUAL EXPERIMENTATION AMONG HETEROSEXUALS

The importance of sexual fantasy in relationship to interpersonal sexual experience is illustrated by sexual experiences of identical twin men that occurred during early adolescence. The sexual histories of these boys were studied as part of a research project carried out by RCF (Friedman, 1988).

The sexual incident in question concerned the conduct of a group of boys in an automobile. As many boys stuffed themselves into a small car as the car could contain. Heterosexual pornographic magazines were distributed, and the boys masturbated themselves and each other—while looking at depictions of nude women. One twin was exclusively heterosexual. Even though he achieved orgasm by being masturbated by a friend, the experience for him was heterosexual. The magazine imagery that conformed to his inner fantasy life was of the opposite sex. He imagined himself sexually involved with the model. The other twin was gay, however, and for him the experience in the automobile was deeply homoerotic. He paid no attention to the pornographic imagery but, rather, attended to his inner fantasies, which were brought to life by the sexual activity enacted in the car.

The story of the twins illustrates that erotic fantasy programming shapes the way in which males interpret sexual context. It is also an example of sexual activity carried on between heterosexual boys. Such activity is common but tends to be interpreted according to preexisting sexual fantasy profiles. Thus (contrary to myths about homosexuality), adolescent boys who experiment with mutual masturbation do not tend to be "drawn into" homosexual orientation later in life.

Men and women develop similarly in many ways, but differently in others. An important difference is that men are more likely to value homosexual phenomena negatively than women are. Clarification of the psychology of homophobia in heterosexual men helps place this phenomenon in perspective. It is important to emphasize that our entire discussion in this chapter is culture bound. Our experience has primarily been with American patients, and our observations about development are based on studies largely carried out in Northern America or Western Europe. This point bears particular salience in our consideration of the negative value attributed by many men and toward phenomena they perceive to be homosexual or feminine, in others and in themselves. Attitudes toward homosexuality differ between societies and across historical epochs. In ancient Greece, for example, homosexual activity was not condemned. In fact, a specific type of relationship between an adolescent boy and an older man was considered the ideal embodiment of passionate love (Dover, 1989).

HOMOPHOBIA IN HETEROSEXUAL MEN

Albert, a 45-year-old executive, requested help because of anxiety and depression associated with separation from his wife of 10 years. The partners had lost a sense of intimate connection with each other as each had become more and more professionally successful. During the year prior to the separation, each had become involved with other sexual partners. To his surprise, Albert, who prided himself on not being "possessive," found that he was jealous. He realized that it was "irrational" to object that his wife, a 40-year-old lawyer, was not monogamous, as he himself was not. He felt that his "feelings and thoughts were not on the same page." Intellectually, he believed that the same rules should govern the sexual behavior of both partners in a marriage, but his emotions responded as if this were not the case.

To his consternation and for the first time in his life, Albert was unable to perform sexually with extramarital partners. Typically, he experienced loss of sexual desire and of his erection just as the couple was about to have intercourse. He then felt deeply ashamed and puzzled. He decided that the reason for his difficulty might be "physical," but he was embarrassed to discuss sex with his family physician.

Albert discussed these symptoms and difficulties during his first consultation visit. Not until the second session, however, and only upon tactful probing by the therapist, did he reveal that something else was troubling him as well. More or less coincident with the other difficulties, he began to ruminate that he might be gay. Ego-alien thoughts of being homosexual produced distress and occurred despite the fact that Albert's history of erotic fantasy and activity was entirely heterosexual.

During his life Albert had had 10 sexual partners, all women. With the exception of his wife, all had been involved with him prior to his marriage. He had first engaged in sexual intercourse at age 17 with a high school girlfriend. Of his 10 partners, Albert had been in love with 1 and involved in intimate monogamous relationships with 4 others. The remaining encounters were casual. Albert dated the onset of his sexual desires/ fantasies to about age 6 or 7. The object of his erotic desires had always been female. He began masturbating at age 12, and masturbatory fantasies were always of women, usually classmates and movie stars. During the year prior to his consultation, the very time when he worried that he might be homosexual, he continued to masturbate regularly, and his fantasized object was always female. From young adulthood on, Albert had been interested in pornography to some degree, always heterosexual. Given that Albert's sexual history had always been exclusively heterosexual, he was understandably confused that he was concerned about being homosexual for no apparent reason.

Albert was treated with supportive psychotherapy, and he and his wife responded positively to marital therapy. They reconciled and resumed satisfying sexual activity. Albert, who had never experienced sexual symptoms with his wife, gave up extramarital sexual activity. His worries about being homosexual faded away.

Discussion

Albert had grown up in a sexist, blue-collar environment. The values of his adulthood and his childhood were quite different. Having enjoyed an excellent university education and traveled widely, Albert prided himself on being humanistic and cosmopolitan. However, at an unconscious level, he tended to endorse the sex-role stereotypes that he had been raised with. Despite the fact that he did not consider himself homophobic, nonetheless, imagining himself as homosexual was unacceptable. In fact, Albert considered the imagery and meaning of male homosexuality as representing masculine inadequacy. To Albert, "I am homosexual" symbolically meant "I am a weak, unmasculine man." Albert had (unconsciously) concluded that his wife had rejected him because he was not sexually adequate. He suffered a sense of competitive defeat because of his (unconscious) conviction that his wife's lovers were better men than he was. His dread that he was not "a real man" seemed to be confirmed by his difficulty performing sexually with other women. Albert represented his feeling poor masculine self-esteem with a thought, "I am homosexual." The thought took the form of an obsessional worry: an ego-alien, repetitive, irrational idea.

It was not necessary during Albert's treatment to make his unconscious irrational ideas conscious. What was crucial, however, was for the therapist to understand that Albert was deeply insecure about his masculinity and that his homosexual thoughts symbolically represented this insecurity. In Albert's case, couples' therapy and individual supportive therapy led to marital reconciliation and symptom improvement. Other patients with this type of symptom often require additional forms of treatment. For example, in some cases, an obsessional worry such as Albert's may be part of a more pervasive obsessional personality disorder. These patients might experience diverse nonsexual obsessions and compulsions and their treatment generally involves pharmacological treatment with serotonin selective reuptake inhibiting drugs, in addition to psychotherapy. Still other patients require exploratory psychotherapy. In these instances, the unconscious connections between the patient's irrational fears and conscious experience are explored as part of the therapeutic process.

Although guidelines for the different types of therapeutic strategies that help different types of patients are not possible in this chapter, a good rule of thumb is for the therapist to attempt to provide the intervention that will produce the greatest therapeutic effect with the least cost—personal and financial—to the patient. For example, in Albert's case, the fact that his symptom remitted with supportive interventions led to the therapeutic decision that prolonged insight-oriented therapy was not indicated— at least at this time.

PSEUDOHOMOSEXUAL ANXIETY: A PSYCHOANALYTIC CONCEPT PROPOSED IN THE 1950s

The psychoanalyst Lionel Ovesey was the first to clarify the reasons that men whose erotic programming is heterosexual nonetheless may experience thoughts, sometimes in the form of worries, that they might be homosexual (Ovesey, 1969). Ovesey, who studied the dreams, associations, and symptoms of his patients, suggested that some men symbolically represented conflicts about power and dependency in the form of homosexual imagery. Feelings of competitive defeat in struggles with other men were often depicted as homosexual imagery in the man's fantasy life and dreams. For example, Ovesey reported the dream of a man who felt intimidated by his boss:

> I tore into his office madder than hell. He was sitting behind his desk. This time I was really going to tell him. He looked up and said, "What in hell do you want?" I just stood there and couldn't say anything. Then I turned around, but instead of walking away, I crawled away on my hands and feet with my ass up in the air. (1969, p. 40)

Ovesey collected a number of examples of such cases and suggested mechanisms by which some men represented competitive failure in the unconscious part of their minds: "I am a failure = I am not a man = I am castrated = I am a woman = I am a homosexual" (1969, p. 57). Thus, in the clinically disturbed group of patients he discussed, three different types of ideas were condensed in the minds of the patients: (1) ideas about masculine adequacy in terms of competitive success or failure, (2) ideas about gender identity/gender role, and (3) ideas about sexual orientation.

Homophobia in Heterosexual Men

Ovesey discussed his patients many years ago. Today these men would be considered homophobic. In fact, unconscious homophobia is sometimes expressed by heterosexual men, even when these men do not consider themselves homophobic at a conscious level. At the time Ovesey discussed the phenomena he termed *pseudohomosexual*, homosexuality itself was considered pathological. Most therapists considered it to be the end result of developmental derailment. Today we know that these ideas were invalid. It is important therefore to distinguish homosexual worries and fears of heterosexual men from the motivations of those who are gay. Because of social conflict surrounding all aspects of discussion about homosexuality, this point bears particular emphasis. In gay men, homosexual motivation is not based on a sense of defect or inadequacy.

Representations of the self as unacceptably unmasculine or feminine are not uncommon among clinical populations of heterosexual men, although there are no epidemiological studies that suggest how frequently this occurs. This being the case, we have no way of knowing whether the frequency of such phenomena has decreased in response to the 1974 depathologization of homosexuality and to the generally diminished sexism over the last several decades.

The question arises, why should men who are not gay sometimes represent themselves as being homosexual when they are anxious or depressed? A developmental perspective sheds light on this. We have observed that the developmental roots of male homophobia are in mid- and late childhood (Friedman & Downey, 2000a). During this phase of life, children tend to move out of the social world of their families and into that of peers. Peer play is a crucially important mode of social interaction of older children. Studies of children in many societies indicate that mid- and late-childhood peer play tends to be sex-segregated. Boys tend to play with boys and girls with girls (Friedman & Downey, 2002; Maccoby, 1998). Although there are many exceptions to this general tendency, studies of children throughout the world indicate that in all societies in which free play during late-childhood has been investigated, sex-segregated play is the rule. Juvenile play is a core building block of late-childhood peer culture.

The developmental psychologist Eleanor Maccoby has observed that the peer cultures that are formed by boys and girls are quite different. Understanding this difference is important for understanding the origins of homophobia in boys.

Boys' groups tend to be more aggressive, competitive, xenophobic, and hierarchically structured than girls' groups are. Juvenile-aged boys tend to be intolerant of cross-gender behavior, and those that are perceived as feminine are often abused or ostracized. From the perspective of juvenile-aged boys, traits that are viewed as being feminine are valued negatively, whether they occur in others or in oneself. To be considered girl-like is to be devalued in juvenile male peer culture. The difference between the sexes in value assigned to cross-gender behavior at this age is illustrated in the meanings that are commonly assigned to terms denoting such behavior. "Sissy" has a negative connotation, whereas "tomboy" does not.

The sex stereotyping that commonly occurs during late childhood is not an invariate phenomenon. Many boys are tolerant and accepting. Extreme reactions are much more common than most adults would like to believe, however. Some men leave homophobic attitudes and values behind as they grow older. Others, however, who belong to specific pathological subgroups, are likely to activate the childhood roots of their masculine insecurity under stress. Their negative self-images, expressed in symbolic terms, may best be understood as an adult manifestation of internalized homophobia that has persisted since late childhood. This phenomenon remains to be adequately studied, and it is possible that the pathological subgroups alluded to previously are heavily weighted toward boys who come from home environments of abuse, neglect, extreme psychopathology of the caretakers, or any combination of these.

DEVELOPMENTAL DIFFERENCES BETWEEN THE GENDERS

In this chapter we have discussed commonly occurring homosexual phenomena in heterosexual people. During childhood, girls and boys often participate in sexual play and exploration with members of the same sex. Sometimes such activity involves mutual masturbation and sometimes masturbation in groups, as occurred in the twins whom we discussed earlier. There is no evidence that such activity influences children to become gay or lesbian later in life, and in fact most grow up to become heterosexual.

Understanding psychosexual developmental differences between boys and girls, men and women, provides a useful context for placing homosexual phenomena in heterosexual patients in a therapeutically useful framework. Boys tend to be more uniform with respect to psychodevelopmental milestones than girls and women are. In boys, sexual fantasies are experienced during a range from 4 to 12 years old. Boys begin to masturbate during mid- and late childhood and early adolescence. Interpersonal sexual activity tends to occur during adolescence and early adulthood. During men's entire lives, the sexual activity that they engage in tends to be in keeping with fantasies experienced during childhood. Most men are sexually attracted exclusively to women, a small minority (1–2%) exclusively to men, and an additional 5% more or less to both sexes (Friedman & Downey, 1994, 2000b). Because American society has no bisexual social niche, some men in the latter group label themselves heterosexual and some gay. (Some privately consider themselves bisexual, of course.) There is no relationship between the objects of a person's sexual desires (men, women, or both) and psychopathology. Thus, we believe that no health value should be assigned to being heterosexual, gay/lesbian, or bisexual, no matter how these terms are defined.

Subgroups of girls appear to follow different time lines with respect to the earliest occurrence of sexual fantasies, masturbation, interpersonal sexual activity, and self-labeling as heterosexual or lesbian. In many girls the time table sequences are similar to those of boys. In others, however, including those discussed in this chapter, they are not. One reason for this concerns sex differences with respect to plasticity of the erotic object. In most men, sexual fantasies are inclusionary and exclusionary. Stimuli outside of a person's sexual profile are experienced as neutral. Men who are exclusively heterosexual, for example, are not sexually interested in imagery that arouses gay men, and vice versa. Heterosexual women, much more frequently than men, appear to have the capacity for homoerotic desire to emerge during adulthood in certain conducive situations, such as a deep intimate relationship or as a function of intense political convictions. We suspect that this occurs partly because plasticity, with respect to erotic imagery, is part of the "hardwiring" of the brains of women (for reasons that are outside the scope of this article).

Another difference between the sexes concerns the value attributed to feminine versus masculine traits. Women and girls appear to be more tolerant of cross-gender behavior in themselves and others. Boys and men are often intolerant of perceived unmasculine or feminine behavior in themselves, as well as other boys. This may take the forms of symptoms of *internalized homophobia* in heterosexual men. When this occurs, the man labels himself "homosexual" in a symbolic and devaluing way—to connote a sense of masculine inadequacy. The psychotherapeutic treatment of such men requires empathic exploration of the underlying causes of their gender/role insecurity.

Even though gay men and lesbians are different in many respects, they are similar in others. For example, many have been or are married. Many a clinician has been surprised to discover that a person who is stably married and organized around traditional "family values" is also actively involved in sexual/love relationships with a partner of the same sex. Sometimes these relationships are secret—the person is in the closet. Sometimes, however, the person may be "out" (e.g., out of the closet), to greater or lesser degree, and carry out personal lives in different sexual/romantic spheres successfully. The most important guideline we offer therapists to be helpful to patients in this situation is to be nonjudgmental. Sexual value systems of therapists vary widely but include many who endorse monogamy, "honestly" conforming to one's perceived sexual orientation, or both. Thus, people whose lovers are of the same gender "should be" gay; people whose lovers are of the opposite gender "should be" heterosexual. Therapists who attempt to impose their personal value systems on patients are likely to be unhelpful and may even be harmful. People take many different pathways toward finding fulfillment in love and passion during their lives, and therapists must respect these differences, no matter how anxiety-provoking this may be.

CONCLUSION

Exposure to homosexual experiences and activities among heterosexual people can provoke considerable anxiety in clinicians. Our own experience has been instructive in that regard. We have found it helpful to have regular discussions with each other in which we review our clinical work. We have found that honest and detailed discussions of clinical process with a trusted colleague diminishes countertransference responses, including those provoked by homosexual phenomena in heterosexual patients. Although our personal peer-review experience has involved a dialogue between therapists of different genders, we believe that many different structures for peer discussion may be helpful.

The material that we have presented in this chapter was selected for many reasons. Two of the most important are that the clinical situations we have discussed are common and that we have found that they often stimulate defensive responses in therapists. This chapter was written in the hope that awareness of homosexual phenomena in heterosexual patients will diminish countertransference responses and will facilitate therapeutic work.

ANNOTATED BIBLIOGRAPHY OF OUR PUBLICATIONS

Friedman (1988). This book integrated sexual science with psychoanalytic developmental theory. It reviewed the psychoanalytic literature in detail and demonstrated that a commonly accepted paradigm that homosexuality is inherently pathological was supported neither by scientific sexology nor by the psychoanalytic literature itself. *Male Homosexuality: A Contemporary Psychoanalytic Perspective* extensively discussed bisexuality. It provided clinicians with a way of conceptualizing the psychodynamics of gay, heterosexual, and bisexual men who had Axis I and Axis II psychiatric disorders.

Friedman and Downey (2002). In this book we discussed sexual orientation in men and women and concentrated on research and clinical material presented during the past decade. Little of the material we considered was discussed in Friedman's earlier book on male homosexuality. The first half of the book is developmental, and we explained the basis for conceptualizing female sexual orientation as part of the psychology of women and male sexual orientation as a dimension of the psychology of men. We also discussed the origins of male homophobia in late childhood. The clinical section "Sexual Orientation and Psychoanalysis" was devoted to understanding and treating homophobia and internalized homophobia. Although the scientific and clinical sections of our book are integrated, each part stands on its own. Clinicians interested in the psychodynamic aspects of homophobia, for example, can read this part of the book separately.

Friedman and Downey (1994). This was a "Special Article" for the *New England Journal of Medicine,* in which we discussed the epidemiology, endocrinology, genetics, and psychological aspects of homosexuality.

Friedman and Downey (2000a and b). These articles on sexual fantasy, development, and gender-role psychology are reproduced and elaborated on in our book.

REFERENCES

American Psychiatric Association. (1994). *Diagnostic and Statistical Manual of Mental Disorders* (4th ed.). Washington, DC: Author.

Billy, J. O. G., Tanfer, K., Grady, W. R., & Klepinger, D. H. (1993). The sexual behavior of men in the United States. *Family Planning Perspectives, 25,* 52–60.

Dover, K. J. (1989). *Greek Homosexuality.* Cambridge, MA: Harvard University Press.

Downey, J. I., & Friedman, R. C. (1998). Female homosexuality: Classical psychoanalytic theory reconsidered. *Journal of the American Psychoanalytic Association, 46*(2), 471–506.

Friedman, R. C. (1988). *Male Homosexuality: A Contemporary Psychoanalytic Perspective.* New Haven, CT: Yale University Press.

Friedman, R. C., & Downey, J. (1994). Special Article: Homosexuality. *New England Journal of Medicine, 331,* 923–930.

Friedman, R. C., & Downey, J. I. (2000a). The psychobiology of late childhood: Significance for psychoanalytic developmental theory and clinical practice. *Journal of the American Academy of Psychoanalysis, 28*(3), 431–448.

Friedman, R. C., & Downey, J. I. (2000b). Psychoanalysis and sexual fantasies. *Archives of Sexual Behavior, 29*(6), 567–586.

Friedman, R. C., & Downey, J. I. (2002). *Sexual Orientation and Psychoanalysis: Sexual Science and Clinical Practice.* New York: Columbia University Press.

Kernberg, O. (1975). *Borderline Conditions and Pathological Narcissism.* New York: Jason Aronson.

Laumann, E. O., Gagnon, J. H., Michael, R. T., & Michaels, S. (1994). *The Social Organization of Sexuality: Sexual Practices in the United States.* Chicago: University of Chicago Press.

Maccoby, E. E. (1998). *The Two Sexes: Growing Up Apart, Coming Together.* Cambridge, MA: Harvard University Press.

Ovesey, L. (1969). *Homosexuality and Pseudohomosexuality.* New York: Science House.

Chapter Seventeen

Understanding Transgendered Phenomena

Friedemann Pfäfflin, MD

INTRODUCTION

As a medical student I appreciated the opportunity to regularly assist a famous psychiatrist, Eberhard Schorsch, at the Institute of Sex Research at Hamburg University, Hamburg, Germany. At that time in his career, Dr. Schorsch was almost exclusively active in forensic psychiatry. He saw the most extraordinary people who had committed serious crimes, in order to prepare psychiatric expert evaluations for courts. During his examinations of criminals, for example, who had committed sexual murders, he enabled his patients to talk by being reserved, treading softly, and listening attentively. The patients themselves, their lawyers, the courts, and the public often became aware of the motives for and circumstances of the patients' horrible deeds, and the psychiatrist was admired for his capacity to create such insight.

However, in the case of the first patient with transsexual symptoms whom I saw with him, Dr. Schorsch's typical engaging reserve gave way to total passivity. The patient talked almost unendingly—without appearing to need a stimulus. Dr. Schorsch never interrupted him, even when it was apparent that my mentor did not get a single answer to any of his questions. It was as if the patient was allowed to talk into empty space. The patient did not appear at the next session. When this same pattern of psychiatric passivity repeated itself with the second and third transsexual patient, I asked Dr. Schorsch about the reasons for his different behavior with these patients. I recognized that I had strongly identified with the patients and what I perceived to be their feeling of being at a total loss because of the doctor's lack of response.

He told me that he could only minimally relate to the patients' wish for "sex change" and "not much could be done anyway." "Certainly, it is true that only in Casablanca, Morocco, where most European transsexuals go, is sex reassignment surgery frequently performed. The chances of success are not great and the University Clinic of Hamburg does not have sufficient personnel to tackle this difficult problem. This is in contrast to the United States where the situation is more advanced, with a number of large gender identity clinics." The psychiatrist suggested that if I was interested, I could do a clinical attachment there. Following this suggestion, I spent several weeks at the Johns Hopkins University Gender Identity Clinic in Baltimore, which, since 1965, had been the first American university clinic to carry out "sex changes." Along with John Money, John K. Meyer, and their coworkers, I was able to talk to a large number of patients who sought assessments, therapy, or follow-up. I was amazed to observe how openly patients with transsexual symptoms were received. I was also fascinated by the patients themselves and developed a great interest in sex and gender issues. Later, back in Germany, I held a position as assistant under Schorsch and since then have dedicated most of my professional life to transsexuals, transgenderists, and related issues.

DIFFERENT RESPONSES BY MENTAL HEALTH PROFESSIONALS

The psychiatrist's and my responses to the confrontation with a person's wish to change his or her sex mark two extremes of possible reactions: overengagement on my side, total detachment on the psychiatrist's side. Obviously, there is something very irritating about such a wish. It seems hard to remain neutral, to listen, to watch, and to develop empathy before taking refuge in activism. This is true for friends, partners, and relatives, and it is true for the professionals, too, who are sought out by transgender patients. Three additional examples of first encounters may illustrate the diversity of possible reactions to such irritation.

A Dramatic Encounter

A famous sexologist once described his first encounter with a transsexual patient. It occurred during a time when public reports on transsexualism and transgenderism were not yet available and most physicians had never heard of such phenomenon. According to the information he had received from his receptionist, he was expecting a male patient and was thunderstruck when a beautiful lady entered his office, pulled a gun out of her handbag, aimed at him, and said, "If you don't issue a referral to the surgeon for sex reassignment surgery immediately, I will shoot you."

It is hard to conceive of a more dramatic first encounter between a patient and a doctor. When trying to imagine yourself in such a situation, what do you experience? Fear? Anxiety? Horror? What would you have done? Would you have knocked the gun out of her hand without hesitation, because you are trained in self-defense? Would you have cried for help? Would you have tried to escape? Or would you politely have offered her a seat in a perfect reaction formation? One may think of many different reactions.

To calm you down: There is ample evidence that the story is completely fictitious. The colleague is in good health. One might ask even more so what caused him to publish the event and what he wanted to convey with the story. I have no doubts that he was horrified when confronted with the transsexual desire. In addition, it seems remarkable that he exclusively blames the patient for causing this horror. But what was it that frightened him so much, when the story is but a fantasy? Might it be possible that he was, due to his own unresolved conflicts, deeply afraid of women so that he could conceive of a woman only as an aggressive phallic being, as a *pistolièra*?

An Administrative Solution

A family doctor saw a male patient with the same request as the fictitious patient just mentioned, the only difference being that this man uttered his request with a very low voice and pleadingly, not demandingly. The doctor was so touched by this and by the patient's depressive state and obvious suffering that she felt incited to immediately take action. She sent him to me with a letter: "Dear colleague, the patient wants a sex reassignment. Please let me know if the health insurance will pay for the operation and if I will be liable when recommending such a treatment. I also need information on how much estrogen material [sic!] has to be injected."

The doctor thus tried to solve the crisis that she experienced when confronted with the patient's desire by means of administrative steps. That the man had come and said, "I cannot be a man, please help me, I cannot stand it any longer, I cannot live like that," seemed to have moved her so much that she threatened to become depressed herself and counteracted this by resorting to an administrative solution. She took his wish at face value, without exploring it in more depth and even without asking me to do this. Her irritation and her doubts were expressed only indirectly in her seemingly neutral question; whether or not she might be liable.

Taking Time and Reflecting on One's Irritation

The third example I owe to a psychotherapist who is strongly opposed to sex reassignment and who hoped to get out of the affair by telling his patient after the first encounter that he did not want to refer the patient to a surgeon but would be willing to find another doctor or an institution with more experience in handling transgender problems that might help. Between the intake and the second interview, he busily inquired about alternative treatment centers, discussed the case with many colleagues, and, during that discussion, became increasingly uncertain as to why he wanted to get rid of this patient so quickly. He realized that he was both made uneasy and fascinated by the patient.

He opened the second interview by explaining that he had used the time to ponder the first one, and that he had decided that *he* would not help the patient find a surgeon. Instead, he would like to offer the patient the opportunity to discuss his wish for sex reassignment surgery and any doubts he might have about such a treatment. The patient's expression froze. To prevent the patient from leaving angrily, the therapist continued talking by referring to a remark of the patient's during the first interview. "You said that you made up your mind that you needed sex reassignment surgery to 99.5%. I want to know how large the remaining half percent was."

Hesitantly, the patient nodded, thus indicating at least partial agreement. The therapist explained that he thought he was able to help the patient best in his search for certainty by keeping a neutral stance and not taking the side of encouraging or discouraging his wish for surgery. Instead, the psychotherapist wanted to support the patient in finding certainty for himself. With this empathic intervention he respected his own limits but, at the same time, opened a wide space that allowed the patient to explore his wishes in great detail and to engage in a very fruitful psychotherapy, in which he resolved a deep depression underlying his transsexual symptoms.

TRANSGENDERISM:
A CHALLENGE TO THOSE WHO ARE NOT TRANSGENDERED

The wish to change one's own sex is a challenge to most people, not only to mental health professionals. Most people feel and experience themselves as either male or female, and never in their lives would they waste a thought on a life in the cross-gender role. Women are proud of their femaleness and especially of those body parts and functions that constitute this femaleness. The same holds true for men. They are usually proud of their male genitals, their deep voice, and their ability to grow a beard, even if they may not like to actually grow a beard. People see themselves as males or females, and they want to be mirrored in the eyes of others in their respective sex and gender. The sex of a person is not just a bodily attribute, but it usually constitutes the person as a whole. In addition, it is a signal to others and contributes to a large extent to the kind and quality of interactions, attachments, and relationships that people may establish during their lives.

Being confronted with somebody who does not share this pride in his or her own bodily outfit is experienced by most people as an attack against their own identity. Automatically, they try, as is usually the case in conversations, to identify with the other person's wish, and they rapidly come to the conclusion: "That, I would never want to do. For me, it would be the worst thing I can think of." For transgendered people, such a reaction may be a source of great distress. They also want to be acknowledged and mirrored in the eyes of their beholders in the same way that they see themselves.

THE TRANSGENDERED PHENOMENON: WHAT IS IT?

During the 1980s, *transgenderism* slowly became an umbrella term for a variety of transitional lifestyles between the traditional dichotomous extremes of being either male or female. The word *lifestyle* may not exactly be the proper term for all the phenomena involved, but for an introduction it may serve to at least superficially describe what this chapter is about.

The term *transgenderism* was coined in an attempt to leave the limitations of a clinical and medical interpretation behind and to promote a broader understanding of transitional or in-between states that have their own pride. Some of these states might best be understood and helped clinically. Others never cross the clinical threshold. They unfold in individual or social activities beyond clinics and treatment centers.

The term *lifestyle* conjures up in many people the connotation of free choice. Some *transgenderists* may claim that for themselves, too. They have chosen to permanently live either in the opposite gender role or somewhere in-between the extremes of stereotypical maleness and femaleness, and they are happy with it.

Others have the feeling of being trapped in the wrong body—for example, a male body, but that they really are female, or vice versa. They suffer from the discrepancy of their gender identity and their cross-sexual bodily outfits. They cannot help feeling different. They do not experience a free choice but instead an irresistible urge to change, or they have changed their bodies with the help of medication and surgery, so that their bodies fit their gender identities. Traditionally, this phenomenon is called *transsexualism*.

Again, others switch clothes and gender roles temporarily. Some of them are sexually excited when doing so; others are not. Sometimes cross-dressing is sexually exciting, and the fascination for cross-dressing vanishes rapidly after the person has had an orgasm. Then, the individual feels ashamed and does not want to have anything to do with it any longer. But the desire and the urge for it return, and the story starts all over again. In many biographies sexual excitement plays an important role only initially, but this excitement fades away over the course of time. This phenomenon is usually called *transvestism*.

There are transitions between all three phenomena. Somebody may start as a transvestite and end up as a transgenderist or a transsexual. Nobody can really foretell which route and which developmental path an individual may eventually take.

ETHNOLOGICAL PARALLELS

Transgenderism was observed in many cultures, although it had other labels and often a different significance. Ethnologists of the 18th and 19th centuries described transgenderists in native American cultures as *berdache*, an inappropriate name that in fact was derived from Arabian and French words for male prostitutes in the old Arabian world. In some of the more than 130 North American Indian cultures, *berdaches* were believed to have spiritual powers and thus had an outstandingly honored social position and sometimes the function of a witchdoctor. But this was not true for all Indian cultures. Today, the term *berdache* is no longer used. Instead, one talks of the *two-spirit* or the *two-spirited* phenomenon,[1] although some cultures know of more than two genders. In the Amarete culture in the Andes mountains in Bolivia, for instance, a gender proliferation is found, and a person may have up to 10 different gender roles, some of which are permanent, whereas others are dependent on the land one owns, on the office one holds, or on what one does. They are not combined with transvestism.[2]

Similar yet different phenomena as transgenderism in the Western world were found in other parts of the world, for example, the *hijras* in India, the *kahtoey* in Thailand, the *mak nyahs* in Malaysia, and the *kushra* in Pakistan. The main differences between these phenomena and Western transgenderism can be attributed to Western individualism. Historians found forerunners of the phenomenon in earlier epochs—for example, in the 17th and 19th centuries in the Netherlands and in France, and even in old mythology.

WHY ALL THOSE NAMES AND CATEGORIES?

One might wonder why we cannot do with just one name for a variety of similar phenomena. When a new term is coined, it is usually due to the awareness that interests of special subgroups need to be addressed. The famous German sexologist Magnus Hirschfeld, a protagonist of the gay liberation movement at the end of the 19th and the beginning of the 20th century, coined the term *transvestism* in 1910,[3] at a time when the gay liberation movement was at risk of failing. Some noblemen with close connections to the German Kaiser Wilhelm II were convicted of homosexual acts, then still a felony. One faction, oriented toward an idealized Greek type of socially well-adjusted lifestyle, therefore feared the failure of its attempts to abolish criminal sanctions against gay men if homosexualism included so-called effeminate styles, drag queens, fags, and so forth. Hirschfeld reacted by presenting a two-volume monograph with the title *Die Transvestiten* (The Transvestites), thus creating a new category apart from homosexuality. The book contained biographies of people, many of whom would now be characterized as having transsexualism or transgenderism.

Transvestite remained the leading term for cross-dressing men, less frequently for women, until the 1960s, regardless of whether these persons changed their roles only temporarily, wanted to live permanently in the opposite sex and gender role, or wished for hormonal and surgical treatment. Hirschfeld had also first mentioned the term *transsexualism* in 1923 in passing.

That this term, *transsexualism*, became a category of its own was mainly due to the availability of hormonal and surgical sex reassignment. More or less silently, such operations had been performed in Europe in rare cases since 1912. The general public learned about such interventions only in the early 1950s, when information about the famous case of the former American GI Christine Jorgensen spread like wildfire around the globe—it was the time when television was becoming widespread. With the foundation of the first Gender Identity Clinic at the Johns Hopkins University Clinic in Baltimore, Maryland, in 1965, such interventions were groundbreaking and controversial and in some settings eventually became accepted treatments.

To justify medical treatments, you need, first of all, a proper medical diagnosis. The term *transvestism* was not suitable for this purpose, because it implied such a wide range of behaviors, some of which were even criminalized in some states of the United States. An alternative was needed. Focusing on cases of severe suffering, Harry Benjamin (1966)[4] presented his monograph *The Transsexual Phenomenon,* demonstrating that transsexualism was a medical problem that had to be tackled. The diagnosis transsexualism was born. In 1980 it was included in the *Diagnostic and Statistical Manual* of the American Psychiatric Association. In 1991, the International Classification of Diseases, edited by the World Health Organization, adopted it and closely connected the diagnosis with hormonal and surgical treatment, as if the diagnosis automatically implied one specific form of treatment.

Gender identity clinics and other treatment centers developed admission criteria for sex reassignment. To be on the safe side, they selected patients for whom they expected the best prognosis and the least amount of trouble. In some clinics the admission rate was much lower than 10 percent of applicants. All applicants had to undergo diagnostic psychiatric procedures, but they often did not want to comply with these. They defined their problem as a mistaken body, not a sick mind. They did not want to be labeled psychiatric patients. Why should they attend psychotherapy when there were hormones and surgery? That was what they wanted. And they wanted to live freely and proud, without having to submit to psychiatric and medical requirements. That was the background for the birth of the term and the movement of *transgenderism*. Thus, most transgenderism escapes clinical awareness and is studied instead by anthropologists and sociologists.[5]

As a reaction, the *Diagnostic and Statistical Manual* of the American Psychiatric Association dropped the term *transsexualism* altogether in its 4th edition (1994) and now prefers the diagnosis Gender Identity Disorders, leaving open what kind of treatment might be appropriate.

CLINICAL PRESENTATIONS

There remains, however, a large number of persons who seek psychological and medical support. The way in which they present their distress to clinicians varies widely. Only few cases are as spectacular as the three mentioned previously.

There are clients who avoid mentioning their main complaint and instead present totally inconspicuous wishes. For instance, they just regularly come to the doctor's office to pick up the prescription for their spouses for hormonal contraception. The doctor has no suspicion whatsoever that they take the pills themselves. Others come with minor cosmetic complaints. They may ask for a hair transplant because they are going bald at their temples. Or they may ask for a cartilage shaving of a prominent Adam's apple or nose surgery, presenting these complaints as isolated aesthetic problems and independent of any gender-identity conflict. I have seen patients who had up to 10 such minor surgical interventions, sometimes even mammoplasty, in young women who had not spoken a single word about their major gender problem before they finally came to my office. Again, others may come depressed or with suicidal ideation, not revealing the true cause of their distress. With patients who survived a severe suicide attempt, the mental health professional should always consider that a gender-identity problem may be an underlying conflict.

Most patients are much more straightforward. Well informed—and sometimes also misinformed—by self-help organizations or by Internet contacts, they immediately voice what they want. They may or may not be willing to discuss the services they request. Frequently, they are much better informed than are providers. The mental health professional is well advised to be respectful of the patient's information. A lot may be learned from patients. Listening closely to what the patient complains about, reports, and requests usually gives enough clues as to how to proceed. Immediate referral to a specialist may be, as shown in two of the previously mentioned examples, an all-too-hasty decision. In time you, too, will become an expert by listening and learning from patients. Most of what I know about transgendered people I learned from them, not from books. The most abruptly broken-up patient–provider interactions I heard about from patients, as well as from therapists, were due either to the lack of willingness to listen or to prejudice derived from reading the wrong material about transvestism, transsexualism, and transgenderism on the part of the providers. By wrong material, I mean all psychological and medical literature on the three topics that focuses only on severe pathology, points at major deficits (both of which, of course, may be found), and neglects the resources and creative forces of patients. Many providers underestimate the competence of their clients and overestimate their own competence. It's no use trying to hide one's ignorance and inexperience or seeking to cover it by pseudocompetence. The patient will not return for a second appointment if treated in this way. When one does not know an answer to a patient's question, it is preferable to admit that and to explore, together with the patient, where an adequate answer may be found.

FORMS IN MALES AND FEMALES

Although males and females usually have the common aim of changing their sex, they clearly differ in their ideas of what this might mean.

Males

Some males would already be satisfied if something could be done about their deep voices and their beards. The greatest desire for others is to grow breasts, and they may not be interested in getting rid of genitals that they still frequently use to get pleasure out of masturbation. Still others clearly want to have a vagina, and some would even like to get a transplant of a uterus and of ovaries, to be able to become pregnant and give birth to a child. In ongoing contacts one may observe that such wishes surface step by step, with the patient first checking whether the mental health professional has an open ear for them. On other occasions the full scope is demanded from the very beginning.

Among transgendered males the variety of desires and behaviors is, according to all reports and the evidence in the literature, much greater than in females. Often they contact a mental health professional only when they have already taken many steps by themselves—for example, adoption of a female first name, cross-dressing in public and at the workplace, and perhaps even intake of female hormones. They want to demonstrate how sure they are, and they want to safeguard themselves against critical and doubtful questions they expect from the mental health professional. Others are very shy and full of doubts, have not yet thought about a cross-gender first name, and fear very much being ridiculed by family members, friends, and colleagues when they reveal secret desires. They may need a lot of time, and also encouragement, to deal with their doubts.

Comorbidity may be absent, or it may catch the eye from the onset of the first contact. Depending on what kind of complaints come to the fore, the mental health professional should make his choice as to what to focus on first. Suicidal ideation and behavior always have to be dealt with first. Antisocial acting out and psychotic disorders must also be taken seriously and taken care of. But these are rather rare exceptions, not the rule.

Adult patients present at all ages, some very young, others as husbands and as fathers of children, and some even after retirement. The follow-up literature suggests that late onset has a poorer prognosis for passing in the new gender role. Although this may be statistically valid, there are exceptions. The gender team in Amsterdam operated on a 78-year-old man and said it was a success. I have seen a number of men in their 50s and 60s who waited until their children had grown up and had their own families before they dared to consult a mental health professional about their long-lasting distress. Despite having had a hard time, they had not wanted to burden beloved family members. Usually, these patients did extremely well after sex reassignment.

When I started to work with transsexuals, it was a rule in the clinic where I worked not to accept a married person for sex reassignment. First, the marriage needed to be divorced. I regularly invited the wives and learned that quite a few loved their partners and wanted to stay with them even if they moved on to become women socially, as well as somatically. Apart from the financial disadvantages a divorce would bring about, there was no real rationale for demanding that a couple get a divorce. The first such couple whom I met in 1974, parents of three then small girls, are still together and send me a Christmas card every year. Now they are over 70 years old and are happy to assist in rearing their grandchildren. About one fifth of the more than 1,000 transsexual patients whom I have accompanied, mostly for longer periods, were still or had been married (some several times) and had fathered children. It was not infrequent that spouses supported their husbands and stayed together with them.

As an aside, it may be mentioned that admission rules in specific treatment centers contribute to the clinical variety of patients who are seen there, to a large extent. When the Johns Hopkins University Clinic started its gender identity program, sexually active patients were excluded. The administration, as well as the staff of the program, feared public opposition to the treatment if persons engaging actively in heterosexual or homosexual promiscuity, paraphilic activities, or any combination of these were included. At the beginning of the Australian treatment programs for transsexuals, the staff also adhered to this rule and, therefore, did not see sexually active transsexuals. That shaped the conceptualization of transsexualism for quite a while. Transsexuals thus were characterized as asexual persons. Whoever did not fulfill this admission criterion was, in turn, labeled a nontranssexual, not a true transsexual or a secondary transsexual. Clinical practice and research in other centers of the world demonstrated how artificial such categorizations are. Transgendered persons show the same variety of sexual conduct as do all other people, from being very shy and chaste to being extremely sexually active.

Sometimes transgender issues gain importance during a couple's separation conflict. It may be the wife who complains about the man's increasing preference for cross-dressing. But such an increase may also be a man's reaction to his wife's tendencies to act more independently or even to separate from him. I usually offer couple sessions in such situations, to resolve the partner conflict first. The status of the transgender issue that caused the patient or the couple, respectively, to ask for a consultation is often better understood when the more urgent issue of staying together or separation has been discussed.

Females

The group of females with transgenderism and transsexualism seems to be more homogenous than the male group. On an average they come about 5 to 7 years earlier in life for their first consultation, often before the age of marriage. Only a very small number does get married, and very few give birth to a child. Their aversion against sexual intercourse with a man is usually so profound that they do not give way to respective invitations and sometimes get pregnant only in the course of a rape, which certainly contributes to strengthening the aversion. In most cases their tomboyish and masculine behavior is recognized early by family members, by peers, and by teachers but is often not accepted by the family. Severe comorbidity is less frequent compared to that of males. When not accepted as males, that is, in the way they see themselves, some resort to drug and alcohol addiction and are very happy when the staff of an addiction center where they end up first explores the real background for their addiction and supports them in living their desired lives.

WHAT SHOULD BE OFFERED AT THE INTAKE INTERVIEW?

Understanding transgendered phenomena, as suggested in the heading of this chapter, is a hard task. When I was still a student, one of my professors gave me the advice: "If you want to become a researcher, don't try to understand and explain schizophrenia or some topic as large as that. Restrict yourself to describing what you can observe, and investigate more specific questions with small groups of patients."

Within the consultation hour, I never want to understand transsexualism or transgenderism. Rather, I want to understand the person I am talking with now. Some clinicians think that when they have seen one transsexual, they have seen all of them and know all about the phenomenon. They suggest that it is always the same story. What may be true about such an observation is that there are certain patterns and slogans—for example, "Since I can remember, I have wanted to be a {boy/girl}"—that reoccur. But it is always a different story and an individual person. Similarly, one might say that falling in love regularly follows the same patterns. Yet every lover would rightfully protest and characterize his specific condition as singular.

Some patients do not present as persons but as types, calling themselves just "trans" or "transsexual." By dropping this name, everything, they think, should be clear. I often get mail from all over the world, whose authors write, "I am trans. Please give me an appointment for an operation." I am not a surgeon, but even if I were, I would probably become as depressed as I do as a psychotherapist when reading such mail. When somebody reduces his whole life, his whole person, and his whole individuality to such a label, I think this is depressing. At the same time, I feel that I am being reduced to a slot machine, where you insert the trans coin and pull out some genitals. The richness of the human being and of existential interaction is thus lost, and it is my feeling that it has to be regained first, no matter what the practical treatment consequences might be.

If it is not obvious at first glance whether I am talking to a man or a woman, as judged from outer appearance, I usually ask the person how he or she wants to be addressed, and I comply with those wishes. Only on very rare occasions did I experience such a deep discrepancy between the appearance of the patient and her or his wish to be addressed with the cross-gender pronoun that it seemed necessary to dedicate some time to clarify the unease stemming from the discrepancy. As in all other clinical interviews, it is essential that the patient, as well as the therapist, feel at ease when talking to each other.

I would like to give a paradoxical recommendation to those mental health professionals who for the first time encounter a transgendered person: See yourself as a discoverer who has just found a treasure. Yet keep in mind King Solomon's saying that there is nothing new under the sun. That will keep you enthusiastically engaged and, at the same time, modest. You do not have to immediately publish a single case study, taking pride in explaining the whole phenomenon and sometimes even the whole transgendered world. Many other authors have done that. It usually was at the expense of the patient, who then experienced himself as being—and actually was—used for other purposes and thus dropped out of treatment. There are so many crude theories about transsexualism and transgenderism that it is no surprise that many patients prefer to avoid contact with mental health professionals. You should take an invitational stance toward the patient, and both of you will profit from it.

WHAT SHOULD NOT BE OFFERED

Do not put yourself under pressure to offer the patient so-called deep interpretations in the first session, by explaining the logic of his transgender development from inborn conditions, unconscious early childhood experience, and family structure. Apart from the fact that the patient in all likelihood has pondered these issues many a time without finding satisfactory explanations, such effort usually is in vain and produces at best rationalizations without explanatory power. They may satisfy the clinician, but usually not the patient.

Similarly, it is of little use to confront the patient with the fact that after a sex change, he will not be able to have children or might be exposed to social discrimination. Again, others have told him that long ago, he has often thought about it or even experienced it, and it causes him great distress. That is why he is consulting you. The famous late director of the gender identity program at Charring Cross Hospital in London wrote in a survey about his work that a person with transsexualism will never become a full member of the opposite sex and that a former man, after a sex change operation, will be but a castrated man.[6] Fortunately, such crude utterances are now history, but, unfortunately, they still have repercussions in the legislation of the United Kingdom, which to the present time does not allow a post-op person with transsexualism to get married in his new gender role.

Instead of continuing this list of absurdities, it may be useful to know some general rules for positively handling transgender issues. You will find more about such rules in the following paragraph.

STANDARDS OF CARE

When sex reassignment was still a controversial issue, doctors were afraid to offend generally accepted customs and to go against laws protecting the integrity of a healthy person; for example, laws prohibiting castration. Naturally, they wanted to be on the safe side, and they also wanted their patients to be on the safe side. They did not want to be seen as quacks, especially as there is a lot of quackery around for rare conditions that are unknown to many health professionals.

Against this background it was essential to formulate standards of care for the treatment of people with transsexualism. People with transvestism consulted mental health professionals only occasionally, as one usually does not need psychological or medical advice on how to cross-dress. When it comes to sex change, however, one does need to be helped, as it is impossible to manage it all on one's own.

Such standards were first formulated in 1979. In reverence of Harry Benjamin, the author of the first monograph on transsexualism, they were later called the Harry Benjamin International Gender Dysphoria Association's *The Standards of Care for Gender Identity Disorders* (SOC), and they were regularly updated. The two most recent versions are freely accessible in the Internet.[7] It is worthwhile to read both versions, to get a notion of the shifts of emphasis at different times and of what is generally accepted in the scientific and clinical community. But don't forget: Standards are guidelines, and they should not be used as cookbooks that don't allow any latitude. As cookbooks they give a good orientation for the beginner. The art of cooking allows for variations and refinements. And many transgendered persons want to determine their own routes. As a co-traveler, the mental health professional may get to know fascinating parts of inner and outer worlds yet unknown to him when he is open to individual route planning, as long as it is not hazardous. As a responsible person, he will take care of himself, as well as of the patient.

As guidelines, the SOC found international recognition and distribution, although, in some other countries, various medical and psychological committees issued their own standards, and in other countries even the legislative or administrative bodies or the courts regulate the access to sex change.

OUTCOME OF TREATMENT: SURPRISES

Provided proper treatment is offered, the outcome is usually favorable. One should talk of *outcome* in plural, however, as there are a number of different possible outcomes. Some patients will, with or without ongoing counseling or psychotherapy, reconcile with their primary bodily outfit and the appropriate gender role. For others this is impossible, and they will move on. They might stop at any stage in-between the two extremes, or they might progress to a full sex change.

Mental health professionals should not kid themselves about knowing the long-term outcome when meeting a transgendered person for the first time or about knowing what would be best for this person. I remember a number of first encounters when I thought, Why not prescribe cross-sex hormones? Or even, Why not send this patient immediately to the surgeon, if he so wishes? The respective patients were so overwhelmingly convincing in their appearance in the desired gender role, and their histories seemed so coherent and typical that it did not seem to make sense to further explore the conditions of their everyday lives and to encourage them to expose themselves to what the Standards of Care call the Real Life Experience.

On the other hand, I saw persons of whom I could not conceive ever passing successfully in the desired gender role because their stature, their large hands and feet, their prominent chin, their dark beard, and their deep voice contributed to such a striking appearance that they would always attract undue attention.

In both instances, I repeatedly witnessed surprising developments. Some of the initially perfect people with transsexualism gave up their wish to live as females and, in the long run, settled as males. On the other hand, some of the seemingly unsuited candidates finally found peace in the new gender role and are getting on quite well. Transgenderism and transsexualism are first and foremost inner conditions, and these inner conditions are decisive for what might be best for the patient. To judge patients according to stereotypes of how a woman should look does not do them justice.

OUTCOME OF TREATMENT: STATISTICS

During the economic recession of the 1980s, it suddenly became an issue in my country of whether health insurance companies were obliged to pay for sex reassignment or not. They had paid earlier with little ado, as there were not so many cases, and most of the patients had gone abroad for surgery—mainly, to Morocco—and had paid for it out of their own pockets. In 1980, a new law was passed in Germany, allowing change of first name and of legal sex. It was discussed widely, and the public feared that a large number of persons would now want to have sex reassignment surgery. Insurance companies feared the costs and suddenly started to refuse reimbursement. Quite a few patients went to court. Expert witnesses were called in, among them a famous forensic psychiatrist who regularly wrote that the outcome of sex reassignment was extremely poor and that there were many regrets.

When I was also called in as an expert to promote some of my patients' claims, I started to study the evidence. Together with a colleague, Astrid Junge, we evaluated more than 75 reviews and individual follow-up studies after sex reassignment surgery from the international scientific literature published between 1961 and 1991, covering more than 3,000 persons after sex reassignment surgery.[8] The results were encouraging and proved that this treatment had been scientifically evaluated more thoroughly than were quite a number of other treatments generally accepted in various fields of medicine.

Seven factors of effectiveness were identified through international clinical research between 1961 and 1991: (1) the patient's continuous contact with a treatment center, (2) cross-gender living or real-life experience, (3) cross-hormone treatment, (4) counseling and psychotherapy, (5) surgery, (6) quality of surgery, and (7) legal acknowledgment of sex change.

On an average, about two-thirds of the individual samples had improved on most measures applied in the different studies; close to one-third had not impressively changed, neither to the worse nor to the better; and only a few had worsened. The latter is, of course, an appalling outcome, as is the 1 to 2 percent of patients who regretted sex reassignment in the long run.

REGRETS

It is tragic when people find out only after sex reassignment surgery that the route they have taken was misleading. It is tragic for patients, as well as for those mental health professionals who were involved in their treatment. I know for sure of two of my patients with whom this occurred, and we still have regular contact. Both clearly emphasize that at the time when they made the decision for the operation, they believed they had no alternative. I cannot but agree with them, although I am aware of shortcomings of the treatment, be it poor surgical results or neglect of the fact that one of these patients skipped many appointments in psychotherapy, always having "good reasons," but without us reflecting what may have been concealed behind such good reasons.

I got to know some post-op patients who had been treated elsewhere only many years after they had returned to their former gender roles and were now asking for my advice on whether they should go for surgical restitution, usually a rather futile undertaking. Their suffering affected me very much, and at first glance I thought it would last forever. But even then, exploring their histories and their former striving to have surgery usually revealed biographical constellations and inner worlds that allowed one to understand that what they had done had been necessary for them at the time they did it. In all but one case, lasting reconciliation was achieved.

ETIOLOGY: LOOKING BACK OR LOOKING
IN THE HERE AND NOW AND INTO THE FUTURE

The reader might be astonished to find a paragraph on etiology only so late in the chapter. When therapists are interviewed by journalists or asked by spouses, parents, and other relatives of transgendered persons, the first questions asked are "Where does it come from?" "What are the causes?" and "How do you explain the trans-phenomenon?" Intentionally, I postponed these questions here.

First of all, would it make a difference for your present contact with your patient if you knew the answer(s)? There are many phenomena of which we do not know the causes. And even if we knew them, nobody can change the past. Patients sit in front of you and want to be relieved from their distress. They do not want an academic discussion of causes, elaborate as these may be. They wants to have their problems solved now.

Second, if your argument is that you want to know the causes for the sake of prevention, do you really want to prevent people from becoming transgendered? The same etiological discussion was expanded endlessly with homosexuality. What argument should we use to prevent men from wanting to be gay and women to be lesbian?

When voiced by family members, especially parents, the causal questions, even if formulated in the same words as the journalists', have a different underlying melody: "Who is responsible and who can be blamed?" Under such circumstances, I regularly say, "It's certainly not your fault. Your son (or daughter) is not here to blame you but to solve his (or her) own problem."

Third, science gives some answers to the etiological questions and sums them up in one single phrase: "There are many factors that may contribute to a transgender development, for example, genetics and environment." This seems to be a convenient and comprehensive answer, and yet it does not explain anything. Of course, this summary may be fanned out and differentiated in more detail. Let's take environment: Is it the intrauterine hormonal environment or the medication that the pregnant mother might have taken? Is it trauma at birth? Having been an unwanted child? The position in the sibling order? Conscious or unconscious wishes of the parents to have a child of the opposite sex? Having been teased as a toddler for certain play and toy preferences? The list could be continued endlessly. The same is true for the genetic or anlage perspective: Is there a chromosomal deficiency, a mutation, and a cell count difference in certain regions of the brain, a hormonal imbalance? Again, these are but a few examples.

Interesting as each of these questions may be, it is rather unlikely that you will ever be able to adequately solve them for your individual patients. Discussing their lives with them, in great detail, however, you might get a hint as to where to put greater emphasis in individual cases if patients are interested in finding an answer. Most answers will stay hypothetical, though, as long as you have the patients in treatment.

Instead of looking back and asking where the present condition may have come from, you and the patient may use your time more efficiently by asking where it leads to or, more precisely, where the patient wants to go. Together, you may explore patients' anxieties with which they stop themselves from doing what they allegedly want to achieve so urgently, as well as explore their fears and doubts; provide information on what realistic perspectives there are; and support them in their resources. I have often observed that patients first have to have the experience of being supported by the mental health professional in their present crisis, before they feel safe enough to explore such luxurious questions as those about the precursors of their condition.

IS PSYCHOTHERAPY A PREREQUISITE?

In the beginning of sex reassignment surgery this intervention was justified as a last resort, after all other—at that time, often very drastic—psychiatric treatments (e.g., electroshock, lobotomy, long-term hospitalization in closed wards) had failed. In the 1970s and 1980s, when sex reassignment surgery became available in many parts of the world and could not be denied as a helpful form of treatment any longer, some renowned psychotherapists in North America and in Europe started a campaign against such "mutilating interventions," as they preferred to call sex reassignment. After they had lost the battle between the alternatives of either psychotherapy or hormones with surgery, they finally had to give in. Some of them then argued that somatic treatment should be offered only when the failure of a psychotherapeutic attempt had been demonstrated. This line of argumentation is a kind of *hara-kiri*. As long as patients know they will get what they want only by letting the therapist fail, one can predict the outcome. And a psychotherapist whose explicit intentions are counter to those of the patient has no chance and even deprives the patient of considering alternative routes.

Psychotherapy is one of the factors of effectiveness in regard to a good outcome for sex reassignment surgery, granted that it is started and pursued open-mindedly. The more that I, as a therapist, want patients to give up their wish for sex reassignment, the less I give patients a chance to arrive at this decision. In contrast, when I am open for all options, including surgery, patients have a chance to find the route appropriate for themselves.

ARE TRANSGENDER PHENOMENA MENTAL HEALTH ISSUES?

There is a twofold answer to this. They are not, considering the varieties of lifestyles throughout space and time. When an employer asks me, and when the patient has given written informed consent for my response, I will explain that, usually, a transgender phenomenon does not interfere with job performance and effectiveness.

The second half of the answer is, yes, they are. When an individual is distressed by a transgender issue, it is legitimate and also reasonable to consult a mental health professional and have counseling or psychotherapy. If it should turn out during such work that this individual needs hormone treatment and sex reassignment surgery, then there is a medical indication and the treatment should be covered by health insurance.

CHILDREN, YOUTHS, AND ADOLESCENTS

Not all, but many transgendered persons report having felt different from very early on or for as long as they can remember. When in the 1960s clinical reports appeared about very young cross-dressing children, clinicians and scientists thought they had found transsexuals *in statu nascendi*. These children seemed to confirm the adult transsexuals' retrospective reports. Evidently, more research was needed, and two clinicians and scientists, Green and Stoller, started a prospective study following up these children for nearly 20 years.[9] Alas, it turned out that most of these children turned out to become homo- or heterosexual, not transgendered.

Most of the children of this sample had behaved so extremely that they were identified as clinical cases and brought by their parents for diagnostics and therapy. It is, however, not uncommon that children, for certain periods of time, may prefer cross-gender typical toys and plays, wear mothers' or siblings' clothes, and take cross-gender roles in role-plays, such as father, mother, and child. Mostly, these are transient phenomena, in which the children explore their gender roles without yet being fixed to either gender role. Most parents do not take it all too seriously but enjoy the playfulness and exploratory behavior of their children.

In some children such behavior persists; in others, it comes to the fore only around puberty. Many a time it is acted out only secretly and, when detected by parents, often a critical event, it results in punishment of and shame for the child. In some families, such an event is then denied and is never again openly discussed, but its dynamics remain powerful under the cloak of superficial harmony and silence.

The problem is rarely unveiled to the mental health professional, but if it is, it happens in two typical ways. There are parents who want you to "cure the child from his deviant behavior," at the same time denying all possible conflicts within the family. Alternatively, parents bring their child of 7 or 12 years to demonstrate how cute the child is in the cross-gender role and ask you to start hormone treatment.

Both alternatives are challenging. I have not worked in child and adolescent psychiatry and psychotherapy but was repeatedly contacted by such parents and their children, as there is a great lack of specialists in the field. I felt great pity for these children, posing like dolls in the hands of their parents and sometimes like weapons between conflicting parental parties. Almost automatically, I found myself on the side of the child and felt impulses to rescue the child from these parents. Parents will sense such a partiality immediately and may withhold the child from further contact. It is therefore essential to find a balance, both reflecting the parents' needs and respecting their defense mechanisms. It is a delicate situation, usually easier to handle when working in a team with family therapists. As those are not readily available everywhere, the focus should lie on establishing and fostering contact, to be able to further explore the family situation and to possibly refer these families to more experienced specialists.

In the last 15 years some centers have specialized in treating children, youths, and adolescents with gender identity disorders, for example, in Toronto, Canada; London, the U.K.; and Utrecht, the Netherlands. There are now reports showing that cross-gender identity may actually be fixed in some adolescents long before they reach legal maturity. These kids and their parents should be encouraged to have the child enroll in school in the desired gender role. For some adolescents it may even be indicated to give medication to cause pubertal delay. The rationale for this is that they, as adults with transsexualism, will otherwise have to undergo costly and painful electrolysis of their facial hair, long vocal training if their voice has already broken, and other interventions that will not be necessary if they do not develop the full somatic characteristics of their primary sex.

For the handling of these problems, the Royal College of Psychiatrists in London has issued guidelines in 1998, which meanwhile have been incorporated into the latest version of the *Standards of Care* of the Harry Benjamin Gender Dysphoria Association.

PATIENCE

Patient and *patience* have, as words, the same root. As psychologists and medical doctors, we are trained to work quickly and effectively and to provide solutions for many seemingly and not infrequently really unsolvable problems. *Efficiency* is the magic word in modern medicine, although, in the long run, we are not as efficient as we claim to be. All of our patients, as well as we ourselves, will eventually be hauled in by death.

In working with transgendered people, I have experienced many a dramatic situation, and sometimes I was as desperate as my patients were. I remember a young girl who had just finished high school and came for a sex change. Her parents knew about her visit—she needed their insurance card for admission to the outpatient clinic where I worked—and sent me a registered letter prohibiting my treating her. Threateningly, they announced their visit to my office and canceled it for trivial reasons. The patient herself did not want to convey much of her inner world and was angry with me for insisting on regular visits for at least 1 year before making a decision for hormone treatment. At that time, this was the rule in the clinic. She came once a month—that was the maximum amount of closeness she could bear—before hormone treatment was started. But she appreciated that I intervened at the national admissions office for medical students and attested her a case of hardship so that she could enroll as a medical student, which otherwise would not have been possible due to the very poor marks with which she had left high school. Twice, she failed the preliminary exams for medical students because of an insurmountable disgust and uneasiness she experienced in the anatomical lecture theater. Again I intervened to get special permission for her to take the exams a third time. Thereafter, she had surgery, with poor results. The surgeon illegally experimented on her, clipping the operation sutures on the right breast and sewing them on the left one, to find out which side would give better results. Then, she had a legal sex change.

From then on, this individual, now male, became a fairly good student, simultaneously engaging in the student's organization and in various committees of the faculty. He took his final exams, got married to a colleague, and managed to work in a number of clinics without anybody knowing of his past. That was extraordinary and owed to his ability to give plausible explanations for his scars at the medical examinations when starting a new job. He became a consultant in psychiatry and a psychotherapist, very effective and respected as a forensic psychiatrist by staff as well by patients. About 15 years after our first encounter, he contacted me again and asked for continuing psychotherapy, as he was now prepared to look into his history. We worked for 3 years, and he had to travel a whole day for the appointments. During this psychotherapy, I learned a lot about his family background and severe traumas the patient had suffered, including nearly being killed. Retrospectively, he reflected that had it been possible to reveal all of this 15 years earlier and to work it through, the route to sex reassignment surgery possibly could have been circumvented. At the same time he was convinced that 15 years earlier, it would have been impossible for him to talk about specific events. A lot of mourning was necessary, to say good-bye to lost alternatives and to parents who were both loved and hated. Now, he is content with what he has achieved.

CONCLUSION

My almost 30 years of continuous work with transgendered persons have not resulted in fatigue. For me, it is as fascinating as on the first day. Every person is a new challenge, and taking up this challenge is usually rewarding. To embark on a new encounter is like embarking on a journey to new shores, with new riddles to be solved and new treasures to be found.

NOTES

1. Lang, S. (1998). *Men as Women, Women as Men: Changing Gender in Native American Cultures.* Austin: University of Texas Press. Sabine Lang gives an excellent survey of the history and various interpretations of transgender phenomena in native American cultures.
2. Rösing, I. (2001). *Religion, Ritual und Alltag in den Anden. Die zehn Geschlechter von Amarete, Bolivien* (Religion, Ritual and Everyday Life in the Andes Mountains in Bolivia). Berlin: Dietrich Reimer Verlag. This book by Ina Rösing, an anthropologist of Ulm University, has not been translated into English yet. It would be worthwhile, as the author is a pioneer in exploring hitherto unexplored cultures in Asia, as well as in South America.
3. Hirschfeld, M. (1910). *Die Transvestiten. Eine Untersuchung über den erotischen Verkleidungstrieb mit umfangreichem casuistischem und historischem material* (The Transvestites. An Exploration of the Erotic Instinct to Cross Dress, including many case histories and historical material). Berlin: Alfred Pulvermacher & Co. This path-breaking book also has not yet been translated into English. Readers who want to know more about the early history of transsexualism may have a look into the *International Journal of Transgenderism*, accessible free of charge on the Internet. There you will find my article: "Sex Reassignment, Harry Benjamin, and Some European Roots" (http://www.symposion.com/ijt/ijtc0202.htm).
4. Benjamin, H. (1966). *The Transsexual Phenomenon. A Scientific Report on Transsexualism*

and Sex Conversion in the Human Male and Female. New York: Julian Press. An electronic version of this out-of-print book is accessible free of charge in the book section of the *International Journal of Transgenderism* on the Internet (http://www.symposion.com/ijt/).

5. Ekins, R., & King, D. (2001). Transgendering, migrating and love of oneself as a woman: A contribution to sociology of autogynephilia. *International Journal of Transgenderism, 5*(3). (http. //www.symposion.com/ijt/ijtvo05no03_01.htm). You will find more references in this article if you are interested in the sociology and anthropology of transgenderism.

6. Randell, J. (1969). Preoperative and postoperative status of male and female transsexuals. In R. Green & J. Money (Eds.), *Transsexuals and Sex Reassignment* (pp. 355–381; here p. 375). Baltimore: Johns Hopkins University Press.

7. *International Journal of Transgenderism* (http://www.symposion.com/ijt/). The most recent version, the 6th version, is found in vol. 5, no. 1, 2001; the previous version, the 5th version, in vol. 2, no. 2, 1998.

8. Pfäfflin, F., & Junge, A. (1992). Nachuntersuchungen nach Geschlechtsumwandlung. Eine kommentierte Literaturübersicht 1961–1991. In F. Pfäfflin & A. Junge (Eds.), *Geschlechtsumwandlung. Abhandlungen zur Transsexualität* (pp. 149–457). Stuttgart – New York: Schattauer. An English translation of this chapter is found in the book section of the *International Journal of Transgenderism*, accessible free of charge on the Internet: F. Pfäfflin & A. Junge, Sex reassignment. Thirty years of international follow-up studies: A comprehensive review, 1961–1991 (http://www.symposion.com/ijt/).

9. Green, R. (1974). *Sexual Identity Conflict in Children and Adults.* London: Duckworth. Meanwhile, a number of new studies of children and adolescents with gender identity conflicts have been published, e.g. D. Di Ceglie & D. Freedman. (1998). *A Stranger in My Own Body. Atypical Gender Identity Development and Mental Health.* London: Karnak Books. See also P. Cohen-Kettenis & F. Pfäfflin. (2003). *Transgenderism and Intersexuality in Childhood and Adolescence: Making Choices.* Thousand Oaks, CA: Sage.

Chapter Eighteen

Men Who Are Not in Control of Their Sexual Behavior

Al Cooper, PhD

I. David Marcus, PhD

OVERVIEW

Perhaps the title of this chapter should be "Men who speak with their penises." In our work with sexual compulsivity, we find that sexual behavior is a powerful way that many men communicate the storms and solaces of their internal world. Although dreams may be the golden road to the unconscious, sexual behavior is the fast track to unspoken, perhaps unrealized, feelings. Our work draws passion from how the treatment of sexual behavior so often leads into explorations of how people pursue their needs in a world that can be unyielding, find acceptance in a world that can be disparaging, and find control in a world that can be disempowering. Although we tire of teaching men simple behavioral fixes like the squeeze technique, the treatment of sexual compulsivity cuts to the heart of how feelings affect lives. Its treatment is often the story of how those who feel unacceptable find some resolution to the perhaps universal need to feel accepted. However, sexual compulsivity is typically deeply entrenched and difficult to change, so its treatment is best suited to clinicians who are willing to jog, rather than those who must sprint. In this type of work, we find patients whose emotional vulnerability belies their superficial presentation. These men are often very high functioning in many areas and present with a powerful facade. But beneath this presentation, they have feelings of shame and inadequacy and a sense of being out of control. They hurt and they turn to sex as a panacea for their pain. Sexual compulsivity seems more prevalent now than ever. One reason is that the Internet, with its Triple A engine of access, affordability, and anonymity (Cooper, 1998), has introduced millions of people to a venue where the most explicit and varied sexual fantasies can be accessed all too easily, leading some men down the slippery slope of compulsivity.

Freed from its traditional role of procreation, sex is the climax that releases tension, the surrender that eases control, and the control that binds anxiety. So tightly bound to a man's sense of self, powerfully yielding both intrinsic and utilitarian needs, sexual behavior is sensitive to psychic pressures both past and present. A man gets all this with a rush that comes for some in the pursuit of a partner, for others in the seduction, and for yet others in the climax, leading many of our patients to report an exhilaration, a high that is difficult to match in more stable relationships. With such psychological and physiological payoffs, many of these men center large parts of their lives around preparing for, engaging in, and covering up their sexual activities. We have patients who use the high to self-medicate, to break through their pervasive malaise, to experience some vitality in their lives, and to distract themselves from uncomfortable emotions. Sexual compulsivity is a quasiconnection with another person in a ritualized, constricted, and "safe" manner. Our job is to offer the patient a "real" relationship where emotions are exposed, engaged, and tolerated; where superficial and damaging highs are replaced by a satisfaction that endures, so that looking in the mirror is a more pleasant activity. The patient's inclination is to focus on how others see him and to seek acceptance from the outside; we encourage him to focus on how he sees himself.

In this chapter, we assert that one essential way of viewing sexual compulsivity is as a relationship disorder. Therefore, a supportive and nurturing relationship is the ideal vehicle for change, in that it gives the patient the opportunity to increase his own capacity to engage in healthy relationships. When we are successful, we help the patient deal with barriers to intimacy and to ultimately replace narrowly defined sexual "relationships" with more authentic and multidimensioned relationships. Through our acceptance, he finds his own acceptance. Levine (1992) points to the mechanism of this change, noting that "When psychological intimacy occurs, we begin to weave the (other) person into our selves." The single healthy relationship that psychotherapy provides may not be sufficient, but it is often a critical first step to increasing the patient's tolerance of intimacy. As Leedes (2001) observes, "As many as 95% of sexual addicts are unable to form close attachments" (p. 218). We believe that it is this lack of safe interpersonal connection that drives much of the behavior of sexually compulsive men. In our treatment, we work to form an honest relationship with the patient, in which he tolerates vulnerability in the service of forming a new relationship template that invokes soothing instead of pain. This understanding is consistent with the view that sexual compulsivity is often a disorder of intimacy (Adams & Robinson, 2001; Schwartz & Masters, 1994). In this chapter, we discuss a treatment program that involves a careful evaluation, then a midtreatment interval in which the core issues coalesce, and, finally, how we help these men become conscious of and competent to understand the issues that they must face in the future. It is our hope that you gain a sense of the process we use in treating men who have lost control over their sexual behavior, as well as some of the potential complexities and therapeutic errors commonly seen in working with this population.

WHAT IS SEXUAL COMPULSIVITY?

By "sexual," we mean more than just intercourse. Sexual behaviors include but are not limited to masturbating, viewing pornography, engaging in fetishism (e.g., becoming sexually aroused by inanimate objects like shoes), and chatting on the Internet or the phone. Sexual compulsivity can involve paraphilic (e.g., socially deviant) or nonparaphilic behaviors, or both. Although we prefer the term *sexual compulsivity*, rather than *sexual addiction* (see Goodman, 2001, for a discussion of these terms), the *Diagnostic and Statistical Manual of Psychiatric Disorders* (*DSM*) criteria of "dependence" is often used as a model to define this disorder. That is, an individual can be diagnosed with sexual compulsivity when his or her sexual behavior interferes with social, recreational, or occupational responsibilities; when repeated efforts to stop or decrease the behaviors have been unsuccessful; when the individual spends increasing and excessive amounts of time, money, or both on these activities; and when increased frequency, intensity, or both of sexual behavior is required to reach the same level of arousal. Another practical way to determine if the behavior is problematic is to explore whether it positively or negatively affects important relationships. However, because denial is so often a feature of sexual compulsivity, these patients may underreport difficulties. Therefore, we seek collateral information, as well as keep a keen eye on how the patient acts in our relationship with him.

ONLINE SEXUAL COMPULSIVITY

Sexual compulsivity is not limited to and does not even need to include face-to-face contact with another person. The Internet is the activity of choice for many men (Cooper, 2000). For instance, Delmonico and Carnes (1999) found that 65% of subjects who scored high on the Sexual Addiction Screening Test (SAST) also reported problems with their Internet sexual activity.

Online sexual activities (OSA) include but are not limited to looking at erotic pictures or videos, reading sexual material, engaging in sexual chat, exchanging explicit sexual e-mails or pictures, sharing sexual fantasies while both people masturbate, and looking for people with whom to engage in various offline sexual activities. The Triple A engine of the Internet gives men with prior problems controlling their sexual behavior an ideal venue to pursue these proclivities. It also creates problems for some individuals that they would not otherwise have had.

Internet sexuality, like other forms of sexuality, is best viewed as falling along a continuum, ranging from life-enhancing (Cooper, Scherer, & Marcus, 2002) to problematic (Cooper, Scherer, Boies, & Gordon, 1999). Evidence suggests that most of those who visit Internet sexual sites do so in a recreational way and do not experience negative consequences (Cooper, Boies, Maheu, & Greenfield, 1999). For most people, online activities are sexual in an entertaining way, like viewing a Victoria's Secrets catalogue, rather than in a genital- or orgasm-focused way. However, a significant minority does become entangled in problematic usage that leads to serious adverse consequences in those individuals' lives.

Three ways that users engage in online sexual pursuits have been proposed (Cooper, Putnam, Planchon, & Boies, 1999). The first type includes recreational or nonpathological users. As noted previously, some Internet users access sexually explicit materials due to curiosity, novelty, or entertainment and do not find the material to be problematic. Individuals who have a preexisting propensity toward sexual compulsivity are the second type of Internet users. They may have an already established pattern of unconventional sexual practices, such as a preoccupation with pornography, multiple affairs, or sex with several or anonymous partners. A third type of Internet users does not have a history of sexual compulsivity. It appears that these are the people who may never have had difficulty with sexual compulsivity if it were not for the Internet. They may have had a latent vulnerability, but their internal resources and impulse control were sufficient to resist temptation until faced with the power of the Triple A Engine.

Engaging in OSA is so solitary and secretive an activity, it can easily be hidden from us. To address the patient's reluctance to disclose, we ask detailed questions that cover three areas. First, what types of sites does the patient seek? We include what type of activities he engages in, the kind of pictures he likes, and the people with whom he chats. Second, what are the reasons for the patient's sexual surfing? Recent research found (Cooper, Griffin-Shelley, Delmonico, & Mathy, 2001) that engaging in OSA to cope with stress, as well as participating in activities online that would not be engaged in offline, are two particular risk factors correlated with online sexual problems, so clinicians are wise to include these two data-driven questions in their assessment. The third question is how much time does the patient engage in OSA each week? Cooper, Delmonico, and Burg (2000) found that those who are involved with OSA for 1 hour or less per week rarely find it to have an adverse effect on their lives, whereas those who engage in OSA 11 or more hours a week are more likely to have a problem.

TRANSFERENCE AND COUNTERTRANSFERENCE

Transference and countertransference are complex constructs, and their definitions— let alone, how to effectively incorporate them into therapy—are controversial. Basically, the *experience* of countertransference is that the patient invokes feelings, fantasies, thoughts, and, potentially, actions in us. This provides critical information, because it offers a sense of how others feel in their dealings with the patient, as well as what he is "pulling" from people. The central issues that these men struggle with (e.g., control, dependency, aggression, shame) are not dissimilar from our own. Therefore, based upon the current state of our lives, history, and experiences, a range of powerful feelings might be stirred. For us, as for them, the key is to avoid suppressing or judging our feelings. Instead we try to be conscious, to understand, and then be in a position to use these feelings as a facilitative force in the therapy. For instance, sexually compulsive men often feel out of control, so they will find a multitude of direct and indirect ways to control other people, including us. Nobody likes feeling controlled, so we may experience anger. If we are not tuned into ourselves, the anger may prevent us from being empathetic or cause us to be more rigid and confrontational. Conversely, if we are aware of our anger and what is happening in the therapy that is catalyzing it, we can explore how and why the patient needs control in that moment. Fear of intimacy is another emotional theme we find with these patients. In the room, this fear may be manifested by the patient keeping a distance through talking about issues that are not particularly relevant, by not wanting to talk at all, or by presenting with bland affect. In these situations, it is easy for us to feel bored. This is a common countertransference reaction. We find ourselves thinking about what to have for dinner, instead of about the patient. We may even dread the next session with the patient. However, if a session is boring, we have reason to believe that the patient is probably not engaged. Well, *that* is interesting. Here he is paying us money and investing his time, and he is not engaged. If we are unconscious of the countertransference, we decide to play "chicken." If we are conscious of the countertransference, we ask why.

So, if we attend to our own feelings and work them out in our own therapies and consultations, we can inform the client of these in a helpful manner that allows him to know how he affects others. In this way, countertransference provides exceptional information about the patient. Because sex is so provocative, clinicians who treat sexual disorders are especially vulnerable to difficulties with countertransference. We may feel that the man's behavior is wrong and that he should adhere to nicer sex. As Carnes (1989) aptly notes, "All professional helpers bring a set of beliefs to the problem of sexual addictions—beliefs forged out of experience, culture, and professional training. Given this, therapists need to be aware that they may have beliefs that limit their understanding and acceptance of sexual addiction" (p. 41).

We find that transference and countertransference dynamics can be particularly charged when the gender and other physical attributes (e.g., ethnicity) of the therapist match the sexual preference of the patient. For sexually compulsive men whose sexual preferences include women, expect that he will sexualize a female therapist, which then plunks them both right into the middle of his "stuff." If a male therapist is treating a patient whose object choice is other men, a similar reaction is expected. For instance, the patient may describe a sexual dream or fantasy he had of the therapist. How much detail the patient chooses to use and the energy that he brings to the session may tread a fine line between what is therapeutically helpful and what is sexually acting out with the therapist. Sexual experiences are complex and conflicted for these men, and they often react to these situations with desire, shame, and dread. As if this is not enough, the patient may become angry with the therapist for "causing" him to have these feelings. This is a transference reaction. At these moments the therapist is not *a* woman, she is the patient's wife or mother, or all the women throughout his life who have rejected him. What the therapist sees is flirtatious behavior, devaluing behavior, and then withdrawal. Depending upon prior life experiences, this may trigger feelings from rage to self-deprecation in the therapist. The therapist's feelings may become so powerful that she loses awareness of how they influence her responses to the patient. But, again, remember that how the patient treats the female therapist is a template for how he treats all women. As with any transference reaction, it may be uncomfortable, but it is not good or bad. The best way to handle the reaction is to be aware of what is happening and to help the patient see how he contributes and what it serves for him. The timing of the interpretation is critical. Be wary about interpreting too early, particularly if it is a means to avoid your own feelings. If we expect the patient to linger in feelings, then we must be able to linger with them as well. Still, it is important to interpret any clear boundary infractions (e.g., late payments, addressing the therapist in an overly familiar manner, trying to extend the session) early and often. If the patient does not feel that his message is being received, he may escalate until he obtains the reaction to which he is accustomed. Commenting on the patient's behavior and asking him directly about it makes it part of the therapy and also gives the patient the opportunity to understand what he is doing and why. The clues to how the patient's transference will develop can be predicted by looking at his history. For example, if historically he acts out to protest not feeling in control, then we would expect that the times he experiences lack of control in the therapy (e.g., when an appointment time is changed, when he experiences strong emotion) will be the times that he displays his typical defense.

PREVALENCE

Societal stressors are becoming more intense, and sexual behavior is working double-time to ameliorate all of life's woes. Pornography is estimated to be an $8 billion a year industry (Byrne & Osland, 2000). Prostitution is estimated to average 1.5 million customers a week and to be a $14 billion annual business. Three of four family-hour programs on TV contain some sexual content, and 61% contain sexual behavior, averaging 8.5 sexual interactions per hour (Freeman-Longo & Blanchard, 1998). Several years ago, the National Council on Sexual Addiction and Compulsivity estimated that 6 to 8 percent, or 16 to 21.5 million Americans, are addicted to sex (Amparano, 1998). We have found that the rate jumps to as high as 17% for online sexual problems (Cooper, McLoughlin, & Campbell, 2000). However, both online and offline prevalence rates are difficult to determine because people with these issues are often fearful of the reactions of others and are more likely to hide the frequency and details of their behavior.

There is a dearth of studies that have examined socioeconomic, cultural, racial, and sexual orientation factors in regard to sexual compulsivity. Clinical experience suggests that beyond the estimated 4:1 ratio of men to women, sexual compulsivity is an equal opportunity employer that is influenced but not limited by cultural and ethnic factors. With the space limitations we can only offer some thoughts on the most common presentations and treatment challenges with these men. We suggest that you take the basic ideas offered here and modify them as needed to deal with the range of people that you will see in your practice.

COMORBIDITY

It is rare that an individual will engage in only one type of sexually compulsive behavior. There may be a favorite, but most men find more than one way to "scratch their itch." Often, the presenting issue that is caught is only the tip of the iceberg, and the most shameful activities are hidden the deepest, so stay curious. Furthermore, other types of addictive behaviors (e.g., alcoholism) frequently coexist and may trigger, disinhibit, or help cover sexual compulsivity. Sexual compulsivity may also be entwined with Axis I conditions, such as mood or anxiety disorders. Although these comorbid conditions must be treated, simply attributing sexual compulsivity to another disorder can be a mistake and the sexual behavior must be specifically assessed.

ETIOLOGY

For men who are affectively illiterate, issues concerning anxiety and control play central roles in sexual compulsivity and its treatment. Often, anger underlies sexual behavior and takes the form of "eroticized rage," lying latent until triggered by what Carnes has termed *catalytic events* (1989, p. 56). This point of view is consistent with a diathesis-stress model, in which an individual has an underlying vulnerability to certain types of sexual behavior (Kafka, 2000). We find that many of our patients have difficulty knowing what to do with their own aggressive urges and oscillate, often unconsciously, between passive and aggressive expressions.

In terms of sexual compulsivity, the events often tap into core issues, such as feeling abandoned, unloved, out of control, or simply unacceptable. Other common background factors in individuals who cannot control their sexual behavior include early crossing of normative sexual boundaries via direct (e.g., being sexually abused by an adult) or indirect (e.g., hearing about or seeing a parent's sexual exploits) means, not experiencing another person as a source of soothing, low self-esteem related to abusive childhood experiences (physically, sexually, emotionally, or any combination of these), problematic masculinity introjects, and difficulties with social interactions and relationships. In addition to psychosocial factors, Kafka (2000, 1997) notes a relationship between sexual disinhibition and decreased serotonin.

TREATMENT OPTIONS

Although this chapter focuses on individual psychotherapy, we follow the lead taken by Kafka (2000), in his discussion of nonparaphilic hypersexuality, that effective treatment involves "a multimodal approach, utilizing behavioral, psychodynamic, group, psychoeducational and pharmacological treatments." The research also seems to support that treatment has the best chance of success when it is part of an integrated program offered by those with at least some specialized training in this area (Freeman-Longo & Blanchard, 1998). A comprehensive program will typically also require family or couples' therapy, or both. In addition, we believe that some type of group therapy is a critical component of treatment. (For an in-depth discussion of our group therapy model, see Line & Cooper, 2002.) In certain situations, medications can be an effective adjunct to treatment, to either address comorbid conditions, reduce the amount and urgency of sexual thoughts, or ameliorate sexual disinhibition (Kafka, 2000). And, finally, when the patients' sexual behaviors are dangerous to themselves or others, experienced as especially out of control, particularly refractory to treatment, or any combination of these, inpatient and residential programs can be considered (see www.ncsac.org, for a list of programs).

TREATMENT

Evaluation/Early Treatment

In the waiting room, Kevin casually leafs through a magazine. Sitting up-right and stiff, he does not move when I call his name. As I walk back to the office, I notice that he has not followed and wonder whether he heard me. Just when I am about to go back, he ambles in and sits in a chair instead of on the couch. He immediately addresses me by my first name and says, "I have a few questions to ask." After I answer those that seem appropriate (those needed for him to give informed consent to the treatment), Kevin plainly states that his wife is considering leaving him unless he seeks help. He states that he had a brief affair with a woman he met on an airplane. He has stopped that "thing" but his wife is still upset because she also found a few "porn sites" on their computer.

When asked about whether he has had prior affairs, Kevin asks, "What do you mean by affairs?" When I clarify, he says that he isn't sure. When I ask him to guess how many, he replies, "Hundreds." He says that he does not consider them affairs because it is only sex, not love. During the history taking, Kevin details multigenerational promiscuity. He recalls how his single mother had numerous men coming over to the house at all times and how his grandmother not only talked often about sex and wore skimpy clothing but also encouraged Kevin to walk naked around the house. His father died before his second birthday, so the men his mother had over were his most common masculine contacts. When asked what part of sex he enjoys the most, Kevin looks confused and, for a fleeting moment, vulnerable. He pauses as though gathering his response and finally says, "It's funny . . . but I don't enjoy sex that much." When I ask what part of being with sexual partners he does enjoy, he says, "The yes. I love it when they indicate we've got something going." Before leaving, Kevin smiles and comments on the fact that I work late and that I must be very dedicated.

Our treatment methodology for sexual compulsivity is psychodynamic in nature. As Goodman (2001) notes, "The primary goals of psychodynamic psychotherapy in the treatment of addictive disorders are to enhance individuals' self-regulation and to foster their capacity for meaningful interpersonal connections" (p. 208). We divide our treatment into the evaluation, which often merges into beginning treatment; midtreatment; and the "end game," which involves termination, transition into a different type of treatment, or both.

Our evaluations typically last two to three sessions. We have four goals for the evaluation: to get a sense of the patient's issues, letting him know that we "see" him and are not repelled; to allow the patient to experience our style to see if it works for him (it is essential that he knows that he has some control); to reposition and reframe the issues from "you must stop" to "you can regain as much control as you want"; and to establish a treatment contract with the patient. Starting with the evaluation and continuing through treatment, we focus upon the 3 Rs of therapy: relationship, resistance, and reality. Let's walk through our evaluation sessions, working toward our goals while paying attention to the 3 Rs.

Relationship

We want to reiterate that in our thinking, sexual compulsivity is a relationship disorder, and, therefore, the path to change lies in forming an authentic relationship with the patient. Our relationship with the patient is a real-time example of his universe of relationships. It is easy to believe that we are going to be buffered from the chaos common in the patient's interpersonal life. However, such an assumption obstructs the clearest window into the patient's world. Not only does our relationship with the patient teach us how he attempts to use people in his life, but his descriptions of his day-to-day relationships warn us of the potential traps in our relationship with him. Cues about each individual's themes start from the moment of first contact: what he wears, where he sits in the waiting room, how he walks into the office, and how he addresses and treats us.

Establishing trust is one of the first challenges we find in building a relationship with these men; its waxing and waning course is a central issue throughout treatment. Typically, sexually compulsive men trust no one, including themselves, so why should they trust us? The earliest seed of their potential trust is planted by explicitly establishing a solid therapy frame that includes "rules," such as the frequency of sessions, the fee, and cancellation policies. When working with these men, we bring out our best confidentiality speech, emphasizing its importance and making clear any limitations, both for their sake and to remind ourselves. Sexually compulsive men look for chinks in the trust, and a little lapse or contradiction is not soon forgotten. We are very conscious of what we say and the words we use. If there is an unexpected change in the patient's behavior, we take note of it and usually comment because waiting may result in not seeing him again. Remember that the M.O. of these patients is to have shallow relationships in which they never truly reveal themselves. When emotions get intense or if there is a feeling of not being safe, these men will leave us as quickly as their last sexual partner.

During the evaluation sessions, we try to communicate to the patient that we see beneath his presentation, that we see and can tolerate his "true self." We have found three central relationship themes or fears to be common among men who are sexually compulsive: the fear of intimacy, which is the fear of truly being seen or known; the fear of losing control, which includes feeling strong emotions such as sadness, anger, or love; and the fear of being alone, alternating with the fear of trusting enough to open up. These fears are not mutually exclusive and their concurrent presentation makes for complex cases. For instance, a man may be fearful of being truly known because he feels so fundamentally bad but may also feel unable to tolerate the emotions involved in being intimate. In the patient's relationship with the therapist, who serves as "participant observer" (Strupp & Binder, 1984), the relationship themes are observed, noted, and experienced by both the therapist and the patient. So one of the critical tasks of the evaluation is to pay attention to our internal tugs. We acknowledge these realities to demonstrate that we understand, offering hope that we might be able to help find a way out of the downward spiral that brought him into treatment. By the end of the evaluation, we give the patient a brief summary of the issues we see, the type of treatment we recommend, and a reasonable set of early treatment goals.

As sexual compulsivity has effectively soothed anxiety, self-loathing, and other strong feelings for many years, it is not easily given up. At times its benefits outweigh its risks, especially when the patient finds that the world is not kind in its response to the pain he causes. Thus the typical reactions of others often send these men scurrying back to their acting out, creating a vicious cycle. If patients believe that the therapist's goal is to simply eliminate their behavior and leave them "without," they will at least emotionally leave. Similarly, if there is a sense of zero tolerance, then patients may feel defeated when the inevitable "slip" occurs and may find therapy to be another situation in which they have no control and will fail. We want these patients to learn how to *feel and acknowledge* emotions, especially success. Therefore, we lean toward the patient's subjective sense of success as an early treatment goal. We want him to concretely define conditions that, if achieved, he will describe as successful. We do not view the elimination of sexual urges, adaptive or otherwise, as a criterion for success. These patients may have some degree of problematic urges, fantasies, and thoughts for quite some time, if not forever. Another goal is to notice and understand these urges without acting upon them. Our belief is that as the "true" meaning of the urges become clearer, their compelling nature will loosen its hold on the patient, allowing him to substitute more adaptive behaviors.

With Kevin, a theme of control became evident in how slowly he left the waiting room and where he sat. We pay attention to how his behaviors feel to us. Already Kevin has opened the blinds to his internal world, and we must take note of what we see. He minimizes the power differential by using the therapist's first name, finding a way to make the relationship feel more equal. The signals already point to a man who feels desperately out of control and who struggles to hold onto what remnants he can. There is no room for vulnerability in Kevin's world, and this theme will inevitably and repeatedly emerge during treatment. As the session ends, Kevin is almost flirtatious in his consistent attempts to erode boundaries. In some ways, the therapist is his next conquest.

Resistance

Resistance is inevitable in all therapy. The patient's presenting complaint serves some purpose and attempts will be made to maintain his status quo. Patients attempt to ward off unacceptable thoughts and feelings and to form an unconscious "compromise between the forces that are striving toward recovery and the opposing ones" (Freud, 1912). Great apprehension about coming into treatment intensifies the resistance. Patients are terrified at the prospect of changing their behavior, as well as by the fear that they might not be able to. The disadvantages of being in treatment seem vast and immediate, whereas the advantages appear small and uncertain. To get a sense of how intense their resistance will be, we ask why the patient has come to seek treatment. As with Kevin, these men rarely seek treatment on their own accord. Usually, another person (e.g., his partner, employer, legal system) demands that the patient enter treatment. Few experiences can be as unsettling for them as seeking psychological help. The less they want to be in our office, the stronger will be the overt and covert efforts to leave. Even those who appear to be motivated will have ambivalence, and it is critical to get it put on the table. Remember, sexually compulsive men are adept at keeping relations superficial, and they will find reasons to leave just when the experience deepens, so don't wait until that point to "predict the flight."

To help us learn how an individual's resistance may manifest, we ask about other relationships. We ask what did and did not work in any prior therapy relationships. We ask about how well family relationships did or did not meet his needs. And, of course, we ask about his romantic and sexual relationships. Understanding the past gives us an educated guess as to what the patient will do in our relationship as it evolves. In terms of romantic relationships, it is helpful to ask the patient if he leaves or does he push the other person away so that he is left. Is there a final contact, an explosive scene, or does he just disappear? What emotion arises that provides the "final straw" and the impetus to go? Missed appointments may be our version of missed trysts. Attempts to keep the therapy brief will be our one-night stand. If he reports that he frequently feels disappointed and betrayed, he is likely to find what we say to be simplistic, off the mark, or otherwise disappointing. If he has found his relations to be not exciting or fulfilling enough, he is also likely to find the therapy to be insufficient or not satisfying enough. In fact, it is not uncommon for these patients to "cheat" on us, getting a bit more on the side by seeing another therapist at the same time that they find our therapy "not satisfying enough." Of course, in this process, the patient is only partially engaged, so with us, as with many others, his dissatisfaction can be a self-fulfilling prophecy. Look for possible parallels in the therapy and talk about them early and often.

The resistance also manifests in the relational themes we mentioned. We frequently find that competitive themes emerge, and the patient may assert his superiority in dress, manner, and what *he chooses* to discuss. The therapeutic frame is another likely medium in which to enact these issues, and there may be testing around appointment times or cancellation policies. With female therapists, resistance may manifest in sexual themes, sometimes violent fantasies, involving the therapist or with the patient objectifying the therapist by being patronizing or commenting on the therapist's attire or physical appearance. We often find ourselves having strong countertransference reactions as the patient brings us into his world, so consultation can be extremely helpful during this time.

Treat resistance with respect. The patient protects himself because he feels some combination of shame, disapproval, and guilt. He believes that if we see him, we will feel toward him as he feels toward himself, so he needs to remain hidden in his sexual cave. Typically, the patient supports his resistance with a multitude of cognitive distortions regarding the seriousness of the situation and how likely he will be able to resolve it on his own. Part of Kevin's resistance is evident in how he asks questions and what is meant by "affairs." It is also evident in how he initially minimizes his behavior before being flip, never actually focusing on what he has done.

Reality

Reality involves both understanding and helping the patient understand the "facts" of his life. Sexually compulsive men are masters in maintaining an image. But they do not realize the harm their behavior causes. However, the painful feelings are a self-fulfilling prophecy because they motivate him to act out with people he does not care about and to remain distant from those for whom he does care. A critical first step is for him to acknowledge that he emotionally hurts himself and others. As an alliance is established, we work to help the patient understand how his *compulsive* sexual behavior has undermined his ability to enjoy life and to have fulfilling relationships. We help him glimpse a new reality through our relationship with him.

The past is another aspect of the patient's reality, so, during the evaluation, we take careful psychosocial and sexual histories. Patients may attempt to gloss over critical facts of past relationships, so we slow them down by sifting through the details, dragging our feet as we learn about salient aspects of the past. The sexual history includes sexual themes in his family of origin ("How did your family discuss sex?"), his first sexual experiences, what he likes and dislikes about sex, and performance differences between when the patient masturbates and has sex with another person. We help him look at historical patterns and to begin untangling the whys of his behavior.

When evaluating the patient, we also pay close attention to what parts of the sexual relationship (e.g., the chase, the courtship, the infatuation, the climax) turn him on. We seek the gravitational pulls that draw him to acting out again and again. For patients who are dysphoric and empty, the intensity of sexual activity penetrates their malaise. Some revel in the initial acceptance by another person, with sex being the ultimate decree of "You're okay." Some want to be controlled. Others are drawn to the conquest. Some patients have a repetition compulsion and need to know that they can meet another's needs. Once they have, they devalue the person and thus "undo" the success, resulting in their needing to find a new object. Break it down. What are the critical components? But allow people to be complex. Often their behavior is multidetermined. For Kevin it was primarily "the yes," the sense of being accepted by another.

There is also a practical, nuts-and-bolts aspect to reality that involves two components: the severity of the compulsivity and its repercussions. Understand severity as the full spectrum of activities in which the patient participates, how long he has been engaging in them, how much time he spends on them, how much risk he puts himself and others in (e.g., whether or not he uses a condom or engages in high-risk sexual activities). As noted previously, men who present with sexual compulsivity often exhibit more than one sexual issue, so you need to again be very specific and detailed in your inquiries. For example, in our clinic the Internet almost always exists as *one* of the sexually compulsive behaviors with which a patient presents. Learn the age at which the first affair occurred, the first use of prostitution, and the first use of sexual magazines or videos. What does he use when he masturbates and what is his favorite fantasy? Ask how much time he spends on each activity (in his mind, as well as in reality). As therapy progresses, ask these questions again, because the answers will change as he feels more comfortable. Sex is like a Rorschach, and a man's specific activities of choice reveal a wealth of information about him. Kevin's reality lies in multigenerational sexual compulsivity. He competed with many men and what he had to offer his mother was not good enough. Even the relationship with his grandmother, a traditional source of comfort, confused him and made it appear that his value was in his sexuality. We glimpsed his reality when he responded to what part of sex he enjoyed most.

At the end of the evaluation, we ask the patient how the evaluation felt to him and how it was to work with us. Be suspicious of overly positive feedback and probe for doubt, discomfort, and dislike. These are expected reactions around issues as sensitive as sexuality, and our encouraging their verbalization helps the patient learn that we can tolerate his emotions. Next, we summarize some of the primary issues and defenses and acknowledge how these have both protected and limited the patient in important ways. Finally, we make treatment recommendations regarding whom to see (are we the best choice?), what kind of therapy program is most appropriate, and what kind of major challenges he is likely to face. The breadth of the recommendations will increase with experience. Only make those with which you feel comfortable, and consult if you are not sure. If the patient pushes you for quick responses, allow yourself to get back to him. His rush is part of his acting out. Your job is to make the best, not the quickest, recommendations. We end with the establishment of a specific treatment contract that includes the frequency of the treatment and the *minimum* number of sessions. We usually ask the patient to commit to at least 10 sessions, after which we ask him and ourselves whether we are on the right track and determine what, if any, modifications are needed. Agreeing upon a specific number of sessions is important for several reasons. It gives the patient a sense of control, it helps him understand that he will not be in therapy forever, and it helps keep him in treatment when he wants to leave.

Midtreatment

The relationship themes first elucidated during the evaluation unfold during midtreatment, which we roughly understand as sessions 10 to 24. We shift from a more structured, content-oriented style to a less structured, process-oriented format. Midtreatment means that at the end of the evaluation, we have recommended treatment with us, that the patient has accepted this recommendation, and that we have progressed through the first agreed-upon time period. Reminiscent of rapprochement, during midtreatment patients often vacillate between feeling very close to and distant from us. One issue that seems to arise particularly often, but by way of patients' partners, is how focused the therapy is on the sexual issues. We find that there is a curvilinear relationship between treatment and the amount of time spent specifically discussing the patient's sexual issues. Initially, some focus is required to understand the behavior, and most men quickly give up at least portions of their sexually compulsive behaviors. For each portion, there is a loss, perhaps analogous to a mourning, as a central part of the patient's life is disavowed. There may even be physiological withdrawal, with symptoms similar to depression, as the man loses the high that had held so much value. As treatment progresses, this process continues, but the focus on the sexual behavior tends to decrease as relationship issues come to the fore. Toward the end of this phase of treatment, the focus returns as the understandings gained are applied to the patient's sexual behavior. We find that three interdependent themes predominate during this period: the patient seeking immediate relief while we try to strengthen the alliance, keeping the patient in treatment, and dealing with shame. Let us look at these one by one.

Establishing an Alliance/Establishing Immediate Relief

> *During session #7, Kevin tells me that psychotherapy is a soft science and there are no clear indications that it works. "Either way," he says, "You get your money." I ask him how it feels to tell me that. He pauses and says, "I don't mean to hurt your feelings, but you want me to be honest and that's honest." I ask him to consider how he felt before he came in and whether he feels better now. He says, "Probably, but nobody can tell by looking at me." When I point out that he is learning to trust his own feelings, Kevin pauses, looking stunned, before he says, "What a foreign concept."*

As emphasized earlier, we approach treatment as a relationship that ultimately invokes the dynamics of the patient's world of relationships. When the therapeutic relationship, the alliance, is strong and the therapist aware, it provides a safe forum for the patient to play out his issues, seeing them more clearly and perhaps practicing some new options. Psychotherapy takes time and produces emotional turmoil for the patient. The alliance is the glue that allows the patient to stick to treatment when every one of his protective impulses says, "Get out." You can help him and can strengthen the alliance by staying focused on his concerns. It is easy to have the agendas of others (partners, children, colleagues) in your mind when conducting any therapy and especially this type of work. But if the patient feels judged, dismissed, or uncared for, he will be gone.

Anxiety often mounts as he experiences the should-I-go or should-I-stay dilemma. One way that the patient can escape is by holding us responsible for his change, asking for immediate relief. This is a perfect solution for him. If the therapist fails to "fix him," the patient can leave knowing that he tried to get help, but the lousy therapist failed, so how could he possibly change? This creates a therapeutic dilemma: If we do not respond to his requests for help, the alliance and, by association, the entire therapy is at risk. If we do jump into problem solving by offering solutions, we become vulnerable to an array of therapeutic landmines. For instance, if we give homework, the patient may find that he cannot do it and thus is failing the therapist. Sexually compulsive men are used to letting people down. Their interpersonal landscape is littered with ruined relationships and disappointed people. How can this time be different if we allow him to set us up as the demanding authority? Control comes into play here. Just as some patients will usurp it wherever they can, others will continually struggle with deferring, defying, or both. So, what do we do?

Remember that in addition to the immediate demands of the patient, there is a level of relational reenactment occurring. He wants us to make him feel better. It might be better to turn the responsibility back by asking him what kind of homework he thinks would be helpful. He will resist by saying, "You're the expert." That's fine. Allow him to express his anger and disappointment. At these times it is critical to know that the patient's desire to get needs met yesterday is a way to avoid painful affects, hopping from experience-to-experience and never lingering long enough to feel. If the patient could take a pill to fix everything, he would. As he pushes us for quick resolution, it is easy to doubt our ability to help. But notice how the patient's world invades ours. These men tend to be an "I need it now" type of group, and although their problems are years in the making, they want these fixed in days or weeks. The awareness that our feeling of not being good enough may be part of the patient's transference keeps us from overreacting. These patients often believe that nobody has or can fully satisfy their needs—including the therapist. One key to successful treatment is not to problem solve with the patient when he wants relief but instead to help him see how he holds others responsible for his feelings, then consider ways that he can take care of himself. By increasing self-control, he will be less compelled to control others, and underlying feelings of shame will be ameliorated by a new sense of competence.

Therefore, when we feel pushed by the patient to fix things *for him* now, we first explore what waiting feels like. We empathize that he must be exhausted from needing to rush all the time. Learning that he can tolerate some degree of discomfort, anxiety, and dissatisfaction is often a surprising and even reassuring experience. The patient experiences alternative ways to deal with both conscious and unconscious feelings, rather than taking immediate action. He learns that after an initial increase in discomfort, talking helps.

Having said all this, we must add that there are circumstances when providing some short-term symptom relief is indicated. To this end, some focused behavioral interventions may be helpful. However, as we are pointing out, the potential impact on the overall treatment and long-term effects need to be carefully considered. The framing of any homework assignment helps to avoid these traps. Turn the responsibility back by asking what kind of homework he thinks would be helpful and how he might achieve it. Another idea for more concrete patients is to give a menu of interventions from which to choose. These may include talking to a friend, going to an on- or offline 12-step meeting, journaling his thoughts and feelings, or engaging in some alternative pleasurable activity so that he can pass through the vulnerable moment without incident. Once the patient makes a decision about what he wants to try, we use lines such as, "Are you sure you are ready to give yourself that assignment?" Then, proactively, we explore feelings that may arise should the patient not complete the assignment. Again, predicting can be a valuable tool here. You can use the interpersonal theme and pull upon historical information to help the patient examine the reasons that he has *let himself down* in the past and ways he might prepare for that possibility this time. Another way to efficiently impart practical information and simple exercises is to recommend one of the self-help books, tapes, videos, or websites dealing with these issues. This keeps us in a supportive role that strengthens the alliance.

Keeping the Patient in Treatment

> *Kevin misses session #14 without a call, then returns the next week only to say that he has decided to end therapy because he "has nothing else to talk about and feels better." I recall that during the last session, for the first time, I had discussed his father in depth.*

As noted previously, in many cases, the relationship that we forge with the patient will be the most honest, intimate, revealing relationship he has ever had. Because of this, the patient will work hard to escape because being "seen" is so frightening and leaves him so vulnerable. But as his relationship deepens with us, he feels the emotions against which he so diligently defended. As he feels them, fears emerge as to how deep or bottomless the emotions may be. There is often an all-or-nothing quality to the psychic life of these men, and a hint of sadness or anxiety portends a terrifying loss of control and torrent of affect.

To help the patient have enough confidence in his ability to not be overwhelmed by his emotional experiences and to minimize his attempts to escape treatment, it is important to be aware of the patient's pace. Before going into dark places, ask "headlight" questions such as "What would it be like to talk about that?"; "What will happen in here when you want to cry?"; "How might we each feel about you when you reveal that?"; and "What might be the most frightening part of telling me about this?" These questions prepare the patient to discuss difficult issues and provide him with that needed sense of control.

Working Through Shame

> *Kevin looks different as he presents for his rescheduled session #14. Instead of sitting back confidently on the couch, with his legs casually crossed, he perches at the edge. As opposed to his usual unflinching gaze, his eye contact is fleeting and he looks like a scared little boy. During the session, he talks about the pain of hurting his wife and how he increasingly feels that he is not a real man, because he "let down a good woman." At the end of the session, as he stands up, Kevin blurts out, "I want you to know that as a teenager, I had sex with another boy."*

No matter how defended, there is always some element of shame in sexually compulsive men. As Adams and Robinson (2001) note, shame is the "primary feeling the addict is trying to medicate, rework and compensate for" (p. 26); we find that sexually compulsive men are subject to intense shame and self-castigation, which are both causes for and products of their sexual compulsivity.

Expressions of shame tend to emerge later in the therapy because they both require and elicit deep vulnerability. The patient must trust us to be "safe" as previously unmentioned memories are finally discussed. Shame can change the very way the patient interacts with us. Whereas in the evaluation phase the interactions may feel like sparring matches, as themes of control and power predominate, there is a palpable difference when the patient becomes more vulnerable. We expect longer pauses and increased sensitivity to our nonverbal responses, as he tries to discern our judgments. Often we ask him what response he anticipates and wonder whether he expects us to judge him as he judges himself.

To complicate matters, men in this society have learned that they should not express certain emotions, so the very feelings dislodged by the therapy can intensify the shame. Sadness, especially if it involves crying, is a usual suspect, though fear and, in some cases, unexpected anger can also produce shame. In this way, many men who have lost control of their sexual behavior experience shame as a meta-emotion, an emotional response to other feelings. They are adept at judging and have strong beliefs about what feelings are tolerable. As one of our patients stated, "I'm afraid of the emotions. Fear is the doubt that anyone will like the real person behind the façade. The difficulty comes from accepting myself, warts and all."

It is not unusual for the patient to again lose control of his sexual behavior during this period, though sometimes it is not as severe (e.g., the person is able to limit his behavior to online sexual activities). Although initial gains are commonly made during the beginning of treatment, the shame generated by uncovering feelings and their attendant memories produces the exact type of affective responses that the sexual behavior warded off in the first place. Remember that the patient engaged in his sexual behavior for a reason, and, in many respects, the behavior worked all too well. Prediction decreases the element of surprise and allows the therapist to say, "You just had a slip. If we can understand it, it will be an isolated event—a lapse not a relapse." This is a time when we might recommend that the patient increase the number of people he has told about his issues and garner more support. Alternatively, he might consider increasing the frequency of his therapy and adding other adjunctive supportive activities that might not already be in place, such as group or couples' therapy.

THE END GAME/TRANSITION

Kevin discusses the day his mother died. She was on a trip abroad and died unexpectedly after, he believes, not receiving adequate medical care. Kevin has told this story before but always with anger. Today he looks sad. I comment on the sadness and he cries. In nearly a year of treatment, this is the first time he has cried. I ask what it's like to cry in front of me and he

says, "I'm scared to death. I'm scared you'll be angry or tell me to stop it."
I sit quietly as Kevin recounts the phone call informing him of his mother's
death, having to go through her clothes, never being able to say good-bye,
and his new recognition of how alone he was during that time. When I
observe that he stayed sad throughout the story, that he kept going, he
exhales and says, "That stuff has been in there a long time. It feels good to
tell you about it."

Knowing when to end treatment is perhaps the most difficult decision to make when treating these men. At some point, therapy moves from problem-oriented, in which treatment is necessary condition for change, to self-growth, in which treatment is an optional condition for change. For termination to be indicated, the patient must display significantly greater comfort and understanding in his feelings and the dynamics of relationships. He must truly have his behaviors under control, so that he experiences himself for what may be the first time. He looks less to others for approval and can tolerate strong emotion. When the question of ending treatment arises, his task is to slow down and look at his feelings, whereas our task is to respect his growing ability to make healthy autonomous decisions and to allow him to leave without having to destroy the relationship. Stopping treatment too early or too late both run risks, with the former leading to quick relapse and the latter perhaps fostering dependence. Although we believe that frequent consultation is very helpful with these patients, this is an especially critical time to get a fresh view on a case. When deciding whether to end treatment, we use several criteria; whether the patient can use relationships to bolster his own self-soothing, how well he can feel his emotions and be more present in his life, and if he seems to have a realistic idea of the course ahead.

Soothing, Not Using

One termination criterion we use is whether the patient seems to have learned that relationships can be soothing instead of using, that being with another person actually makes him feel better. We echo Leedes's (2001) assertion that "As comfort towards interpersonal relationships increases, the power of objectified fantasies is diminished" (p. 223). Sexually compulsive men tend to view interpersonal relationships as a means to an end, as a tool to fix their needs. The other person is little more than a prop. In this relationship model, there is little risk because there is little investment. The relationships are inherently limited and typically are ways to keep feelings limited in terms of amount and scope. Conversely, the therapeutic relationship involves vulnerability and feeling more than they are comfortable with. It is safe enough to make a greater investment. Having stayed in the room, engaged the process, the patient has had to feel feelings previously avoided and has endured the pain necessary to get to the benefits of a relationship. He has learned how it feels to be emotionally connected to another person and how sharing feelings is profoundly soothing, which was previously unimaginable for someone who had been deprived of this experience. As Levine (1992) explains, "psychological intimacy soothes the soul . . . both people feel an inner peace" (p. 45). Once the patient has experienced the benefits of relating to another person, relationships outside the room feel different. Suddenly, he notices what it feels like to be distant from his partner. He is aware of when there is and is not emotional connection. He does not have to rely on the extremely limited, sex-focused interactions on which he had been scraping by. He is no longer satisfied with "just sex."

Feeling Emotions

Throughout this chapter, we have emphasized the importance of creating an environment safe enough for our patients to experience their emotions. The capacity to tolerate emotions and attain some degree of mastery with them is a critical component of relapse prevention and termination. Because we view sexually compulsive behaviors as an indirect expression of affect, we feel more comfortable ending a therapy if the patient displays more direct expression. It is common in the start of treatment to hear a patient make statements like, "Let me think how I feel." Toward the end, patients will pause, clearly paying attention to the area below their head. Whereas in the beginning of treatment, we might see incongruent emotional expressions (e.g., laughing when reporting sadness), expressions tend to be more congruent at the end. In addition, when considering termination, look at the emotional amplitude. Although we see more restricted expressions in the beginning, it is more common to see the patient cry and raise his voice as therapy progress. And, once again, look to your internal barometer and what you feel in the relationship. Though the patient may not be entirely comfortable with strong affects, does he at least engage them? Note how Kevin spontaneously acknowledges that he is "scared to death" and cries. He certainly does not enjoy the feelings but also does not minimize them.

The Course Ahead

If termination is indicated, we try to help the patient realistically appraise the course ahead—the likely challenges to be faced, the potentials for relapse, and red flags pointing to a need to resume treatment. It is also important to predict and explore the many difficult feelings that are inherent in returning to therapy. Sometimes with those least likely to ask for help, scheduling "check-in" sessions far in advance helps them to feel the therapist's presence more constantly even prior to the visit. In those cases where the patient is determined to leave without as much progress as is optimal, we need to keep in mind that it is better to lose the battle than the war. Thus, even when a bit premature, a planned and discussed, rather than an impulsive and conflicted, ending greatly increases the likelihood that the patient will return if necessary.

Relapse is a key hazard on the road ahead. The patient will have urges to act out again. As we noted in the evaluation, urges to be sexually compulsive may occur for many years or even throughout the patient's life. If he becomes self-punitive over a slip, he is much more vulnerable to relapse. Blaming the slip on personal weakness, having it be the catalyst for a cycle of self-criticism and castigation, can become a self-fulfilling prophecy. However, if he notices the urges and wonders, "Why now?" they may not turn into a tailspin. The goal is to understand. Even if a patient does "slip," we encourage him to view that as a reasonable mistake in learning how to maintain self-control. Part of relapse prevention is learning to accept mistakes. Of course, the exact nature of the slip is critical and, although therapeutically we may understand it, the patient's partner may not. Here, a few sessions of couples' therapy may help them both decide on the severity of the episode and whether they can get back on track with a limited number of "booster sessions," or if a resumption of ongoing treatment is necessary.

SUMMARY

Since the time we wrote this chapter and the time you read it, each of us has become better at the process we just explained. Start now and you will be better later. Just like our patients, we will never be perfect or truly finished; therefore, we, too, must learn to value the journey as much as the outcome. We recognize that accompanying these men is not easy, particularly as our treatment approach requires us to keep our head and heart amidst raw, primitive emotions. Do not be overly concerned with mistakes; we make many mistakes and you will, too. If the patient feels let down, he feels let down. We accept his feelings and try to understand the parallels to other relations in his present or past, as well as allowing ourselves to admit when he has tapped into another of our own personal tangles. If the difficulties can be tolerated, we have the opportunity to accompany the patient through some of the most intense issues of being human. Whether you have a seamless or patchwork course of treatment, the relationship with the patient is real. By maintaining a caring relationship through both easy and difficult disclosures, there is an amelioration of his fears of being seen and the drive to stay hidden. He learns to experience a wider range of deeper emotions and to be in control of, instead of being controlled by, them. Paradoxically, the patient may find that what he has so assiduously avoided is what he needs the most. He replaces despair with hope. Both patient and therapist must be willing to experience the risks and rewards of being intimately involved with another person for there to be a real relationship. When this happens, it allows the patient to introject a bit of the therapist, and thus he is changed forever. This is quite a weighty responsibility, but it is not a one-way street, as we are also forever changed by our relationship with him.

REFERENCES

Adams, M. A., & Robinson, W. R. (2001). Shame reduction, affect regulation, and sexual boundary development: Essential building blocks of sexual addiction treatment. *Sexual Addiction and Compulsivity, 8,* 45–78. Excellent article, especially regarding how attachment affects the capacity to tolerate affect, a skill so critical to sexually compulsive men.

American Psychiatric Association. (1994). *Diagostic and Statistical Manual of Mental Disorders* (4th ed.). Washington, DC: Author.

Amparano, J. (1998, September 25). Sex addicts get help *The Arizona Republic*, p. A1.

Byrne, D., & Osland, J. A. (2000). Sexual fantasy and erotica/pornography: Internal and external imagery. In *Psychological Perspectives on Human Sexuality*. New York: Wiley.

Carnes, P. (1989). *Contrary to Love: Helping the Sexual Addict.* New York: Bantam. Carnes is one of the leaders of the field, and this is one of the core books on these issues.

Cooper, A. (1998). Sexually compulsive behavior. *Contemporary sexuality*, *32*(4), 1–3. A brief summary of sexual compulsivity.

Cooper, A. (Ed.). (2000). *Cybersex and Sexual Compulsivity: The Dark Side of the Force.* Philadelphia: Brunner-Routledge. This is a special edition journal with interesting articles related to sexual compulsivity on the internet.

Cooper, A., Boies, S., Maheu, M., & Greenfield, D. (1999). Sexuality and the Internet: The next sexual revolution. In F. Muscarella & L. Szuchman (Eds.), *The Psychological Science of Sexuality: A Research Based Approach* (pp. 519–545). New York: Wiley. A comprehensive book chapter in this human sexuality text on Internet sexuality.

Cooper, A., Delmonico, D., & Burg, R. (2000). Cybersex users and abusers: New findings and their implications. *Sexual Addiction and Compulsivity: Journal of Treatment and Prevention, 7*, 5–29. Research article with findings on online sexual compulsivity.

Cooper, A., Griffin-Shelley, E., Delmonico, D., & Mathy, R. (2001). Online sexual problems: Assessment and predictive variables. *Sexual Addiction and Compulsivity: Journal of Treatment and Prevention, 8*, 267–285. This article provides clinicians with several factors found to be correlated with online sexual problems.

Cooper, A., McLoughlin, I., & Campbell, K. (2000). Sexuality in cyberspace: Update for the 21st century. *CyberPsychology and Behavior, 3*(4), 521–536. Helpful review of online sexuality.

Cooper, A., Putnam, D. E., Planchon, L. A., & Boies, S. C. (1999). Online sexual compulsivity: Getting tangled in the Net. *Sexual Addiction and Compulsivity: Journal of Treatment and Prevention, 6*(2), 79–104. This article discusses assessment and treatment of online sexual problems. Received an award for excellence from the journal.

Cooper, A., Scherer, C., Coralie, R., Boies, S. C., & Gordon, B. L. (1999). Sexuality and the Internet: From sexual exploration to pathological expression. *Professional Psychology: Research & Practice, 30*(2), 154–164. Research article detailing findings of the first large scale study of Internet sexuality, also has some interesting suggestions on implications for public policy.

Cooper, A., Scherer, C., & Marcus, I. D. (2002). Harnessing the power of the Internet to improve sexual relationships. In A. Cooper (Ed.), *Sex and the Internet: A Guidebook for Clinicians.* New York: Brunner-Routledge. This chapter in this new book provides a look at some ways the Internet can be used to facilitate therapy and enhance sexuality.

Delmonico, D. L., & Carnes, P. J. (1999). Virtual sex addiction: Why cybersex becomes the drug of choice. *CyberPsychology & Behavior*, *2*(5). 457–464.

Freeman-Longo, R. E., & Blanchard, G. T. (1998). *Sexual Abuse in America: Epidemic of the 21st Century.* Brandon, VT: Safe Society Press. Excellent book exploring factors contributing to sexual abuse and sexual offenders. Also offers suggestions for treatment; both on an individual, as well as on a societal, level.

Freud, S. (1912). The dynamics of transference. In J. Strachey (Trans. & Ed., 1958), *The Standard Edition of the Complete Psychological Works of Sigmund Freud, 12* (pp. 97–108). London: Hogarth Press.

Goodman, A. (2001). What's in a name? Terminology for designating a syndrome of driven sexual behavior. *Sexual Addiction and Compulsivity, 8*, 191–213. This is article does a very good job of outlining the pros and cons of various terms such as *sexual addiction, sexual compulsion,* and so forth, and the treatment ramifications.

Kafka, M. P. (1997) A monoamine hypothesis for the pathophysiology of paraphilic disorders. *Archives of Sexual Behavior, 26,* 505–526.

Kafka, M. P. (2000). The paraphilia-related disorders: Nonparaphilic hypersexuality and sexual compulsivity/addiction. In S. R. Lieblum & R. C. Rosen (Eds.), *Principles and Practices of Sex Therapy (3rd ed.).* Another leader of the field who also offers many valuable issues to be consider in the assessment and treatment of sexual compulsivity. Kafka's work is another "must read" for clinicians who want to be grounded in the literature.

Leedes, R. (2001). The three most important criteria in diagnosing sexual addictions: Obsession, obsession, and obsession. *Sexual Addiction and Compulsivity, 8,* 215–226, esp. 218. Helpful to read in conjunction with the Goodman article to get a different perspective.

Levine, S. B. (1992). *Sexual Life: A Clinician's Guide.* New York: Plenum. Well-written, comprehensive book on sexuality that outlines several of the most common issues faced by those working in this field.

Line, B., & Cooper, A. (2002). Group therapy: Essential component for success with sexually acting out problems among men. *Sexual Addiction and Compulsivity: Journal of Treatment and Prevention, 9*(1), 15–32. This article provides a very detailed description of a successful group program for men with sexual acting-out issues and would be valuable for clinicians who are interested in starting such a group.

Schwartz, M. F., & Masters, W. H. (1994). Integration of trauma-based, cognitive, behavioral, systemic, and addiction approaches for treatment of hypersexual pair-bonding disorder. *Sexual Addiction and Compulsivity, 1,* 57–76.

Strupp, H. H., & Binder, J. L. (1984). *Psychotherapy in a New Key: A Guide to Time-Limited Dynamic Psychotherapy.* New York: Basic Books. This book does a wonderful job of discussing how the relationship plays out in dynamic psychotherapy. It explains how an individual's history, presenting complaint, and the experience of the therapy relationship combine to provide a powerful tool for change.

Chapter Nineteen

The Paraphilic World

J. Paul Fedoroff, MD

INTRODUCTION

At coffee breaks, cocktail parties, question and answer sessions for the media, or grand rounds, I am frequently asked, "Doctor, what made you decide to devote your life to studying and treating the sort of people you do?" Whenever the question is raised, my thoughts return to one of my first patient encounters:

A financially successful married man with three children presented with an intriguing chief complaint: "concerns about intimacy."

In response to a question about what he meant, he replied, "My wife and I get along fine and our sex life is great. Doctor, I can see you raising your eyebrow. Let me explain. Once or twice a week I leave my office and drive toward home on the expressway. I'll have the radio on and I will be thinking about the events of the day. I never know when it will happen, but, like I said, once or twice a week, a funny thing happens. Without thinking about it, I take a wrong exit. And then it starts. I go into "auto-pilot." I start driving aimlessly until I am lost in a neighborhood I have never been to and to which I would never go. I drive until I am lost and can't remember how I got there. I drive until I see a house with a light on or some sign that someone is home, smoke coming from the chimney, the sight of someone through the blinds, but never with a car in the driveway. This part always feels like it takes forever but never takes long. I am sweating by this time because I know what is coming. By this point there is nothing I can do to stop. I find the right house. I always park right in front of the house and sit there for a minute. The radio is off now. All I can hear is my own breathing. I get out of the car and walk to the front door. I try the door knob. I don't know why, but it is usually open. I go in without knocking or making any noise. I get into the front closet. Most houses like this have front coat closets.

Now the clock is ticking. I strip naked. I am totally sexually excited. I masturbate while I imagine the "lady of the house" walking around. I have never seen any of the women in the houses I have used. I have some thoughts about what she looks like, but what excites me is knowing that the "man of the house" could be home any minute. He is coming home from work, just like me. At any second he could drive up to his house, see my car parked in front, read my license plate, wonder what is going on. Then he will come home and open the door and then the closet door and then . . . I climax. I get dressed in a frenzy. I escape from the house without ever seeing who is in it. I am panicking. What have I done? What will happen if anyone saw me? I jump in the car. Will it start? Will someone hear? I drive off and search frantically for the expressway. There is no radio now. All I hear is my heart pounding. I get frantic, thinking about what could happen. Then I find the ramp back to the expressway. I drive on. I merge with the traffic and I think, "Home free." I always say the phrase "Home free," and then I am totally calm. I made it. I am safe. I drive home and give my wife a big hug and kiss, "Hi, honey, I'm home. How was your day?"

He paused, flushed and short of breath. I asked the obvious question, "Why, sir, do you do this?" His response: "Doctor, I have no idea. It is insane. That is why I came to you. I don't think this is healthy. But doctor, I have to admit. It is the most exciting sex I have ever had in my life. You have to try it!"

If you care for people, regardless of your special area of interest, you will encounter individuals and couples who have sexual interests, behaviors, or both that are as unconventional as the one just described. Some will involve illegal activities (like the present case); most will involve "variations" that although not illegal, create phenomenal distress to the patients and their partners. The purpose of this brief chapter is to introduce the topic of unconventional sexual disorders, technically known as the "paraphilias."

THE PARAPHILIAS

The latest version of the American Psychiatric Association catalogue of psychiatric disorders lists only 10 "paraphilic disorders" (*DSM-IV-TR*, 2000). *The DSM-IV-TR* defines four primary areas in which sexual problems are prominent: sexual dysfunctions, gender identity disorders, sexual orientation problems, and the paraphilias. All four areas are subsumed under the category of "sexual disorders." The *DSM-IV-TR* sexual disorders are summarized in table 19.1.

According to the *DSM-IV-TR*, the essential feature of paraphilic disorders is the presence of "recurrent, intense sexually arousing fantasies, sexual urges, or behaviors generally involving" "nonhuman objects," "the suffering or humiliation of oneself or one's partner," "children or other non-consenting persons," or any combination of these

TABLE 19.1. *DSM-IV-TR* Paraphilia Criteria

Paraphilia	Criteria A*	Criteria B**	Criteria C
Exhibitionism	Exposure of genitals to an unsuspecting stranger	Marked distress or interpersonal difficulty	No criteria
Fetishism	Use of nonliving objects	Significant distress in social, occupational, or other areas of functioning	Objects, not only female clothing or vibrators
Frotteurism	Touching or rubbing against a nonconsenting person	Marked distress or interpersonal difficulty	No criteria
Pedophilia[1]	Prepubescent child	Same as above	Person is at least 16 and at least 5 years older than the child
Masochism	The act (not simulated) of being humiliated, beaten, bound, or otherwise made to suffer	Significant distress or impairment in social, occupational, or other important areas of function	No criteria
Sadism	Acts (not simulated) that involve the psychological or physical suffering (including humiliation) of the victim	Acted on sexual urges with a nonconsenting person or marked distress or interpersonal difficulty	No criteria
Transvestic fetishism[2]	A heterosexual male aroused by cross-dressing	Clinically significant distress or impairment in social, occupational, or other important areas of function	No criteria
Voyeurism	Observing an unsuspecting person	Marked distress or interpersonal difficulty	No criteria
Paraphilia NOS	No criteria	No criteria	No criteria

*"Over a period of 6 months, recurrent, intense sexually arousing fantasies, sexual urges, or behaviors involving . . . "
** "Person has acted on the urges or the fantasies, sexual urges, or behaviors cause . . . "
[1]Pedophilia subtypes: attracted to males; attracted to females; attracted to both; limited to incest; exclusive type; nonexclusive type
[2]Transvestism subtypes: with or without gender dysphoria

for a least 6 months. This definition may seem cumbersome but fortunately can be simplified by noting that paraphilic disorders by the *DSM-IV-TR* definition simply involve sex without the possibility of a consensual, mutually reciprocal relationship.

The criminal paraphilias meet the simplified criteria by virtue of the fact that the sex acts committed by individuals with pedophilia, exhibitionism, voyeurism, and frotteurism are by definition nonconsensual. In the case of pedophilia, children are not legally able to give consent to enter into sexual activities with adults. This point is often lost by people with pedophilia, who attempt to argue that the child had said "yes" or had implied consent by not reporting the abuse.

The etiology of paraphilic sexual disorders is unknown. Given the diverse and variable presentation of the paraphilias, it is unlikely that a single cause will ever be found. In the meantime an analogy may be helpful. We know that every child who undergoes normal embryologic development is born with the potential to speak any language in the world. The language the child eventually speaks is determined by the child's environment—in particular, the language of the child's caretakers. Once the language is learned, it becomes the child's "mother tongue." From that moment on, the mother tongue determines how the child thinks and what languages the child can understand and therefore with whom and in what manner the child interacts. Similarly, when children are born, they have the potential to develop a wide range of sexual preferences. What sexual preference they ultimately develop certainly must be influenced by environmental effects. However, once the preference is "set," it becomes "hardwired" like the child's language. Like the mother tongue, the "mother sexual preference" influences subsequent interests and activities for the rest of each person's life. In the case of language, the mother tongue can be modified by learning new words, new phrases, and when and where to say different things. Even entire new languages can be learned. Sexual preferences, including paraphilic preferences, appear to be similar. They are likely influenced by both biological and environmental factors. Once they are acquired, like language preferences, sexual preferences are very resistant to change. However, modern treatment methods do seem to be effective in influencing how, where, and in what manner sexual preferences are expressed. With this brief introduction, the world of paraphilias will now be reviewed briefly.

Exhibitionism (*DSM-IV-TR* 302.4) and Variations

People with exhibitionism usually expose to adult victims, who, while possessing the ability to consent to sex with the exhibitionist, are not asked. Most people with exhibitionism have no interest in nude beaches or "nudist colonies." There are two reasons. The first is that they find the experience of being naked around strangers to be intensely sexually exciting. Most nude beaches do not encourage overt sexual arousal, so exhibitionists find these locations intensely frustrating. One patient reported an experience in which he had located a "nudist hotel and camp ground." However, when he checked in, he found the idea of walking around other people who were also naked so upsetting that he came out of his room with a towel on. He was promptly evicted due to his "prudishness."

The second reason people with exhibitionism avoid nude beaches is because an essential element of the disorder is that it depends on exposure to victims *who do not consent*. Because people who go to nude beaches are all consenting and insist on being naked, those with exhibitionism find these types of beaches uninteresting. They do not "flash" their spouses. In fact, most people with exhibitionism report that they have no interest in engaging in any further contact or sexual activity with their victims. Most are heterosexual and married, have many victims (often in the 100s), and do not present for treatment until they have been charged.

An exception to the tendency to avoid treatment are people with a variation on exhibitionism, in which there is an interest in "having sex in public" without being seen. Individuals with this paraphilia are sometimes referred to as "public masturbators." They typically seek locations where they can masturbate while fantasizing that they might get caught. The most common location chosen is the car. Some masturbate while driving on the highway; others sit in shopping mall parking lots or hide behind bushes in public parks. People who masturbate in public seem to be more likely to seek help on their own, perhaps because they are less likely to be caught. Typically, they respond to treatment much better, again perhaps due to the fact that they represent a more self-motivated group.

Although people with exhibitionism and those who masturbate in public tend to be creatures of habit, often frequenting the same locations and targeting the same types of victims, the variation between individual exhibitionists is immense. Some expose in order to elicit signs of shock, interest, or arousal. Some expose when they are angry at their spouses. Some only when they are intoxicated. Most in the northern hemisphere expose only during the nonwinter seasons.

A more unusual variation involves men who expose artificial genitalia. The most common pattern in this variant involves stuffing items into their underwear in order to give the appearance that they have larger than normal genitalia and then to observe the reactions of others. This activity seems most common among gay men who seek the attention of other gay men. Sometimes men will purchase artificial female vulvas from sex stores, which are then used to expose. This variation is most common among men with gender identity disorders and often (but not always) is accompanied by cross-dressing. People who expose artificial genitalia are often not charged by police, who prefer to refer them for treatment.

One man was referred by the police, who admitted they were not sure what the charge would be. He had been making random calls to a large fast food restaurant chain, asking for "Brenda" (all names and identifying details in case reports have been altered). When he found a store at which a Brenda answered, he told her there was a package waiting for her in a post box. He gave her his own post box number in the apartment where he lived. When Brenda got off work, she went by the address and found a large envelope in the unlocked post box with the words "PACKAGE FOR PICK-UP" written on it. As per instructions, she took the package home, wondering if this was some store promotion sponsored by the manager of the store where she worked (he had handed her the phone earlier that day). To her horror, when she opened the package she found about 100 close-up photographs of the exhibitionist's penis. She called the police, who had no trouble locating the offender because he had used his own mailbox. However, when they went to arrest him, he denied making any phone calls. When the police told him what had been found in the package, he asked the officers whether it was a crime to leave a sealed envelope containing pictures of one's own penis in one's own mailbox and, furthermore, whether there wasn't some sort of law against removing mail from a stranger's mailbox, as the complainant had done?

When he arrived for assessment and, once he was assured that the usual rules for confidentiality of medical information applied, he was much more forthcoming. He admitted to having planned the package pickup and to having made the phone call. In fact, he said he had made many phone calls and was certain that many women had viewed the contents of his packages. He was somewhat surprised that no one had reported him before. He was asked what else he did for sexual arousal. Again, he expressed surprise, saying that he had been interviewed by others when he was arrested for more conventional exhibitionistic behaviors, and no one had ever considered the possibility that there is more than one way to expose. He said the "package" scheme was a new one and somewhat less interesting than his usual "scheme."

Usually, he would check into a motel. Next, he would place photographs of his penis face-down under each door in the hallway. He would always place a photograph under the door to his own room as well. Next, he would disrobe, sit on his bed, and masturbate. He claimed that he never had to wait long before the event he was waiting for. The Polaroid photo under his door would suddenly be whisked away by someone on the other side of the door. He said that just the sound of the photograph rubbing against the floor was enough to make him climax. He was asked what sorts of things he would think about while waiting for the photo to disappear; we will return to his answer in a moment.

Most people with exhibitionism who come to legal attention are men. However, cases of females with exhibitionism have been reported (e.g., Fedoroff, Fishell, & Fedoroff, 1999). Women are more likely to expose in ways that appear accidental and in situations that reduce the possibility of being alone with the victim. For example, one woman used to disrobe and masturbate in the window of her apartment, with strategically placed lighting. She was self-referred. As is my practice, at the end of my initial consultation I cautioned her strongly against engaging in any further illegal activity. I told her that a condition of any further treatment with me would be that she cease her illegal activities immediately. Upon hearing this, she looked at me quizzically, "And why is that, Doctor?" I explained that treatment would consist of a series of interventions designed to help her to achieve a happy, healthy, fulfilling, and lawful sex life. In order to do this, it would be necessary to stop any unlawful activities immediately. The reason was twofold. First, because the treatment plan would be designed to help her feel comfortable with lawful sex, it would be necessary to find out how she felt when she did not expose. Second, because she was engaging in an illegal sexual activity, she could be arrested, and this would obviously interfere with therapy. She agreed to my conditions because the first reason I gave her made sense. But she added, "I don't think you know much about the law, Doctor. I have been doing what I do for years. I have never gotten a complaint. If I did, and the police showed up at my door, I would tell them that whoever complained must have been spying on me. Who do you think they would arrest?"

Voyeurism (*DSM-IV-TR* 302.82) and Variants

The answer to the question posed by the women with exhibitionism in the proceeding section leads neatly to the paraphilic disorder known as voyeurism. She is correct that the average police officer, faced with the choice of charging a woman with exhibitionism and a man with voyeurism, will select the latter. To be fair, the legal criteria for spying on another person (peeping) do not depend on a diagnosis of voyeurism, which is sexual arousal from "observing an unsuspecting person who is naked or in the process of disrobing, or engaging in sexual activity" (*DSM-IV-TR*, p. 575). As in the case of exhibitionism, the key adjective is *unsuspecting* and therefore nonconsenting.

People who have voyeurism go to great lengths to spy on unsuspecting victims. In a manner analogous to the aversion that people with exhibitionism have of nude beaches, those who have voyeursim do not frequent "strip bars." One patient, again self-referred, told of a strip bar he had found in a large city. He explained that he was in the habit of parking his truck in the back alley behind the bar. With the use of a step ladder that he kept in the back of the truck, he was able to hoist himself up level with a window that allowed him to peer into the change room used by the "dancers." He presented for treatment after he had narrowly avoided being beaten and robbed by a group of criminals who chanced upon him in the back alley on a stormy winter's night.

I asked him whether he had considered the idea of entering the bar through the front door, purchasing a drink, and enjoying the evening from the comfort of a bar stool. His response was immediate, "Doc, the guys who go to strip bars are losers and perverts and drunks. I am not like that. I have no interest in watching a stripper who is just doing it for the money. What I do is different. I get to see them as they really are. That is what turns me on."

This patient's comments highlight the tragedy of all paraphilias, namely, the requirement for nonconsent. What distinguishes people with voyeursim from nonparaphilic people is not the interest in observing naked people (a characteristic technically known as scoptophilia) but rather the interest in observing people who don't know they are being observed. As a result, people with voyeurism do not commonly use conventional pornography ("the models are paid"), spy on their spouses ("I know what he or she looks like"), or pay prostitutes in order to peek at them.

The exceptions to the preceding statement confirm the rule. One married patient drilled holes in the floor below the bathroom adjoining the master bedroom of his house. With the use of an elongated tube, he was able to catch fleeting glimpses of his wife as she brushed her teeth in her nighty. He came for treatment after being caught by his wife when he sneezed.

The remainder of my comments about people with voyeurism are similar to those about exhibitionism. Although individuals with voyeurism have very idiosyncratic voyeuristic routines, the ingenuity of their efforts is breathtaking. A category of voyeuristic activities not available to exhibitionists involves spying on sleeping victims or ones who are rendered incapable of knowing they are being observed, through intoxication. The topic of men who assault sleeping victims has been reviewed elsewhere (Fedoroff et al., 1997). One patient worked at the front desk of a motel. When a woman he was attracted to checked into the motel, he would book her into a room he had specially prepared by drilling a hole in the wall of the adjoining room (which he normally keep vacant). Rather than use the peek hole to spy on the woman's activities, he used the access to determine when she had gone to sleep. He then used his master key to enter her room, carefully uncovered her feet, and masturbated at the foot of the bed before leaving.

Although I am convinced that his interests were primarily voyeuristic and focused on the women's feet (discussed further on), his activities clearly could be interpreted as more sinister. I explained this to the man in question who assured me he was "only a voyeur." He declined treatment. Several years later I received word that he had moved to another location in the United States known for a "get tough" approach to crime. He had been found in a motel room, masturbating at the foot of the bed of a man and woman. Besides receiving a severe beating at the hands of the woman's husband, rather than being charged with voyeurism, he was charged with attempted rape. He remains in custody today.

Fetishism (*DSM-IV-TR* 302.81) and Variants

People with paraphilic fetishes are sexually aroused by "nonliving objects" (*DSM-IV-TR,* p. 570). The most common fetishistic objects are shoes, undergarments, and items made of leather, rubber, or plastic. No one knows why these objects are so popular, but there are obvious possibilities. Fetishistic objects tend to have an "earthy" odor, touch, or both. Although this observation is far from scientifically proven, it can be a useful guide in evaluation. Police were mystified by a culprit who was stealing only bicycle seats. Frequently, he took seats that were less valuable than others nearby. Of more concern was the fact that whenever a seat was stolen, the ofender replaced it with another (often more valuable) seat. The answer came when the man involved confessed that he did not steal randomly. Instead, he would often track a woman whom he saw bike riding for weeks. He would then "borrow" her (bicycle) seat, which he would sniff while masturbating. The paraphilia consisting of arousal from body odors is technically known as "mysophilia." The same phenomena explains why people with a panty fetish are generally more interested in unwashed panties, and those with a shoe fetish are generally more interested in shoes that have been worn.

In a case described previously in the section on voyeurism, the man involved spied on women for the purpose of seeing their feet while he masturbated. He was asked why he didn't simply find a consenting partner, who would comply with his seemingly harmless preoccupation with feet. He explained that he would find it too embarrassing. Fetishes involving preoccupation with objects associated with body odors tend to be met with revulsion. People with fetishes deal with this problem either by focusing their interest on the object (as opposed to the odor) or by resorting to surreptitious means of fulfilling their desires (e.g., stealing the objects, spying on sleeping victims, etc.). Generally, individuals with paraphilic fetishes do not come into conflict with the law unless they steal objects or they frighten people with the intensity of their interests. One patient with a shoe fetish faced harassment charges due to his pattern of buying shoes for the object of his desires, even after she told him she had enough footwear.

A group of paraphilic disorders that is best viewed as a variant of fetishes consists of the "partialism" disorders. Partialism disorders involve a sexual preoccupation with a piece of the human body to the exclusion of all else. The most common of the partialism disorders is foot fetishism. Although partialism is most often described as a fixation on a body part, this is really only half of the problem because these paraphilias are usually accompanied by an idealized idea of what the "perfect" body part would look like. For example, though all people with foot fetishes by definition have a sexual focus on feet, each person has a different special interest. One patient spent most of his waking hours surreptitiously photographing the feet of women whom he saw walking on the street in open-toed shoes. He would then develop the pictures and measure the first (big) and second toes with calipers. His aim was to find a woman whose first and second toes were exactly the same length. Asked what he would do when he found her, his answer was chilling: "I have spent my whole life looking for the perfect foot. When I find it, I would like to cut the two toes off and put them on a chain I would wear around my neck so I could keep them with me forever."

Not all people with fetishes or partialism are criminal or dangerous. In fact, the reverse is true. Many people with fetishes or partialism live healthy, happy lives and consider their unconventional sexual interests or preoccupations to be a "gift," as do their partners. The reason some people with fetishes fail in establishing fulfilling sexual and romantic relationships leads naturally to the next major *DSM-IV* paraphilic disorder.

Transvestic Fetishism (*DSM-IV-TR* 302.3) and Its Variants

Transvestic fetishism is often referred to as transvestism (TV) and is defined as a sexual preoccupation with "cross-dressing" (*DSM-IV-TR*, p. 575). In contrast to most of the *DSM-IV* text that painstakingly avoids "sexist" language, the *DSM-IV-TR* specifically states that only *heterosexual males* can receive a diagnosis of transvestic fetishism. The *DSM-IV-TR* criteria for TV often make accurate diagnosis confusing, so I will briefly review the differential diagnosis. Men wear women's clothing for a variety of reasons. Some have a fetishistic interest in women's lingerie, with no interest in wearing it. Some have gender identity disorder and believe that they are female. Wearing women's clothing helps to support this belief. Some gay men find that they are able to attract the attention of men when they wear women's clothing. Some men wear women's clothing as part of their work apparel (e.g., female impersonators). None of these men would meet the criteria for TV.

However, some men wear women's clothing because they find the activity to be sexually arousing. Only men with this characteristic have TV. Although there appears to be no reason that women who are sexually aroused by wearing men's clothes or gay men who are sexually aroused by wearing women's clothes should not meet the criteria for TV, the remainder of this discussion will deal only with heterosexual men who have TV.

Men with TV almost never present with legal problems, aside from child custody disputes. Instead, they present with marital problems. The marital problems they present with are diagnostic. Typically, they are attracted to women who appreciate their attention to fashion. Men with TV often enter professions in which uniforms are worn (e.g., the military). Sexual relations often involve lingerie that most women find flattering. Although most men with TV are able to transfer their interest in cross-dressing to a fetishistic interest in lingerie, inevitably a moment occurs when the man's wife realizes that the lingerie is more important than she is. Shortly afterward, the man will present for treatment "because my wife thinks something is wrong."

As with all the *DSM-IV-TR* paraphilia diagnoses, variants abound. The most frequent variation involves men with gender identity disorder who report a history of cross-dressing for the purpose of sexual arousal. As the men age, episodes in which they cross-dress, masturbate, reach orgasm, and then quickly change back to their regular clothing become less frequent. The episodes are replaced by hours and days in which they cross-dress and then engage in nonsexual activities. Often, the activities involve stereotypical "female" activities such as housework. Men who follow this pattern have been labeled "aging transvestites" and are identified in the *DSM-IV-TR* taxonomy as "transvestic fetishism with gender dysphoria." Men with TV also vary in terms of the items they wear, the conditions in which the items are worn, and what they think about or are trying to achieve while cross-dressing.

Transvestic fetishism is associated with sexual masochism and autoerotic self-asphyxia (also known as hypoxyphilia). Autoerotic self-asphyxia is a syndromic condition in which sexual arousal is obtained by restricting breathing, often by strangulation. Strangulation is obviously a dangerous activity, so it is important to always ask about hypoxyphilia when assessing men with TV. The attitude that a patient has toward the act of cross-dressing sometimes provides a clue because men with TV who also meet criteria for sexual masochism, autoerotic self-asphyxia, or both tend to treat cross-dressing as an act of humiliation. In contrast, men with "aging transvestism" or gender dysphoria tend to idealize women and regard cross-dressing as an act of "self-actualization."

Sexual Masochism (*DSM-IV-TR* 302.83) and Variants

Sexual masochism is defined as sexual arousal from "the act (not simulated) of being humiliated, beaten, bound or otherwise made to suffer" (*DSM-IV-TR*, p. 573). A secondary criteria (associated with many psychiatric disorders) is that the problem is sufficiently severe to cause "clinically significant distress or impairment in social, occupational, or other important areas of functioning" (*DSM-IV-TR*, p. 573). Together with sexual sadism (discussed further on), there are few psychiatric disorders in which the second criterion is so important. This is because there is a vocal and highly political community of people with interest in precisely the activities listed in the first criterion that insists their interests and activities are "safe, sane, and consensual." These people dissociate themselves from individuals who would meet the second criteria, by insisting that their interests and behaviors enhance, rather than interfere with, their lives and relationships. Individuals in this community frequently state that the most dangerous people in a group that insists it is "safe, sane, and consensual" are "unstable masochists." They argue that this is because in a consensual relationship, the "masochist" or submissive member is the one who determines the limits and therefore holds the true control over what happens. People with masochism rarely seek professional help due to conflict with the law. As with most of the noncriminal paraphilias, they are more likely to seek help when they have marital problems or concerns about self-harm.

One patient presented with a concern that he was "too submissive." His wife confirmed his concern. She said that she was sexually sadistic but had become worried that her husband was attempting to push her into being more "cruel" than she wanted to be. Although this patient's interests and behaviors easily met the primary criteria for masochism (interest in humiliation, being bound, and being made to suffer), in therapy, he frequently argued that it was his wife's failure to be sufficiently sadistic that caused their marital discord. His wife confirmed that he provided well for his family and was an excellent father. In this case there was never any question of his masochist interests interfering with any aspect of this life besides his marriage.

Sometimes the diagnosis is easier to make. A successful businessman was referred by his physician due to concerns about his wish to be "tortured and castrated by a dominatrix." He had been seeking a "professional dom" who would be willing to castrate him without anesthetic. He was aware that the procedure could lead to his death. Fortunately, every professional dominatrix had so far refused, questioning his ability to consent and, by implication, his sanity.

In a similar case a 70-year-old man was referred by his urologist. He had sought the assistance of the urologist for the purpose of being castrated. He had no gender identity problems. In fact, he had been examined by a well-known expert in gender identity disorders years previously and was turned down for gender identity treatment of any type. On examination, the patient explained that whenever he masturbated, he would bind his testes tightly with wire and then hit them with a hammer. He found this extremely sexually arousing. In spite of this preoccupation, he had an otherwise normal life. He had married, had children, and had become a grandfather. Now that his children were grown, he stated that he wanted to fulfill his lifelong dream of being castrated.

Because this man did not have a gender identity disorder and because selective serotonergic medications have been reported to sometimes be effective in alleviating violent paraphilic fantasies, a pharmacological treatment was offered. He was prescribed fluoxetine and told to return in 6 weeks. He did so. On his second visit he was asked whether he still wanted to pursue castration. He replied, "That is the craziest idea I have ever had." He said that he not only did not want castration, he no longer had any interest in hitting his testes, and his sexual relations with his wife were better than they had ever been. He was followed for 2 years and showed no evidence of a return of masochistic interests.

Sexual Sadism (*DSM-IV-TR* 302.84) and Variants

The diagnostic criteria for sexual sadism include "sexual arousal from the psychological or physical suffering (including humiliation) of the victim" (*DSM-IV-TR*, p. 574). As with sexual masochism, Criterion B specifies that the sadistic urges have been acted upon or that "the urges or fantasies cause marked distress or interpersonal difficulty" (*DSM-IV-TR*, p. 574). Unlike sexual masochism, Criterion B explicitly states that the requirements can be fulfilled by acting on the urges with a "nonconsenting person." The difference between the *DSM-IV-TR* criteria for sexual masochism and those for sexual sadism illustrates a conundrum. What happens if a person with sadism meets one with masochism who is willing to consent to more than the sadistic person is willing to do? This is more than an academic problem and occurs frequently. The couple described previously (under Masochism) is an example of this situation. The husband had an extreme degree of masochism and pushed his wife to engage in more severe "punishments" than she was willing to inflict. Furthermore, she insisted that she was aroused only by consensual sexual activities with her husband. Her husband was primarily aroused by the idea that his wife would one day take their sexual activities to a level to which he could not consent. He indicated that one of the main reasons he loved and stayed with his wife was her "sadistic" nature. Therefore, although the wife considered herself sadistic and although she did engage in apparently sadistic activities with her husband, the question arises as to whether she would meet the technical *DSM-IV* criteria for sexual sadism because she engaged only in consensual activities and because her "sadistic" activities enhanced, rather than detracted from, the marital relationship.

Other cases are much easier to diagnose. One unemployed man was referred by his probation officer after he was released from prison. He had been convicted of sexually assaulting (raping) a woman in a subway. The sexual assault was brutal and involved a great deal of unnecessary force. During the rape, he told the woman that he had been following her for days and knew where she lived. He told her he was HIV-positive and was not using a condom (although in fact he did use one and was not in fact infected). During his assessment, this man readily admitted that he was aroused by the fear he was able to provoke in his victim. A diagnosis of sadism was confirmed by his response to a standard diagnostic question: "Imagine two doors. Behind Door A is a woman who wants to have sex with you. Behind Door B is her identical twin who does not want to have sex with you. Assuming there are no legal consequences, which door do you go through?" He answered that the consenting woman behind Door A would hold no interest for him, "I only get aroused when I am with a woman who resists. I would go through Door B."

There are many varieties of sadism which vary along the orthagonal dimensions of aggression, cruelty, and assertiveness. Although there is a tendency to think of people with sadism as aggressive, cruel, and assertive, it is also possible for an individual who is gentle, kind, and passive to meet the criteria for sexual sadism. An example would be the wife in the couple described previously. Although she and her husband both described her as sadistic, her sexual activities were not characterized by overt aggression. For example, her preferred "foreplay" involved suspending her eagerly consenting husband from a hook in the basement and blindfolding him. She would then leave the house and go shopping. Her husband would have no idea when or if she would return and could exercise his fantasy of being in a nonconsensual scenario.

The man convicted of rape and the wife just described could hardly be more different. What is similar is the need for both people to be in control, dominant, or both. It is probably the need for control that is most important in individuals with sadism. In fact, even "sadists" who are completely law-abiding and interested only in consensual encounters show a dependence on control. Paradoxically, the more sadistic an individual is, the more dependent that person will be and therefore the less absolute control he or she will have. People with extreme sadism are difficult to distinguish from those with extreme masochism. For this reason it is sometimes useful to think of sadism and masochism as points on a circle, rather than as disorders at opposite ends of a linear continuum.

For example, imagine a man and women who go into a restaurant together. The gentleman picks up the menu and orders a meal for both of them. Suppose he finds the act sexually arousing. Is he sadistic or masochistic? The answer depends on the context. If, prior to entering the restaurant, he ordered the woman to remain silent and to accept whatever he decided she could eat, sexual sadism would be likely. On the other hand, what if, prior to entering the restaurant, the woman had told him that she did not want to have to say a word? What if she expected him to order exactly what she wanted and to pay for it? In this case a diagnosis of sexual masochism in the man would be more likely. The point is that the same behaviors have different diagnostic significance, depending on the context. In fact, most restaurant dates, that are eminently sensuous, are neither sadistic nor masochistic.

Frotteurism (*DSM-IV-TR* 302.89) and Variants

Frotteurism is defined as sexual fantasies, urges, or acts that involve touching and rubbing against a nonconsenting person (*DSM-IV-TR*, p. 570). It is the only paraphilia in which the most frequent incidence of paraphilic acts occurs between the ages of 15 and 25. It is rare to find individuals who prefer frotteuristic acts over all other sexual activities. Rather, frotteuristic activities tend to be crimes of opportunity (e.g., rubbing against victims on crowded subway trains) or examples of social incompetency. People who are socially incompetent are more likely to have mental retardation, developmental delay, brain damage, or severe social phobia.

One specific disorder frequently associated with frotteurism is Asperger's syndrome.

Asperger's syndrome is a developmental delay disorder characterized by social incompetence. People with Asperger's syndrome are unable to accurately interpret nonverbal social communication. As a result, they often misunderstand or misinterpret the steps necessary before engaging in intimate physical contact with another person. Their behaviors are asocial, rather than antisocial, in nature.

Similarly, individuals with brain damage (particularly those with frontal-parietal lesions) can become disinhibited. A specific syndrome known as "utilization phenomenon" has been described, in which people with brain lesions will interact with objects in the environment (including people), with no awareness of how inappropriate the behavior is.

A middle-aged, never-married laborer was referred by his family doctor. His job involved working with heavy machinery in total isolation. He lived by himself. He had some hearing impairment due to his work with noisy machinery. This man was preoccupied with the idea of touching the breasts of a woman who lived in his town. Although he had never spoken to the woman, he felt that she was the "woman of [his] dreams." No amount of discussion could convince him that he would be wise to speak with the woman before making any attempt to touch her. He had never had a girlfriend or ever been in a romantic relationship with anyone. He was a virgin. On examination he was found to have severe social phobia, with likely mild mental retardation.

In another case, the wife of an executive called my office at 5 P.M. Her husband had recently begun treatment for exhibitionism. She explained that her husband had left for work as usual that morning. At 4:45 she received a call from her husband from within one of the city jails. He was released from custody on bail the next day and reported promptly for reassessment.

He explained that he had left home for work as usual. However, on the train he had spotted an attractive woman. He managed to maneuver himself behind her and rub his groin against her while pretending to read a newspaper. He ejaculated. His victim had become aware of his surreptitious activities and at the next station reported his behavior to the transit authorities. They radioed the train conductor, who placed an inspector in the man's car. He was arrested at the next stop and taken directly to jail.

He stated that he had not exposed himself. However, he admitted to having engaged in frotteuristic activities that he had never previously disclosed. Though admitting that he had been sexually aroused by the events in question, he felt that the primary motive had been anxiety related to problems at work.

This case is presented to highlight two points. The first is the change in the attitude of law enforcement toward frotteuristic activities. In the past, these were more or less ignored. More recently, law enforcement agencies and, in particular, public transportation authorities have acted on these activities with much more concern. Frotteurism is a criminal paraphilia that needs to be taken seriously.

The second point is that frotteurism often occurs in conjunction with other paraphilias, in particular, exhibitionism and voyeurism. These paraphilias (frotteurism, exhibitionism, and voyeurism) have been referred to as *courtship disorders*. Paraphilic rape is sometimes also included as a courtship disorder. The theory behind courtship disorders is that some individuals get "fixated" on one stage of normal courtship: viewing the object of desire (voyeurism), touching or kissing the object of desire (frotteurism), disrobing in front of the object of desire (exhibitionism), and eventual sexual relations (paraphilic rape). Although the fact that voyeurism, exhibitionism, and frotteurism often occur together argues against the theory that men with courtship disorders are fixated on a single point in conventional courtship, the idea that these are people who have difficulties achieving or maintaining traditional romantic relationships suggests an important area for attention in treatment (see further on).

Pedophilia (*DSM-IV-TR* 302.2) and Variants

People with the diagnosis of pedophilia are defined as having sexual fantasies, urges, or activities involving sex with a prepubescent child. The person must be at least 16 years of age and at least 5 years older than the child. People in "late adolescence involved in an on-going relationship with a 12 or 13 year old child" are specifically excluded (*DSM-IV-TR*, p. 572). Aside from transvestic fetishism, in which a subtype with gender dysphoria is listed in the *DSM-IV-TR* criteria, pedophilia is the only paraphilia in the *DSM-IV-TR* with multiple recognized subtypes. These are "sexually attracted to males," "sexually attracted to females," "sexually attracted to both (males and females)," "limited to incest," "exclusive type (attracted only to children)," and "nonexclusive type."

An analysis of the *DSM-IV-TR* diagnostic criteria reveals several important premises. First, a diagnosis of pedophilia cannot be assigned to a child. This is because it is now recognized that children have sexual interests, and "sex play" between same-aged children is recognized as common and normal.

A middle-aged men with pedophilia who had multiple convictions was referred by his parole officer. He explained that he had been orphaned when he was very young, due to a car accident. He had been placed in a foster home and subsequently transferred to a "boys training school" in another country. The discipline was harsh. Because he had no one to look after him, he befriended some of the older boys, who offered him protection and privileges in exchange for sex. He said he didn't like it at first but found that life in the institution was safer when he was allowed to hang around the older boys. "Time went on and I grew up. When I was 13, I started to help the new boys who were just arriving. It just seemed natural that sex would be involved. That was the life I knew. But I know I am different. When my friends started to be interested in girls and older women, I didn't change. I was still interested in boys around age 8. I guess I never grew up."

Contrary to expectations, this patient never endorsed the idea that his pedophilic interests were the result of childhood trauma or abuse. He described his encounters with older boys in the most positive terms. He had no interest in or experience with anal sex. His activities involved only him performing fellatio on other males. Although he freely admitted that his interest in boys was sexually motivated, he claimed that he also had nonsexual interests in boys: "I prefer being with children. Adults smoke and drink. They sit around and complain. Children are full of life and fun. They don't have bad habits."

People with pedophilia frequently report a sense of being more easily accepted by children. Another patient was referred after being convicted of performing oral sex on a 16-year-old youth. He had been a teacher in the school that the 16-year-old had attended. The sexual event had happened during the summer holiday. An extensive police investigation had failed to uncover any other sexual assaults on any other students over the teacher's 25-year career. On examination, the teacher admitted to being aroused by "young males" but denied interest in prepubescent children. He had never been in a romantic relationship with anyone at any time in his life. Further inquiry revealed that he had never had sex with anyone besides the victim. Asked why, he replied, "I have a very small penis. I was always afraid if I got involved with someone my own age, they would see it and laugh at me. I decided if I did something with someone who was inexperienced, I could get away with not showing my penis."

This theme of being uncomfortable about initiating sex with age-appropriate partners is surprisingly common. Sometimes it is part of a recognition by patients that they have a paraphilia; sometimes it is due to poor self-esteem or body image. Older textbooks often say that people who commit sex offences always understate the number of victims they have had and imply that men with (for example) pedophilia by definition have many victims. Although this is certainly the case in many instances, people who have pedophilia, but with no victims, are becoming much more common in forensic clinics. The reason is twofold. The first is that word is beginning to get out that there is effective treatment available. The second and more important reason is that people with pedophilia are now being arrested in increasing numbers because they access child pornography sites on the Internet. In many cases, although the offender has hundreds or thousands of images or video clips of children on his computer, extensive investigation fails to reveal any victims in the community. "Victimless" people with pedophilia represent a new group that is likely to become increasingly common and about which almost nothing is known.

Paraphilias Not Otherwise Specified (*DSM-IV-TR* 302.9) and Variants

This is the ubiquitous *DSM-IV-TR* catch-all category for everything that doesn't fit into the categories reviewed previously. The *DSM-IV-TR* specifically lists sexual arousal from telephone scatalogia (obscene phone calls), necrophilia (corpses), partialism (body parts), zoophilia (animals), coprophilia (feces), klismaphilia (enemas), and urophilia (urine). However, the list is far from exhaustive.

Two diagnostic questions arise. The first is, how detailed should the taxonomy of paraphilias be? The second question, which follows, is how should paraphilia diagnoses be assigned. Concerning the first question, it is obvious that the variety of stimuli and activities that can be associated with sexual arousal is virtually limitless. Does it make sense to attempt to catalogue every specific variation? For example, one patient's wife reported that her husband had a bizarre pattern of sexual behavior. Whenever they went to their cottage, he would venture into the woods by himself with a jar of honey. He was in the habit of smearing the honey on his exposed penis. He would then allow mosquitoes to repeatedly bite his penis. This had the effect of causing his penis to swell. He claimed that the sensation of having intercourse with his wife with his inflamed penis was extremely enjoyable. Although behaviors like this have been described with other insects, is this worth naming?

Concerning the second question, does it make sense to list every activity or interest as a separate paraphilia? The literature on this question has been somewhat acrimonious. On the one hand are advocates of a detailed listing of each act as a separate disorder. On the other are advocates of the idea that each individual has an idealized "love map" and that once the love map is identified, the activities that the person engages in are better viewed as the modus operandi, rather than as specific disorders. The *DSM-IV-TR* requires that each paraphilia be listed separately. Although this certainly makes sense, it is important to distinguish between activities that are sexually arousing in themselves and activities that are in aid of a more important sexual preference or paraphilia.

For example, one patient was sexually interested in prepubescent girls. His pattern was to frequent schoolyards with a camera. He would begin taking pictures of his intended victim. He would convince her to return to his apartment, where he would expose himself and convince the victim to disrobe. Finally, he would convince the victim to lie in a coffin that he kept in his bedroom so he could take "pictures to remember her by." He always let the victim go. What is the diagnosis? One group would categorize his paraphilias as voyeurism (arousal from spying on an unsuspecting victim), exhibitionism (exposing himself to a nonconsenting victim), pedophilia (sexual arousal from a prepubescent child), and a necrophilia (sexual arousal from corpses). When he was interviewed, he admitted that his fantasies involved torture (sexual sadism) and dismemberment (apotomophilia).

ASSESSMENT AND TREATMENT

Assessment and treatment of paraphilic disorders are two large and rapidly evolving areas. No attempt will be made to fully deal with them here. Instead, I will broadly outline "rules" that may be of some assistance to professionals who provide care for people with paraphilias but who do not have specialized training in this area.

1. **Do be explicit about whom you are working for.**
   Sadly, people rarely seek help for sexual problems until they think they have no choice. It is very important at the beginning of any assessment to establish why this person has sought help from you at this time. Besides asking the person, a quick guide is to ask yourself, "Who is paying for this assessment?" and "To whom will I be reporting the results of this assessment?" If a third party has retained you (e.g., lawyer, children's aid society), you should make sure that the person you are assessing knows this.
2. **Do be honest about the limits of confidentiality.**
   Every province and state in North America has laws requiring that professionals

disclose known abuse of children who are identifiable. Although the specifics of the requirements vary between jurisdictions, the principle that professionals must act if a child is at risk is universal. It is important to be honest about your moral, professional, and legal obligations.

3. **Do not refer someone for the purpose of fulfilling your duty to report.**
   If you discover that an adult is molesting an identifiable child, you must report the fact without delay. Referring the person to an "expert in sex abuse" does not discharge your duty. In addition, the fact that you did not file a report promptly can convey the false impression that child abuse is not an emergency or that reporting is only an optional activity.

4. **Do get as much information as possible.**
   Sex is complicated. It usually involves more than one person. The more you know, the better. If there are legal documents (e.g,. disclosure of the alleged activities) or previous assessments, ask for them. Many professionals are sometimes confused about their ethical obligations in this area. Though the rules of confidentiality forbid disclosure of information unless a child is at risk (see 2.), nothing forbids a professional from listening to information provided by others. If your patient's wife calls you because there is something she thinks you should know, listen to her. You may not tell her anything about her husband without permission, but there is no reason why you can't collect information from her. In general, whenever a person has a legal sexual partner, it is worthwhile, with permission, to interview the partner in person.

5. **Do forbid illegal activity.**
   If patients disclose that they are engaging in illegal sex acts (e.g., exposing), tell them they must stop immediately. Do not accept the excuse that they are "out of control and can't help it." One man in treatment for exhibitionism was certainly persistent. On one occasion he had exposed on the courthouse steps, having just come from an arraignment for a new set of charges. He said he simply could not resist exposing himself. It was pointed out that he had somehow managed to avoid exposing himself while he was before the judge. In fact, he had also managed to arrive for treatment, get past the office staff, and sit through an hour-long session without succumbing to the "irresistible" urge to expose himself. On reflection, he agreed. In this context he was started on medication for the purpose of lessening his discomfort at not exposing but not for the purpose of "making him stop" exposing, which he accepted was his responsibility.

6. **Do not try to be a police detective.**
   Your job is to assess and treat people who seek your help for specific problems. Although it is important to be thorough and to critically evaluate all the information you can get (see 4.), you are not a detective. Nor are you a judge. If you pretend that you are, you will make therapeutic mistakes. On this topic, some therapists believe it is essential that people with paraphilias (particularly, criminal paraphilias) fully disclose every offense they have ever committed or have thought of committing. This is a waste of time. In the case of people with exhibitionism who may have thousands of victims, it is not only a waste of time, it is impossible. Instead,

focus on what is happening in the present. There is rarely a lack of material, and it represents issues about which something can be done.

7. **Do not get distracted.**

    People with paraphilias often want to talk about everything but the problem. Do not get distracted. Once the diagnosis is made, focus on the presenting problem. Every person with a paraphilia has a story about how he or she got that way. One exhibitionist explained that his problem began one day that was clearly and indelibly etched upon his mind: "It was a beautiful day and I was sitting by myself in the park on a bench, masturbating. Suddenly, the most beautiful woman I have ever seen came right up to me and said she wanted to have sex with me. Ever since then, I haven't been able to stop exposing myself. I just can't forget how exciting that afternoon was." This account was spontaneously presented as an explanation for why he had exhibitionism. Amazingly, it had never occurred to him that the fact that he was masturbating in broad daylight on a park bench suggested that he was at least predisposed to exhibitionism prior to that day. In general, it is impossible to know whether or not some recalled incident that the patient thinks explains his or her condition even occurred. As a rule, time spent reviewing childhood events in search of an explanation for current paraphilic activities is time taken from ending the misery caused by the paraphilia in the present.

8. **Do not tell someone you just met that he or she is incurable.**

    Rule #8 may seem obvious but is routinely broken by professionals who should know better. The fact is that most people with paraphilic disorders who receive modern treatment get better. Even the most severely disturbed sex offenders, as a group, do extremely well. The average published rate of relapse for sex offenders is below 14%, making the success rate for the treatment of paraphilias in general better than almost any other psychiatric condition (e.g., Hanson & Bussiere, 1998). Why is there a widespread myth about the dismal prognosis for paraphilias? There are several reasons, but probably the most important is the fact that people who get better never tell anyone. In contrast, the people who recidivate are often reported in the media and are rarely forgotten. By analogy, bacterial pneumonia is a highly treatable and curable disease. However, in every major city, every day, people die from this disease. They die because they have comorbid conditions or because they did not receive adequate treatment. Even so, medical students are not taught that pneumonia is incurable, and they are not trained to tell people they can't be cured, just before sending them to specialists. If the media ran headlines every time someone died from pneumonia, it is likely the public would start to believe the disease was incurable, especially if people never reported it when they got better. Clearly, not everyone with pneumonia or a paraphilia is treatable, but telling people they are incurable before treatment begins is counterproductive.

9. **Do not limit your treatment options or goals.**

    Professionals who treat individuals with paraphilias are blessed with a wide variety of effective treatment options. A major mistake is to get locked into a single-treatment paradigm. What works for one patient will be utterly ineffective for the next. This is not the fault of the treatment, the therapist, or the patient. The prob-

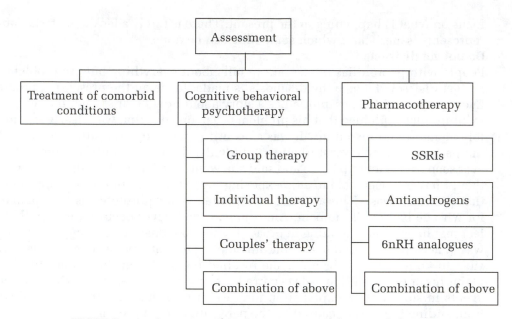

FIGURE 19.1. Summary of Treatment Protocol for Paraphilias

lem is that no two people are the same. One treatment protocol is summarized in Figure 19.1.

The first step is to conduct a thorough assessment. This should include obtaining as much collateral information as possible, particularly if there are forensic issues. The aim of the assessment should be not only to diagnose any paraphilic disorders correctly but also to rule out disorders that can masquerade as paraphilic disorders (e.g., organic syndromes, obsessive-compulsive disorders, personality disorders) and to identify comorbid disorders (e.g., substance abuse). The next step is to review the findings with the individual seeking treatment. Next, treatment options should be reviewed and agreed upon. Though many people with paraphilias find group therapy extremely beneficial, for some, particularly those with anxiety disorders or attention deficit disorders, group therapy is aversive. The specific form of treatment should be individualized so that the treatment is seen as helpful, rather than simply as a form of punishment. Other formats for psychotherapy include individual and couples' therapy, and the choice of one therapy format does not preclude the use of others simultaneously or sequentially.

The risks and benefits of pharmacotherapy should be reviewed. Several good reviews of the pharmacological options are available (e.g., Bradford & Greenberg, 1996). Most patients elect starting with a selective serotonin reuptake inhibitor (SSRI) (Fedoroff, 1995). There is no evidence that one is better than another, but some patients certainly fail to respond to one SSRI but do very well on another. Choice of a specific SSRI should therefore be on the basis of side effects. One important side effect to watch for is inhibited orgasm. Often patients with paraphilic disorder will report a normalization of their paraphilic interests until they begin to experience inhibited orgasm. The onset of this disorder is often accompanied by a return to paraphilic fantasies and behaviors, which defeats the purpose of treatment. Because the side effect of inhibited orgasm caused by SSRI medications is dose dependent, reducing the dosage of the SSRI is often more effective than increasing it.

Some patients require pharmacological inhibition of all sexual interest (normal and paraphilic), at least temporarily. Generally, patients will choose antiandrogen medications for this purpose. Physicians in the United States are currently limited to medroxyprogesterone acetate that can be given either orally or by weekly injection. In Canada, cyproterone acetate is also available in oral or intramuscular formulations. Both of these medications decrease serum testosterone levels, and patients often report an accompanying decrease in their sexual interest.

A third approach involves gonadotropin release hormone (GnRH) analogues such as leuprolide or gosserelin. These medications are available only in intramuscular injection formulations. They act centrally on the pituitary-hypothalamic axis to decrease the production of gonadotophic hormones. Treatment with these medications results in a dramatic diminution in testosterone blood levels and appears to decrease sexual desire of all types. The primary problematic side effects caused by all medications that decrease testosterone are osteoporosis and menopausal-like symptoms (e.g., "hot flashes"). The other important difficulty in using GnRH analogues is the high cost associated with these medications.

Concerning goals, therapists often aim too low. The goal for every patient should be the establishment of a lawful, happy, fulfilling sex life within the context of a meaningful and balanced lifestyle. This should be the aim of every psychotherapeutic intervention. You should not keep this secret from the patient. Patients will work hard if the goal is worthwhile. In contrast, patients will not be enthusiastic about treatment that aims to end their sex life, end their "denial," or prove that they belong in jail.

10. **Do be systematic.**
In planning treatment, identify measurable objectives. For example, there is no point in putting someone on an antiandrogen if the person has no sexual desire and no opportunity to have sex, because there is no way of knowing if the treatment is effective. Begin with a reasonably comprehensive treatment program. If needed, add one new intervention at a time. Explain to the patient that each time a new intervention is added, we will learn something that will make the next intervention more effective. For example, if a patient finds that he drinks more alcohol when he can't cross-dress, substance abuse treatment may be indicated. If he finds that he get depressed, interventions aimed at depression would make more sense.

An important new trend in the management of criminal paraphilic disorder is the use of rating instruments based on actuarial statistical assessments of sex offenders followed up over time. Although actuarial methods are obviously of little use in dealing with individual cases, they can be helpful in objectively highlighting patients who require more intensive therapy. The three most widely used actuarial instruments are the Hare Psychopathy Checklist Revised (HPCL-R) (for review, see Hare, Clark, Grann, & Thorton, 2000), the Violence Risk Appraisal Guide (VRAG), and the Sex Offender Risk Appraisal Guide (SORAG) (Quinsey, Harris, Rice, & Cormier, 1998). Only the SORAG has been specifically designed to predict risk of reoffense for sex offenders. It, like the VRAG and HPCL-R, is heavily weighted to measure criminal and antisocial behaviors. Paradoxically, the current actuarial data suggest that the best predictors of future criminal sexual behavior are indicators of criminal propensity, rather than sexual deviation itself.

11. Do consult.

Most people with paraphilias neither seek nor receive treatment. This is a shame because most paraphilias can be successfully managed by nonspecialized professionals. However, specialized clinics are able to offer more sophisticated assessments and to advise in treatment planning. For example, penile plethysmography testing (PPT) is often useful in assessing sexual response patterns and response to therapy. In PPT, changes in penile blood flow are dynamically measured while the patient is presented with auditory or visual stimuli. Though the test is not designed to determine "guilt or innocence," it can be a helpful addition to a full evaluation (Blanchard, Klassen, Dikey, Kuban, & Blak, 2001). Specialists in the assessment and treatment of paraphilic disorders are always delighted to be consulted, particularly because the field is developing so rapidly.

SUMMARY AND CONCLUSIONS

This chapter began with the question: "What made you decide to devote your life to studying and treating the sort of people you do?" It should be clear to you, having reviewed the topic, that the only common feature among people with paraphilias is that they have problems due to unconventional sexual interests. Not all paraphilic interests are criminal, and even among people with criminal sexual interests, not all act on their criminal interests. Treatment of paraphilic disorders is usually successful and rewarding. Patients, their spouses, and even their victims are grateful. It is hard to imagine a more intellectually interesting or professionally rewarding endeavor.

But perhaps the last words should go to the 70-year-old masochistic grandfather described earlier in this chapter:

> All my life I was an outsider. I had an interest that I knew was a disease, but I couldn't tell anyone. I couldn't get any help. It separated me from my friends, my family, my wife. If I had known I was not alone and that there was treatment, I would have lived a different life. Now I am free of the disease. I may be old now, but I know the rest of my life will be better than the first 70 years. I just can't help thinking how many other people

*there are like me out there. Please tell your doctor friends to keep asking
their patients about their sex problems. You will save a lot of lives if you do.*

REFERENCES

Classification and Assessment

American Psychiatric Association. (2000). *Diagnostic and Statistical Manual of Mental Disorders* (4th ed., text rev.). Washington, DC, Author. The "bible" for psychiatric classification of psychiatric disorders in North America. Although the I*nternational Statistical Classification of Diseases and Related Health Problems* (*ICD-10*) probably retains preeminent international acceptance, the *DSM-IV* is fully compatible. The "text revision" form of the *DSM-IV* retains identical diagnostic criteria to that of the *DSM-IV* but has added minor text revisions in the accompanying diagnostic preamble.

Blanchard, R., Klassen, P., Dickey, R., Kuban, M. E., & Blak, T. (2001). Sensitivity and specificity of the phallometric test for pedophilia in non admitting sex offenders. *Psychological Assessments, 13,* 118–126. One of the best published assessments of the usefulness of a very specialized test instrument.

Fedoroff, J. P. (1995). Antiandrogrens vs. serotonergic medications in the treatment of sex offenders: A preliminary compliance study. *The Canadian Journal of Human Sexuality, 4,* 111–122. A comparison of compliance and acceptance of serotonergic and antiandrogen medications, showing that serotonergic medications are much more frequently selected by sex offenders.

Fedoroff, J. P., Brunet, A., Woods, V., Granger, C., Chow, E., Collins, P., & Shapiro, C. (1997). A case-controlled study of men who sexually assault sleeping victims. In C. Shapiro & M. Smith (Eds.), *Forensic Aspects of Sleep*, New York: Wiley. An article describing a series of men who assaulted sleeping victims, in which several motivations and subtypes are identified.

Fedoroff, J. P., Fishell, A., & Fedoroff, B. (1999). A case series of women evaluated for paraphilic sexual disorders. *The Canadian Journal of Human Sexuality, 8,* 127–140.

Hare, R. D., Clark, D., Grann, M., & Thorton, D. (2000). Psychopathy and the predicative validity of the PCL-R: An international perspective. *Behavioral Sciences and the Law, 18,* 623–645. This is only one of many articles by Dr. Hare that is worth reviewing, in order to appreciate the influence that psychopathy has on the expression of sexually deviant interests.

Money, J. (1986). *Lovemaps.* New York: Irvington. Lovemaps is arguably the masterpiece work by a scholar who has written on virtually every aspect of human sexual behavior. *Lovemaps* fully describes an explanatory and descriptive theory of paraphilias.

Von Krafft-Ebig, R. (1965). *Psychopathia Sexualis.* New York: G. P. Putnam's Son's. This is the original and one of the most comprehensive attempts to catalogue the range of (criminal) sexual behaviors. It was originally published in 1886 in Latin. The cited edition is the first fully translated English edition. It is worth reading to appreciate the fact that most of the sex crimes reported in the media as "crimes of the century" were equaled by those of criminals of previous centuries.

Treatment

Bradford, J. M. W., & Greenberg, D. M. (1996). Pharmacologic treatment of deviant sexual behavior. In R. C. Rosen, C. Davis, & H. Ruppel Jr. (Eds.), *Annual Review of Sex Research* (Vol. 7, pp. 283–306). One of the best (and most comprehensive) reviews of the developing field of pharmacological treatments of paraphilic disorders.

Hanson, R. K., & Bussiere, M. T. (1998). Predicting relapse: A meta-analysis of sexual offender recidivism studies. *Journal of Consulting and Clinical Psychiatry, 66,* 348–362. At the time of writing, the most comprehensive meta-analysis of sex offender recidivism studies.

Laws, D. R. (Ed.). (1989). *Relapse Prevention with Sex Offenders.* New York: Guilford. This is a classic book, which has launched the preeminent nonpharmacological therapy for sex offenders. Based on the "relapse prevention" (RP) therapy techniques used with great success in the management of patients with substance abuse, RP therapy remains a mainstay in the treatment of individuals with paraphilic disorders.

Marshall, W. L., Fernandez, Y. M., Hudson, S. M., & Ward, T. (Eds.). (1998). *Sourcebook of Treatment Programs for Sex Offenders.* New York: Plenum. Another encyclopedia of resources. This text reviews a wide variety of treatment programs. Details about treatment methodology and results, accompanied by extensive contact information, make this text indispensable.

Quinsey, V. L., Harris, G. R., Rice, M. E., & Cormier, C. A. (1998). *Violent Offenders: Appraising and Managing Risk.* Washington, DC: American Psychological Association. A tour de force by a dedicated research team that takes a "radical" actuarial approach to the prediction of sex offender recidivism. Though widely criticized, it is certainly the most credible argument for an actuarial method of predicting potential for recidivism. This book lists the items for the VRAG and SORAG and provides scoring instructions.

Schwartz, B. K., & Cellini, H. R. (Eds.). (1995). *The Sex Offender: Corrections, Treatment and Legal Practice.* Kingston, NJ: Civic Research Institute. One of a series of edited texts that thoroughly summarizes the field. For a full review of these two volumes, see: Fedoroff, J. P. (1998). The sex offender (volumes I & II), edited by B. K. Schwartz & H. R. Cellini. *Journal of Sex & Marital Therapy.*

Schwartz, B. K., & Cellini, H. R. (Eds.). (1997). *The Sex Offender: New Insights, Treatment Innovations and Legal Developments.* Kingston, NJ: Civic Research Institute.

Part Five

BASIC YET
TRANSCENDENT MATTERS

Chapter Twenty

Therapeutic Weaving: The Integration of Treatment Techniques

Stanley E. Althof, PhD

By training and degree I am a clinical psychologist, yet my colleagues often refer to me as a sex therapist or sexologist. My preferred identity as psychologist is important because it anchors me in two complementary worlds, that of the clinician who treats men, women, and couples with sexual problems and that of the scientist who studies the effects of innovative sexual pharmacological treatments on the patient and partner's sexual function, psychological well-being, and relationship. As such I serve as a consultant to several pharmaceutical companies, helping them design clinical trials and develop new assessments of quality-of-life outcomes. These assessment scales measure the impact of medical interventions on multiple dimensions of a couple's lives. This area of inquiry is much more interesting to me than simply testing the efficacy of a drug on genital function.

I also work in two very different settings: a private group mental health practice that specializes in marital and sexual problems and an outpatient hospital-based urology practice. In my private practice, I see men and women in individual, couples', and group therapy, some briefly and some for several years. In the urology practice, I see men once for a consultation session prior to their visit with the urologist. In that consultation, I try to identify obstacles that may limit their response to medical intervention. I also offer coaching to restart long dormant sexual lives and make referrals for those couples who require more extended psychological intervention for psychotherapy. Working in both settings has taught me many valuable lessons on integrating therapies. My goal here is to teach you the value of thoughtful integration in order to enable you to help your patients with sexual problems.

I will tell you about three aspects of integration. Mostly, I will focus on the integration of pharmacological treatments with psychotherapy for male sexual dysfunction, because, presently, there are no FDA-approved pharmacological interventions for women. To a lesser extent I will discuss integrating different ideological orientations (e.g., psychodynamic approaches with behavioral techniques) and multiple modalities of psychotherapy (e.g., individual, marital, and group treatment).

ON INTEGRATING PHARMACOTHERAPY AND PSYCHOTHERAPY

The philosopher Yogi Berra's comment "It seems like déjà vu all over again" reminds me that we have been here before. In mainstream psychiatry during the 1970s, a battle was waged between psychiatrists and psychoanalysts. Analysts insisted that psychotropic medication interfered with the purity of their analysis and would detract from recovery. Psychiatrists argued that analysts deprived patients in desperate need of medication of readily available relief. Two decades later, the pendulum still moving, we heard from the prominent psychopharmacologists that medication was the foundation of treatment. They deemphasized psychotherapeutic interventions so much that many psychiatric institutions dramatically diminished the opportunities of their trainees to learn how to conduct psychotherapy. Today the pendulum has returned to a more centrist position. Patients can be treated with medication and psychotherapy, rather than with either alone, without an ideological battle.

Several well-controlled studies demonstrated that patients diagnosed with diverse psychiatric conditions (depression, schizophrenia, post-traumatic stress disorder, etc.) benefit significantly more from combined psychological and pharmacological approaches than from either modality alone (Keller et al, 2000; Nathan & Gorman, 2002). I contend that this is also true for sexual medicine, although we do not as yet have any prospective controlled studies to support my assumption. Pharmacological interventions that restore sexual function have restimulated the ideological battle. Pharmacotherapists are upbraided for ignoring the important, complex psychosocial dilemmas faced by patients and couples. Advocates of psychotherapeutic approaches are challenged for using costly, time-consuming methods that lack evidence of efficacy—particularly in the long term. It should not surprise you that I believe both sides are wrong, disrespectful of one another, and narrowly rigid in perspective. Each fails to appreciate how an integrated treatment, thoughtfully administered, can provide a synergistic solution (Althof, 1998; Perelman, 2001; Rosen & Leiblum, 1995).

Integrated treatments, however, are more challenging to plan and conduct than are discrete treatments and they typically require a mental health professional. Before I discuss this, I want to remind you of two points. First, psychotherapy is basically an intuitive, individual art, rather than a manualized cookbook that instructs all therapists to perform in the same way. Second, I want to caution you about the concept of clinical success with sexual problems.

SEXUAL SUCCESS

To be effective in enabling patients to make love, we clinicians need to broaden our perspective from believing we need to provide patients with adequate genital functioning to appreciating the context in which couples live. Outcomes conceived solely in terms of women's facility in achieving coital orgasm, men's prowess at delaying ejaculation, the buckling force of an erection, blood flow through the vagina, or the frequency with which partners bring their bodies to one another are far too narrow and mechanistic criteria for success. Successful sexuality outcomes require attending to the complex interplay between the biological, psychological, and relational components of individuals' and couples' lives. It is not solely how many orgasms individuals achieve; it is their satisfaction and sense of psychological and relational well-being that constitute success.

Success often requires that the therapist help the individual or the couple to overcome a variety of psychosocial barriers to lovemaking. Throughout this discussion, I will return to my notion that such barriers have three levels of severity or complexity, which are

1. No or insignificant barriers preventing the couple from making excellent use of the medical intervention;
2. Mild to moderate barriers; or
3. Profound psychological/interpersonal difficulties that will render any treatment ineffective.

Each level leads to an alternative treatment plan. In scenario one, we generally encounter a couple with a high-quality relationship. Although the partners may be struggling with a sexual dysfunction, they continue to be affectionate and maintain noncoital sexual play. One or both have realistic expectations about treatment. They value their return to a satisfying sexual life. In such ideal circumstances, pharmacotherapy, whether targeted at her or at him, most likely will reverse the sexual symptoms. Nothing more than a medical prescription and succinct advice about how to best use the drug is usually necessary.

In scenario two, which is the most frequently encountered situation, we meet a couple who has been sexually abstinent for an extended period of time. The partners' expressions of affection have dwindled. At least one person is mildly depressed and uncertain how to restart lovemaking. Brief, directed coaching is often helpful in improving this couple's sexual life. You also need to suggest techniques for talking calmly about both partners' wish to resume a sexual life and for ensuring that they are prepared emotionally. You may need to address one or both partners' depression, attend to performance anxiety, or inquire about any physical obstacles—such as vaginal dryness—that might diminish the quality of their sexual experiences. You must speak realistically about treatment, as well as provide guidance about how to best use the pharmacological intervention. With sildenafil, for instance, this means you have to instruct them to avoid eating fatty meals before taking the drug and to wait 45 minutes before beginning lovemaking. You also may need to help them fashion a romantic ambience. Do not forget to schedule a follow-up appointment to evaluate their progress.

In scenario three, the more complicated situation, we perceive profound psychological or interpersonal difficulties (or both) with one or both partners and intuitively recognize that the obstacles are too great to be surmounted with medication alone. Their individual psychological and interpersonal terrains are not adequately prepared to make use of effective medical treatments— even if the partners emphasize that their goal is to resume lovemaking. Here are some of the obstacles that you may notice: poorly managed or unresolved anger, power and control issues, abandonment concerns, broken attachments, substance abuse, serious depression, contempt, and disappointment. These psychological states, complicated by prolonged sexual abstinence, have to be addressed prior to, or during, the pharmacological treatment intervention, in order for the couple to achieve emotional satisfaction from sex.

Similarly, when these couples voice unrealistic expectations, saying or implying, "With a restored erection lovemaking will be more frequent," or "I will feel more lovable/successful in life, " or "This will cure my marital woes," be wary! These expectations usually prove to be highly unrealistic. When they are inevitably not realized, the patient will announce, "It didn't work." Disappointed patients rarely ever say, "I had unrealistic expectations."

Patients may avoid telling you the complete story when they have disguised or hidden (conventional and unconventional) sexual arousal patterns. Examples include the married woman who is intensely attracted to only women; the man who has no sexual desire for his unattractive wife; or the man who does not acknowledge his sexual arousal to young children, to sadomasochistic behaviors, or to flashing. Any of these arousal patterns are very likely to interfere with therapeutic success, as I broadly define it. Each requires your curiosity and tactful questioning.

RESISTANCE TO USING EFFECTIVE TREATMENTS

Actually, only a small percentage of men and women with sexual problems seek pharmacological treatment, and a large percentage of those who do discontinue it. This initially shocked me. I did not understand it; today it feels as if I always know why. The answer is to be found in the psychoanalytic concept of resistance. In the next several pages, I will try to make the concept of resistance very clear.

Erectile dysfunction illustrates this well. In the past we attributed the high dropout rate to the objectionable nature of the treatment itself—having to self-inject the penis, for example. We thought the introduction of sildenafil (Viagra), an efficacious and safe oral agent, would dramatically decrease the discontinuation rate (Goldstein et al., 1998). All PDE5 inhibitor drugs, like sildenafil, tadalafil*, and vardenafil* (respectively, Viagra, Cialis*, and Levitra*) restore erections in approximately 70% of men. Nonetheless, approximately 50% of men still discontinued treatment. The men who drop out say, "Doctor, it doesn't work!" Consider Ralph with me.

Ralph, a 45-year-old divorced man, told me that he has suffered from erectile dysfunction for 3 years. It began toward the end of his marriage and continues with a woman he now dates. After being given 50 mg of

---

*Not currently FDA approved

sildenafil by his family practice physician, he "took it out for a successful test drive" with masturbation and found he could obtain a firm, long-lasting erection. However, when he attempted to be sexual with his girl-friend, he "couldn't get his engine started." Ralph was genuinely puzzled and was ready to discontinue the drug, as well as any form of lovemaking.

No significant medical factors accounted for Ralph's dysfunction—no illness, drugs, surgeries, or history of smoking. His firm morning and masturbatory erections suggested that the etiology of his dysfunction was psychogenic.

In fact, Ralph had lost his sexual confidence and developed intense performance anxiety. We discovered that he did not become sexually aroused because he was too busy watching and worrying about his erectile performance. I explained that sildenafil did not automatically induce erections but only helped facilitate them when the man was sexually or mentally aroused. I suggested that when taking the drug he should focus on sensuous feelings, mental and physical, (e.g., the sensations of touching and being touched) and to try to avoid negative fearful thoughts about losing his erection or watching his performance.

When Ralph returned the following week he said, "I feel like I won the Daytona 500." His performance anxiety began to diminish, allowing us to focus in therapy on the painful experience of his fear and to understand the protective nature of the dysfunction. He and I came to call his erectile problem "his friend." My goals were to restore Ralph's confidence and to wean him from sildenafil after he thoroughly understood his interpersonal anxiety.

MEDICAL INTERVENTIONS FOR ERECTILE DYSFUNCTION

You need to know the medical treatments available for restoring erectile function, but I want you to keep in mind my mantra: Giving men firm erections is relatively straight-forward these days; getting them to make use of these regularly in lovemaking is much more complicated. The medical options currently available include oral PDE5 inhibitors, sublingual apo-morphine (Uprima˚), intracavernosal injections (Edex and Caverjet), intraurethral therapy (MUSE), vacuum tumescence devices, topical ointments (Nexpro˚), penile prosthesis, and vascular surgery.

The introduction of sildenafil in 1998 forever changed the treatment landscape. Currently, over 90% of men are treated with PDE5 inhibitors for their erectile dysfunction. The PDE5 class of drugs is efficacious with erectile problems of differing etiologies and is relatively safe (the only contraindication is with concomitant nitrate use).

Today, family practice physicians are the principal caretakers of men with erectile dysfunction, whereas urologists see the more problematic cases. Mental health clinicians rarely see men or couples with this problem, initially. Unfortunately, the primary care physician and the urologist too often obtain a limited, organ-focused history that

˚Not currently FDA approved

fails to reveal to the doctor one or more of the following obstacles to recovery, all of which contribute to the varying levels of complexity in each case:

1. The previously mentioned patient variables of performance anxiety, depression, unrealistic expectations, or unconventional sexual arousal patterns
2. Partner variables such as her health, disinterest in resuming lovemaking, or vaginal atrophy
3. Interpersonal variables such as the quality of the couple's relationship
4. Sexual variables such as duration of sexual abstinence or previously incompatible sexual interests
5. Contextual variables such as current life stresses with finances, children, parents, or occupation

These five obstacles are the source of either the patients' resistance to beginning to use a medical intervention or their dropping out soon after they have begun. When we invoke the concept of resistance, we mean that something unsaid—occasionally unconscious, but usually simply not clarified with the therapist—is more powerful than the wish to resume sexual activity with their partners. The "something" is almost always one of these five matters.

Let me give you a portrait of the prototypical man with erectile dysfunction (ED) who comes to our urology practice. In your practice you will see many variations of this theme. Generally, this 54-year-old married man has waited 2 years before seeking evaluation. During this time he has developed feelings of inadequacy, performance anxiety, partner resentment, and depression. He has begun to go to sleep either earlier or later than his wife. He has told her that he is too tired or too busy to make love; sometimes he blames his age, saying, "Look dear, I'm not 25 anymore." His goal was to avoid embarrassment or outright failure. Some years earlier, he began to notice his less-than-firm erections. He felt reluctant then to initiate lovemaking as frequently as usual. Soon lovemaking mysteriously disappeared. He now has no desire for sexual activity and has become overly involved with work, television, volunteer efforts, or the children. Affectionate touching has also disappeared—anything that might remotely be perceived by his partner as an invitation to lovemaking is avoided.

His wife has begun to wonder, "Does he still love me?" "Is he having an affair?" "Is he still attracted to me with the weight I've gained over the years?" or "Is sex over in our relationship?" She may have colluded with him by avoiding sex play, in order to lessen her pain of feeling rejected. Their relationship now feels disconnected to her without lovemaking and affection. She is probably experiencing her husband as somewhat down, irritable, preoccupied, or defensive.

Although most men come for evaluation at the behest of their partners, others seek treatment without telling their partners. I have seen many men who choose not to tell their wives about having received sildenafil from their physician. They come home and display to their partners, without prior discussion, their newfound erection. This unexpected performance is unsettling to the wife, and she feels an amalgam of amazement, anger, dismay, and anxiety: "Can I get ready for this again?" "Will this erection really last?" "I was hoping we were past this." He, too, of course, is anxious about his performance. If she discovers that he has taken sildenafil, she may feel betrayed and believe that his arousal was due to the medication and not to her. But even if told about his use of sildenafil, the wife may find that menopausal-induced lubrication and arousal difficulties cause intercourse to be uncomfortable. The sexual experience for each of them is disappointing, and thus his newfound sexual enthusiasm wanes.

At a follow-up visit the man, as expected, will tell his physician that the sildenafil "did not work." You and I would hope that he would realize that the formidable barriers of fear and anxiety grown during his years of avoidance and failure were too difficult for he and his wife to overcome. But this never happens. In order to enable sildenafil to "work," the partners now need our help in overcoming these unrecognized, intransigent blocks to their lovemaking—their resistance.

This "typical case" illustrates five sources of psychological resistance that can converge to defeat ED treatment: (1) the length of time the couple has been asexual before seeking treatment, (2) the man's nonverbal approach to resuming a sexual life with his partner, (3) the female partner's physical and emotional lack of readiness to resume lovemaking, (4) the meaning to each partner of using a medical intervention to enable intercourse, and (5) the negative quality of the nonsexual aspects of the relationship (Althof, 2002).

My prototypical case portrays two people who are comfortably heterosexual and conventional in their sexual longings. Of course, not everyone fits this mold. Two other issues are important to consider when treating with PDE5 inhibitors. First, these drugs require that the man experience arousal with his partner. If he finds his partner unattractive, sildenafil will not induce a genital response. And second, if his sexual preference is for something other than conventional lovemaking (e.g., a sadomasochistic encounter), he is not likely to generate an erection with his partner under conventional circumstances. Let me tell you about John, who illustrates those men who wish to be potent with their wives but have primarily unconventional sexual fantasies.

> He is a 35-year-old accountant who sought marital treatment because he and Megan, his wife of 8 years, were having difficulty conceiving a child. Actually, this was not accurate because they were not having sexual intercourse. John would find excuse after excuse to avoid being sexual. When Megan insisted, John could not achieve or sustain his erection. Their physician had prescribed sildenafil, to no avail.
>
> In my first individual meeting with John, he spoke of his "Internet addiction." He said he spends several hours a day engaging in "cybersex" with women. Without using sildenafil, he achieves firm erections and orgasms easily, as long as the women follow his sadomasochistic script. Megan has no interest in sadomasochism and refuses to participate in even the mildest behaviors suggested by John.
>
> During their courtship John had been interested in Megan as a sexual partner and was able to perform reliably. Over time, though, his interest in conventional sexuality waned. Megan has grown increasingly frustrated, especially as other members of her family became pregnant.
>
> During treatment John became increasingly aware of the cost of his

> *Internet addiction. Megan, who initially perceived John's time on the com-*
> *puter as excessive but "as a harmless activity that most guys engage in,"*
> *now has become aware of the psychological and relational consequences*
> *of his behavior. John, struggling to stop his Internet behavior, is trying to*
> *develop more interest in conventional lovemaking. Megan alternates be-*
> *tween being supportive and feeling betrayed and cheated.*

Obviously, sildenafil could not provide the sexual arousal necessary for John to make love to Megan. The goal of this integrated treatment was to help John and Megan understand the origins of his unconventional wishes. For John this would diminish somewhat the power of the fantasies, and for Megan it would help her not to personalize the rejection she experienced. John feels relieved about not having to keep his sexual life a secret; Megan is still struggling to come to terms with what she now knows about John.

John and Megan's situation also raises the third question I promised to discuss with you—namely, integrating treatment modalities. Consider now whether you would recommend that the partners be seen in separate individual therapies, would recommend treatment for only John, or would see both of them individually and together martially. In answering this question, consider that one vital goal of helping John is to increase the ratio of his conventional to unconventional longings.

PSYCHOTHERAPY FOR ERECTILE DYSFUNCTION

The simple focus of psychotherapy for this condition is to identify and work through the barriers or resistances to lovemaking. Generally, we "work through" these resistances by conducting a brief symptom-focused therapy, with an emphasis on the "here and now." My psychotherapies, whether conducted alone or combined with medical interventions, focus on helping the man or the couple to (1) express and accept difficult feelings regarding onerous life circumstances, (2) find new solutions for old problems, (3) surmount barriers to psychological intimacy, (4) increase communication, (5) lessen performance anxiety, (6) transform destructive attitudes that interfere with lovemaking, and (7) modify rigid sexual repertoires. Patients come to understand how the dysfunction serves as their "friend" by protecting them from confronting unpleasant dilemmas (Althof, 2000).

Many sophisticated individuals believe in what I label the mechanistic theory of arousal (Zilbergeld, 1999), namely, that the penis should erect under any circumstance. We therapists need to be very clear that this is not true. What is important is how partners feel about each other, the circumstances of their lives, and the conditions under which they make love, which all influence their degree of arousal. This seems simple and obvious, but many couples fail to appreciate this straightforward truth.

Here is a case example of how a young patient and I worked through his inhibition to feeling pleasure.

> *Joe is a 24-year-old computer science student who received sildenafil at*
> *the Health Service after complaining of several "failures" with his new*

girlfriend. Although he succeeded in having intercourse with sildenafil, Joe sought me out because he did not want to be dependent on the drug— although he could not be successful without it. We both recognized that the etiology of his ED was psychogenic.

He had been raised in a very religious home where sexuality was never discussed. In high school he felt a combination of envy and disgust at his peers who were talking about trying to get laid. He saw himself as morally superior to those who were engaging in sexual play. He did not date and rarely masturbated. Although he attended a very liberal college, his sexually negative attitude did not abate. He had two separate long-term relationships, in which he attempted to have intercourse but was unable to do so. In graduate school this pattern continued.

We focused on two issues: developing a more prosexual attitude and helping him overcome his performance anxiety. He now wanted to change his sexual attitudes, and his girlfriend was very supportive. I urged him to be more selfish and to focus on what felt good to him. I told him that such selfishness would not displease his girlfriend in the least because it would allow her to feel that she was a source of his pleasure to him. Concentrating on his girlfriend's arousal distracted him from his own arousal. Very quickly, he was able to engage in lovemaking on his own for the first time.

Joe continued to make excellent progress until he failed a final exam. He was so disappointed with himself that he when tried to make love that night, his ED returned. The next day he took sildenafil, to "reset the system."

Joe's idea of using sildenafil as a "reset button" was intriguing. He used it whenever he encountered a difficult moment to "reset" himself sexually. Then he had no problem for several weeks. The "resets" became fewer and less frequent and ultimately were not necessary.

RAPID EJACULATION

Rapid ejaculation (RE), also known as premature ejaculation, is the most common of male sexual dysfunctions. It appears that close to 30% of men struggle with controlling the timing of their ejaculation (Lauman, Paik, & Rosen, 1999). However, my experiences, in both urology and mental health practices, show that relatively few patients seek treatment for this problem.

There has been a subtle shift in the methods used to help men with RE. For many years treatment consisted of only psychological/behavioral paradigms; 10 years ago we began to use the side effects of some drugs as well. No medication has yet been FDA-approved for this indication, although several are in the clinical trial stage. The antidepressants (e.g., paroxetine, sertraline, fluoxetine, and clomipramine), topical ointments (e.g., SS-cream* or lidocaine), PDE5 inhibitors, or combinations of these delay the orgasmic reflex. Double-blind, placebo-controlled studies with clomipramine and with

---

*Not currently FDA approved

the major SSRIs, using strict dosages in carefully selected populations, have repeatedly demonstrated that these agents are efficacious in delaying ejaculation (Althof, 1995). I suggest you read Dr. Waldinger's excellent chapter 15 in this book for more information on pharmacological treatments.

Treatments utilizing combinations of fluoxetine and lidocaine or paroxetine and sildenafil have also been reported to delay ejaculation (Montorsi et al., 2001). More research on the efficacy and safety of these combination treatments is necessary.

The principal controversy in treating rapid ejaculation with SSRIs is about the method of dosing: daily versus "as needed." There are data supporting both positions, but no agreed-upon scientifically derived guidelines exist.

SS-cream* is a newly developed topical agent made from the extracts of nine natural products, which is to be applied to the glans penis 1 hour before sexual intercourse (Choi et al., 2000). In placebo-controlled, double-blind studies this compound significantly improved ejaculatory latency and sexual satisfaction. The side effects include mild local burning and mild pain. There are also several anecdotal reports that lidocaine improves ejaculatory latency. However, one should be aware that any topical ointment may permeate vaginal tissues as well and may result in unwanted side effects for the partner.

Sildenafil, in two independent studies, has been shown to significantly improve ejaculatory latancy (Abdel-Hamid, El Naggar, & El Gihany, 2001; Chen, Greenstein, Mabjeesh, & Matzkim, 2001). None of the men in these studies had erectile dysfunction. The mechanism underlying a sildenafil-induced delay in ejaculation is unknown.

My experience in treating men for rapid ejaculation with pharmacological agents is similar to treatment of ED—patients discontinue therapy. In the short-term, patients are satisfied, but as they try to wean themselves off the medication or stop altogether, they find themselves returning to baseline ejaculatory latency. Sustained pharmacological delay of ejaculation clearly does not result off-medication in long-term improved ejaculatory latency.

PSYCHOLOGICAL INTERVENTION

Having reviewed the benefits and limitations of RE medications, I would like to provide a cursory overview of psychological interventions and then return to the topic of combined therapies. Beginning in the early 1970s with Masters and Johnson's publicized treatment of RE, an array of individual, conjoint, and group therapy approaches integrating behavioral strategies, such as stop-start, the squeeze technique, progressive sensate focus exercises, masturbatory exercises, and "quiet vagina" with the female astride, became the treatments of choice for RE (Althof, 1995).

The stop-start procedure involves the man repeatedly being brought to high levels of excitement, initially by hand stimulation, which stops prior to ejaculation (Semans, 1956). This pause presumably allows the man's arousal to decrease, thereby delaying orgasm. This exercise is repeated several times, after which the man is permitted to ejaculate. Subsequently, Masters and Johnson (1970) modified the procedure and re-

*Not currently FDA approved

named it the "squeeze technique." Their modification requires that the partner cease stimulation and squeeze the glans penis. This results in a delay of ejaculation and a partial loss of erection.

"Quiet vagina" is an elaboration of the stop-start maneuver that involves intercourse. The woman sits astride or lies on top of the man and, without any thrusting or movement, envelopes his penis in her vagina. The aim of this exercise is to desensitize the man to the wet, warm sensations of the vagina. After the man can master "quiet vagina" for a prolonged period of time, movement is slowly introduced and controlled by the female. The man directs her to stop when he believes his excitement approaches his ejaculatory threshold. The couple then sits or lies quietly until his arousal decreases, whereupon the partners resume the exercise and proceed to his orgasm.

Sensate focus exercises were designed to heighten the man's awareness of his arousal level and to decrease his performance anxiety by eliminating the demand characteristics of the usual sexual experience. In a slow, graduated fashion, the man and his partner take turns giving and receiving pleasure by touching. Initially, the touching is restricted to nongenital/nonbreast stimulation; no intercourse is allowed. The restricted areas are then pleasured as well. The assumption is that as higher levels of arousal are tolerated without ejaculation, a man will learn how to put off having his orgasm.

It is crucial for the therapist to monitor closely the partners' needs and responses during this therapy. Partners must not be made to feel used; their involvement in this retraining program should be acknowledged as an investment in the couple's future sexual life. Also, the therapist needs to keep a keen eye on both patient and partner for the emergence of any resistances that may sabotage the treatment, such as the woman deliberately stroking her partner's penis after he says "stop" or the patient blaming her for his lack of control.

Levine (1992) advocates an integrated approach, where the man or the couple seeks to understand the hidden meaning(s) of the rapid ejaculation, to appreciate the interference of performance anxiety, and, when ready, to embark on a series of behavioral tasks. He cautions clinicians to be aware of the man's or the couple's need for a symptom and of how rare it is to find "simple cases" of rapid ejaculation.

INTEGRATING PHARMACOTHERAPY AND PSYCHOTHERAPY FOR RAPID EJACULATION

Patients in my practice have contradictory goals. They wish to rapidly gain control over their ejaculation but do not want to be dependent on medication in the long term. Therefore, I often begin men on a medication and work simultaneously with the man, the couple, or both psychotherapeutically to help them understand the need for and the meaning of the symptom. Then I teach the man or the couple skills to delay ejaculation.

Consider Pete, a 35-year-old macho construction worker, who comes to our mental health practice seeking treatment for recently acquired rapid ejaculation. In the past he had several sexual partners and remembers

having good control with them. However, with his new girlfriend he ejacu-
lates within 15 seconds of penetration and feels like he has no ejaculatory
control.

Immediately, I am curious about this new relationship in which he
developed this sexual problem. I invite him to tell me about her. She is in
her early 30s, was never married, and is described as extremely beautiful.
Also, she is college educated and the CFO of a local company. He feels
"intimidated by her; she is the dominant force in the relationship." He
then recalls that several years ago he dated another woman whom he also
described as more "dominant" in the relationship. Not surprisingly, he
experienced rapid ejaculation with her as well.

Clearly, Pete suffers from a high degree of performance anxiety and
feels unmasculine with this new girlfriend. Though he wishes for a quick
fix, he is hesitant to take medication because this, too, would be "unmanly."

Together, we agree that medication, in the short term, might help di-
minish performance anxiety. We also decide to meet weekly to discuss his
concerns with dominance/submission and masculinity and to help him
develop behavioral skills that will enable him to regain ejaculatory control.

Would you be surprised to learn that as Pete's "performance" improved, and as he gained ejaculatory control, the relationship deteriorated?

WHEN IS PHARMACOTHERAPY INDICATED?

Of course, treatment decisions are ultimately up to our patients, but let me offer some guidelines on deciding which treatment for which patient is appropriate under what circumstances. The lifelong versus acquired classification of RE is now the most useful marker for formulating treatment recommendations. I believe the ideal candidate for drug therapy might be a man with several years of sexual experience and a lifelong pattern of rapid ejaculation, who is free of substance abuse, depression, and psychosis and is capable of developing stable, satisfying nonsexual relationships. This is similar to the ideal scenario described for men with ED.

In contrast, for a man with a relatively recent onset of acquired rapid ejaculation, who has some degree of psychological mindedness but little sexual experience, pharmacological interventions should not be the first line of consideration. Initially, reassurance and education should be offered, with the expectation that in time these men will develop increased self-confidence and the ability to control ejaculation.

Whether it is a lifelong or an acquired condition, be very cautious offering drug therapy alone to men when you suspect that their symptom reflects intrapsychic or interpersonal conflict. Rapid symptom removal may disrupt the individual's or the couple's equilibrium and may result in the development of other psychological problems. I base this caution on actual experiences with a small number of patients for whom treatment unfortunately resulted in destructive acting out.

Finally, be careful not to collude with the patient's unrealistic expectations of boundless intercourse ability, as these idealized fantasies are based on ignorance and may reflect unresolved psychological concerns. There are situations when it is appropriate for us to decline to treat a patient.

INTEGRATED TREATMENTS FOR FEMALE SEXUAL DYSFUNCTION

It is quite possible that by the time this chapter is published and you read it, an effective pharmacological intervention for female sexual dysfunctions will have been developed. At the present moment, however, no pharmacotherapy has established efficacy for lifelong hypoactive sexual desire (HSD) disorder, female sexual arousal disorder, or orgasmic disorder. This may be because we are still struggling to develop a paradigm that truly reflects the complexity of female sexual response. The Kaplan model of sexual response—that is, of sexual desire leading to arousal, followed by orgasm—has come under intense criticism for its neglect of women's sexual priorities and experiences (Tiefer, 1991). Newly proposed models describing female sexual response support that it is not a mirror image of male response, subjectively, objectively, or developmentally (Basson, 2000). At this point, without a theoretical model that accurately reflects women's sexual responses, treatment interventions are unlikely to yield positive results.

My expectation is that efficacious pharmacological interventions for women will be centrally acting—that is, will work directly on the brain. This is in contrast to the PDE5 drugs for men, which target the genitals themselves. The prime candidate to restore diminished sexual drive in women is an androgen. Clinical trials are presently underway to test the effectiveness of testosterone, using different delivery systems. As yet there is no proven pharmacological candidate for female sexual arousal disorder or orgasmic disorder.

A recent study reported that sildenafil was no more successful in restoring sexual function in a group of women experiencing arousal disorder and hypoactive sexual desire disorder than was placebo (Basson et al., 2002). And a recent single-blind multisite study found that bupropion increased several indices of libido in females with idiopathic hypoactive sexual desire disorder (Segraves, Croft, Kavoussi, & Ascher, 2001). Although this study suggested some promise for bupropion, bear in mind that it was a single-blind study and that, historically, women show very high placebo response rates to sexual medication, up to 50% in some randomized, double-blind clinical trials. To me, this is further evidence that the brain, not the female genitals, is the most important sexual organ. It also suggests that psychological treatment, when competently conducted, may be most helpful. This has been already established in the treatment of orgasmic disorders and of HSD secondary to marital discord. No evidence for the successful treatment of arousal disorders or for lifelong hypoactive sexual desire disorder has been found.

It is difficult to discuss the use of medical interventions for female sexual dysfunction because none have demonstrated efficacy. If a drug were to become available eventually, I would posit the same three-tiered model of severity previously discussed for

men. Namely, in the ideal situation all that may be necessary would be pharmacotherapy with appropriate follow-up. In the typical scenario, where integrated treatment strategies are necessary because biopsychosocial obstacles combine to precipitate
and maintain the symptom, a combined treatment would be in order. In the complicated scenario, where psychological or interpersonal obstacles or both are prominent,
an admixture of individual and couples' therapy will be necessary prior to considering
pharmacological intervention.

> *Joan came to see me because she wanted to begin androgen therapy for
> low sexual desire. She was perimenopausal and had heard on television
> that androgen could quickly remedy her problem. She had little interest
> in lovemaking with her husband of 4 years and felt under pressure from
> him to fix herself. Joan felt that it was a marital obligation to be ready
> sexually whenever he wanted, and she minimized her need for affection
> and intimacy.*
>
> *When I took her sexual history, she reported that she had lost her
> sexual desire toward the end of her first marriage. She regained it again
> when she met her current husband. However, within 6 months of marriage
> she again lost interest in lovemaking. Her husband had no interest in par-
> ticipating in therapy and was disappointed that she did not come home
> with the drug in hand.*
>
> *I thought androgen supplementation was ill advised because it rein-
> forced her belief that she was the problem; instead, she was turned off
> sexually because of her disappointments in the marriage. On her own,
> Joan began to read self-help books and asked her husband to read them as
> well. She tried to encourage him to be more affectionate and intimate.*

This story does not have a happy ending. And I do not believe that androgen would
have been the magic bullet. Joan eventually recognized the limitations of her marriage
and reframed her sexual disinterest as a reflection of the contextual issues in her life.
She is less self-blaming now but is uncertain how to resolve her interpersonal dilemma.

THE PRESCRIPTION OF BEHAVIORAL TASKS

I promised to discuss strategies for combining different theoretical techniques when
conducting sex therapy. Let's think about how to accomplish this task. For those of you
like myself, with a psychodynamic orientation, insight has been traditionally viewed
as the most powerful agent of change in psychotherapy. This idealized perspective is
both incorrect and excessively narrow in scope. Insight is useful but not sufficient in
overcoming sexual problems. It is the judicious integration of carefully selected behavioral tasks with insight that facilitates the resolution of the dysfunction. In truth, there
is much overlap in specialized forms of treatment. For example, most patients are likely
to do as well with a cognitive, as with a psychodynamic or behavioral, therapist.

Sex therapy has always employed behavioral tasks to (1) overcome performance anxiety, (2) aid diagnostic assessment and clarification of underlying dynamics, (3) alter previously destructive sexual interactions, (4) confront resistances in each partner, (5) alleviate a couple's anxiety about physical intimacy, (6) dispel myths and educate patients regarding sexual function and anatomy, (7) counteract negative body image concerns, and (8) heighten sexuality.

In the era of Masters and Johnson (1970s), we routinely began sex therapy by prescribing behavioral tasks. We believed that these exercises alone would rapidly resolve the sexual dysfunction. Rather than cure, to our surprise and dismay, these tasks often uncovered previously unrecognized or unidentified resistances in one or both partners. These days we are inclined to delay the prescription of behavioral tasks until after the major therapeutic issues have been worked through, (e.g., until trust begins to develop). By waiting, we provide the patient or the couple with a way to master the assignment and move forward. Behavioral exercises given too early in treatment may precipitate resistances. Though the discovery of resistance may be enlightening, it can sometimes negatively disrupt the treatment, causing patients to terminate therapy and to feel hopeless about recovery.

The best-known and most frequently prescribed behavioral task is termed *sensate focus*. It is a progressive, in vivo desensitization exercise designed to help patients achieve the three requirements necessary for a good sexual life, that is, willingness, relaxation, and sensuality. I described much of it in the section on rapid ejaculation. You can find an excellent, more detailed description in *The New Sex Therapy* (Kaplan, 1974). Although you should become acquainted with the standardized instructions, I do not want you to become locked in to them. Rather than be formulaic, one needs to be creative and sensitive to both partners' anxieties regarding sexual intimacy. I routinely modify the experience to accommodate those couples who are too shy, embarrassed, or anxious for the conventional exercise. I may have them begin by holding hands in the dark in bed, dressed in pajamas. I have suggested to others that they start by taking a bubble bath and washing one another's backs.

Other behavioral sex therapy tasks include guided fantasy and directed masturbation. On occasion I suggest guided fantasy to individuals who have difficulty becoming aroused or to those who are preoccupied with obsessive thoughts of failure. I suggest directed masturbation to women to help them arouse themselves and achieve orgasm. Again, the overarching principle for incorporating behavioral exercises into an ongoing treatment is patient readiness. Too much, too early can be counterproductive. I believe it is better to err on the side of slowness.

WHICH MODE OF TREATMENT FIRST?

Now that we have thought about combined pharmacological and psychological treatments and the integration of different ideological orientations and techniques, I want to discuss strategies for psychological treatment planning. After describing John and Megan, I asked you to think about how to decide among several psychotherapeutic modalities: individual therapy for one or both partners, conjoint or couples' treatment, or a mixture of all of them simultaneously. Now I will give you my opinions.

Treatment recommendations are influenced by our values and prejudices regarding ideology and treatment modality, as well as by insurance limitations. Current research data are not sophisticated enough to predict which patient with what specific disorder will do best with a particular therapist who engages in a certain form of treatment.

This does not imply that we should not be thoughtful about offering alternatives to patients, as if it really made no difference. Rather, we should recognize the limitations of our knowledge and skills and appreciate that some of what we do is more intuitive than scientific. Given this caveat, some suggestions for treatment planning follow. Remember, it is ultimately the patient who makes the final decision to accept or reject our plans.

I believe as well that it is inadvisable for the therapist to switch treatment modalities midtherapy—that is, begin individual therapy with the man and then switch to conjoint treatment with the couple or to see one individual alone and the partners together in conjoint therapy. When a relationship is first formed between the male patient and his therapist, the partner may feel that an alliance exists between them against her. If the therapist endeavors to be sensitive to the partner's feelings, the patient may then feel abandoned. Although not a strict rule, it is generally advisable for us to restrict treatment to one modality with a patient.

GUIDELINES FOR RECOMMENDING TREATMENT

If the sexual dysfunction is lifelong, I generally recommend individual therapy. This decision is based on the assumption that lifelong dysfunctions are an intrapsychic developmental failure, rather than an interpersonal problem. These individuals also frequently have severe character pathology. Lifelong dysfunction is often the end result of unresolved gender identity, sexual orientation, or paraphilic conflicts.

Individual treatment lends itself to the intensive exploration of early life events and intrapsychic dilemmas. It allows a deeper understanding and working through of the obstacles to establishing a comfortable sexual self. These issues are more difficult to explore and to resolve in a couples' treatment format. Not only does the presence of others dilute the focus, but patients are often reluctant to share these concerns with partners.

However, when a man with lifelong dysfunction has limited psychological reflectiveness and is markedly inarticulate, estranged from his emotional life (e.g., he is markedly schizoid or alexythymic), or both, individual treatment is ill advised. In these situations, if there is a partner, I ask her to join us. She is often aware of pertinent family events and can help the patient talk more easily about aspects of himself that would remain obscure in individual treatment.

I recommend conjoint treatment for those patients with acquired sexual dysfunctions who have viable relationships. Acquired dysfunction suggests that the patient has successfully traversed developmental hurdles to establish a comfortable sexual self. Moreover, the symptom is generally rooted in the present or recent past and is not an outgrowth of early childhood issues. In fact, the dysfunction often represents both partners' shared solution to some aspect of their relationship.

The exceptions to the guideline of "conjoint treatment for acquired dysfunction" are the single individuals without partners or with uncommitted partners and the couple whose relationship has deteriorated so much that both partners cannot work productively with one another. Although the lack of involvement in a relationship does present clear limitations for therapy, the patient can nonetheless benefit. When a patient is having sex with someone, the question that arises is whether the partner is committed or not. Meeting with each partner alone is helpful in making this determination. Each may articulate an ambivalence about the future of the relationship, indicating that conjoint treatment may not be appropriate. I generally attempt to see dysfunctional couples in a conjoint format first but employ more structure than usual. If this proves unworkable, I refer them for individual treatment to help prepare for the possibility of couples' treatment in the future.

Sometimes a married man with no desire to make love to his wife wants treatment in order to be sexual with his lover. These situations present an ethical dilemma to the therapist. My stance allows me to see these men in individual treatment but not in conjoint therapy with their lovers or wives. I think that such major secrets are ultimately destructive. I cannot, in good conscience, see both partners while holding one's secret in confidence.

CONCLUSION

I hope you will be able to put the ideas in this chapter to good use. Believe me when I tell you that helping men and women with their sexual lives is very rewarding work. You can do this!

The principle points I would like you to remember are that combined therapy is generally more helpful than either psychotherapy or pharmacotherapy alone. And that the essence of the psychological intervention is to help patients overcome obstacles that interfere with their making effortless use of a medical intervention. Finally, when necessary, thoughtful integration of different modalities of treatment and techniques will increase the power of your interventions and help men and women to achieve improved sexual, emotional, and relational satisfaction.

REFERENCES

Abdel-Hamid, I. A., El Naggar, E. A., & El Gilany, A. H. (2001). Assessment of as needed use of pharmacotherapy and the pause-squeeze technique in premature ejaculation. *International Journal of Impotence Research, 13*(1), 41–45.

Althof, S. (1995). A new method of treating rapid ejaculation: Drug therapy. *Psychiatric Clinics of North America, 3,* 85–94. A review paper on the pharmacological treatment of rapid ejaculation.

Althof, S. (1998). New roles for mental health clinicians in the treatment of erectile dysfunction. *Journal of Sex Education and Therapy, 23,* 229–231.

Althof, S. (2000). Erectile dysfunction: Treatment of men and couples. In S. Lieblum & R. Rosen (Eds.), *Principles and Practices of Sex Therapy* (3rd ed., pp. 242–275). New York: Guilford.

Everything you always wanted to know about conducting psychotherapy with men and couples with ED.

Althof, S. E. (2002). When an erection alone is not enough: Biopsychosocial obstacles to lovemaking. *International Journal of Impotence Research, 14*(Suppl. 1), S99–S104.

Basson, R. J. (2000). The female sexual response: A different model. *Journal of Sex & Marital Therapy, 26,* 26–51. This paper generated a great deal of excitement for its intimacy-based model of female sexual response.

Basson, R. J., McInnes, R., Smith, M., et al. (2002). Efficacy and safety of sildenafil citrate in women with sexual dysfunction associated with female sexual arousal disorder. *Journal of Women's Health and Gender-Based Medicine, 11*(4), 367–377.

Chen, J., Greenstein, A., Mabjeesh, N. J., & Matzkin, H. (2001). Role of sildenafil in the treatment of premature ejaculation. *International Journal of Impotence Research, 13,* S48.

Choi, H. K., Jung, G. W., Moon, K. H., Xin, Z. C., et al. (2000). Clinical study of SS-cream in patients with lifelong premature ejaculation. *Urology, 55*(2), 257–261.

Goldstein, I., Lue, T., Padma-Nathan, H., Rosen, R., et al. (1998). Oral sildenafil in the management of erectile dysfunction. *New England Journal of Medicine, 338,* 1397–1404. First paper published reporting on the clinical trial results of sildenafil.

Kaplan, H. (1974). *The New Sex Therapy.* New York: Brunner/Mazel. Another classic volume in sex therapy. Describes Dr. Kaplan's methods of treatment.

Keller, M. B., et al. (2000). A comparison of nefazodone, the cognitive-behavioral analysis system of psychotherapy, and their combination for the treatment of chronic depression. *New England Journal of Medicine, 342,* 1462–1470.

Laumann, E. O., Paik, A., & Rosen, R. C. (1999). Sexual dysfunction in the United States: Prevalence and predictors. *Journal of the Americal Medical Association, 281*(6), 537–544. Best article documenting prevalence of sexual dysfunction among U.S. men and women and important medical and psychosocial factors associated with each dysfunction.

Levine, S. (1992). *Sexual Life, a Clinicians Guide.* New York: Plenum. An excellent, easy-to-read book for clinicians and patients regarding multiple aspects of sexual life.

Masters, W., & Johnson, V. (1970). *Human Sexual Inadequacy.* Boston: Little Brown. A classic volume in the history of sex therapy. Describes their treatment approach and outcome results.

Montorsi, F., Salonia, A., Zanoni, M., Deho, S. G., et al. (2001). Premature ejaculation: A prospective study comparing paroxetine alone vs. paroxetine plus sildenafil. Preliminary results. *International Journal of Impotence Research, 13,* S48.

Nathan, P. E., & Gorman, J. M. (Eds.). (2002). *A Guide to Treatments That Work* (2nd ed.). New York: Oxford University Press.

Perelman, M. A. (2001). The impact of the new sexual pharmaceuticals on sex theapy. *Current Psychiatry Reports, 3,* 195–201.

Rosen, R., & Lieblum, S. (1995). Treatment of sexual disorders in the 1990s: An integrated approach. *Journal of Consulting & Clinical Psychology, 63*(6), 877–890.

Segraves, R. T., Croft, H., Kavoussi, R., & Ascher, J. A. (2001). Bupropion sustained release (SR) for the treatment of hypoactive sexual desire disorder (HSDD) in nondepressed women. *Journal of Sex & Marital Therapy, 27*(3), 303–316.

Semans, J. (1956). Premature ejaculation: A new approach. *Southern Medical Journal, 49,* 353–358.

Tiefer, L. (1991). Historical, scientific, clinical and feminist criticisms of "The Human Sexual Response Model." *Annual Review of Sex Research, 2,* 1–23. An articulate and scholarly article critical of the current female sexual response models.

Zilbergeld, B. (1999). *The New Male Sexuality.* New York: Bantam. The most widely read book for the lay public and professionals on male sexual dysfunction. A classic!!

Chapter Twenty-One

Recognizing and Reversing Sexual Side Effects of Medications

R. Taylor Segraves, MD, PhD

INTRODUCTION

I first became aware of the problem of treatment noncompliance because of drug-induced sexual side effects while working in a psychopharmacology clinic in Veteran's Administration Hospital 16 years ago. I noted that a large number of my patients were discontinuing psychiatric drugs prematurely and were being rehospitalized because of illness relapses. Subsequently, I discovered that one of the reasons for their discontinuing medications against my advice was that the drugs I had prescribed were causing sexual problems. Until that time, it had never dawned on me to inquire if these drugs might have sexual side effects. These side effects were not discussed in psychopharmacology texts. At that time, there was minimal published information on this issue. I became fascinated with the issue and have continued to study it in my clinical practice and in clinical trials. I am pleased to have this opportunity to share one of my life's major interests with you. I will start with two brief patient stories.

Case 1

Mrs. D., a 35-year-old, vice president of a medium-sized community bank, had consulted a psychotherapist because of fatigue, insomnia, appetite loss, indecisiveness, and hopelessness. The managed-care company referred the patient to a psychiatrist for evaluation for pharmacotherapy of depression and approved six sessions of psychotherapy with a counselor. The psychiatrist began the patient on fluoxetine (Prozac). In psychotherapy sessions with her counselor, she discussed her difficulties balancing the time demands of being a wife, a mother, and a successful businesswoman and her sense of guilt that she might be sacrificing her family for her career. Her mood gradually improved, she became more efficient at work, and she began to enjoy her free time with her family. The managed-care company did not approve further psychotherapy sessions. After a few months, the psychiatrist received a telephone call from the husband, saying that his wife needed to be seen immediately, as she had mentioned thoughts of suicide. The psychiatrist asked if she was still on fluoxetine. Her husband replied that his wife had discontinued fluoxetine after about 3 months, as she was feeling much better and was having trouble reaching orgasm. The patient had not mentioned this problem to her counselor or her psychiatrist.

Case 2

Mr. T. is a 42-year-old man who lived in a supervised psychiatric group home and was followed by a psychotherapist. A primary care physician monitored his medications, while his psychotherapist focused on social skills training and problems of living. He was stabilized on haloperidal (Haldol) but would occasionally become noncompliant and have to be rehospitalized. The reason for his medication noncompliance was initially unclear. One day he asked his psychotherapist about sildenafil (Viagra). The therapist inquired about the reason for his interest and discovered that the patient had experienced erectile problems since starting haloperidal. The therapist suspected that the man's partner was a prostitute and informed the patient about the importance of safe sex. The therapist then called the primary care physician, explained the situation, and asked if a sildenafil prescription should be considered. The primary care physician said, "Insurance will never pay for it. But I have samples." In the next session the patient stated that the primary care doctor agreed to save sildenafil samples for him. He was happy about that. The patient did not seem to want to discuss the matter further, then added, "It's nice to feel normal. I know that normal people don't hear voices, but they do have sex!" The therapist noted that the patient was more self-confident than usual. The patient has remained treatment compliant and has not been rehospitalized since being given sildenafil samples.

Personal Dignity and Sexual Dysfunction

I am presenting these two case vignettes to illustrate several points. Regardless of their social strata, patients may prefer to become medication noncompliant rather than brave the social discomfort of volunteering to discuss their sexual activities with a therapist or physician. My clinical impression is reinforced by the fact that studies in the United States, Great Britain, and Spain have shown that only one third of patients experiencing sexual side effects on drugs volunteer this information to their physicians without being asked directly. During an acute illness episode, sexual function may become relatively unimportant. However, upon recovery, sexual function may assume a greater importance and the sexual dysfunction may be an unspoken cause of medication non-compliance. I also want to emphasize that we cannot assume that sexual function is unimportant to a patient with a psychotic disorder. We should never underestimate the desire to feel normal among patients with severe psychiatric disorders.

My plan for this chapter is to review the major classes of drugs associated with sexual side effects and their medical management. I will end with a discussion of the medical management of low libido.

DIAGNOSIS OF DRUG-INDUCED SEXUAL DYSFUNCTION

Relatively Straightforward Situations

The diagnosis of drug-induced sexual dysfunction is based on a careful sexual history after good clinician–patient rapport has been established. In a healthy male patient with good premorbid sexual function, the recognition of drug-induced sexual dysfunction can be relatively easy. Typically, drug-induced sexual dysfunction begins within weeks of drug initiation or a dose increase. The disorder is also usually present in all sexual situations. Problems with erection, ejaculation, and orgasm occur in masturbatory, as well as partner-related, activities. A decrease in libido includes a decrease in sexual fantasies and thoughts. The diagnosis is confirmed if a trial off medication restores pretreatment sexual function. Exactly the same guidelines apply to women patients.

Complicated Situations

Diagnosis is complicated if the disease being treated is also associated with sexual dysfunction. Examples of psychiatric diseases associated with sexual dysfunction include bipolar disease, depression, anxiety disorders, anorexia, and schizophrenia. A large number of physical diseases are associated with sexual problems and include hyperlipidemia, diabetes mellitus, multiple sclerosis, and renal failure. Diagnosis is also complicated when the sexual side effect occurs gradually during long-term therapy. Here are two examples of drugs with sexual side effects that may not be evident until months of therapy: digoxin (Lanoxin) and carbamezapine (Tegretol). Evaluation is complex when less than normal function preceded treatment of the medical disorder. For example, it is clear that decreased libido is part of the depressive syndrome and can precede treatment of depression, as well as be worsened by some pharmacological interventions.

PSYCHIATRIC DRUGS ASSOCIATED WITH SEXUAL DYSFUNCTION

A large number of drugs have been associated with sexual dysfunction. Probably, most evidence concerning sexual side effects of drug usage concerns psychiatric drugs. One reason for the existence of this knowledge base in psychiatry is that several large pharmaceutical companies have used the relative absence of sexual side effects of their product to competitively market their agents. Their marketing efforts have educated physicians about drug-induced sexual side effects. Sexual side effects appear to be common with most classes of psychiatric drugs.

The magnitude of the effect of antidepressant drugs on sexual function was not appreciated until these drugs had been in active clinical practice for a number of years. Many common sources of information about the incidence of sexual side effects were usually inaccurate. In particular, information in the *Physicians Desk Reference* concerning sexual side effects of drugs is inaccurate because the listed side effect data were based on clinical trials in which direct inquiry was not used.

Detecting Drug-Induced Sexual Dysfunction

Differentiation of drug-induced sexual dysfunction from other causes of sexual difficulties in psychiatric patients can be difficult. The etiology of difficulties with libido can be especially difficult to determine, as disturbances of libido can be part of the symptomatic presentation of major depressive disorder and are common in anorexia nervosa and some anxiety disorders. Similarly, the emotional problems that prompted the prescription of psychiatric drugs may have by themselves put additional strain on interpersonal relationships. These resultant interpersonal problems may in turn cause sexual difficulties. Ultimately, a careful history will provide clues as to the etiology of the sexual difficulty. Most drug-induced sexual difficulties occur at the initiation of drug therapy or with dose increases. In addition, the problems will manifest themselves in all situations, not just in partner-related activity. Ultimately, return of function with a trial off the drug, successful use of an antidote, or switching to an alternative agent with resultant normal function will provide presumptive evidence that the problem was drug-induced. In split treatment, the psychotherapist may have better rapport with the patient and be better able to detect drug-induced sexual dysfunction than would the prescribing psychiatrist. Some psychiatrists may feel threatened when a nonphysician detects a drug side effect that they overlooked. A nonthreatening way to transmit the information to the physician is to send an e-mail stating that the patient discussed a new onset sexual problem with you because he or she was embarrassed to discuss this directly with the psychiatrist. Tell the psychiatrist that you would appreciate the physician's opinion as to whether the difficulty could be drug-induced.

Antidepressants

Serotonergic antidepressants, especially the selective serotonin reuptake inhibitors (SSRIs), are associated with orgasm or ejaculatory delay and decreased libido. Some studies suggest that a small subgroup of men on some SSRIs experience erectile failure. Most but not all studies have found that the frequency of sexual side effects is higher in

TABLE 21.1. **Serotonergic Drugs Associated With Orgasmic Dysfunction**

Citalopram	(Celexa)
Clomipramine	(Anafranil)
Escitalopram	(Lexapro)
Fluvoxamine	(Luvox)
Fluoxetine	(Prozac)
Paroxetine	(Paxil)
Sertraline	(Zoloft)
Venlafaxine	(Effexor)

men than in women. It is unclear whether this is a true sex difference or an artifact of how the data were collected. A partial list of serotonergic antidepressants associated with sexual dysfunction is listed in table 21.1. It is important to remember that monoamine oxidase inhibitors and tricyclic antidepressants are also associated with orgasm delay.

SSRIs

The most common sexual side effect of the serotonin reuptake inhibitors is ejaculatory and orgasm delay. Among the SSRIs, this is most common with paroxetine (Paxil), fluoxetine (Prozac), and sertraline (Zoloft). In fact, this side effect has been used by some clinicians to treat premature ejaculation. Approximately 30–40% of patients on SSRIs experience some orgasmic delay with these agents. Citalopram (Celexa) and fluvoxamine (Luvox) have the lowest incidence of orgasmic dysfunction. Around 20% may report decreased libido.

Other Antidepressants

Controlled evidence suggests that clomipramine (Anafranil), a tricyclic antidepressant with strong serotonergic activity, creates the most ejaculatory delay of any of the tricyclic antidepressants. Venlafaxine (Effexor), which acts as a serotonin reuptake inhibitor at low dosages, appears to have an intermediate effect on orgasm. Mirtazapine (Remeron) may have a lower incidence of sexual dysfunction than other antidepressants have, but this has not been confirmed in controlled studies to date. Bupropion (Wellbutrin) and nefazodone (Serzone) clearly have extremely low rates of causing sexual dysfunction. Table 21.2 lists the antidepressants with minimal sexual side effects.

I actively monitor and treat antidepressant-induced sexual side effects to encourage treatment compliance in depressive disorder, a possibly lethal and often recurrent disorder. Some evidence suggests that insufficient treatment may increase the liklihood of recurrence. Depression severely distresses relationships. This is a critical issue because the social support of an intimate sexual relationship may facilitate recovery. One

TABLE 21.2. Antidepressants With Minimal Sexual Side Effects

Minimal or no sexual side effects
      Bupropion   (Wellbutrin)
      Nefazodone   (Serzone)

SSRIs with the least sexual side effects
      Citalopram   (Celexa)
      Fluvoxamine   (Luvox)

Antidepressant suspected to have a low incidence of sexual dysfunction
      Mirtazapine   (Remeron)

clearly wishes to restore sexual intimacy as soon as possible to a relationship that is already stressed by nonsexual factors.

MANAGEMENT OF ANTIDEPRESSANT-INDUCED SEXUAL DYSFUNCTION

A variety of strategies has been employed to manage antidepressant-induced sexual dysfunction. Occasionally, dose reduction can alleviate sexual side effects without causing a return of depressive symptoms. Some clinicians have advocated "drug holidays"— for example, taking several days off medication for sexual activity, then a resumption of taking the antidepressant. This strategy has three important drawbacks: (1) Timing of sexual activity on a limited scheduled basis creates a sense of artificiality that many couples find unpleasant. (2) Suggesting drug holidays might inadvertently encourage treatment noncompliance. The patient may conclude that if skipping the drug for sex is safe that he or she no longer needs to take the drug on a continuous basis. (3) Some agents, such as venlafaxine (Effexor) and paroxetine (Paxil), can be associated with unpleasant withdrawal effects that may be misdiagnosed as the "flu." Drug holidays should not be used with these agents.

Drug substitution can be employed. I usually substitute bupropion (Wellbutrin) or nefazodone (Serzone) in place of the agent that caused sexual dysfunction. If an SSRI is required, citalopram (Celexa) or fluvoxamine (Luvox) may be substituted for fluoxetine (Prozac), sertraline (Zoloft), or paroxetine (Paxil). Citalopram (Celexa) and fluvoxamine (Luvox) have a lower incidence of sexual dysfunction than do the other SSRIs. This method is limited by the fact that all antidepressants do not have the same efficacy in all patients, and different drugs may vary in their side effect profiles and ability to treat comorbid conditions. For example, I would not substitute bupropion for fluoxetine in a patient with major depressive disorder and panic disorder, as bupropion is not effective against panic disorder. One would use caution in switching from sertraline (Zoloft) to fluvoxamine (Luvox) or nefazodone (Serzone) in a patient on multiple pharmacological agents, as fluvoxamine and nefazodone have different drug–drug interactions than sertraline has.

Use of Antidotes

A number of antidotes to antidepressant-induced sexual dysfunction have been reported in the literature. I will discuss the antidotes that have been proved effective in double-blind studies and then discuss antidotes that are used in clinical practice but have not been established by double-blind studies. Controlled studies have demonstrated that 50–100 mg of sildenafil (Viagra) is effective in reversing erectile and ejaculatory problems that are caused by SSRIs. To date, there are no controlled studies of sildenafil for this purpose in the female. Controlled study has demonstrated that 60 mg of buspirone (Buspar) for 2 weeks will reverse SSRI-induced sexual dysfunction in 60% of patients of both sexes. Some of the most commonly prescribed, but not scientifically proven, antidotes are bupropion (Wellbutrin), yohimbine (Yocon), and cyproheptadine (Periactin). Case reports suggest that the addition of low doses of nefazodone (Serzone) or mirtazapine (Remeron) may reverse SSRI-induced sexual dysfunction, although this has not been demonstrated in double-blind studies.

The adverse effects of SSRIs on sexual function are hypothesized to be mediated by the serotonin 5-HT$_{2a}$ receptor. Nefazodone and mirtazapine both block this receptor. These drugs would be expected to be effective on theoretical grounds. However, very few compounds have been tested in controlled studies. Management strategies for SSRI-induced sexual dysfunction are listed in table 21.3. Antidotes of proven efficacy for SSRI-induced sexual dysfunction are listed in table 21.4.

Tranquilizers

Most of the minor tranquilizers, such as clonazepam (Klonopin), alprazolam (Xanax), chlordiazepoxide (Librium), chlorazepate (Tranxene), diazepam (Valium), and lorazepam (Ativan), have been reported to cause sexual problems, especially ejaculatory and orgasmic delay. The effect of diazepam on orgasm delay has been demonstrated in a controlled double-blind laboratory study in women. Lorazapam (Ativan) has been reported to be useful in the treatment of premature ejaculation. It is not clear whether certain benzodiazepines are worse than others in their adverse sexuality effects.

TABLE 21.3. Management of SSRI-Induced Sexual Dysfunction

Dose reduction
Drug holidays
Drug substitution
Antidotes

TABLE 21.4. Antidotes of Proven Efficacy

Buspirone	(Buspar)
Bupropion	(Wellbutrin)
Sildenafil	(Viagra)

Antipsychotic Drugs

Antipsychotic drugs have also been implicated in causing sexual dysfunction. Patients taking antipsychotic drugs are reluctant to volunteer the presence of drug-induced sexual side effects to their physicians. The extent to which antipsychotic drug-induced sexual dysfunction contributes to treatment noncompliance is unknown. Several investigators have postulated that antipsychotic drugs that cause prolactin elevation are more likely to cause decreased libido and erectile dysfunction than the prolactin-sparing antipsychotics are. Most of the aliphatic, piperidine, and piperazine phenothiazines have been reported to cause ejaculatory and erectile problems. The few studies that included females found that female patients report anorgasmia on these agents. Examples of these agents include chlorpromazine (Thorazine), thioridazine (Mellaril), mesoridazine (Serentil), trifluoperazine (Stelazine), fluphenazine (Prolixin), perphenazine (Trilafon), perchlorperazine (Compazine), chlorprothixine (Taractan), and thiothixine (Navane). The exact frequency of these side effects is unclear. However, one study with thioridazine found that approximately 40% of patients experienced both erectile and ejaculatory problems. Other tradtional antipsychotics, such as haloperidal (Haldol), pimozide (Orap), loxapine (Loxitane), and molindone (Moban), have been associated with erectile difficulties. The newer antipsychotics, appear to have lower incidences of sexual dysfunction, with the possible exception of risperidone (Risperidal). Olanzapine (Zyprexa), quetiapine (Seroquel), and ziprazodone (Geodon) appear to have a very low incidence of sexual dysfunction. Case reports and clinical series suggest that drug substitution or the addition of sildenafil is usually sufficient to reverse antipsychotic drug-induced sexual dysfunction. Some clinicians have advocated the use of dopaminergic agents such as bromocriptine and amantadine (Symmetrel). Cabegoline (Dostinex) has also been reported to reverse sexual side effects caused by antipsychotic drugs that elevate prolactin. Antipsychotic drugs with minimal sexual side effects are listed in table 21.5. The commonly used antidotes for antipsychotic drug-induced sexual dysfunction are listed in table 21.6.

TABLE 21.5. Antipsychotics With Minimal Sexual Problems

Olanzapine	(Zyprexa)
Quetiapine	(Seroquel)
Ziprazodone	(Geodon)

TABLE 21.6. Antidotes for Antipsychotic-Induced SD

Amantadine	(Symmetrel)
Bromocriptine	
Cabegoline	(Dostinex)
Sildenafil	(Viagra)

Priapism

It is important to remember that many of the antipsychotic drugs have been associated with priapism, a prolonged erection that can be painful and can result in permanent erectile dysfunction. If a patient reports erections that persist for several hours after ejaculation without additional stimulation, it would be prudent to consider switching to a different agent. Priapism is a medical emergency and should be treated immediately to prevent permanent damage to the corpora cavernosa. Clitoral priapism can also occur and can be quite painful. It does not appear to cause permanent damage. Drugs reported to be associated with priapism are listed in table 21.7.

Mood Stabilizers

Evidence regarding the incidence of sexual problems on lithium carbonate and other mood stabilizers is unclear. Mania is associated with increased libido, so it is difficult to ascertain whether decreased libido on mood stabilizers is due to treatment of mania or a drug-induced difficulty. The available evidence suggests that lithium may have

TABLE 21.7. Psychiatric Drugs Thought to Cause Priapism

Buspirone	(Buspar)
Chlorpromazine	(Thorazine)
Clozapine	(Clozaril)
Fluphenazine	(Prolixin)
Haloperidol	(Haldol)
Mesoridazine	(Serentil)
Molindone	(Moban)
Olanzapine	(Zyprexa)
Perphenazine	(Trilafon)
Riseridone	(Risperdal)
Thiothixine	(Navane)
Thioridazine	(Mellaril)
Trazodone	(Desyrel)

adverse effects on libido and erectile function in some patients. Some reports suggest that lithium plus benzodiazepines may have unusually frequent adverse effects on sexual function. Among anticonvulsants frequently used in psychiatric practice, gabapentin (Neurontin) has been reported to be associated with ejaculatory delay. Whether other anticonvulsants are associated with sexual problems is unclear.

Other Drugs

Most of the antihypertensive agents have been reported to cause erectile problems. There has been minimal study of the effects of such agents in women. Sildenafil appears capable of reversing these side effects in most patients. Case reports suggest that a large variety of other drugs, such the gastrointestinal drugs metoclopromide (Reglan) and cimetidine (Tagamet), the antifungal agent ketoconazole (Nizoral), and antiarrthymic agents such as disopyramide (Norpace), propafenone (Rythmol), amiodarone (Cordarone), and sotalol (Betapace), may be associated with erectile dysfunction. Other drugs reported to be associated with erectile dysfunction include digoxin and many of the hypolipidemic drugs, such as clofibramate (Atromid-S), gemfibrozil (Lopid), lovastatin (Mevacor), pravastatin (Pravachol), and simvastatin (Zocor). As cardiovascular disease and hyperlipidemia are associated with erectile dysfunction, it is unclear whether the relationship between cardiovascular drugs and sexual problems is causal. Isolated reports suggest that sildeanfil will reverse most forms of drug-induced erectile problems. Whether sildenafil will reverse drug-induced female sexual dysfunction is unclear. A partial list of other drugs possibly causing sexual dysfunction is listed in table 21.8. It should be emphasized that the evidence concerning these relationships is mainly from case reports and may prove false.

TABLE 21.8. Other Drugs That Cause Sexual Dysfunction

Amiodarone	(Cordarone)
Cimetidine	(Tagamet)
Clofibrate	(Atromid-S)
Disopyramide	(Norpace)
Gemfibrozil	(Lopid)
Ketoconazole	(Nizoral)
Lovastatin	(Mevacor)
Metoclopromide	(Reglan)
Propranolol	(Inderal)
Propafenone	(Rythmol)
Pravastatin	(Pravachol)
Sotalol	(Betapace)
Simvastatin	(Zocor)

Cancer Treatment

Both chemotherapy and radiation therapy of cancer are associated with problems with libido, erection, and lubrication. The precise agents responsible are difficult to identify, as most cancer chemotherapy regimes contain numerous agents. Many of these are neurotoxins or induce menopause. An increased frequency of sexual problems is found in survivors of most types of cancer. The most widely studied group of cancer patients is those with breast cancer. Many young women experience early menopause and suffer severe dyspareunia because of fragility of the vaginal epithelium and decreased capacity to lubricate when sexually aroused.

Whether estrogen replacement is safe in this population is unknown. Some clinicians feel that the suspected risk of estrogen therapy is more than offset by the real improvement in quality of life that estrogen replacement provides. I find it important to remember that loss of libido in patients with breast cancer is not necessarily the result of altered body image but may be the result of the toxicity of chemotherapy itself.

DRUG TREATMENT OF LOW LIBIDO

Treatment of low libido varies according to etiology. Low libido due to psychological and interpersonal problems should be treated by psychotherapy. Drug-induced libido difficulties should be managed by drug substitution or the use of antidotes. Now I want to share with you my thoughts about the problem of low libido of unknown etiology or low libido from hormonal difficulties.

Men

A number of drug treatments for low libido have been proposed. Androgen replacement in hypogonadal men is a well-established intervention. Current evidence indicates that a certain minimal level of androgen, perhaps between 200 to 450 ng/ml, is sufficient to restore normal sexual activity. Supraphysiological doses above that level are without much benefit. In most cases of hypogonadism, the clinician needs to first establish if the problem is gonadal failure or is due to a lesion of the hypothalamic-pituitary system. The usual laboratory screening tests include serum testosterone, serum hormone binding globulin, luteinizing hormone (LH), follicle stimulating hormone (FSH), and prolactin. If low free testosterone is found with high LH and FSH, one can usually safely conclude that the problem is gonadal failure and can treat with hormone replacement. Low testosterone in the presence of low LH and low FSH indicates that further evaluation of the pituitary-hypothalamic system is necessary. For example, it is possible that a tumor is responsible for gonadal failure in such cases.

Hormone replacement can be administered via transdermal systems, a gel applied to the skin, oral methyltestosterone, or testosterone enanthate injection. With all methods, it is necessary to obtain a baseline serum-free testosterone level. This is repeated after treatment to establish the proper dosage. Most clinicians prefer either testosterone gel or transdermal systems. Hepatic toxicity has been reported with oral methyltestosterone. Testosterone enanthate produces a supraphysiological level that falls to nearly hypogonadal levels prior to the next injection. The transdermal system and testosterone gels produce levels that approximate normal testosterone production. The starting dose of the transdermal system is usually the 5mg system. The starting dose of testosterone gel is either the 25 or the 50 mg system. If one treats a patient with testosterone, routine monitoring of serum lipids, hematocrit, and prostate specific antigen is necessary, as testosterone may alter blood lipids adversely, increase erythropoeisis, and possibly worsen the prognosis with prostate carcinoma.

Women

A fairly large number of clinicians in many different countries are using androgen supplementation in females with complaints of low libido. The indications for this treatment, its long-term effects, and the normal levels of androgen in females are not well established. A number of studies have indicated that supraphysiological levels of testosterone in females will increase libido. There is minimal evidence that variations of testosterone within normal limits have a clinically meaningful effect on libido in the female. Some studies have found that increases of testosterone within normal limits have the same effect on libido as placebo. As female testosterone is approximately one tenth the value of testosterone in the male, some clinicians recommend diluting testosterone gel from 25 mg to .25 mg. It should be emphasized that neither the efficacy nor the safety of this approach has been proved.

There have been a number of studies of the effects of peripheral vasodilators (for example, sildenafil) on female arousal and libido. In general, these studies have demonstrated that peripheral vasodilators increase lubrication without having a beneficial effect on sexual pleasure or desire. Some women report unpleasant increased sensation with sildenafil use. A number of case reports suggest that some antidepressants may increase libido. One controlled single-blind study of nondepressed women in good relationships found that bupropion sustained-release increased various signs of libido. This effect was attributed to bupropion's effect on dopamine reuptake. The dosage used was 300 mg per day. A history of seizures or serious head injury is a contraindication to the use of this compound. This effect of bupropion is now being investigated in a double-blind multi-enter study.

CONCLUSIONS

I have been fortunate to have been involved in the study of drug effects on sexual functioning for almost 2 decades. I have been delighted to watch the knowledge in this previously neglected area expand rapidly. We now know that a number of psychiatric and nonpsychiatric drugs cause sexual side effects, and these side effects contribute to treatment noncompliance. In most situations, we can use alternative agents or anti-dotes to reverse drug-induced sexual dysfunction. The study of drug treatment of low libido is still in its infancy. I expect to see knowledge in that area expand rapidly in the next decade.

I feel that our future challenge will be to determine when and how to use pharma-cological agents for sexual problems and when to combine them with psychotherapies. I also have the good fortune to be in an academic center and to see practice patterns change. It is rewarding to see the psychiatrists of tomorrow now inquire about sexual side effects and try to find ways to minimize these problems that contribute to non-compliance. This is so different than it was just 16 years ago.

REFERENCES

Aizenberg, D., Sigler, M., Zemishlany, Z., & Weizman, A. (1996). Lithium and male sexual func-tion in affective disorder. *Clinical Neuropharmacology, 19,* 515–519. This is one of several clinical series finding suggestive evidence that lithium carbonate may induce sexual prob-lems. Thirty-five men with bipolar disease, who were on lithium and euthymic, were ques-tioned regarding their sexual activity. Approximately 20% reported decreased sexual thoughts and difficulty with erectile function while on lithium.

Aizenberg, D., Zemishlany, Z., Dorfman-Etrog, P., & Weizman, A. (1995). Sexual dysfunction in male schizophrenic patients. *Journal of Clinical Psychiatry, 56,* 137–141. The authors sys-tematically investigated the presence of sex dysfunction in 20 drug-free patients with schizo-phrenia, 51 schizophrenic patients receiving treatment, and 51 normals. Comparing the treated to the nontreated group, the authors hypothesized that treatment may impair sexual function. They also suggested that schizophrenia may be associated with diminished li-bido.

Davis, A. R. (2000). Recent advances in female sexual dysfunction. *Current Psychiatry Reports, 2,* 211–214. Science trails hope.

Ferguson, J. M. (2001). The effects of antidepressants on sexual functioning in depressed outpa-tients: A review. *Journal of Clinical Psychiatry, 62,* Suppl. 3, 22–34. The author reviews the published double-blind studies and clinical series concerning the effects of antidepres-sants on sexual function. The data are consistent in finding that serzone and bupropion have the lowest rates of sexual dysfunction.

Gelenberg, A. J., Delgado, P., & Nurnberg, G. (2000). Sexual side-effects of antidepressant drugs. *Current Psychiatry Reports, 2,* 223–227. Another demonstration of the SSRI problem.

Guay, A. T. (2001). Advances in the management of androgen deficiency in women. *Medical Aspects of Human Sexuality, 1,* 32–38. A urological approach to hypoactive sexual desire.

Gutierrez, M., & Stimmel, G. (1999). Management and counseling for psychotropic drug-induced sexual dysfunction. *Pharmacotherapy, 19,* 823–832. This paper summarizes strategies to treat antipsychotic-induced sexual dysfunction and discusses possible mechanisms by which antipsychotic drugs might adversely affect sexual function. They recommend dose reduc-tion, drug holidays, and antidotes such as amantadine, cypropheptadine, and sildenafil.

Hummer, M., Kemmler, G., Kurz, M., Kurzthaler, I., Oberbauer, H., & Fleischbach, W. W. (1999). Sexual distrubances during clozapine and haloperidol treatment for schizophrenia. *Ameri-can Journal of Psychiatry, 156,* 631–634. This is the report of a prospective study of the development of sexual dysfunction in patients with schizophrenia treated with either haloperidal or clozapine. Both drugs initially had a high incidence of sexual side effects that remitted over 2–3 months.

Jensen, J., & Lendorf, A. (1999). The prevalence and etiology of impotence in 101 male hypertensives. *American Journal of Hypertension, 12,* 271–275. Erectile dysfunction is a high-prevalence problem among hypertensives.

Keene, L., & Davies, P. (1999). Drug related erectile impotence. *Adverse Drug Reactions Toxicology Review, 18,* 5–24. This paper is a comprehensive review of the data associating erectile dysfunction with various medications.

Kennedy, S., Dickens, S. E., Eisfeld, B. S., & Bagby, R. M. (1999). Sexual dysfunction after antidepressant therapy in major depression. *Journal of Affective Diseases, 56,* 201–208. Sexual dysfunction adds to the already high sexual burden of depression.

Kotin, J., Wilbert, D. E., Verburg, D., & Soldinger, S. (1976). Thioridazine and sexual dysfunction. *American Journal of Psychiatry, 133,* 82–85. A classic paper: 60% of patients taking thioridazine had sexual dysfunction.

Landen, M., & Erisson, E. (1999). Effect of buspirone on sexual dysfunction in depressed outpatients treated with selective serotonin reuptake inhibitors. *Journal of Clinical Psychiatry, 19,* 268–271. The authors reanalyzed data on the efficacy of buspirone in augmenting the antidepressant effect of citalopram and paroxetine. They found that the addition of 20 to 60 mg of buspirone was effective in reversing SSRI-induced sexual dysfunction in 60% of patients. The effect was usually noted by the end of the first week of antidote therapy.

Montego, A. L. (2001). Incidence of sexual dysfunction associated with antidepressant agents: A prospective multicenter study of 1,022 outpatients. Spanish working group for the study of psychotropic-related sexual dysfunction. *Journal of Clinical Psychiatry, 62,* Suppl. 3, 10–21. This study is important because of the number of patients involved, the fact that standardized assessment was utilized in multiple centers, and the fact that the ratings took place in normal clinical practice. Over 1,000 patients were studied. Both sexes were represented in the study. The serotonin reuptake inhibitors were found to be associated with some form of sexual dysfunction in about 50% of the patients studied. Mirtazapine and mirtazapine had very low rates of sexual dysfunction.

Mortimer, J. E., Boucher, L., Knapp, D., Ryan, E., & Rowland, J. (1999). Effect of tamoxifen on sexual function in patients with breast cancer. *Journal of Clinical Oncology, 17,* 1488–1492. Sexual life often deteriorated during and following treatment of brest cancer.

Nurnberg, H. G., Hensley, P. L., Lauriello, J., & Bogenschutz, M. P. (2001). Sildenafil treatment of antidepressant-associated sexual dysfunction: A 12 case treatment replication in a naturalistic setting. *Primary Psychiatry, 8,* 69–78. This dissertation was the stimulus for a double-blind placebo-controlled trial.

Rothschild, A. J. (2000). Sexual side effects of antidepressants. *Journal of Clinical Psychiatry, 61,* Suppl. 11, 28–36. The author reviews the data concerning antidepressant-induced sexual dysfunction and the medical management of this condition—dosage reduction, drug holidays, changes in time of dosing, and the use of antidotes.

Salerian, A. J. (2000). Psychotropic-induced sexual dysfunction in 31 women and 61 men. *Journal of Sex & Marital Therapy, 26,* 133–140. In this large clinical series, the author found that 50–100 mg of sildenafil was effective in reversing sexual dysfunction induced by antipsychotics, lithium, benzodiazepines, and antidepressants.

Segraves, R. T., Croft, H., Kavoussi, R., Ascher, J., Batey, S., Foster, V., Bolden-Watson, C., & Metz, A. (2001). Bupropion sustained release (SR) for the treatment of hypoactive sexual desire disorder (HSDD) in nondepressed women. *Journal of Sex & Marital Therapy, 27,*

306–316. In this multisite single-blind study, women with idiopathic acquired HSDD were treated with 300 mg bupropion for 8 weeks. Interview ratings of desire for sexual activity, sexual thoughts, and sexual arousal all doubled during bupropion treatment.

Segraves, R. T., Kavoussi, R., Hughes, A. R., Batey, S. R., Johnston, J. A., Donahie, R., & Ascher, J. A. (2000). Evaluation of sexual functioning in depressed outpatients: A double-blind comparison of sustained-release bupropion and sertraline treatment. *Journal of Clinical Psychopharmacology, 20,* 122–128. In a randomized, double-blind multicenter trial, the effects of bupropion and sertraline on sexual function were studied using standardized clinical interviews. As early as the end of the first week, there was a significant difference between the two drugs. Sertraline was associated with more sexual dysfunction than bupropion was. The major effect of sertraline was on orgasm and ejaculatory function. It also had adverse effects on libido, erections, and vaginal lubrication.

Tran, P. V., Hamilton, S. H., Kuntz, A., Potvin, J., Andersen, S., Beasley, C., & Tollepson, G. (1997). Double-blind comparison of olanzapine versus risperidone in the treatment of schizophrenia and other psychotic disorders. *Journal of Clinical Psychopharmacolgy, 17,* 407–418. An international multicenter, double-blind, parallel-group comparison of olanzapine and risperidone was conducted. The incidence of sexual dysfunction was much lower on olanzapine than on risperidone. The major sexual dysfunction caused by risperidone was ejaculatory delay. Risperidone also caused more elevation of prolactin.

Waldinger, M. D. (1998). Effect of SSRI antidepressants on ejaculation: A double-blind placebo-controlled study with fluoxetine, fluvoxamine, paroxetine, and sertraline. *Journal of Clinical Psychiatry, 18,* 274–281. The effects of various serotonin reuptake inhibitors on ejaculation were studied in men with rapid ejaculation. Efficacy was monitored by the partner using a stopwatch during coitus. Paroxetine had the greatest effect in delaying orgasm.

Chapter Twenty-Two

Sexual Potentials and Limitations Imposed by Illness

William L. Maurice, MD, FRCPC

Sexuality is such a fundamental part of all our lives that it is hard to imagine this area to be unaffected by mental disorders of any kind.

Affected? Certainly! Limited? Absolutely (although in varying degrees, depending on the patient and the disorder)! Erased? Not from what I hear from patients who have a severe mental illness!

And yet, the topic of sexuality arises so infrequently in the assessment of mentally ill patients.

In order to give you, the reader, a flavor of stories I hear, I will describe six patients in this chapter (without their real names), whom I've seen as the Sexual Medicine expert in a citywide mental health service. Patients (or, more properly, their sexual concerns) are, of course, "the problem," but, equally, so is the "system," which does little to encourage the identification and treatment of these concerns. These are the reasons why we developed a specialized clinic within the mental health service where sexual problems could be addressed and where we always include the patient's primary therapist in visits.

I have no expectation that mental health professionals (MHPs) will exactly imitate what I do when I meet a patient—either as a result of reading this chapter or of watching me conduct a consultation. After all, it took me years of experience to get to the point where I could talk with patients about this sensitive subject with the same neutrality that others have in talking about an injured arm, kidney disease, or an episode of depression.

Nevertheless, many MHPs tell me that they extract portions of what they see me do and productively apply these in their clinical practice, to enable their patients to safely maximize their sexual potential. My goal with readers of this chapter is to assist you to do the same.

PROBLEM #1: THE PATIENT

Patient #1: Jim, a 47-year-old man with a 15-year history of schizophrenia, was referred to me because of "premature ejaculation" and "erections that were not firm." He had read a brochure concerning a "sex" clinic while in the waiting room of the mental health center and asked his primary therapist for referral. Jim provided only superficial information regarding his sexual concerns to his therapist. No details were available prior to the first visit with me.

Jim lived with his family of origin, worked part time as a janitor, was maintained on risperidone (2 mg/day), had never used street drugs, only occasionally used alcohol in the past, smoked one package of cigarettes/day since his late teens, and had always been in good physical health.

Jim's sole current sexual activity was masturbation, which occurred a few times each week. He had experienced intercourse three times in his life and only with prostitutes, the last being about 1 year prior.

Jim's level of sexual desire had diminished in recent years. He reported sexual thoughts several times each week, whereas about 5 years ago, these had been daily experiences. Erections with masturbation and in the morning had also lessened; they were now 5/10 (on a scale where 0 meant that his penis was entirely soft and 10 meant it was full and firm). The last time he experienced 9 or 10/10 was about 15 years prior. Ejaculation and orgasm (he had no concern about the latter) took place regularly about 2 minutes after he began stimulating himself. Ejaculation occurred more quickly than he thought was "normal." He had considerable warning that ejaculation was imminent and made no attempt to delay it from happening. Jim was under the impression from watching sexually explicit videos that the process should take much longer.

Jim's principal sex-related diagnoses were (1) possible Hypoactive Sexual Desire Disorder; (2) Erectile Dysfunction (ED), acquired (vs. life-long) and generalized (vs. situational); and (3) unrealistic expectations concerning the timing of ejaculation and orgasm.

Recommendations concerning ED included a physical exam (his family doctor indicated that no abnormalities were apparent), a lab exam, and possible use of sildenafil (Viagra). I attempted to reassure him (by way of educational intervention) concerning his experience with ejaculation and orgasm.

The only abnormal values on the lab exam were very high lipid levels. I referred him to the dietician associated with the mental health service, in an attempt to institute a low-fat diet, and asked him to return to his family doctor for continuing care of his elevated lipids. In addition, I answered Jim's many inquiries concerning male and female genital anatomy and physiology (using diagrams and rubber models), as well as his questions about "normal" sexual and emotional aspects of relationships.

Jim's ED was successfully treated with Viagra, samples of which were obtained from the drug company. Diminished sexual desire and "premature ejaculation" ceased to be concerns following our discussion. He was pleased with the outcome of the consultation and agreed that a fourth visit was unnecessary.

Patient #2: Rosalyn, a 32-year-old married woman, presently euthymic but with an 11-year history of one depressive period and many manic episodes, was referred to me because of intrusive and disturbing sexual thoughts. She had discussed these thoughts in detail with her primary therapist; he suggested referral to the Sexual Medicine Consultation Clinic.

Rosalyn lived with her husband in a one-bedroom apartment (they had been married 8 years), did not work, was maintained on carbamazepine, had never used street drugs, used alcohol only occasionally, never smoked cigarettes, had never been pregnant (neither she nor her husband wanted to have children), and was in good physical health.

Rosalyn had no concerns about her own or her husband's sexual function, but this was not equally true about her view of their sexual practices. They experienced a variety of sexual activities, all of which many people would consider to be mainstream.

Nevertheless, and unbeknownst to her husband, she ruminated about certain sexual acts that she found objectionable, based on religious ideas, as well as on statements made by family members when she was a child. Most recently, her preoccupation was with what she thought to be her husband's desire for anal intercourse, which, in fact, had never taken place between the two of them. Past history revealed that she had been anally, orally, and vaginally raped in her teens on several occasions.

Rosalyn's current sexual thoughts seemed to be related to her past history of sexual assault, family-of-origin issues, and the inability to be candid about sexual matters with her husband. After she and I explored the first two issues in several visits, I included her husband in the next session. He convincingly stated that he had much concern about his wife's history of sexual assault and had no inclination to force her into any form of sexual activity that she found unacceptable. Specifically, he stated that he was not at all interested in anal intercourse and attempted to reassure her generally that he found their sexual experiences enjoyable and sufficient. Her sexual concerns lessened considerably.

Six months later, she returned in a similar state of mind, but this time her focus was on oral sexual activity. In telephone discussions, her psychiatrist and I considered the notion that she might be experiencing obsessive-compulsive symptoms that might benefit from a more specific form of treatment. In fact, she was given an anti-obsessive medication. At follow-up 1 year later, she had no sexual obsessions.

PROBLEM #2: THE SYSTEM

Sexuality in the Rehabilitation of Patients with Mental Illness

Given the acceptance of attending to sexual issues in the rehabilitation of patients with a chronic and severe *physical* disability, I have often wondered why this same focus has been so minimal in the care of those with a chronic and severe *mental* disability (Szasz, 1989). To me, attitudes toward sexuality in the mentally ill seem similar to those that existed in the early days of attention to sexual issues in people with a physical illnesses (Anthony, Cohen, Farkas, & Gagne, 2002). In that era, health professionals seemed to assume that patients should be so grateful for the help they were already receiving that they should not expect to have their sexual concerns addressed as well.

In fact, there *have* been two sex-related areas where the mental health system has become more mindful: medication side effects and sexually transmitted diseases (STDs, especially HIV/AIDS). We have been concerned about drugs because of their potential interference with compliance. Likewise, we have been attentive to STDs because of wanting to protect those under our care from the negative impact of chronic physical illnesses (Kelly, Murphy, & Bahr, 1992). As important as these two areas are, our sex-related focus has been selective and idiosyncratic; it has not spread to other sexual topics.

The mental health response to the issue of STD exposure has often been to place condoms in the washrooms of mental health centers. Though potentially helpful, condoms in the washrooms are not enough. Providing condoms may make us mental health professionals feel better, because we can think that we are actually *doing* something in the area of safer sex to help our patients. And although condoms in the washrooms no doubt send an important message, they might also be seen as the mental health equivalent of the embarrassed doctor who only provides patients with a book to read when they bring up a sexual problem.

Though the practical value of free condoms may be limited, they are symbolically connected with the rehabilitation of patients with a serious and chronic mental disorder. Condoms convey the message that "the system" considers some aspects of sexuality important in patients' care. Furthermore, free condoms transmit the notion that mending must take place in an environment that is safe and that the concept of safety includes sexual safety. Talking about the details of acquiring and preventing STDs is best accomplished within the context of talking about sexual matters generally. When an MHP accepts this thesis, sexuality can join other issues such as housing, transportation, and vocational rehabilitation in the list of goals for the care of the mentally ill.

MELDING THE TWO PROBLEMS: THE SEXUAL MEDICINE CONSULTATION CLINIC

While a resident in psychiatry 3 decades ago, I had the extraordinary experience of completing an elective in Masters & Johnson's clinic (then known as the Reproductive

Biology Research Foundation). Since then, most of my focus has been on the subspe-cialty of sexual medicine (Maurice, 1999). I have spent 30 years talking with individu-als and couples about sexual matters. The kinds of sexual problems experienced by my patients have mostly been in the area of sexual dysfunctions, rather than paraphilias or gender identity disorders—the three major categories of sexual and gender problems listed in *DSM-IV-TR* (American Psychiatric Association, 2000). (Paraphilias involve atypical forms of sexual behavior, such as men becoming sexual excited when dressing in women's underwear; in the case of gender identity disorders, men want to become women or vice versa, sometimes to the point of asking for a sex-change operation.) Apart from their sexual dysfunctions, most of my patients have been psychiatrically well. To be sure, many have been unhappy in varying degrees about the connection between their sexual difficulties and their relationship with a partner, or the link be-tween their problems and associated physical disorders.

Because I wanted to return to my roots as a psychiatrist, I decided about 5 years ago to spend part of my time applying my knowledge and skills in sexual medicine to patients with a chronic and severe form mental illness. The development of the Sexual Medicine Consultation Clinic (SMCC) took place in the context of a large (over 6,000 patients and staffed by more than 200 health professionals), highly organized (eight teams), and praised outpatient service that takes care of the needs of severely psychiat-rically ill patients in the City of Vancouver—the Vancouver Community Mental Health Service (VCMHS) (Torrey, Bigelow, & Sladen-Dew, 1993). As far as we know, the SMCC is unique, in the sense of being a dedicated sexual medicine clinic within a larger mental health service.

When a patient/client/consumer (all three words are used by different health pro-fessionals working in the service—I personally use the first because of habit) is ac-cepted to one of the teams that comprise VCMHS, he or she is assigned a psychiatrist and a "primary therapist." The former manages biomedical aspects of treatment and, depending on needs, sees the patient occasionally, and the latter (usually a social worker) sees the patient much more frequently and handles psychosocial issues.

I formed the SMCC together with a psychologist-colleague who was also interested in assisting psychiatric patients with their sexual difficulties. He had published a book in Punjabi about sexual issues (Singh & Kaam, 1993). The SMCC is permanently based at the location of one of the teams, although services are available to all of VCMHS; it operates one half-day each week; and patients are seen by referral and only from within the service.

Two preconditions exist for referrals: (a) the primary therapist accompanies the patient to *all* visits, and (b) the psychiatric disorder is under control.

> *Patient #3: Carl, a 38-year-old man with schizophrenia since his late teens, was referred because of trouble with "sexual arousal." His primary thera-pist referred him, hoping that "sex" was one of the problems that could be solved.*
>
> *Carl was on disability income, did not work, lived in a group home, did not use street drugs, had a past history of excessive alcohol use, smoked*

one package of cigarettes each day, and had not been on medications for many years but in recent weeks had been treated with olanzapine.

Carl had a profound thought disorder and frequently switched topics. I had extreme difficulty understanding his current sexual concerns and his past sexual history.

Through the fog of Carl's history, I thought that he might have experienced sexual intercourse in recent years with many different partners. Therefore, I suggested to him and his family doctor that he have an HIV test. The result was negative.

In my consultation report, I suggested to the referring primary therapist and psychiatrist that I might be more helpful if the evaluation of Carl's sexual concerns took place sometime in the future when I could more clearly understand what he was saying.

I accept referrals of patients with any type of sexual difficulty. In practice, however, most are related to two problems: sexual dysfunction and having unsettling sexual thoughts.

Patient #4: Don was 23 years old and had had schizophrenia for 4 years. His main sexual worry was that others thought that he was gay, and he wondered whether this was accurate. Don had mentioned his concern about being homosexual to his primary therapist on several occasions.

Don was living in a group home with four other men, had a part-time janitorial job, was maintained on risperidone, had used alcohol and street drugs for several years in his teens but not recently, smoked one package of cigarettes/day, and was in good physical health.

In talking with Don about sexual orientation, it became clear to me that his many past sexual experiences with partners had been only with women, he had no sexual desire for men, his sexual fantasies were entirely heterosexual, and he enjoyed watching only heterosexual events when viewing sexually explicit videos.

After asking many pertinent questions about his orientation, I categorically stated to him that he was heterosexual, rather than bisexual or exclusively gay. On the second visit he said that he was pleased with the outcome of the first and that he was thinking of this matter much less often. The eventual disappearance of concern about sexual orientation was confirmed when I spoke with his primary therapist 6 months later.

Our experience tells us that on almost all occasions, patients, rather than the MHP, initiate the discussion of a sexual problem with the rehabilitation team. Consistent with that observation, I find that the patient's most recent *psychiatric* assessment (which we always obtain *before* the first visit), contains little or no sex-related detail, apart from the main sexual problem—generally, because the area has not so far been included in the patient's rehabilitation plan. I also know that sex-related questions are not usually part of the primary therapist's history taking, the main reason being that so often the health professional does not know what to do with the answers.

When we originally began seeing patients in the SMCC, it became evident that they welcomed the opportunity to talk about their sexual troubles. We guessed that they likely would have done so previously with their primary therapist or psychiatrist, had they been asked relevant questions. Because we were initially unsure whether patients would be unwilling to talk about sexual issues because of their concerns about privacy, we also worried that the presence of the primary therapist might hamper the process. Our misgivings turned out to be a nonissue. Having a familiar and trusted person present (the primary therapist) when talking to a stranger (myself) about this most personal subject was more crucial to the patient than facing me without any apparent support.

From our point of view, the presence of the primary therapist was advantageous for two additional reasons. First, watching us ask detailed sex-related questions as we explored concerns, completed an assessment, and established a treatment plan provided a continuing education experience for that health professional. Second, the presence of the referring person underlined the notion that he or she retained primary responsibility for the continuing care of the patient.

The process that we follow is such that the first visit or two consist of detailed history taking, obtaining health-related information from the family doctor, and ordering relevant laboratory tests. In the assessment, emphasis is given to the sexual concern, rather than to the psychiatric disorder, because the latter information is not the reason for the referral and, in any case, has already been thoroughly explored and is well-documented. We always include a review of the patient's current medication regimen in the initial visit because of our experience that changes in drugs often take place in the interval between initiation of the referral and the consultation. As well, we appreciate the great impact that medications used in psychiatry have on sexual function (Crenshaw & Goldberg, 1996).

Patients are seen in the SMCC as long as all parties see potential value in continued visits. In practice, this typically means between one and six visits. Fewer visits are necessary if we can quickly determine that it is desirable for the patient to be referred to another sex specialist with different skills.

> *Patient #5: Kerrie, a 28-year-old woman with a history of episodes of depression since her midteens, was referred because of a long history of confused feelings about both her sexual orientation and her gender identity. She was on disability income, did not use alcohol or drugs, did not smoke cigarettes, and was in good physical health. She had been on various antidepressants at different times but was not on any medications at the time of evaluation.*
>
> *In the past, Kerrie had cut her hair in a traditionally masculine way and had dressed in male clothing. More recently, she described allowing her hair to grow and dressing in a more feminine manner. In contrast, she described feelings and fantasies in which she was more masculine. She*

felt "in drag" when out in public and wearing more traditionally feminine clothing. When asked to describe her fantasies, she categorized them as "male–female."

Over the course of two visits, much information was obtained about Kerrie's growth and development, her past sexual experiences with both men and women, and her objectives in wanting to talk with us (not to find a method for obtaining sex reassignment surgery, but rather to help clarify her orientation and gender status). A referral was made to a well-established gender clinic in Vancouver. One year later she was still in psychotherapy.

More visits are generally required when patients experience a change in sexual function since becoming ill, or when they want to talk about a long-standing concern that predated the onset of their psychiatric disorder.

Patient #6: Mike was a 50-year-old man of Irish heritage who had had a bipolar disorder since age 32, for which he was currently taking valproic acid. He said that he had never had a close relationship with anyone in his life and that he had never had "even a heartbeat" when it came to women. He was on disability income, did not drink alcohol or use drugs, and had smoked one package of cigarettes each day since his teens.

Mike described having had a great deal of concern in the past about being homosexual but having "come to terms with it now." He was still in anguish, however, over not having had a child and not having ever had a close relationship with another man because of the dual fears of rejection and of being infected with HIV.

Mike's elementary and high school experience had been at a private Catholic school. In the past (and the present) he felt considerable guilt about his homosexuality, sexual fantasies about men, and experience with masturbation and felt that it would all "lead to hell."

Over the course of five visits and in contrast to his past experience with MHPs, Mike was pleased about being able to discuss sexual issues openly. He was encouraged to be more candid about sexual matters with his primary therapist. Such discussions had, in fact, taken place in the intervals between visits.

Explanations for a change in sexual *function* are often difficult to establish and require multiple visits. Patients will frequently attribute such problems to the use of medications. But the story is often more complex. Drugs may indeed be a central determinant when, for example, orgasm is delayed or absent (in men or women). But they are more likely to be only one of several elements when trying to understand the reason for diminished sexual desire. When erectile problems exist, the same factors that explain the high prevalence of this problem in the general population also become evident with mentally ill patients—high blood lipid levels, high blood pressure, cigarette smoking, diabetes, and abnormal levels of testosterone and prolactin. Impaired insight, which so often accompanies schizophrenia and bipolar illness may not permit a patient to understand that the lack of the capacity to experience intimate relationships may limit the treatment of a sexual function difficulty of any kind.

SEX AND INTIMACY

The words *sex* and *intimacy* are often confused with one another, as if they were the same. Indeed, some years ago one heard those words used as synonyms; that happens even occasionally now. But they are *not* equivalent and the distinction is important, although difficult to define. Intimacy refers to relationships that are more than transient and includes such issues as the individual's capacity to identify, understand, and exchange feelings with another person—feelings that may be sexual but that encompass the whole panoply of connections between two people. "The word intimacy conjures up notions of familiarity, understanding, affection, and privacy" (Levine, 1992). *Sex* and *sexuality,* on the other hand, are much more specific and relate to feelings, thoughts, and actions that are sexual and that may or may not involve another person. In humans, sex is a biological attribute that has psychosocial ramifications, whereas intimacy is a psychosocial attribute that may have biological ramifications.

So many patients with severe and chronic mental illness have intimacy problems as part of their disorder. In the same way that sex and intimacy are different, so, too, are sex problems and intimacy problems. MHPs are equipped to deal with the latter, and such problems do not require referral to a "sex expert."

The roots of intimacy difficulties are in the patient's past. In our zeal to deal with here-and-now issues, we are liable to forget the possible implications of such a past. This part of the patient's life needs to be thoroughly explored, because it might well have included turmoil in his or her family of origin, as well as a dearth of love and nurturing connections, which are so often a rehearsal for love relationships later in life. Likewise, the patient's past may not have included the experimental love and sexual relationships of adolescence, in which so much learning takes place about oneself and others. One of the consequences of the absence of adolescent experiences is missed opportunities to learn about biopsychosocial aspects of sexuality in the opposite sex. As a result, knowledge of basic facets of opposite-sex anatomy and physiology are often deficient and therefore need to be part of any treatment intervention.

SEXUAL PROBLEMS AND ATTITUDES TO MEDICATIONS

MHPs tend not to take the initiative in asking questions about medication side effects but rather respond when a patient raises the subject. Besides learning of that dynamic from patients many years ago, more recently I observed six psychiatry residents while they practiced interviewing patients in preparation for specialty oral exams. In the 12 interviews that I watched, only one candidate ever asked anything about drug side effects (or, in fact, about anything related to sexual matters), and he had previously worked in the Department's Sexual Medicine Clinic!

Could it be that MHPs avoid asking about medication sexual side effects because we don't want patients to connect sexual problems with their drugs and therefore stop using their medications? This notion might be similar to the discredited idea of not asking a patient about suicide because it might suggest that notion to them. In fact, the patient grapevine is such that patients are well versed in medication side-effect information, including those drugs that affect sexual function, long before this might be discussed with a MHP.

Sometimes it becomes clear to everyone involved with a patient that sexual function problems result from medications and that various strategies such as switching were either unwise or ineffective. Contrary to what many expected, patients have often told us that they would prefer to use psychiatric drugs and bear the consequences of continuing sexual function deficits if the alternative meant the possibility of experiencing another episode of illness.

THE SEXUALITY AGENDA IN THE CLINICAL PRACTICE OF GENERALIST MHPS

When considering the addition of an inquiry into sexual issues in the assessment of a new patient, MHPs have three choices:

A. Ask no questions.
B. Ask one or two general screening questions.
C. Ask a thorough set of specific screening questions that covers most potential sexual problems.

Whereas C is best from the patient's point of view, our experience tells us that usually A occurs. The choice is really between A and B. Given the vulnerability of the mentally ill to STDs and especially HIV/AIDS, the absence of *any* "sex" questions in a new assessment represents an ethical puzzle (perhaps even an ethical violation) for the MHP.

One or two sex-related questions are better than none and are easily integrated into an assessment. If only one question is asked, the best one is: "Do you have any sexual concerns?" However, many MHPs are more comfortable if that question is preceded by a general permission-oriented question: "Is it okay if I ask you a few questions about sexual matters? (Maurice, 1999)"

I am more inclusive in my own assessments. I attempt to cover seven sex-related areas. Screening questions about each of these seven areas could easily be asked by any MHP at appropriate places in the first few visits with a new patient.

1. Does the patient have a *sexual symptom of a psychiatric disorder* (depression and diminished sexual desire are common examples) or if there is a sexual concern, did it precede the onset of the psychiatric illness?

2. Is there any sex-related facet of the patient's *personal and social history* (e.g., sexual assault) that might help to explain current sexual concerns?
3. Are there *reproductive consequences* (especially to women) to the patient's illness? Examples include the effect of pregnancy on the patient's illness or the effect of the illness on the patient's pregnancy, the ability of the patient to manage child care, and the use of birth control.
4. Are the patient's *sexual practices* such that there are STD-related consequences to the person's psychiatric disorder? (Recent literature has emphasized the vulnerability of mentally ill patients to HIV/AIDS.) (Sohler, Colson, Myer-Bahlbarg, & Susser, 2000)
5. Are there any *sex-related aspects of the patient's general concerns* in addition to his or her psychiatric disorder—whether or not one preceded the other? Examples include sexual dysfunctions, gender identity concerns, or paraphilias (previously known as perversions).
6. Is there any sex-related aspect of the patient's *mental status* (such as thoughts of sexual aggression or violence)?
7. Is the patient receiving any *medications* that might interfere with sexual function?

MHPs COMMENT ABOUT THEIR PROFESSIONAL EXPERIENCE WITH SMCC REFERRALS

I talked with two MHPs (a man and woman) who had referred many patients to the SMCC and asked them for their comments, some of which follow:

What were the benefits to you of referring your client to the SMCC and participating in the assessment?

It opens up the dialogue between me and the client. . . . It gives permission to the client to open the topic with me and vice versa. . . . There is role modeling. . . . I watch how you phrase questions and open up topic areas. . . . It makes me ask questions more clearly. . . . I ask questions about sex more often after a session with you.

Were there any "downsides" for you or the clients?

Clients have found the experience to be surprisingly easy, (whereas) I have less choice. . . . I find that I'm fairly comfortable talking about sexuality with a friend or a partner, but in a professional setting it's like talking in public . . . so the way I talk makes a difference. The occasional client has said he didn't want me involved, but when you insisted, it didn't seem to be a problem for the person at the time or even afterward.

What did the clients think of the experience?

They normalized the experience quite quickly. . . . They were interested in what was explained. . . . Worries were dispelled. . . . There was an improvement in sexual problems . . . some hope for the future. . . .

RESULTS OF A NEEDS SURVEY OF MHPs ON SEXUAL ISSUES

In the SMCC's first year, we conducted a needs survey of all the MHPs who worked for VCMHS, in an attempt to find out the sexual concerns of their patients, how MHPs managed those problems, and what sort of assistance the professionals wanted. The results of the survey were informative. I will share some of them with you.

The response rate was more than 50%, especially when we left out the workers who saw only children and older persons. Of the 80 respondents who saw only adults, there were 55 social workers and nurses and 25 physicians (psychiatrists and family doctors). Forty-six of the respondents were women and 34 were men.

One of the questions asked was "What kind of sexual concerns have your *male* clients discussed with you?" The most common answers were (with the number of responses in brackets after the item): erection dysfunction (58), STDs (28), ejaculation/orgasm dysfunction (25), and sexual orientation (25).

We asked a similar question concerning reports of sexual concerns by *female* clients and the most common answers were sexual assault/abuse (47), loss of sexual desire (40), and STDs/AIDS/safe sex (32).

Thus, men seemed to focus more on their sexual *function*, whereas women were more concerned about their own sexual *behavior* and that of others. In spite of those issues, 75% of MHP respondents reported that they either never or infrequently asked questions of anyone concerning sexual function in the first few visits with a new patient. Likewise, 40% of MHP respondents either never or infrequently asked questions of women concerning sexual assault in that same time frame (although a minority [20%] routinely did).

We concluded that there was a great discrepancy between the sexual function concerns of male clients and the extent to which MHPs initially asked about those issues. Similarly, we came to the same understanding in relation to women clients and the subject of sexual assault.

SUMMARY OF THE MAIN POINTS

My experience in the care of men and women with sexual concerns in the context of severe and chronic mental illness has taught me that in such individuals

- *Sexual problems* in general occur at least as commonly as in the population at large.
- Specific *sexual function difficulties* occur much more than in the general population because of the medications that are used to treat serious psychiatric disorders.
- *Sexuality difficulties* generally are extremely common because mental illness often impairs the patient's ability to establish and maintain intimate relationships.
- *Adult sexuality* is problematic, partly because the intimate family relationship rehearsals of childhood often did not occur or were distorted, and, likewise, experimental love relationships that are a normal part of adolescence usually did not occur.
- *Knowledge of sexual anatomy and physiology, as well as of the intricacies of sexual*

relationships, is often deficient—somewhat similar to what may be found in adults who have physical developmental problems beginning in childhood.

- *Erectile function* is often impaired for similar reasons to those in the general population and especially because poverty is rampant in this group, which, in turn, results in poor diet, atherosclerosis, and interference with the function of many body organs.
- *Absence of initiation of discussion of sexuality issues by the treatment team* results in an inability to fill patient knowledge deficits and repair sex-related damage.
- *MHPs infrequently ask* men about sexual function difficulties and women about their history of sexual assault within the first few visits, in spite of the fact that many clients have concerns in these areas.
- *Attitudes toward partner-related and solo sexual activity* among health professionals involved in their care are often such that in the absence of a partner, discussion of sex-related issues is not felt to be a priority. The implication seems to be that solo sexual activity, as well as sex-related thoughts and feelings (apart from acts), are not worthy of attention.
- *In the assessment of sexual difficulties* the patient's psychiatric status must be in good control.
- *Reassurance about sexual concerns* can sometimes have a powerful impact.

MHPs have much work to do in helping to identify and treat sexual difficulties in their patients. Although mental health systems do not encourage MHPs to integrate sexual issues into a rehabilitation plan, comprehensive care of patients demands exactly that.

I hope I was able to illustrate to you through the six case histories that sometimes (not always) and in varying degrees, MHPs can be quite helpful to patients distressed about their sexual problems. Rarely does one factor explain everything about the origin of a particular sexual problem. The impact of a serious psychiatric disorder on a patient's capacity for intimate relationships and the treatment of that illness are intertwined and connected to yet other, more concrete, issues, like diet.

Although talking about sexual matters is, by itself, almost always helpful and sometimes all that is needed, timing is important. Sometimes it is better to delay discussion of sexual issues in the course of an illness, though most of the time, this is not so. MHPs can easily integrate the topic of sexuality into their initial visits with new clients by simply asking if they have any sexual concerns. Some MHPs are more comfortable with a preliminary permission-oriented question. I ask more specific questions, covering a wide range of potential sexual problems, than do most MHPs, and I encourage the reader to borrow some of these.

EPILOGUE

In the days of the mental hospital, sexual issues were ignored until patients ended up in bed with one another. In the days of deinstitutionalization, HIV/AIDS, Viagra, and the Internet, there is no way that mental health professionals could convincingly say that they are providing comprehensive care to patients without also addressing their sexuality in a manner that is explicit, skillful, regular, and accepting,

REFERENCES

American Psychiatric Association. (2000). *Diagnostic and Statistical Manual of Mental Disorders* (4th ed., text rev.). Washington, DC: Author.

Anthony, W., Cohen, M., Farkas, M., & Gagne, C. (2002). *Psychiatric Rehabilitation* (2nd ed.). Boston: Center for Psychiatric Rehabilitation. An excellent, comprehensive, up-to-date, and easy-to-read (sidebars and chapter summaries) outline of current concepts in psychiatric rehabilitation.

Crenshaw, T. L., & Goldberg, J. P. (1996). *Sexual Pharmacology: Drugs that Affect Sexual Function.* New York: W. W. Norton.

Kelly, J. A., Murphy, D. A., Bahr, G. R., et al. (1992). AIDS/HIV risk behavior among the chronic mentally ill. *American Journal of Psychiatry, 149,* 886–889.

Levine, S. B. (1992). *Sexual Life.* New York and London: Plenum.

Maurice, W. L. (1999). *Sexual Medicine in Primary Care.* St. Louis: Mosby. The first half of the book is entirely devoted to sex-related interviewing and history taking, the second half to reviews of sexual dysfunctions, and the appendices to, for example, sex-related drug side effects and reading suggestions for patients.

Singh, R., & Kaam, Vigyan. (1993). *A Two-Part Series on Adult Sex Education in the Punjabi Language.* Burnaby: Punjabi Press.

Sohler, N., Colson, P. W., Myer-Bahlbarg, F. L., & Susser, E. (2000). Reliability of self-reports about sexual risk behaviors for HIV among homeless men with severe mental illness. *Psychiatric Services, 51*(6), 814–816.

Szasz, G. (1989). Sexuality in persons with severe physical disability: A guide to the physician. *Canadian Family Physician, 35,* 345–351.

Torrey, E. F., Bigelow, D. A., & Sladen-Dew, N. (1993). Quality and cost of services for seriously mentally ill individuals in British Columbia and the United States. *Hospital and Community Psychiatry, 44,* 943–950.

Chapter Twenty-Three

Understanding and Managing Professional–Client Boundaries

S. Michael Plaut, PhD

I n the normal course of doing our work, we are likely to meet colleagues, students, or clients to whom we are sexually attracted. This is not only normal, but if we are truly honest with ourselves, our caring for and about people probably has a lot to do with why we do what we do for a living. We are given the rare privilege of sharing in the intimacies of strangers. The vulnerability inherent in a client sharing his or her private stories and feelings with us may have a powerful meaning to us and thus evoke feelings in us. How we handle these feelings is one of the great challenges for the health-care professional, especially those in the mental health professions. If these feelings are unrecognized, denied, or mishandled, we may cross what are considered to be appropriate provider–client boundaries. Such boundary crossings may occur in many ways, ranging from social contact outside the practice setting to excessive personal disclosure to overt sexual contact.

What are appropriate provider-client boundaries? Do these differ in various situations? Why are boundaries important? What can we do to help ensure that appropriate boundaries are maintained?

In this chapter, I will share with you some of what I have learned about these questions during 2 decades of reading, teaching, and consultation. For simplicity, I will typically use the word *client* to refer to anyone over whom we may have professional responsibility—patient, student, supervisee, or employee. Occasionally, I will use more specific terminology.

HOW I GOT INVOLVED IN THIS AREA AND WHY I HAVE CONTINUED MY INVOLVEMENT

Like many other aspects of my career, my involvement in the area of professional–client boundaries was, to some extent, an accident. From 1982 to 1985, I served on and chaired the Maryland State Board of Examiners of Psychologists. One of my predecessors on the board had told me that my experience would put me in touch with the "soft underbelly of psychology." She couldn't have been more correct. During those 3 years, for example, I saw no less than 12 disciplinary cases involving alleged sexual involvement with clients.

Two things intrigued me about these cases. First, we were very awkward in addressing them. It was an era when professional bodies were seeing an increasing number of sex-related allegations and realized that they had to take them seriously. Previously, licensing boards did not always have a good track record of responsiveness to such allegations. During the 1980s, an increasingly vocal body of consumers called for criminalization of sexual boundary violations, in part because the professional boards were insufficiently responsive.

Second, I initially found it hard to understand the ambivalence of the victims in pursuing their cases. I learned that much of their reluctance was related more to the real or anticipated pain of pursuing the case itself, than to any real concern about its validity. I saw that the betrayal of trust represented by a sexual boundary violation often led to severe consequences for the client, including estrangement from loved ones, depression, and occasionally suicide (Plaut, 1995).

In working on the rehabilitation of professional offenders since that time, I have seen that the consequences for them are often severe as well. Sexual boundary violations are now taken very seriously by most health professions, especially in recent years, as victims have become more vocal and licensing boards more responsive. Serious violations may result in license revocation, with no possibility of reapplication, and notification of boards in other states of the board's action. In some cases, an offender may have his or her license suspended and be asked to complete an intensive rehabilitation program. Such a program typically includes psychiatric evaluation, therapy, and education, all at the offender's personal expense and with periodic reports made to the board (Plaut, 2001). A subsequent period of probation may involve limited practice and clinical supervision. However, the impact on an offender might include, in addition to whatever sanction may be imposed by a licensing board, divorce, dismissal from group practices, loss of hospital privileges and insurance coverage, high legal bills, and an uncertainty about how to behave toward clients in the future.

I also learned that as a profession, we were not doing nearly enough to prepare our students to competently manage psychological intimacy in the professional setting. I learned that the mental health professions were not alone in having to address boundary considerations; boundary issues were a concern in all helping professions (Peterson, 1992). Mental health professionals may play at least four roles in addressing boundary issues—as teachers, therapists, consultants, or licensing board members. We are not simply potential offenders.

As a result of my experiences, I became committed to at least teaching about this important issue to my own medical students. After leaving the board, I continued to consult on cases brought to health professions boards in Maryland and other states. I have been writing, lecturing, and working with both victims and offenders. From 1994 to 1996, I had the honor of chairing a governor's task force on the issue in the State of

Maryland. This role enabled me to become even better acquainted with how the issue was being seen and addressed in various segments of our society (Plaut & Nugent, 1999).

This area is a difficult and often painful one to work in. As time has gone on, it has found me more than I have sought it out. And yet my commitment to teaching remains. I continue to learn more about this critical and complex subject as I confront new situations in myself or in others. I am pleased to have this opportunity to share with you some of the things I have learned.

AREAS OF CONCERN

As I thought about this assignment and sketched out my notes, four major considerations emerged: (1) the nature of and basis for our obligation to our clients; (2) how we conceptualize provider–client boundaries; (3) how and why we and our professions decide where appropriate boundaries ought to be; and (4) our own self-awareness, level of comfort, and coping mechanisms.

I will first briefly outline each of these considerations. Later, I will discuss them in greater detail. Rather than emphasizing what may be considered right or wrong, I will discuss the behaviors that promote either an optimal or an inappropriate professional–client relationship and the processes of deciding where boundaries ought to be.

Our Obligation to Our Clients

Although a part of our relationship to our clients may involve caring, empathy, or touch, there is a level of separateness and objectivity that is critical to an effective clinical, teaching, or supervisory relationship. Part of the need for that separateness is inherent in the power given to us by clients because of our knowledge, skills, and judgment. Excessive intimacy is thus likely to be considered a breach of trust on the part of the professional, regardless of who initiates a boundary crossing. Certain characteristics of either provider or client may lead to boundary crossings that are counterproductive to an effective professional relationship.

Conceptualization of Professional–Client Boundaries

The level of intimacy between professional and client exists on a continuum or a spectrum. The location of appropriate boundaries along that spectrum differs for different professional–client situations. Appropriate boundaries may be defined differently for a patient versus a student, a psychologist versus a dentist, or even with one patient versus another patient. One of the most important challenges of professional life is learning how to decide where boundaries ought to be. The decision is based on knowledge of laws, ethical standards, local practices, occasional consultation with colleagues, and, ultimately, our own good judgment.

How and Why Professional Standards Are Determined: The Focus on Sexual Involvement

Despite the existence of a spectrum of intimacy, there has been a strong focus, both in the professions and in the public sector, on sexual intimacy between professional and client. This emphasis is related to the symbolic nature of sexual intimacy in our lives and the level of harm that so often results from sexual contact in the professional setting. Sexual misconduct is not defined only as sexual intercourse; it consists of a broad range of sexual behaviors.

Coping Strategies

Our ability to set and maintain appropriate boundaries depends to a great extent on our ability to be aware of our own needs and vulnerabilities. Mental health professionals must consider the human tendency to rationalize inappropriate behaviors that serve personal interests, rather than serve the client's welfare. We need to be aware of our inner messages, the red flags that signal progressive boundary crossings—the proverbial "slippery slope"—and we need to nurture our own personal relationships and support systems.

Dr. J

> Dr. J was a psychologist in private practice who also ran an employees assistance program (EAP) for a local business concern. Mr. S was referred to Dr. J when his supervisor was concerned about his job performance. Mr. S disclosed that he was having serious marital problems that were affecting his ability to concentrate on his work. Dr. J began seeing the couple in therapy.
>
> Ms. S was a nurse who was severely depressed, had a history of childhood sexual abuse, had made a previous suicide attempt, and showed clear characteristics of borderline personality disorder. This was her second marriage, the first having ended in divorce 5 years earlier. After meeting with the couple for a few sessions, Dr. J felt that he could be of help to Ms. S and that Mr. S was not being as understanding or supportive as he might have been to her situation. Dr. J suggested that he continue to see Ms. S alone and that they meet in his private office instead of at the EAP office.
>
> As their work progressed, Dr. J began to be increasingly aware of his attraction toward Ms. S. He disclosed to Ms. S that he was also experiencing marital difficulties and that he was feeling very depressed. He occasionally called her at home to see how she was doing. He gave her a card on her birthday. Ms. S also expressed feelings of attraction to Dr. J, and their conversations in therapy became increasingly personal in nature.

Ms. S was very sympathetic to and supportive of Dr. J's situation, and she hugged him at the end of a session, telling him how much more cared for she felt by him than by her husband. Over the next few sessions, the hugs evolved into long embraces, kisses, exchanges of gifts, and expressions of love for one another. They began to meet outside of therapy sessions. Dr. J invited Ms. S to his apartment, where they had sexual intercourse. He told Ms. S that he could lose his license for getting involved with her. He insisted on total secrecy about the relationship, to which she readily agreed. These meetings in the office and at Dr. J's apartment continued for several months. Office appointments were scheduled at the end of the day when they could be alone without time constraints.

Ms. S initiated divorce proceedings, expecting that Dr. J would do likewise, as he had promised. Dr. J began to feel trapped by Ms. S's expectations and her constant need for attention. At one point he felt so depressed that he asked Ms. S to drive him to the hospital. At the hospital, he told her that he saw no alternative but to end their relationship. She was devastated, felt angry and betrayed, and eventually filed a complaint with Dr. J's licensing board. After a hearing, the board revoked Dr. J's license. She also filed a civil action, which was in progress at the time of the hearing. As part of the civil case, a psychiatrist interviewed Ms. S at length. The pain of having to relive her experience yet again, coupled with her continuing psychiatric problems, was too much for her to bear— she took her own life a month after the psychiatric interview.

A local TV program highlighting the problem of sexual exploitation by therapists discussed the Dr. J case, which was now a matter of public record. Dr. J's attorney made three arguments to support his license reinstatement: (1) Dr. J had made sincere voluntary efforts to rehabilitate himself through therapy and education; (2) the relationship with Ms. S had been his only violation; (3) Ms. S was just as responsible for the sexual relationship, as she was herself a health professional and "should have known the rules."

A psychologist who had been involved in Dr. J's case was also interviewed on the TV program. Soon thereafter, the psychologist received an anonymous phone call from a woman who insisted that she, too, had been intimately involved with Dr. J at one time, but had been reluctant to come forward. When Dr. J later asked the psychologist for a letter in support of his relicensure, the psychologist told him about the phone call and said that he felt obligated to report that incident in any letter to the board. After consulting with his attorney, Dr. J asked the psychologist not to write the letter.

A number of aspects of this case are typical of sexual boundary violations. Not only was the patient especially vulnerable because of her psychiatric condition, her childhood sexual abuse, and her current marital problems, but the therapist was vulnerable because of his marital problems and depressed state. Rather than seek professional assistance, he reached out to his patient, who began to provide him with the support that she deserved from him. Rather than apologize to her for his initial boundary crossing and try to repair the therapeutic relationship, he became increasingly involved with her, providing her with the caring that she should have been getting from her husband. Dr. J set the stage for a sexual relationship by dismissing the husband from therapy and then moving the therapy to the isolation of his private practice. When Dr. J realized that the relationship was not helpful to either of them, he had already caused irreparable damage to his patient, who had once again been victimized—this time by the person she was trusting to help her out of her vicious cycle. He might have ended their professional relationship before they engaged in genital sex and referred her to another therapist with full rights of disclosure. Even then, however, he had still violated appropriate professional–client boundaries in the therapeutic context, and a continuation of their intimate relationship might still have had the same unfortunate consequences and have been taken just as seriously by the licensing board. In the resolution of the case, itself a difficult experience for Ms. S, the defense attorney blamed her for violating boundaries that should have been maintained by the therapist, causing even greater stress on the patient. When all was over and done with, the violation and the succeeding events not only failed to serve any therapeutic value, but arguably cost Ms. S both her second marriage and her life.

OUR OBLIGATION TO OUR CLIENTS

We may all have different reasons for having entered a helping profession. Our clear professional obligation is to put our clients' needs above our own. With regard to boundary issues, this means finding a balance between caring, closeness, availability, and intimacy, on one hand, and distance and objectivity, on the other.

I once worked on a rehabilitation assignment with a chiropractor who had become sexually involved with one of his patients. He told me that when he entered the profession, he expected that he would one day "adjust his future wife." Clearly, this expectation of intimacy with a patient had contributed to his current problems with his licensing board. Functioning in a professional setting with such an expectation in mind cannot help but compromise one's clinical priorities.

A central and often misunderstood concept about boundaries has to do with the power that we have as helping professionals. The relationships we have to our clients are often referred to as trust-based relationships. Our clients come to us because they trust our knowledge, skill, and judgment. The power we have is power they give to us, not necessarily power that we assume on our own. We need to accept the fact that we are very likely to have influence on our clients far beyond our intentions or awareness.

Because of the power differential that is inherent in the helping relationship, it is considered impossible for clients to give truly informed consent to a serious boundary violation, sexual contact in particular (Plaut, 1995). Whether such a boundary crossing is requested by the client or by the provider, it is therefore the provider who is expected to maintain appropriate boundaries (Feldman-Summers, 1989).

As we are all aware, our clients are vulnerable not only because of the very nature of the helping relationship, but they may bring other vulnerabilities to the clinical setting as well. They may not have supports in their personal lives, they may have been psychologically or sexually abused, or they may be grateful to us for something we have provided for them that no one ever has. As a result, they may ask for more closeness from us, personal information, a longer period of assistance, or contact outside the professional setting. Complicating such requests may be a need for intimacy that we may have in our personal lives, especially when we have experienced a loss, or when we are having difficulties in our own primary relationships.

As ironic as it may sound, part of our role as helper, whether as clinician, teacher, or parent, is helping our charges get to the point that they don't need us any more, rather than to providing excessively for their needs (Kopp, 1976). The trainees of a child psychiatrist colleague would sometimes express a desire to continue to care for a child or an adolescent beyond what was pragmatic in a given clinical setting. He would ask them, "How big is your basement?" Our own need to be needed can lead us to do things for our clients that do more to serve our own needs than theirs and may exceed either what is practical or what is in the client's best interest in the long term.

A second trait that we often see in professionals who violate professional boundaries is the sense of entitlement that comes with the privilege of being a recognized, licensed professional. This may lead one to feel that he or she is above the need to observe certain rules, standards, and courtesies. Often in these cases, professional power and status inflame preexisting personality vulnerabilities and deficits. At its extreme, such people are serial offenders who may never appreciate the consequences of their actions. However, the assumption that "rank has its privileges" can never be said to apply to an ethical obligation.

A dentist was disciplined by his licensing board for inappropriately touching a patient while she was under the influence of nitrous oxide during a dental procedure. After completing a board-imposed rehabilitation program, he was found to have made unwanted advances to a number of additional patients, as well as employees. The investigation of those allegations disclosed that he was also violating Occupational Health and Safety Administration (OSHA) standards in his practice, even while under observation. Clearly, this was a person who flaunted authority in many respects and continued to do so, despite warnings and disciplinary action.

Senior professionals must be role models for those coming behind them. Thus, our obligation to maintain appropriate boundaries with clients in the clinical setting also extends to our students and to clinical supervisees (Bridges, 1999). Like many other aspects of professionalism and ethics, the issue of professional–client boundaries has often been ignored in professional education. Our teaching needs to go beyond the simple admonition "Don't have sex with your clients." Nor will abstract discussions of transference and countertransference alone help students to understand the realities of everyday boundary challenges. Students need to struggle with some of the more subtle boundary challenges that we face every day (Bridges, 1995). This needs to be an open issue, and we, as teachers and supervisors, need to be able to discuss openly the dilemmas we so often face ourselves. Finally, we need to model appropriate boundaries in our own behavior. This means not only that we maintain boundaries with our own clients in the clinical setting, but also that we do so with our students and trainees (Plaut, 1993).

THE SPECTRUM OF PROVIDER–CLIENT BOUNDARIES

It is typical to discuss professional–client boundaries as being of two types—sexual and nonsexual. Virtually all health professions prohibit the crossing of sexual boundaries, although definitions of sexual misconduct differ somewhat (Bisbing, Jorgenson, & Sutherland, 1995; Plaut & Nugent, 1999). The second, nonsexual type relates to what the ethics of the American Psychological Association (1992) and the National Association of Social Workers (1993) call *dual* or *multiple relationships*. These are situations in which a professional has two or more simultaneous professional relationships (e.g., both therapist and teacher) or both a professional and a personal relationship with a client at the same time. Ethical codes about such relationships are rather flexible and are influenced by contextual factors. Examples of professional–personal dual relationships might include such things as treating a family member, employing a client in one's practice, giving or accepting gifts, hugging clients, or socializing with clients.

Are dual relationships wrong? A few authors have expressed the opinion that they are always wrong. To be sure, it is well known that certain kinds of nonsexual boundary crossings have a tendency to precede or accompany sexual boundary violations. These may include, for example, disclosure of personal problems by a therapist, exchanges of greeting cards or expensive gifts, or planned contact outside the therapeutic setting. However, a realistic consideration of dual relationships makes it quickly apparent that avoiding all dual relationships is neither possible nor necessarily advisable. Gutheil and Gabbard (1993) distinguish between boundary crossings and boundary violations. For example, casual exchange of gifts may fit a social norm, whether in a given culture or a given clinical setting, such as homemade cookies brought in for the clinical staff or even for a given professional at a holiday time. However, an expensive or very personal gift may be presented with a very different intent or expectation. Similarly, Bridges (2001) explores ways in which personal disclosure may serve the therapeutic relationship, whereas in some circumstances it may represent an excessive level of intimacy.

Speaking from a purely clinical and ethical point of view, one might say that a boundary crossing constitutes a violation if it compromises professional effectiveness. This might occur by confusing the client about the role of the professional, reducing the professional's ability to make decisions that reflect the client's welfare rather than his own, or reinforcing a client's expectation of a personal component to the relationship.

It may be easier to understand this distinction by realizing that there are certain differences in such practices among the various professions, depending in large degree on what is expected in that profession (Peterson, 1992). For example, dentists often treat members of their immediate families. Physicians are not supposed to do so (Council on Ethical and Judicial Affairs, 1998). Certain physicians may socialize to some degree with their patients, but mental health professionals typically do not. However, there may be differences even within professions as to what may be considered appropriate behavior. One might not consider boundary issues to be very important for, say anesthesiologists, who tend not to develop close, enduring relationships with their patients. However, this may be quite different for the anesthesiologist who runs a chronic pain clinic, where regular contact may occur over a period of time and where clients may be especially grateful for the relief that the physician has given them.

Dual relationships are often unavoidable in what are called "closed systems" (White, 1997). For example, those of us who work in hospitals may often treat patients who are also employees of that hospital. In a small town, one's client may be encountered in a supermarket, at a party, or at a religious institution more frequently than would happen in larger urban areas. In such situations, the professional may sometimes have to make a special effort to keep professional and personal aspects of a relationship separate and to realize when objective decision making may be compromised.

Some professionals may expect the profession to provide definite rules about such issues. However, we are not always talking here about what is right and what is wrong, but about what constitutes good clinical judgment. This may vary somewhat, from one clinical situation to another, and is a special challenge in a closed system.

A somewhat extreme but poignant example of this was seen in the experience of Dr. Jerri Nielsen, the physician who recounted her experiences at the South Pole in the book *Ice Bound* (2001). During her year in isolation with about 40 other workers, she served as the only trained health-care provider, her responsibilities ranging from planning social events, to maintaining psychological well-being and morale, to doing root canals. However, the very survival of this small, isolated group of people required a high level of interaction and interdependence. Excessive aloofness on Dr. Nielsen's part might actually have compromised trust, and the consequent isolation of the physician might have reduced her own morale and thus her clinical effectiveness.

Yet the dilemma presented by this situation was not an easy one. At one point in the book she writes, "The terror of a doctor in Antarctica is that one of your friends (and that includes everyone) will be seriously sick or injured and there won't be much you can do about it" (p. 149). At another point in the book, Dr. Nielsen tells about learning of her own diagnosis of breast cancer in a rather impersonal e-mail message from a pathologist in the United States. She writes, "The next thing I remember from that morning was seeing one of the carpenters lying on the cart in Biomed. While examining him, I realized from the expression on his face that he could tell something wasn't right with me. For once I couldn't summon up the impassive mask that I always wore when I saw my patients. There was no way I could hide my feelings from him, or any friend at the Pole. We were too connected by now, like cells in a simple organism. He deserved to know what was wrong. 'I just found out that I have cancer.' The patient got up from the bed and held the doctor" (p. 258). Although one might try to prevent such a role reversal in the "real world," it was virtually unavoidable in this setting.

If we are not sure how to handle a given dilemma in our own environment, there are three ways we can get help. First, there may be policies or informal guidelines about dual relationships that exist in a given clinical situation—about accepting gifts in a clinic or hospital, for example. Second, it is always advisable to consult with one or more trusted colleagues about an ethical dilemma or a situation about which one has questions or doubts. Third, we can be honest with ourselves about our motivation for crossing a boundary or not doing so. Finding that balance between overinvolvement and an insensitive aloofness is one of the central challenges of a professional–client relationship. We are paid and recognized for our good judgment, as much as we are for our knowledge and skill.

The Internet is a relatively new boundary challenge. There are times when a client will contact me by e-mail with an insurance question, a change of appointment, or a need for clarification of a homework assignment. I have found these communications to be useful and more efficient than phone contacts because of our relative accessibility. However, when clients use e-mail to raise serious clinical issues, or when a person I don't know who lives some distance from me discovers me on the Internet and wants to discuss her sexual relationship with her therapist in great detail, I ask myself two questions: To what extent is this communication in the person's best interest? And is this an appropriate use of my professional time?

HOW AND WHY PROFESSIONAL STANDARDS ARE DETERMINED: THE FOCUS ON SEXUAL INVOLVEMENT

Where boundaries need to be set depends on the nature of the professional–client relationship and the risk of harm when they are crossed. Just as governments set speed limits because of the risk of danger when these are exceeded on a given type of road, so each profession needs to assess for itself the risk to clients of certain kinds of professional behavior. When the State of Maryland decided in 1998 to require that all health occupation boards define sexual misconduct in their regulations, each profession was permitted to define it in its own way, following guidelines that had been recommended by a governor's task force 2 years earlier (Plaut & Nugent, 1999). After a thorough review of the literature, the task force defined sexual misconduct in three ways:

1. *Sexual activity in the context of a professional evaluation, procedure, or other service to the client.* This kind of behavior is typically seen in the medical, rather than in the psychotherapeutic, setting and might include such things as excessive genital stimulation during a pelvic or genital exam, draping techniques that leave the patient unnecessarily exposed, or genital exams that are not clinically justifiable.
2. *Sexual activity on the pretense of therapeutic intent or benefit.* Such behaviors might include asking a client to disrobe or to masturbate during a psychotherapy session in the interest of "getting in touch with one's body or sexual feelings," or sponsoring nude hottub sessions for groups of clients. A provider may sexualize the clinical setting by using humor inappropriately, often with good intent. A chiropractor, whose patient could not raise his leg in a range of motion test, said, "Can't get it up, eh?" Such a comment would not sit well with many patients, especially one who happened to be experiencing erectile dysfunction! An acupuncturist required all of his female patients to disrobe to their panties, regardless of the procedure he was plan-

ning to do. He "justified" this behavior by imbedding this practice in a consent form that all patients signed before their first appointment.

3. *"Sexually exploitative relationship."* This consists of an ongoing intimate relationship between provider and client, perhaps of the type that would be called an "affair" between truly consenting partners. However, because of the power differential and the inability to consent, discussed earlier, such relationships are typically considered exploitative by their very nature.

Those of us in the mental health professions are certainly aware of the vulnerability of many of our clients to exploitation and the tendency of sexual abusers to rationalize their behavior. Our professions have decided that the frequency of violations and risk of harm are great enough that these behaviors need to be formally proscribed. This is not a recent occurrence, although the problem had been largely ignored until the last 20 years or so. The original version of the Hippocratic Oath prohibits sexual intimacies between physician and patient, "man or woman, free or slave."

Some may feel that for a profession to set boundary standards denies a constitutional right to freedom of association. However, as an assistant attorney general I once worked with put it, when we accept a license to practice, we trade certain personal freedoms for the standards of our profession. In this case, those standards are based on what is likely to be either beneficial or harmful to our clients.

Because of the lasting effects of the transferential aspects of the professional relationship and the fact that a client who has terminated therapy might need to return at a later time, the mental health professions also proscribe sexual contact with clients for at least 2 years after a professional relationship has been terminated. In most cases, it is probably best to follow the standard of the psychiatry profession, "Once a patient, always a patient."

Even when genital sexual involvement begins after termination of a formal professional relationship, one might wonder what thoughts, fantasies, verbal exchanges, or personal disclosures by the therapist occurred during therapy sessions. Did these behaviors serve the client well in the long run, or did they serve only to set the stage for further, more intense, intimacy? Despite the technical definition of sexual behavior that may be necessary to legally codify such acts, the individual therapist might do well to consider something like Shaw's (1997) definition of infidelity in deciding whether an inappropriate line is being crossed. She writes, "Infidelity consists of taking sexual energy of any sort—thoughts, feelings, and behaviors—outside of a committed sexual relationship in such a way that it damages the relationship, and then pretending that this drain of energy will affect neither the partner nor the relationship, as long as it remains undiscovered."

For purposes of defining professional–client sexual boundaries in a functional sense, I would recast Shaw's definition as follows: "Sexual exploitation consists of taking sexual energy of any sort—thoughts, feelings, and behaviors—into a professional–client relationship in such a way that it does not serve the therapeutic needs of the client, and then pretending that this misdirected energy will affect neither the client nor the relationship, as long as it remains undiscovered."

COPING STRATEGIES

As implied by my recasting of Shaw's definition of infidelity, our approach to boundary issues will not be most effective if it derives only from a commitment to following "the rules." Rather, a constructive and contextual approach to boundaries is based on a professional considering what is best for the relationship with a client and for the client's ultimate welfare. Furthermore, there generally are no specific rules except with regard to the most flagrant boundary violations, sexual intimacy in particular. Most of the time, boundary decisions are based on good judgment, rather than on firm standards.

Given that commitment, how do we address boundary challenges on a day-to-day basis? First, we need to realize that we will and do face boundary challenges each day of our professional lives. Most of these are subtle, such as whether or not to accept the gift of homemade cookies, but many are not. I offer six suggestions for effectively addressing these challenges.

1. Be Aware of Your Own Inner Experience

Probably the most effective signal that a boundary crossing is potentially problematic is the response that a situation arouses within us. We need to be in touch with these feelings and to address them honestly (Rutter, 1989, 1997).

For example, when I am with a female colleague whom I find attractive, how willing am I to bring my wife into our conversation when it might be otherwise natural to do so in the context of the conversation? When I walk down a corridor and see a group of medical students coming toward me, does my eye contact focus equally on male and female students in the group? To the extent that it does not, what is the real significance of that difference? When I encounter any woman in the professional setting, to what extent do I see her as a colleague, student, or patient worthy of my respect and to what extent do I see her as a potential intimate partner, even if only in fantasy?

Whenever we consider crossing a boundary with a client, be that patient, student, or secretary, we might go through a thought process that I call "progressive boundary analysis." What would be the impact of this boundary crossing on the client? On our relationship? On the environment in which we work? Is it likely to lead to further boundary crossings? If so, how would I handle it?

There is a frequent tendency to rationalize our behavior when it comes to sexual boundary violations. Offenders often hide behind the reproductive definition of sex as vaginal intercourse. Thus, one may claim that one hasn't had sex unless one ejaculates. A psychiatrist I interviewed for the Maryland Board of Physician Quality Assurance insisted that he had not had sex with his patient and in fact couldn't, as he was hypertensive and couldn't maintain an erection. I asked him if there had been genital contact between him and his patient, and he went on to describe their activity in that regard. A minister in whose case I was involved convinced his female parishioner that he wouldn't be betraying his wife if they limited their activity to oral sex.

One useful way to prepare for boundary challenges is to engage in a process that is sometimes called "behavioral rehearsal." Bridges (1995) has described her use of case vignettes in discussing countertransference issues with psychiatry residents. In my own teaching, I use one- or two-line open-ended descriptions of nonsexual boundary issues to stimulate thought and discussion (Plaut, 1997). I might say, for example, "Your client has just lost her job and you are in need of a receptionist." Would you hire a client—or even a former client—as a receptionist under any circumstances? Why or why not? As you consider how you would address this situation, to what extent do age, gender, or level of attractiveness of the client enter into your considerations? If you did hire this person, what might be the possible consequences? What if she performed inadequately as an employee while still being your patient? How would you handle it? Considering such hypothetical situations openly and honestly can only encourage us to look at ourselves more closely in the process and to be better prepared for issues that may actually arise in practice.

2. Acknowledge Sexual Feelings and Advances of Clients for What They Are

Even in a purely medical setting, such as a hospital, it is easy to see why a patient might develop feelings toward a health professional. The clinical setting is isolating, patients feel frightened and vulnerable, and a health professional may have provided a greater level of empathy and caring than anyone in the patient's personal life. Therefore, a patient's reaching out is more likely a symbolic gesture than one based on any real knowledge of the person for whom he or she has feelings. It is important that the provider acknowledges these feelings, maintains a balance between caring and professional objectivity, and confronts such feelings only if they persist and obstruct the provider's ability to provide appropriate care (Assey & Herbert, 1983). If we find that patients or students appear to be making advances toward us on a frequent basis, we may need to make an honest appraisal of our dress, the scents we wear, and the nonverbal signals we may be giving our clients, asking for honest feedback from colleagues as necessary.

Erotic feelings toward a psychotherapist are not only likely to be more intense, but these feelings may provide some of the basis for a successful therapeutic outcome. As Levine (1992, p. 216) has put it, "Why should a patient not love a therapist who consistently provides a high quality affective connection, calm clear thinking, and a reliable interest in the patient's happiness?" We are, in fact, "paid for our ability to deal with our temptations, fantasies, and arousal with apparent calm [p. 220]. When patients let their therapist know about their love, they expect to be helped to benefit from it. Sexually offending therapists often rationalize their sexual behavior with the patient as being for the patient's benefit. In the regression of therapy, patients may request and accede to the therapist's sexual advance. Even as it is occurring, most patients know that it is improper" (p. 222).

Managing such erotic feelings requires a careful balance of closeness and separateness on the part of the therapist. Levine (1992, pp. 226–229) describes the case of his patient Bea, who had repeatedly expressed intense and persistent erotic feelings toward him in therapy. She once presented him with a necktie at Christmas, which he accepted "after much conflict." Two months later, after dishonestly delaying her normal appointment so that her next session occurred on Valentine's Day, she presented him with a box of chocolates and an expensive pen. Despite her acknowledging the love and desire for a sexual relationship that were imbedded in these gifts, Dr. Levine refused them. She was mortified and upset for weeks over her humiliation. By holding the line and allowing the patient to express her love in a safe environment, this recently divorced woman who could not feel sexual interest in her husband, eventually came to feel safe with a man. "And this," she said as her therapy terminated, "has been worth everything to me."

3. Know the Risk Factors That Lead People to Rationalize Boundary Violations

A number of authors have discussed the phenomenon called the "slippery slope" (Strasburger, Jorgenson, & Sutherland, 1992). The concept is based on observations that there are certain nonsexual boundary crossings that very frequently precede or accompany sexual boundary crossings. Among these are excessive personal disclosures, exchange of personal gifts, problems in the primary relationship of one or both parties, and contact outside the normal professional setting. An awareness of these and other risk factors may help a therapist prevent more serious problems down the road.

4. Nurture Your Own Personal Life and Relationships

White (1997) has described a phenomenon called "organizational incest." All of us, he says, need to find nurturance in our personal lives, in the form of relationships, hobbies, vacations, and so forth. There needs to be a balance between the professional and the personal aspects of our lives. To the extent that boundaries between our personal and professional lives become less permeable, our professional, social, and sexual energy may tend to become increasingly focused within the "organizational boundary" (figure 23.1). This can happen whether the "organization" is a therapist–client dyad or an entire hospital or clinic. By seeing to our personal needs and relationships and keeping personal and professional priorities in balance, we maintain sufficient boundary permeability, and we are thus less likely to exercise our personal needs within the professional realm.

Probably the most frequent evidence of organizational incest in cases of sexual boundary violations is that the professional offender is typically having problems in his or her primary relationship. The intimate relationships of professionals are often at risk because of our frequent tendency to be overcommitted to professional priorities at the expense of partner and family (White, 1997). Attending to personal relationships and keeping them in balance with our professional lives deserves special attention throughout our careers.

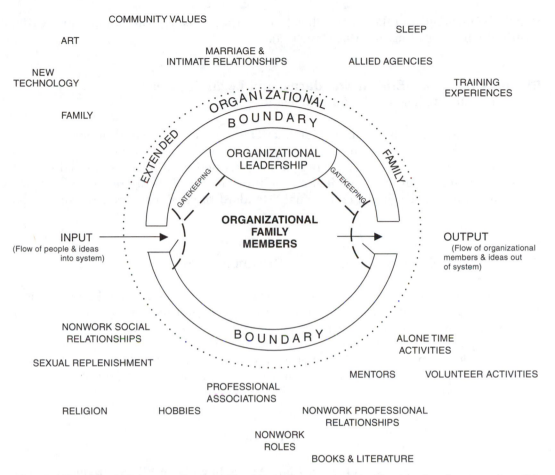

Figure 23.1. Our ability to easily cross boundaries between our professional and personal worlds will prevent excessive professional, social, and sexual energy from being expended within the "organizational boundary," as often happens in a closed system. Adapted from *The Incestuous Workplace: Stress and Distress in the Organizational Family* by William L. White. Copyright 1997 by Hazelden Foundation. Reprinted by permission of Hazelden Foundation, Center City, MN.

Writer Joan Anderson, in her autobiographical book *A Year by the Sea* (1999), describes having dinner at her cottage on Cape Cod with an unnamed middle-aged psychotherapist from the Boston area who was working on the topic of professional–client boundaries. She quotes him as saying, "I might be attracted to a 21-year-old client, not an unusual occurrence for a man of my age, and yet if I acted on my lustful fantasies there might be all hell to pay. But simply denying these thoughts is sheer repression. I might have had to turn off such thoughts when I was newly married and we were raising our children, but now I have more freedom and will gain nothing from denying my fantasies. Rather, it behooves me to bring them to the surface, look at what

I might be missing, and then move ahead to incorporate, say, more passion in my life, within the bounds of my marriage" (p. 115).

5. Know the Laws, Ethical Standards, and Local Policies Related to Professional Boundaries

Although I have said that boundary standards are more often based on good professional judgment than they are on rules, we must always be aware of the consensus within our profession, as well as laws in our jurisdiction of practice, formal ethical standards, and institutional policies and traditions in our place of practice. Every professional situation requires a consensual "standard of care" of which we should be aware.

6. Consult a Colleague When Ethical Dilemmas Arise

A critical risk factor that is seen in almost every case of sexual misconduct by professionals is that the offender has never discussed his or her boundary dilemmas with anyone else. This might not be surprising after sexual contact has begun. However, one cannot help but wonder how many sexual boundary violations might be prevented if a therapist who felt attracted to a client or who was unsure how to address the attraction to him expressed by a client had the courage to simply seek some grounding from a trusted colleague.

CONCLUSION

Situations like the one involving Dr. J and Ms. S have been all too frequent in the service professions. Such events not only reflect a failure of the professional's responsibility, but they can cause severe consequences to the client, the professional, others in their lives, and the level of public trust in our professions. We can better serve our public and our clients by understanding what our obligations are as professionals, depending on peer or professional support when we need it, nurturing our personal needs in our personal world, and taking seriously the spectrum of risk factors that can lead to boundary violations. Most of all, we must remember that we are paid and trusted to operate on the sometimes precarious balance between an uncaring aloofness and a level of intimacy that harms more than it helps.

In 1983, the commencement address at the University of Maryland, Baltimore, was given by the noted Washington attorney and then owner of the Baltimore Orioles, the late Edward Bennett Williams. After receiving his honorary degree, he gave an address about professionalism, inviting his "classmates" to join him on a crusade to preserve what he considered to be an endangered species—the CI or Caring Incorruptible. In two words, Williams was able to touch on the core of professionalism—client-centered service in an atmosphere of inviolable trust. I believe that this is a worthy objective for all of us as we pursue our clinical careers.

REFERENCES

American Psychological Association. (2002). *Ethical Principles of Psychologists and Code of Conduct.* Washington, DC: Author. http: www2.apa.org/ethics/code2002.doc_Toc21796696.

Anderson, J. (1999). *A Year by the Sea: Thoughts of an Unfinished Woman.* New York: Random House.

Assey, J. L., & Herbert, J. M. (1983). Who is the seductive patient? *American Journal of Nursing, 4,* 531–532.

Bisbing, S. B., Jorgenson, L. M., & Sutherland, P. K. (1995). *Sexual Abuse by Professionals: A Legal Guide.* Charlottesville: MI. This is the "legal bible" of the field, covering criminal, civil, and administrative (licensing board) laws and practices. Well-written by three of the leading attorneys in the field, one of whom is also a psychologist, supplements are published periodically to update the material.

Bridges, N. A. (1995). Managing erotic and loving feelings in therapeutic relationships: A model course. *Journal of Psychotherapy and Practice Research, 4,* 329–339. Bridges teaches at the Harvard Medical School and the Smith School for Social Work and has developed an interactive model of teaching about professional–client boundaries that encourages students to grapple intensively with issues of countertransference. She has written a number of thoughtful, insightful papers, replete with excellent case examples.

Bridges, N. A. (1999). The role of supervision in managing intense affect and constructing boundaries in therapeutic relationships. *Journal of Sex Education and Therapy, 24,* 218–225.

Bridges, N. A. (2001). Therapist's self disclosure: Expanding the comfort zone. *Psychotherapy, 38,* 21–30.

Council on Ethical and Judicial Affairs, American Medical Association. (1991). Sexual misconduct in the practice of medicine. *Journal of the American Medical Association, 266,* 2741–2745.

Council on Ethical and Judicial Affairs, American Medical Association. (1998). *Code of Medical Ethics: Current Opinions.* Chicago: Author.

Feldman-Summers, S. (1989). Sexual contact in fiduciary relationships. In G. O. Gabbard (Ed.), *Sexual Exploitation in Professional Relationships* (pp. 193–209). Washington, DC: American Psychiatric Press. This is one of a number of chapters in the Gabbard volume, which is one of the key resources in this field. The author provides an excellent discussion of the issues of power and vulnerability in professional relationships.

Gutheil, T. G., & Gabbard, G. O. (1993). The concept of boundaries in clinical practice: Theoretical and risk management dimensions. *American Journal of Psychiatry, 150,* 188–196.

Kopp, S. (1976). *If You Meet the Buddha on the Road, Kill Him.* New York: Bantam.

Levine, S. B. (1992). *Sexual Life: A Clinician's Guide.* New York: Plenum. In his own inimitable style, Levine has given the health professions his own perspectives on love, intimacy, and sexuality. He has suggested ways in which we can facilitate those critical aspects of human life in our own patients and perhaps in ourselves as well.

National Association of Social Workers. (1993). *NASW Code of Ethics.* Washington, DC: Author.

Nielsen, J., with Vollers, M. (2001). *Ice Bound: A Doctor's Incredible Battle for Survival at the South Pole.* New York: Hyperion.

Peterson, M. R. (1992). *At Personal Risk: Boundary Violations in Professional Relationships.* New York: W. W. Norton. While the bulk of the literature in this area focuses on psycho-therapeutic relationships, this book is a comprehensive treatment of professional–client relationships that includes various kinds of professional relationships in various gender combinations.

Plaut, S. M. (1993). Boundary issues in teacher–student relationships. *Journal of Sex & Marital Therapy, 19,* 210–219. Available at: http://www.advocateweb.org/hope/teachms.asp

Plaut, S. M. (1995). Informed consent for sex between health professional and patient or client. *Journal of Sex Education and Therapy, 21,* 129–131. Available at: http://ww.advocateweb.org/hope/informedconsent.asp. This short paper was written as a tongue-in-cheek effort to capture the impact on the patient of sexual involvement with a therapist. It has probably had the greatest impact of any paper written by the author in this area. The website from which it can be obtained is an excellent resource for articles, support groups, chat rooms, and other information about sexual exploitation by professionals.

Plaut, S. M. (1997). Boundary violations in professional-client relationships: Overview and guidelines for prevention. *Sexual and Marital Therapy, 12,* 79–96.

Plaut, S. M. (2001). Sexual misconduct by health professionals: Rehabilitation of offenders. *Sexual and Relationship Therapy, 16,* 7–13.

Plaut, S. M., & Nugent, C. D. (1999). The Maryland task force to study health professional–client sexual exploitation: Building understanding and facilitating change through collaboration. *Journal of Sex Education and Therapy, 24,* 236–243.

Rutter, P. (1989). *Sex in the Forbidden Zone.* New York: Fawcett Crest. Rutter has given us two excellent books on professional–client boundaries—one focusing on sexual exploitation, the other on sexual harassment. Though his Jungian approach leads him to focus almost exclusively on the male as offender and the female as victim (which, in fact, is the case most of the time), his impassioned and well-informed discussion is compelling.

Rutter, P. (1997). *Understanding and Preventing Sexual Harassment.* New York: Bantam Books.

Shaw, J. (1997). Treatment rationale for Internet infidelity. *Journal of Sex Education and Therapy, 22,* 29–34.

Strasburger, L. H., Jorgenson, L., & Sutherland, P. (1992) The prevention of psychotherapist sexual misconduct: Avoiding the slippery slope. *American Journal of Psychotherapy, 46,* 544–555. The authors are psychiatrists and attorneys, and their paper focuses on the non-sexual aspects of professional–client relationships that tend to precede or accompany more intimate relationships between provider and client.

White, W. L. (1997). *The Incestuous Workplace: Stress and Distress in the Organizational Family.* Center City, MN: Hazelden Foundation. White's book, originally published in 1986, highlights the tendency for institutional systems to close themselves to outside influences, a phenomenon that is characteristic of therapists who become overinvolved with clients.

ACKNOWLEDGEMENT

The author is indebted to Nancy A. Bridges, Catherine D. Nugent, and Judith M. Plaut for their comments on the manuscript.

Chapter Twenty-Four

Sexual Trauma

Barry W. McCarthy, PhD

I am a clinical psychologist with subspecialties in sex therapy, sexual trauma, and couple therapy. The field of sexual trauma is one of the most controversial and conflictual in mental health. Traditionally, sexual abuse was treated as a "shameful secret." Now some theorists and clinicians believe that sexual trauma, especially repressed memories of child sexual abuse, are the main cause of severe adult psychopathology.

In this chapter, I hope to present a model for conceptualizing, assessing, and treating sexual trauma that addresses and honors the problem without making it the controlling self-definition for the individual or the couple. It is important to be aware that negative sexual experiences, sexual abuse, and sexual trauma are extremely common. I believe (McCarthy, 1986) that negative sexual experiences are an almost universal occurrence for both females and males, whether occurring in childhood, adolescence, young adulthood, or adulthood.

My theoretical orientation is primarily social learning, and my clinical orientation is based on cognitive-behavioral therapy. My therapeutic goal is to help individuals and couples see themselves as "responsible survivors," rather than as "passive, shameful victims," on one extreme, or as "angry victims whose lives and sexuality are controlled by sexual trauma," on the other extreme. In working in sexual trauma field, I try to be respectful of individual, couple, value, and cultural differences. The sexual trauma field lacks well-validated assessment, intervention, and effectiveness data. In part, this is caused by the powerful emotional, political, and value issues generated by sexual trauma (Rind, Tromovitch, & Bauserman, 1998). And in part because there are so many factors that affect how the individual and the couple deal with sexual trauma that we clinicians need to be modest in generalizing about the effectiveness of our models and interventions. One size does *not* fit all.

In their first therapy session, couples where one or both partners have a sexual abuse history ask whether the best treatment approach would be individual, couples', or group therapy. They wonder whether the focus should be on their sexual relationship or if they first need to deal with the effects of sexual trauma. This uncertainty is not unique to them; the same questions are a matter of disagreement and controversy in the professional literature. Specialists in the area of therapy with adults who have a history of sexual trauma disagree conceptually and clinically on how to best assess and treat the problem. A colleague and I (McCarthy & Sypeck, in press) have proposed a model for assessment and treatment that emphasizes couples' sex therapy. Our model is based on three core concepts:

1. In addition to the major traumatic sexual experiences of child sexual abuse, incest, and rape, there are a number of other negative sexual experiences, including being sexually humiliated or rejected; dealing with an unplanned pregnancy or a sexually transmitted disease; feeling guilt about masturbation or sexual fantasies; being exhibited to, peeped on, or rubbed against; receiving obscene phone calls; or being sexually harassed, all of which can cause sexual trauma.
2. Child sexual abuse can result in a range of adolescent and adult sexual symptoms. These are caused not just by the abusive incident, but, just as important, by how it was processed and dealt with at the time and how it is incorporated into adult sexual self-esteem.
3. Effective treatment requires careful consideration of individual, relational, cultural, and value factors.

In this chapter, I will share with you in some detail the history of a couple and of two individuals I have treated using the model. I hope this will give you a way of thinking about and intervening with adults who present with a history of negative sexual experiences, sexual abuse, and sexual trauma.

CASE—CHRIS AND STEVEN

When Chris and Steven presented for therapy, they were a deeply ambivalent and demoralized couple. For the past 8 months Chris had been attending an Incest Survivors self-help group based on the book Courage to Heal *(Bass & Davis, 1988). She had been sexually abused by one of her brothers and was not sure whether she had also been abused by the father, uncles, other males, or any combination of these men. Steven had initially been supportive but was now frustrated by Chris's anxiety and depression and blamed her for the nonsexual state of their 4-year-old marriage. Steven felt that Chris was only marginally involved in parenting their 18-month-old son, that she was so caught up in exploring past abuse that she had no energy left for the marriage or for parenting. Chris felt that Steven was her worst critic. She felt emotionally alienated from him and reported severe inhibited sexual desire.*

Two years earlier, Chris and Steven had consulted their minister and attended a couples' retreat. Afterward, they consulted a marriage therapist for five sessions but felt that there was no clear direction or therapeutic focus. Although they were committed to the marriage, their marital bond was badly stressed. They were stuck in a cycle of blame and counterblame, with increasing frustration and alienation. Chris shifted from self-blame to blaming Steven. Steven was disappointed in Chris, the marriage, and the absence of sex.

In our first meeting, I proposed a four-session assessment contract (initial couple interview, each has an individual history-taking session, and then a feedback session). I evaluate individual, relational, medical, situational, and sexual factors so that I can propose a therapeutic plan (McCarthy, 2000a). They agreed and were hopeful that I would provide guidance and direction.

The initial couple session is important in establishing a prime concept in sex therapy—that sexuality is a couple issue. This is quite different from the medical model, which looks at the problem primarily as an individual issue and strives to ensure the proper diagnosis so that the right medication or intervention can be prescribed. The sex therapy model is a one-two combination of personal responsibility for sexuality (including dealing with past sexual trauma) and being an intimate team (including being partners in healing).

The conjoint session focused on Chris and Steven's views of the sexual problem and on Chris's trauma history. Their marital commitment, motivation for change, and attitude toward therapy were explored. Each signed release of information forms to discuss past treatment with the marital therapist. Chris signed a release for me to contact her Incest Survivors sponsor by phone to obtain the sponsor's perceptions of Chris's progress in the program.

The next step in the assessment process is to conduct individual sexual histories. I begin the individual session by saying, "I want you to be as frank and honest as possible about your sexual development and experiences, both positive and negative. At the end I'll ask you to flag sensitive or secret material you do not want shared with your spouse. I will respect that and will not share anything without your permission, but I need to know as much as possible in order to help you resolve the sexual problem." I structure the sexual history chronologically, moving from questions that provoke less anxiety to those that are more anxiety-provoking. My first question is how the person learned about sexuality. This allows me to explore family, religious, educational, peer, and cultural influences.

It is important that we clinicians ask about child sexual abuse, incest, and rape, as well as a range of other negative sexual experiences. These include having an unwanted pregnancy; contracting a sexually transmitted disease; being caught masturbating; guilt about sexual thoughts or fantasies; being sexually rejected or humiliated; having an unsuccessful or painful first intercourse; being exhibited to, peeped on, or rubbed against; receiving obscene phone calls; or being sexually harassed. We are not just trying to establish whether an incident occurred; we want to explore the client's thoughts, feelings, and experiences at the time of the incident;

learn whether it was dealt with or kept secret; and inquire as to how the experience was incorporated into the person's sexual self-esteem. Once you establish how old the person was when he or she left home, ask the open-ended question, "As you think back on your childhood and adolescence, what was the most confusing, guilt-inducing, or traumatic experience that occurred?" One in four people, especially males, will disclose an experience not discussed in the chronological review.

For Chris, reviewing psychological and sexual experiences and carefully exploring both negative and positive reactions were very different than what occurred in the self-help group. The developmental focus allowed her to more fully and objectively assess sexual learnings, including abusive incidents. This was in contrast to the Incest Survivors group, which was highly emotional, with the focus on confronting denial, shame, and pathology. Chris realized that the most stressful thing about her childhood was not sexuality but how the situation degenerated when her father and uncles became drunk, with threats of violence and chaos. She remembered emotionally and physically clinging to her two older brothers for comfort. The oldest brother would leave, making Chris more dependent on the brother who was 3 years older. It was with this brother that the sexual abuse incidents occurred. Although the sexual touching was confusing and negative, it was not physically forced. The brother orally stimulated Chris's genitals and then she manually stimulated him to orgasm. This scenario occurred two to three times a month over a 4-year period beginning when Chris was 7. The sexual abuse ended after the brother was beaten up by the father and two uncles in a conflict not involving sexuality. This led to the brother being removed from the home by social service authorities. Chris never discussed sexual abuse incidents with the brother or anyone else. In our session, Chris realized that her fear about her father, her uncles, and their friends revolved primarily around alcohol and violence, not sexuality. A second individual session with Chris completed her sexual history, solidified the developmental insights, and focused on her adult sexual conflicts.

Steven's sexual history did not contain sexual abuse incidents but revealed that he had felt humiliated by male relatives' jokes about his masturbation habits. Steven felt sensitized to rejection in dating situation, which generalized to feelings of rejection with Chris. Steven felt that he was a sexually inadequate, unattractive man.

In the young adult and marriage phases of the sexual history, I explore a range of issues, including positive and negative experiences with dating, how the two met and began their sexual relationship, when their best and worst sexual experiences occurred, what each person values most about the marriage, and what changes the client wants from the spouse and marriage. I carefully inquire about sensitive issues such as masturbation, affairs, dysfunctional sex, compulsive sexuality, and sexual secrets.

Toward the end of the sexual history, I ask, "As you review your entire life, what is the most confusing, negative, traumatic, or guilt-inducing sexual experience you had?" About one in four people then disclose an additional sensitive or traumatic experience.

At the end of the session, when I ask if there is any material that should not be shared with their spouse, 75 to 85 percent of people specify something. After a brief discussion of the motivation for keeping it secret, a number of clients readily agree to share this sensitive or secret material. I am a proponent for the value of sharing past traumatic sexual experiences (McCarthy, 2002b). Most spouses are empathic, supportive, and willing to be "partners in healing" (Maltz, 2001). When it is the male who has been sexually traumatized, the wife is usually eager to be an intimate, supportive partner. The clinician and the couple need to be aware that too much caring and sympathy can inadvertently result in anti-erotic feelings.

What can you do when the client does not want a secret shared? You cannot break your promise nor can you coerce the person. What you can do is to help the person carefully consider the costs and benefits of keeping sensitive material secret. It is usually easier and more therapeutic to share past secrets, such as guilt over compulsive masturbation or shame about having been sexually abused. The typical fear is that the spouse will be harsh or rejecting. That is possible, but it is much more likely that the spouse's empathy and support will increase. The client comes to understand the potential benefits, as well as the psychological and sexual costs to him or her, of keeping the secret.

The harder issue is a present secret, such as a compulsive Internet sexual pattern, an extramarital affair, or having talked to a lawyer about divorce. The core issue is whether the client is motivated to change and whether there is a genuine commitment to revitalizing the marital and sexual bond. For example, if the person is unwilling to give up the affair, couples' sex therapy will be a sham contract. In that case, I tell the couple that I recommend against sex therapy at this time and offer an alternative such as individual therapy, relationship therapy, or divorce therapy. In cases where the person agrees to share the secret or the sensitive material, it is important to be sure that it is motivated not by hostility or blaming but by the willingness to share a vulnerability or a trap so that the couple can work toward rebuilding marital and sexual intimacy.

The final step in the assessment process is the feedback session. This is usually scheduled as a double session and is the core component in sex therapy. The feedback session provides three vital elements to the couple: a new understanding of the sexual problem, a therapeutic plan, and the first homework exercise.

The feedback session was quite impactful for Chris and Steven. Steven had only a vague sense of Chris's past sexual trauma. He felt shut out when Chris was involved with the 12-step program. Rather than being a partner in healing, Steven felt that as a male he was indicted as being part of the problem and perhaps as a perpetrator.

For the first time, Chris was able to discuss traumatic childhood experiences and feelings in a way that Steven could understand, which increased his empathy. Chris believed that the core issues of the abuse had been identified. Chris felt that being in the Incest Survivors group had increased her consciousness of sexual victimization and supported her in giving voice to her concerns. However, she had outgrown the usefulness of the group. The pressure from Chris's sponsor and from the group spokeswoman to search out other repressed memories was confusing and stressful. She felt that the 12-step approach was too focused on past pathology. Chris believed that she needed to focus on psychological and sexual healing, which was best done in couples' sex therapy.

PROCESS OF COUPLES' SEX THERAPY AND SEXUAL TRAUMA

The clinician's role is to keep the couple focused and motivated to move through the therapeutic process to a successful resolution. This means the person sees herself and acts as a survivor, not a victim. This enables her to take back responsibility for and control of her sexuality. When she is able to experience desire, arousal, orgasm, and satisfaction and view sexuality as voluntary, pleasure-oriented, mutual, and intimate, she is no longer controlled by the trauma. She is a proud survivor, not a passive or angry victim. The couples' task is to develop a sexual style that is comfortable and functional for both people. The spouse is a "partner in healing." Sexuality nurtures and energizes their martial bond.

The focus of their sex therapy was on sexual desire. A crucial technique was that Chris could veto any sexual activity she found anxiety-provoking or anti-erotic; Steven was to honor her veto. It is very difficult to say "yes" to pleasure-oriented sexuality unless you can say "no" to aversive sexuality. Rather than the veto ending a sexual interaction and thus reinforcing avoidance, Chris would request a comfortable, sensual way to remain connected to Steven. They reported a poignant example where Chris was feeling responsive to Steven's manual genital stimulation. As her arousal increased, she impulsively said, "Go down on me." When he did, she experienced a flashback to the childhood experience with her brother, "froze up," and began to shake. Steven stopped even before she said anything. Rather than being apologetic or angry, Steven asked how he could be of help. She asked to move to the trust position that they had established as part of the couple exercises on revitalizing sexual desire (McCarthy & McCarthy, 2002). The position they used had Chris lie in Steven's arms with her head on his chest, listening to his heartbeat. When she felt reconnected and stable, they resumed manual stimulation and kissing but refrained from oral sex.

Sex therapy involves monitoring attitudes, behavior, and feelings and individualizing sexual exercises dependent on feedback from the couple. Progress is seldom linear. A major function of the exercises is diagnostic—to identify anxieties, inhibitions, lack of comfort or skill, or any combinatioon of these. It is critical that the therapist and each member of the couple reinforce healthy attitudes and behaviors to build an intimate, mutual, pleasure-oriented couple sexual style. Both spouses need to be aware of vulnerabilities and sensitivities caused by the victimization experience. For example, a woman who was raped by a fellow employee has been sensitized to distrust male sexual behavior and to be hypervigilant about a male's hidden sexual agenda. It is crucial that her husband respect her veto and not have ambiguous or hidden sexual agendas. Although this is necessary to heal from the trauma, it is not enough. The couple needs to establish inviting sensual and erotic scenarios. The spouse with a history of sexual trauma learns to value comfortable, mutual, pleasure-oriented marital sexuality.

RELAPSE-PREVENTION STRATEGIES AND TECHNIQUES

Relapse prevention is an integral component of couple sex therapy and is especially important for clients who were sexually traumatized. Relapse-prevention strategies and techniques are built into comprehensive sex therapy and are implemented after termination of formal therapy. Relapse prevention has four components. The first is dealing with thoughts, feelings, and experiences regarding past trauma. The second is maintaining a comfortable, functional couple sexual style. For Chris, this meant being able to recall and process the sexual trauma with Steven and her minister in a manner that honored the reality of the experiences, with the attendant feelings of psychological pain and confusion. Chris felt that she had dealt with the trauma, accepted the experiences, and took pride in being a survivor. As Chris said, "It was a sad, painful chapter in my life, but it does not control my life. I appreciate the present chapter so much more." When Chris has flashbacks, thoughts, or feelings about child sexual abuse, she accepts these without panicking, avoiding, or feeling out of control. She has mastered the skill of emotional regulation.

When Chris processes traumatic material with Steven, it is outside the context of their sexual relationship. Although it has not happened in months, Chris knows that if she felt uncomfortable, she could veto an activity and Steven would honor it and switch to their trust position. Chris realizes that she will never feel totally comfortable with her trauma history but is confident that it no longer controls her or their marital sexuality.

A third element in relapse prevention is to maintain positive, realistic sexual expectations. This begins with us—our realistic expectations for the couple. A healthy expectation is that 40 to 50 percent of sexual encounters will be positive for both spouses, 20 to 25 percent will be quite good for one and okay for the other, 20 to 25 percent will be okay, and 5 to 15 percent of sexual encounters will be mediocre, dissatisfying, or dysfunctional (McCarthy, 1999). It is particularly important that the partners not overreact to their occasional dissatisfying or dysfunctional experiences. In Chris and Steven's case, their ability to joke about a disappointing experience and reconnect in a day or two when both are receptive and responsive is a major marital resource.

The fourth key to relapse prevention is not to take marital sexuality for granted or treat it with benign neglect, but to devote the time and psychological energy to keeping sexuality vital and satisfying. Chris and Steven planned a sensual date every 2 months, with the understanding that it would not result in intercourse. They planned a couple weekend away twice a year and would discuss special romantic and erotic times. They built bridges to sexual desire, instead of settling into a mechanical sexual routine. Chris very much appreciated Steven's acknowledging how much he values the marriage and her psychological and sexual growth.

TYPES OF CLIENT PRESENTATIONS

Whether presenting for individual, couples', or sex therapy, usually the person does not view sexual trauma as the primary problem. Many clients present with sexual trauma issues minimized or denied, although increasing numbers view sexual trauma as a major deficit or a causal factor in their psychological, relationship, or sexual problems. I try to help the client assess the individual and couple attitudes, behaviors, and emotions that could be subverting psychological, relational, or sexual functioning. The therapeutic concept that guides me is to honestly deal with the past trauma in a caring, respectful manner and to honor its impact, rather than denying, on one extreme, or giving it controlling power, on the other extreme. The client needs to be comfortable in sharing experiences, perceptions, and feelings. Our role as clinicians is to clarify experiences and feelings so that the client can confront past issues in a therapeutic manner. This frees the person to devote the energy to succeed, using the adage "Living well is the best revenge." This requires the careful exploration of past trauma so that the guilt, shame, or sense of deficit is resolved.

COPING WITH ABUSE AND INCORPORATING
A TRAUMA HISTORY INTO SEXUAL SELF-ESTEEM

I find the concept of three levels of victimization a helpful way for me to think of assessing and coping with abuse. The "Levels of Victimization" concept has been of help to many clients. The levels are:

1. The abuse incident(s) itself
2. How the abuse was dealt with at the time
3. How the abuse is incorporated into adult self-esteem

The second and third levels of victimization are often more damaging than the abuse itself was (McCarthy, 1997). Traditionally, abuse was treated as a "shameful secret," where the child (or adult) told no one. The stress of keeping it secret and having an unprocessed and unintegrated part of the person's life often generated anxiety, depression, alcohol or drug abuse, eating disorders, or sexual dysfunction. In addition, a minority of males cope with their abusive experiences by adopting a "super macho" approach of being sexually aggressive. The man then becomes a perpetrator, creating more victims, usually female. As a culture, we cannot return to the era of silence and denial.

Yet now the most frequent cultural reactions are neither helpful nor therapeutic. The abuse is disclosed but not dealt with well. Often a multitude of conflicting sources are involved—social workers, ministers, guidance counselors, police, trauma experts— who focus on the abuse from their disparate perspectives. The child is barraged by a confusing panoply of questions, suggestions about what happened, what to do, and what it means to be abused. Especially when police and attorneys are involved, the situation becomes adversarial and the child feels stigmatized. People, including family and friends, gossip about the incidents. The child's needs for privacy and support are overruled. The abuse becomes the defining event of the year or of her entire childhood. In my view, the pendulum has swung too far from denial to definition (McCarthy, 1992).

A POSITIVE MODEL OF DEALING WITH SEXUAL ABUSE

What is the therapeutic ideal in dealing with abusive or traumatic sexual experiences? The child would disclose the abuse to a trusted adult who was empathic and listened for the child's needs. These needs include stopping the abuse, understanding it so that the child does not feel blamed or guilty, getting the perpetrator to take responsibility, and getting the perpetrator to apologize (Saywitz, Mannarino, Berliner, & Cohen, 2000). Many, if not most, children want to maintain a nonabusive relationship with the perpetrator. We clinicians want to help the child to develop a positive understanding of sexuality so that intimacy, touching, and sexuality are separate from sexual abuse. Such positive intervention protects the person from feeling like a sexual victim and reinforces the message of being a proud survivor, where sexuality can play a positive role in her adult life and intimate relationship.

DEALING WITH A RANGE OF SEXUAL TRAUMA HISTORIES

People report a range of sexual victimization experiences and present these quite differently in therapy (Haugaard, 2000). The factor that contributes most to traumatizing feelings is whether physical violence was involved. Most child sexual abuse and incest does not involve physical force. One of the reasons that rape, especially stranger rape, is so impactful is the fear of injury or death. For many middle-class adolescents and young adults, rape is their first experience with physical violence. The combination of violence and sexuality has a multiplicative effect in terms of trauma; it overwhelms the coping capacities of the victim.

A second variable influencing trauma is the violation of the trust bond. Contrary to popular mythology, most incidents of sexual abuse involve a perpetrator the child knows, not a stranger. Most perpetrators are males. The closer the relationship—brother, minister, counselor, or grandfather—the more impactful, because it violates a close trust bond and the expectation of protecting the child emotionally. Father–daughter incest is extensively written about because it is such a monumental violation of trust.

A third variable is whether abuse is ongoing or is limited to a single incident. Ongoing abuse is more impactful, especially when it is intermittent and unpredictable. Predictable abuse is psychologically painful, but the child knows what to expect and passively goes along with it. In unpredictable, intermittent abuse the child is unsure of what is happening and is more likely to blame herself, feeling that she could control the abuse if she did something or had not done something else. This erroneous cognition that the child is to blame or has the power to stop the abuse adds to her sense of shame and guilt. In fact, the responsibility for abuse is always the adult's, not the child's.

The child's gender is another important variable. Male children feel embarrassed about and deny abuse. Most perpetrators for both boys and girls are male. Most of the cultural focus and literature emphasize abuse of female children. Sexual abuse is not supposed to happen to males, so male victims feel more stigmatized and shameful about their abuse. They deny it to themselves longer and are fearful that it means they are homosexual or that abuse will make them homosexual.

CASE—TIM

Incestuous sexual behavior is significantly higher in blended families, cohabiting families, and families where there is alcohol or drug abuse (Finkelhor, Hotaling, Lewis, & Smith, 1990). Tim was 7 when his mother remarried, 8 when sexual abuse began, 10 when anal intercourse began, and 14 when the marriage ended. Tim never told his mother or anyone else about the sexual abuse. Male children are less likely to disclose abuse and are more likely to deny or minimize its impact.

Tim presented for therapy at 24, dragged in by his girlfriend of 4 months for treatment of ejaculatory inhibition. She had taken an undergraduate human sexuality course and was the first woman to confront Tim that he had a sexual dysfunction. Previously, Tim had bragged about how he was a stud who pleased women because he could "go all night." Male friends envied Tim because more than 50% of adolescent males experience premature ejaculation as do 30% of adult males (Laumann, Paik, & Rosen, 1999). In the sexual performance contest, Tim was viewed as a winner.

Tim did not have difficulty ejaculating during masturbation when he used pornographic videos, Internet stories, or fantasies where the theme was dominance and submission, specifically spanking the woman until she bled, and then he ejaculated. Tim had never been orgasmic in any type of partner sex.

Unfortunately, the girlfriend had a hidden agenda. She delivered Tim to therapy and then broke up the relationship to return to a previous boy-

*friend. Tim felt duped and angry. If I had tried to focus on sexuality is-
sues, Tim would have left therapy. Instead I helped Tim process his feelings of being betrayed. It was helpful to have him write a letter to the
ex-girlfriend (which he did not send), expressing his hurt and angry feelings. This allowed Tim to represent himself well and to realize he deserved to be treated better than that. In therapy Tim admitted that he felt
powerful and in control of the sexual performance scenario, even though
he was cheating himself from sexual pleasure.*

*After five sessions, Tim was ready to participate in a comprehensive
sexual history assessment. He did not disclose the incestuous activity until
after the question "What was the most confusing, negative, traumatic, or
guilt-inducing experience you had in childhood or adolescence?" Tim said
that if the clinician had not asked that specific question, he would not
have volunteered about sex with the stepfather. Tim had not known how
to process these incidents at the time and still could not at age 24. It was
very hard for Tim to admit that he had been sexually abused. Even harder
was admitting that as an adult, he had a sexual dysfunction that was in
part caused by the abuse. Tim explored other causal factors, including his
compulsive masturbation pattern and narrow use of pornography with a
single fantasy theme. Tim became aware that the focus on performing for
the woman, as opposed to valuing intimate, interactive sexuality, was self-
defeating. To deal with ejaculatory inhibition, Tim would need to emotionally open and see the woman as an intimate ally. Being sexually open
and vulnerable with a woman was a psychological challenge for Tim.*

*In reviewing the sexual incidents with the stepfather, a source of great
embarrassment and ambivalence was that Tim regularly attained orgasm
when he was in the receiving role in anal intercourse. Tim asked, if he was
orgasmic how could it be abuse? Did this mean he was gay? Why could he
not have an orgasm with a woman? Tim had a range of conflicting feelings. It was important to identify the feelings, but even more important to
formulate a way of understanding the sexual abuse that was acceptable to
Tim and that allowed him to begin resolving intimacy and sexuality issues in his adult life.*

*In addition to processing the abusive experiences during therapy, Tim
did writing exercises between sessions. The first assignment was writing
the positives and negatives from the sexual abuse incidents. The value of
between-session exercises is that they made personal and concrete the
issues raised in therapy. Tim was genuinely surprised by how long the list
of negatives was and how many self-defeating beliefs he had regarding
trust and sexuality. He listed only one positive—his commitment to never
again be sexually victimized. The therapist reinforced that this was a
strength. Tim tried to delve more deeply into the list of negatives. This
resulted in an empowering insight—Tim wanted to maintain a dominant
role with women, including ejaculatory inhibition, so that he would not*

be vulnerable to being hurt. In exploring the negative functions of pornography with violence and domination themes, Tim realized that this protected him against being victimized by using the "macho extreme" of the perpetrator. Tim cried as he said that this was not him. Tim was committed to not hurting anyone, sexually or otherwise. A powerful healing cognition is "The abuse cycle will stop with me." The commitment is to not create further victims.

Tim read two popular male victim self-help books but did not find them helpful. Likewise, he attended two male victimization self-help groups but found he did not respect nor could he identify with these men. This is as common a response as appreciating self-help groups or writings. Clinicians need to be aware of and respectful of a patient's response to self-help programs and bibliotherapy. For some people, self-help programs are integral to their healing process; for others, the chance to tell their stories and realize they are not alone is therapeutic, but continued group involvement or reading is not helpful (after 2 weeks or 2 months they receive maximum benefit). For a third group, self-help programs are of no value or can even be harmful. One size does not fill all.

For Tim, individual therapy and between-session cognitive and writing exercises were powerful and therapeutic. He agreed to throw out and delete all the pornography with the domination–submission and spanking themes. Tim began to use a variety of erotic fantasies with themes that were transferable to couple sexuality. He broke the pattern of compulsive masturbation, masturbating only when feeling erotic. He did not masturbate out of habit, as a tension reducer, or as a mood regulator. Tim focused on identifying "orgasm triggers" that could be utilized in partner sex.

In an ideal case, Tim would have found a new partner he was comfortable with, attracted to, and trusted so that he could share the abuse history and work together with that person to overcome the ejaculatory inhibition (Perelman, 2001). However, the ideal partner did not appear. Tim did write out his criteria for a healthy, intimate relationship and internalized the concept of sharing pleasure, rather than of performing for the woman. I hope that in the future he will be able to put this into practice. Tim might well seek couples' therapy but not until he is in a serious intimate relationship.

CONCEPTUAL AND EMOTIONAL CONTROVERSIES REGARDING SEXUAL TRAUMA

The issue of sexual trauma, especially recovered memories of child sexual abuse, is one of the most controversial in all of mental health (Knapp & Ven de Creek, 2000). Courtois (2000) provides helpful clinical guidelines with the intention of making this a less political and litigious issue. It is necessary to address sexual trauma from a therapeutic perspective, using professionally validated guidelines for assessment and treatment. Anger generated by the adversarial legal system often results in revictimizing the person. Even when there is a monetary settlement, the promised sense of validation and closure does not result. The clinician can be a therapeutic advocate for the client but is on dangerous ground when he attempts to be a legal advocate. The therapeutic strategy is to help people see themselves as survivors and retake control of their lives and their sexuality. Creating a frustrated or angry victim is countertherapeutic.

One component of the cognitive-behavioral approach is to confront people labeling sexual victimization as the main event of their childhoods (or lives). Self-esteem should not be defined by a negative "I came from an incest family," "My sexuality was stolen by the rapist," or "Sexual harassment caused me to change my career." This does not help in dealing with the trauma; instead, it gives the trauma unnecessary control of the person's life. It is the difference between honoring past victimization in a manner that allows the person to take pride in being a survivor, as opposed to being the passive, shamed victim, on one extreme, or an angry, bitter victim, on the other extreme (Bartoi & Kinder, 1998). My wife and I (McCarthy & McCarthy, 1993) presented a model of confronting the victim role that emphasized

1. Careful exploration of past and present attitudes, behavior, and emotions about the sexual victimization;
2. Realization that the responsibility for the abuse lies with the perpetrator, that guilt and shame are inappropriate and self-punitive;
3. Acceptance of the incident and its repercussions, realizing that one has coped and survived in the best way one could, given the resources available to one at the time; and
4. Commitment to lead one's life as a proud survivor and to enjoy a psychologically, relationally, and sexually healthy life.

Here is an example of how I use these four concepts in therapy.

CASE—KAREN

Karen was a 26-year-old college graduate who presented for individual psychotherapy with a combination of anxiety, depression, career dissatisfaction, and low self-esteem. In the second session, while exploring her psychological history, Karen revealed that a year and a half ago she experienced an acquaintance rape. Karen said that this caused a great deal of stress at the time, but she had dealt with it. How can the clinician explore this issue?

I asked open-ended questions about Karen's sex education (both formal and informal) and what she had learned about sexual assault (rape). Like many young women, Karen believed the misinformation that the most common type of rape was by a stranger, using a weapon. In fact, Karen's

*experiences fit the norm—it was a man she knew through work friends;
they had both been drinking, which impaired perception and judgment;
neither a weapon nor physical force was used; and the initial touching
had been consensual. When Karen said, "no," and tried to end the encounter, he overpowered her and intercourse occurred. He denied that
there was anything wrong and did not believe there was a problem, much
less that this had been a date rape. Karen did not go to a hospital nor did
she seek medical treatment. She was taking the birth control pill so was
not worried about pregnancy and, although concerned, did not seek out
STD/HIV testing. Karen did talk with siblings and other friends about the
sexual incident but had not discussed it with work friends. She avoided
any contact with the man, and when his name came up, she would leave
the room.*

*Karen had a number of psychological concerns; healing from the rape
was not a stated concern. I encouraged Karen to have an HIV test and STD
screen. When the results came back negative, Karen was visibly relieved.*

*The prime theme in therapy was to increase Karen's self-efficacy and
for her to be an active problem-solver, especially in terms of her career
and living situation. This theme generalized to physical health—specifically, joining an exercise group, which both improved her mood and resulted in a moderate, sustained weight loss. Enhancing self-efficacy was
the context in which sexuality and the rape incident was explored. Karen
was tired of the dating scene and especially of sexual games. Her goal was
to marry and have children, but she felt demoralized about finding a life
partner. The rape was a shadow over Karen's sense of self-esteem and
included the feeling that she did not deserve a successful relationship or a
sexual life.*

*Karen blamed herself, at least in part, for the rape. She felt that she
had led the man on by being drunk and vulnerable. She wanted to keep
the incident from coworkers because she feared being stigmatized and
judged. The incident lowered her self-esteem and feelings of attractiveness,
while increasing her cynicism about men and sexual relationships. Paradoxically, she felt guilty that it had not affected her sexual responsiveness.*

I felt that Karen was self-punitive and had not incorporated any positive learning
or empowering motivation from the rape experience. A motivating cognition for survivors of rape is "Living well is the best revenge." Together, Karen and I assessed what
had happened in an objective and aware manner, with the focus on learning what
would make her less vulnerable in the future. I suggested that Karen not "pile on"
negative judgments of herself. She needed to acknowledge that he was responsible for
the sexual assault, not her. I reinforced Karen for retaining her capacity for desire,
arousal, and orgasm. It was good that she retained her sexual responsivity. Cognitive
restructuring was utilized to reinforce the image of Karen as a proud survivor who took
back control of her body and her sexuality from the rapist.

The most impactful intervention was a cognitive exercise to learn a process for choosing an intimate partner. This involved listing specific positive characteristics she needed in a man and in a relationship, as well as awareness of "poisons" or fatal flaws that would subvert a relationship. By engaging in this exercise, Karen became aware of how the rape experience exacerbated her tendency to see herself as undeserving and to settle for men she did not respect or trust. Karen decided to set a "higher screen" for dating and not waste her time on "second-class" partners. Karen shared her newly structured story of the acquaintance rape with her minister. She received both spiritual forgiveness and reassurance of being in God's good graces. Karen decided that she would share the acquaintance rape experience with a new partner but not until she was seriously involved. She would not be apologetic or defensive but would make him aware of specific sensitivities and of her need to feel safe, especially of her need for his willingness to honor a "no" from her.

THERAPIST ISSUES IN DEALING WITH SEXUAL TRAUMA

Sexual trauma work is personally challenging, as well as stressful, for the therapist. Some clinicians decide to refer these cases, because they either are not interested in the topic or do not have proper training or skills, or the topic raises personal issues and anxieties that are too disruptive. Just as in other areas of mental health, it is an unrealistic demand that a therapist be skilled and comfortable with all kinds of therapy, all types of issues, and all types of clients (Meichenbaum, 1994). Most clinicians can gain the knowledge and skills and can successfully monitor their anxieties so that they are able to work in the fascinating and complex area of sexual trauma. Helping people process sexual trauma and feel and behave like survivors is challenging and satisfying.

As a psychologist who conducts a clinical practice, teaches, and writes about sexual trauma and sexual dysfunction, I believe that sexual behavior is multicausal and multidimensional, with large individual, relational, value, and cultural differences. I also believe that clinicians need to develop a set of therapeutic strategies and techniques that they feel comfortable with and competent in, but also be willing to attend to the complexity of each individual and couple. The reality of the clinical case is more important than theory or even of empirically validated guidelines. The sexual trauma area clearly needs improved scientific research and empirically validated protocols, but even with these resources the clinician will still be challenged by the complexity of individual and couple cases.

A prime therapeutic challenge is to maintain the stance of being supportive and respectful when dealing with the emotionally charged issues surrounding sexual trauma. Involved, caring clinicians are not, nor should they be, value-free, but they do honor the experiences and values of the client. One of the more powerful therapeutic approaches is *Emotionally Focused Couple Therapy* (Johnson, 2002).

The person wants empathy and respect, not sympathy or feeling that she is so deficient that she needs to be taken care of. Clients want the clinician's caring, but, even more, they want professional feedback on how to deal with trauma and lead their lives as survivors. Many clinicians err in giving so much emphasis to exploring feelings of victimization that they do not allow healing to occur or allow assuming responsibility for the self in the present. Other clinicians find the careful exploration of the trauma too painful or do not want the client to "whine," so they treat abuse issues in a cursory manner. Clinicians need to be comfortable with the material, so they are empathic, are respectful, and can help clients deal with traumatic feelings and experiences. Most important is to promote personal self-efficacy, which enhances psychological and sexual functioning.

SUMMARY

Clinical work in the area of sexual trauma is too common and too important to leave to subspecialists. To work effectively in the sexual trauma field, the clinician needs to be comfortable and skilled in individual therapy, couples' therapy, and sex therapy, in addition to sexual trauma. The clinician must be willing to explore attitudes, experiences, and feelings about the sexual trauma, at the time and in retrospect. Sexual trauma is dealt with as an important part of the person's developmental history, neither a shameful secret nor a defining characteristic. In this chapter we have discussed Chris, whose experience with brother incest created a marital situation that generated sexual dysfunction; Tom, whose prolonged stepfather victimization led to ejaculatory inhibition; and Karen, whose date rape generated mood, self-esteem, and self-regulation problems. This illustrates the potential multidimensional effects of abusive and traumatic sexual experiences.

Two therapeutic guidelines are of prime importance. First is helping people see themselves as survivors, not as victims. This includes their seeing sexuality as a positive, integral component of themselves and seeing themselves as people with a commitment to live their lives in a manner that promotes self-respect. Second, intimate sexuality is experienced as voluntary, mutual, and pleasure-oriented. When people are able to experience sexual desire, arousal, orgasm, and satisfaction, they have taken back control of their bodies and their sexuality. Sexuality is a positive part of their lives and their intimate relationships. I find helping individuals and couples deal with sexual trauma personally and professionally challenging but very worthwhile.

REFERENCES

Bartoi, M., & Kinder, B. (1998). The effects of child and adult sexual abuse on adult sexuality. *Journal of Sex & Marital Therapy, 24*, 75–90. A well-controlled, empirical study that demonstrated the quite variable effects of sexual abuse on adult sexual attitudes and functioning. The importance of this study was that it challenged the popular and professional misconception that severe effects of sexual abuse were universal and inevitable.

Bass, E., & Davis, L. (1988). *The Courage to Heal.* New York: Harper and Row.

Courtois, C. (2000). The aftermath of child sexual abuse. In L. Szuchan & F. Muscarella (Eds.), *Psychological Perspectives on Human Sexuality*. New York: Wiley.

Finkelhor, D., Hotaling, G., Lewis, L., & Smith, C. (1990). Sexual abuse in a national sample of adult men and women. *Child Abuse and Neglect, 14*, 19–28.

Haugaard, J. (2000). The challenges of defining child sexual abuse. *American Psychologist, 55*, 1036–1039. This article spells out many misconceptions and overgeneralizations about child sexual abuse. Haugaard proposes a more specific, operational, and multidimensional approach to defining and measuring types of sexual abuse.

Johnson, S. (2002). *Emotionally Focused Couple Therapy With Trauma Survivors*. New York: Guilford. Johnson utilizes a challenging, alternative therapeutic approach to couples' therapy with trauma survivors. She employs emotionally focused therapy and, via case vignettes, vividly illustrates the multicausal, multidimensional aspects of trauma on the person and the couple.

Knapp, S., & Ven de Creek, L. (2000). Recovered memories of childhood abuse. *Professional Psychology, 31*, 365–371. The issue of recovered memories of childhood sexual abuse is one of the most political, value-laden, and emotionally charged in mental health. This thoughtful article attempts to treat the issues with the complexity they deserve and proposes a professional consensus on understanding and treating trauma in a therapeutic manner.

Laumann, E., Paik, A., & Rosen, R. (1999). Sexual dysfunction in the United States. *Journal of the American Medical Association, 281*, 537–544.

Maltz, W. (2001). *The Sexual Healing Journey*. New York: Harper-Collins. The writings of Wendy Maltz, about individuals and couples dealing with the aftermath of sexual abuse and trauma, are the most empathic and humane in the entire field. She suggests a healing approach that is applicable to both individuals and couples. Her concept of the spouse as a "partner in healing" is particularly valuable.

McCarthy, B. (1986). A cognitive-behavioral approach to understanding and treating sexual trauma. *Journal of Sex & Marital Therapy, 12*, 15–19.

McCarthy, B. (1992). Sexual trauma. *Journal of Sex Education & Therapy, 18*, 1–10.

McCarthy, B. (1997). Therapeutic and iatrogenic interventions with adults who were sexually abused as children. *Journal of Sex & Marital Therapy, 23*, 118–125. It is crucial to realize that well-intended therapeutic concepts and interventions can cause iatrogenic damage to the individual and the couple. Therapeutic guidelines are proposed to differentiate helpful and potentially harmful interventions. Case examples are used to illustrate the adult sexual healing process.

McCarthy, B. (1999). Relapse prevention strategies for inhibited sexual desire. *Journal of Sex & Marital Therapy, 25*, 297–303.

McCarthy, B. (2002a). Sexuality, sex therapy, and couple therapy. In A. Gurman & N. Jacobsen (Eds.), *Handbook of Couple Therapy* (3rd ed.). New York: Guilford. This chapter is an in-depth exploration of the issues in contemporary couple sex therapy, using a range of sexual dysfunction examples. The cognitive-behavioral approach of taking personal responsibility, being an intimate team, and integrating of intimacy, pleasuring, and eroticism is described.

McCarthy, B. (2002b). Sexual secrets, trauma, and dysfunction. *Journal of Sex & Marital Therapy, 28*, 353–359.

McCarthy, B., & McCarthy, E. (1993). *Confronting the Victim Role*. New York: Carroll & Graf.

McCarthy, B., & McCarthy, E. (2002). *Sexual Awareness: Couple Sexuality for the Twenty-First Century*. New York: Carroll & Graf. This book includes the range of couple sexual exercises from nongenital and genital pleasuring, to enhancement exercises for building bridges to sexual desire and eroticizing marriage, to exercising for overcoming male and female dysfunction.

McCarthy, B., & Sypeck, M. (in press). Childhood sexual trauma. In D. Snyder & M. Whisman (Eds.), *Treating difficult couples*. New York: Guilford.

Meichenbaum, D. (1994). *A Clinical Handbook/Practical Therapist Manual for Assessing and Treating Adults with Post-Traumatic Stress Disorder (PTSD)*. Waterloo, NT, Canada: Institute Press.

Perelman, M. (2001). Integrating sildenafil and sex therapy: Unconsummated marriage secondary to ED and RE. *Journal of Sex Education and Therapy, 26*, 13–21.

Rind, B., Tromovitch, P., & Bauserman, R. (1998). A meta-analytic examination of assumed properties of child sexual abuse using college samples. *Psychological Bulletin, 124*, 22–53. This is arguably the most politically controversial study ever published in a scientific journal, at least in mental health. It is a meta-analysis of college student samples and reactions to sexual abuse. The authors suggested that some adult–adolescent sexual experiences were consensual and nonharmful, which led to the creation of a congressional resolution attacking the study and the American Psychological Association.

Saywitz, K., Mannarino, A., Berliner, L., & Cohen, J. (2000). Treatment for sexually abused children and adolescents. *American Psychologist, 55*, 1040–1049. A thoughtful review of treatment strategies and techniques for treating children and adolescents. Good treatment at the time reduces the likelihood of adult psychological and sexual symptoms.

Chapter Twenty-Five

The Effects of Drug Abuse on Sexual Functioning

Tiffany Cummins, MD
Sheldon I. Miller, MD

Editor's Note

Despite the high prevalence of substance abuse in Western cultures and the sexual difficulties of many of those who are addicted, few professionals have devoted themselves to understanding the interactions between sexual function and the chronic use of drugs of abuse. When we wanted to draw attention to this neglected topic, we turned to an alcoholism expert, Sheldon I. Miller, MD, professor of psychiatry and chairman at Northwestern University School of Medicine. Dr. Miller agreed to take responsibility for this chapter under the condition that he could use it as an opportunity for an advanced resident to write the chapter. He chose Tiffany Cummins, a 4th year resident at Northwestern Memorial Hospital in Chicago. Dr. Cummins is a graduate of Tulane University School of Medicine. It is our hope that this chapter will assist our readers to recognize both what is known and how much there is yet to be learned about the subject. Dr. Cummins has told us how developing this chapter has changed her views on substance-abuse treatment. We hope that this chapter will inspire others to be curious about the sexuality of their addicted patients. We have another hope as well: that Dr. Cummins's excellent work will inspire other young professionals to be scholarly about neglected subjects.

INTRODUCTION

Drugs and sex have been linked throughout recorded history. Man seems to have been constantly searching for a substance that would alter his sexual drive and performance. Myths and claims—most unsubstantiated—abound. Despite the high level of interest in this subject, however, limited effort seems to have been made to scientifically study it until the latter half of the 20th century. Unfortunately, the focus had moved away from the topic by the early 1980s (Buffum, 1982). As a consequence, though our understanding of neurobiology has become more sophisticated during the last 15 years, it has not been applied to the subject of drugs and sex.

Even the data that do exist are not entirely reliable. The validity of research-derived information about the impact of drugs of abuse on sexual function is limited because of many methodological obstacles, such as the following:

1. The sexual effects of substances on other animal species are often quite different, making it difficult to extrapolate from animal research.
2. Given the cultural expectations of the libido-enhancing effects of certain drugs, it is not usually possible to separate psychological expectancy effects from true pharmacological effects. Unfortunately, placebo-controlled studies in this area are especially rare.
3. Clinical observations of patients with substance-abuse disorders are complicated by the tendency of substance users to use multiple substances, which can contaminate data.
4. The substance use itself may lead to erroneous subjective reports. For example, chronically inebriated alcoholics are often unaware of their sexual dysfunction. They honestly report no dysfunction; their partners often report the opposite.
5. Substance users often also suffer from serious character pathology. This increases doubt about the trustworthiness of their subjective reports.
6. It is often difficult to substantiate such subjective reports with objective evidence, especially in women, whose sexual responses are less obvious and less well understood.
7. Researchers may be reluctant to administer (or even to tacitly accept the self-administration of) potentially harmful substances to human subjects, especially ones who may become pregnant. (Possibly as a result of this and the previous obstacle, female subjects have not been included in the majority of studies, leaving data unbalanced).

We're writing this chapter to exhort clinicians (including ourselves) to address the issue of sexuality when treating patients and to encourage researchers to resume work on the subject. After the 1970s, the mental health field seemed to forget that people are more than just heads! Most of us realize how closely sexual function is related to mental illness and probably remember to ask depressed people (for example) about their sex lives, but we almost never ask people who abuse substances. All too often, we tend to focus on the most obvious presenting problems and forget to look beyond them. Clearly, while a patient is delirious from alcohol withdrawal and tied to his hospital bed, your immediate aim is to detoxify him safely. After discharge, your goal is preventing relapse and then maintaining sobriety. But do we ever get around to assessing his overall satisfaction with the other facets of his life? When do we ask about sex? After all, sex is a basic human function and of great importance to most people, though they probably won't bring it up. This is unfortunate, because sexual function is intimately related to substance abuse. If a man had been using heroin to treat his premature ejaculation, for example, is he more likely to relapse? If a woman is unable to tolerate sex when sober, will she maintain her sobriety? If we hope to address our patients' substance abuse issues, we have to remember that they are more than just substance abusers. They are complex beings, and we must treat them as such. Okay, we're off our soapbox.

Now, for the subject of this chapter—the following is a synopsis of our knowledge to date on the effects of substance abuse on sexual function.

THE SEDATIVE/HYPNOTICS—ALCOHOL, BENZODIAZEPINES, BARBITURATES, GHB, AND OTHERS

This is a large and widely used class of drugs. Some, such as benzodiazepines and phenobarbital, have legitimate medical uses. Others, such as GHB, an anesthetic, do not (at least, not in the United States). All of them depress (decrease activity in) the central nervous system (CNS). The first part of the brain to be affected is the reticular activating system. In so doing, these drugs tend to relax the user, even to the point of sleep. The CNS depressant effects of all these drugs can be additive, making them lethal if their combined effect depresses the breathing center of the brainstem. With the exception of alcohol, we could find little data on the sexual effects of these drugs. Therefore, we will restrict our discussion to alcohol.

Alcohol

Ethyl alcohol has been in use for thousands of years, presumably since man found that drinking rancid grape juice made him feel funny. Alcohol affects sexual functioning in many ways. It decreases inhibitions, allowing the user to think sexual thoughts or to behave sexually. Those with considerable guilt feelings about sex may experience an even greater increase in arousal. Alcohol has been extolled as an aphrodisiac, though its deleterious effects on performance are common knowledge, as described by Shakespeare in *Hamlet*: "It provokes and unprovokes: it provokes the desire, but it takes away from the performance."

Alcohol's libido-enhancing effects may largely stem from the expectations of the subject and the settings in which alcohol is consumed. For instance, imagine that Mr. Frank N. Beans has made plans to meet his buddies on a Friday night. He spends an hour selecting his outfit (brand-new T-shirt, acid-washed jeans), styling his mullet hairdo, and spritzing on his Player cologne before he heads over to the Get Lucky tavern. He is primed to feel randy before the beer even hits his lips!

Effects in Men: To illustrate the effects of expectancy, a study was done in which male subjects were given either alcohol or tonic water. Those who were told they had received alcohol reported higher levels of arousal, whether or not they had actually been given alcohol (Wilson & Lawson, 1976). At blood alcohol levels below 5 mg%, expectation plays a large role in determining the user's response. Above this level, the pharmacological effects of the alcohol begin to play a more dominant role. To study these effects, Farkas and Rosen (1976) hooked 16 male college students up to penile strain-gauges, turned on some adult movies, and started feeding the men alcohol. At 25 mg%, tumescence (the increase in size of the penis when erect) increased slightly, whereas at 50 and 75 mg%, maximal tumescence decreased. At levels of 100 mg% and above, erections are almost completely eliminated. In addition, the amount of time required to achieve the erection lengthens with increasing blood alcohol levels. (FYI: The legal limit in Illinois is 85 mg%.)

> *Ted, aged 30, had relapsed for 2 years after 6 months of sobriety. He had been suffering from erectile failure during attempts at intercourse since the age of 18. Consumption of two six-packs of beer a day had also begun at age 18. When not drinking, Ted was able to masturbate with full erection and complete ejaculation. It had never occurred to him that he had not been drinking while masturbating and had always been drinking when with women. He developed severe performance anxiety, which hampered his ability to have intercourse during his first 6-month recovery period (Schuster, 1988)*

The length of time before orgasm and ejaculation occur also rises with increasing blood alcohol levels. Some men who suffer from premature ejaculation may exploit this effect.

Chronic use of alcohol can cause prolonged sexual impairment. Many alcoholics have organic erectile dysfunction and sterility. Evidence suggests that the breakdown in the system can occur at three levels: the testes, the liver, and the nerves.

Testes. Alcohol limits the production of testosterone by Leydig cells in the testes by two mechanisms—by inhibiting 17-alpha-hydroxyprogesterone aldolase (an enzyme involved in the formation of testosterone) and by using up nicotine-adenine dinucleotide (NAD). NAD is necessary for the oxidation of alcohol to acetaldehyde by ethanol dehydrogenase, and for the subsequent oxidation of acetaldehyde to acetate. The transformation of pregnenolone to testosterone also requires NAD.

Ethanol dehydrogenase, one of the enzymes mentioned in the last paragraph, is also required to convert retinal to retinol, the form of vitamin A necessary for sperm production. But if alcohol dehydrogenase is busy breaking down alcohol, it won't have time to convert retinal to retinol, and sperm can't be properly formed.

Initially, alcohol leads to fewer fully mature, well-formed spermatozoa. (In fact, sperm samples taken after acute alcohol consumption revealed spermatozoa with curled tails, distended midsections, and broken-off heads!) As a result, fewer spermatozoa are found in the tubules, which back up with immature spermatids. These subsequently degenerate, leaving the tubules a veritable ghost town!

Chronic exposure to alcohol damages the tubular germinal epithelium (the section of the testes where immature sperm first sprout) and decreases the diameter of the seminiferous tubules where sperm mature. Alcohol may also produce scarring of the vas deferens (the tube through which sperm exit the testes), which could cause an obstruction. Because the seminiferous tubules make up about 85–90% of the testicular volume, this scarring, along with decreases in seminiferous tubule diameter and Leydig cell damage, causes testicular atrophy. Testicular atrophy has been found in 70–80% of chronic alcoholic men.

Liver. When the liver is damaged by chronic alcohol ingestion, the activity of two enzymes, alpha-5-reductase and aromatase, increases. Alpha-5-reductase is the first enzyme to break down testosterone to dihydrotestosterone; aromatase completes the conversion of testosterone to estrogen. At the same time, the liver develops a decreased ability to take female hormones, like estrone, and weak androgens, like androstenedione, out of circulation. Androstenedione may then be converted to estrone at a peripheral site in the body, producing an even greater overabundance of estrogen. In addition, some data suggest that alcoholic men have an increased response to normal levels of estrogen. As a result of these mechanisms (along with testicular dysfunction), feminization may occur. Of note, feminization—breast enlargement, decreased face and body hair, and prostate shrinkage—is associated with high rates of erectile dysfunction.

Nerves. Data suggest that chronic alcohol use can damage the peripheral nervous system. About one third of alcoholic men develop peripheral neuropathy, with sensory loss and motor weakness in the extremities, similar to that found in diabetics. Presumably, this neuropathy could lead to decreased genital sensitivity. Alcohol also affects the autonomic nervous system (the part of the nervous system that controls unconscious bodily processes). Erectile dysfunction could result from the disruption of the reflex arcs that mediate erections.

The prevalence of sexual dysfunction among male alcoholics is high. In one study of inpatients enrolled in an alcohol detoxification program, 75% reported having sexual dysfunction within the preceding 6 months; 66% of them were still sexually dysfunctional up to 9 months after treatment (Fahrner, 1987). Another study reported a 54% frequency of erectile impotence in alcoholics compared to 28% for nonalcoholics (Whalley, 1978). A large study found 8% of chronic alcoholics to be impotent. Half of them had not regained erectile capability after years of sobriety, although they still expressed a strong desire for sex (Lemere & Smith, 1973).

Effects in Women. In some respects, alcohol similarly affects men and women. Low-dose alcohol tends to increase libido. Few objective studies of sexual arousal in women exist, in part because women's arousal is more difficult to measure. Wilson and Lawson (1976) used vaginal photoplethysmography (a technique for measuring genital blood flow) with 16 nonalcoholic women. They demonstrated decreased vaginal blood flow with increasing blood alcohol levels (even though the subjects reported increased arousal) and increased time to orgasm. Later work has found that time to orgasm increased, whereas vaginal blood volume and subjective orgasmic intensity decreased in moderately to highly intoxicated women. However, some report greater arousal and orgasmic pleasure.

Chronic alcohol use also affects women's reproductive systems. Beckman (1979) found that 51% of alcoholic women had "menstrual or other female problems," compared to 36% for controls. (However, the incidence among psychiatric patients was 54%, suggesting that alcohol may not be the sole factor responsible.) A Yugoslavian study found that approximately two-thirds of female alcoholics had signs of ovarian dysfunction. Nine percent had the onset of menopause prior to 40 years of age, a frequency that is more than double their general population's prevalence of premature menopause (Moskovic, 1975). Autopsy studies of alcoholic women of reproductive age have demonstrated few corpora lutea, consistent with ovulatory failure. Alcoholic women can suffer from defeminization, as evidenced by the breast, uterine, and vaginal wall atrophy. They have greater difficulty in conceiving and in carrying pregnancies to term.

Alcohol is associated with women's sexuality in less direct ways. A higher than average percentage of female alcoholics were sexually abused in their youth. Plus, the abuse tends to have been more violent and of greater duration and to have begun earlier than was the sexual abuse of nonalcoholics. A large percentage of alcoholic women who were sexually abused score very high on measures of guilt associated with sex. They may be using alcohol as a kind of escape from these feelings. Alcoholic women also have a higher incidence of rape as adults. In part, this might stem from being in bars alone at night and from men's perceptions of them as more vulnerable and less worthy of respect. Response to such types of trauma ranges from sexual avoidance to promiscuity. Overall, alcoholic women have more sexual partners and are less likely to practice safe sex. Alcoholic women are much more likely to have had a sexually transmitted disease (Beckman & Ackerman, 1995).

> There was a childlike, innocent quality to Margaret's presentation. She was 30 but appeared 15 years younger. She casually mentioned that she had been raped when intoxicated on numerous occasions. She went to bars in neighborhoods away from her home and hitched rides when the bars closed. Rape was deserved, Margaret thought, because, after all, "I am an alcoholic." When sober, Margaret didn't want to be touched by anyone and flinched if a patient or staff member of either gender came within 2 feet of her. She said that she felt permanently contaminated and hopeless. Her heterosexual adjustment prior to the onset of alcoholism was hard to assess because Margaret had been suspended from private schools four times since the age of 14 for drinking. She had never had a boyfriend and could not picture herself attached to anyone. (Schuster, 1988)

OPIOIDS/NARCOTICS—HEROIN, METHADONE, MORPHINE

Heroin has no legitimate uses in the United States, but many other opioids are widely used to relieve pain. They all promote relaxation and a sense of well-being and can lead to sleep and respiratory depression in high doses.

Effects in Men. Narcotics affect all stages of male sexual function. Although very small doses may increase libido by disinhibition, narcotic intoxication generally decreases desire. Cushman (1972) found that 61% of heroin addicts reported impaired libido (0% in the controls), 39% reported erectile dysfunction (7% in the controls), and 70% had delayed ejaculation (0% in the controls). The prevalence of loss of sex drive among methadone users has been reported to range from 6% to 100%. Erectile failure in methadone users ranges from 6 to 50%. Retarded ejaculation occurs in 5–22%.

Premature ejaculation is common in addicts undergoing withdrawal. This may simply be an effect of the withdrawal, or it may reflect predrug functioning. Premature ejaculation is far less common while on heroin, however.

Sperm motility and quantity of ejaculate are considerably lower among heroin and methadone users. Methadone reduces fertility more than heroin does; in one study, men on methadone maintenance did not father any children, though they had fathered 53 total children beforehand. Heroin users, on the other hand, remained fertile.

Although the mechanisms of the previous effects are not certain, hormones are likely to be involved. The ventral and medial hypothalamus, which controls the pituitary, contains numerous opiate receptor–binding sites and high levels of endogenous opiates. Naturally occurring opioids exert a constant inhibitory effect on the hypothalamic-pituitary axis. Narcotic drugs produce a similar effect.

Opioids inhibit LHRH, which causes a decrease in LH, which causes a decrease in testosterone. Similar depression of testosterone and LH, with associated sexual dysfunction, has been reported with codeine, propoxyphene, methadone, and oxycodone. Thus, sexual dysfunction among narcotics users is thought to be the result of action on the central nervous system and not directly on the genitals.

> *Example: After his large morning fix of heroin, which used most of his day's supply, he was, at first, impotent. Then, during the day, he developed erections but could not ejaculate. Later, libido increased and normal responsiveness developed until in the early evening his potency was excellent with optimal ejaculatory time. During the evening, his sexual reflexes became quicker and ejaculatio praecox was the rule. During the night, the run-down of drugs in his system was associated with spontaneous ejaculations. The same cycle repeated itself every 24 hours. The partners programmed their love life accordingly. (Parr, 1976)*

Effects in Women: Bai et al. found that 60% of female heroin users noted decreased libido (compared to before heroin use) (Bai, Greenwald, Caterini, & Kaminetzky, 1974). Sexual activity was also lowered. When switched to methadone, 10 claimed an increase in libido and some claimed an increased enjoyment of sex. In women with dyspareunia, heroin may increase sexual enjoyment because of its anxiety and pain-relieving properties.

Chronic narcotic use also affects women's reproductive function. Users commonly experience diminished or absent menstrual periods, miscarriages, and infertility. Heroin frequently induces abnormal menstrual cycles and termination of it allows normal cycles to return. Amenorrhea began, on the average, about 17 months after initiation of heroin use. After withdrawal, periods returned about 1.8 months later. Women on methadone have reported regularized menses.

STIMULANTS—COCAINE, AMPHETAMINES, MDMA

The stimulants do just that—they stimulate the user, causing increases in heart rate, blood pressure, and alertness. Large doses can lead to severe anxiety and paranoia, along with heart attacks and strokes (Kloner & Rezkalla, 2003). Despite these potential adverse effects, the stimulants are widely used (both legitimately and illegitimately). Amphetamines come in the form of "crystal meth," "ice," "speed," and "uppers." The route of administration, dose, and social setting play a large role in determining a user's sexual response to amphetamine. IV users may substitute mutual injections with a partner for sex. This route has led to reports of immediate spontaneous erections and immediate orgasms in women. The sexual effects of orally ingested amphetamine are more subtle; low doses can increase libido in both sexes, help sustain erections in men, and bring about multiple orgasms (Parr, 1976). Higher oral doses may cause erectile failure and delay or prevent orgasms.

Amphetamine affects multiple neurotransmitter systems in the CNS. It releases norepinephrine, blocks the uptake of norepinephrine and serotonin, and, most important, acts on the dopaminergic system. Initially, amphetamine causes a rapid release of dopamine. With repeated use, the reserves of dopamine are depleted. Some think that the initial flood of dopamine is responsible for the increase in libido. Peripherally, amphetamine stimulates alpha-adrenergic receptors, which might facilitate multiple orgasms or shunt blood away from the genitalia. Beta-adrenergic stimulation by amphetamine may shunt blood away. As amphetamine is long-acting, these effects could presumably last for several hours.

Amphetamine may create behaviors that the person would not usually engage in, such as group sex, fetishism, homosexuality, or bestiality.

> *Example: In three cases parents complained that their sons had, on returning home in amphetamine intoxication, openly masturbated. "He sat down in front of the television, opened his trousers and started playing with himself. His sister was in the room; he didn't seem to know we were there." (Scott & Willcox, 1965)*

Cocaine

Cocaine is a stimulant with effects similar to those of amphetamine. However, unlike amphetamine, its effects wear off in 5 to 15 minutes. Cocaine has variable effects on orgasm and erectile function (Siegel, 1977). Multiple orgasms have been reported with cocaine intoxication, but delays in orgasm and erectile failure have also been reported. Multiple orgasms and spontaneous erections after IV injection of cocaine have been described, but, generally, intravenous use is associated with decreased interest in sexual activity. Low-dose intranasal use (1 to 4 grams per month) seems to increase sexual stimulation without significant dysfunction.

Increased prolactin levels have been found in patients who abuse cocaine, presumably secondary to dopamine depletion. Elevated prolactin levels are commonly associated with infertility, menstrual irregularities, and decreased libido, though no specific data exists on cocaine users with elevated prolactin levels.

> *Example: A 24-year-old woman, with a long history of polydrug use, reported that she tried every drug there is, "but cocaine free base got a hold of me." She would smoke every 5 minutes for several days at a time and reported hallucinations and paranoid ideation. She attempted suicide by cutting her wrists but found that the razor blade she used had been too dulled from chopping cocaine. . . . "Every day is a hassle to live out. . . . I'm not a happy person, nothing will make me happy. I can't relate even to my children, coke is more important. Cocaine is my relationship, I can't have a relationship. I can't have an orgasm anymore. . . . When I take a hit, it's like I'm in love, but I've never been in love that good."*

> *Example: A 33-year-old man had been a cocaine abuser for 8 months. He administered the substance intranasally up to several times a day. He described an active, functional sex life before the cocaine abuse. Sexual indifference and the inability to maintain an erection developed after 6 months. His sexual interest decreased further in association with increased prolactin levels after abrupt abstinence from cocaine in the hospital. Bromocriptine . . . was started on day 30, and sexual interest returned. He experienced a nocturnal ejaculation on day 32, his first one since age 15. On follow-up, he reported a return to normal sexual function.*

MDMA—"Ecstasy"

3,4-methylenedioxy-methamphetamine, also known as "Ecstasy," is derived from amphetamine and structurally resembles both its parent and the hallucinogen mescaline. The latter may explain the fact that MDMA has psychedelic properties similar to those of LSD. Many users claim that MDMA has the ability to produce feelings of love for one's sexual partner, but it is hard to understand why Ecstasy would be any more of a love potion than would other amphetamines of similar molecular structure. Ecstasy can also cause nausea and vomiting and an intense desire to defecate ("disco dump").

MDMA seems to enhance the sensual aspects of sex, possibly due to the increased feelings of emotional closeness (which may be interpreted as love). In a study of 20 males and 15 females, 95% of men and 100% of women reported increased sexual desire after MDMA. Around 91% reported increased satisfaction, and 80% of men and 40% of women reported a delay in orgasm. The orgasm was perceived to be more intense by 85% of the men and 53% of the women (Zemishlany, Aizenberg, & Weizman, 2001). Problems in achieving orgasm while under its influence were reported by 62% of men and 17% of women in another study, but 4 women claimed that orgasms were easier to achieve. Responses regarding erection were mixed: 46% said it decreased their ability to achieve an erection, whereas 4% said it increased it; 69% said MDMA increased their ability to delay ejaculation (Buffum & Moser, 1986).

Users often report that under the influence of MDMA, they engage in sexual acts they wouldn't ordinarily engage in (including dangerous or illegal acts), which suggests both a decrease in inhibition and impaired judgment. In one study of gay men at circuit parties, unsafe sex was associated with frequent use of Ecstasy (Mattison, Ross, Wolfson, & Franklin, 2001).

Tobacco

Tobacco's effects are largely influenced by expectation and setting. Think of the film noir starlet, holding a cigarette between manicured fingers while smoke swirls in the dimly lit bar. . . . However, tobacco's actual effects on sexual function are not positive. Smoking acutely causes constriction of blood vessels in the penis. Chronic, long-term smoking can contribute to generalized atherosclerosis and atherosclerosis of the genital blood supply. Mannino, Klevens, and Flanders (1994) found that tobacco smoking was associated with a 50% increased incidence of self-reported impotence, even when risk factors (vascular disease, marital status, abuse of other substances, age, hormonal factors, race, and psychological factors) were adjusted for. Sperm motility may be decreased in smokers, and heavy smoking may impair men's fertility.

Women's sexual function is also adversely affected by tobacco. Higher infertility rates, perhaps due to poor embryonic implantation in the endometrium, and early menopause have been reported. An inverse dose-response relationship between the number of cigarettes smoked per day and the age of menopause has been documented (Kaufman, Slone, Rosenberg, Miettinen, & Shapiro, 1980).

HALLUCINOGENS—LSD, PCP, MESCALINE, KETAMINE, HALLUCINOGENIC MUSHROOMS, AND OTHERS

The primary effects of these drugs are thought disturbance and perceptual changes. Although users commonly report thinking about sex while under the influence, the idea of actually accomplishing the act can seem ridiculous. All the data are anecdotal. We'll just briefly touch on two of the most well-known hallucinogens: LSD and PCP.

LSD ("Acid")

Some users report no sexual feelings at all, whereas others report deeply moving sexual-emotional experiences.

> *"To make love on acid is to make perfect love and gain protoplasmic unity."*
> *"When I come (on LSD), my whole soul and body seem to fuse with my partner."*

> *One mature man of undoubted virility became impotent with his newly married wife following one horrendous LSD trip. Under the influence of the drug, he hallucinated her as a shark, and thereafter this image was repeated whenever he attempted intercourse with her.*

PCP ("Angel Dust")

Phencyclidine was initially developed as a dissociative anesthetic, but because it was found to cause unmanageable agitation, it has no legitimate uses. It causes disinhibition and pain reduction. Recreational and light chronic users tend to report a decrease in sexual feelings but no dysfunction. However, 50% of heavy chronic PCP abusers report feeling more sexual after PCP use. Both males and females describe prolonged orgasm with decreased intensity. As the dosage is increased or if the drug is used chronically, reports of erectile or ejaculatory impairment, or both tend to occur.

> *A 20-year-old homosexual male came to the Haight-Ashbury Free Medical Clinic acutely intoxicated with PCP. He had been smoking the drug three times per day for 6 months. He found that whenever he tried to discontinue using PCP, he developed depression with significant cognitive impairment. He indicated that when he first began using PCP, it enhanced his sexual pleasure by producing disinhibition. However, as his dosage of PCP escalated and his usage pattern became daily, he found that he had a decrease in sexual desire with some ejaculatory failure. He retained the ability to get an erection but in the middle of the sex act, he would "space out and forget what he was doing." At the time of the interview, he had significant depression and cerebral dysfunction and his level of sexual activity approached zero. This was substantially below his level of sexual activity before PCP use (Smith, Buxton, & Moser, 1980).*

Some reports have described homosexual men who used PCP in association with "fisting" (a sex act in which one person inserts his fist into his partner's rectum). It was primarily used by the "fistee" to disinhibit and relieve pain.

OTHER DRUGS

Volatile Nitrates (Amyl Nitrate or "Poppers")

These are vasodilators, some of which had been used in the treatment of angina. They are also used for the enhancement of sexual pleasure, especially among gay males (Goode & Troiden, 1979). The usual pattern of use is for one or both partners to inhale the drug during intercourse, often simply to release inhibitions. Amyl nitrate is also thought to relax the anal sphincter to facilitate anal intercourse and is reputed to prolong orgasm, or the perception of orgasm. Its use at circuit parties is also associated with unsafe sex (Mattison et al., 2001).

> Example: "Amyl gives an engorgement of my genitals, a sense of merging with my partner. It heightens my body response and body rhythm. It plays a primary role in the erotic turn-on while I'm able to space-off into the complete pleasure of sensuality."

(Amyl nitrate is contraindicated in the use of any phosphodiesterase inhibitor.)

THC (The Active Ingredient in Marijuana, Hashish, etc.)

Tetrahydrocanabinol has properties of the stimulants, hallucinogens, and sedatives. Marijuana usage is undeniably associated with increased sexual activity for many people. Low to moderate doses may enhance sexual function. In one study, 68% of the males and 40% of the females stated that the quality of their orgasm was enhanced by marijuana. Overall, 75% of males and 90% of females indicated that feelings of sexual pleasure and satisfaction were increased (Halikas, Weller, & Morse, 1982). Our clinical experience supports these data—most of the users of low-dose marijuana whom we've seen praise its effects on their sexual function. None have reported a deleterious effect.

High, chronic doses, however, have been reported to cause both decreased libido and inability to perform. Ascetics in India use large doses of hemp drugs to destroy their sexual appetite.

Data on THC's effects on hormones are inconsistent. Kolodny, Masters, Kolodner, and Toro (1974) found decreased testosterone levels in a study of 20 men who had been smoking marijuana at least 4 times a week for 6 months. However, this was not replicated in other studies. Research on LH and FSH levels has also failed to turn up any abnormalities. Several studies found decreased sperm counts in men after heavy marijuana use (Hembree, Zeidenberg, & Nahas, 1976; Kolodny et al., 1974). Because these decreases in sperm count were not associated with significant changes in serum testosterone, luteinizing hormone, or follicle-stimulating hormone levels, the authors proposed that the observed decreases in sperm count were due to direct suppressant actions of the THC on the germinal epithelium. There are also some reports of decreases in sperm motility and changes in sperm morphology (shape/structure) accompanying marijuana use. In all the studies, the sperm returned to baseline within several months after marijuana use ceased.

There are minimal data on the effects on women's sexual function. One study found that marijuana users had 2-day shorter menstrual cycles, compared to nonusers, and had more anovulatory cycles. Levels of LH, FSH, estrogen, and progesterone did not differ from those of nonusers. However, prolactin levels were significantly lower and testosterone levels were significantly higher in users (Kolodny, Webster, Tullman, & Donrbush, 1979). What this suggests is unclear.

SUMMARY

It seems that sex, drugs, and rock-n-roll are not always such a swingin' threesome. However, reliable data are scant. Unfortunately, research on the subject has tapered off, though drug use has not. Why is this? There isn't much funding from the government to go around. Pharmaceutical companies have little reason to invest in studies on drugs of abuse. Inpatient chemical dependence treatment programs have dried up (until recently, these made cheap and relatively well-controlled environments in which to do studies). Finally, it's likely that many researchers, like the general public, have adopted a harsher stance on drug use (compared to the more liberal '60s and '70s). The public is less sympathetic to substance abusers and less enthusiastic about studying this population. If we're going to treat substance abuse, however, we have to understand its effects, including those on sexual function.

REFERENCES

Bai, J., Greenwald, E., Caterini, H., & Kaminetzky, H. (1974). Drug-related menstrual aberrations. *Obstetrics and Gynecology, 44,* 713–719.

Beckman, L. J. (1979). Reported effects of alcohol on the sexual feelings and behavior of women alcoholics and nonalcoholics. *Journal of Studies on Alcohol, 40,* 272–282.

Beckman, L. J., & Ackerman, K. T. (1995). Women, alcohol, and sexuality. In M. Galanter (Ed.), *Recent Developments in Alcoholism* (Vol. 12: *Women and Alcoholism*). New York: Plenum.

Buffum, J. (1982, January–June). Pharmacosexology: The effects of drugs on sexual function, a review. *Journal of Psychoactive Drugs, 14*(1–2). This article is a brief summary of the effects of drugs on sexual function, including drugs of abuse and a wide variety of prescription medications. Succinct and to the point, it devotes only a few paragraphs to each drug but conveys the important facts. It also directs the reader to relevant major studies.

Buffum, J., & Moser, C. (1986, October–December). MDMA and human sexual function. *Journal of Psychoactive Drugs, 18*(4), 355–359.

Cushman, P. (1972). Sexual behavior in heroin addiction and methadone maintenance. *New York State Journal of Medicine, 72,* 1261–1265.

Fahrner, E. M. (1987). Sexual dysfunction in male alcohol addicts: Prevalence and treatment. *Archives of Sexual Behavior, 16,* 247–257.

Farkas, G. M., & Rosen, R. C. (1976). Effect of alcohol on elicited male sexual response. *Journal of Studies on Alcohol, 37*(3), 265–272.

Goode, E., & Troiden, R. R. (1979, August). Amyl nitrite use among homosexual men. *American Journal of Psychiatry, 136,* 8.

Halikas, J., Weller, R., & Morse, C. (1982). Effects of marijuana use on sexual performance. *Journal of Psychoactive Drugs, 14*(1–2).

Hembree, W. C., Zeidenberg, P., & Nahas, G. G. (1986). Marihuana's effects on human gonadal function. In G. G. Nahas (Ed.), *Marihuana: Chemistry, Biochemistry and Cellular Effects* (p. 521). New York: Springer Verlag.

Kaufman, D. W., Slone, D., Rosenberg, L., Miettinen, O. S., & Shapiro, S. (1980). Cigarette smoking rage at natural menopause. *American Journal of Public Health, 70,* 420–422.

Kloner, R. A., & Rezkalla, S. H. (2003). Cocaine and the heart. *New England Journal of Medicine, 348*(6), 487–488.

Kolodny, R. C., Masters, W. H., Kolodner, R. M., & Toro, G. (1974). Depression of plasma testosterone levels after chronic intensive marijuana use. *New England Journal of Medicine, 290,* 872–874.

Kolodny, R. C., Webster, S. K., Tullman, G. D., & Donrbush, R. I. (1979). Chronic marihuana use by women: Menstrual cycle and endocrine findings. Paper presented at the New York Postgraduate Medical School 2nd Annual Conf. Marihuana, June 28–29.

Lemere, F. & Smith, J. W. (1973). Alcohol induced sexual impotence. *American Journal of Psychiatry, 130,* 212–213.

Mannino, D. M., Klevens, R. M., & Flanders, W. D. (1994). Cigarette smoking: An independent risk factor for impotence? *American Journal of Epidemiology, 140*(11), 1003–1008.

Mattison, A. M., Ross, M. W., Wolfson, T., & Franklin, D. (2001). Circuit party attendance, club drug use, and unsafe sex in gay men. *Journal of Substance Abuse, 13,* 119–126.

Moskovic, S. (1975). Uticaj hronicnog trovanja alkoholom na ovarijunsku disfunkciju. *Srpski Arhiv a Celokupno Lekarstvo,* 751–758.

Parr, D. (1976). Sexual aspects of drug abuse in narcotic addicts. *British Journal of Addiction, 71,* 261–268.

Schuster, Carlotta. (1988). Alcohol and sexuality. *Sexual Medicine,* Volume 7. New York: Praeger. Dr. Schuster's book is quite useful to the reader who is interested not only in biological data but also in sociological and psychological data. She includes sections on sexual deviance and criminal behavior among alcoholics and separately considers male and female, heterosexual and homosexual, alcohol users. Her plentiful case examples illustrate the interpersonal conflicts caused by substance abuse. Although the book primarily focuses on alcohol, it includes a very brief synopsis of other drugs of abuse.

Scott, P. D., & Willcox, D. R. C. (1965). Delinquency and the amphetamines. *British Journal of Psychiatry, III,* 865–875.

Siegel, R. K. (1977). Cocaine: Recreational use and intoxication. In R. C. Petersen & R. C. Stillman (Eds.), *Cocaine: 1977.* NIDA Research Monograph 13. Rockville, MD: NIDA.

Smith, D. E., Smith, N., Buxton, M. E., & Moser, C. (1980). PCP and sexual dysfunction. *Journal of Psychedelic Drugs, 12,* 3–4.

Whalley, L. J. (1978). Sexual adjustment of male alcoholics. *Acta Psychiatrica Scandinavia, 58,* 281.

Wilson, G. T., & Lawson, D. M. (1976). Expectancies, alcohol, and sexual arousal in male social drinkers. *Journal of Abnormal Psychology, 85*(6), 587–594.

Wilson, G. T., & Lawson, D. M. (1976). The effect of alcohol on sexual arousal in women. *Journal of Abnormal Psychology, 85*(3), 489–497.

Zemishlany, Z., Aizenberg, D., & Weizman, A. (2001) Subjective effects of MDMA ("Ecstasy") on human sexual function. *European Psychiatry, 16,* 127–130.

Author Index

Subject Index

Note: *Italicized* page numbers indicate a figure or table.